B. Péroche
H. Rushmeier (eds.)

Rendering Techniques 2000

Proceedings of the Eurographics Workshop
in Brno, Czech Republic,
June 26–28, 2000

Eurographics

SpringerWienNewYork

Prof. Bernard Péroche, PhD
Ecole Nationale Superieure des Mines de Saint Etienne
Saint Etienne, France

Holly Rushmeier, PhD
IBM TJ Watson Research Center,
Hawthorne, NY, USA

© 2000 Springer-Verlag/Wien
Printed in Austria

Typesetting: Camera-ready by authors
Printing: Novographic, A-1238 Wien
Binding: Papyrus, A-1100 Wien

Graphic design: Ecke Bonk

Printed on acid-free and chlorine-free bleached paper

SPIN: 10770704

With 250 partly coloured Figures

ISSN 0946-2767
ISBN 3-211-83535-0 Springer-Verlag Wien New York

Preface

This book contains the proceedings of the 11th Eurographics Workshop on Rendering, which took place from the 26th to the 28th of June, 2000, in Brno, Czech Republic. Over the past 10 years, the Workshop has become the premier forum dedicated to research in rendering. Much of the work in rendering now appearing in other conferences and journals builds on ideas originally presented at the Workshop.

This year we received a total of 84 submissions. Each paper was carefully reviewed by two of the 25 international programme committee members, as well as external reviewers, selected by the co-chairs from a pool of 121 individuals (The programme committee and external reviewers are listed following the contents pages). In this review process, all submissions and reviews were handled electronically, with the exception of videos submitted with a few of the papers (however, some mpeg movies were also sent electronically).

The overall quality of the submissions was exceptionally high. Space and time constraints forced the committee to make some difficult decisions. In the end, 33 papers were accepted, and they appear here. Almost all papers are accompanied by color images, which appear at the end of the book. The papers treat the following varied topics: radiosity, ray tracing, methods for global illumination, visibility, reflectance, filtering, perception, hardware assisted methods, real time rendering, modeling for efficient rendering and new image representations. Each year, in addition to the reviewed contributions, the workshop includes invited presentations from internationally recognized experts. This year we were pleased to have Robert Shakespeare (University of Indiana) and Heinrich Bülthoff (Max-Planck-Institute) as invited speakers. As in previous years, we expect these proceedings to become an invaluable resource for both rendering researchers and practitioners.

We wish to thank the organizing chairman Pavel Zemcik and his colleagues at the Department of Computer Science and Engineering, Faculty of Electrical Engineering and Computer Science, Brno University of Technology, for their help in the production of the proceedings, and for taking care of all the local organization aspects of the workshop. We also want to acknowledge IBM for contributing financial support, SGI-Silicon Graphics for technical support, Jihomoravská Plynárenská a.s. (South Moravian Gas Corporation) and Minolta for cooperation and Camea spol. s r.o. for contributing to the preparation of the workshop.

Finally, we wish to thank all of the authors who submitted their work to the workshop, and the programme committee members and external reviewers for all the time and energy they invested in the review process. We were impressed with both the quality of the submissions, and the quality of the reviews evaluating the papers. We are proud to present the results of this process in the form of this book.

Bernard Péroche
Holly Rushmeier

June, 2000

Contents

VIII

International Programme Committee

External Reviewers

Maneesh Agrawala
Antonio Augusto de Souza
Fausto Bernardini
Volker Blanz
Emilio Camahort
Min Chen
Johan Claes
Katja Daubert
Yoshinori Dobashi
Fredo Durand
Paul Fearing
Neil Gatenby
Andrew Glassner
Stephen Gortler
Chuck Hansen
Heinrich Hey
Isabelle Icart
Jim Klosowski
Justin Legakis
Reto Lütolf
Ignacio Martin
Michel Meriaux
Lázló Neumann
Tomoyuki Nishita
Eric Paquette
Ingmar Peter
Jan Přikryl
Amela Sadagic
Gernot Schaufler
Francisco Seron
Claudio Silva
Peter-Pike Sloan
Cyril Soler
James Stewart
Yinlong Sun
Joelle Thollot
Kei Nam Tsoi
Thomas Vetter
Ben Watson
Alexander Wilkie
Peter Wonka
Yizhou Yu

Daniel Aliaga
Kavita Bala
Martin Blais
Stefan Brabec
Marie-Paule Cani
Franklin Cho
Michael Cohen
Xavier Decoret
Iddo Drori
Phil Dutre
Jim Ferwerda
Sherif Ghali
Guy Godin
Eduard Gröller
John Hart
Nicolas Holzschuch
Jan Kautz
Michael Kowalski
Jerome Lengyel
Bill Mark
Ioana Martin
Gary Meyer
Fabrice Neyret
Marc Olano
Gustavo Patow
Matt Pharr
Ravi Ramamoorthi
Mateu Sbert
Hans-Peter Seidel
Guoqiang Shan
Maryann Simmons
Philipp Slusallek
Marc Stamminger
Eric Stollnitz
Frank Suykens
Robert Tobler
Jack Tumblin
Marie Luce Viaud
Daniel Weiskopf
Michael Wimmer
Andrew Woo

Ian Ashdown
Philippe Bekaert
Edwin Blake
Chris Buehler
Alan Chalmers
Per Christensen
Cyrille Damez
Paul Diefenbach
Reynald Dumont
David Ebert
Jean-Dominique Gascuel
Djamchid Ghazanfarpour
Amy Gooch
Pascal Guitton
Jean-Marc Hasenfratz
John Hughes
Alexander Keller
William Leeson
David Luebke
Stephen Marschner
Ann McNamara
Tsoi Nam
Shaun Nirenstein
Marc Ouellette
Frederic Perez
Pierre Poulin
Claudio Rocchini
Stephan Schaefer
T. Sellares
Harry Shum
Mel Slater
John Snyder
Michael Stark
Wolfgang Stürzlinger
Lázló Szirmay-Kalos
Nicolas Tsingos
Carlos Ureña
Bruce Walter
Harold Westlund
Tien-Tsin Wong
Steve Worley

Author Index

Measuring Visual Shape using Computer Graphics Psychophysics

M. S. Langer   H. H. Bülthoff

Max-Planck-Institute for Biological Cybernetics, Tübingen, Germany
www.kyb.tuebingen.mpg.de/bu
{michael.langer, heinrich.buelthoff}@tuebingen.mpg.de

Abstract. This paper reviews recent psychophysical methods that have been developed for measuring the perceived shape of objects. We discuss two types of shape ambiguities that exist for many objects – a depth reversal ambiguity and an affine ambiguity. We show that people perceptually resolve these shape ambiguities by making strong prior assumptions the object.

1   Introduction

When we open our eyes and look at the objects around us, we typically feel confident that we can judge the 3-D shapes of the objects we see. The pattern of light that is reflected from these objects depends on several independent factors, however: the shape of the objects, the material of the objects and the light field surrounding the objects. The human visual systems is somehow able to disentangle these factors, and produce a coherent percept of an object from of an image. We would like to understand better how the visual system achieves such coherent percepts. To do so, we must develop methods for measuring what people actually perceive when they look at objects.

In this paper we are concerned mostly with the perception of object shape, rather than perception of lighting or material. The main question we address is how one can experimentally measure perceived shape using psychophysical methods. By "psychophysical," we mean that we treat a person's visual system as a black box: an instrument for measuring some physical property of the world, in this case the shape of objects. Using psychophysics, we would like to characterize this instrument in terms of its biases, noise properties, etc. Psychophysics is to be distinguished from methods that study the neural implementation of perception, such as functional magnetic resonance imaging (fMRI), electro– or magneto–encephalography (EEG or MEG), or single cell electrophysiology.

We invite people "off the street" – so–called "naive observers" – and ask them specific questions about the 3-D shapes that they see when they look at pictures of objects. Naive observers are usually willing to give an hour of their time for such experiments. Our challenge is, given that hour, which objects should we show the observers and which questions should we ask in order to measure the perceived shape? In this paper, we review some of the psychophysical approaches typically taken and some of the findings. We concentrate on methods that have used computer graphics - hence the phrase "computer graphics psychophysics."

Why is this psychophysical research relevant to computer graphics rendering? The basic answer is that, even though observers are remarkably good at perceiving object shape, they nevertheless suffer from certain fundamental limitations which are inherent in the vision problem, namely, a image of an object does not uniquely determine the shape, material, and illumination of that object. We can show using psychophysical methods that observers get around these limitations by making very strong prior assumptions about the object and scene, and stick to these assumptions even in the presence of contradictory image information. These assumptions are remarkably consistent from observer to observer. These results are relevant for computer graphics since, by understanding better the prior assumptions that observers make, we will be better able to render images in a manner that is consistent with these assumptions.

This paper consists of two parts. First, we review several psychophysical methods that have been used to measure perceived shape. Second, we discuss two inherent ambiguities in the perception of object shape and how observers resolve these ambiguities by making prior assumptions about what they are looking at.

2 Measuring perceived shape

2.1 Single point

A common method for measuring perceived shape is to mark a single point on a surface and to ask an observer about the shape of the surface at that point. Is the surface slanted to the right or to the left? Is the surface curved or flat? If it is curved, is it elliptical or hyperbolic [MKK96]? Is the point on a hill or in a valley [LBss]? Such judgments can be made very quickly, typically in one second or so even by naive observers, and so an observer can make such judgments at a rate of several thousand per hour.

2.2 Pair of points

Observers might be shown instead a pair of points and asked to discriminate the depth of these points, *i.e.* to judge which point is further away from the eye [TR89, KvDK96, LBss]. Pairs of points can also be used to measure how well observers can discriminate the relative orientation of two nearby points [TN95, NT96, RTY95].

2.3 Binocular depth probe

One can use a binocular probe to measure perceived depth directly. An observer may be presented with a rendered image monocularly, and a point probe binocularly. The binocular disparity of the probe – that is, the difference in the image positions of the probe in the two eyes — provides a depth cue for the observer [Gre70]. Observers are asked to judge whether the probe is in front of or behind the surface [SB87], or are asked to manipulate the perceived depth of the probe interactively until the probe appears to lie on the surface [BM88]. The binocular disparity value at which the probe appears to lie on the surface is then a direct measure of perceived depth at that point (see also [KKT+96]). By sampling the perceived depth values over the surface, one obtains an estimate of the perceived depth map. This depth map may be thought of as a z–buffer (to borrow computer graphics jargon). It is a depth may that is registered with the intensity image.

One limitation of a binocular depth probe is that the probe may perceptually interact with the surface [BM88]. For example, when the depth of the probe is manipulated interactively, the probe can perceptually stick to the surface and stretch or compress the perceived surface in depth as the stereo disparity of the probe is varied. Such interactions between the probe and the image should be avoided if possible.

2.4   Depth gradient probe

Surface depth is an important property of perceived shape. However, depth information is often not directly available in the image. Cues such as texture and shading reveal information about the depth gradient of a surface rather than about the absolute depth [Ste83]. For example, under collimated lighting, shading depends on the local surface normal direction relative to the light field in which the surface is embedded.

One method for measuring the depth gradient on a surface is to show observers a *graphical probe* such as an ellipse. Observers are asked to fit this ellipse to the surface by imagining that the ellipse is a disk that is lying on the surface. The ellipse may be superimposed on the image [SB87] or it may be shown alongside the image [MT86, MLM97]. Using a mouse, the observer may manipulate the aspect ratio and the 2-D orientation of the ellipse until the perceived disk appears to be co-tangent to the surface [KvDK92]. The aspect ratio and orientation of the ellipse then provide a direct measure of the perceived depth gradient at that point. The perceived depth gradients may be sampled over the image and from these samples one can obtain an estimate of the global surface depth map via numerical integration.

While the depth gradient probe is a very useful tool for measuring perceived shape, it too has limitations. One limitation is that the probe itself might not be perceived correctly. That is, one cannot assume that the observer's settings of an ellipse provide a "readout" of the perceived depth gradient at a point. There are two issues here. First, perceiving the orientation of a graphical probe is itself a perceptual problem that the visual system must solve, and there is no reason to assume that every observer solves this problem correctly *e.g.* without systematic biases [MLM97]. Second, the perceived orientation of the probe may interact with the perceived orientation of the image, similar to the interaction found in the stereo probe case. These limitations need to be explored further before we can be certain of how to interpret the data obtained with such probes.

2.5   Global shape probe

An alternative method for measuring global surface shape is to show observers two surfaces and ask them to decide whether the shape of the two surfaces match [BM90, RB00]. The surfaces may be presented simultaneously and rendered with different visual cues, for example, with different albedo patterns or under different lighting. One surface might be shown monocularly and the another binocularly. Finally, one surface might be viewed from the front and compared to a profile slice [TM83, TA87].

3   Ambiguities in shape perception

Now that we have discussed some of the methods commonly used for measuring perceived shape, let us discuss some of the ambiguities in the shape perception problem and some of the strategies that the visual system uses to resolve these ambiguities.

Consider an object with Lambertian reflectance. We allow the albedo **a** to vary from point to point on the surface. Suppose the object is illuminated by a collimated light source in direction **L**. Let **N** denote the unit surface normals. The image **I** may be represented as the product,

$$\mathbf{I} = \mathbf{a}\,\mathbf{L}^T\,\mathbf{N}. \qquad (1)$$

Observe that the right hand side of Equation (1) has three independent variables, whereas the left side has only a single variable. Given the variables on the right hand side, it is easy to compute the left hand side. This is the graphics problem. The vision problem is harder. Given the left hand side, the visual system tries to compute what it can about the variables on the right hand side.

It should be clear to the reader that it is impossible to solve the vision problem exactly since there are more unknown variables on the right hand side of Equation (1) than there are known values on the left hand side. And yet, the visual system somehow manages to compute something about the right hand side, since otherwise how would the visual system be able to judge object shape? Let us address what the visual system can compute about the right hand side by trying to understand the ambiguities that are present in Equation (1) and how the visual system resolves these ambiguities.

3.1   Ambiguity 1. Depth reversal

One well known ambiguity is that, if the surface depth map $z(x,y)$ is inverted,

$$z(x,y) \rightarrow -z(x,y)$$

and the light source direction $\mathbf{L} = (l_x, l_y, l_z)$ is reflected about the line of sight

$$(l_x, l_y, l_z) \rightarrow (-l_x, -l_y, l_z),$$

then the same image $\mathbf{I}$ is obtained. (We are assuming orthographic projection here.) This depth reversal ambiguity has been known for centuries [Rit86, Bre26].

The depth reversal ambiguity suggests that objects should flip-flop in depth. This is not what we perceive, however, when we look at typical objects. Rather, object shapes are typically perceived to be stable. What strategies does the visual system use to resolve this depth reversal ambiguity?

One strategy is to use information in the image that is not captured by Eq. (1). For example, cast shadows are not captured by Eq. (1) and can be used to determine the direction of the source and thereby resolve the depth reversal ambiguity [BBC84, EKK93]. A second source of information is binocular stereo. Even the sign of stereo disparity is sufficient for resolve the depth reversal ambiguity [HB93]. Familiarity with the object is an important factor. A hollow mask of a face will typically be seen incorrectly as a convex face [Luc16].

A second strategy is to make prior assumptions about the object or scene. For example, the visual system can make assumptions about the lighting. One well-known assumption is that the light source is above the line of sight rather than below the light of sight [Bre26, Rit86]. The assumption is a natural one since the sun is typically above the line of sight. Another assumption about the lighting, which applies for animation sequences, is that the light source is stationary [KMK97]. Other assumptions concern the surface geometry. For example, it has been shown that a floor orientations are preferred over ceiling orientation, that is, the visual system prefers to interpret the surface as if it is viewed from above rather than from below [RT90]. Again this is a natural assumption. We tend to see more floors than ceilings and we tend to see the tops of objects more than the bottoms of objects. A second assumption about surface geometry is that the surface bounds a globally convex object, *i.e.* the surface is the boundary of a solid object rather than the interior of a hollow mould or shell. This too is a natural assumption. Most objects seen in isolation are solid rather than shell-like.

Which of the many strategies do observers use to resolve the depth reversal ambiguity? Let us present an example of how we can address this question using computer graphics psychophysics. Figure 1 shows two rendered images of smooth bumpy surfaces. The surfaces have uniform Lambertian reflectance and are rendered using RADIANCE [War94]. One of the surfaces is a concave hemi-cylinder and the other is a convex hemi-cylinder. Although the depth reversal ambiguity applies to these surfaces in theory, the reader will note that the surfaces do not flip-flop in depth. Rather, there is a compelling sense of the shape of the surface, in particular, which points are local hills and which points are the local valleys. One can imagine answering questions about the depth gradient or the curvature at isolated points in the image. Although the depth reversal ambiguity implies that one should *not* be able to answer such questions, it is clear that we are able to answer them. What strategies does the visual system use to solve this shape perception problem?

Let us describe an experiment we recently carried out to answer this question. The experiment used many surfaces similar to those in Figure 1. Half of the surfaces were concave hemi-cylinders and the other half were convex hemi-cylinders. Each surface was rendered under two different lighting conditions. The source was either slightly above the line of sight or was slightly below the line of sight. Images were presented on a monitor in a dark room and viewed monocularly on a CRT from a distance of 80 cm. This provided the correct perspective. A small black probe was superimposed on each image and the observer was asked to judge whether the probe was on a local hill or in a local valley, one of these answers being correct in each case. Each observer made 512 of such judgments. To test the possible assumptions that observers were making to resolve the depth reversal ambiguity, we used three independent conditions. (1.) The light source was either above the line of sight or below it. (2.) The probe was either above or below the horizontal mid-line of the object, and hence was either on a floor–like or a ceiling–like region of the surface. (3.) The surface was either globally convex (a solid) or globally concave (a hollow shell). We balanced the conditions such that each of the eight combinations ($2 \times 2 \times 2$) was tested 64 times.

Percent correct scores are shown in Figure 1. We see that each of the three assumptions played a role. Observers scored highest if the light was from above, if the surface had a floor orientation near the probe, and if the surface was globally convex. Performance fell off as each of these assumptions was violated. It was interesting to note that performance overall was at chance (48 % correct). This indicates that shadows and perspective information were not used in the task. Rather, observers performed the task as if this information was not present in the image.

3.2   Ambiguity 2. Affine invariance

A second general ambiguity was discovered recently by researchers in computer vision [BKY97]. Consider the following affine transformation of a surface depth map,

$$z(x, y) \rightarrow \lambda z(x, y) + \mu x + \nu y, \qquad (2)$$

where $\lambda > 0$. This transformation corresponds to a depth scaling plus an additive slanted plane. Depth is compressed if $\lambda \in (0, 1)$ and expanded if $\lambda > 1$, and the μ and ν variables define the slant of the added depth plane.

When the depth map is transformed as above, the unit surface normals undergo a transformation point-wise,

$$\mathbf{N} \rightarrow \frac{1}{\| \mathbf{G} \mathbf{N} \|} \mathbf{G} \mathbf{N}$$

where

$$\mathbf{G} = \begin{pmatrix} \lambda & 0 & -\mu \\ 0 & \lambda & -\nu \\ 0 & 0 & 1 \end{pmatrix}.$$

6

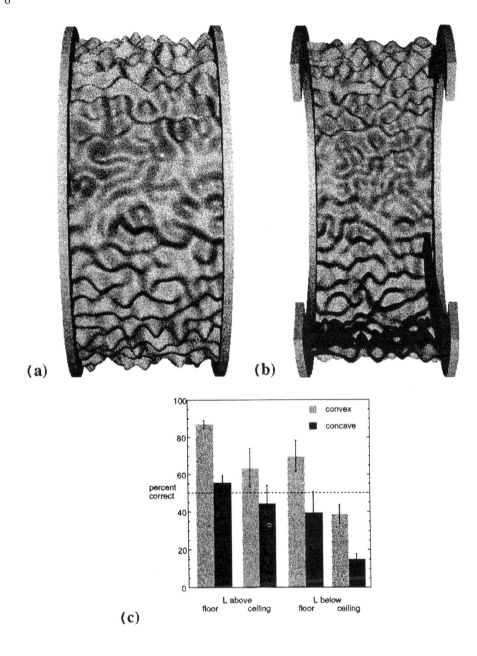

Fig. 1. Two surfaces are shown (a.) a globally convex surface illuminated from above (b.) a globally concave surface illuminated from below. Nine observers judged whether isolated points on many such surfaces were "on a hill" or "in a valley." (c.) Percent correct scores were higher when the light source is from above, when the surface is convex, and when the point lies on a floor–like region of the surface. Error bars show the standard error of the mean of observer's scores for each of the eight combinations of conditions.

If we also consider a transformation of the light source vector,

$$\mathbf{L} \rightarrow (\mathbf{G}^{-1})^T \mathbf{L}$$

and a transformation of the albedo

$$a \rightarrow \parallel \mathbf{G}\,\mathbf{N} \parallel a$$

then it is easy to show that these transformed variables yield exactly the same image $\mathbf{I}$ as the original object. Remarkably, this affine transformation of the object and lighting leaves the shadowed regions of the surface unchanged (see [BKY97] for a proof). This implies that the affine ambiguity holds for an arbitrary sum of collimated light sources, not just for a single collimated source. To summarize, we have that for any surface seen under orthographic projection, there is a family of affine related surfaces that produce exactly the same images.

This affine ambiguity appears to be related to a recent psychophysical finding that used depth gradient probes to recover global depth maps by integration. It was found that, although the depth maps of different observers were dissimilar in an absolute Euclidean sense, they were very similar in an affine sense [KvDK92]. One observer's depth map could be fit to another observer's depth map quite well by an affine transformation such as Eq. (2).

How do observers choose among the family of affine-related surfaces when perceiving the surface shape? Several possibilities come to mind. If the object is a familiar shape such as a human figure then observers might perceive a shape that is consistent with the many other human figures that have been seen before. Such prior information about shape may be learned from observer movement and stereo vision. For example, it has been demonstrated using a computational model that knowledge of 200 face shapes can be used to reconstruct the shape of a new face, from only a single image [BV99]. Other prior assumptions about shape might be used as well. Bilateral symmetry may be preferred, especially if the object is an animal. Observers might also prefer surfaces in which the albedo variation is minimal. A surface whose albedo is constant might be preferred over one in which the albedo is varying.

One strategy for which there is considerable evidence is that observers have a bias to see darker points as further away. Such a bias for dark-means-deep has been observed in several studies that examined local shape perception [CK97, LBss]. The bias seems to extend from local shape to global shape perception as well. One study that reconstructed a depth map from local depth gradients found that the overall slant of the surface varied by ±4 degrees as the light source direction was moved. When the source was above and to the left, the upper–left part of the surface appeared closer to the observer than when the light source was from the lower–right, in which case the lower right part of the surface appeared closer to the observer [KvDCL96]. The dark–means–deep bias is a natural one to make, in the sense that indentations of a surface tend to be dark because they tend to lie in shadow [LZ94] whereas protrusions tend to be bright because they are fully illuminated. Further studies are needed of course to explore other strategies observers use for resolving the affine ambiguity.

8

4 Discussion

When talking about *the shape* that an observer perceives when looking at an object, one needs to keep several issues in mind. The retina does not sample all visual directions uniformly but rather the sampling density is greatest near the line of sight. Thus for a single glance at an object, observers process some image regions much more than others. Observers can compensate for this limitation to some extent by making eye movements to explore the various parts of an image. However, one should not get the idea that there is a single high resolution z-buffer in the brain in which observers piece together the local shapes computed from each glance. Rather, as observers explore an image with eye movements, much of the information about surface shape that is computed in one glance is lost in the next. The depth maps that are computed by the experimenter from a set of measurements of perceived depth gradients (recall Sec. 2.4) should not be taken literally as a readout of the brain's z-buffer. Rather, they should be regarded as a way of studying how perceived shape varies *e.g.* as a function of the observer or as a function of an independent scene variable such as light source direction.

These issues raise a host of questions. What strategies do observers use to actively explore an image with eye movements? How are perceived shapes (or surface materials) retained and integrated from one eye movement to the next? Such questions can be addressed, in principle, by tracking eye movements and by changing the images in a systematic way in real time as an observer actively explores an image. Such studies are at the forefront of computer graphics psychophysics and are just now getting underway. In the coming years we will surely see several exciting new approaches to measuring perceived shape. These approaches will take us closer to our goal of understanding what observers perceive when they look at graphically rendered images. They should also provide key insights into how we can render images so that observers see what we want them to see, rather than what their brains want them to see.

References

BBC84.   K. Berbaum, T. Bever, and C.S. Chung. Extending the perception of shape from known to unknown shading. *Perception*, 13:479–488, 1984.

BKY97.   P. Belhumeur, D. Kriegman, and A. Yuille. The bas-relief ambiguity. In *Proceedings of the IEEE Conference on Computer Vision and Pattern Recognition*, pages 1060–1066, San Juan, Puerto Rico, June 1997.

BM88.   H. Bülthoff and H. Mallot. Interaction of depth modules: Stereo and shading. *Journal of the Optical Society of America*, 5:1749–1758, 1988.

BM90.   H. Bülthoff and H. Mallot. *AI and the eye*, chapter Integration of stereo, shading, and texture, pages 119–146. Wiley, 1990.

Bre26.   D. Brewster. On the optical illusion of the conversion of cameos into intaglios and of intaglios into cameos, with an account of other analogous phenomena. *Edinburgh Journal of Science*, 4:99–108, 1826.

BV99.   V. Blanz and T. Vetter. Morphable model for the synthesis of 3d faces. In *SIGGRAPH Conference Proceedings*, pages 187–194, 1999.

CK97.   C. G. Christou and J. J. Koenderink. Light source dependence in shape from shading. *Vision Research*, 37(11):1441–1449, 1997.

EKK93.   R. Erens, A. Kappers, and J. J. Koenderink. Perception of local shape from shading. *Perception and Psychophysics*, 54(2):145–156, 1993.

Gre70.   R. Gregory. *The Intelligent Eye*. MacGraw-Hill, New York, 1970.

HB93.   H. Hill and V. Bruce. Independent effects of lighting, orientation, and stereopsis on the hollow-face illusion. *Perception*, 22:887–897, 1993.

KKT⁺96.   J. J. Koenderink, A. M. L. Kappers, J. T. Todd, J. F. Norman, and F. Philips. Surface range and attitude probing in stereoscopically presented dynamic scenes. *Journal of Experimental Psychology: Human Perception and Performance*, 22:869–878, 1996.

KMK97.   D. Kersten, P. Mamassian, and D. C. Knill. Moving cast shadows induce apparent motion in depth. *Perception*, 26(2):171–192, 1997.

KvDCL96. J. J. Koenderink, A. J. van Doorn, C. Christou, and J. S. Lappin. Perturbation study of shading in pictures. *Perception*, 25(9):1009–1026, 1996.

KvDK92.   J. Koenderink, A. van Doorn, and A. Kappers. Surface perception in pictures. *Perception and Psychophysics*, 52(5):487–496, 1992.

KvDK96.   J. J. Koenderink, A. J. van Doorn, and A. M. L. Kappers. Pictorial surface attitude and local depth comparisons. *Perception and Psychophysics*, 1996.

LBss.   M. S. Langer and H. H. Bülthoff. Depth discrimination from shading under diffuse lighting. *Perception*, 2000 (in press).

Luc16.   M. Luckiesh. *Light and shade and their applications*. Van Nostrand, 1st edition edition, 1916.

LZ94.   M. Langer and S. Zucker. Shape-from-shading on a cloudy day. *Journal of the Optical Society of America A*, 11(2):467–478, 1994.

MKK96.   P. Mamassian, D. Kersten, and D. Knill. Categorical local-shape perception. *Perception*, 25:95–107, 1996.

MLM97.   P. Mamassian, M. S. Landy, and L. T. Maloney. Global shape and surface orientation. *Investigative Ophthalmology and Visual Science*, 1997.

MT86.   E. Mingolla and J. Todd. Perception of solid shape from shading. *Biological Cybernetics*, 53:137–151, 1986.

NT96.   J. F. Norman and J. T. Todd. The discriminability of local surface structure. *Perception*, 25:381–398, 1996.

RB00.   J. C. Rodger and R. A. Browse. Choosing rendering parameters for effective communication of 3d shape. *IEEE Computer Graphics and Applications*, 2000.

Rit86.   D. Rittenhouse. Explanation of an optical deception. *Transactions of the American Philosophical Society*, 2:37–43, 1786.

RT90.   F. R. Reichel and J. T. Todd. Perceived depth inversion of smoothly curved surfaces due to image orientation. *Journal of Experimental Psychology: Human Perception and Performance*, 16(3):653–664, 1990.

RTY95.   F. D. Reichel, J. T. Todd, and E. Yilmaz. Visual discrimination of local surface depth and orientation. *Perception and Psychophysics*, 57(8):1233–1240, 1995.

SB87.   K. Stevens and A. Brookes. Probing depth in monocular images. *Biological Cybernetics*, 56:355–366, 1987.

Ste83.   K. Stevens. Slant-tilt: the visual encoding of surface orientation. *Biological Cybernetics*, 46:183–195, 1983.

TA87.   J. Todd and R. Akerstrom. Perception of three-dimensional form from patterns of optical texture. *Journal of Experimental Psychology: Human Perception and Performance*, 13(2):242–255, 1987.

TM83.   J. Todd and E. Mingolla. Perception of surface curvature and direction of illumination from patterns of shading. *Journal of Experimental Psychology: Human Perception and Performance*, 9(4):583–595, 1983.

TN95.   J. T. Todd and J. F. Norman. The visual discrimination of relative surface orientation. *Perception*, 24:855–866, 1995.

TR89.   J. Todd and F. Reichel. Ordinal structure in the visual perception and cognition of smoothly curved surface. *Psychological Review*, 96(4):643–657, 1989.

War94.   G. J. Ward. The radiance lighting simulation and rendering system. *Computer Graphics*, pages 459–472, July 1994.

Metropolis Light Transport for Participating Media

Mark Pauly   Thomas Kollig   Alexander Keller

ETH Zürich   University of Kaiserslautern
pauly@inf.ethz.ch   {kollig, keller}@informatik.uni-kl.de

Abstract. In this paper we show how Metropolis Light Transport can be extended both in the underlying theoretical framework and the algorithmic implementation to incorporate volumetric scattering. We present a generalization of the path integral formulation that handles anisotropic scattering in non-homogeneous media. Based on this framework we introduce a new mutation strategy that is specifically designed for participating media. Our algorithm includes effects such as volume caustics and multiple volume scattering, is not restricted to certain classes of geometry and scattering models and has minimal memory requirements. Furthermore, it is unbiased and robust, in the sense that it produces satisfactory results for a wide range of input scenes and lighting situations within acceptable time bounds.

1 Introduction

Many global illumination algorithms have been developed for solving the light transport problem, yet the majority of these methods focuses on scenes without participating media. Volumetric effects due to clouds, fog, smoke or fire can greatly enhance the realism of a rendered image, however, and in many applications are the decisive factor of the simulation. Visibility analysis for traffic or building design, fire research, flight simulation, and high-quality special effects in animation systems all rely on a realistic depiction of volumetric phenomena [Rus94].

Global illumination algorithms for participating media can be classified according to the directional behaviour (isotropic/anisotropic, single/multiple scattering) and spatial variation (homogeneous/inhomogeneous) of the supported media. Finite element methods for isotropic scattering include zonal methods [RT87] and other extensions to the classical radiosity approach, such as hierarchical radiosity [Sil95, Bha93]. Anisotropic scattering was modeled deterministically using spherical harmonics [KVH84], discrete ordinates [LBC94] and point collocation [BT92]. All these algorithms require some discretization of the volume or the directional space into finite elements and compute the interactions between these elements. Thus excessive amounts of memory are required to effectively capture sharp discontinuities of the illumination (e.g. caustics) or uneven directional distributions (e.g. glossy reflections).

Monte Carlo methods are a promising alternative and have been used extensively in global illumination. In the context of participating media, various extensions to existing Monte Carlo approaches have been proposed. Pattanaik and Mudur [PM93] presented a Monte Carlo light tracing algorithm that generates random walks starting from the light sources. They sample interaction points in the volume according to the transmittance of the medium. Lafortune and Willems [LW96] improved on this approach by creating paths both from the light sources and the eye and combining all valid connections between these paths in a multiple sample estimate [VG95]. This led to a bidirectional path tracing algorithm for non-emitting media. A two-pass algorithm based on photon density estimation was presented by Jensen and Christensen in [JC98]. Although simple and efficient the method suffers from various artifacts (e.g. blurred shadow and caustic borders) and requires substantial amounts of memory for difficult lighting situations. In [VG97] a new global illumination algorithm was proposed, the Metropolis light transport (MLT) algorithm. This first application of the Metropolis sampling technique [MRR+53] to the field of computer graphics resulted in a versatile Monte Carlo method for image synthesis.

In this paper we show how the MLT algorithm can be extended to include volumetric scattering. Section 2 briefly reviews the fundamental equation governing the equilibrium distribution of light in scenes with participating media. In section 3 we extend the path integral framework and show how it can be applied to solve the light transport problem. Section 4 is concerned with different aspects of sampling and presents an improved ray marching algorithm. Rendering with the Metropolis light transport algorithm is described in section 5, where we introduce a new mutation strategy for participating media. We present our results in section 6 and draw the conclusions in the final section.

2 Light Transport for Participating Media

We consider the radiance distribution in a finite volume $\mathcal{V} \subset \mathbb{R}^3$. $\partial \mathcal{V}$ is the boundary of $\mathcal{V}$, i.e. a finite set of surfaces describing the objects of the scene. The space between objects is denoted by $\mathcal{V}^0 := \mathcal{V} \setminus \partial \mathcal{V}$, and can be filled with participating media. According to the theory of radiative transfer [Cha50], the equilibrium distribution of radiance L in $\mathcal{V}^0$ is given by the *global balance equation*

$$\omega \cdot \nabla L(x,\omega) = L_{e,\mathcal{V}^0}(x,\omega) + \sigma_s(x) \int_{S^2} f_p(\omega,x,\omega') L(x,\omega')\, d\omega'$$
$$- \sigma_a(x) L(x,\omega) - \sigma_s(x) L(x,\omega). \tag{1}$$

It describes the spatial variation of radiance due to emission, in-scattering, absorption and out-scattering. $L_{e,\mathcal{V}^0}$ is the volume emittance function that defines volumetric light sources such as fire or plasma. S^2 is the unit sphere of all directions, σ_s and σ_a are the scattering and absorption coefficients, respectively, and f_p is the phase function, which describes the scattering characteristics of the medium. If f_p is independent of direction, we have isotropic scattering, which is analogous to perfectly diffuse reflection on surfaces. If σ_a and σ_s are independent of position, we have a homogeneous medium. To obtain a complete description of L in $\mathcal{V}$ we need to specify the boundary conditions for $x \in \partial \mathcal{V}$, given by the *local scattering equation*

$$L(x,\omega) = L_{e,\partial \mathcal{V}}(x,\omega) + \int_{S^2} f_s(\omega,x,\omega') L(x,\omega') \cos \Theta_x\, d\omega', \tag{2}$$

where f_s is the bidirectional scattering distribution function (BSDF), Θ_x is the angle between ω' and the surface normal in x, and $L_{e,\partial \mathcal{V}}$ defines the emittance on surfaces. We now derive the Fredholm integral equation of the second kind, describing the light transport in the presence of particpating media. The resulting integral equation will be solved using the Neumann series. Incorporating the boundary conditions (2) into equation (1) [Arv93] yields the integral equation

$$L(x,\omega) = \tau(x_{\partial\mathcal{V}},x)L(x_{\partial\mathcal{V}},\omega) \tag{3}$$

$$+ \int_{x_{\partial\mathcal{V}}}^{x} \tau(x',x)\left[L_{e,\mathcal{V}0}(x',\omega) + \sigma_s(x')\int_{S^2} f_p(\omega,x',\omega')L(x',\omega')d\omega'\right]dx',$$

where $x_{\partial\mathcal{V}} := h(x,-\omega) \in \partial\mathcal{V}$ is the closest surface point from x in direction $-\omega$ determined by the ray casting function h. Equation (3) expresses radiance as the sum of the exitant radiance at $x_{\partial\mathcal{V}}$ and the accumulated emitted and in-scattered radiance between $x_{\partial\mathcal{V}}$ and x. These components are attenuated by the path transmittance

$$\tau(x,x') := e^{-\int_x^{x'} \sigma_e(x'')dx''},$$

which accounts for absorption and out-scattering with the extinction coefficient $\sigma_e := \sigma_a + \sigma_s$. We define the *incident surface emittance* (with $x_{\partial\mathcal{V}}$ as above) as

$$L_{i,\partial\mathcal{V}}(x,\omega) := \tau(x_{\partial\mathcal{V}},x)L_{e,\partial\mathcal{V}}(x_{\partial\mathcal{V}},\omega),$$

the *incident volume emittance* as

$$L_{i,\mathcal{V}0}(x,\omega) := \int_{x_{\partial\mathcal{V}}}^{x} \tau(x',x)L_{e,\mathcal{V}0}(x',\omega)dx',$$

the *surface light transport operator* as

$$(\mathbf{T}_{\partial\mathcal{V}}L)(x,\omega) := \tau(x,x_{\partial\mathcal{V}})\int_{S^2} f_s(\omega,x_{\partial\mathcal{V}},\omega')L(x_{\partial\mathcal{V}},\omega')\cos\Theta_{x_{\partial\mathcal{V}}}d\omega',$$

and the *volume light transport operator* as

$$(\mathbf{T}_{\mathcal{V}0}L)(x,\omega) := \int_{x_{\partial\mathcal{V}}}^{x} \tau(x',x)\sigma_s(x')\int_{S^2} f_p(\omega,x',\omega')L(x',\omega')\,d\omega'dx'.$$

Using these definitions we can rewrite equation (3) in operator notation as

$$L = \underbrace{(L_{i,\partial\mathcal{V}} + L_{i,\mathcal{V}0})}_{=:L_i} + \underbrace{(\mathbf{T}_{\partial\mathcal{V}} + \mathbf{T}_{\mathcal{V}0})}_{=:\mathbf{T}}L,$$

which clearly exhibits the Fredholm integral equation structure. Given that $\|\mathbf{T}^\alpha\| < 1$, $\alpha \in \mathbb{N}$, which holds for all physically valid scene models where no perfect reflectors or transmitters exist, the Neumann series can be applied:

$$L = \sum_{j=0}^{\infty} \mathbf{T}^j L_i = \sum_{j=0}^{\infty} (\mathbf{T}_{\partial\mathcal{V}} + \mathbf{T}_{\mathcal{V}0})^j (L_{i,\partial\mathcal{V}} + L_{i,\mathcal{V}0})$$

$$= L_{i,\partial\mathcal{V}} + L_{i,\mathcal{V}0} + \mathbf{T}_{\partial\mathcal{V}}L_{i,\partial\mathcal{V}} + \mathbf{T}_{\mathcal{V}0}L_{i,\partial\mathcal{V}} + \cdots \tag{4}$$

3 Generalized Path Integral Formulation

To generate an image of size M we need to compute a set of measurements $I_1,\ldots,I_M$, where each I_j corresponds to a pixel value. By defining a set of sensor responsivity

14

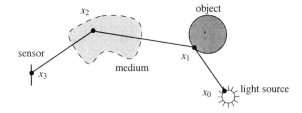

Fig. 1. A typical transport path, defined as an ordered sequence of vertices. In this example, x_0, x_1 and x_3 are on surfaces ($\in \partial \mathcal{V}$), while x_2 is in the volume ($\in \mathcal{V}_0$). The path $\bar{x} = x_0 x_1 x_2 x_3$ thus has the characteristic $l = 1011_b = 11$, i.e. $\bar{x} \in \Omega_3^{11}$.

functions[1] $W_e^{(j)}$, we can express I_j as a scalar product in the *measurement equation*

$$I_j := \int_{\mathcal{V} \times S^2} W_e^{(j)}(x, \omega) L(x, \omega)\, d\omega\, dV(x). \tag{5}$$

In order to apply the Metropolis sampling algorithm, we need to represent I_j as a path integral. This formulation has been introduced in [VG97] for scenes without participating media. We now generalize this scheme, i.e. we define the path space and the measurement contribution function not only for interaction points on surfaces but also for points in the volume.

3.1 Path Space, Measure and Characteristic

A light transport path $\bar{x}$ of length k is represented by $k+1$ vertices x_i, and is classified according to its *path characteristic* $l \in \mathbb{N}$, which determines whether vertices are in the volume or on a surface. For this purpose, let $b_i(l) \in \{0, 1\}$ represent the value of the i-th bit of the binary representation of l, such that b_0 denotes the least significant bit. We define the path characteristic l of a path $\bar{x}$ such that $b_i(l) = 1$ if vertex x_i is on a surface and $b_i(l) = 0$ if x_i is in the volume. The set of all paths of length k with charateristic l is then given as

$$\Omega_k^l := \left\{ \bar{x} = x_0 x_1 \cdots x_k \,\middle|\, x_i \in \begin{cases} \partial \mathcal{V} & \text{if } b_i(l) = 1 \\ \mathcal{V}^0 & \text{if } b_i(l) = 0 \end{cases} \right\},$$

for $1 \le k < \infty$ and $0 \le l < 2^{k+1}$ (see figure 1). A measure μ_k^l on Ω_k^l is defined by

$$\mu_k^l(D) := \int_D \prod_{i=0}^k d\mu_{k,i}^l(\bar{x}),$$

where $D \subseteq \Omega_k^l$ and

$$d\mu_{k,i}^l(\bar{x}) := \begin{cases} dA(x_i), & \text{if } b_i(l) = 1 \\ dV(x_i), & \text{if } b_i(l) = 0 \end{cases}$$

---

[1] These define the response of the sensor, e.g. a film plane, to light incident upon it.

for a path $\bar{x} = x_0 \cdots x_k$. Now we can define the *path space*

$$\Omega := \bigcup_{k=1}^{\infty} \bigcup_{l=0}^{2^{k+1}-1} \Omega_k^l,$$

as the set of all finite-length paths with the associated *path space measure*

$$\mu(D) := \sum_{k=1}^{\infty} \sum_{l=0}^{2^{k+1}-1} \mu_k^l(D \cap \Omega_k^l).$$

3.2 Measurement Contribution Function

The measurement contribution function can be defined directly in terms of paths and path vertices by transforming the integration domain of the inner integration of equation (3) from $\mathcal{S}^2$ to $\mathcal{V}$. The corresponding conversion of measures is reflected in the generalized geometric term[2]

$$G(x \leftrightarrow y) := V(x \leftrightarrow y) \frac{D_x(y) \cdot D_y(x)}{\|x - y\|^2} \tau(x \leftrightarrow y),$$

where $D_x(y) := |\omega_{xy} \cdot \hat{n}(x)|$, if $x \in \partial\mathcal{V}$. ω_{xy} is the unit direction vector from x to y and $\hat{n}(x)$ the surface normal in x. For $x \in \mathcal{V}^0$ we set $D_x(y)$ equal to one. $D_y(x)$ is defined symmetrically. The visibility function $V(x \leftrightarrow y)$ is one if x and y are mutually visible, i.e. if the connecting ray is not blocked by an object, and zero otherwise. We define the measurement contribution function as

$$f_j(\bar{x}) := L_e(x_0 \to x_1)G(x_0 \leftrightarrow x_1) \cdot \tag{6}$$

$$\cdot \left[\prod_{i=1}^{k-1} (\hat{f}(x_{i-1} \to x_i \to x_{i+1})G(x_i \leftrightarrow x_{i+1}))\right] \cdot W_e^{(j)}(x_{k-1} \to x_k),$$

where $\bar{x} = x_0 \dots x_k$,

$$L_e(x \to x') := \begin{cases} L_{e,\partial\mathcal{V}}(x \to x') & x \in \partial\mathcal{V} \\ L_{e,\mathcal{V}^0}(x \to x') & x \in \mathcal{V}^0 \end{cases}$$

and

$$\hat{f}(x \to x' \to x'') := \begin{cases} f_s(x \to x' \to x'') & x' \in \partial\mathcal{V} \\ \sigma_s(x')f_p(x \to x' \to x'') & x' \in \mathcal{V}^0 \end{cases}.$$

Now we can insert the Neumann series (1) into the measurement equation (5), yielding

$$I_j = \sum_{k=1}^{\infty} \sum_{l=0}^{2^{k+1}-1} \int_{\Omega_k^l} f_j(\bar{x})d\mu_k^l(\bar{x}) = \int_{\Omega} f_j(\bar{x})d\mu(\bar{x}). \tag{7}$$

Each integral over Ω_k^l of the above equation corresponds to exactly one addend of equation (4). In physical terms, f_j describes the differential flux that is transported along a path towards pixel j. Equation (7) defines a measurement as an integral over the infinite-dimensional path space. This allows for a whole new set of integration techniques to be applied for solving the light transport problem in the presence of participating media.

---

[2]We use the common arrow notation for specifying a direction. The $\leftrightarrow$ symbol indicates symmetry of the arguments.

4 Sampling

In order to evaluate the path integral (7) we need to build transport paths with respect to an appropriate probability density function (pdf). We split the generation of paths into an alternating sequence of scattering and propagation events: A scattering event chooses a direction at a given vertex x by sampling according to the phase function f_p (for $x \in \mathcal{V}^0$) or the BSDF f_s (for $x \in \partial \mathcal{V}$). A propagation event determines the next interaction point x' in a given direction ω starting from x. This is done by sampling the distance d between x and x' according to the path transmittance τ. The pdf of the whole path is then simply the product of all scattering and propagation pdfs, as these are independent of each other.

4.1 Line Integral Computation

Propagation in the absence of participating media is straightforward, as the new interaction point is uniquely determined by the ray casting function h. If a ray passes through a medium, we generate the next interaction point with the inversion method [HM72], and we obtain an expression for the distance d by normalizing, integrating and inverting τ.

Homogeneous Media. The homogeneous case is simple, because here we have the explicit expression $d = -\ln(1 - \xi)/\sigma_e$, where ξ is a uniformly distributed random variable in $[0, 1)$. All we need to do is compare the sampled d with the distance s to the closest surface point $x_{\partial \mathcal{V}}$. If $d < s$, we set $x' := x + d \cdot \omega$, otherwise we choose $x' := x_{\partial \mathcal{V}}$ and adapt the probability density accordingly.

Inhomogeneous Media. These require more work, since we need to compute d from the implicit equation $\ln(1 - \xi) = \int_0^d \sigma_e(x + t\omega)dt$. This is done with a *ray marching* algorithm [PH89], which accumulates σ_e along the ray (x, ω) until the threshold $\ln(1 - \xi)$ is reached or the surface point $x_{\partial \mathcal{V}}$ is hit. In effect, a ray marching algorithm approximates a one-dimensional integral by dividing the ray into a number of disjoint segments and evaluating σ_e at certain points within each segment. *Equidistant sampling* traverses the ray with constant stepsize Δ, which produces visible artifacts due to aliasing, as depicted in figure 2 (a). The explanation for the layers in the cloud is simple: Light is emitted downwards from the light source at the ceiling and hits the cloud. As the traversal of the cloud data[3] starts at the top surface of its cubic bounding box, the interactions in the medium occur roughly within the same horizontal layers, whose vertical spacing is determined by the size of the ray segments Δ. Consequently, different transport paths that contribute to the same pixel are correlated. These effects can be eliminated by randomly perturbing the sample point within each ray segment, a method known as *jittering*. This leads to *stratified sampling*, a Monte Carlo technique for numerical integration. While stratified sampling reduces aliasing (see figure 2 (b)), it is not a particularly efficient sampling method for this kind of integration problem. Monte Carlo integration is particularly suitable for high-dimensional integrals with discontinuities in the integrand. Here we have a one-dimensional, rather smooth continuous function, favouring deterministic approaches. Therefore we have implemented a combination of equidistant and stratified sampling. Instead of using independent random samples in each ray segment, we choose an initial random offset that is applied to all subsequent

---

[3]We store inhomogeneous media on a three-dimensional grid with intermediate values being computed through tri-linear interpolation.

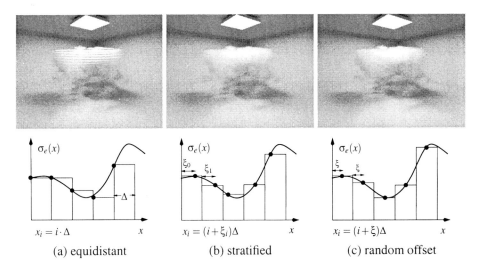

Fig. 2. Different ray marching strategies. The lower picture shows the sampling method, illustrated for box integration. In the upper row is an image generated with this method. Equidistant sampling clearly reveals aliasing artifacts which are no longer visible in the randomized versions of the ray marching algorithm.

samples of the current ray (see 2 (c)). This breaks the correlation of different transport paths (and hence reduces aliasing) but keeps the integration essentially deterministic and thus more efficient. In general we found an efficiency gain of 30-45% for random offset sampling as compared to stratified sampling. Since about 25% of the total computation time of figure 2 are spent on sampling the medium, this leads to an essential decrease in overall rendering time of about 10% for this scene. The samples generated this way can be used as input for an adaptive ray marching scheme as used in [JC98].

5 Rendering

In [VG97] Veach and Guibas presented the Metropolis Light Transport (MLT) algorithm for scenes in vacuum. We have extended this approach to incorporate participating media, based on the generalized version of the path integral as defined in section 3. MLT makes use of the *Metropolis sampling algorithm* [MRR$^+$53], a very powerful method for the simulation of random variables. The basic idea is to generate a random walk $\bar{x}_0, \bar{x}_1, \ldots$ through the path space Ω and deposit a certain constant amount of energy at each pixel a path passes through. The desired image is obtained by distributing the paths proportionally to their contribution to the final image. Metropolis sampling generates this distribution by first proposing a mutation of the current path and computing the corresponding acceptance probability α. Sampling α then determines whether the mutated path is accepted or rejected as the next sample of the random walk. Note that the paths generated this way are correlated, which allows various forms of coherence to be exploited. On the other hand we are faced with a potential increase in variance as compared to independent sampling.

MLT requires an initialization step which determines the total image brightness and generates the seed path for the Markov chain of paths. Similar to [VG97], our initialization uses bidirectional path tracing, which we extended to incorporate participating media [LW96]. A more detailed description of Metropolis sampling and its application to evaluate the path integral can be found in [Vea97].

5.1 Mutation Strategies

Generating a new mutation and computing the corresponding acceptance probability is central to the MLT algorithm. We use a set of different mutation strategies for this purpose and randomly select one of them to create the proposed mutation.

1. *Bidirectional mutations* delete a contiguous section of the current path and replace it with a new path section by appending vertices to both ends of the created subpaths. Adapting the bidirectional mutation strategy described in [VG97] to our generalized path integral framework is straightforward, so we omit a detailed discussion here.

2. *Perturbations* exploit the fact that small variations to the path most likely lead to similar image contributions and hence a high acceptance probability. We distinguish two types of perturbations:

    (a) *Scattering perturbations* displace the direction vector at a certain vertex,
    (b) *Propagation perturbations* displace the interaction point along a certain ray segment.

    The mutated path is then created by retracing the original path, while preserving the path characteristic. In a sense, scattering and propagation perturbations are complementary. The first perturbs a direction hoping to obtain a similiar interaction point, while the latter perturbs an interaction point hoping to obtain a similar direction. The idea of both is to sample path space locally. Once an important path has been found, neighboring paths are explored as well. This is especially beneficial for bright areas of the image, such as caustics. Another important feature of perturbations is that they alter the image location. This leads to a better distribution of paths over the image plane and significantly reduces the variance of the generated images.

We have implemented two scattering perturbations: *Sensor perturbations* alter the location on the image plane[4] and retrace the path towards the light source. This mutation strategy combines the lens and multi-chain perturbations of [VG97]. *Caustic perturbations* retrace the path towards the eye, after perturbing the direction vector of the second path edge from the eye.

Propagation Perturbation. This mutation strategy is specifically designed for participating media. Let $\bar{x} = x_0 \ldots x_k$ denote the current transport path, where x_0 is a point on a light source and x_k is a point on the sensor. Similarly, $\bar{y} = y_0 \ldots y_k$ is the proposed mutation of $\bar{x}$. If x_{k-1} is an interaction point in the medium, i.e. $x_{k-1} \in \mathcal{V}^0$, this vertex is displaced along the line from x_{k-2} to x_{k-1} to obtain y_{k-1}. This new vertex is then connected with the eyepoint to determine the new sensor location y_k. x_{k-1} is moved a distance D in either direction along $x_{k-2}x_{k-1}$ according to the pdf

$$p(D) \propto \frac{1}{D}, \quad D \in [D_{min}, D_{max}],$$

---

[4]We use the common pinhole camera model, specified by an eye point and an image plane, such that each point of the image plane corresponds to exactly one pixel of the final image.

where D_{min} and D_{max} specify the minimal and maximal distance, respectively (see figure 3). If y_{k-1} falls outside the medium, or $x_{k-1} \notin \mathcal{V}^0$ the mutation is rejected, i.e. its acceptance probability is set to zero. Note that propagation perturbation is computationally very cheap as it only requires one occlusion test to check whether the connection with the eyepoint is unobstructed.

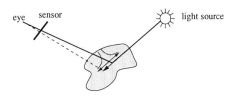

Fig. 3. Propagation perturbation. The interaction point is spatially displaced according to the indicated distribution.

6 Simulation Results

We have implemented our version of the MLT algorithm based on the experimental ray tracing kernel McRender [Kel98], which supports fast BSP ray intersections and occlusion testing. We use a convex combination of Schlick's base functions to model the phase function of the medium, as described in [BLSS93]. The BSDF is modeled with an extension of Ward's reflection model [War92] for isotropic scattering, which includes singular scattering. These scattering models allow a new direction to be generated with the inversion method, which is essential for efficient sampling.

As a minor optimization we estimate paths of length one, i.e. directly visible light sources, with standard ray tracing techniques. Explicit direct lighting calculation has not been implemented so far and it might be worthwhile to incorporate methods such as those described in [War91] or [SWZ96]. This should lead to significant efficiency gains for scenes dominated by direct light. The pinhole camera model imposes some constraints on the use of perturbation strategies, e.g. the caustic perturbation is not effective for caustics seen through a mirror. For the case of a more general camera model with a finite aperture the perturbation strategies can easily be adapted so that such situations are covered. If the light source and the camera aperture are small, however, paths that contain two or more singular scattering interactions separated by a diffuse interaction are not handled well by the MLT algorithm. When perturbing a direction vector (in either direction) and re-tracing the path, the diffuse interaction point will move. From this displaced position we will most likely not hit the sensor respectively the light source, because we must enforce a singular scattering to preserve the path characteristic. Thus the acceptance probability will be low on the average, leading to increased variance. All images were rendered on a single processor HP C3000 with a PA 8500 CPU at 400 MHz. We have only used scenes without surface textures so that the Monte Carlo variance (i.e. noise) and illumination details can be observed more clearly.

Figure 4 (see the color page) features a rendered cloud lit by an approximation of the CIE clear sky model. Figure 5 shows a test scene with a difficult lighting situation. The room is entirely illuminated by indirect light passing through the half-open door. Note that the light source is located at the far end of the adjacent room, i.e. no light can reach the eye without being scattered at least twice. The scene contains glossy surfaces, e.g. the floor, transparent objects, e.g. the glass ball, and an inhomogeneous medium "streaming" through the door. Most other existing global illumination algorithms would perform poorly in this scene. Bidirectional path tracing, for instance, creates transport paths by connecting subpaths that start both from the eye and from the light sources. Most of these connections will be blocked, however, which leads to increased noise in the image. The photon map method [JC98] fails for this scene, because most photons will be located in the adjacent room and thus cannot contribute to the radiance estimate. Here, even the importance driven generation of the photon map [PP98] does not help, because the door slit is too narrow for a sufficient number of photons to pass through (see [KW00] for a detailed discussion of these topics). Metropolis light transport is far superior in this setting. The locality of the perturbation strategies leads to a better coverage of the relevant transport paths. The image of figure 5 is 720 by 576 pixels and has been rendered with 700 mutations per pixel in approximately 6 hours. Note that the table legs are thin metal plates angled towards the center of the table, which explains the different extends of the shadows. MLT will in general perform better if substantial amounts of the transport paths with a high image contribution are clustered in a "small region" of path space. The strong correlation of subsequent samples of the random walk ensures that these regions are sampled adequately.

Figures 6 to 8 show different views of a realistic architectural model with more than 240,000 geometrical primitives and various surface materials. These images clearly demonstrate the robustness of the Metropolis light transport algorithm for participating media in complex environments. The night scene of figures 6 to 8 illuminated by spotlights and street lamps contains more than 700 area light sources and illustrates that MLT easily handles scenes with many light sources. In figure 6 the church is surrounded by a thin homogeneous medium, simulating a foggy atmosphere. This image is 720 by 490 pixels and has been generated with 640 mutations per pixel in 15 hours. Figure 7 shows an example of a volume caustic, created by light being focused from the glass sphere of the sculpture into the medium. This image was rendered in 18 hours with 640 mutations per pixel at 720 by 576 pixels. In Figure 8 the homogeneous medium has been replaced by a cloud modelled with a very large inhomogeneous medium. Using 640 mutations per pixel the image has been rendered in 8 hours at 380 by 490 pixels.

7 Conclusions

We have presented an extension of the Metropolis light transport algorithm that provides a physically-based simulation of global illumination for radiatively participating media. Using an improved version of ray marching, the algorithm handles inhomogeneous media with multiple, anisotropic scattering and can simulate volumetric effects such as volume caustics and color bleeding between media and surfaces. The results show that high quality images are obtained, even for difficult lighting situations, such as strong indirect light or large numbers of light sources.

Since Metropolis light transport is based on point sampling, no discretization of the scene geometry or the directional space is necessary and no memory-intensive data structures are required. This makes the algorithm suitable for complex scenes, e.g. models represented procedurally, by fractals, or acyclic graphs. Furthermore, it easily supports participating media that are defined implicitly or by procedural models. Parallelizing the algorithm is straightforward, e.g. different processes compute separate images that are then averaged to obtain the final result.

We believe that many optimizations of the algorithm are still possible. For instance, different mutation strategies are selected randomly according to a discrete pdf that assigns a constant weight to each mutation strategy. The optimal values for these weights strongly depend on the specific scene, however. For several test scenes (e.g. simple scenes like the cornell box) best results were obtained by weighting the perturbations a hundred times stronger than bidirectional mutations. In these cases the average acceptance probability α for bidirectional mutations is high enough to guarantee an even sampling of all paths $\bar{x}$ with $f_j(\bar{x}) > 0$. Yet in other scenes, e.g. figure 5, bidirectional mutations will on average produce a much lower α. So weighting the perturbations a hunderd times stronger leads to an uneven sampling, as the space of paths is not adequately covered. For the scene of figure 5, for instance, single vertices of the path degenerate to point light sources because their probability of becoming mutated is too low. These vertices located in the adjacent room result in sharp shadow boundary artifacts instead of yielding the correct smooth illumination transition. In order to avoid such severe artifacts a balanced pdf is much more appropriate. All images in this paper have been rendered with equal weights, as we found this to be the most robust setting in general. We are currently working on a heuristic for adaptively determining these weights, which will further increase efficiency.

The propagation perturbation is just one possible mutation strategy that is specifically designed for participating media. Other variations are conceivable, e.g. swapping from the medium to a surface and vice versa.

Acknowledgements

The authors would like to thank Gerald Maitschke at Compaq Computers for supporting this research work by the donation of an Alpha Workstation. Special thanks go to Christa Marx for the models rendered on the colorpage.

References

Arv93.   J. Arvo, *Transfer Functions in Global Illumination*, ACM SIGGRAPH '93 Course Notes - Global Illumination, 1993, pp. 1–28.

Bha93.   N. Bhate, *Application of Rapid Hierarchical Radiosity to Participating Media*, Proceedings of ATARV-93: Advanced Techniques in Animation, Rendering, and Visualization (1993), 43–53.

BLSS93.   P. Blasi, B. Le Saec, and C. Schlick, *A Rendering Algorithm for Discrete Volume Density Objects*, Computer Graphics Forum (Eurographics '93) **12** (1993), no. 3, C201–C210.

BT92.   N. Bhate and A. Tokuta, *Photorealistic Volume Rendering of Media with Directional Scattering*, Third Eurographics Workshop on Rendering (1992), 227–245.

Cha50.   S. Chandrasekhar, *Radiative Transfer*, Clarendon Press, Oxford, UK, 1950.

HM72.   E. Hlawka and R. Mück, *Über eine Transformation von gleichverteilten Folgen II*, Computing (1972), no. 9, 127–138.

JC98.   H. Jensen and P. Christensen, *Efficient Simulation of Light Transport in Scenes with Participating Media using Photon Maps*, SIGGRAPH 98 Conference Proceedings (Michael Cohen, ed.), Annual Conference Series, ACM SIGGRAPH, Addison Wesley, July 1998, pp. 311–320.

Kel98.   A. Keller, *Quasi-Monte Carlo Methods for Photorealistic Image Synthesis*, Ph.D. thesis, Shaker Verlag Aachen, 1998.

KVH84.   J. Kajiya and B. Von Herzen, *Ray Tracing Volume Densities*, Computer Graphics (ACM SIGGRAPH '84 Proceedings) **18** (1984), no. 3, 165–174.

KW00.   A. Keller and I. Wald, *Efficient importance sampling techniques for the photon map*, Interner Bericht 302/00, University of Kaiserslautern, 2000.

LBC94.   E. Languenou, K. Bouatouch, and M. Chelle, *Global Illumination in Presence of Participating Media with General Properties*, Fifth Eurographics Workshop on Rendering (1994), 69–85.

LW96.   E. Lafortune and Y. Willems, *Rendering Participating Media with Bidirectional Path Tracing*, Rendering Techniques '96 (Proc. 7th Eurographics Workshop on Rendering) (1996), 91–100.

MRR⁺53.   N. Metropolis, A. Rosenbluth, M. Rosenbluth, A. Teller, and E. Teller, *Equation of state calculations by fast computation machines*, Journal of Chemical Physics **21** (1953), 1087–1092.

PH89.   K. Perlin and E. Hoffert, *Hypertexture*, Computer Graphics (SIGGRAPH Journal, vol. 23), 1989, pp. 253 – 262.

PM93.   S. Pattanaik and S. Mudur, *Computation of Global Illumination in a Participating Medium by Monte Carlo Simulation*, The Journal of Visualization and Computer Animation **4** (1993), no. 3, 133–152.

PP98.   I. Peter and G. Pietrek, *Importance driven Construction of Photon Maps*, Rendering Techniques '98, 1998, pp. 269–280.

RT87.   H. Rushmeier and K. Torrance, *The Zonal Method for Calculating Light Intensities in the Presence of a Participating Medium*, Computer Graphics (ACM SIGGRAPH '87 Proceedings) **21** (1987), no. 4, 293–302.

Rus94.   H. Rushmeier, *Rendering Participating Media: Problems and Solutions from Application Areas*, Fifth Eurographics Workshop on Rendering (1994), 35–56.

Sil95.   F. Sillion, *A Unified Hierarchical Algorithm for Global Illumination with Scattering Volumes and Object Clusters*, IEEE Transactions on Visualization and Computer Graphics **1** (1995), no. 3.

SWZ96.   P. Shirley, C. Wang, and K. Zimmerman, *Monte Carlo Techniques for Direct Lighting Calculations*, ACM Trans. Graphics **15** (1996), no. 1, 1–36.

Vea97.   E. Veach, *Robust monte carlo methods for light transport simulation*, Ph.D. thesis, Stanford University, 1997.

VG95.   E. Veach and L. Guibas, *Optimally Combining Sampling Techniques for Monte Carlo Rendering*, SIGGRAPH 95 Conference Proceedings, Annual Conference Series, 1995, pp. 419–428.

VG97.   E. Veach and L. Guibas, *Metropolis light transport*, SIGGRAPH 97 Conference Proceedings (Turner Whitted, ed.), Annual Conference Series, ACM SIGGRAPH, Addison Wesley, August 1997, pp. 65–76.

War91.   G. Ward, *Adaptive Shadow Testing for Ray Tracing*, 2nd Eurographics Workshop on Rendering (Barcelona, Spain), 1991.

War92.   G. Ward, *Measuring and Modeling Anisotropic Reflection*, Computer Graphics (SIGGRAPH 92 Conference Proceedings), 1992, pp. 265 – 272.

Editors' Note: see Appendix, p. 391 for colored figures of this paper

Density Control for Photon Maps

Frank Suykens, Yves D. Willems

Department of Computer Science, K.U. Leuven, Belgium
franks,ydw@cs.kuleuven.ac.be

Abstract.   The photon map method allows efficient computation of global illumination in general scenes. Individual photon hits, generated using Monte Carlo particle tracing, are stored in the maps and form a geometry independent representation of the illumination. Two important issues with the photon map are memory requirements to store the photons and the question how many photons are needed for an accurate representation of illumination in a certain scene. In this paper we introduce a method to control the density of photon maps by storing photons selectively based on a local required density criterion. This reduces memory usage significantly since in unimportant or over-dense regions less photons are stored. Results for caustic photon maps and global photon maps representing full illumination show a decrease in number of photons of a factor of 2 to 5. The required density states how accurate the photon map should be at a certain location and determines how many photons are needed in total. We also derive such a criterion based on a novel path-importance-based first pass, taking some steps towards solving the difficult 'how many photons' question.

1 Introduction

Computing global illumination solutions for general scenes is a difficult job. Scenes can be very complex, and the materials used can have arbitrary reflection and refraction properties.

Pure Monte Carlo methods, like path tracing[11] or bidirectional path tracing[12, 20], are capable of computing light transport for such general scenes. They do not store any information in the scene and are therefore capable of rendering very complex geometry. However, not storing the illumination means that it has to be recomputed every time when needed. This can be very inefficient for example for multiple indirect reflections and caustics (or caustics seen through a mirror for bidirectional path tracing).

Two-pass and multi-pass methods address this problem by computing and storing illumination in the scene in one or more preprocessing passes. A final Monte Carlo (or ray-tracing) pass can use this illumination information. In this context, radiosity and light maps[1] have often been combined with ray-tracing[3, 16] or (bidirectional) path tracing[19].

An interesting two-pass algorithm and storage method that uses photon maps was proposed by Jensen[6, 7, 10]. In an initial Monte Carlo particle tracing pass, a number of photons are traced through the scene and stored individually in a kd-tree. To reconstruct radiance at a certain point the nearest photons are located and used in a radiance estimate. Usually a separate high-density caustic photon map for direct visualization is used next to a global photon map for efficiently computing indirect light. The next section gives a more detailed overview of this algorithm.

An advantage of this method is that the storage is independent of the geometry, but rather dependent on the illumination complexity. The method accommodates general material properties and includes all possible global illumination effects.

Disadvantages are the large memory requirements for storing the photons and the more expensive radiance reconstruction (e.g. compared to radiosity) because the nearest photons must be located among all the stored photons. Another difficulty with photon maps is that it's hard to know how many photons should be used for a particular scene in order to get a sufficient accuracy. In most current implementations this number is set by the user, and dependent on his know-how of photon maps and global illumination.

In this paper we introduce density control for photon maps. Photons are only stored in a photon map when a certain required density criterion is not yet met, otherwise their energy is distributed among the nearest neighbors. This approach has two main advantages:

- The density of photon maps can be controlled locally in the scene. Less photons are stored in over-dense or unimportant regions. This can reduce memory requirements quite effectively.
- Introducing the concept of required density, offers an interesting framework for error control in photon maps. Since the density of photon maps is related to their accuracy, a high density should be chosen for important regions in the scene. The required density can be chosen arbitrarily and can be based on principles like view importance, relative error, visual masking by textures, ...

The method is applied first to caustic photon maps and a simple convergence criterion for these maps is presented. A second application uses a novel view-importance-based first pass to determine required densities for global photon maps. The required densities are large for important parts of the scene and the real density of the global map matches closely due to the selective storage.

Both approaches significantly decrease memory requirements and, maybe even more important, they take steps to letting a user choose a more scene-independent accuracy, rather than the number of photons. However many interesting extensions are possible within this framework, and further research is needed to put it to full use.

Another approach to control the density of photon maps, was presented by Peter and Pietrek [15]. They use an importance map to guide more photons to visually important regions in the scene. The photon map is then used for importance sampling in a standard path tracing pass. Their resulting photon maps however contain a mixture of high- and low-powered photons, which can result in higher variance when reconstructing illumination[8]. Our approach offers a more localized control over the density and results in a more smoothly varying photon energy.

The next section describes the current photon map algorithm in more detail establishing some terms and notation. Section 3 describes the new method for selectively storing the photons in the photon map. Section 4 proposes a required density heuristic for the global photon map and the results obtained. Section 5 presents conclusions.

2 Photon Maps

This section briefly describes the standard photon map method as presented by Jensen in [6]. More detailed information can be found in his paper(s).

It is a two-pass method, where in the first pass a high-density caustic map and a lower density global photon map are constructed by tracing particles or photons from the light sources. Photons are only stored on diffuse (D) and (slightly) glossy surfaces (G). The caustic map contains photons that have been reflected specularly (S) a number of times, storing $(L(S)^+(D|G))$ paths. The global photon map stores an approximation to the full global illumination solution ($L(D|G|S)^*(D|G)$ paths).

For each photon i the energy or flux Φ_i, the incoming direction ω_i and the location p_i are stored. From the photon map, reflected radiance L_r can be estimated at a position x on a surface in a direction ω by locating the nearest M photons around x:

$$L_r(x,\omega) \approx \tilde{L}_r(x,\omega) = \sum_{i=1}^{M} f_r(x,\omega_i,\omega) \frac{\Phi_i}{\pi r_M^2(x)}$$

with f_r the BRDF and $r_M(x)$ the maximum distance between x and its M nearest photons. This corresponds to nearest neighbor density estimation[17], where a sphere is expanded to find the nearest neighbors. To efficiently find nearby photons, they are stored in a (possibly balanced) kd-tree.

The second pass is a stochastic ray-tracing pass, that uses the photon maps in different ways. Suppose a path is traced from the eye e and hits a surface in x. In x direct illumination is computed and the caustic map is visualized directly, because caustics are hard to compute using stochastic ray-tracing. For other indirect illumination, scattered rays are spawn say to a point y on another surface. If a diffuse or glossy bounce is made in x, the radiance approximation using the global photon map is used in y. For a specular bounce the same procedure is repeated for y as was done for x.

Advantages of the photon map method are:

- The method includes all possible global illumination effects.
- Storage of photon maps is independent of geometry, allowing it to be applied to very complex scenes.

Our current implementation of the photon map method includes both the caustic and global photon map. For the radiance estimates the number of photons M was set to 50. Some differences with Jensen's method are that we don't (yet) balance our kd-tree, use Ward's irradiance caching [21] for indirect diffuse illumination nor use importance sampling for directions based on the global photon map [5]. These are all optimizations for the second rendering pass to speed up computations. Our rendering pass therefore can take several hours to compute a final image. However in this paper we focus on the construction of the photon maps, and our techniques can be combined with these optimizations without major change.

3 Selective Storage of Photons

When constructing photon maps, the photons are emitted from the light sources according to the emitted radiance distribution. Scattering on surfaces is performed according to the physics involved (proportional to BRDF times cosine). As a result the flux of each photon is the same in case of a single wavelength [8]. Differences can occur when using multiple wavelengths at once (e.g. an RGB color per photon), or when sampling the exact underlying physics is not possible (e.g. analytical sampling of BRDF times cosine impossible).

This way of constructing the maps results in a photon density that follows the illumination intensity in the scene. Brightly lit regions correspond to a high density of the map. A high density also corresponds to a high accuracy when estimating radiance.

However, in very bright regions (e.g. the center part of caustics) the density might be much higher than needed, while other parts (e.g. outer part of caustics, visually important parts of the scene) can have a lower density. To increase the density for these parts, more photons must be shot, but a large percentage will again be stored in the already bright regions.

This observation has lead to the basis of our method: Photons are still generated as before, but storage is controlled using a local required density criterion. If the density is already sufficient, the photon is not stored but its power is distributed over previously stored nearby photons. The next section describes this more formally while section 3.2 describes application to caustics.

3.1 A method for selective storage and redistribution

Suppose we have traced a new photon k to a position x on a surface. Suppose also we can evaluate a certain required density $D_r(x)$ that gives us a measure of how dense the photon map must be at x for accurate reconstruction. Note that in our current method the required density is only dependent on the position, which is sufficient for storage on diffuse and not too glossy surfaces. However if desired, it is possible to adapt all proposed methods to take the incoming directions of the photons into account.

To determine whether or not we want to keep the photon, we estimate the current photon map density $D_c(x)$. This can be done by locating the M nearest photons and evaluating:

$$D_c(x) = \frac{M}{\pi r_M^2(x)}$$

An acceptance probability P_{acc} can now be defined as a function of the density ratio: $s(x) = (D_c(x)/D_r(x))$. For P_{acc} we have tried a step function ($s(x) \leq 1$ accept, otherwise distribute) and a translated cosine, both with good results.

If the photon is accepted it is stored in the photon map, otherwise it's power must be accounted for somehow to keep the global flux in the map consistent with the flux emitted from the light sources.

One simple (and unbiased) way to do this, is to modify the power of accepted photons by $1/P_{acc}$[1], which corresponds to a form of Russian Roulette. However this can lead to huge photon powers and we noticed a significant variance increase in the reconstruction.

Better results were obtained by distributing the photon power over its nearest neighbors. This can be justified as follows:

If we would have stored the photon k then reconstruction of radiance using M+1 photons at x would be:

$$\tilde{L}_r(x,\omega) = \frac{\sum_{i=1}^{M} f_r(x,\omega_i,\omega)\Phi_i + f_r(x,\omega_k,\omega)\Phi_k}{\pi r_M^2(x)}$$

Note that $r_M(x)$ without k stored is equal to $r_{M+1}(x)$ when k is stored, since k is located in x.

Now since we don't store the photon the power of the other photons must be adjusted, so that the reconstruction in x would deliver the same result:

$$\tilde{L}_r(x,\omega) = \frac{\sum_{i=1}^{M} f_r(x,\omega_i,\omega)(\Phi_i + \Delta\Phi_{k,i})}{\pi r_M^2(x)}$$

Different choices for $\Delta\Phi_{k,i}$ can be made depending on f_r and the distance of x to photon i:

---

[1] For this method the acceptance probability may never become zero

- $f_r(x, \omega_i, \omega)$: To get an equal reconstruction $\tilde{L}_r(x, \omega)$ in x, $\Delta\Phi_{k,i}$ should be zero when f_r is zero because these photons do not contribute to $\tilde{L}_r$. Currently the angle between ω_i and the normal n_x in x is used to determine whether $\Delta\Phi_{k,i}$ should be zero (i.e. for a non-transparent material, $\Delta\Phi_{k,i} = 0$ when $cos(\omega_i, n_x) \leq 0$). [2]
- Distance to x: The distribution of the photon power can be seen as applying a low-pass filter (or as splatting). The dependence of $\Delta\Phi_{k,i}$ on the distance to x determines the filter kernel. We distribute the power equally over the affected photons to keep the photon powers homogeneous which, as said, is beneficial for the reconstruction.

So to summarize, we choose:

$$\forall i, cos(\omega_i, n_x) > 0 : \Delta\Phi_{k,i} = \Phi_k/M'$$

with M' the number of photons that have a cosine > 0.

Of course the radiance estimate at other locations than x, will give a slightly modified result. But since the current density is high enough anyway, this averaging can be expected not to introduce artifacts (if the required density does not change too abruptly).

Note that the selective storage requires estimation of the map density during its construction. We store the photons directly in an unbalanced kd-tree so that the lookup is efficient. Before the final rendering pass this tree can be balanced for even faster access.

We now have a method to control the density of photon maps based on a required density D_r. This density can be chosen arbitrarily, depending on the application, providing a flexible density control framework.

3.2 Application: Caustic maps

The selective storage was first tested on a caustic map. In this application the required density D_r for the caustic map is simply chosen to be constant (currently set manually). Caustic photons are then traced through the scene as usual, but the stored density will be limited.

One useful observation is that if the illumination at a certain location is much larger than the caustic map contribution alone, the caustic map does not have to be as accurate since relative errors will be small. From this observation we derived a simple convergence criterion for the caustic map at x: The ratio D_c/D_r is multiplied by a factor dependent on the relative contribution of the caustic radiance $\tilde{L}_c$ compared to the global radiance $\tilde{L}_g$ (which also includes the caustic radiance):

$$C(x) = \frac{D_c(x)}{D_r(x)} F(\tilde{L}_g/\tilde{L}_c)$$

If $C(x) > 1$ the caustic map can be considered converged at this point. Currently F is chosen by hand, and good results were obtained by taking a power of two or three for F. For the radiance reconstructions ($\tilde{L}_g$ and $\tilde{L}_c$) an outgoing direction must be known. We chose it equal to the normal in x. For diffuse surfaces this direction is unimportant, but for glossy materials other choices may be better.

---

[2] Another approach could be to choose a larger delta for photons with a direction similar to the distributed photon. This might be better for non-diffuse brdf's but at the cost of a less smoothly varying photon power.

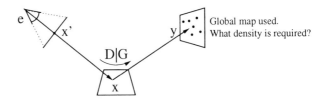

Fig. 1. Illumination from diffuse or glossy reflection is computed using a radiance estimate at y from the global photon map.

Figure 5 shows a scene with a glass egg lit by two light sources. Caustics can be seen to the left and right of the egg. For this image D_r was set to 80000 photons/m^2. There are about 92.000 photons stored in the caustic map using density control. Without this control 190.000 photons would have been stored, while there are no differences in the resulting images. Constructing the density controlled caustic map required 145 seconds (SGI Octane, 195MHz R10000), while constructing the normal caustic map (190.000 photons) required 90 seconds. The extra time is spent in the look-ups needed for the density estimates. This overhead, however, is not a problem since the final rendering is orders of magnitudes slower.

Figure 6 visualizes $C(x)$ (set to $(\tilde{L}_g/\tilde{L}_c)^3$) for this scene. Blue color indicates that $D_c \geq D_r$. This is were the memory is gained. Green color indicates that $D_c < D_r$ but $C(x) > 1$, which means the caustic map is considered converged. Red color means that more photons are needed. Some variance near this regions can be seen in the image.

We also continued the caustic map construction until all regions were converged. This required about 195.000 photons, while without density control 730.000 photons would be stored. So a factor of 2 to 4 can be gained easily (Actually an arbitrary factor can be gained since the number of photons using density control is limited.)

4   A required density estimate based on importance

The selective storage allows the photon map density to be adapted to a certain local required density criterion. Many choices, depending on the application, are possible and in this section we develop a three-pass view-importance-based method that gives a heuristic for the required density of global photon maps. The main idea is that when the final stochastic ray-tracing pass is computed for a certain camera position, the global map density should be high were the contribution to the error of a pixel in the image might be large.

View-importance has been used in many other algorithms, for example to drive a refinement criterion[18] or to direct more paths to important parts of the scene[14, 2]. Lischinski et. al.[13] presented a hierarchical radiosity method with error-driven refinement (also using importance) that considered the effect of interactions on the *total error*.

Our method is derived for eye paths exy of length two (see figure 1), meaning that in x a diffuse or glossy bounce has taken place and the global map is used in y. Extension to longer paths is discussed further on.

4.1 Importance and error

When an image is rendered, the estimated flux Φ_j (or average radiance) of a pixel j will exhibit a certain error E_j, that should be limited depending on the desired image quality. The error E_j is an integral over points x' on the pixel j of the error ϵ on the incoming radiance L:

$$E_j = \int_{A_j} dA_j W_e(e \to x')\epsilon(e \leftarrow x')$$

W_e is the emitted potential[3]. It includes a weighting factor for the camera model used in order not to burden the equations. Note that x' can be replaced by x in this equation.

This equation can be expanded to an integral over surfaces A_y [4] where the global map is used to approximate radiance:

$$E_j = \int_{A_j} dA_j W_e(e \to x) \int_{A_y} dA_y f_r(e, x, y)G(x, y)\epsilon(y \to x) \tag{1}$$

$\epsilon(y \to x)$ is the error made by approximating $L(y \to x)$ with a global map estimate $\tilde{L}(y \to x)$ and $G(x, y)$ is the geometric term: $cos(n_x, x \to y)cos(n_y, y \to x)/\|y - x\|^2$. This equation relates the pixel error to the reconstruction error using the global map at indirectly visible surfaces. Note that E_j does not represent the total error of the pixel because direct light, caustic maps and specular reflected light are not taken into account.

There is a close relation between $\epsilon(y \to x)$ and the density of the photon map (higher density, lower error). This relationship is discussed in section 4.2. Now we want to find a suitable value for ϵ throughout the whole scene, so that we can derive a required density for constructing the global map.

A first assumption is that the error $\epsilon(y \to x)$ is independent of the direction in y. This is no problem for diffuse surfaces but may break down for highly glossy materials. An $\epsilon(y)$ can now be defined as the reconstruction error of the global map in any direction. The error contribution $\delta_j(y)$ made by $\epsilon(y)$ to the total pixel error E_j can now be written as:

$$\delta_j(y) = \frac{dE_j}{dA_y} = \int_{A_j} dA_j W_e(e \to x)f_r(e, x, y)G(x, y)\epsilon(y) \tag{2}$$

We want the error $\epsilon(y)$ to be small if it contributes more to the error of the pixel. Note that this corresponds exactly to the notion of importance. Choosing a constant allowable error δ for any y and j [5], an upper bound for the error in y on a surface is now a minimum over all pixels j of δ divided by the importance of j in y (so that the maximum error in y is determined by the pixel with maximum importance):

$$\epsilon(y) \leq MIN_j \left(\frac{\delta}{\int_{A_j} dA_j W_e(e \to x)f_r(e, x, y)G(x, y)} \right) \tag{3}$$

---

[3] As importance corresponds to flux, potential corresponds to radiance.

[4] The integral is expressed over the area measure dA_y, since the density of the photon maps is also expressed in terms of area.

[5] Actually $E_j = \int_{A_y} dA_y \delta_j(y) = \delta A_y$ with A_y the area seen indirectly through pixel j. This area can be conservatively approximated by for instance the total area of the scene, giving a fixed relationship between the pixel flux error E_j and δ.

30

Fig. 2. Importance of a single **Fig. 3.** Importance of the whole **Fig. 4.** Path based importance pixel (indicated by the white screen for surfaces indirectly approximation for a pixel. Note dot) for surfaces indirectly visible through the screen. the similarity with the real pixel visible through the pixel. Single pixel importances are importance. underestimated.

To compute this upper bound the importance solution for every pixel j is needed separately. Since this is infeasible, most importance based algorithms choose to compute importance for the whole screen at once ($A_j \rightarrow A_{screen}$). This, however, averages the pixel importances, underestimating the typical localized importance of these pixels. Figure 2 and 3 show an example of this difference. In figure 2 the indirect importance of the indicated pixel is visualized, while figure 3 shows the total screen importance. The importance of the wall near the pixel is too low because it is unimportant for many other pixels.

We take a different approach by reducing the pixels to an infinite small size. An upper bound can now be expressed as a minimum over a screen position x' (removing the integral over A_j):

$$\epsilon(y) \leq MIN_{x'} \left(\frac{\delta}{A_{pix} W_e(e \rightarrow x) f_r(e, x, y) G(x, y)} \right) \qquad (4)$$

Note that we include a pixel area factor (A_{pix}) to get results of equal magnitude as in equation (3). It can also be viewed as if the integral in (3) was approximated by one sample x'.

In order to be able to evaluate $\epsilon(y)$ during photon map construction, we introduce a first pass that shoots particles (or importons [15]) from the eye into the scene and stores the upper bound at hit points on the indirectly visible surfaces.

It is important to note that equation (4) does not contain any integrals anymore, so shooting the importons is not a form of Monte Carlo integration, but an arbitrary way to sample a 4D function dependent on x' and y. The generating pdf's are not taken into account and reconstruction of the function can be done by interpolation. This function can be evaluated for the individual paths and we will refer to it as the *path-importance function*.

Since we need the minimum over x' we do not need to store the x' position. $\epsilon(y)$ can be reconstructed by locating nearby importons and *taking the minimum of their values* (A possible variant could take the distance to y into account to get a smoother function).

Figure 4 shows a reconstruction of the maximum importance ($\sim 1/\epsilon$) over x' for one pixel of interest. A good match is obtained with the pixel importance shown in figure 2.

The incoming direction of importons is currently ignored, but could be used for a directional maximum error estimate.

4.2 Error and Density

$\epsilon(y)$ gives us an estimate of the upper error bound allowed in y. To derive the required density $D_r(y)$ at y we need to find the relationship between ϵ and D_r.

This is a difficult question and currently we assume them to be inverse proportional to each other:

$$D_r(y) = \frac{C}{\epsilon(y)}$$

If the allowable error is large, a lower density can be tolerated. The constant C is combined with the other constants in ϵ, into one *accuracy parameter* α of the algorithm, so that:

$$D_r(y) = \alpha \cdot MAX_{x'}(W_e(e \to x)f_r(e, x, y)G(x, y))$$

The parameter α determines the number of stored photons needed in the scene.

This parameter is currently chosen manually and a more detailed analysis of the error vs. density relation is definitely necessary. However, most important is that the constant(s) will be virtually independent of the scene (or at least easily derived from it), since the allowable pixel error and the relation local error - local density are isolated into a manageable form.

4.3 Longer paths

The allowable reconstruction error $\epsilon(y)$ was derived for paths of length two, assuming a diffuse or glossy bounce in x. However it can happen that the global map is used after more than one bounce (e.g. if a specular surface is hit first). Longer paths (e.g. $exzy$) introduce extra integrals over intermediate vertices (z) into the error bound equation.

Accurate evaluation of these integrals for every importance path would be infeasible, and therefore we believe more in a crude but conservative approximation, so that a path-importance function can easily be evaluated for longer individual paths also.

Two common cases where longer paths occur are:

- **Specular bounces:** Integrals introduced by specular bounces are very sharply peaked and can be approximated by a single sample. However convergence or divergence of light rays is not taken into account when using importance functions based on single paths. An interesting approach here would be to incorporate ray differentials, a way to track pixel footprints during ray tracing[4], into the importance evaluation. Our current implementation does not yet deal with specular surfaces in the importance-driven required density case.
- **Corners:** As can be seen in figure 4, pixels near a corner require a very high density on the adjacent wall, because a small area on this wall has a big influence on the pixel error. Jensen recognized this problem and uses an additional bounce when the distance between two path vertices is too small [6]. We have experimented with a crude approximation to the integral one such bounce introduces. A detailed analysis would lead too far, but results were promising and the required density in corners is effectively reduced.

Currently we are investigating techniques to generalize the single-path-importance evaluations so that, when the required density would be too high, automatically extra bounces are introduced. The distinction between specular, glossy or diffuse or corner distance thresholds would not be needed anymore. We believe generalizing ray differentials to arbitrary brdf's would be interesting for this but, as Igehy says, this is still an open question[4].

4.4 Results

We implemented the importance-based required density method into RenderPark[6] and tested it on a number of scenes.

The accuracy parameter α was chosen by hand (10000 was used) for one scene and, as was expected, also gave good results for other scenes. Scenes contained diffuse, some glossy but no specular surfaces. We tested relatively simple scenes, but the method is expected to scale just as well as the standard photon map method.

In a first pass the required density was computed for a certain view using the path-importance-based technique. Figure 8 shows a false-color overview of the computed required density. Blue corresponds to a low density while red is a very high density (a log scale is used). A minimum required density is used if the importance is too low. This explains the constant blue color in unimportant parts of the scene. Due to the glossy desk-pad a higher density is required on the cylinder and parts of the wall. About 80.000 importons were stored in the map, but this number could have been reduced, since many of them corresponded to a lower required density than our minimum.

Using the computed required density, a global photon map was constructed using density control. Figure 9 shows the actual density of the global photon map used to render the image in figure 7. This global map contained only 40.400 photons, while without importance based density control 290.000 photons would have been stored.

Note that the glossy reflections on the desk-pad are using the global map directly from the cylinder and wall. The density there is adequate for these reflections.

Some interesting points learned from the experiments were:

- Not all regions have enough photons according to the required density. However the image shows no artifacts, so probably our accuracy is even set a bit too high or the density-error relationship should be tuned.
- Since we emit photons in the same way as with the standard photon map method, dark regions can require a large number of photons to be traced before they contain enough photons. However the storage remains limited whereas in the standard method this regional density would be infeasible. Importance sampling when emitting photons as in [15] might also be useful to guide photons where more density is needed. However the time to construct the photon maps is in any case still much smaller than the time taken by the final rendering pass.
- We noticed some bias in the reconstruction when a very low-density region with higher powered photons meets a very high-density region, similar to the blurring of caustic borders when using the caustic map. Jensen's technique to reduce caustic blurring[9] could also be used here, or one could try to get a smoother transition from low to high densities. However, it seemed not necessary for the images we rendered.

A few more general remarks about the method:

- The importance-based derivation of the required storage accuracy could also be used for other algorithms, typically other final gathering approaches.
- A similar method could be derived to estimate the required density for the directly visualized caustic map. However the handling of specular bounces should be further developed first.
- As with any importance-based method, the view-independence of, in this case, the global photon map is lost.

---

[6]RenderPark is a physically based rendering system available at www.cs.kuleuven.ac.be/~graphics

5 Conclusion

This paper presented a method to control the density of photon maps. A technique was introduced to selectively store photons in a photon map, while ensuring a correct illumination representation in the map. Storage can be significantly reduced in over-dense or unimportant regions. Benefits of the original method, like the ability to handle complex geometry and materials are preserved.

The decision to store photons is based on a required density criterion, which provides a flexible framework for density control of photon maps. We have applied it to caustic maps and derived a convergence criterion for these maps. Storage gains of a factor 2 and more were obtained.

Also a novel path-based-importance first pass was used to derive the required density for global maps. Dense storage was only necessary in important parts of the scene, leading to less photons in the map. An accuracy parameter can be specified rather than determining the number of photons in the map. This takes us a step closer to answering the 'how many photons' question, a step that might even be more important than the storage reduction.

Although good results were obtained much more research is needed to tune the density control framework and to put it to full use. We assume that the error of recon-struction is simply proportional to the inverse density of the map. However much more advanced relations should be investigated using more scene information, for example:

- The actual illumination could be taken into account. For smoothly varying illumin-ation a high density may not be necessary for a high accuracy or on the other hand a very bright area might have a significant influence although importance is low. Note that these approaches would require a simultaneous construction of illumin-ation and required density maps, since they need each others information.
- Visual masking by high frequency textures or color saturation after tone mapping can reduce the needed density.
- Storage on glossy surfaces could greatly benefit from a directional required density criterion.

Currently we use a fixed number of nearest photons in the reconstruction. A very interesting extension would be to include this number into the framework, for example by adjusting it when the required density is not reached somewhere.

Some other points for future research are the generalization of the path-based im-portance to arbitrary paths and the use of importance sampling to guide photons to regions were more density is needed. Extending the density control to volume photon maps [10] for participating media is also possible.

Acknowledgments

This research was supported by FWO Grant #G.0263.97

References

1. James R. Arvo. Backward Ray Tracing. In *ACM SIGGRAPH '86 Course Notes - Developments in Ray Tracing*, volume 12, August 1986.
2. Philip Dutre and Yves D. Willems. Potential-Driven Monte Carlo Particle Tracing for Diffuse Environments with Adaptive Probability Density Functions. In P. M. Hanrahan and

W. Purgathofer, editors, *Rendering Techniques '95*, pages 306–315, New York, NY, 1995. Springer-Verlag.

3. Paul S. Heckbert. Adaptive radiosity textures for bidirectional ray tracing. *Computer Graphics*, 24(4):145–154, August 1990.

4. Homan Igehy. Tracing ray differentials. *Computer Graphics*, 33(Annual Conference Series):179–186, 1999.

5. Henrik Wann Jensen. Importance driven path tracing using the photon map. In P. M. Hanrahan and W. Purgathofer, editors, *Rendering Techniques '95*, pages 326–335 326–335. Springer-Verlag, New York, 1995. also in Proceedings of the Sixth Eurographics Rendering Workshop, 1995 (Rendering Techniques '95, Springer Verlag).

6. Henrik Wann Jensen. Global illumination using photon maps. In Xavier Pueyo and Peter Schröder, editors, *Eurographics Rendering Workshop 1996*, pages 21–30, New York City, NY, June 1996. Eurographics, Springer Wien. ISBN 3-211-82883-4.

7. Henrik Wann Jensen. Rendering caustics on non-lambertian surfaces. *Computer Graphics Forum*, 16(1):57–64, 1997. ISSN 0167-7055.

8. Henrik Wann Jensen. A practical guide to global illumination using photon maps. In *ACM SIGGRAPH '99 Course Notes - Unpublished*, chapter 7, pages 1–72. 1999.

9. Henrik Wann Jensen and Niels Jørgen Christensen. Photon maps in bidirectional Monte Carlo ray tracing of complex objects. *Computers and Graphics*, 19(2):215–224, March–April 1995.

10. Henrik Wann Jensen and Per H. Christensen. Efficient simulation of light transport in scenes with participating media using photon maps. In *Computer Graphics (ACM SIGGRAPH '98 Proceedings)*, pages 311–320, 1998. r.

11. J. T. Kajiya. The rendering equation. In *Computer Graphics (SIGGRAPH '86 Proceedings)*, volume 20, pages 143–150, August 1986.

12. E. P. Lafortune and Y. D. Willems. A theoretical framework for physically based rendering. *Computer Graphics Forum*, 13(2):97–107, June 1994.

13. Dani Lischinski, Brian Smits, and Donald P. Greenberg. Bounds and Error Estimates for Radiosity. In *Computer Graphics Proceedings, Annual Conference Series, 1994 (ACM SIGGRAPH '94 Proceedings)*, pages 67–74, 1994.

14. S. N. Pattanaik and S. P. Mudur. Adjoint equations and random walks for illumination computation. *ACM Transactions on Graphics*, 14(1):77–102, January 1995.

15. Ingmar Peter and Georg Pietrek. Importance driven construction of photon maps. In G. Drettakis and N. Max, editors, *Rendering Techniques '98 (Proceedings of Eurographics Rendering Workshop '98)*, pages 269–280, New York, NY, 1998. Springer Wien.

16. Peter Shirley. A ray tracing method for illumination calculation in diffuse specular scenes. In *Proceedings of Graphics Interface '90*, pages 205–212, Toronto, Ontario, May 1990.

17. B.W. Silverman. *Density Estimation for Statistics and Data Analysis*. Chapmann and Hall, New York, NY, 1986.

18. Brian E. Smits, James R. Arvo, and David H. Salesin. An importance-driven radiosity algorithm. *Computer Graphics*, 26(2):273–282, July 1992.

19. F. Suykens and Y. D. Willems. Weighted multipass methods for global illumination. In *Computer Graphics Forum (Proc. Eurographics '99)*, volume 18, pages C–209–C–220, September 1999.

20. Eric Veach and Leonidas J. Guibas. Optimally Combining Sampling Techniques for Monte Carlo Rendering. In *Computer Graphics Proceedings, Annual Conference Series, 1995 (ACM SIGGRAPH '95 Proceedings)*, pages 419–428, 1995.

21. Gregory J. Ward, Francis M. Rubinstein, and Robert D. Clear. A Ray Tracing Solution for Diffuse Interreflection. In *Computer Graphics (ACM SIGGRAPH '88 Proceedings)*, volume 22, pages 85–92, August 1988.

Editors' Note: see Appendix, p. 392 for colored figures of this paper

Weighted Importance Sampling Techniques for Monte Carlo Radiosity

Philippe Bekaert*, Mateu Sbert° and Yves D. Willems*

* Department of Computer Science, Katholieke Universiteit Leuven
Celestijnenlaan 200 A, B-3001 Leuven, Belgium
e-mail: Philippe.Bekaert@cs.kuleuven.ac.be

° Institut d'Informàtica i Aplicacions, Universitat de Girona
Lluis Santaló s/n, E 17071 Girona
e-mail: mateu@ima.udg.es

Abstract. This paper presents weighted importance sampling techniques for Monte Carlo form factor computation and for stochastic Jacobi radiosity system solution. Weighted importance sampling is a generalisation of importance sampling. The basic idea is to compute a-posteriori a correction factor to the importance sampling estimates, based on sample weights accumulated during sampling. With proper weights, the correction factor will compensate for statistical fluctuations and lead to a lower mean square error. Although weighted importance sampling is a simple extension to importance sampling, our experiments indicate that it can lead to a substantial reduction of the error at a very low additional computation and storage cost.

1 Introduction

The Monte Carlo method [6] is a method of last resort for solving difficult mathematical problems such as high-dimensional integration and the solution of very large systems of linear equations. In the context of radiosity, it has been applied with success – and sometimes is the only feasible method – for computing the light flux emitted by surface patches, for form factor computation, for the solution of the radiosity system of equations and in a per-pixel final gather pass after radiosity computations [3].

The basic idea of the Monte Carlo method is to formulate the solution of a problem as the expected value of a random variable. By sampling this random variable and computing the mean of the samples, an estimate for the solution is obtained. These estimates will in general deviate from the true solution because of statistical fluctuations. In Pattanaiks random walk radiosity algorithm [10] for instance, light particle paths are simulated according to the physical laws of light emission and scattering in a scene. The light flux emitted by each patch is closely related to the expected number of visits of such light particle paths to each patch. In an actual simulation, some patches will be visited too often and others too few times. This can result in disturbing noisy artifacts in the computed images.

The mean square error (MSE) of the Monte Carlo estimates is proportional to the variance (if finite) of the random variable and inverse proportional to the number of samples. In order to reduce the expected error in the estimates by a factor K, K^2 times more samples need to be taken. Because the convergence rate is so low, a lot of research in Monte Carlo has focussed on the development of techniques to transform a basic Monte Carlo estimator into an equivalent one with lower variance, yielding lower expected error for fixed number of samples. Such transformations are called variance reduction techniques. Some well-known variance reduction techniques are importance sampling (IS), multiple importance sampling (MIS) [17] and the use of control variates.

This paper introduces a generalisation of IS, called weighted importance sampling (WIS) [11, 14, 15], that has not been applied before in the field of rendering. In WIS, one basically tries to predict to what extent the mean of a set of samples will deviate from the true solution of a problem. This is done by accumulating sample weights during importance sampling. The sample weights are the ratio of two probability distribution functions (pdf's): a *source* pdf and a *target* pdf. The source pdf is used for generating the samples. In WIS, it needs to be known only up to a constant factor. The target pdf serves to diagnose statistical fluctuations. It can be a pdf for which no practical sampling algorithm exists as long as it is properly normalised. Eventually, a correction factor is computed based on the accumulated weights. With proper weights, the product of the IS estimate and the correction factor will be closer to the true solution. In Pattanaiks particle tracing algorithm [10] for instance, WIS could be used in order to predict to what extent each patch is visited too often or too few times and to correct the resulting flux estimates accordingly. Alternatively, WIS has been presented [11, 14] as a technique to simulate the effect of using a good, but impractical, pdf by means of cheap samples.

The paper is organised as follows: first (§2), we present WIS as introduced in [11, 14, 15] and present the key how to make it effective in the context of rendering. In subsequent sections (§3 and §4), the application of WIS to Monte Carlo form factor computation and to stochastic Jacobi radiosity [7, 9, 3] is proposed. Our experiments (§5) suggest that WIS can yield speed-ups of about one order of magnitude in the latter application.

2   Weighted importance sampling

Weighted importance sampling. Consider the integral θ of a function $f(x)$ over a domain D:

$$\theta = \int_D f(x)dx.$$

Consider also two pdf's: $q(x)$ ("source" pdf) and $p(x)$ ("target" pdf). $p(x)$ and $q(x)$ are positive everywhere and normalised over D. For WIS, their ratio $p(x)/q(x)$ shall also be strictly positive and bounded. Then, the integral above can be written as:

$$\theta = \int_D \frac{f(x)}{p(x)}\frac{p(x)}{q(x)}q(x)dx = \int_D \frac{f(x)}{p(x)}w(x)q(x)dx \quad \text{with} \quad w(x) = \frac{p(x)}{q(x)}.$$

The basic idea of WIS is to consider the ratio $w(x)$ as a weight for samples drawn according to the source pdf $q(x)$. The expected weight $E_q[w]$ of the samples equals 1:

$$E_q[w] = \int_D w(x)q(x)dx = \int_D \frac{p(x)}{q(x)}q(x)dx = \int_D p(x)dx = 1.$$

For N samples drawn according to $q(x)$, it can be shown that the following is an asymptotically unbiased ("consistent") estimator for θ [11, 14, 15]:

$$\sum_{s=1}^N \frac{f(x_s)}{p(x_s)}\frac{w(x_s)}{\sum_{s=1}^N w(x_s)} = \frac{\sum_{s=1}^N f(x_s)/q(x_s)}{\sum_{s=1}^N p(x_s)/q(x_s)} = \frac{1}{N}\sum_{s=1}^N \frac{f(x_s)}{q(x_s)} \times \frac{N}{\sum_{s=1}^N w(x_s)} \approx \theta.$$

$$(1)$$

Interpretation. The middle expression in (1) shows the form by which WIS was introduced in [11, 14, 15]. The leftmost expression indicates how the estimator can be interpreted as a "mimicking" of the effect of using the target pdf p by using samples drawn according to another, more practical, pdf q. The weights w compensate for sampling the "wrong" pdf. They are large if a sample x_s would be generated with high probability according to p and conversely. The rightmost expression clarifies how WIS can be viewed as an a-posteriori modification of IS: the usual IS estimate

$$\frac{1}{N} \sum_{s=1}^{N} \frac{f(x_s)}{q(x_s)} \approx \theta \qquad (2)$$

is corrected by the ratio of the expected sum of the sample weights (equal to N) over the sum of the weights of the actual samples. If $p(x) = q(x)$, traditional IS results.

Error analysis. If $f(x)/q(x)$ is bounded and $w(x) = p(x)/q(x)$ is bounded away from zero, it can be shown [11, 15] that the MSE ε^2 (bias + variance) asymptotically, for large number of samples N, is given by:

$$\varepsilon^2 \approx \frac{1}{N} \int_D \left(\frac{f(x)}{q(x)} - \theta \frac{p(x)}{q(x)} \right)^2 q(x)dx. \qquad (3)$$

The MSE will be zero if $p(x) = f(x)/\theta$ is the ideal pdf for IS, regardless of what source pdf q is used for drawing samples.

In general, WIS yields biased estimates for a finite number of samples. The bias β however vanishes rapidly, as $1/N$. Asymptotically [11]:

$$\frac{\beta^2}{\varepsilon^2} \leq \frac{1}{N} \int_D \left(w(x) - 1 \right)^2 q(x)dx. \qquad (4)$$

The integral on the right hand side is the variance of the weight distribution.

Regardless of any bias, the decision whether to use the weighted or non-weighted IS estimates can be made in the end, based on a-posteriori estimates for the total MSE. For a sufficiently large number of samples N, we will compare

$$\varepsilon_{\text{WIS}}^2 \approx \frac{1}{N} \int_D \left(\frac{f(x)}{q(x)} - \theta \frac{p(x)}{q(x)} \right)^2 q(x)dx \quad \text{with} \quad \varepsilon_{\text{IS}}^2 \approx \frac{1}{N} \int_D \left(\frac{f(x)}{q(x)} - \theta \right)^2 q(x)dx. \qquad (5)$$

Locally weighted importance sampling. In rendering, one typically needs to compute a set of integrals with identical integrand but with different, disjunct, domain $D_i \subset D$, rather than a single integral. For instance, one needs to compute the flux through all virtual screen pixels or the flux emitted by a set of patches rather than a single pixel or patch. Such integrals could be written as

$$\theta_i = \int_{D_i} f(x)dx = \int_D f(x)\chi_i(x)dx = \int_D \frac{f(x)\chi_i(x)}{p(x)} \frac{p(x)}{q(x)} q(x)dx \qquad (6)$$

where $\chi_i(x)$ is the characteristic function of D_i (1 if $x \in D_i$ and 0 otherwise). Straightforward application of WIS then however results in a correction factor that is identical for all domains $D_i \subset D$ and that is based on irrelevant samples (in other domains $D_j, j \neq i$). An example will be given in §4.2.

The key to making WIS effective in such situations is to consider the normalised restriction to D_i of the pdf's $p(x)$ and $q(x)$:

$$p_i(x) = \frac{p(x)\chi_i(x)}{\int_{D_i} p(x)dx} \quad ; \quad q_i(x) = \frac{q(x)\chi_i(x)}{\int_{D_i} q(x)dx} \tag{7}$$

The integrals (6) can then also be written as:

$$\theta_i = \int_D \frac{f(x)\chi_i(x)}{p_i(x)} \frac{p_i(x)}{q_i(x)} q_i(x)dx.$$

Taking N samples x_s in D according to q as before, the integrals can be estimated as

$$\frac{\sum_s f(x_s)\chi_i(x_s)/q_i(x_s)}{\sum_s p_i(x_s)/q_i(x_s)} = \frac{1}{N} \sum_s \frac{f(x_s)\chi_i(x_s)}{q(x_s)} \times \frac{N \int_{D_i} p(x)dx}{\sum_s \chi_i(x_s)p(x_s)/q(x_s)} \approx \theta_i. \tag{8}$$

The correction factor on the right hand side now depends only on the samples x_s that fall within the sub-domain D_i. Asymptotically, the MSE (3) is given by

$$\varepsilon_i^2 \approx \frac{1}{N_i} \int_{D_i} \left(\frac{f(x)}{q_i(x)} - \theta_i \frac{p_i(x)}{q_i(x)} \right)^2 q_i(x)dx \tag{9}$$

with $N_i \approx N \int_{D_i} q(x)dx$ the number of samples that fall within D_i.

3 Monte Carlo form factor integration by weighted uniform area sampling

The patch-to-patch form factor F_{ij} between two surfaces S_i and S_j is the average point-to-patch form factor $G_j(x)$ between points $x \in S_i$ and S_j:

$$F_{ij} = \frac{1}{A_i} \int_{S_i} G_j(x)dA_x \tag{10}$$

$$G_j(x) = \int_{S_j} G(x,y)\mathrm{vis}(x,y)dA_y = \int_{\Omega_j(x)} \frac{\cos\theta_x}{\pi}\mathrm{vis}(x,y(\Theta_x))d\omega_{\Theta_x}. \tag{11}$$

$G(x,y)$ is the unoccluded point-to-point form factor:

$$G(x,y) = \frac{\cos\theta_x \cos\theta_y}{\pi r_{xy}^2}.$$

$\mathrm{vis}(x,y)$ takes the value 1 if the points x and y are mutually visible and 0 otherwise. $\Omega_j(x)$ is the solid angle subtended by S_j on the hemisphere above $x \in S_i$, disregarding occlusions. θ_x and θ_y are the angle between a line connecting the points $x \in S_i$ and $y \in S_j$ and the surface normal at x and y respectively. r_{xy} is the distance between x and y. Θ_x is a direction from x to S_j and $y(\Theta_x)$ the point on S_j pointed to by Θ_x.

The outer integral (10) can be estimated by uniform area sampling of points $x \in S_i$. For the inner integral (11), the following sampling strategies can be considered:

1. **Uniform area sampling:** the corresponding pdf (conditional on $x \in S_i$) is

$$p^A(y|x) = \frac{1}{A_j}. \tag{12}$$

Uniform area sampling is cheap, but the variance of the resulting patch-to-patch form factor estimator can be arbitrary large. For abutting patches, it is infinite, meaning that the MSE may not decrease by taking more samples [3];

2. **Uniform direction sampling [1]:** The corresponding pdf is

$$p^D(\Theta_x|x) = \frac{1}{\Omega_j(x)} \quad \Leftrightarrow \quad p^D(y|x) = \frac{1}{\Omega_j(x)} \frac{\cos\theta_y}{r_{xy}^2}. \tag{13}$$

Uniform direction sampling is significantly more expensive than uniform area sampling, but the variance of the patch-to-patch estimator is always bounded and lower [3];

3. **Cosine-distributed direction sampling:** The corresponding pdf is

$$p^C(\Theta_x|x) = \frac{\cos\theta_x}{\pi\tilde{G}_j(x)} \Leftrightarrow p^C(y|x) = \frac{G(x,y)}{\tilde{G}_j(x)} \text{ with } \tilde{G}_j(x) = \int_{S_j} G(x,y)dA_y. \tag{14}$$

$\tilde{G}_j(x)$ is the unoccluded point-to-patch form factor from x to S_j and can be evaluated analytically [2]. The variance can be up to 4 times lower than with uniform direction sampling, but there exist no robust algorithms to sample cosine-distributed directions towards arbitrary spherical triangles.

Weighted uniform area sampling. WIS allows to mimic the effect of cosine-distributed direction sampling by means of cheap uniform area sampling. In order to do so, (12) is used as the source pdf q and (14) as the target pdf p in (1). The resulting estimates for the inner integral (11) are:

$$\tilde{G}_j(x) \frac{\sum_{s=1}^{N} G(x,y_s)\text{vis}(x,y_s)}{\sum_{s=1}^{N} G(x,y_s)} \approx G_j(x).$$

If S_j is fully visible from x, the ratio of sums in this expression will equal 1. It will equal 0 in case of full occlusion. With partial occlusion, it will be between 0 and 1, regardless of the distance between x and y_s, which appears in the denominator of the point-to-point form factors $G(x,y_s)$. For nearby points, this point-to-point form factor can become arbitrary large, but large factors in the numerator will be compensated by equally large factors in the denominator. There is only a bias in case of partial occlusion.

Because the ratio of sums in the above expression is bounded by 1, the variance of the corresponding patch-to-patch form factor estimator is bounded as well, even for abutting patches, although uniform area sampling is used.

By weighting w.r.t. $G(x,y)$, statistical fluctuations in the distance between the sample points x and y and in the angles θ_x and θ_y are compensated for. It is possible to do so because the normalisation of $G(x,y)$ is known.

Some experimental results, supporting our claims, are presented in figure 1.

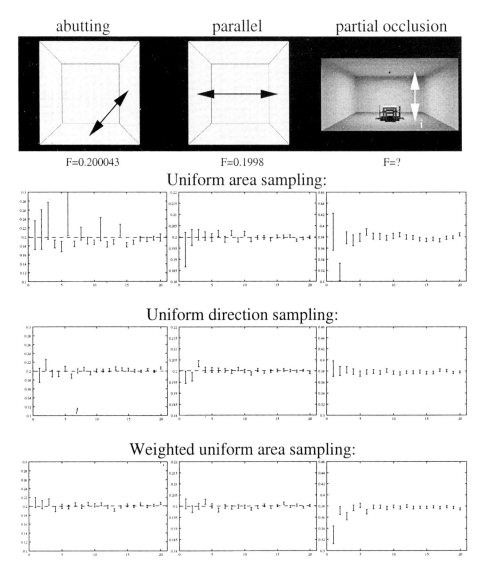

Figure 1. Results obtained with weighted uniform area sampling for computing patch-to-patch form factors. The graphs show the average and the standard deviation after 100 runs with $N \times N$ samples each, as a function of N. In each run, N sample points are chosen uniformly on the receiver patch. The point-to-patch form factors from these points to the source patch are computed using N random samples on the source patch each. In all three cases, weighted uniform area sampling performs similarly to uniform direction sampling and significantly better than uniform area sampling. In the partial occlusion example (right column), a slight bias is visible when the number of samples is low.

4 Radiosity system solution using stochastic Jacobi iterations

In the remainder of this paper, we will discuss the application of WIS to the solution of the radiosity system of equations using a stochastic adaptation of the Jacobi iterative method [7, 9, 8]. The radiosities B_i of the patches in a scene can be obtained by solving the following system of equations in the power $P_i = A_i B_i$ of the patches:

$$P_i = \Phi_i + \sum_j P_j F_{ji} \rho_i. \tag{15}$$

Φ_i denotes the self-emitted power by patch i, ρ_i is the reflectivity and F_{ji} the form factor.

In the classical Jacobi iterative method, a sequence of approximations $P_i^{(k)}, k = 0, 1, \dots$ for P_i is constructed by repeated application of (15), filling in a current approximation $P^{(k)}$ in the right hand side in order to obtain the next approximation $P^{(k+1)}$. The self-emitted power distribution can be used as an initial guess: $P_i^{(0)} = \Phi_i$.

4.1 Stochastic Jacobi radiosity

Neumann [7] proposed to estimate the sums (15) by means of the Monte Carlo method. These sums can also be written as

$$P_i' - \Phi_i = \sum_{j,k} P_j F_{jk} \rho_k \delta_{ki}$$

where δ_{ki} is Kroneckers delta function (1 if $k = i$ and 0 otherwise). These sums can be estimated by randomly sampling terms (j, k) according to some probability distribution p_{jk}. The average quotient of the selected terms over the probability by which they are selected yields an estimate for $P_i' - \Phi_i$:

$$\frac{1}{N} \sum_{s=1}^{N} \frac{P_{j_s} F_{j_s, k_s} \rho_{k_s} \delta_{k_s, i}}{p_{j_s, k_s}} \approx P_i' - \Phi_i. \tag{16}$$

Two common choices for p_{jk} are:

1. **Local lines [7, 9]:** First, a patch j is selected with probability proportional to its power P_j. Next, a patch k is selected conditional on j by tracing a ray with uniformly chosen origin on j and cosine distributed direction. The nearest patch k hit by such a ray is selected with probability equal to the form factor F_{jk}. The combined probability is

$$p_{jk} = \frac{P_j}{P_T} F_{jk} \quad \text{with} \quad P_T = \sum_j P_j. \tag{17}$$

The estimates (16) in this case are:

$$\frac{P_T \rho_i}{N} \sum_s \delta_{k_s, i} \approx P_i' - \Phi_i. \tag{18}$$

It suffices to count the number N_i of rays hitting each patch i. The relative number of hits yields an estimate for the non-self-emitted "output" power distribution. The variance for N samples is [3]:

$$V[P_i' - \Phi_i] = \frac{1}{N}\left(P_T \rho_i (P_i' - \Phi_i) - (P_i' - \Phi_i)^2\right). \tag{19}$$

2. **Global lines and global ray bundles (transillumination method) [12, 7, 16]:**
   These techniques result in line segments connecting patches j and k with probability

$$p_{jk} = \frac{A_j}{A_T} F_{jk} \quad \text{with} \quad A_T = \sum_j A_j. \tag{20}$$

Such line segments are generated at a lower cost, but they are worse distributed than local lines. For an equal amount of line segments, the variance of the resulting power estimates will be higher.

4.2 Globally weighted stochastic Jacobi radiosity

WIS can be used to mimic the effect of local lines with cheaper global lines. The weighted power estimates are obtained by substituting the integral $\int_D$ in (1) by double sums $\sum_{j,k}$ over pairs of patches, $f(x)$ by $P_j F_{jk} \rho_k \delta_{ik}$, the target pdf $p(x)$ by (17) and the source pdf $q(x)$ by (20):

$$(18) \times \frac{N}{\sum_s B_{j_s}/B_{av}} \approx P_i' - \Phi_i. \tag{}$$

B_{j_s} is the radiosity of the patch on which the s-th shot ray originated. $B_{av} = P_T/A_T$ is the average radiosity in the scene. The correction factor is the same for all patches i in the scene. It cannot take away the visually disturbing uncorrelated deviations from the true "output" power on the patches in the scene. Better, individual, correction factors per patch are obtained by using locally weighted importance sampling.

4.3 Locally weighted stochastic Jacobi radiosity

The sub-domains D_i in stochastic Jacobi radiosity correspond to the sets of pairs of indices (j, k) with fixed $k = i$. In order to apply (8), we need to know the normalisation of the restricted target pdf p_i over such sub-domains. This normalisation is not known a-priori for local lines (17), since it corresponds to the incident power on patch i. For global lines (20) in a closed environment however:

$$\sum_{j,k} \frac{A_j}{A_T} F_{jk}\delta_{ki} = \frac{A_i}{A_T}\sum_j F_{ij} = \frac{A_i}{A_T}. \tag{21}$$

Using therefore (20) as the "target" pdf p, and (17) as the source pdf q in (8), the following estimates result:

$$(18) \times \frac{N}{\sum_s \delta_{k_s,i}\frac{A_{j_s}}{A_i q_{j_s}}} \approx P_i' - \Phi_i, \tag{22}$$

with $q_j = P_j/P_T$ the probability of shooting a local line originating at patch j.

4.4 Error analysis

In order to determine whether or not the weighted estimate will be better than the non-weighted estimate, we need to calculate the MSE according to expression (9).

The restricted pdf's (7) and sample weights are:

$$\left.\begin{array}{rclcl} p^i_{jk} & = & \frac{A_j}{A_i}F_{ji}\delta_{ik} & = & F_{ij}\delta_{ik} \\ q^i_{jk} & = & \frac{P_j F_{ji}\rho_i}{P'_i-\Phi_i}\delta_{ik} & = & \frac{\rho_i F_{ij}B_j}{B'_i-E_i}\delta_{ik} \end{array}\right\} \Longrightarrow w^i_{jk} = \frac{p^i_{ji}}{q^i_{ji}} = \frac{B'_i-E_i}{\rho_i B_j} \quad (23)$$

The weights w^i_{ji} correspond to the ratio of irradiance (incident radiosity) on i over the radiosity emitted by other patches j from which i receives illumination.

By straightforward calculation, it can be shown that the MSE of the weighted estimate (22) equals

$$\varepsilon^2_i = \frac{1}{N}\rho_i P_T(P'_i-\Phi_i)V[w]. \quad (24)$$

where $V[w]$ is the variance of the weights (23):

$$V[w] = \sum_j \frac{(p^i_{ji})^2}{q^i_{ji}} - 1 = \sum_j F_{ij}\frac{B'_i-E_i}{\rho_i B_j} - 1 \quad (25)$$

Assuming a sufficiently large number of samples, the weighted estimate will probably be more accurate than the non-weighted estimate if (24) is smaller than the MSE (19) of the non-weighted estimator. This is the case if

$$\frac{V[w]}{1-\frac{P'_i-\Phi_i}{\rho_i P_T}} < 1 \quad (26)$$

In the other case, the non-weighted estimate can be expected to have lower error. The ratio (26) also indicates how many more or less samples are needed with WIS compared to IS in order to obtain the same MSE level.

4.5 Implementation

The incorporation of WIS in stochastic Jacobi radiosity requires a simple extension of the basic algorithm [9, 3]:

1. Shoot N rays as explained in §4.1 (local lines), accumulate:
   - the number N_i of rays hitting each patch i;
   - the sum of the weights associated with incident rays, $W_i = \sum_s A_{j_s}/A_i q_{j_s}$.
   - the sum of the square weights $Z_i = \sum_s (A_{j_s}/A_i q_{j_s})^2$.

2. Compute the "output" power estimates as before, using expression (18):

$$\rho_i P_T \frac{N_i}{N} \approx P'_i - \Phi_i \quad (27)$$

3. Compute

$$\left(\frac{N_i}{N}\right)^2\left[\frac{Z_i}{N_i}-\left(\frac{W_i}{N_i}\right)^2\right] \approx V[w] \quad ; \quad 1-\frac{N_i}{N} \approx 1-\frac{P'_i-\Phi_i}{\rho_i P_T}.$$

If the ratio as indicated in (26) is smaller than 1, multiply (27) with N/W_i.

4.6 Hierarchical refinement

It is straightforward to incorporate WIS in hierarchical stochastic Jacobi radiosity [4, 3]. While shooting rays, ray counts and weights are accumulated on every element in the hierarchy. A contribution to a parent element counts as a fractional contribution to each of its children elements, proportional to the ratio $A^{\text{child}}/A^{\text{parent}}$ of the surface area of the child and parent element. After shooting the rays, the counts and accumulated weights are pushed down to the leaf elements as follows:

$$N_i^{\text{child}} \leftarrow N_i^{\text{parent}} \times A^{\text{child}}/A^{\text{parent}}$$
$$W_i^{\text{child}} \leftarrow W_i^{\text{parent}}$$
$$Z_i^{\text{child}} \leftarrow Z_i^{\text{parent}} \times A^{\text{parent}}/A^{\text{child}}$$

Radiosity estimates are then computed on the leaf elements as explained in §4.5.

5   Discussion and empirical results

Discussion. Expression (26) indicates that weighting will be beneficial on patches which are sufficiently uniformly illuminated. In the extreme case that the radiosity emitted by all patches j surrounding a patch i is equal, the theory predicts a zero MSE. We have tested this in a labyrinth like environment, in which the sum of the reflectivities and self-emitted radiosities were made equal to 1 for all patches: $E_i + \rho_i = 1, \forall i$. In a closed environment, the radiosities B_i themselves will then also be equal to 1, regardless of the geometry. The error in such an environment can be measured accurately, by comparing with the known analytic solution. We observed that the error decreased very rapidly to insignificant levels.

Weighting is not beneficial for strongly directional incident radiance, for instance due to small bright light sources in an otherwise dark environment. In such cases however, weighting still may be beneficial in indirectly lit regions or after a first shot [13, 5]. Our algorithm includes a criterion to decide a-posteriori whether or not weighting will be beneficial. This decision is made for each patch in the scene individually so that weighting will only be applied in those parts of the scene where a gain is predicted. If weighting is not beneficial, the non-weighted radiosity estimate is displayed.

The additional computation cost for weighting is negligible. Storage requirements are slightly higher, due to the need to store the accumulated weights and square weights (two floating point numbers per patch). This is a very low price for the benefits of weighting.

Empirical results. The figures 2-4 (separate page) show one simple environment in which extensive numerical comparisons have been performed. The shown scene consists of 3250 patches. The average reflectivity is about 0.7. Figure 5 illustrates the incorporation of WIS in hierarchical stochastic Jacobi radiosity (§4.6). In figure 5, only indirect illumination was computed using stochastic Jacobi radiosity. This took about 2 minutes on a 195 MHz R10000 SGI Octane workstation. Hierarchical refinement resulted in about 30,000 elements. Direct illumination was computed using stochastic ray tracing. Our findings can be summarised as follows:

- Weighting can yield a well visible reduction of noisy artifacts (compare indirectly lit regions in figure 2);

- There is a bias at low number of samples indeed. The bias vanishes rapidly, except in the neighbourhood of "black" surfaces (the scene cannot be considered closed in this case) and also on patches exhibiting shadow leaks (see figure 3 at the bottom of the hand-like sculpture and also figure 5 on the ceiling near the lights). Weighting compensates for shadow leaks because the element area cancels in numerator and denominator of the weighted radiosity estimates;
- For a sufficient number of samples, the predicted speed-up corresponds well with the observed speed-up. The middle image of figure 4 shows the average speed-up observed in 100 runs with 250 rays per patch. The speed-up was measured by comparing with a reference solution, obtained with 100,000 rays per patch;
- Hierarchical refinement results in small elements near the shared edge of abutting patches and in corners. Due to their small area, such elements can exhibit a high variance. Weighting suppresses this variance well (figure 5) because such elements typically receive the illumination from a small number of nearby elements, on which the illumination varies only little;
- There can be an objectionable bias and discrepancy between the predicted and observed speed-up when the number of incident rays is very low (just a few). Clustering reduces this problem but does not always eliminate it. More robust benefit prediction techniques at very low number of samples need to be developed in future research.

Comparison with multiple importance sampling (MIS) [17]. MIS is a powerful, unbiased and reliable technique to combine samples drawn from several different pdf's. WIS is biased (but consistent) and requires that only a single pdf, the source pdf, be sampled. The target pdf can be a pdf which is impractical to sample (as in §3). MIS requires that all pdf's be properly normalised. In WIS, the normalisation of the source pdf q is not required. Finally, unlike MIS, WIS can lead to perfect estimation (for an environment with perfectly uniform illumination for instance). Combinations of MIS and WIS are possible. This could for instance be used to obtain weighted energy transfers in both directions over each shot ray [3, §11.2].

6   Conclusion

This paper introduced WIS as a simple, but potentially very powerful, extension of IS. We have studied its application to form factor computation and to stochastic Jacobi radiosity. In order to make it effective, WIS was extended so that "local" correction factors can be obtained. Weighting must be used with care however: with inappropriate weights, an actual increase of the variance may result instead of a reduction. We showed how practical heuristics can be developed in order to determine locally when or where weighting will be beneficial. In cases where it is not beneficial, the penalty is very low: the additional computation time and storage cost introduced by weighting are very low. Experiments show that there is good agreement between theory and practice and suggest that substantial speed-ups are possible.

Possible areas for future research, besides more reliable benefit prediction at very low number of samples, include the development of several variants of the proposed algorithms: weighting global lines instead of local lines, the incorporation of view-importance sampling, the extension to higher order radiosity approximations [3] .... Finally, WIS may be beneficial as well in other Monte Carlo rendering algorithms, such as final radiosity gathers and path tracing.

46

Acknowledgements

The first author acknowledges financial support by the research fund of the K.U.Leuven. Additional support has been received in the context of a Catalan-Flemish Joint-Action of the CUR-Generalitat de Catalunya (ABM/acs/ACI98-19). Thanks to Frank Suykens for discussions and to the anonymous reviewers for their constructive remarks.

References

1. J. Arvo. Stratified sampling of spherical triangles. In *Computer Graphics Proceedings, Annual Conference Series, 1995 (ACM SIGGRAPH '95 Proceedings)*, pages 437–438, August 1995.
2. D. R. Baum, H. E. Rushmeier, and J. M. Winget. Improving radiosity solutions through the use of analytically determined form-factors. In *Computer Graphics (SIGGRAPH '89 Proceedings)*, volume 23, pages 325–334, July 1989.
3. Ph. Bekaert. *Hierarchical and Stochastic Algorithms for Radiosity.* PhD thesis, Katholieke Universiteit Leuven, December 1999.
4. Ph. Bekaert, L. Neumann, A. Neumann, M. Sbert, and Y. D. Willems. Hierarchical Monte Carlo radiosity. In *Rendering Techniques '98 (Proceedings of the 9th. Eurographics Workshop on Rendering)*, pages 259–268. June 1998.
5. F. Castro, R. Matinez, and M. Sbert. Quasi-Monte Carlo and extended first-shot improvement to the multi-path method. In *Proc. Spring Conference on Computer Graphics '98*, pages 91–102, Bratislava, Slovakia, April 1998. Comenius University.
6. M. H. Kalos and P. Whitlock. *The Monte Carlo method.* J. Wiley and sons, 1986.
7. L. Neumann. Monte Carlo radiosity. *Computing*, 55(1):23–42, 1995.
8. L. Neumann, A. Neumann, and Ph. Bekaert. Radiosity with well distributed ray sets. *Computer Graphics Forum*, 16(3):C261–C270, 1997. Proceedings of Eurographics '97.
9. L. Neumann, W. Purgathofer, R. Tobler, A. Neumann, P. Elias, M. Feda, and X. Pueyo. The stochastic ray method for radiosity. In P. Hanrahan and W. Purgathofer, editors, *Rendering Techniques '95 (Proceedings of the Sixth Eurographics Workshop on Rendering)*, July 1995.
10. S. N. Pattanaik and S. P. Mudur. Computation of global illumination by Monte Carlo simulation of the particle model of light. *Proceedings of the Third Eurographics Workshop on Rendering*, pages 71–83, May 1992.
11. M. J. D. Powell and J. Swann. Weighted uniform sampling – a Monte Carlo technique for reducing variance. *J. Inst. Maths. Applics.*, 2:228 – 236, 1966.
12. M. Sbert. An integral geometry based method for fast form-factor computation. *Computer Graphics Forum*, 12(3):C409–C420, 1993.
13. M. Sbert. *The use of global random directions to compute radiosity — Global Monte Carlo techniques.* PhD thesis, Universitat Politècnica de Catalunya, Barcelona, Spain, November 1996.
14. J. Spanier. A new family of estimators for random walk problems. *Journal of the Institute of Mathematics and its Applications*, 23:1 – 31, 1979.
15. J. Spanier and E. H. Maize. Quasi-random methods for estimating integrals using relatively small samples. *SIAM Review*, 36(1):18–44, March 1994.
16. L. Szirmay-Kalos and W. Purgathofer. Global ray-bundle tracing with hardware acceleration. In *Rendering Techniques '98 (Proceedings of the 9th. Eurographics Workshop on Rendering)*, pages 247 – 256. June 1998.
17. E. Veach and L. J. Guibas. Optimally combining sampling techniques for Monte Carlo rendering. In *SIGGRAPH 95 Conference Proceedings*, pages 419–428, August 1995.

Editors' Note: see Appendix, p. 393 for colored figures of this paper

Fast Global Illumination Including Specular Effects

Xavier Granier[1], George Drettakis[1] and Bruce Walter[2]

[1] iMAGIS-GRAVIR/IMAG-INRIA
iMAGIS is a joint research project of CNRS/INRIA/UJF/INPG
[2] Cornell Program of Computer Graphics
E-mail: {Xavier.Granier|George.Drettakis}@imag.fr, bjw@graphics.cornell.edu

Abstract.
Rapidly simulating global illumination, including diffuse and glossy light transport is a very difficult problem. Finite element or radiosity approaches can achieve interactive simulations for some classes of diffuse-only scenes, but more general methods are currently too slow and too noisy for interactive use.
We present a new method which seamlessly integrates particle tracing (for non-diffuse transport) into the gather step of hierarchical radiosity (for diffuse transport) to efficiently handle all types of light transport chains. Our integrated approach results in rapid, good visual quality solutions. This is achieved using a radiosity algorithm producing smooth, noise free simulation of diffuse light transfers, and an integrated particle trace for rapid, high quality specular reflections such as caustics.
Using our system, users can interactively visualize and manipulate small environments with global illumination including specular effects. Such general lighting effects can also be simulated for larger environments, albeit at a higher computational cost. Our system can also treat scenes which are lit mainly by indirect lighting, which is very hard using previous methods. With our method, smooth transition from fast, low quality to slower high quality solutions is possible.

1 Motivation

Simulating global illumination is essential for realistic rendering of virtual environments. The incorporation of indirect lighting effects in particular can be very important for many classes of scenes. For diffuse-only scenes, recent radiosity techniques can achieve interactive speeds with moving objects. Real environments however are rarely completely diffuse, and the use of such simulations results in images which are missing many important non-diffuse or glossy effects. The algorithms which treat specular or glossy effects (e.g., caustics) are still too slow and too noisy for interactive applications which require overall high visual quality. Non-diffuse light exchanges contain highly directional components, and are thus unsuitable for discrete, finite-element type methods. As a consequence, they are often treated by stochastic methods or multi-pass approaches, which combine finite element and stochastic solutions. Both are generally too slow to interactively handle dynamic scenes. The former suffer from objectionable noise artifacts while the latter are usually limited in the effects or the environments they can simulate, and often require a series of complex steps to treat all light paths.

The goal of our work is to provide fast, high quality global illumination simulation including both glossy and diffuse effects. We achieve this by integrating hierarchical radiosity with clustering which efficiently treats global diffuse light transfer, with particle tracing for non-diffuse transfers. The integration is simple, and uses the rich light path information in the form of hierarchical radiosity links, to guide and accelerate particle tracing. The result is rapid and complete simulation of all light paths.

For simple scenes, our algorithm allows interactive viewing (as fast as 2 frames/sec.) of a global illumination solution including both global diffuse illumination and moving caustic effects (see Fig. 1). Our algorithm can also treat more complex scenes, albeit at a higher computational cost. The difficult case of scenes lit primarily by indirect light is also handled well. Finally, it has a built-in quality control mechanism, which allows smooth transition from fast, lower-quality solutions to more expensive high quality lighting simulations by shifting computations higher or lower in our hierarchy.

Fig. 1. Two frames from an interactive session using our new algorithm. The ring moves to the right at 2 frames/sec. (SGI R10k workstation). Note the cardioid caustic from the glossy ring.

1.1 Previous Work

In what follows we use Heckbert's [11] regular expression notation for light paths and light transport. L is used for the light, E the eye, S a non-diffuse transfer, D a diffuse transfer, while "*" represents zero or more bounces, "+" at least one bounce and "|" is the "or" operator. Thus for example LD^*E are light paths leaving the light, bouncing off zero or more diffuse objects and arriving at the eye. These paths are well treated by radiosity. All possible light paths can be described by $L(D|S)^*E$.

A vast amount of research has been performed on global illumination and combined glossy/diffuse transfer. For example, many different pure Monte Carlo techniques have been proposed (e.g., see [30] for an overview), though these are currently still too slow or too noisy to achieve the level of interactivity that we require.

For diffuse-only transfer, radiosity methods (e.g., [8, 4]) can produce high-quality images. In particular hierarchical radiosity with clustering (HRC) [24, 21] can simulate radiosity for large environments rapidly. One advantage of radiosity (as any diffuse-only $L(DS)^*DE$ solution) is that the result of the simulation can be interactively visualized for walkthroughs on graphics hardware, and in some cases interactive updates can be made [6]. We will draw heavily on HRC. The important steps and structures of HRC which we will be using are reviewed in Fig. 2.

Since the advent of radiosity methods, several solutions have been proposed to add non-diffuse transfer. One approach is to store directional finite elements on patches. From the earliest such work [12] to the most recent [26] using clustering and wavelets, the storage required for directional discretisation makes these methods unusable for complex scenes which contain highly directional glossy effects such as caustics. Continuous representations (e.g., [22]) also require large numbers of base coefficients, leading to the same problem. To avoid the problem of storing directional finite elements, three point methods (e.g., [1]) have been proposed. However, these still suffer from

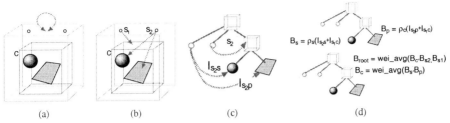

Fig. 2. Basic steps of the hierarchical radiosity algorithm: *Initialization:* the scene, consisting of a sphere and a polygon, contained in a cluster c, and two light sources. Initially there is a *self link* to the root cluster. For each iteration we perform three steps.(a) *Refinement:* a link is created between source s_1 and c, and s_2 is linked to the sphere s and the polygon p. (c) *Gather:* irradiance is gathered over the links, resulting in the values I_{s_2s} (s_2 to s) and I_{s_2p} (s_2 to p) shown in the graph representation of the hierarchy. (d) *Push-pull:* First the irradiance values are pushed to the leaves, where radiosity is set by reflecting the irradiance using reflectance ρ (top). The radiosity values are then pulled up the hierarchy by area weighted averages to maintain consistency (bottom).

a severe k^3 link storage requirement where k is the number of input elements. As a consequence they are restricted to very simple scenes. Dumont et al. [7] trade memory for time by applying a shooting approach based on the link hierarchy and removing links on the fly. This reduces the memory requirement to quadratic, but increases the computation time. Another recent approach is three-point clustering [27]; although its memory requirements are modest compared to diffuse HRC, very fine subdivision of link space is required to get high frequency results such as caustics. Such results are thus very costly both in time and storage.

Extended form-factors have been introduced to take specular transfers into account, in the context of multi-pass radiosity-style algorithms. Limitations such as planar only mirrors [31], or specular-only non-diffuse transfers [23] are often imposed however.

Wann Jensen has introduced the Photon Map (e.g., [13]), which uses particle or photon tracing for all light transfers including diffuse. His method can quickly compute direct caustics (i.e., caustics caused by a light source directly), but requires a costly gather step to compute other transport paths adequately. Despite acceleration using irradiance gradients [35], the gather is still too slow for interactive use.

Density estimation [33] is another closely related approach. As with Photon Maps, all light transfer is performed with particle tracing. However viewing can be performed using a decimated mesh on graphics hardware or using ray-tracing to account for the additional paths from the eye to one or more specular surfaces to the light or a diffuse surface. We will adopt a similar approach for viewing.

Combined multi-pass radiosity/Monte Carlo methods have been proposed (e.g., [20, 2, 14, 19, 17]) but do not fully take advantage of the information provided by one pass to guide and thus accelerate the next. The approaches of Shirley [20] and Chen et al. [2] are precursors to our work in that they also identified the advantage of using radiosity for diffuse illumination. However, since these methods clearly separate the different types of transfers (e.g., specular reflections are treated as a separate process), they often require complex additions and subtractions of light in the various passes to avoid double counting of light transfers. In addition, these methods are based on progressive refinement radiosity, which cannot efficiently treat complex scenes in which indirect lighting is predominant. Secondary light-source reclassification [2] becomes prohibitively expensive when many patches are secondary emitters with about the same power. In contrast, we will be using hierarchical radiosity with clustering, which deals with these configurations efficiently. Some attempts have also been made for interactive display of globally illuminated scenes [29, 32].

Finally, it is worth mentioning that specific methods have been developed for the rendering of caustics which are one of the more beautiful lighting phenomena (e.g., [5, 36]). However, they do not treat the entire breadth of all light transfers.

2 Overview

In our new algorithm, we start by building the cluster hierarchy as in HRC. Refinement proceeds by examining each link (see Fig. 2), and deciding whether to refine based on the chosen criterion. During gather, we check each link: for links leaving diffuse objects and arriving on specular objects, diffuse to specular transfers are performed by particle tracing. The use of the link structure restricts the number of particles emitted since we only sample a limited part of space. It also substantially accelerates particle tracing itself by accurate visibility classification. Particles are then propagated into the environment both by reflection and refraction.

The iteration is completed by updating the hierarchy: first particles are placed at an appropriate level in the hierarchy, then the contribution of particles is added to the diffuse light at the leaves of the hierarchy, and all transfers to diffuse surfaces are thus recorded.

This tightly-coupled loop is particularly effective, for all $L(D|S)^*DE$ light transfer. To display, we first perform a reconstruction step generating a smooth representation of radiosity on surfaces. We can then either interactively visualize the result using graphics hardware, or ray-trace. Interactive visualization includes specular reflections such as caustics and direct shadows, as in Fig. 1. Paths or partial paths of the form $(L|D)S^+E$ can be included using ray-tracing.

The main contribution of our approach is to seamlessly integrate hierarchical radiosity with clustering (HRC) and particle tracing for the first time. The integration is clean and simple, and naturally accounts for all light paths. In contrast to previous approaches, HRC results in efficient, noise free simulation of diffuse transfer and can handle complex, indirect diffuse/specular configurations. The result of this approach is very rapid simulations of all light paths, which for simple scenes permit interactive updates, including high-frequency specular reflections such as caustics. We also treat more complex scenes at a higher, but reasonable computational cost, and handle the difficult case of scenes lit mainly by indirect light. Our algorithm also has a built-in quality control mechanism allowing smooth transition from fast, low-quality solutions, to slower but higher-quality simulations.

In the following we first present the new integrated HRC and particle tracing algorithm, we discuss reconstruction approaches followed by the presentation of our results for interactive rendering and simulations for more complex scenes. We then discuss future work and conclude.

3 Integrating HRC and Particle Tracing

As mentioned above, we will be using particle tracing to simulate glossy transfer across links arriving at glossy objects. To do this, we first introduce a modified gather step. During this step particles are emitted to simulate glossy transfer. Gathering is followed by a modified push step in which we decide where to place particles into the hierarchy. Since particles are emitted across the restricted space defined by a link, special care is needed to choose the number of particles as well as the power assigned to each.

We start our algorithm like HRC, by first constructing the cluster hierarchy using the approach presented in [3]. We then initialize the system with the root self-link [21]. To account for non-diffuse transfer, we store BSDF's (bidirectional scattering distribution function) for the non-diffuse objects [30]. We use a mixed diffuse/specular model of [16], which randomly decides whether a reflection will be glossy or diffuse, based on the percentage of diffuse/specular reflection defined by the material property. A cluster containing specular objects is considered non-diffuse.

3.1 Iterative Step

Refine/Gather and Particle Trace. We use an energy refinement criterion, BFA, where B is radiosity, F is the form-factor, A is equivalent area or *area factor* (which is area for surfaces and $4kV$ for volumes or clusters), and k is an equivalent extinction coefficient and V is volume [21]. If the quantity BFA over a link is greater than a threshold, the link is refined, incurring subdivision where necessary. Once the refinement has placed links at the appropriate level of the hierarchy, we traverse the element hierarchy. At each receiving element, we visit each link and gather irradiance from the linked elements.

If the receiving end of a link is a non-diffuse surface, we trace particles across the link to track the light that is scattered non-diffusely. The particle generation is restricted to particles which are emitted from the source end of the link and which will initially strike the receiver. Particles are emitted across the link, which is the region of space defined by the two elements. This is further described in Section 3.2.

Particles are immediately reflected at the receiving element. For clusters, we intersect with the contents of the cluster and perform the reflection with the object or polygon hit. For objects/surfaces we simply reflect via the associated bidirectional scattering distribution function (BSDF). Particles are then propagated for subsequent bounces until they are absorbed, hit a diffuse surface or exit the scene. Particle hits are stored on all objects excluding the first hit (since this transfer is accounted for by the radiosity system). Using the link hierarchy for reflection or transmission other than the first emission could be possible; the naive approach of searching the hierarchy and finding the appropriate link however has currently proven to be too expensive compared to the benefits. We discuss this further in Section 6 on future work. This process, reflection and propagation, is performed iteratively until all particles have been absorbed or have hit a diffuse surface.

Particle Placement and Push Pull. After propagation, particles are stored at the top level of the object intersected (i.e., a polygon, sphere etc.). Specular effects are often high frequency (similar to shadows for example), and thus can require fine meshing to be correctly represented. We will be using the particles to reconstruct irradiance [13, 11] arriving at a surface; our goal is to perform hierarchical reconstruction (see Section 4). As a result it is important to appropriately choose the level at which we place particles. Placing the particles at too low a level causes visible noise, while placing them too high blurs out high-frequency specular reflection details.

Intuitively, we need to identify regions where many particles are concentrated. In such regions, we want to place particles at an appropriate level in the hierarchy, to ensure that the underlying specular effects are well-represented. This is done using a criterion based on a "spread factor"; we push particles down the hierarchy when a concentration of powerful particles occurs over an area which is small compared to the equivalent area of the element being considered.

We traverse the element hierarchy, and at each element, we have n particles, each

52

carrying ϕ_i power and located at position $\mathbf{x}_i$. We define a "center" c as the power-weighted average position of the set of particles and "spread factor" SF:

$$c = \frac{\sum_n \phi_i \mathbf{x}_i}{\sum_n \phi_i}, \quad SF = \frac{\sum_n \phi_i |c - \mathbf{x}_i|^2}{\sum_n \phi_i} \tag{1}$$

If A is the area factor (see definition of Section 3.1 above) of the element, we test if: $\pi SF \leq \zeta A$ **and** $\sum_{i=1..n} \phi_i \geq \varepsilon$, where ζ determines the percentage spread we try to achieve. We typically use $\zeta = 0.5$. Intuitively, the condition is satisfied when there is a large concentration of particles with high energy compared to the area of the element under consideration. If the condition is false, particles are placed at the current level. Otherwise the particles are pushed further down the hierarchy. This will result in additional subdivision of the hierarchy of elements if necessary, thus automatically adapting the mesh to high frequency specular reflections. Note however that links remain at the level defined by refinement, and thus the additional subdivision does not impact the cost of the diffuse part of the radiosity iteration.

Each element has a irradiance I_d from the diffuse gather across its links and a number, n, of particles, each with power ϕ_i. At each level of the hierarchy with equivalent area A, irradiance I becomes: $I = I_d + \frac{\sum_n \phi_i}{A}$. This can be seen as a coarse multi-level smoothing reconstruction of particle irradiance. At the leaves radiosity is then set to $B = \rho I$, in the same manner as for diffuse radiosity. This results in a constant radiosity value per leaf element. Radiosity is then pulled up the hierarchy for light transfer consistency in subsequent iterations.

Note that we can accumulate particle irradiance, by averaging over the irradiance contributed from each iteration. We have found that this typically improves the quality of specular reflection (caustics in particular), since it reduces noise.

3.2 Particle Emission

An important part of the process described above is the transmission and reflection of particles. We first explain how we estimate the non-diffuse flux across a link using particle emission. The fact that we restrict particle emission to the space defined by the link requires special treatment.

In general, the flux leaving element S is given by the following integral:

$$\Phi_S = \int_S \int_{\Omega_s} L(s, \omega) < \omega \cdot n_s > d\omega ds, \tag{2}$$

where S is the source (emitter), Φ_S is the exiting flux of S, s is a point on S, Ω_s represents all directions leaving s, ω is a direction, n_s is the normal at s and $L(s, \omega)$ is the radiance leaving s in direction ω, and $< \cdot >$ is a dot product.

We stochastically estimate this integral by tracing n_p particles into the environment. These particles are emitted according to a probability density function (pdf), $p(s, \omega)$. Following standard Monte-Carlo methodology [30, 34], the power associated with the emitted particles is given by:

$$\phi(s, \omega) = \frac{L(s, \omega) < \omega \cdot n_s >}{n_p \, p(s, \omega)} \tag{3}$$

We change notation to consider the radiance $L(s, r)$ leaving point s on element S arriving at point r on the receiver element R, and perform the appropriate change of variables. Using the notation of Sillion [21], for the case of clustering the flux between two generic hierarchical elements can be written:

$$\Phi_{RS} = S_R S_S \int_S \int_R L(s,r) \frac{\tau R_r E_r}{\|s-r\|^2} dr\, ds \qquad (4)$$

Where "receiver factor" R_r is 1 for clusters and $\cos\theta_i$ for surfaces, the "emitter factor" E_r is 1 for clusters and $\cos\theta_o$ for surfaces, S_S, S_R are scale factors to account for the volumetric case, which are 1 for surfaces and $\frac{1}{4}$ for clusters [21]; finally τ is the absorption factor for participating media. The quantities $\cos\theta_i$, $\cos\theta_o$ are the cosine of the angle of the normal at the surface and the direction of propagation for the emitter and receiver respectively.

For the case of radiosity, $L(s,r) = \frac{B_S}{\pi}$, and Eq. (4) becomes $\Phi_{RS} = B_S F_{RS} A_R$ (B_S is the radiosity of S and F_{RS} is the unoccluded form-factor between R and S; A_R is the equivalent area of R as defined before in Section 3.1 [21]). If we estimate the flux with n_{RS} particles carrying constant power ϕ_{ct}, we have $\Phi_{RS} = n_{RS}\phi_{ct}$ and thus:

$$n_{RS} = \frac{B_S A_R F_{RS}}{\phi_{ct}} \qquad (5)$$

For a given link from S to R, are the quantities in Eq. (5) are known: form-factor, area-factor and source radiosity. Using Eq. (3) and (4) we define the following *pdf*:

$$p(s,r) = \frac{L(s,r) S_R S_S \tau R_r E_r}{\|s-r\|^2 \Phi_{RS}} \qquad (6)$$

To use this *pdf*, we should first choose a point s_0 with a given *pdf* $p'(s)$ on the sender and then find the conditional probability $p''(r|s = s_0)$ on the receiver. In the general case this proved to be impractical. As an approximation, we sample the elements R and S uniformly $p(r) = \frac{1}{\mu(R)}$ $p(s) = \frac{1}{\mu(S)}$. The measure $\mu()$ we use is area for surfaces and volume for clusters.

We can now determine the power ϕ_{rs} we assign to each particle, given the uniform sampling we use on S and R:

$$\phi_{rs} = \frac{L(s,r) S_R S_S \mu(R)\, \mu(S)\tau R_r E_r}{\|s-r\|^2 n_{RS}} \qquad (7)$$

Some of the particles may be absorbed or reflected diffusely if the receiver has both diffuse and non-diffuse components in its BSDF. Such transfers have already been accounted for by the diffuse (non-particle) transfer across links, and thus we disregard them. We only propagate and store particles which are reflected non-diffusely.

3.3 Accelerated computation

The refinement process provides information about visibility which we use to accelerate particle emission. By using an appropriate object representation for non-planar surfaces, we also achieve significant savings and better quality. Finally, when modifying a scene dynamically, we limit the amount of recomputation. We discuss all of these improvements next.

Visibility classification. We use shaft culling [9] for visibility classification in our approach. For a given link, we determine the list of potential blockers across the link. Bounding boxes are opened at the first level if they overlap the shaft, bounding boxes outside the shaft are removed from the list and bounding boxes entirely contained in the shaft are never opened.

Total visibility, i.e., a completely unblocked transfer between two elements is determined exactly and efficiently if the blocker list is empty. Blocker lists are maintained during recursive refinement for additional acceleration. When transferring particles across a totally visible link, no visibility tests or ray casts need be performed saving much unnecessary computation. If the blocker list is not empty then the visibility factor between elements is computed by ray-tracing as in traditional HRC (e.g., [10]).

Object representation. In order to handle objects such as spheres, cylinders and cones, we use an object representation in our HRC system. This is similar in spirit to [28, 18], in that for the purposes of the radiosity solution, the objects are not explicitly subdivided beforehand, lowering the number of primitives.

All intersection calculations are performed using the untesselated objects which results in significant times savings and improves the quality of the shadows and caustics.

Motion update acceleration. When we move an object (which can also be a source), we maintain the subdivided hierarchy. Once the motion is complete, we traverse the hierarchy, recomputing visibility for all links. We then re-shoot particles across links (we do not accumulate particle irradiances over iterations in this case). The "unoccluded form-factor" estimations are recomputed only for links leaving or reaching the moving object. To achieve better update rates, we limit the number of rays used to compute visibility between elements.

4 Reconstruction and Rendering

As described previously, the push step reconstructs the irradiance due to particles at the different levels of the hierarchy, smoothing the results in the process. These values are thus pushed down the element hierarchy, resulting in a constant radiosity value per leaf patch. To display a smooth solution a supplementary reconstruction step is required. Once this step is complete, we can either render directly using the graphics hardware (but missing the $(L|D)S^+E$ paths) or use ray-tracing which captures all paths.

In traditional radiosity systems, extrapolation is performed to the vertices of the patches, requiring the maintenance of a restricted tree during subdivision. As a first preliminary solution, we reconstruct on a "grid", which is separate from the element hierarchy. The grid is represented as a collection of *display polygons*. For a quadrilateral for example, we create a regular grid of display polygons, each having the size of the smallest subdivided element. For other objects (e.g., spheres or cylinders), specific parameterizations are used.

Our current solution starts by assigning the constant radiosity value of the corresponding patch to each display polygon. Smoothing is then performed by assigning the average radiosity value of the neighboring display polygons to each vertex. We can iterate to perform higher-order smoothing, by first assigning the average radiosity of all vertices to each polygon, and again assigning the average of the patch neighbor radiosities to each vertex. Evidently, a more involved reconstruction scheme (e.g., [15]) could be adapted to our needs (see also Section 6).

Once the reconstruction has been performed, we can directly render the polygons of the grid, or a texture generated directly from these polygons. The only missing paths are $(L|D)S^+E$, that is paths leaving the eye, hitting at least one specular surface and then hitting either a diffuse surface or a light source.

To render these, we use ray-tracing. We first identify pixels which correspond to specular surfaces, and then perform ray-tracing only for these pixels (Monte-Carlo or distributed ray-tracing could also be used). When a ray hits a diffuse surface, the smoothed radiosity value is used directly. To optimize this we actually render the diffuse component in hardware, and then add in the ray-traced $(L|D)S^{+}E$ contributions. To find the corresponding grid element efficiently, we associate them to the hierarchical radiosity elements. The value returned is interpolated appropriately in the interior of the display polygon.

5 Results

All results are on an R10000 (200Mhz) SGI Origin 2000.

Interactive Rendering for Simple Scenes. We have already shown the results of interactive rendering in Fig. 1. Note that only the diffuse component of each object is being shown, using hardware rendering, explaining the dull appearance of the ring. Fig. 5 shows other examples (Fig. 5-8 are in the colour section). Quicktime movies of interactive sessions can be found at:
http://www-imagis.imag.fr/Publications/xgranier/EGWR00.

Quality Control. The iterations are governed by the following three parameters: (i) the threshold ε for the *BFA* refinement criterion. This controls the level of the links in the hierarchy, and thus the accuracy of the diffuse illumination, as in HRC; (ii) the minimum area, which is the size of the minimal element of the element hierarchy. This influences the subdivision due to diffuse light as well as the additional subdivision due to particle push; (iii) the ϕ_{ct} parameter, which controls the number of particles used as discussed above (Section 3.2). The lower ϕ_{ct}, the larger the number of particles sent over a link (see Eq. (5)).

In Fig. 3, we show the effect of varying the ϕ_{ct} parameter. Note that the quality quickly improves without significant overhead in time. The rightmost image is shown as an example of the quality our system can provide.

| 4 sec/1200 particles | 5 sec/7800 particles | 15 sec/81800 particles |

Fig. 3. Effect of varying the ϕ_{ct} parameter. We show the number of particles used to generate each image and the time required for two iterations. The minimum area parameter is fixed. Images rendered in hardware.

Complex and indirectly lit scenes. In Fig. 4 we show a modified version of the conference room scene from Greg Ward-Larson's material geometry format (mgf) test scenes. The model is quite complex (19,000 primitives corresponding to 150,000 polygons if tesselated naively). Due to memory limitations we have computed a coarse solution, but some caustic effects are perceptible.

In Fig. 6, we show a modified version of the Soda Shoppe scene (also an mgf test scene). We have reduced the size of the light sources and added a number of blue glass spheres to clearly demonstrate caustic effects. The scene contains about 1779 primitives (cylinders, spheres, rings and polygons); when initially tesselated to depth five, the input scene contains 80,000 polygons. Note that in a moderate amount of time (17 min 22 sec), we have a number of basic caustic effects. Images of Fig. 6 and Fig. 7

Fig. 4. A coarse solution of a modified version of the conference room scene, light simulation took 4 min 27 sec. (left) General view (right) closer view of the table. Ray-tracing took ∼ 4 min.

were ray-traced at 1980 x 980 resolution in about 4 minutes. Our final image ray-tracer uses the bounding box hierarchy of clusters, and is particularly slow. In both the Soda Shoppe and the conference room, many surfaces (floor, tabletops etc.) have materials with specular components, and thus contribute to non-diffuse transfer.

In Fig. 7(left), we show the same scene, but we have replaced the large direct lights with 12 small polygonal lights pointing to the walls. In a progressive refinement context, this would be very hard to treat, even using secondary source reclassification, since a very large number of patches would be characterized as important secondary sources, resulting in the need for a large number of iterations. Note that the simulation time (9 min 2 sec) is in the same order of magnitude as that for direct lighting.

Informal comparison to Particle Tracing. As an informal comparison we have computed the indirect lighting Soda Shoppe scene in Fig. 7(right) using standard particle tracing [34]. We use the same reconstruction as in our method for fairness of comparison. We have placed our solution computed in about the same time side-by-side. As we can see, the main problem with the particle tracing solution is noise.

Interactive Viewing and the Render Cache. We have integrated our method with the Render Cache [32] for interactive display. This approach allows interactive visualization of ray tracing algorithms. Our algorithm is particularly well suited to this approach, since for diffuse surfaces we render the radiosity directly. An example of its use is shown in Fig. 8 and in the Quicktime movies on the web site.

6 Conclusions

We have presented a novel global illumination algorithm which computes both glossy and diffuse lighting in a seamless, integrated manner.

We have achieved this by integrating particle tracing for glossy transport into the hierarchical radiosity gather step. The radiosity system efficiently simulates all diffuse light interactions. In addition, the link hierarchy it builds encodes considerable structural information about the flow of light in the environment. We exploit this information to guide and accelerate the particle emission that simulates the non-diffuse light interactions. This allows us to simulate all types of light path chains including specular reflection (e.g., caustics) without the high cost and noisy results of using particle tracing for all interactions.

Our integrated approach efficiently treats the case of mainly indirect lighting, including specular reflections. It also permits a smooth transition between coarse but fast solutions and more expensive but higher quality ones, without sacrificing the completeness of our light simulation. A suitable reconstruction step is performed which allows interactive visualisation of diffuse light with specular reflections including complex caustics, and interactive dynamic updates for simple scenes. More complex scenes can also be treated at reasonable cost. For higher quality images, ray tracing can be used to correctly visualize non-diffuse surfaces, and this can even be done interactively for low resolutions using the Render Cache.

Future Work. One limitation of our method is that if high frequencies exist locally in models with large differences of scale, it is hard to avoid explosion in the number of mesh elements. The solution to this will inevitably lead to a separate reconstruction process for low-frequency (mainly diffuse) lighting interactions, and high-frequency (mainly specular) phenomena such as caustics. We are developing a multi-level reconstruction algorithm for the low frequency interactions, while high-frequency effects can be treated by some form of "caustic maps" or textures. For diffuse light transfer, the HRC hierarchy can be used throughout (by averaging the map contents), and thus the caustic maps will be only used for display.

We have performed initial experiments using visual importance [25] to refine the scene locally. However, we need to further develop the concepts, in particular for more complex scenes and the particle tracing part of the algorithm.

We are also investigating better dynamic updates using techniques similar to those of [6]. As with importance, the particle tracing phase needs to be adapted so that work is localized correctly. We are confident that we will be able to achieve interactive object motion within even moderately complex scenes such as those shown here.

Currently, link information is used only for the first segment of a diffuse-specular light path. Use of this information for subsequent bounces is clearly worth investigating.

Acknowledgments

This work was supported in great part by the ESPRIT Open LTR project #35772 SIMULGEN 2. Thanks to P. Poulin for numerous discussions and lots of advice, and to F. Neyret and F. Durand for re-reading the paper.

References

[1] L. Aupperle and P. Hanrahan. A hierarchical illumination algorithm for surfaces with glossy reflection. In *Proc. SIGGRAPH'93*, Annual Conference Series, pages 155–162, 1993.

[2] S. E. Chen, Holly E. Rushmeier, G. Miller, and D. Turner. A progressive multi-pass method for global illumination. In *Computer Graphics (SIGGRAPH '91)*, volume 25, pages 165–174, July 1991.

[3] P. H. Christensen, D. Lischinski, E. J. Stollnitz, and D. H. Salesin. Clustering for glossy global illumination. *ACM Trans. on Graphics*, 16(1):3–33, January 1997.

[4] M. F. Cohen, S. E. Chen, J. R. Wallace, and D. P. Greenberg. A progressive refinement approach to fast radiosity image generation. In *Computer Graphics (SIGGRAPH 88)*, volume 22(4), pages 75–84, August 1988.

[5] S. Collins. Adaptive splatting for specular to diffuse light transport. *5th EG Workshop on Rendering*, pages 119–135, June 1994. Darmstadt, Germany.

[6] G. Drettakis and F. Sillion. Interactive update of global illumination using a line-space hierarchy. In *Proc. SIGGRAPH'97*, Annual Conference Series, pages 57–64, August 1997.

[7] R. Dumont, K. Bouatouch, and P. Gosselin. A progressive algorithm for three point transport. *Computer Graphics Forum*, 18(1):41–56, March 1999.

[8] C. M. Goral, K. K. Torrance, D. P. Greenberg, and B. Battaile. Modelling the interaction of light between diffuse surfaces. In *Computer Graphics (SIGGRAPH'84)*, volume 18(3), pages 213–222, July 1984.

[9] E. A. Haines and J. R. Wallace. Shaft culling for efficient ray-traced radiosity. *2nd EG Workshop on Rendering (Photorealistic Rendering in Computer Graphics)*, 1994.

58

[10] P. Hanrahan, D. Salzman, and L. Aupperle. A hierarchical radiosity algorithm. In *Computer Graphics (SIGGRAPH '91)*, volume 25, pages 197–206, July 1991.

[11] P. S. Heckbert. Adaptive radiosity textures for bidirectional ray tracing. In *Computer Graphics (SIG-GRAPH'90)*, volume 24, pages 145–154, August 1990.

[12] D. S. Immel, M. F. Cohen, and D. P. Greenberg. A radiosity method for non-diffuse environments. *Computer Graphics (SIGGRAPH'86)*, 20(4):133–142, August 1986.

[13] H. Wann Jensen. Global illumination using photon maps. In *7th EG Rendering Workshop, "Rendering Techniques '96*, pages 21–30. EG, Springer Wien, June 1996.

[14] A. Keller. Instant radiosity. In *Proc. SIGGRAPH'97*, Annual Conference Series, pages 49–56, August 1997.

[15] L. Kobbelt, M. Stamminger, and H-P. Seidel. Using subdivision on hierarchical data to reconstruct radiosity distribution. *Computer Graphics Forum*, 16(3):347–356, August 1997. Proc. of EG '97.

[16] E. P. Lafortune and Y. D. Willems. Using the modified phong reflectance model for physically based rendering. Technical Report CW 197, Dept. of Computing Science, K.U. Leuven, November 1994.

[17] L. Neumann. Monte Carlo Radiosity. *Computing*, 55(1):23–42, 1995.

[18] S. Schäfer. Hierarchical radiosity on curved surfaces. In *EG Workshop on Rendering 1998, "Rendering Techniques '98"*, pages 187–192. EG, Springer Wien, June 1997.

[19] P. Shirley. Radiosity via Ray Tracing. In *Graphics Gems II*, pages 306–310. Academic Press Professional, Boston, MA, 1991.

[20] P. Shirley. A ray tracing method for illumination calculation in diffuse-specular scenes. *Graphics Interface '90*, pages 205–212, May 1990.

[21] F. X. Sillion. A unified hierarchical algorithm for global illumination with scattering volumes and object clusters. *IEEE Trans. on Visualization and Computer Graphics*, 1(3):240–254, September 1995.

[22] F. X. Sillion, J. R. Arvo, S. H. Westin, and D. P. Greenberg. A global illumination solution for general reflectance distributions. In *Computer Graphics (SIGGRAPH'91)*, volume 25(4), pages 187–196, July 1991.

[23] F. X. Sillion and C. Puech. A general two-pass method integrating specular and diffuse reflection. In *Computer Graphics (SIGGRAPH'89)*, volume 23, pages 335–344, July 1989.

[24] B. Smits, J. Arvo, and D. P. Greenberg. A clustering algorithm for radiosity in complex environments. In *Proc. SIGGRAPH'94*, Annual Conference Series, pages 435–442, July 1994.

[25] B. E. Smits, J. R. Arvo, and D. H. Salesin. An importance-driven radiosity algorithm. In *Computer Graphics (SIGGRAPH'92)*, volume 26, pages 273–282, July 1992.

[26] M. Stamminger, Annette Scheel, X. Granier, F. Perez-Cazorla, G. Drettakis, and F. X. Sillion. Efficient glossy global illumination with interactive viewing. *Graphics Interface '99*, pages 50–57, June 1999.

[27] M. Stamminger, P. Slusallek, and H-P. Seidel. Three point clustering for radiance computations. In *9th EG Workshop on Rendering, "Rendering Techniques '98"*, pages 211–222. Springer Wien, 1998.

[28] M. Stamminger, P. Slusallek, and H-P. Seidel. Bounded radiosity - illumination on general surfaces and clusters. *Computer Graphics Forum*, 16(3):309–318, August 1997.

[29] W. Stürzlinger and R. Bastos. Interactive rendering of globally illuminated glossy scenes. In *8th EG Workshop on Rendering, "Rendering Techniques '97"*, pages 93–102. Springer Wien, June 1997.

[30] E. Veach. *Robust Monte-Carlo Methods for Light Transport Simulation*. PhD thesis, Stanford University, 1997. http://graphics.stanford.EDU/papers/veach_thesis/.

[31] J. R. Wallace, M. F. Cohen, and D. P. Greenberg. A two-pass solution to the rendering equation: A synthesis of ray tracing and radiosity methods. In *Computer Graphics (SIGGRAPH '87)*, volume 21, pages 311–320, July 1987.

[32] B. Walter, G. Drettakis, and S. Parker. Interactive rendering using the render cache. In *10th EG Workshop on Rendering, "Rendering Techniques'99"*. Springer Wien, June 1999. Granada, Spain.

[33] B. Walter, P. M. Hubbard, P. Shirley, and D. P. Greenberg. Global illumination using local linear density estimation. *ACM Trans. on Graphics*, 16(3):217–259, July 1997.

[34] B. J. Walter. *Density estimation techniques for global illumination*. PhD thesis, Cornell University, 1998. http://www.graphics.cornell.edu/pubs/1998/Wal98.html.

[35] G. J. Ward and P. Heckbert. Irradiance gradients. *3rd EG Workshop on Rendering*, pages 85–98, May 1992.

[36] M. Watt. Light-water interaction using backward beam tracing. In *Computer Graphics (SIGGRAPH 90)*, volume 24(4), pages 377–385, August 1990.

Editors' Note: see Appendix, p. 394 for colored figures of this paper

Virtual Occluders: An Efficient Intermediate PVS representation

Vladlen Koltun   Yiorgos Chrysanthou   Daniel Cohen-Or

Tel Aviv University   University College London   Tel Aviv University

Fig. 1. A virtual occluder (the red and white rectangle) represents aggregate occlusion from a region.

Abstract. In this paper we introduce the notion of virtual occluders. Given a scene and a viewcell, a virtual occluder is a view-dependent (simple) convex object, which is guaranteed to be fully occluded from any given point within the viewcell and which serves as an effective occluder from the given viewcell. Virtual occluders are a compact intermediate representation of the aggregate occlusion for a given cell. The introduction of such view-dependent virtual occluders enables applying an effective region-to-region or cell-to-cell culling technique and efficiently computing a potential visibility set (PVS) from a region/cell. We present a technique that synthesizes such virtual occluders by aggregating the visibility of a set of individual occluders and we show the technique's effectiveness.

1 Introduction

Visibility algorithms have recently regained attention in computer graphics as a tool to handle large and complex scenes, which consist of millions of polygons. Twenty years ago hidden surface removal (HSR) algorithms were developed to solve the fundamental problem of determining the visible portions of the polygons in the image. Today, since the z-buffer hardware is the de-facto standard HSR technique, the focus is on visibility culling algorithms that quickly reject those parts of the scene which do not contribute to the final image.

Conventional graphics pipelines include two simple visibility culling techniques: view-frustum culling and backface culling. These visibility techniques are local in the sense that they are applied to each polygon independently of the other polygons in the scene. Occlusion culling is another visibility technique in which a polygon is culled if it is fully occluded by some other part of the scene. This technique is global and thus far more complex than the above local techniques.

Apparently, occlusion culling techniques and hidden surface removal techniques are conceptually alike and have a similar asymptotic complexity. However, to apply an occlusion culling technique as a quick rejection process, it must be significantly more efficient than the hidden surface removal process. The answer is the use of conservative methods in which for a given scene and view point the conservative occlusion culling algorithm determines a superset of the visible set of polygons [3, 15, 9]. These methods yield a potential visibility set (PVS) which includes all the visible polygons, plus a small number of occluded polygons. Then the HSR processes the (hopefully small) excess of polygons included in the PVS. Conservative occlusion culling techniques have the potential to be significantly more efficient than the HSR algorithms. It should be emphasized that the conservative culling algorithm can also be integrated into the HSR algorithm, aiming towards an output sensitive algorithm [14, 23]. A good overview of most recent culling techniques can be found in [17].

To reduce the computational cost, the conservative occlusion culling algorithms usually use a hierarchical data structure where the scene is traversed top-down and tested for occlusion against a small number of selected occluders [9, 15]. In these algorithms the selection of the candidate occluders is done before the online visibility calculations. The efficiency of these methods is directly dependent on the number of occluders and their effectiveness. Since the occlusion is tested from a point, these algorithms are applied in each frame during the interactive walkthrough.

A more promising strategy is to find the PVS from a region or viewcell, rather than from a point. The computation cost of the PVS from a viewcell would then be amortized over all the frames generated from the given viewcell. Effective methods have been developed for indoor scenes [2, 20, 12, 1], but for general arbitrary scenes, the computation of the visibility set from a region is more involved than from a point. Sampling the visibility from a number of view points within the region [13] yields an approximated PVS, which may then cause unacceptable flickering temporal artifacts during the walkthrough. Conservative methods were introduced in [7, 18] which are based on the occlusion of individual large convex objects. In these methods a given object or collection of objects is culled away if and only if they are fully occluded by a single convex occluder. It was shown that a convex occluder is effective only if it is larger than the viewcell [7]. However, this condition is rarely met in real applications. For example the objects in Figure 2 are smaller than the viewcell, and their umbra (with respect to the viewcell) are rather small. Their union does not occlude a significant portion of the scene (see in (a)), while their aggregate umbra is large (see in (b)). Recently, new conservative methods are emerging [19, 11, 22] which apply occlusion fusion based on the intersection of the umbrae of individual occluders.

In this paper we present a novel way of representing and computing the visibility from a viewcell. For that purpose, we introduce the notion of virtual occluders. Given a scene and a viewcell, a virtual occluder is a view-dependent (simple) convex object, which is guaranteed to be fully occluded from any given point within the viewcell and which serves as an effective occluder from that viewcell. Virtual occluders compactly represent the occlusion information for a given cell. Each virtual occluder represents the aggregate occlusion of a cluster of occluders. The introduction of such view-dependent virtual occluders enables one to apply an effective region-to-region or cell-to-cell culling technique and to efficiently compute the PVS from a region or a cell. Figure 1 depicts a virtual occluder that aggregates occlusion of four columns in the Freedman Museum model. On the right, the scene is shown from above. The virtual occluder is the vertical rectangle placed behind the furthest column. On the left, a view is shown from inside the region for which this virtual occluder was computed. The virtual occluder is completely occluded behind the columns (which are rendered transparent, for the sake of demonstration). We present a technique that synthesizes such virtual occluders by aggregating the occlusion of a set of individual occluders and show its effectiveness. It should be mentioned that the term "virtual occluders" was independently used in [16] with a different meaning.

The rest of the paper is organized as follows: We give an overview of the method in Section 2, as well as summarizing its main contributions. In Section 3 we describe the algorithm for constructing the set of virtual occluders. The results and their analysis are presented in Section 4, and we conclude in Section 5.

2 Overview

The virtual occluders are constructed in preprocessing. For simplicity in the discussion we assume regular partitioning of the scene into axis-aligned box-shaped cells. However, this is not inherent to our algorithm, which may handle any partitioning of the scene into cells of arbitrary non-convex shape. This algorithm is applied to a given viewcell and constructs a set of virtual occluders that effectively represents the occlusion from this cell. It yields a large, dense set of potential virtual occluders. From this set, an effective small sorted subset is selected and stored for the on-line stage. Since the virtual occluders are large, convex and few, the PVS of the associated viewcell can be quickly constructed by applying a simple and effective culling mechanism similar to [7, 18].

The PVS of a viewcell is constructed only once before the walkthrough enters the cell, by culling the scene against the virtual occluders. The frame-rate of the walkthrough is not significantly interrupted by the visibility determination, since the cost of constructing the viewcell's PVS is amortized over the large number of frames during the walk through the cell. Note that one of the advantages of our method is that it generates large effective occluders and thus enables the use of a larger viewcell, which further reduces the relative cost of computing the PVS. The main advantages of the presented method can be summarized as follows:

Aggregate occlusion. Each virtual occluder encapsulates the combined contribution of a cluster of occluders. This results in the ability of culling larger portions of the scene-graph using just a single virtual occluder. Moreover, a small set of virtual occluders faithfully represents the occlusion from a viewcell.

Accuracy. The presented method for constructing virtual occluders is an object-space continuous method. Their shape and location are not constrained by a space partition of the scene (e.g., quadtree or kd-tree). The placement of the virtual occluders adapts to the scene and not to an independent fixed subdivision This leads to accuracy and thus a stronger conservative visibility set.

Speed. Since the number of per-viewcell virtual occluders is small, the visibility culling process is faster. The virtual occluders occlude more than the individual objects, and are thus able to cull larger cells of the scene-graph. This results in a highly reduced amount of computation at run-time for each viewcell.

Storage size. Given a viewcell and a small set of virtual occluders, the PVS can be computed on-the-fly during the walkthrough. This avoids storing the PVS but rather a small set of virtual occluders, which requires less space. This is vital since the potential visibility sets of all viewcells of a complex scene tend to be too large for storage (see Section 4).

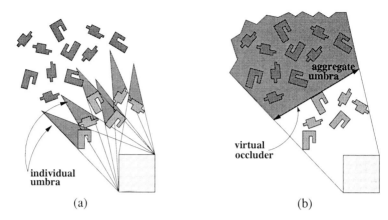

(a)   (b)

Fig. 2. The union of the umbrae of the individual objects is insignificant, while their aggregate umbra is large and can be represented by a single virtual occluder.

There are various applications that can benefit from virtual occluders. All of them exploit the fact that the cost of computing the conservative visibility set can be amortized over several frames. Rendering the scene consists of three processes:

1. computing the viewcell virtual occluders;
2. computing the viewcell PVS;
3. rendering the PVS.

The first process is computed offline, while the other two online. We can consider a rendering system, which is conceptually partitioned into a client and a server. The server can compute the virtual occluders in a preprocess and store them in a spatial data structure. During the walkthrough, the client uses the virtual occluders to compute the PVS. The PVS must be readily available for the real-time rendering of the scene. This requires the system to precompute the PVS of nearby viewcells before the walkthrough enters those viewcells. As mentioned in the introduction, a remote walkthrough application necessarily requires the computation of a from-region PVS to avoid the latency problem [8].

3 Constructing the Virtual Occluders

In this section we show how to construct a set of virtual occluders that represents the aggregate occlusion from a given viewcell. We first describe the algorithm in 2D and then extend it to 3D in the next subsection. The algorithm description is visualized with a set of illustrations: Figure 2 shows the viewcell in yellow and a set of occluders. The umbrae of the individual occluders is illustrated in 2 (a), showing that the occlusion of the individual objects is insignificant. Nevertheless, the aggregate occlusion of these objects is much larger, as can be seen in 2 (b). To construct virtual occluders that effectively capture the aggregate occlusion we use the following algorithm: (1) select a set of seed objects, (2) build a set of virtual occluders from a given seed and the cluster of objects around this seed and (3) decimate the initial dense set of virtual occluders to a cost effective smaller set. The exact definitions and details as applied for a given viewcell are elaborated below.

The set of seed objects is defined according to the solid-angle criterion [15] defined from the viewcell center. Objects with a large solid-angle are likely to be effective occluders from the given viewcell and thus included in a cluster of occluders that builds up larger occlusion. The seed object in Figure 3 is colored in light blue. It should be noted that the algorithm is not sensitive to the accuracy of the definition of the set of seed objects. However, the more seeds used, the better the set of virtual occluders is in terms of its effectiveness (less conservative).

For a given seed object we now construct an aggregate umbra starting from its own umbra and augmenting it with the occlusion of its surrounding objects. First, the two supporting lines that connect the viewcell and object extents build the initial umbra. An initial virtual occluder is placed behind the object in its umbra (see Figure 3 (a)). Now, let us first assume that during this process one of the supporting lines is defined as the *active supporting line* while the other remains static (the active supporting line is drawn in purple). If the active line intersects an object, then this object is a candidate to augment the umbra. If the candidate object intersects the umbra of the seed object, then it augments the umbra and the active line shifts to the extent of the inserted object (see Figure 3 (b)). By iteratively adding more and more objects the umbra extends, and gets larger and larger. There are cases where a candidate object does not intersect the current umbra, but can still augment it. To treat these cases we define and maintain the *active separating line(polyline)* (colored in red).

Initially, the active separating line is defined between the seed object and the viewcell (in the standard way [9]). Then objects which intersect the active separating line redefine it to include the new objects and the separating line becomes a polyline. In Figure 3 (b) we can see that object 2, which intersects the active supporting line, but not the active separating line, cannot contribute its occlusion to the augmented umbra before the contribution of object 3 is considered. As illustrated in Figure 3 (b), object 3 intersects the active separating line and thus redefines it to the polyline shown in Figure 3 (c). Then, object 2 intersects both active lines, augments the aggregate umbra and extends the virtual occluder further (3 (d)). Formally, let us define the evolving aggregate umbra U, the active supporting line P, and the active separating polyline Q. Given an object B:

1. If B intersects U then B updates U, Q and P, and a new virtual occluder is placed behind B.
2. If B intersects only Q then Q is updated to include B.
3. If B intersects both Q and P then B updates U, Q and P, and the furthest virtual occluder is extended to the new location of P.

Once no more objects intersect the active lines, the static line on the other side is activated, the process is repeated for the other side aiming to further augment the umbra by adding objects from the other side of the seed object. In our implementation both left and right separating lines are maintained active and the insertion of objects can be on either side of the umbra. Thus, the initial active supporting and separating lines are as shown in Figure 4. Note that in case 2 above, B has to be above the opposite active polyline.

Since a virtual occluder is placed behind all the individual occluders that make it up, as it grows bigger it also grows further away from the viewcell. For this reason we periodically 'dump' some of the intermediate virtual occluders into the dense set.

This aggregate umbra algorithm bears some conceptual similarity to algorithms that compute shadow volumes from an area light source [4, 5], or even to discontinuity meshing methods [10, 6]. However, here we have two important advantages. First,

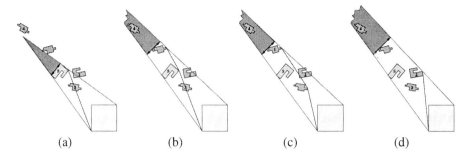

Fig. 3. Growing the virtual occluders by intersecting objects with the active separating and supporting lines. (see color plates)

the aggregate umbra does not necessarily have to be accurate, but conservative, and can thus be calculated significantly faster than area shadow algorithms. The other advantage lies in the effectiveness of the aggregation. While shadow algorithms detect additional objects that intersect an umbra and expand it, they don't make full use of the separating lines. See the example in Figure 5, even if the polygons are processed in front-to-back order, none of the shadow methods successfully merge the umbrae into one, in contrast to the method presented here.

After a dense set of virtual occluders is computed, it is sufficient to select only a small subset of them for the on-line stage. This saves the per-cell storage space and accelerates the process of computing the cell visibility set. The idea is that the subset can represent the occlusion faithfully, since there is a large amount of redundancy in the dense set. In practice, we have found that just less than ten virtual occluders per cell are sufficient to represent the occlusion effectively.

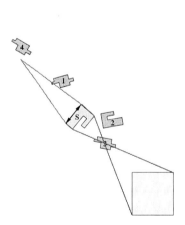

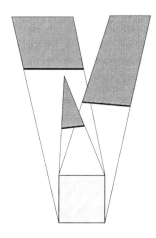

Fig. 5. Current shadow algorithms do not necessarily aggregate the occlusion.

Fig. 4. The active lines are processed on both sides simultaneously.

The greedy algorithm that is used to select this subset is described in Figure 6. Figure 9 shows a subset of virtual occluders selected by the algorithm. The key observation behind this algorithm is that the addition of a virtual occluder to the subset is a tradeoff

- the additional virtual occluder improves the PVS by occluding some part of the scene, but the down-side is that the process of computing the PVS takes longer with a bigger set of virtual occluders. Therefore the algorithm selects the most effective occluders one by one, until the addition of another occluder is not cost effective since the occlusion contributed by it is not significant enough to justify the enlargement of the subset. A beneficiary consequence of this algorithm is that the final subset is sorted, i.e. the most effective occluders appear first. This will accelerate the PVS construction process. This algorithm of course is non- optimal, but practically, there is no significant difference since conservative occlusion is not sensitive to small details.

```
for each virtual occluder O in the dense set D do
    initialize weight of O
        to the size of the area it occludes.
endfor
repeat
    let V be the virtual occluder with largest weight in D
    if V contributes effectively to occlusion
    then
        add it to the final sorted set
        remove it from D
        for every occluder O in D do
            reduce the weight of O by the size of the
            area occluded both by O and V
        endfor
    else
        output the final set, and exit
    endif
endrepeat
```

Fig. 6. Algorithm for selecting a sorted effective subset from a dense set of virtual occluders.

3.1   Treating 3D Cases Using a 2.5D Visibility Solution

Above we have described the algorithm in 2D. Extending the algorithm to handle arbitrary 3D scenes entails considerable increase in its complexity and running time. Fortunately, in practice, full 3D visibility culling is not always necessary. When dealing with typical (outdoor and indoor) walkthroughs, 2.5D visibility culling is almost as effective but much faster. Moreover, in these cases a simpler implementation of the technique significantly accelerates the process, while losing insignificant conservativeness.

The 2.5D visibility problem is reduced to a set of 2D problems by taking numerous slices of the scene at different heights. Farther buildings appear lower from the viewcell, and therefore the slices can not be horizontal in the original scene. To perform the slicing in a way that takes perspective into account, we lower each vertex in the scene proportionally to its distance from the viewcell (in this case, the distance to a point in the viewcell that is farthest from it). After this adjustment, horizontal slices of the scene are representative in terms of occlusion, i.e. if an object is occluded in a 2D slice of a given height, it is guaranteed to be occluded in 3D up to this height.

For each slice we run the 2D algorithm that constructs virtual occluders. These virtual occluders are extended from the ground up to the height of the slice. This yields a dense set of virtual occluders of different heights. The degree to which this representation is conservative, depends on the discretization resolution. This approach is conservative, because in 2.5D, if a vertical object (e.g. virtual occluder) is completely occluded by other objects at a given height, it is guaranteed to be occluded by them at all smaller heights as well.

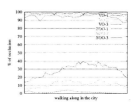

# slices	% of occlusion
5	97.27
4	96.91
3	96.21
2	94.52
1	72.07

Fig. 7. The occlusion as a function of the number of height slices.

Fig. 8. A comparison between the occlusion of individual occluders and virtual occluders. The graph displays the percentage of occlusion for all viewcells along a path across the London model. Different colors correspond to different cell sizes. Red corresponds to cells of size 160x100 meters; green for 320x200 meters; blue for 640x400. (see color plates)

The discretization does not necessarily lead to a loss of precision. In practice it is enough to construct virtual occluders at only a small number of "interesting" heights. There is a tradeoff between the precision and the processing time. As a heuristic strategy, a height-histogram of the scene is quantized and analyzed to select an appropriate number of heights for slicing the scene. The histogram of heights is constructed by considering the perspective-adjusted heights of the scene, as seen from the cell. In practice, five or less slices provide sufficiently good results, as shown in Section 4. In should be emphasized that the virtual occluders are conservative by nature and the effectiveness of the method is not sensitive to small details of the occluders.

4 Results

We have implemented the described algorithms in C-language using the OpenGL libraries. The tests described below were carried out on an SGI InfiniteReality, with a 196Mhz R10000 processor. We have tested the method on two highly complex scenes. One is a model of London, accurately depicting an area of 160 sq. kilometers (some parts are shown in Figures 9 and 12). The model was created from detailed maps provided by Ordnance Survey, and consists of over 250K objects having more than 4M vertices. The other model is the Freedman virtual museum, which spans an area of approximately 50,000 sq. feet, and consists of about a thousand objects having altogether 85K vertices (see Figure 10).

Figure 8 shows how the aggregate umbra of the virtual occluders improves the performance compared to an occlusion culling based on individual objects, for three different cell sizes. Each line shows the percent of occlusion along a long path around the city. We see that as the viewcells get larger the effectiveness of the individual occluders sharply decreases, compared to the effectiveness of using virtual occluders. We see that for large viewcells the occlusion of individual buildings is on average less than two percent of the scene, while virtual occluders occlude more than 85%. For smaller cells the occlusion by virtual occluders is on average more than 98%. An example of the effectiveness of virtual occluders can be seen in Figure 9. Note that the vast majority of the occluded objects are culled by the eight virtual occluders, while only an insignificant fraction of the scene can be culled by individual objects. Figure 11 shows a view of London with a virtual occluder (colored in red) with respect to a viewcell (marked in light green). The buildings that are occluded by this virtual occluder are colored in blue.

Fig. 9. A top view of central London. Virtual occluders (in red) are placed around the viewcell (red square). The blue buildings are those occluded by the virtual occluders and the green ones are those occluded by individual buildings. Only a small set of buildings remains potentially visible (colored in black) after using just eight virtual occluders. (see color plates)

The Museum model is an example of a sparse model, where less occlusion is present from any given region. In our tests, we have found that no object occludes other objects in the scene single-handedly. Nevertheless, more than 50% of the scene are usually found occluded, when virtual occluders are used. In this case, the virtual occluders faithfully represent the little occlusion present, despite the sparse nature of the scene and the ineffectiveness of its individual objects.

Table 1 shows the effectiveness of a small set of virtual occluders in terms of their occlusion. We can see that using just five virtual occluders already provides an effective occlusion of 95% of the London model. The use of more than ten virtual occluders does not contribute much to the occlusion. This means that in terms of per-viewcell storage space the virtual occluders are by far more economical than naive storage of the viewcell PVS list. A virtual occluder is a vertical quadrilateral, represented by opposite corners, which can be represented by only five values (the 2D endpoints and its height). These coordinate values can be quantized to one byte each, since the effective occlusion of the virtual occluder is not sensitive to its fine sizes. Thus, storing ten virtual occluders per viewcell requires just fifty bytes. A different way to deal with the problem of PVS storage was presented in [21], where a sophisticated compression scheme was described.

Figure 7 shows how the slicing resolution affects the conservativeness of the virtual occluders. The table shows the size of the PVS as a function of the number of slices. We see that the size of the PVS is improved greatly by taking only two slices. Using more than five slices does not yield a significant reduction in the size of the PVS.

For an average viewcell, it takes about a minute to produce the dense set of virtual

68

# VO	% of occ.	δ	PVS (#vertices)
1	43.73	43.73	2607241
2	72.05	28.31	1295049
3	86.93	14.88	605592
4	93.92	6.98	281713
5	95.91	1.99	189508
6	96.52	0.61	161244
7	96.77	0.25	149660
8	96.95	0.18	141320

# VO	% of occ.	δ	PVS (#vertices)
1	18.64	18.64	69424
2	34.94	16.30	55515
3	46.16	11.22	45941
4	51.95	5.79	41001
5	56.62	4.67	37016
6	60.92	4.30	33346
7	62.14	1.22	32305
8	63.22	1.08	31384

Table 1. The magnitude of occlusion as a function of the number of virtual occluders saved for real-time use. A small number of virtual occluders represent most of the occlusion. The upper table shows results for the London model, and the lower for the Freedman Museum model.

occluders and their decimation into an effective small set. Once the virtual occluders are given, the time spent on the computation of the PVS is negligible provided the scene is traversed hierarchically in a standard top-down fashion (the PVS is rapidly computed by treating the virtual occluders as strong occluders [7]). In fact, virtual occluders can be used from any point in the viewcell as effective from-point occluders. By performing from-point visibility culling using the precomputed virtual occluders, a refined visibility set can be obtained in each frame.

5   Conclusion

We have presented the new concept of virtual occluders as a means for representing the aggregate occlusion of groups of objects. They can have forms other than the one presented, but the idea is that they are an effective intermediate representation of the occlusion from a cell. One of their important features is that they are ordered in terms of importance. This provides an efficient culling mechanism since the visibility test of each object is applied first with the most effective occluders. Only those few objects that are not culled by the first most effective virtual occluders are tested against the rest of the occluders down the ordered list.

It is important to note that in the London model the buildings are fairly simple and consist of a relatively small number of polygons. This means that level-of-detail techniques (LOD) cannot help much in rendering such a huge model. Thus, occlusion culling is a vital tool for such walkthrough application. In other cases a scene can consist of some very detailed geometric models. This would require incorporating dynamic LOD techniques, image-based rendering and modeling, and other acceleration techniques to handle rendering the potential visibility sets.

6 Acknowledgements

This work was supported by a grant from the Israeli Ministry of Science and by a grant from the Israeli Academy of Sciences (center of excellence). We like to thank Ordnance Survey and the COVEN ACTS project for providing us with the London data and also Anthony Steed for his valuable help with the rendering. We thank the anonymous referees for the constructive comments.

References

1. Michael Abrash. *Zen of Graphics Programming*. Coriolis Group Books, second edition, 1996.
2. J. Airey, J. Rohlf, and F. Brooks. Towards image realism with interactive update rates in complex virtual building environments. *ACM Siggraph Special Issue on 1990 Symposium on Interactive 3D Graphics*, 24(2):41–50, 1990.
3. J. Bittner, V. Havran, and P. Slavik. Hierarchical visibility culling with occlusion trees. In *Proceedings of Computer Graphics International '98*, pages 207–219, June 1998.
4. A. T. Campbell, III and D. S. Fussell. An analytic approach to illumination with area light sources. Technical Report R-91-25, Dept. of Computer Sciences, Univ. of Texas at Austin, August 1991.
5. N. Chin and S. Feiner. Fast object-precision shadow generation for area light sources using BSP trees. In *ACM Computer Graphics (Symp. on Interactive 3D Graphics)*, pages 21–30, 1992.
6. Y. Chrysanthou. *Shadow Computation for 3D Interaction and Animation*. PhD thesis, Queen Mary and Westfield College, University of London, February 1996.
7. Daniel Cohen-Or, Gadi Fibich, Dan Halperin, and Eyal Zadicario. Conservative visibility and strong occlusion for viewspace partitionin of densely occluded scenes. *Computer Graphics Forum*, 17(3):243–254, 1998. ISSN 1067-7055.
8. Daniel Cohen-Or and Eyal Zadicario. Visibility streaming for network-based walkthroughs. *Graphics Interface '98*, pages 1–7, June 1998. ISBN 0-9695338-6-1.
9. Satyan Coorg and Seth Teller. Real-time occlusion culling for models with large occluders. *1997 Symposium on Interactive 3D Graphics*, pages 83–90, April 1997. ISBN 0-89791-884-3.
10. G. Drettakis and E. Fiume. A fast shadow algorithm for area light sources using backprojection. In Andrew Glassner, editor, *ACM Computer Graphics*, pages 223–230, July 1994.
11. Frédo Durand, George Drettakis, Joëlle Thollot, and Claude Puech. Conservative visibility preprocessing using extended projections. *To appear in the proceedings of SIGGRAPH 2000*, 2000.
12. T.A. Funkhouser. Database management for interactive display of large architectural models. *Graphics Interface*, pages 1–8, May 1996.
13. Craig Gotsman, Oded Sudarsky, and Jeffry Fayman. Optimized occlusion culling. *Computer & Graphics*, 23(5):645–654, 1999.
14. Ned Greene and M. Kass. Hierarchical Z-buffer visibility. In *Computer Graphics Proceedings, Annual Conference Series, 1993*, pages 231–240, 1993.
15. T. Hudson, D. Manocha, J. Cohen, M. Lin, K. Hoff, and H. Zhang. Accelerated occlusion culling using shadow frusta. In *Proceedings of the 13th International Annual Symposium on Computational Geometry (SCG-97)*, pages 1–10, New York, June4–6 1997. ACM Press.
16. F.A. Law and T.S. Tan. Preprocessing occlusion for real-time selective refinement. In *ACM Symposium on Interactive 3D Graphics*, pages 47–53, April 1999.
17. Tomas Moller and Eric Haines. *Real-Time Rendering*. A. K. Peters Limited, 1999.

70

18. Carlos Saona-Vazquez, Isabel Navazo, and Pere Brunet. The visibility octree: A data structure for 3d navigation. *Computer & Graphics*, 23(5):635–644, 1999.
19. Gernot Schaufler, Xavier Decoret, Julie Dorsey, and Francois Sillion. Conservative volumetric visibility with occluder fusion. *To appear in the proceedings of SIGGRAPH 2000*, 2000.
20. Seth J. Teller and Carlo H. Sequin. Visibility preprocessing for interactive walkthroughs. *Computer Graphics (Proceedings of SIGGRAPH 91)*, 25(4):61–69, July 1991. ISBN 0-201-56291-X. Held in Las Vegas, Nevada.
21. Michiel van de Panne and A. James Stewart. Effective compression techniques for precomputed visibility. In *Eurographics Workshop on Rendering*, pages 305–316, June 1999.
22. Peter Wonka, Michael Wimmer, and Dieter Schmalstieg. Visibility preprocessing with occluder fusion for urban walkthroughs. In *proceeding of Eurographics Workshop on Rendering*, June 2000.
23. H. Zhang, D. Manocha, T. Hudson, and K. Hoff. Visibility culling using hierarchical occlusion maps. In *Computer Graphics (Proceedings of SIGGRAPH 97)*, pages 77–88, 1997.

Fig. 10. A ray-traced view over the Freedman virtual museum with the ceiling removed. The yellow square in the bottom is the viewcell and the red and white rectangle is one of the virtual occluders.

Fig. 11. A viewcell and one of the corresponding virtual occluders (the long red rectangle piercing through the buildings). The buildings that are occluded by this virtual occluder are colored in blue. (see color plates)

Fig. 12. A view over a part of the London model.

Editors' Note: see Appendix, p. 395 for colored figures of this paper

Visibility Preprocessing with Occluder Fusion for Urban Walkthroughs

Peter Wonka, Michael Wimmer, Dieter Schmalstieg

Vienna University of Technology

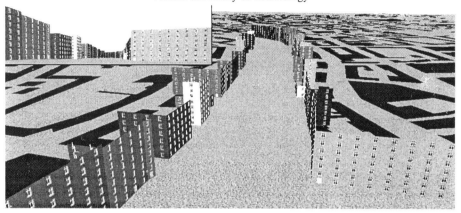

Figure 1. Views from the 8 million polygon model of the city of Vienna used in our walkthrough application. The inset in the upper left corner shows a typical wide open view, while the large image shows the portion of the scene rendered after occlusion culling. Note how occlusion fusion from about 200 visible occluders allows to prune over 99% of the scene.

Abstract. This paper presents an algorithm for occlusion culling from regions of space. It is conservative and able to find all significant occlusion. It discretizes the scene into view cells, for which cell-to-object visibility is precomputed, making on-line overhead negligible. Unlike other precomputation methods for view cells, it is able to conservatively compute all forms of occluder interaction for an arbitrary number of occluders. We describe an application of this algorithm to urban environments. A walkthrough system running an 8 million polygon model of the city of Vienna on consumer-level hardware illustrates our results.

Keywords. Visibility determination, occlusion culling, occluder fusion, urban walkthroughs

1 Introduction

Applications of visual simulation, such as architectural walkthroughs, driving simulators, computer games, or virtual reality require sufficiently high update rates for interactive feedback. While update rates starting from 10 frames per second (fps) are often called interactive, they are rarely considered satisfactory. To avoid temporal aliasing, true real-time behavior requires update rates equivalent to the monitor refresh rate, i. e. 60 Hz or more.

For very large databases, this kind of performance cannot be achieved with hardware acceleration alone, but must be assisted by algorithms that reduce the geometry to be rendered to a tolerable amount. A popular means is occlusion culling, which quickly prunes large portions of the scene. Visibility calculations for a *single viewpoint* have to be carried out online and infer significant runtime overhead. Moreover, in a typical single-CPU system, online processing time must be shared with other tasks, such as rendering and collision detection. Therefore it is useful to calculate visibility for a region of space (*view cell*) in a preprocessing step.

1.1   Motivation

Occlusion culling shares many aspects with shadow rendering. Occlusion culling from a view cell is equivalent to finding those objects which are completely contained in the umbra (shadow volume) with respect to a given area light source. In contrast to occlusion from a point, exact occlusion culling for regions in the general case (or its equivalent, shadow computation for area light sources) is not a fully solved problem. Two main problems impede a practical closed-form solution:

- The umbra with respect to a polygonal area light source is not only bounded by planes, but also by reguli, i. e. ruled quadratic surfaces of negative Gaussian curvature [4][21]. Such reguli are difficult to store, intersect etc.

- The maximum number of topologically distinct viewing regions constitutes the so called *aspect graph* [7][14], which is costly to compute ($O(n^9)$ time [7]). For applications such as radiosity, a more practical approach is the *visibility skeleton* [5]. However, the algorithmic complexity and robustness problems of analytic visibility methods impede their practical use for large scenes.

For visibility from a point, the joint umbra of many occluders is the union of the umbrae of the individual occluders, which is simple to compute. In contrast, for view cells, the union of umbrae is only contained in the exact umbra, which also depends to a great extent on contributions of merged penumbrae (see Figure 2). While umbra information for each occluder can be described by a simple volume in space ('in/out'-classification for each point), penumbra information also has to encode the visible part of the light source, making it hard to find a practical spatial representation. Therefore a general union operation for penumbrae is not easily defined.

Although an approximation of the umbra from multiple occluders by a union of individual umbrae is conservative, it is not sufficiently accurate. There are frequent cases where a significant portion of occlusion coming from occluder fusion is missed, making the solution useless for practical purposes. In particular, we distinguish between the cases of connected occluders, overlapping umbrae, and overlapping penumbrae (see Figure 2 (a), (b) and (c) respectively).

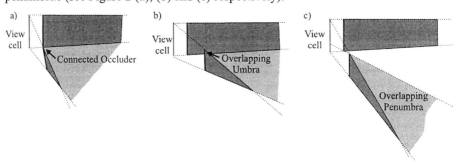

Figure 2. Different types of occluder interactions (illustrated in 2D). Individual umbrae (shaded dark) cover only a small area, while the occluders jointly cover a large unbounded area (shaded light).

This paper describes a fast, conservative occlusion culling algorithm that solves the aforementioned problems. It is based on the idea that conservative visibility for a region of space can be calculated by *shrinking* occluding objects and *sampling* visibility from points on the boundary of the region. Thus, conservative visibility for each cell can be computed as a preprocess, and visibility determination consumes no time during actual walkthroughs. This approach has several essential advantages:

Occluder Fusion: Our technique places no inherent restriction on the type of occluder interaction. Fusion of occluder umbrae[1] and even penumbrae is implicitly performed. This includes the hard case where individual umbrae of two occluders are disjoint (see Figure 2 (c)). We also discretize umbra boundaries, which are typically made up of reguli (curved surfaces). Other published algorithms do not currently handle such cases of occluder interactions.

Conservativity. Our method never reports visible objects as invisible. While some authors argue that non-conservative (approximate) visibility *can* be beneficial, it is not tolerable for all applications.

Note that while occlusion culling can typically speed up rendering by orders of magnitude, no visibility algorithm alone can guarantee sufficiently high frame rates. If the complexity of visible objects is too high, occlusion culling has to lay a good foundation for further simplification techniques like level of detail and image-based rendering.

1.2   Related Work

Several methods were proposed to speed up the rendering of interactive walkthrough applications. General optimizations are implemented by rendering toolkits like Performer [15] that aim for an optimal usage of hardware resources. Level of detail (LOD) algorithms [9] are very popular in urban simulation [11], because they do not need a lot of calculation during runtime. With image-based simplification, coherent parts of the scene are replaced by impostors (textured quadriliterals [17][18] or textured depth meshes [19]).

Occlusion culling algorithms calculate a conservative estimation of those parts of the scene that are definitely invisible. Final hidden surface removal is usually done with a z-buffer. A simple and general culling method is view frustum culling, which is applicable for almost any model.

Occlusion culling from a point can be calculated in image space [8][25] or geometrically [1][3][10]. The implementation presented in this paper makes use of graphics hardware to calculate occlusion. We use the concept of *cull maps*, which have recently been proposed by Wonka and Schmalstieg [23] for online occlusion culling of city-like scenes.

To calculate occlusion for regions, a general method is to break down the view space into cells and precompute for each cell a set of objects that are potentially visible (potentially visible sets, PVS). For general scenes, visibility precomputation can

---

[1] The umbra with respect to a view cell is the region of space from where no point of the view cell can be seen, whereas the penumbra is the region of space from where some, but not all points of the view cell can be seen.

become quite costly with respect to time and memory, but for certain scenes, like terrains [20] or building interiors [22] it is possible to use the a priori knowledge about the scene structure for visibility calculation. Cohen-Or et al. [2] show an algorithm for densely occluded scenes that does not make use of occluder fusion.

Several view cell visibility methods with occluder fusion have only recently been proposed. Durand et al. [6] position six planes around a view cell and project occluders on those planes. To calculate conservative occlusion they define an extended projection for occluders and occludees. Schaufler et al. [16] perform occluder fusion by extending occluders in an octree into octree nodes already found occluded. Koltun et al. [12] calculate large cross sections through the shadow volume from a view cell and use them as virtual occluders during online occlusion culling.

1.3   Organization of the paper

The remainder of the paper is organized as follows. Section 2 introduces the main idea of how to calculate occluder fusion for the region visibility problem. Section 3 describes how we apply the algorithm to urban environments. Results are shown in section 4, and section 5 contains a discussion of our algorithm in comparison with other methods. Section 6 concludes the paper and shows avenues of future research.

2   Occluder Fusion

This section explains the main idea of our algorithm: visibility can be calculated fast and efficiently for point samples. We use such point samples to calculate visibility for a *region* of space. To obtain a conservative solution, occluders have to be shrunk by an amount determined by the density of point samples.

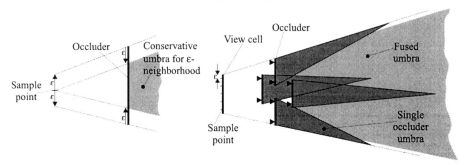

Figure 3. *Left*: Occluder shrinking: By considering an occluder after shrinking it by ε, the umbra from a point sample provides a good conservative approximation of the umbra of the original occluder in a neighborhood of radius ε of the sample point. *Right*: The fused umbra from the 5 point samples shown in Figure 4 is the intersection of the individual umbrae (shaded light). It is here compared to the union of umbrae from the original view cell (shaded dark). As can be seen, point sampling computes superior occlusion and only slightly underestimates exact occlusion.

2.1   Occluder fusion by occluder shrinking and point sampling

As can be concluded from the examples in Figure 2, occluder fusion is essential for good occlusion culling, but difficult to compute for view cells directly. To incorporate the effects of occluder fusion, we present a much simpler operation, which can be constructed from point sampling (for clarity, our figures show simple 2D cases only).

Our method is based on the observation that it is possible to compute a conservative approximation of the umbra for a view cell from a set of discrete point samples placed on the view cell's boundary. An approximation of actual visibility can be obtained by computing the intersection of all sample points' umbrae. This approach might falsely classify objects as occluded because there may be viewing positions between the sample points from where the considered object is visible.

However, *shrinking* an occluder by ε provides a smaller umbra with a unique property: An object classified as occluded by the shrunk occluder will remain occluded with respect to the original larger occluder when moving the viewpoint no more than ε from its original position (see Figure 3, left side).

Consequently, a point sample used together with a shrunk occluder is a conservative approximation for a small area with radius ε centered at the sample point. If the boundary of the original view cell is covered with sample points so that every point on its boundary is contained in an ε-neighborhood of at least one sample point, an object lying in the intersection of the umbrae from all sample points is therefore occluded for the original view cell (including its interior).

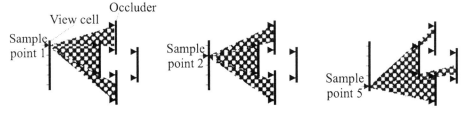

Figure 4. When performing point sampling for occlusion after occluders have been shrunk (as indicated by small triangles), all four occluders can be considered simultaneously, cooperatively blocking the view (indicated by the shaded area) from all sample points.

Using this idea, multiple occluders can be considered simultaneously. If the object is occluded by the joint umbra of the shrunk occluders for every sample point of the view cell, it is occluded for the whole view cell. In that way, occluder fusion for an arbitrary number of occluders can be performed (see Figure 4 and Figure 3, right side) using two main approaches:

- If a PVS is available for every sample point of a view cell, the PVS for the view cell can be calculated as the union of all individual PVS (this approach is independent of the algorithm used to calculate point visibility).

- If umbra information is stored explicitly as a volume during the point visibility algorithm, a joint umbra volume for the view cell can be calculated by intersecting the umbra volumes of all sample points (this approach might be more efficient, depending on the data structure used in the point visibility algorithm). The PVS for the view cell is then obtained by testing objects against this joint umbra.

While the method is conservative and not exact in that it underestimates occlusion, the fact that an arbitrary number of occluders can cooperate to provide occlusion helps to find relevant occlusion as long as ε is small in relation to a typical occluder.

In general, the exact amount by which a *planar* occluder (e.g., a polygon) has to be shrunk in each direction is dependent on the relative positions of sample point and occluder. If we consider a *volumetric* occluder, however, it can be shown that shrinking this volumetric occluder by ε provides a correct solution for an arbitrary volumetric view cell (see the appendix for a formal proof of this fact). Therefore, the occlusion culling problem can be solved using occluder shrinking and point sampling.

2.2 Implications of occluder shrinking

Since occluder shrinking need only be applied once during preprocessing for each occluder, the actual visibility computation is efficient for each view cell.

Note that while the algorithm apparently discretizes the view cell, it actually discretizes the complicated occluder interactions (Figure 2), i.e., including merged penumbrae and umbra boundaries defined by reguli. This principle makes it possible to compute occlusion from simple and fast point sampling.

2.3 Algorithm Overview

In the following, we outline the preprocessing algorithm:

1. Subdivide environment into view cells, choose ε.

2. Shrink occluders to yield conservative visibility with respect to ε.

3. For each view cell:

    4. Determine a sufficient number of sample points for that view cell.

    5. Calculate visibility for each sample point.

    6. Calculate view cell visibility (merge PVS or intersect umbra volumes of sample points)

3 Application to Urban Environments

Using the occluder shrinking principle explained in the last section requires a great amount of point sampling. Our implementation builds on the occluder shadow work explained in [23] and thus operates on city-like scenes (2.5D). It makes use of graphics hardware, which allows for fast calculation of individual point samples.

Because of the 2.5D property of occluders, any object found visible from one particular point is also visible from all locations above this point. This implies that sample points need only be placed on the edges of the top of the view cells.

While this type of environment may appear restrictive, it is suitable for the applications we have in mind (urban walkthroughs, driving simulation, games) and typically provides a large amount of occlusion. We made the following choices in our implementation:

3.1 Subdivision into View Cells

For our system we chose to use a constrained Delaunay triangulation of free space. The actual view cells are found by erecting a prism above each triangle of the triangulation.

3.2 Occluder Shrinking

In 2.5D, occluders can be arbitrary discontinuous functions $z = f(x,y)$ with compact support. Occluders must be given as a triangular irregular network, with heights assigned to the vertices of the triangles and possibly with discontinuities. We use a simple geometric algorithm to shrink occluders by the required amount.

3.3 Occluder selection

Typical models of urban environments consist of a large number of small triangles. Instead of using those triangles directly, our modeling system automatically extracts and stores building facades as occluders, a feature that cannot be assumed to be available in a general application. Occluders obtained this way correspond to a subset of the visual hull (i.e., the maximal object that has the same silhouettes and therefore the same occlusion characteristics as the original object, as viewed from all view cells [13]). Therefore, we do not need to consider irregular features of the facade like doors or windows. Our system handles arbitrary 2.5D-occluders, i.e., heightfields. The footprint of the occluder may be (and usually is) concave.

3.4 Optimizations

To accelerate preprocessing for urban environments, we extended the frame buffer algorithm from [23] with two major extensions (see [24] for details concerning implementation issues):

1. The point visibility algorithm explicitly stores umbra information in a frame buffer section. We use stencil buffer operations available on current graphics hardware to incrementally intersect umbra volumes from all sample points of a view cell. Only the joint umbra needs to be read back from the frame buffer.

2. For rapid preprocessing of large scenes, rasterizing *all* occluders to obtain a close approximation of exact visibility is not feasible. Quick rejection of large portions of the scene including the contained *occluded occluders* is essential. To achieve this goal, we employ a hierarchical approach.

4 Implementation and Results

A walkthrough system using the techniques outlined in this paper was implemented in C++ and OpenGL. All tests reported here were run under Windows NT on a Pentium-III 650MHz with 1GB RAM and a GeForce 256 graphics accelerator.

4.1 Preprocessing

A model of the city of Vienna with 7,928,519 polygons was used throughout testing. It was created by extruding about 2,000 building block footprints from an elevation map of Vienna, and procedurally adding façade details such as windows and doors (Figure 7, also on the color plate). One building block consists of one up to ten connected buildings. Note that each building block was modeled with several thousand polygons (3900 on average). Building blocks were further broken down into smaller objects (each consisting of a few hundred polygons) which were used as primitives for occlusion culling.

82,300 view cells were considered. The sample spacing constant ε was set to 1m, which led to the use of 6-8 sample points per view cell edge on average. Preprocessing took 523 minutes. 54 % of the preprocessing time was spent on reading back umbra information from the frame buffer.

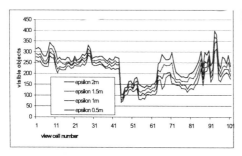 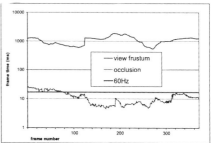

Figure 5. *Left*: Influence of various values of sample spacing (ε) on occlusion quality. Plotted is the number of visible objects (y-axis) against the view cells visited in the test walkthrough. *Right*: Frame times of occlusion culling vs. view frustum culling for the walkthrough. Note that frame times are plotted on a log scale to fit two orders of magnitude into the diagram.

4.2   Quality

We experimented with different settings for sample spacing (ε). Figure 5 (left side) shows the results for various choices of ε. As can be seen, larger values of ε also yield acceptable occlusion, allowing to handle larger models. On average, our algorithm identifies 99.34% (~1:150) of the scene as occluded. While these numbers are representative for a real-world data set, arbitrary occlusion ratios can be generated by increasing the depth complexity of the model. More interesting is the fact that the absolute numbers of occluders that contribute to occlusion is about 200 on average for our test model, which is quite high. See section 5.2 for a discussion of this fact. Figure 1 demonstrates the effect of occluder fusion.

4.3   Real-time rendering

To assess real-time rendering performance, precomputed occlusion was used to speed up rendering of a prerecorded walkthrough of the model, which was 372 frames long and visited 204 view cells. The model consumed approximately 700 MB and was fully loaded into main memory before the beginning of the walkthrough. Occlusion information (object IDs of potentially visible objects for each view cell) consumed 55 MB and was also fully loaded. Standard optimizations like triangle stripification, backface culling, compiled vertex arrays or display lists and static state sorting were used.

We measured frame times for two variants
- Full occlusion culling
- View frustum culling as a reference measurement

Occlusion culling provided an average speed-up of 93.78 over view frustum culling. Figure 5 (right side) shows the frame times from our walkthrough for occlusion culling vs. view frustum culling (logarithmic scale). Note that the desired 60Hz are achieved for the second part of the walkthrough (dense occlusion), while the first part (wide open view) would require further optimizations (e. g. impostors).

5 Discussion

5.1 Comparison

Competitive methods for view cell visibility have only recently been investigated independently by other authors. We are aware of two approaches: both require that an occluder intersects the accumulated umbra of previously considered occluders for occluder fusion to occur. Schaufler et al. [16] extend blockers into areas already found occluded, while Durand et al. [6] project occluders and occludees onto planes with new extended projections from volumetric view cells.

While these methods work in full 3D, they only consider a subset of occluder interactions handled by our method. Since their spatial data structure only represent *umbra* information, they cannot handle cases such as Figure 2 (c), for example, where the *penumbrae* of two occluders can be merged, even though there is no joint umbra. In most cases, missing such types of occluder interaction will cause a larger number of objects to appear in a PVS than necessary.

We found that complex shadow boundaries arise already in simple cases. Even in 2.5D, a simple occluder with non-convex footprint gives rise to so-called 'EEE event surfaces' [5], ruled quadric surfaces incident on three edges in the scene. Those event surfaces bound the umbra due to the occluder, but are usually not considered in other methods. Our approach discretizes such boundaries through point sampling, which gives a good approximation of the real umbra.

We believe that discretizaton is a reasonable trade-off between correctness and efficiency: our method implicitly handles all types of occluder interactions, and if we decrease ε, our method converges to a correct solution.

Although the idea of occluder shrinking and point sampling is applicable in 3D, the large number of point samples required would make a straightforward implementation rather slow.

5.2 Selection of occluders

Several algorithms achieve good results with a heuristic to select a set of occluders that is most likely to occlude a big part of the scene [3][10]. However, we have found that the number of occluders that contribute to occlusion is typically quite large (as indicated by results presented in section 4.1). Even missing small occluders can create holes that make additional objects visible. Therefore, all visible occluders should be considered for visibility calculations.

Using a large number of occluders requires significant computational effort. However, our preprocessing times are reasonable even for large scenes because the only geometric operation, occluder shrinking, needs to be performed only once during preprocessing. In our implementation, per view cell operations almost fully leverage the speed of current rasterization hardware, so we can calculate and render up to several hundred thousand occluder shadow polygons per second.

6 Conclusions and Future Work

Visibility preprocessing with occluder fusion is a new method for accelerated real-time rendering of very large urban environments. While it cannot compute exact visibility, no simplifying assumptions on the interaction between occluders or heuristics for occluder selection are necessary. Through point sampling, the proposed algorithm approximates actual umbra boundaries due to multiple occluders more exactly than previous methods, leading to better occlusion.

The measured number of occluders that contribute to occlusion (~200 on average) leads us to believe that simultaneous consideration of a large number of occluders is indeed crucial for achieving significant culling in hard cases where large open spaces are visible. The frame rates from our walkthrough, which are closely below or above the desired 60Hz, show that no significant time is available for on-line occlusion calculation, and that precomputed occlusion is necessary for true real-time performance.

Future work will focus on constructing suitable image-based representations for areas of the city where visibility preprocessing alone is not sufficient to guarantee a frame rate above 60 Hz. The restriction to volumetric occluders could be resolved with the introduction of view-dependent occluder simplification.

Acknowledgements

This research is supported by the Austrian Science Fund (FWF) contract no. p-13867-INF. The authors would like to thank Fredo Durand and Gernot Schaufler from MIT for fruitful discussions, Martin Held and Xinyu Xiang from Stony Brooks for their triangle stripper and triangulation code, Alan Murta from the University of Manchester for a polygon clipper, and Gerald Hummel from TU Vienna for support with the city model.

References

[1] J. Bittner, V. Havran, P. Slavík. Hierarchical Visibility Culling with Occlusion Trees. Computer Graphics International 1998 Proceedings, pp. 207-219, 1998.

[2] D. Cohen-Or, G. Fibich, D. Haperin, E. Zadicario. Conservative Visibility and Strong Occlusion for Viewspace Partitioning of Densely Occluded Scenes. Computer Graphics Forum (Proceedings of EUROGRAPHICS'98), 17(3), pp. 243-253, 1998.

[3] S. Coorg, S. Teller. Real-Time Occlusion Culling for Models with Large Occluders. Proceedings of the Symposium on Interactive 3D Graphics, pp. 83-90, 1997.

[4] F. Durand. 3D Visibility. Analytical Study and Applications. PhD thesis, IMAGIS-GRAVIR/IMAG-INRIA, Grenoble, France, 1999.

[5] F. Durand, G. Drettakis, C. Puech. The Visibility Skeleton: A Powerful and Efficient Multi-Purpose Global Visibility Tool. SIGGRAPH 97 Conference Proceedings, pp. 89-100, 1997.

[6] F. Durand, G. Drettakis, J. Thollot, C. Puech. Conservative Visibility Preprocessing using Extended Projections. To appear in SIGGRAPH 2000 Conference Proceedings.

[7] Z. Gigus, J. Canny, R. Seidel. Efficiently computing and representing aspect graphs of polyhedral objects. IEEE Transactions on Pattern Analysis and Machine Intelligence, 13(6), pp. 542-551, 1991.

[8] N. Greene, M. Kass. Hierarchical Z-Buffer Visibility, SIGGRAPH 93 Conference Proceedings, pp. 231-240, 1993.

[9] P. Heckbert, M. Garland. Survey of Polygonal Surface Simplification Algorithms. Multiresolution Surface Modeling (Course 25), SIGGRAPH, 1997.

[10] T. Hudson, D. Manocha, J. Cohen, M. Lin, K. Hoff, H. Zhang. Accelerated Occlusion Culling using Shadow Frusta. 13th International Annual Symposium on Computational Geometry (SCG-97), pp. 1-10, 1997.

[11] W. Jepson, R. Liggett, S. Friedman. An Environment for Real-time Urban Simulation. Proceedings of the Symposium on Interactive 3D Graphics, pp. 165-166, 1995.

[12] V. Koltun, Y. Chrysanthou, D. Cohen-Or. Virtual Occluders: An Efficient Intermediate PVS Representation. To appear in Eurographics Rendering Workshop 2000.

[13] A. Laurentini. The visual hull concept for silhouette-based image understanding. IEEE Transactions on Pattern Analysis and Machine Intelligence, 16(2), pp. 150-162, 1994.

[14] H. Plantinga, C. R. Dyer. Visibility, Occlusion, and the Aspect Graph, IJCV(5), No. 2, pp. 137-160, 1990.

[15] J. Rohlf, J. Helman. IRIS Performer: A High Performance Multiprocessing Toolkit for Real-Time 3D Graphics. SIGGRAPH 94 Conference Proceedings, pp. 381-395, 1994.

[16] G. Schaufler, X. Decoret, J. Dorsey, F. Sillion. Conservative Volumetric Visibility with Occluder Fusion. To appear in SIGGRAPH 2000 Conference Proceedings.

[17] G. Schaufler, W. Stürzlinger. A Three-Dimensional Image Cache for Virtual Reality. Computer Graphics Forum (Proceedings of EUROGRAPHICS'96), 15(3), pp. 227-235, 1996.

[18] J. Shade, D. Lischinski, D. Salesin, T. DeRose, J. Snyder. Hierarchical Image Caching for Accelerated Walkthroughs of Complex Environments. SIGGRAPH 96 Conference Proceedings, pp. 75-82, 1996.

[19] F. Sillion, G. Drettakis, B. Bodelet. Efficient Impostor Manipulation for Real-Time Visualization of Urban Scenery. Computer Graphics Forum (Proceedings of EUROGRAPHICS'97), 16(3), pp. 207-218, 1997.

[20] A. Stewart. Hierarchical Visibility in Terrains. Eurographics Rendering Workshop 1997, pp. 217-228, 1997.

[21] S. Teller. Computing the antipenumbra of an area light source. Computer Graphics (SIGGRAPH 92 Conference Proceedings), vol. 26, pp. 139-148, 1992.

[22] S. Teller, C. Sequin. Visibility preprocessing for interactive walkthroughs. Computer Graphics (SIGGRAPH 91 Conference Proceedings), vol. 25, pp. 61-69, 1991.

[23] P. Wonka, D. Schmalstieg. Occluder Shadows for Fast Walkthroughs of Urban Environments. Computer Graphics Forum (Proceedings of EUROGRAPHICS'99), pp. 51-60, 1999.

[24] P. Wonka, M. Wimmer, D. Schmalstieg. Visibility Preprocessing with Occluder Fusion for Urban Walkthroughs. Technical Report TR-186-2-00-06, Vienna University of Technology, 2000.

[25] H. Zhang, D. Manocha, T. Hudson, K. E. Hoff. Visibility Culling Using Hierarchical Occlusion Maps. SIGGRAPH 97 Conference Proceedings, pp. 77-88, 1997.

82

Appendix: A proof for conservative point sampling

Let an occluder O be an arbitrary connected subset of R^3. A *shrunk occluder* O' is a subset of O so that for all points $A \in O'$: $|B-A| \le \varepsilon \rightarrow B \in O$.

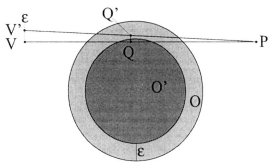

Figure 6. Any point P hidden by a shrunk occluder O' from V is also hidden by the original occluder O from any point V' in an ε-neighborhood of V.

Theorem: Any point P that is occluded by O' seen from a sample point V is also occluded by O from any sample point V' with $|V'-V| \le \varepsilon$ (see Figure 6).

Proof: Assume there is a V' for which P is not occluded by O. Then any point along the line segment V'P must not be contained in O. Since P is occluded, there is at least one point $Q \in O'$ along the line segment VP. VV'P form a triangle and $|V'-V| \le \varepsilon$, so there must be point Q' along V'P with $|Q'-Q| \le \varepsilon$. By definition, all points within an ε-neighborhood of Q are contained in O, so Q' is contained in O. Therefore P cannot be visible from V'. q.e.d.

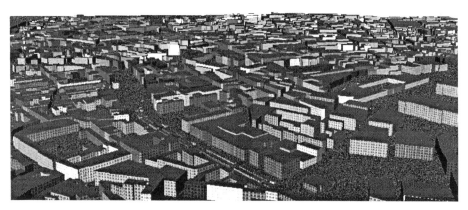

Figure 7. Overview of the 8 million polygon model of the city of Vienna used as a test scene. Note that the city is modeled in very high detail – every window, for example, is modeled separately with 26 polygons

82

82

82

Editors' Note: see Appendix, p. 396 for colored figures of this paper

Real-Time Rendering of Densely Populated Urban Environments

Franco Tecchia

Laboratorio Percro - Scuola Superiore S. Anna, Pisa, Italy

Yiorgos Chrysanthou

Department of Computer Science, University College London, London, UK

Abstract. In this paper we present some preliminary results concerning a real-time visualisation system for densely populated urban environments. In order to be able to render the large number of humans, we developed a method based on Image-Based Rendering techniques. To allow them to move freely in the city while avoiding collisions against the environment and other humans, we developed a simplified collision test that makes use of the graphics hardware to quickly generate a discretization of the environment. Although our research is at an early stage, the results are already quite promising; we are able to render in real-time a virtual city with thousands of walking humans on a standard PC. Several avenues for further investigation are finally proposed.

1 Introduction

Recently we have seen the appearance of many geometric models of towns and cities around the world with an enormous number of potential applications. There has been a lot of work in accelerating the rendering of such models. Many different techniques have been used such as visibility culling [3] and image based rendering [7, 12], to the point where we can now render quite substantial models in real-time. At UCL we have a polygonal model of London that covers a large portion of the city, 160 km in total, with some parts of it modelled in great detail. This model was originally developed through the COVEN project [4] for use in various VR simulations. However, without any humans populating it, it did not look very realistic. Our overall objective is to render in real-time the virtual model of London, simulating also the crowd and traffic of the city. There are several problems to be addressed before this can be realised, such as rendering, simulating the behaviours, avoiding collisions both among the crowd and with the environment. In this paper we will concentrate mainly on fast crowd rendering and collision avoidance, while the implemented behaviour is just random, constrained only by collisions. The algorithms we will describe are better viewed in the context of a level-of-detail system where different techniques are applied in order to produce the best possible image while maintaining a high frame rate. At the lowest level, when the viewer is at some distance above the crowded city and potentially has in view a very large number of objects and moving humans, the techniques described here can be used. As the viewer gets closer some individuals become more visually important but at the same time the number of visible objects becomes smaller. Higher detail solutions should be used as the avatars get too close [15, 13]. In Section 2 we describe the rendering of the avatars and in Section 3 we touch briefly on the collision solution. Some implementation details and results are presented in Section 4 followed by conclusions and some proposals for future directions and improvements.

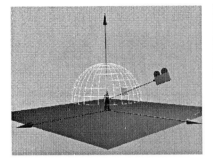 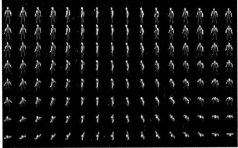

Fig. 1. Discretising the view direction between the object and the viewpoint

Fig. 2. Views of the human from the set of discrete directions

2 Rendering the virtual humans using image based rendering

The main difficulty in the rendering process of the crowd resides in the high number of independent elements to visualise and animate. Clearly using detailed geometric representations will not scale enough. An attractive alternative is the use of image based rendering (IBR) techniques [10, 11]. Aubel et al. [1] applied such ideas recently to virtual humans. However, they use dynamically computed impostors which can only be used for a few frames before being discarded.

The basic idea of our approach is to make use of only one polygon per human, using a pre-computed texture in a way that it shows a good approximation of the human aspect as seen from a given viewpoint. Taking into account that the amount of dedicated texture memory on low-cost workstations is increasing at an exponential rate in the recent years we decided to make wide use of it in order to store a high number of different views of a human character sampled while performing a walking animation. We decided not to use interpolation between views as that would be too cpu-intensive for our purpose. The first phase of the algorithm consists of the generation of a sufficiently large set of sample views of an object. An example is shown in Figure 2.

In our tests we produced 16*8 different images. Each row of images represents the object as seen from 16 different viewpoints at a certain height, rotating around the Y axis. Mirroring them we are able to generate 32 different views of the object with a difference of 11.25 degree one from the other. Each row of images corresponds to a different elevation of the viewpoint. The images, inclusive of the appropriate alpha values, are stored as textures, and the visualisation of every single human is obtained by pasting one of these images to a single polygon having the right orientation toward the camera. This kind of approach might at first appear to be very expensive in terms of memory requirement. Fortunately, when applied to the visualisation of a virtual crowd there are some constraints that allow us to reduce the number of necessary images:

1. In scenes that show a high number of humans, the vast majority of them appear to be far from the viewpoint (see Figures 5 and 6.)
2. Every human can have his own movement direction but the possible rotations of each human is usually limited to the y-axis.
3. We will rarely have a view of some human as seen from below, so we can undersample these views.

At each frame, to select the correct image from the set of the different images available we disctretize the direction between each human and the viewpoint (Figure 1). From this process we get two indices (one referring to the elevation of the viewpoint over the human, and the other referring to the direction around the human) that permit us to select the right row and column of the image stored. Adding an integer number to the column index when retrieving the right image allows us to simulate a rotation of a human around the y-axis with intervals of 11.25 degrees. As the human-camera direction changes we select different images from the set that we have, in order to get the better possible approximation. Storing in the texture memory snapshots from different frames of an animation for the same model and selecting different textures at each frame we are then able to visualise animated figures. The result of the animation can be seen in Figure 6. Our algorithm results to be fast enough to allow the visualisation of virtual environments populated by thousands of humans in real time. Because of the limited number of memorised images and the absence of procedures to warp them, the visualisation turns out to be slightly imprecise. However, when the scene is populated, like in our case, with thousands of animated individuals, or if the viewpoint is sufficiently far, the artifacts becomes hardly noticeable.

3   Collision avoidance using rasterisation

We need to consider two factors for the collision method. The first is the huge number of moving entities and second is the large (and rapidly increasing) complexity of the static model. Thus the algorithm needs to be fast and scalable; ideally the speed of the collision test should not depend on the polygonal complexity of the model. Space discretization methods [8, 9] are probably the most likely to satisfy these criteria. Graphics rasterisation hardware can be used to make the discretisation easy to implement and fast. With an outdoor model such as a city these algorithms are well suited since the environment can be seen as a 2D plan with heights[1]. In [14] we described an approach that takes advantage of that property. Briefly, a *height-map* is created by taking an orthographic rendered view of the static model with the camera looking down from above and then reading the z-buffer. This map constitutes a discreet representation of the height at each point in the environment and is maintained in main memory as an array. At each frame we can test for collision by just mapping the position of each avatar on to this array and comparing the elevation of the avatar against the corresponding value on the height-map. If the difference between them is above a threshold, it means that the step necessary in order to climb up or down from the actual avatar position is too big and we classify the object as "unclimbable" forcing the avatar to change direction. Otherwise we allow the avatar to move to the new position and update its height using the value stored in the height-map. We extend the idea of discretisation to inter-avatar collision, using another map which we call *collision-map*. However this is an integer array and it is not necessarily of the same resolution as the height-map. It is used not only for avoiding direct collision but also for keeping the avatars from coming too close to each other. The allowed proximity is determined by the size of the map pixels. Initially the values of all pixels in the map are set to zero. A pixel with a zero value indicates a free position in space while one with value > 0 is considered occupied (or too close to someone else). For each avatar its position in the map as well as its neighbourhood (the eight positions surrounding it) are found and their value incremented by one. When an avatar is to move, the target position is sampled. If it is already occupied then a different direction has to be chosen, otherwise it is allowed to move there. The move is done in two steps, first the current

---

[1]There are exceptions such as bridges and under-passes but these can be dealt with by adding another 2D level of rasterisation

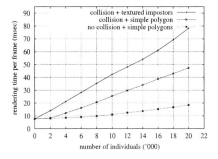 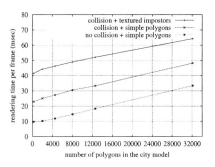

Fig. 3. Time to render against increasing number of particles   **Fig. 4.** Time to render against increasing complexity of the city model

pixel position and neighbourhood are decremented by one and then the new position and neighbourhood are incremented by one. Notice that the neighbourhood of avatars are allowed to overlap (and thus a map pixel might have a value greater than one), however avatar-neighbourhood overlaps are not allowed. In this way avatars can come to within one pixel of the map away but no closer.

4 Implementation and results

We developed the system using a low-end Intel workstation equipped with a 350 MHz PentiumII processor, 256Mb RAM and an OpenGL compliant videocard with 32 MB video memory. We tried to maximise the rendering efficiency on this kind of architecture by following some basic principles. In particular we tried to limit the number of texture changes during the simulation, since this operation is very expensive in terms of time. To achieve this we grouped together all the different view images of an object for each animation frame into one single texture. In our implementation each image has a resolution of 64x64 pixels - we found it to be the best compromise in terms of image quality produced and memory requirements - therefore a single texture of 1024x512 pixels can hold all 16*8 views. The animation stored was composed of 10 different frames of a walking human, produced using two commercial packages: Kinetix 3DStudioMax and MetaCreations Poser. To build the single images we rendered the polygonal version of the humans from the sample directions and then copied every rendered image from the framebuffer into the texture memory, using alpha values for the transparent zones. Since we were not attempting to get the highest precision impostors and in order to reduce memory occupancy we store them with just 16 bits - 5 for each of R, G and B and 1 bit for A. In this way we need 1 Mb of uncompressed texture memory to store each single frame.

To test the system we run two tests, the results of which can be seen in Figures 3 and 4. In both graphs the Y axis shows milliseconds per frame and all three curves include the rendering of the static model and the impostor polygon for each avatar. However for the lower curve both collision and texturing of impostors are turned off, for the middle curve collision is turned on and for the higher one both collision and textured impostors are enabled. For the first test we used a small city model of 2,368 polygons. The aim was to measure the scalability of the method when the number of simulated individuals increases. With the second test we wanted to measure the scalability with regards to the polygonal complexity of the virtual environment. We kept the population steady at 10,000 avatars and varied the static model from a simple box like city block of 267 polygons to a fraction of the London model available here at UCL composed of 32128 polygons. As we can see from both tests we got almost linear curves which re-enforces our argument of scalability for both the avatar rendering and the collision. Just to read out one sample from Figure 3 above, a model with 2,368 polygons using full collision detection and 10,000 textured impostors runs at 25 frames per second.

5 Conclusions and future work

Using the algorithms described it is possible to populate virtual environments with thousands of animated virtual humans in real-time even on low end machines. However there is great scope for extension and improvement.

In terms of rendering, a disadvantage of our algorithm resides in the big amount of texture memory necessary for storing the avatar views. One way to improve the method is rationalising the memorisation process of the set of views in a single texture. The current strategy relies on a regular subdivision of the texture; in this way there is a large portion of unused space in the final image (see Figure 2). An alternative is to use an irregular subdivision of the texture so as to be able to store more views in the same amount of space. We expect that using a smaller portion of the texture will produce also benefits on the fill-rate requirement for the visualisation of the crowd. It would be also very interesting to try our algorithm using some of the devices present on the market that employ compression algorithms on the texture memory; with these devices it is possible to reach compression ratios in the order of 6:1.

At the moment all the avatars have the same colour. One way of avoiding this is to use more than one textured polygon per avatar. For example one for each body member (hand, leg, torso, head), along the spirit of [1]. This will of course increase the rendering time however it has several potential benefits. The different parts could be interchanged between avatars, their colour can be modulated during the frame providing more variety and they can also be packed more tightly saving texture memory.

Adding behaviour would benefit the system immensely; although it can also be quite expensive [15, 13]. At a low level of detail, we can at-least achieve more realistic walking patterns by making use of the pedestrian movement data made available, for example, by the UCL Bartlett School of Architecture [2]. These provide the density of the pedestrians along each pavement at each hour of the day. We can represent the data as colour on polygons corresponding to the pavements. These colour polygons can then be rendered with an orthographic projection to provide a *density-map* of the scene. Avatars could then move and decide their paths after probabilistically sampling this map. Streets will have very low densities thus preventing the avatars from wondering on them. The behaviour of the avatars could be interactively updated by changing the map.

If we are walking at street level then at any moment the largest part of the static and dynamic scene is not visible. There is a variety of efficient algorithms for culling away the hidden static regions. However visibility culling with such a number of dynamic entities is very much an open problem. Extending one of the cell visibility algorithms (eg [6, 5]) seems like a good avenue to follow. Lets assume that we are using the density map described above. At pre-processing the scene and the map are hierarchically subdivided into cells. When the viewer first moves into a region, the culling algorithm is applied which outputs the set of cells which are potentially visible (PVC) while the viewer stays within the region. We can then restrict the simulation to only the avatars within the PVC's. However this will make the number of visible avatars drop to potentially zero if we stay in the same view-region long enough, since some avatars will be moving out of the PVC's but none will be coming in. To eliminate this problem we can again use the density information. During the culling (which happens only once every several frames) we can identify boundaries between visible and non-visible cells. There we can define 'avatar generators' processes which will sample the densities on either side and periodically send in some avatars.

References

1. A. Aubel, R. Boulic, and D. Thalmann. Lowering the cost of virtual human rendering with structured animated impostors. In *Proceedings of WSCG 99*, Plzen, Czech Republic, 1999.
2. Ucl bartlett school of architecture, pedestrian movement project. http://www.bartlett.ucl.ac.uk/spacesyntax/pedestrian/pedestrian.html.
3. Daniel Cohen-Or, Gadi Fibich, Dan Halperin, and Eyal Zadicario. Conservative visibility and strong occlusion for viewspace partitioning of densely occluded scenes. *Computer Graphics Forum*, 17(3):243–254, 1998. ISSN 1067-7055.
4. Collaborative virtual environments project. http://coven.lancs.ac.uk/.
5. Frédo Durand, George Drettakis, Joëlle Thollot, and Claude Puech. Conservative visibility preprocessing using extended projections. *To appear in the proceedings of SIGGRAPH 2000*, 2000.
6. Vladlen Koltun, Yiorgos Chrysanthou, and Daniel Cohen-Or. Virtual occluders: An efficient intermediate PVS representation. In *Proceedings of Eurographics Workshop on Rendering*, 2000.
7. Paulo W. C. Maciel and Peter Shirley. Visual navigation of large environments using textured clusters. In Pat Hanrahan and Jim Winget, editors, *ACM Computer Graphics (Symp. on Interactive 3D Graphics)*, pages 95–102. ACM SIGGRAPH, April 1995. ISBN 0-89791-736-7.
8. Karol Myszkowski, Oleg G. Okunev, and Tosiyasu L. Kunii. Fast collision detection between complex solids using rasterizing graphics hardware. *The Visual Computer*, 11(9):497–512, 1995. ISSN 0178-2789.
9. Jarek Rossignac, Abe Megahed, and Bengt-Olaf Schneider. Interactive inspection of solids: Cross-sections and interferences. *Computer Graphics*, 26(2):353–360, July 1992.
10. Germot Schaufler and Wolfgang Sturzlinger. A three-dimensional image cache for virtual reality. *Computer Graphics Forum*, 15(3):C227–C235, C471–C472, September 1996.
11. Jonathan Shade, Dani Lischinski, David Salesin, Tony DeRose, and John Snyder. Hierarchical image caching for accelerated walkthroughs of complex environments. In Holly Rushmeier, editor, *SIGGRAPH 96 Conference Proceedings*, Annual Conference Series, pages 75–82. ACM SIGGRAPH, Addison Wesley, August 1996. held in New Orleans, Louisiana, 04-09 August 1996.
12. François Sillion, G. Drettakis, and B. Bodelet. Efficient impostor manipulation for real-time visualization of urban scenery. *Computer Graphics Forum*, 16(3):207–218, August 1997. Proceedings of Eurographics '97. ISSN 1067-7055.
13. D.Thalmann S.R. Musse, F. Garat. Guiding and interacting with virtual crowds in real-time. In *Proceedings of Eurographics Workshop on Animation and Simulation*, pages 23–34, Milan, Italy, 1999.
14. F. Tecchia and Y.Chrysanthou. Real-time visualisation of densely populated urban environments: a simple and fast algorithm for collision detection. In *Eurographics UK*, April 2000. to appear.
15. Xiaoyuan Tu and Demetri Terzopoulos. Artificial fishes: Physics, locomotion, perception, behavior. In Andrew Glassner, editor, *Proceedings of SIGGRAPH '94 (Orlando, Florida, July 24–29, 1994)*, Computer Graphics Proceedings, Annual Conference Series, pages 43–50. ACM SIGGRAPH, ACM Press, July 1994. ISBN 0-89791-667-0.

Editors' Note: see Appendix, p. 397 for colored figures of this paper

Guaranteed Occlusion and Visibility in Cluster Hierarchical Radiosity

Luc Leblanc   Pierre Poulin
Département d'informatique et de recherche opérationnelle
Université de Montréal

Abstract.
Visibility determination is the most expensive task in cluster hierarchical radiosity. Guaranteed full occlusion and full visibility can reduce these computations without causing visibility errors. We build a hierarchy of large convex occluders using face clustering. This structure is efficiently exploited to avoid computing visibility between mutually fully occluded scene elements. Used in conjunction with a full visibility culling method, we show improvements on several scenes.

1 Introduction

Cluster hierarchical radiosity [26, 23, 24, 12, 2] possesses attractive theoretical and practical advantages to solve the problem of global illumination. Recently, adapted multiresolution surfaces [34, 6] have been introduced to better control the quantity and quality of energy transfers between surfaces rather than individual polygons or self-occluding volume clusters. While these improvements are essential to provide an increased realism for complex scenes at reduced computation cost, the major cost in these algorithms remains determining the visibility between pairs of elements, whether they are patches (subdivided or not), face clusters, or volume clusters.

In these hierarchical approaches, we can greatly benefit if we can *guarantee efficiently* at the highest possible level of the hierarchy that a pair of elements is mutually fully occluded or fully visible. Then no visibility computations would be required for any pair of children elements derived from these two parent elements. Guaranteed visibility and occlusion ensures no errors are introduced in the energy exchanges. We observed that full visibility and full occlusion can represent a significant proportion of visibility between pairs of elements in a scene. For instance in our test scenes, full visibility varies between 20 and 60% and full occlusion between 40 and 80%.

Guaranteed full visibility has been successfully exploited before by testing a shaft [13] enclosing the pair of elements against bounding volumes of the scene hierarchy. Testing full occlusion of these visibility shafts is more difficult. To be efficient, occluders should be as large as possible. Unfortunately objects in a scene can have complex concave shapes, resulting in difficulties to efficiently guarantee occlusion. Moreover in many scenes, objects are so finely meshed that no single polygon can be considered a good occluder. Algorithms handling the combined occlusion of several polygons have appeared in recent years [27, 10, 21], but they often require an important preprocessing step and a large amount of memory to store the corresponding structures.

In this paper, we fit a set of large convex polygons to handle efficiently the occlusion due to a large mesh of small polygons. Face clustering is first used to determine flat sections in surfaces. Then a small set of large convex polygons (our occluders) are fitted to each flat face cluster to efficiently represent the occlusion. The user can control the minimum size and the number of the occluders. The full occlusion query proceeds by testing the rays bounding the visibility shaft against our convex occluders, themselves organized in a hierarchical structure.

Our results demonstrate that even with a limited number of occluders, we can find a large proportion (40 to 93%) of the full occlusions in several tested scenes. When full visibility is used in conjuntion with full occlusion, we observe reduction of the total rendering time (up to 11 times in our test scenes). Moreover even in scenes with little full occlusions, the cost of testing full occlusion is small enough that it almost never seems to penalize the visibility computations, and if it does, it will be negligible.

Although our visibility determination method is applied here to cluster hierarchical radiosity, its generality indicates it should also provide interesting results in walk-throughs [4, 16] and direct illumination from extended light sources.

In the next section, we briefly classify visibility techniques in the context of radiosity. In section 3, we describe how large convex occluders are extracted from the face clustering of the scene surfaces. Then we present the particularities of our cluster hierarchical radiosity system, before explaining in section 5 how full occlusion and full visibility are implemented in our system. The system has been tested with a wide range of scenes, and section 6 analyses the results. Finally we conclude and present directions for future improvements.

2 Related Work on Visibility Determination for Radiosity

Visibility determination is one of the fundamental problems in computer graphics, and an extensive literature has addressed various aspects of this problem. Many techniques are based on a single viewpoint, and therefore less directly applicable to specific visibility determination between pairs of elements in radiosity algorithms. Due to space constraints, we refer the interested reader to a more comprehensive survey such as the Ph.D. thesis of Durand [7].

We roughly divide the methods into sampled visibility, volumetric visibility, analytical visibility, portals, and occlusion culling. A large class of visibility methods are based on sampled visibility. The most popular of these methods simply shoots a number of rays between the pair of elements [32, 14]. They can prove efficient and their observed accuracy can usually be increased by using more samples, at the additional cost of increased computation time. However they suffer from the lack of bounds on the error of the estimated visibility, leading to potential light or shadow leakages in difficult configurations.

Volumetric visibility [22, 24] associates a density for a volumetric representation of surfaces, and the occlusion is approximated as an attenuation factor. While it provides a general sense of occlusions, the method assumes a uniform distribution of small objects, and therefore fails to accurately represent occlusions that are in nature more directional.

Analytical 3D visibility methods [20, 5, 29, 9] provide the complete and accurate solution to visibility. Unfortunately their algorithmic complexity quickly becomes a serious concern for any practical use in large scenes. Even though some extensions [8] make them more practical, the robustness problems of these methods remain.

Portals [30] offer major gains between elements distributed in separated rooms. If the information about portals is not included into the scene design, methods exist to automatically construct such portals [30, 17]. However portals become inefficient outside typical architectural scenes, within a single room, or as the rooms mutual visibility increases.

Occlusion culling based on a single large convex occluder [19, 4, 15] can eliminate

Fig. 1. Two views of a given level of face clustering applied on a sofa

an important portion of an entire scene in walkthroughs. However one must provide a list of such occluders and this list should depend on the positions of the pair of elements. The preprocessing of visibility using cells [31, 3, 33] allows to identify large occluders with respect to the current cell. However when the scene is mostly constituted of a soup of small polygons, they cannot fuse together these occluders to form a large occluder, and the expected gains are quite reduced.

Recent methods have been presented to extract large occluders from polygonal models. One approach uses simplification mesh techniques preserving occlusion [16]. The resulting occluders are not convex, which is essential in our case to efficiently guarantee full occlusion. Another approach grows octree boxes within closed geometric models [1]. This algorithm is restricted to closed models, which is not always guaranteed in many geometric modelers. Our extraction technique is similar to this one, but is based on a surface rather than a volume. We believe both solutions are useful and should be used in conjunction to identify the best occluders. In fact, these two occluder types can be integrated in our occlusion culling algorithm described in section 5. The next section details our extraction algorithm.

3 Extraction of Large Convex Occluders

Our occlusion culling structure relies on the presence of large occluders in the scene. Unfortunately for many scenes, the only information available is a list of a large number of small polygons, or if we are lucky, a list of objects, each constituted of its list of polygons.

As a preprocessing step, we first need to build a list of "good" convex occluders. To create these occluders, we use face clustering [11] to identify face clusters (a group of adjacent polygons) that are flat and as large as possible. These polygons are projected onto the supporting plane of the face cluster and large rectangles are fitted onto this projection to produce our large occluders.

3.1 Face Clustering

Face clustering [34] was introduced in cluster hierarchical radiosity in order to produce a more accurate energy transfer between clusters of polygons forming a suitable face cluster. We use a similar face cluster hierarchy to extract the list of occluders.

In the iterative construction of the face cluster hierarchy [11], a polygon or a group of polygons (face cluster) that minimizes a certain number of criteria such as adjacency, planarity, smallest perimeter, etc., is added to its corresponding face cluster. At the end of the construction, we have a list of face clusters, each organized hierarchically.

Figure 1 shows two views of a sofa with face clusters of a given level identified by different colors. Note that the face clusters in this figure are not necessarily flat; the face clusters that we use to extract our occluders are flat. We join these face clusters into a hierarchy of volume clusters similarly to the technique of Mueller *et al.* [18].

We consider a good occluder to be planar and as large as possible. Such occluders include floors, walls, doors, desktops, shelves, etc. Therefore, starting from the root of the scene cluster hierarchy, we look if the current face cluster can be a flat and sufficiently large occluder. Volume clusters are simply traversed recursively until face clusters are reached. We check the planarity of a face cluster from its associated cone of normals.[1] If the face cluster is not satisfying, we continue down the hierarchy until we find such face clusters, or until the area of a face cluster is smaller than a user specified fraction of the dimension of the scene.

If a face cluster lies on the contour of the bounding box of the entire scene, such as floors and ceilings in some scenes, this face cluster would not occlude any element, and it is simply removed from the list of occluding face clusters.

3.2 From Face Cluster to Occluder

Once a face cluster satisfies our set of conditions, we must extract a small number of suitable convex flat polygons approximating *conservatively* the occlusion of this face cluster. These polygons will reside on the supporting plane of the face cluster. Because the orientation on the plane influences the size of the extracted occluders, we need to find the 2D bounding rectangle that has the smallest surface. Currently, we simply test a number of orientations (typically 10) and keep the smallest one. More sophisticated schemes could improve this naive solution, but so far, it has proven sufficient. The contour of the face cluster is then projected orthogonally onto this supporting plane and we proceed with our extraction of 2D convex polygons. It is important to note at this point that the projected face cluster can be concave, and even contain holes.

Our extraction algorithm is similar to the extraction in 3D of volume occluders by Andujar *et al.* [1]. However geometric 3D models might not be closed, or individual polygons might be used as objects to represent ceilings or walls. Therefore to remain as general as possible, we decided to work with surfaces.

We first check some simple conditions to determine if the polygon is already simple and convex. If not, we construct a quadtree representing the 2D face cluster. Each quadtree element contains a list of the edges traversing its surface, or if it is empty, its status as interior or exterior of the face cluster.

From this quadtree, we iterate to extract occluding rectangles with the following steps:

1. Find the interior quadtree element with the largest unmarked area.
2. Expand the quadtree element along one of its two axes until the resulting rectangle intersects an edge.[2]
3. Expand similarly the rectangle along the second axis.
4. Mark the quadtree elements completely inside the rectangle so a different initial quadtree element is used in the next iteration.

---

[1] In our current implementation, we consider only almost planar occluders, *i.e.*, for which each polygon has an orientation difference of at most 1 degree, resulting from limited representation or numerical instabilities.

[2] In case the quadtree axes would be slightly misaligned with the face cluster, the expanded rectangle could get stuck with an edge. Shrinking the rectangle along the first axis (typically 1/1000th of its length) gives better results.

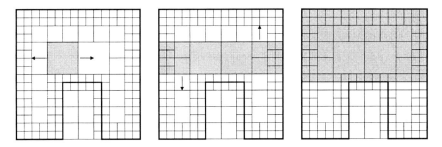

Fig. 2. On the left: largest unmarked interior quadtree element. On the middle and right: the occluding rectangle is expanded along each of its axis.

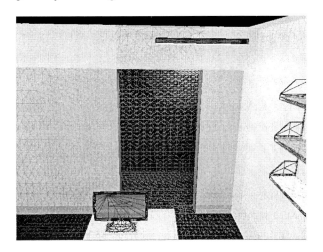

Fig. 3. Extracted large convex occluders in semi-transparent colors over the original mesh of a scene.

The process stops whenever the area of the unmarked quadtree elements is smaller than a specified threshold, or that a given number of rectangles is found. Figure 2 illustrates these steps.

Our occluders are rectangular because they are very simple convex polygons, efficient to intersect, and they are well suited in typical architectural scenes. Our occlusion testing can be easily generalized to any convex polygon, but so far, rectangles have been sufficient.

These rectangles can obviously overlap each other. This is an advantage in our case since we use each of them individually to test against shafts. Each of them should therefore be as large as possible. Another interesting advantage of this extraction technique is that whatever the polygonization of the scene, the extraction of the occluders provides a set of very similar rectangles. Figures 3 and 4 show the extracted occluders for two scenes. In all our test scenes (see Figure 5), the extraction of occluders always took less than 10 seconds on a PC Athlon 600 MHz running linux.

The extracted occluders are kept in a separate hierarchy of bounding volumes aligned on the scene axes. The hierarchy is stored in an array [25] to efficiently access these occluders.

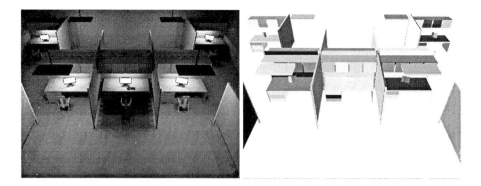

Fig. 4. Original scene and extracted large convex occluders.

4 Cluster Hierarchical Radiosity

This section describes the specificities of the radiosity algorithm we developed.

We implemented our occlusion structure within an algorithm of cluster hierarchical radiosity without links, similar to the one of Stamminger *et al.* [28]. We integrated in this algorithm a simplified version of the face clustering of Willmott *et al.* [34], postponing to a later date the introduction of the notion of "vector-based radiosity" in our system. Face clustering [11] is also used to extract the set of the largest convex occluders. It has shown useful to correct for small inaccuracies in geometric models, thus avoiding undesired cracks.

The scene hierarchy is stored as a binary tree of bounding boxes aligned with the scene axes. It is built with the criteria from Mueller *et al.* [18].

In the radiosity solution, we proceed down the scene hierarchy and shoot radiosity between scene elements starting only at the level of the face clusters or below; we do not currently exchange energy if a volume cluster is involved, although we plan to add it soon to our system. Our oracle uses a BFA refinement criterion, *i.e.*, the shooting radiosity value times the form factor times the area of the face cluster or of the polygon.

We use the technique described by Smits *et al.* [25] when rays need to be shot between two scene elements to test for full occlusion with the bounding segments of shafts or to test partial occlusion [14].

5 Hierarchical Occlusion Culling

In the context of guaranteed occlusion and visibility, we can benefit from the two extreme cases: full visibility and full occlusion.

5.1 Full Visibility

Full visibility has been exploited in a number of visibility techniques. In the case of visibility between two elements (polygons, face clusters, or volume clusters), a shaft [13] between the two elements is constructed from planes, and if no other scene elements lay within the shaft, the two elements are considered fully visible, notwithstanding self-occlusions by the elements.

Our full visibility testing algorithm between two clusters recursively traverses the bounding boxes intersecting the shaft until:

- A bounding box is completely inside the shaft. We can then stop and consider the two elements as not fully visible.
- A bounding box contains a single polygon. We then test if the polygon intersects the shaft and if so, we consider the two elements as not fully visible.

Any bounding box outside the shaft is simply culled without any further processing.

5.2 Full Occlusion

Determining all the visibility events resulting from a combination of several occluders is a complex task. It is much easier to determine if a single convex occluder blocks the entire shaft. This simply corresponds to test all segments bounding the shaft with the occluder. If all the segments intersect the convex occluder, the two elements are guaranteed to not see any portion of each other. If a single segment does not intersect the convex occluder, although another occluder could block the remaining portion of the shaft, we cannot conclude anything except the two elements might be occluded. We then proceed by subdividing the shaft, treating the sub-shafts recursively. If we reached the lowest level in the scene hierarchy, we resort to the traditional solution of generating n rays randomly between the two elements [14] to test for occlusion.

Our occlusion testing algorithm between two clusters follows these steps:

1. A shaft [13] is built from the bounding boxes (aligned on the scene axes) of the two elements.
2. Depending on the configuration, four to eight segments on the contour of the shaft are computed.
3. The shaft is tested with the hierarchy of extracted occluders.

   (a) We cast a segment in the list of occluders.
   (b) For an occluder intersected, we test with all the remaining segments.

      - As soon as one segment does not intersect this occluder, we start again with another occluder of the list.
      - If all the rays intersect this occluder, we have guaranteed full occlusion.

Since many segments must be tested, we implemented an iterative approach [25] to efficiently traverse the scene hierarchy of bounding boxes instead of the conventional recursive approach. We observed a gain of a factor of three to four in speed for this portion of the algorithm.

5.3 Full Occlusion and Full Visibility in Cluster Hierarchical Radiosity

Our cluster hierarchical radiosity algorithm treats light exchanges by going down the hierarchy. Our oracle determines if the light exchange should be computed between the two current elements, or if we should subdivide one of the two elements and test recursively. Light is exchanged only between face clusters or polygons, never at the level of volume clusters. Visibility requests are included within this oracle. The oracle observes the following conditions:

- If the two elements (face cluster or polygon) are considered flat enough, we compute a standard BFA oracle. If the two cones of normals are entirely backfacing each other, we can stop the recursion.

- Visibility between two elements is tested only every four subdivision levels down the hierarchy. This allows the shaft to be sufficiently smaller to increase the probability of full visibility or full occlusion, and this reduces the computation costs. The jump of four levels empirically provided the best trade-offs in our test scenes. A visibility test is always computed when a light exchange is required between two elements.
- Full occlusion is less expensive to compute, so it is treated first. If we detect full occlusion, subdivision is stopped and no light exchanges occur. Because the occluder hierarchy is separated from the scene hierarchy, it becomes inefficient to attempt to traverse the two hierarchies in parallel.
- If full occlusion is not detected, the test for full visibility is computed. Obviously, one would think that if partial occlusion was detected, there is no needs to test for full visibility. However we observed that marking bounding boxes outside the shaft (explained below) is more efficient even if we know there will not be full visibility.
- In case of full visibility, this information is passed down to their children so they are not tested for visibility.
- All the bounding boxes of the scene hierarchy that are detected as outside the current shaft are marked so they are not tested if the shaft is further subdivided.

6 Results

6.1 Statistics on our Test Scenes

The results for the visibility method presented in the previous section are summarized in Table 1. We selected a set of scenes that feature a variety of visibility types. An image of these scenes appears in Figure 5, along with the number of polygons and the number of extracted occluders. Some of these images have been gamma corrected to better display their features.

Scenes A and E feature arrangements of rooms with relatively limited energy exchanges between them, while in scene B, every room can see a good proportion of the others (scene B is constructed from an array of 10×10 rooms). Scene C has a high occlusion factor but is an open room, this configuration being difficult to handle with portals. Scene D is an example of a room with very little occlusion. Finally, scene F is a mix between full visibility and full occlusion.

We tested three schemes. In the *normal* technique, the oracle decides at which level in the hierarchy of clusters the exchange happens. When this level is reached, the visibility coefficient is calculated by ray casting [14]. Eight rays were used for all scenes, except for scene C (10 rays) and scene D (20 rays). In this latter case, 20 rays were used only to compute an image with less noise. The *visibility* technique is the same as the *normal* technique with the addition of the full visibility test. The *occlusion* technique adds the full occlusion test to the visibility technique.

A single pass in radiosity consists of shooting radiosity from the scene onto itself, going down the scene hierarchy with our BFA criteria. One pass corresponds to all direct illumination, two passes to all the first reflections, etc.

The total time is in seconds, and comes from a PC Athlon 600 MHz with 256 MB of memory and running linux.

For every scene, Table 1 gives the number of energy exchanges between the elements (face clusters or polygons) and the number of them fully blocked, that is every rays shot are blocked. The number of rays shot and the number of these rays blocked by full occlusion or partial occlusion are also shown. The number of shafts built represents the number of visibility queries for full visibility and full occlusion.

Full occlusion is divided in two parts. First, the proportion of energy exchanges fully occluded. In fact, this number represents a superset of all the fully occluded exchanges because this statistics relies only on the rays cast. Therefore when all sampling rays are blocked, we consider this exchange as fully occluded while it might not be. The second number represents the proportion of full occlusion detected in comparison with the maximum possible. For instance in scene A, 38% of all exchanges were fully occluded. We detected 73% of these full occlusions, therefore close to 28% of all exchanges. Full visibility is the proportion of exchanges that were calculated without requiring to casting rays because they were detected as fully visible.

6.2 Analysis

As one can see from the timings, the combined visibility methods resulted in speedups ranging from 1.3 to 11 for our test scenes, with a typical acceleration of approximately 2.5. Full occlusion testing is fairly efficient, and only in the second and third passes in scene D did we observe a very slight increase (about 1% of computation time) due to full occlusion testing.

One can note that the gain slightly reduces for indirect lighting. We believe this occurs because these energy exchanges have lower energy and thus are handled at higher levels in the scene hierarchy. As a consequence the relative size of our occluders with respect to the size of shafts tends to diminish, so that full occlusion and full visibility become less frequent.

Although our occluder extraction algorithm does not allow general occluder fusion, as much as 93% (scene F, pass 1) of all occlusions were accounted for by our occluders. Another interesting aspect is that the occlusion test is fairly inexpensive, so that even though scene D has very little occlusion, the full occlusion test had almost no impact on the total time.

The maximal proportion of full occlusions calculated in our test scenes can appear less than what one might expect. For instance, test scene F, pass 1 has a full occlusion factor of 38%. This is explained by the fact that most of the energy exchanges occur nearby the emitter, due to the form factor contribution to the BFA error metrics in the oracle. Therefore many of the light exchanges between distant elements (that would be good candidates for full occlusion) are never considered because of this oracle; these exchanges occur at a higher level in the scene hierarchy.

7 Conclusion

We presented a guaranteed visibility culling algorithm implemented in a cluster hierarchical radiosity algorithm with face clustering. We exploited efficiently full visibility and full occlusion, providing an early stop in visibility determination with no errors. This leads to higher quality energy exchanges at a lower computational cost.

We put emphasis on culling due to full occlusion. Face clustering is used to extract a set of rectangles representing flat sections of surfaces. These rectangles are organized in a hierarchy of occluders for efficient visibility queries with the segments bounding a shaft between two elements. The user can control the size and the number of occluders.

We tested our culling method onto a large set of different scenes, and analyzed the results. In all cases, our structure proved useful, even when full visibility and full occlusion were not apparent. The resulting visibility structures are very simple to build,

Scene Pass	Culling Technique	Total Time (sec)	Energy Exch (M)	Exch Blocked (M)	Rays Shot (M)	Rays Blocked (M)	Shafts Built (M)	Full Occlus. (%)		Full Vis. (%)
A . 1	normal	428	4.7	1.78	37.9	15.8	0			
	visibility	271	4.7	1.78	20.3	15.8	3.0	38	73	46
	occlusion	220	3.4	0.47	9.9	1.9	1.9			
B . 1	normal	382	4.8	2.91	39.0	24.5	0			
	visibility	275	4.8	2.91	27.7	24.5	9.5	61	69	29
	occlusion	173	2.8	0.86	11.3	8.1	3.4			
C . 1	normal	199	1.20	0.64	12.07	6.96	0			
	visibility	141	1.20	0.64	9.80	6.96	0.98	53	81	19
	occlusion	88	0.68	0.13	4.65	1.84	0.44			
C . 2	normal	430	2.40	1.95	23.72	20.84	0			
	visibility	435	2.40	1.95	23.33	20.84	6.96	81	75	2
	occlusion	200	0.93	0.49	8.68	6.45	2.57			
C . 3	normal	532	2.99	2.66	29.90	28.12	0			
	visibility	553	2.99	2.66	29.66	28.07	8.99	88	77	1
	occlusion	228	0.93	0.62	9.14	7.58	3.17			
D . 1	normal	93	0.32	0.05	6.60	1.29	0			
	visibility	28	0.32	0.05	2.88	1.29	0.08	16	40	56
	occlusion	25	0.30	0.02	2.31	0.73	0.07			
D . 2	normal	55	0.23	0.02	4.62	0.85	0			
	visibility	33	0.23	0.02	3.04	0.85	0.18	9	50	34
	occlusion	34	0.22	0.02	2.95	0.80	0.17			
D . 3	normal	44	0.17	0.02	3.38	0.98	0			
	visibility	33	0.17	0.02	2.57	0.98	0.22	12	50	24
	occlusion	34	0.16	0.02	2.48	0.93	0.22			
E . 1	normal	273	2.29	1.41	18.37	12.02	0			
	visibility	158	2.29	1.41	15.14	12.02	1.02	62	81	18
	occlusion	95	1.15	0.27	6.01	2.89	0.47			
E . 2	normal	118	0.98	0.40	7.84	3.74	0			
	visibility	76	0.98	0.40	5.81	3.74	0.74	41	58	26
	occlusion	69	0.75	0.17	3.95	1.92	0.49			
E . 3	normal	89	0.84	0.48	6.70	4.24	0			
	visibility	73	0.84	0.48	5.53	4.23	0.96	57	65	17
	occlusion	59	0.53	0.18	3.08	1.82	0.52			
F . 1	normal	1017	11.13	4.26	89.04	34.30	0			
	visibility	413	11.13	4.26	34.92	34.30	2.28	38	93	61
	occlusion	92	7.15	0.29	3.12	2.50	0.36			
F . 2	normal	639	5.63	2.41	45.06	19.66	0			
	visibility	256	5.63	2.41	21.07	19.66	1.50	43	66	53
	occlusion	139	4.05	0.82	8.36	6.96	1.05			
F . 3	normal	298	2.57	1.12	20.53	9.24	0			
	visibility	126	2.57	1.12	10.11	9.24	0.78	44	53	51
	occlusion	86	1.98	0.54	5.40	4.53	0.66			

Table 1. Full visibility and full occlusion on various scenes

as small as desired, provide interesting speed ups, and produce no visibility errors.

We integrated our culling method in a cluster hierarchical radiosity algorithm, but it should be simple to use it in walkthroughs, in rendering from a given viewpoint, and direct illumination.

We expect also that the method could be exploited in improved radiosity algorithms with exchanges between volume clusters, irradiance vectors, and final gathering.

Other promising directions for future work include the use of volume occluders and directional occluders for curved surfaces.

Acknowledgments. We acknowledge financial support from NSERC and Discreet, a division of Autodesk. We would like to thank Frédo Durand and Filippo Tampieri for helpful comments.

References

1. C. Andújar, C. Saona-Vázquez, and I. Navazo. LOD visibility culling and occluder synthesis. *Computer Aided Design*, 2000. Accepted for publication.
2. P.H. Christensen, D. Lischinski, E.J. Stollnitz, and D.H. Salesin. Clustering for glossy global illumination. *ACM Transactions on Graphics*, 16(1):3–33, January 1997.
3. D. Cohen-Or, G. Fibich, D. Halperin, and E. Zadicario. Conservative visibility and strong occlusion for viewspace partitioning of densely occluded scenes. *Computer Graphics Forum (Eurographics '98)*, 17(3):243–254, 1998.
4. S. Coorg and S. Teller. Real-time occlusion culling for models with large occluders. In *1997 Symposium on Interactive 3D Graphics*, pages 83–90, April 1997.
5. G. Drettakis and E. Fiume. A fast shadow algorithm for area light sources using backprojection. In *Proceedings of SIGGRAPH '94*, Annual Conference Series, pages 223–230, July 1994.
6. R. Dumont and K. Bouatouch. Using levels of detail to speedup radiosity computation. Technical Report RR-3602, INRIA, 1999.
7. F. Durand. *3D visibility, analysis and applications*. Ph.D. thesis, Université Joseph Fourier, Grenoble, 1999.
8. F. Durand, G. Drettakis, and C. Puech. Fast and accurate hierarchical radiosity using global visibility. *ACM Transactions on Graphics*, 18(2):128–170, April 1999.
9. F. Durand, G. Drettakis, and C. Puech. The visibility skeleton: A powerful and efficient multi-purpose global visibility tool. *Proceedings of SIGGRAPH 97*, pages 89–100, August 1997.
10. F. Durand, G. Drettakis, J. Thollot, and C. Puech. Conservative visibility preprocessing using extended projections. In *SIGGRAPH 2000 Conference Proceedings*, Annual Conference Series, July 2000, to appear.
11. M. Garland. *Quadric-Based Polygonal Surface Simplification*. Ph.D. thesis, Carnegie Mellon University, 1999.
12. S. Gibson and R.J. Hubbold. Efficient hierarchical refinement and clustering for radiosity in complex environments. *Computer Graphics Forum*, 15(5):297–310, 1996.
13. E. Haines and J. Wallace. Shaft culling for efficient ray-traced radiosity. In *Eurographics Workshop on Rendering*, 1991.
14. P. Hanrahan, D. Salzman, and L. Aupperle. A rapid hierarchical radiosity algorithm. In *Computer Graphics (SIGGRAPH '91 Proceedings)*, volume 25, pages 197–206, July 1991.
15. T. Hudson, D. Manocha, J. Cohen, M. Lin, K. Hoff, and H. Zhang. Accelerated occlusion culling using shadow frustra. In *Proceedings of the Thirteenth Annual Symposium on Computational Geometry*, pages 1–10, June 1997.
16. F.-A. Law and T.-S. Tan. Preprocessing occlusion for real-time selective refinement. In *1999 Symposium on Interactive 3D Graphics*, pages 47–52, 1999.

17. D. Meneveaux. *Lighting simulation in complex architectural environments: sequential and parallel approaches*. Ph.D. thesis, Université de Rennes I, 1998.
18. G. Mueller, S. Schaefer, and D. Fellner. Automatic creation of object hierarchies for radiosity clustering. In *Pacific Graphics '99*, October 1999.
19. H. Plantinga. Conservative visibility preprocessing for efficient walkthroughs of 3D scenes. In *Proceedings of Graphics Interface '93*, pages 166–173, May 1993.
20. H. Plantinga and C.R. Dyer. Visibility, occlusion, and the aspect graph. *International Journal of Computer Vision*, 5(2):137–160, 1990.
21. G. Schaufler, J. Dorsey, X. Decoret, and F.X. Sillion. Conservative volumetric visibility with occluder fusion. In *SIGGRAPH 2000 Conference Proceedings*, Annual Conference Series, July 2000, to appear.
22. F. Sillion. Clustering and volume scattering for hierarchical radiosity calculations. In *Fifth Eurographics Workshop on Rendering*, pages 105–117, June 1994.
23. F. Sillion, G. Drettakis, and C. Soler. A clustering algorithm for radiance calculation in general environments. In *Eurographics Rendering Workshop 1995*, pages 196–205, June 1995.
24. F.X. Sillion. A unified hierarchical algorithm for global illumination with scattering volumes and object clusters. *IEEE Transactions on Visualization and Computer Graphics*, 1(3):240–254, September 1995.
25. B. Smits. Efficiency issues for ray tracing. *Journal of Graphics Tools*, 3(2):1–14, 1998.
26. B. Smits, J. Arvo, and D. Greenberg. A clustering algorithm for radiosity in complex environments. In *Proceedings of SIGGRAPH '94*, Annual Conference Series, pages 435–442, July 1994.
27. C. Soler and F.X. Sillion. Fast calculation of soft shadow textures using convolution. In *SIGGRAPH 98 Conference Proceedings*, Annual Conference Series, pages 321–332, July 1998.
28. M. Stamminger, H. Schirmacher, P. Slusallek, and H.-P. Seidel. Getting rid of links in hierarchical radiosity. *Computer Graphics Forum (Eurographics '98)*, 17(3):165–174, 1998.
29. A.J. Stewart and S. Ghali. Fast computation of shadow boundaries using spatial coherence and backprojections. In *Proceedings of SIGGRAPH '94*, Annual Conference Series, pages 231–238, July 1994.
30. S. Teller and P. Hanrahan. Global visibility algorithms for illumination computations. In *Proceedings of SIGGRAPH '93*, Annual Conference Series, pages 239–246, 1993.
31. S.J. Teller and C.H. Séquin. Visibility preprocessing for interactive walkthroughs. In *Computer Graphics (SIGGRAPH '91 Proceedings)*, volume 25, pages 61–69, July 1991.
32. J.R. Wallace, K.A. Elmquist, and E.A. Haines. A ray tracing algorithm for progressive radiosity. In *Computer Graphics (SIGGRAPH '89 Proceedings)*, volume 23, pages 315–324, July 1989.
33. Y. Wang, H. Bao, and Q. Peng. Accelerated walkthroughs of virtual environments based on visibility processing and simplification. *Computer Graphics Forum (Eurographics '98)*, 17(3):187–194, 1998.
34. A. Willmott, P. Heckbert, and M. Garland. Face cluster radiosity. In *Eurographics Workshop on Rendering*, pages 293–304, June 1999.

Editors' Note: see Appendix, p. 398 for colored figures of this paper

Parameterized Animation Compression

Ziyad S. Hakura*, Jerome E. Lengyel**, John M. Snyder**

*Stanford University, **Microsoft Research

Abstract. We generalize image-based rendering by exploiting texture-mapping graphics hardware to decompress ray-traced "animations". Rather than 1D time, our animations are parameterized by two or more arbitrary variables representing view/lighting changes and rigid object motions. To best match the graphics hardware rendering to the input ray-traced imagery, we describe a novel method to infer parameterized texture maps for each object by modeling the hardware as a linear system and then performing least-squares optimization. The parameterized textures are compressed as a multidimensional Laplacian pyramid on fixed size blocks of parameter space. This scheme captures the coherence in parameterized animations and, unlike previous work, decodes directly into texture maps that load into hardware with a few, simple image operations. We introduce adaptive dimension splitting in the Laplacian pyramid and separate diffuse and specular lighting layers to further improve compression. High-quality results are demonstrated at compression ratios up to 800:1 with interactive playback on current consumer graphics cards.

1 Introduction

The central problem of computer graphics is real-time rendering of physically illuminated, dynamic environments. Though the computation needed is beyond current capability, specialized graphics hardware that renders texture-mapped polygons continues to get cheaper and faster. We exploit this hardware to decompress animations computed and compiled offline. The decompressed imagery retains the full gamut of stochastic ray tracing effects, including indirect lighting with reflections, refractions, and shadows.

For synthetic scenes, the time and viewpoint parameters of the plenoptic function [1, 23] can be generalized to include position of lights, viewpoint, or objects, surface reflectance properties, or any other degrees of freedom in the scene. For example, we can construct a 2D space combining viewpoint movement along a 1D trajectory with independent 1D swinging of a light source. Our goal is maximum compression of the resulting arbitrary-dimensional *parameterized animation* that maintains satisfactory quality and decodes in real time. Once the encoding is downloaded over a network,

the decoder can take advantage of specialized hardware and high bandwidth to the graphics system to allow a user to explore the parameter space. High compression reduces downloading time over the network and conserves server and client storage.

Our approach infers and compresses parameter dependent texture maps for individual objects rather than combined views of the entire scene, illustrated in Figure 1.

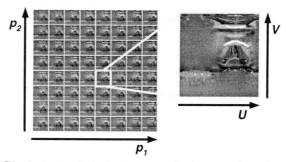

Fig. 1. An 8×8 block of parameterized textures for a glass parfait object is shown. In this example, dimension p_1 represents a 1D viewpoint trajectory while p_2 represents the swinging of a light source. Note the imagery's coherence.

To *infer* a texture map means to find one which when applied to a hardware-rendered geometric object matches the offline-rendered image. Encoding a separate texture map for each object better captures its coherence across the parameter space independently of where in the image it appears. Object silhouettes are correctly rendered from actual geometry and suffer fewer compression artifacts.

Figure 2 illustrates our system. Ray-traced images at each point in the parameter space are input to the compiler together with the scene geometry, lighting models, and viewing parameters. The compiler targets any desired type of graphics hardware by modeling the hardware as a linear system. It then infers texture resolution and texture samples for each object at each point in the parameter space to produce as good a match as possible on

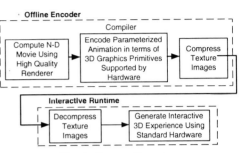

Fig. 2. System Overview

that hardware to the "gold-standard" images. We use pyramidal regularization [20] in our texture inference to provide smooth "hole-filling" for occluded regions without a specialized post-processing pass. Per-object texture maps are then compressed using a novel, multi-dimensional compression scheme that automatically allocates storage between different objects and their separated diffuse and specular lighting layers. The interactive runtime consists of a traditional hardware-accelerated rendering engine and a texture decompression engine that caches to speed decoding and staggers block origins to distribute decompression load.

2   Previous Work

Image-Based Rendering (IBR).   IBR has sought increasingly accurate approximations of the plenoptic function [1, 23], including use of pixel flow [4], and tabulation of a 4D field, called a "light field" or "lumigraph" [18, 10] to interpolate views. Layered depth images (LDI) [30] are another representation of the radiance field better able to handle disocclusions and have found use in the rendering of glossy environments [2]. Extending to a 5D or higher field permits changes to the lighting environment [35, 27]. The challenge of such methods is efficient storage of the high-dimensional image fields.

For spatially coherent scenes, it has been observed that geometry-based surface fields better capture coherence in the light field, achieving a more efficient encoding than view-based images like the LDI or lumigraph [33, 25, 14, 32, 27]. Our work generalizes parameterizations based solely on viewpoint. We also encode an entire texture at each point in parameter space that can be accessed in constant time independent of the size of the whole representation. Other encoding strategies, such as Miller's [25], must visit an irregular scattering of samples over the entire 4D space to reconstruct the texture for a particular view and thus make suboptimal use of graphics hardware.

Another IBR hybrid uses view-dependent textures (VPT) [6, 7, 5] in which geometric objects are texture-mapped using a projective mapping from view-based images. VPT methods depend on viewpoint movement for proper antialiasing - novel views are generated by reconstructing using nearby views that see each surface sufficiently "head-on". Such reconstruction is incorrect for highly specular surfaces. We instead infer texture maps that produce antialiased reconstructions independently at each parameter location, even for spaces without viewpoint change. We also use "intrinsic" texture parameterizations (i.e., viewpoint-independent (u, v) coordinates per vertex given as input on each mesh) rather than view-based ones. We can then capture the view-independent lighting in a single texture map rather than a collection of views to obtain better compression.

Interactive Photorealism. Another approach to interactive photorealism seeks to improve hardware shading models rather than fully tabulating radiance. Diefenbach [8] used shadow volumes and recursive hardware rendering to compute approximations to global rendering. Even using many parallel graphics pipelines (8 for [34]) these approaches can only handle simple scenes, and, because of limitations on the number of passes, do not capture all the effects of a full offline photorealistic rendering, including multiple bounce reflections and refractions and accurate shadows.

Texture Recovery/Model Matching. The recovery of texture maps from images is closely related to surface reflectance estimation in computer vision [29, 22, 39]. We greatly simplify the problem by using known geometry and separating diffuse and specular lighting layers during the offline rendering. We focus instead on the problem of inferring textures for particular graphics hardware that "undo" its undesirable properties, like poor-quality texture filtering. A related idea is to compute the best hardware lighting to match a gold standard [38]. Separating diffuse from specular shading to better exploit temporal and spatial coherence is a recurring theme in computer graphics [36, 26, 16, 19].

Compression. Various strategies for compressing the dual-plane lumigraph parameterization have been proposed. Levoy et al. [18] used vector quantization and entropy coding to get compression ratios up to 118:1 while Lalonde et al. [15] used a wavelet basis with compression ratios of 20:1. Miller et al. [25] compressed the 4D surface light field using a block-based DCT encoder with compression ratios of 20:1. Nishino et al. [27] used an eigenbasis to encode surface textures achieving compression ratios of 20:1 with eigenbases having 8-18 vectors.

Another relevant area of work is animation compression. Standard video compression uses simple block-based transforms and image-based motion prediction. Wallach et al. [37] used rendering hardware to accelerate standard MPEG encoding. Guenter et al. [11] observed that compression is greatly improved by exploiting information available in synthetic animations. Levoy [17] showed how simple graphics hardware could be used to match a synthetic image stream produced by a simultaneously-executing, high-quality server renderer by exploiting polygon rendering and transmitting a residual signal. We extend this work to the matching of multidimensional animations containing non-diffuse, offline-rendered imagery using texture-mapping graphics hardware.

3 Parameterized Texture Inference

To infer the texture maps that best match the input gold-standard rendered frames, we first model the graphics hardware as a large sparse linear system (Section 3.3), and then perform a least-squares optimization on the resulting system (Section 3.4). To achieve a good encoding, we first segment the input images (Section 3.1), and choose an appropriate texture domain and resolution (Section 3.2).

3.1 Segmenting Ray-Traced Images

Each geometric object has a parameterized texture that must be inferred from the ray-traced images. These images are first segmented into per-object pieces to prevent bleeding of information from different objects across silhouettes. To perform per-object segmentation, the ray tracer generates a per-object mask as well as a combined image, all at supersampled resolution. For each object, we filter the portion of the combined image indicated by the mask and divide by the fractional coverage computed by applying the same filter to the object's mask.

A second form of segmentation separates the view-dependent specular information from the view-independent diffuse information for the common case that the parameter space includes at least one view dimension. Figure 3 illustrates segmentation for an example ray-traced image. We use a modified version of Eon, a Monte Carlo distribution ray-tracer [31].

(a) Complete Image   (b) Diffuse Layer   (c) Specular Layer   (d) Diffuse Table Layer   (e) Specular Parfait Layer

Fig. 3. Segmentation of Ray-Traced Images. (a) Complete Image, (b,c) Segmentation into diffuse and specular layers respectively, (d,e) Examples of further segmentation into per object layers.

3.2 Optimizing Texture Coordinates and Resolutions

Since parts of an object may be occluded or off-screen, only part of its texture domain is accessed. The original texture coordinates of the geometry are used as a starting point and then optimized so as to: 1) to ensure adequate sampling of the visible texture image with as few samples as possible, 2) to allow efficient computation of texture coordinates at run-time, and 3) to minimize encoding of the optimized texture coordinates. To satisfy the last two goals, we choose and encode a parameter-dependent affine transformation on the original texture coordinates rather than re-specify them at each vertex. One affine transformation is chosen per object per block of parameter space (see Section 4).

The first step of the algorithm finds the linear transformation, $R(u, v)$, minimizing the following objective function, inspired by [21]

$$R(u,v) = \begin{bmatrix} a & b \\ c & d \end{bmatrix} \begin{bmatrix} u \\ v \end{bmatrix}, \ f(x) = \sum_{\text{edges } i} W_i \left(\frac{s_i - \|R(u_{i_0}, v_{i_0}) - R(u_{i_1}, v_{i_1})\|}{\min\left(s_i, \|R(u_{i_0}, v_{i_0}) - R(u_{i_1}, v_{i_1})\|\right)} \right)^2 \quad (1)$$

where s_i represents the length on the screen of a particular triangle edge, i_0 and i_1 represent the edge vertices, and W_i is a weighting term which sums screen areas of triangles on each side of the edge. At each point in the parameter block, the sum in f is taken over *visible* triangle edges determined by rasterizing triangle identifiers into a zbuffer after clipping to the view frustum.

This minimization choses a mapping that is as close to an isometry as possible by minimizing length difference between triangle edges in texture space and projected to the image. We divide by the minimum edge length so as to equally penalize edges that are an equal factor longer and shorter. $\nabla f(x)$ is calculated analytically for use in conjugate gradient minimization.

In the second step, we ensure that the object's texture map contains enough samples by scaling the R found previously. We check the greatest local stretch (singular value) across all screen pixels in which the object is visible, using the Jacobian of the mapping from texture to screen space. If the maximum singular value exceeds a threshold, we scale R by the maximum singular value in the corresponding direction of maximal stretch, and iterate until the maximum singular value is reduced below the threshold. This essentially adds more samples to counteract the worst-case stretching of the projected texture.

Finally, the minimum-area bounding rectangle on the transformed texture coordinates determines the resulting texture resolution and affine texture transformation.

3.3 Modeling Hardware Rendering as a Linear System

A simple texture inference algorithm maps each texel to the image and then filters the neighboring region to reconstruct the texel's value [22]. One problem with this approach is reconstruction of texels near arbitrarily-shaped object boundaries and occluded regions (Figure 3-d,e). Such occluded regions produce undefined texture samples which complicates building of MIPMAPs. Finally, the simple algorithm does not take into account how texture filtering is performed on the target graphics hardware.

A more principled approach is to model the hardware texture mapping operation in the form of a linear system:

$$
\underbrace{\begin{bmatrix} s_{0,0} \text{ filter coefficients} \\ s_{0,1} \text{ filter coefficients} \\ \vdots \\ s_{m-1,n-1} \text{ filter coefficients} \end{bmatrix}}_{A}
\underbrace{\begin{bmatrix} \left.\begin{array}{c} x_{0,0}^0 \\ \vdots \\ x_{u-1,v-1}^0 \end{array}\right\} \begin{array}{c} \text{level} \\ 0 \end{array} \\ \left.\begin{array}{c} x_{0,0}^1 \\ \vdots \\ x_{\frac{u}{2}-1,\frac{v}{2}-1}^1 \end{array}\right\} \begin{array}{c} \text{level} \\ 1 \end{array} \\ \vdots \\ \left.\begin{array}{c} x_{0,0}^{l-1} \\ \vdots \\ x_{\frac{u}{2^{l-1}}-1,\frac{v}{2^{l-1}}-1}^{l-1} \end{array}\right\} \begin{array}{c} \text{level} \\ l-1 \end{array} \end{bmatrix}}_{x}
=
\underbrace{\begin{bmatrix} s_{0,0} \\ s_{0,1} \\ \vdots \\ s_{m-1,n-1} \end{bmatrix}}_{b}
\qquad (2)
$$

where vector b contains the ray-traced image to be matched, matrix A contains the filter coefficients applied to individual texels by the hardware, and vector x represents the texels from all $l-1$ levels of the MIPMAP to be inferred. Superscripts in x entries represent MIPMAP level and subscripts represent spatial location. This model ignores hardware nonlinearities in the form of rounding and quantization. All three color components of the texture share the same matrix A.

Each row in matrix A corresponds to a particular screen pixel, while each column corresponds to a particular texel in the texture's MIPMAP pyramid. The entries in a given row of A represent the hardware filter coefficients that blend texels to produce the color at a given screen pixel. Hardware filtering requires only a small number of texel accesses per screen pixel, so the matrix A is very sparse. We use hardware z-buffering to determine object visibility on the screen, and need only consider rows (screen pixels) where the object is visible. Filter coefficients should sum to one in any row.

Obtaining Matrix A. A simple but impractical algorithm for obtaining A examines the screen output from a series of renderings, each setting only a single texel of interest to a nonzero value, as follows:

Initialize z-buffer with visibility information by rendering entire scene
For each texel in MIPMAP pyramid,
    Clear texture, and set individual texel to maximum intensity
    Clear framebuffer, and render all triangles that compose object
    For each non-zero pixel in framebuffer,
        Divide screen pixel value by maximum framebuffer intensity
        Place fractional value in A[screen pixel row][texel column]

Accuracy of inferred filter coefficients is limited by the color component resolution of the framebuffer, typically 8 bits.

To accelerate the simple algorithm, we observe that multiple columns in the matrix A can be filled in parallel as long as texel projections do not overlap on the screen and we can determine which pixels derive from which texels. An algorithm that subdivides texture space and checks that alternate texture block projections do not overlap can be devised based on this observation. A better algorithm recognizes that since just a single color component is required to infer the matrix coefficients, the other color components (typically 16 or 24 bits) can be used to store a unique texel identifier that indicates the destination column for storing the filtering coefficient. With this algorithm, described in-depth in [12], the matrix A can be inferred in 108 renderings, independent of texture resolution.

3.4 Least-Squares Solution

Removing irrelevant image pixels from Equation (2), A becomes an $n_s \times n_t$ matrix, where n_s is the number of screen pixels in which the object is visible, and n_t is the number of texels in the object's texture MIPMAP pyramid. Once we have obtained the matrix A, we solve for the texture represented by the vector x by minimizing a function $f(x)$ defined via

$$f(x) = \|Ax - b\|^2, \quad \nabla f(x) = 2A^T(Ax - b) \tag{3}$$

subject to the constraint $0 \leq x_{i,j}^k \leq 1$. Given the gradient, $\nabla f(x)$, the conjugate gradient method can be used to minimize $f(x)$. The main computation of the solution's inner loop multiplies A with a vector x representing the current solution estimate and, for the gradient, A^T with $Ax - b$. Since A is a sparse matrix with each row containing a small number of nonzero elements (exactly 8 with trilinear filtering), the cost of multiplying A or A^T with a vector is proportional to n_s. Another way to express $f(x)$ and $\nabla f(x)$ is:

$$f(x) = xA^TAx - 2x \cdot A^Tb + b \cdot b, \quad \nabla f(x) = 2A^TAx - 2A^Tb \tag{4}$$

In this formulation, the inner loop's main computation multiplies A^TA, an $n_t \times n_t$ matrix, with a vector. Since A^TA is also sparse, though less so than A, the cost of multiplying A^TA with a vector is proportional to n_t. We use the following heuristic to decide which set of equations to use:

if $(2n_s \geq Kn_t)$ Use A^TA method: Equation (4) **else** Use A method: Equation (3)

where K is a measure of relative sparsity of A^TA compared to A. We use $K = 4$. The factor 2 in the test arises because Equation (3) requires two matrix-vector multiplies while Equation (4) only requires one.

The solver can be sped up by using an initial guess vector x that interpolates the solution obtained at lower resolution. The problem size can then be gradually scaled up until it reaches the desired texture resolution. Alternatively, once a solution is found at one point in the parameter space, it can be used as an initial guess for neighboring points, which are immediately solved at the desired texture resolution.

Segmenting the ray-traced images into view-dependent and view-independent layers allows us to collapse the view-independent textures across multiple viewpoints. To compute a single diffuse texture, we solve the following problem:

$$
\overbrace{\begin{bmatrix} A_{v_0} \\ A_{v_1} \\ \vdots \\ A_{v_{n-1}} \end{bmatrix}}^{A'} \begin{bmatrix} x \end{bmatrix} = \overbrace{\begin{bmatrix} b_{v_0} \\ b_{v_1} \\ \vdots \\ b_{v_{n-1}} \end{bmatrix}}^{b'}
\tag{5}
$$

where matrix A' concatenates the A matrices for the individual viewpoints v_0 through v_{n-1}, vector b' concatenates the ray-traced images at the corresponding viewpoints, and vector x represents the single diffuse texture to be solved.

Regularization. One of the consequences of setting up the texture inference problem in the form of Equation (2) is that only texels actually used by the graphics hardware are solved, leaving the remaining texels undefined. To support movement away from the original viewpoint samples and to make the texture easier to compress, all texels should be defined. This can be achieved with *pyramidal regularization* of the form:

$$
f_{reg}(x) = f(x) + \varepsilon \left(\frac{n_s}{n_t} \right) \Gamma(x)
\tag{6}
$$

where $\Gamma(x)$ takes the difference between texels at each level of the MIPMAP with an interpolated version of the next coarser level as illustrated in Figure 4. The objective function f sums errors in screen space, while the regularization term sums errors in texture space. This requires a scale of the regularization term by n_s/n_t. We compute ∇f_{reg} analytically. This regularizing term essentially imposes a filter constraint between levels of the MIPMAP, with user-defined strength $\varepsilon \geq 0$. We currently define Γ using simple bilinear interpolation.

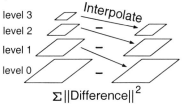

Fig. 4. Pyramidal regularization is computed by taking the sum of squared differences between texels at each level of the MIPMAP with the interpolated image of the next higher level.

3.5 Texture Inference Results

Figure 6 (see appendix) shows results of our least squares texture inference on a glass parfait object. The far left of the top row (a) is the original image to be matched. The next three columns are hardware-rendered from inferred textures using three filtering modes: bilinear, trilinear, and anisotropic.[1] The corresponding texture maps are shown in the first three columns of the next row (b). These three examples did not use pyramidal regularization.[2] Most of the error in these examples is incurred on the parfait's silhouettes due to mismatch between hardware and ray-traced rendering.

---

[1] Results were achieved with the NVidia Geforce chip supporting anisotropy factors up to 2.

[2] Without pyramidal regularization, we find that another regularization term is needed to ensure that the texture solution lies in the interval $[0, 1]$. Refer to [12] for details.

Bilinear filtering provides the sharpest, most accurate result because it uses only the finest level MIPMAP and thus has the highest frequency domain with which to match the original. Trilinear MIPMAP filtering produces a somewhat worse result, and anisotropic filtering is in between. Observe (Fig.6b) that more texture area is filled from the finest pyramid level for anisotropic filtering compared to trilinear, especially near the parfait stem, while bilinear filtering altogether ignores the higher MIPMAP levels. Bilinear filtering produces this highly accurate result *only at the exact parameter values (e.g., viewpoint locations) and image resolutions where the texture was inferred.* The other schemes are superior if viewpoint or image resolution are changed from those samples.

The next two columns show results of pyramidal regularization with anisotropic filtering. Inference with $\varepsilon = 0.1$ is almost identical to inference with no pyramidal regularization (labeled "anisotropic"), but $\varepsilon = 0.5$ causes noticeable blurring. Regularization makes MIPMAP levels tend toward filtered versions of each other; we exploit this by compressing only the finest level and re-creating higher levels by on-the-fly decimation.

Finally, the far right column in (a) shows the "forward mapping" method in which texture samples are mapped to the object's image layer and interpolated using a high-quality filter (we used a separable Lanczos-windowed sinc function). To handle occlusions, we first filled undefined samples with a simple boundary-reflection algorithm. Forward mapping produces a blurry and inaccurate result because it does not account for how graphics hardware filters the textures. In addition, reflection hole-filling produces artificial, high-frequency information in occluded regions that is expensive to encode.

4 Parameterized Texture Compression

The multidimensional field of textures for each object is compressed by subdividing into parameter space blocks as shown in Figure 1. Larger block sizes better exploit coherence but are more costly to decode during playback; we used 8×8 blocks in our 2D examples.

Adaptive Laplacian Pyramid. We encode parameterized texture blocks using a Laplacian pyramid [3] where the "samples" at each pyramid level are entire 2D images. We use standard 2D compression (e.g., JPEG and SPIHT [28] encodings) to exploit spatial coherence over (u, v) space. Each level of the Laplacian pyramid thus consists of a series of encoded 2D images. Parameter and texture dimensions are treated asymmetrically because parameters are accessed along an unpredictable 1D subspace selected by the

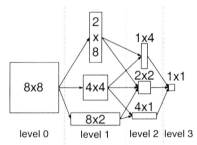

Fig. 5. Adaptive Laplacian Pyramid

user at run-time. We avoid processing large fractions of the representation to decode a given parameter sample by using the Laplacian pyramid with small block size, requiring just $\log_2(n)$ simple image additions where n is the number of samples in each dimension of the block. Furthermore, graphics hardware can perform the necessary image additions using multiple texture stages, thus enabling on-the-fly decompression.

Image coders often assume that both image dimensions are equally coherent. This is untrue of parameterized animations where, for example, the information content in a viewpoint change can greatly differ from that of a light source motion. To take advantage of differences in coherence across different dimensions, we use an *adaptive* Laplacian pyramid that subdivides more in dimensions with less coherence, illustrated in Figure 5. Coarser levels still have 4 times fewer samples.

Automatic Storage Allocation. To encode the Laplacian pyramid, storage must be assigned to its various levels. We apply standard bit allocation techniques from signal compression [9]. Curves of mean squared error (MSE) versus storage, called *rate/distortion curves*, are plotted for each pyramid level and points of equal slope on each curve selected subject to a total storage constraint. We effectively minimize the sum of MSEs across all levels of the pyramid, because a texture image at a given point in parameter space is reconstructed as a sum of images from each level, so an error in any level contributes equally to the resulting error.

There is also a need to perform storage allocation across objects; that is, to decide how much to spend in the encoding of object i's texture vs. object j's. We use the same method as for allocating between pyramid levels, except that the error measure is $A_i E_i$, where A_i is the screen area and E_i the MSE of object i. This minimizes the sum of squared errors on the screen no matter how the screen area is decomposed into objects. When objects have both specular and diffuse reflectance, our error measure sums across these lighting layers, each with an independent rate distortion curve.

5 Runtime System

The runtime system decompresses and caches texture images, applies affine transformations to vertex texture coordinates, and generates rendering calls to the graphics system. Movement off (or between) the original viewpoint samples is allowed by rendering from that viewpoint using the closest texture sample. Higher-order interpolation would improve smoothness at the expense of more texture map accesses.

The texture caching system decides which textures to keep in memory in decompressed form. Because the user's path through parameter space is unpredictable, we use an adaptive caching strategy that reclaims memory when the number of frames since last use exceeds a given lifetime. Images near the top of the pyramid are more likely to be reused and are thus assigned longer lifetimes. See [12] for more details.

If blocks of all objects are aligned, then many simultaneous cache misses occur whenever the user crosses a block boundary, creating a computational spike as multiple levels in the new blocks' Laplacian pyramids are decoded. We mitigate this problem by *staggering* the blocks – using different block origins for different objects.

6 Results

6.1 Demo1: Light × View

Compression Results. The first example scene (Figure 8 in appendix, top) consists of 6 static objects (4384 triangles): a reflective vase, glass parfait, reflective table top, table stand, walls, and floor. The 2D parameter space has 64 viewpoint samples circling around the table at 1.8°/sample and 8 different positions of a swinging, spherical light source. The image field was encoded using eight 8×8 parameter space blocks, each requiring storage 640×480×3×8×8= 56.25MB/block.

Our least-squares texture inference method created parameterized textures for each object. The resulting texture fields were compressed using a variety of methods, including adaptive 2D Laplacian pyramids of both DCT- and SPIHT-encoded levels. To test the benefits of the Laplacian pyramid, we also encoded each block using MPEG on a 1D zig-zag path through the parameter space varying most rapidly along the dimension of most coherence. A state-of-the-art MPEG4 encoder [24] was used. Finally, we compared against direct compression of the original images (rather than renderings using compressed textures), again using MPEG4.

Figure 8 shows the results at two targeted compression rates: 384:1 (middle row) and 768:1 (bottom row). All texture-based images were generated on graphics hardware using 2×2 antialiasing; their MSEs were computed from the framebuffer contents, averaged over an entire block. Both Laplacian pyramid texture encodings (right two columns) achieve reasonable quality at 768:1, and quite good quality at 384:1. The view-based MPEG encoding, "MPEG-view", is inferior with obvious block artifacts on object silhouettes, even though MPEG encoding constraints did not allow as much compression as the other examples.

For MPEG encoding of textures we tried two schemes: one using a single I-frame per block, and another using 10 I-frames. The decoding complexity for 10I/block is roughly comparable to our DCT Laplacian pyramid decoding. Single I-frame/block maximizes compression. The 10I/block MPEG-texture results have obvious block artifacts at both quality levels especially on the vase and background wallpaper. The 1I/block MPEG-texture results are better[3], but still inferior to the pyramid schemes at the 768:1 target as MPEG only exploit coherence in one dimension. Unlike the MPEG-view case, the MPEG-texture schemes use our novel features: hardware-targeted texture inference, separation of lighting layers, and optimal storage allocation across objects.

System Performance. Average compilation and preprocessing time per point in parameter space is shown in Table 1. It can be seen that total compilation time is a small fraction of the time to produce the ray-traced images.

To determine playback performance, we measured average and worst-case frame rates (fps) for a diagonal trajectory that visits a separate parameter sample at every frame, shown in Table 2.[4] The performance bottleneck is currently software decoding speed. Reducing texture resolution by an average of 91% using a manually specified reduction factor per object provides acceptable quality at about 31fps with DCT.

Table 1. Compilation time

texture coord. opt.	1 sec
solving for textures	4.83 min
compression	.58 min
total compilation	5.43 min
ray tracing	5 hours

Table 2. Runtime performance

Encoding	Texture	Worst fps	Average fps
Laplacian	undecimated	2.46	4.76
DCT	decimated	18.4	30.7
Laplacian	undecimated	0.27	0.67
SPIHT	decimated	2.50	5.48

6.2 Demo2: View × Object Rotation

In the second example, we added a rotating, reflective "gewgaw" on the table. The parameter space consists of a 1D circular viewpoint path, containing 24 samples at 1.5°/sample, and the rotation angle of the gewgaw, containing 48 samples at 7.5°/sample. Results are shown in Figure 7 (appendix) for encodings using MPEG-view and Laplacian SPIHT.

In this example, the parameter space is much more coherent in the rotation dimension than in the view dimension, because gewgaw rotation only changes the relatively small reflected or refracted image of the gewgaw in the other objects. MPEG can exploit this coherence very effectively using motion compensation along the rotation dimension, and so the difference between our approach and MPEG is less than in the previous example. Though our method is designed to exploit multidimensional coherence and lacks motion compensation, our adaptive pyramid produces a slightly better MSE and a perceptually better image.

Real-time performance for this demo is approximately the same as for demo1.

---

[3]MSE=25.9 at 768:1 target and MSE=10.1 at 384:1 target compression. See [12].

[4]Measured with Nvidia Geforce 256 chip, 32MB video/16MB AGP memory on Pentium III 733Mhz PC.

7 Conclusions and Future Work

Synthetic imagery can be very generally parameterized with combinations of view, light, or object positions, among other parameters, to create a multidimensional animation. While real-time graphics hardware fails to capture full ray-traced shading effects, it does provide a useful operation for decoding such animations compiled beforehand: texture-mapped polygon rendering. We encode a parameterized animation using parameterized texture maps, exploiting the great coherence in these animations better than view-based representations. This paper describes how to infer parameterized texture maps from segmented imagery to obtain a close match to the original and how to compress these maps efficiently, both in terms of storage and decoding time. Results show that compression factors up to 800:1 can be achieved with good quality and real-time decoding.

Our simple sum of diffuse and specular texture maps is but a first step toward more predictive graphics models supported by hardware to aid compression. Examples include parameterized environment maps, hardware shadowing algorithms, and per-vertex shading models. The discipline of measuring compression ratios vs. error for encoding photorealistic imagery is a useful benchmark for proposed hardware enhancements.

Other extensions include use of perceptual metrics for guiding compression and storage allocation, handling nonrigidly deforming geometry and photorealistic camera models, and automatic generation of texture parameterizations. Finally, we are interested in measuring storage requirements with growing dimension of the parameter space and hypothesize that such growth is quite small in many useful cases. There appear to be two main impediments to increasing the generality of the space that can be explored: slowness of offline rendering and decompression. The first obstacle may be addressed by better exploiting coherence across the parameter space in the offline renderer, using ideas similar to [13]. The second can be overcome by absorbing some of the decoding functionality into the graphics hardware. We expect the ability to load compressed textures directly to hardware in the near future. A further enhancement would be to load compressed parameter-dependent texture block pyramids.

Acknowledgments

Extremely useful advice and discussions were provided by Henrique Malvar, Philip Chou, and Brian Guenter on compression, John Platt on optimization and regularization, and Steve Marschner on solving for texture maps and ray tracing. We thank Anoop Gupta and Turner Whitted for their guidance and support. Peter Shirley's Eon ray tracer was a valuable research tool.

References

1. Adelson, E., and J. Bergen, "The Plenoptic Function and the Elements of Early Vision," In Computational Models of Visual Processing, MIT Press, Cambridge, MA, 1991, pp. 3-20.
2. Bastos, R., K. Hoff, W. Wynn, and A. Lastra. "Increased Photorealism for Interactive Architectural Walkthroughs," 1999 ACM Symposium on Interactive 3D Graphics, April 1999, pp. 183-190.
3. Burt, P., and E. Adelson, "The Laplacian Pyramid as a Compact Image Code," IEEE Transactions on Communications, Vol. Com-31, No. 4, April 1983, pp. 532-540.
4. Chen, S.E., and L. Williams, "View Interpolation for Image Synthesis," SIGGRAPH 93, August 1993, pp. 279-288.
5. Cohen-Or, D., Y. Mann, and S. Fleishman, "Deep Compression for Streaming Texture Intensive Animations," SIGGRAPH 99, August 1999, pp. 261-265.
6. Debevec, P., C. Taylor, and J. Malik, "Modeling and Rendering Architecture from Photographs: A Hybrid Geometry- and Image-Based Approach," SIGGRAPH 96, August 1996, pp. 11-20.
7. Debevec, P., Y. Yu, and G. Borshukov, "Efficient View-Dependent Image-Based Rendering with Projective Texture Maps," In 9th Eurographics Rendering Workshop, June 1998, pp. 105-116.

8. Diefenbach, P. J., Pipeline Rendering: Interaction and Realism Through Hardware-Based Multi-Pass Rendering, Ph.D. Thesis, University of Pennsylvania, 1996.

9. Gersho, A., and R. Gray, Vector Quantization and Signal Compression, Kluwer Academic, Boston, 1992, pp. 606-610.

10. Gortler, S., R. Grzeszczuk, R. Szeliski, and M. Cohen, "The Lumigraph," SIGGRAPH 96, pp. 43-54.

11. Guenter, B., H. Yun, and R. Mersereau, "Motion Compensated Compression of Computer Animation Frames," SIGGRAPH 93, August 1993, pp. 297-304.

12. Hakura, Z., J. Lengyel, and J. Snyder, "Parameterized Animation Compression", MSR-TR-2000-50, June 2000.

13. Halle, M., "Multiple Viewpoint Rendering," SIGGRAPH 98, August 1998, 243-254.

14. Heidrich, W., H. Lensch, and H. P. Seidel. "Light Field Techniques for Reflections and Refractions," In 10th Eurographics Rendering Workshop, June 1999, pp. 195-204, p. 375.

15. Lalonde, P. and A. Fournier, "Interactive Rendering of Wavelet Projected Light Fields," Graphics Interface '99, June 1999, pp. 107-114.

16. Lengyel, J., and J. Snyder, "Rendering with Coherent Layers," SIGGRAPH 97, August 1997, pp. 233-242.

17. Levoy, M., "Polygon-Assisted JPEG and MPEG compression of Synthetic Images," SIGGRAPH 95, August 1995, pp. 21-28.

18. Levoy, M., and P. Hanrahan, "Light Field Rendering," SIGGRAPH 96, August 1996, pp. 31-41.

19. Lischinski, D., and A. Rappoport, "Image-Based Rendering for Non-Diffuse Synthetic Scenes," In 9th Eurographics Workshop on Rendering, June 1998.

20. Luettgen, M., W. Karl, and A Willsky, "Efficient Multiscale Regularization with Applications to the Computation of Optical Flow," IEEE Transactions on Image Processing, 3(1), 1994, pp. 41-64.

21. Maillot, J., H. Yahia, A. Verroust, "Interactive Texture Mapping," SIGGRAPH 93, pp. 27-34.

22. Marschner, S. R., Inverse Rendering for Computer Graphics, Ph.D. Thesis, Cornell University, August 1998.

23. McMillan, L., and G. Bishop, "Plenoptic Modeling," SIGGRAPH 95, pp. 39-46.

24. Microsoft MPEG-4 Visual Codec FDIS 1.02, ISO/IEC 14496-5 FDIS1, August 1999.

25. Miller, G., S. Rubin, and D. Poncelen, "Lazy Decompression of Surface Light Fields for Pre-computed Global Illumination," In 9th Eurographics Rendering Workshop, June 1998, pp. 281-292.

26. Nimeroff, J., J. Dorsey, and H. Rushmeier, "Implementation and Analysis of an Image-Based GLobal Illumination Framework for Animated Environments," IEEE Transactions on Visualization and Computer Graphics, 2(4), Dec. 1996, pp. 283-298.

27. Nishino, K., Y. Sato, and K. Ikeuchi, "Eigen-Texture Method: Appearance Compression based on 3D Model," Proceedings of 1999 IEEE Computer Society Conference on Computer Vision and Pattern Recognition. Fort Collins, CO, June, 1999, pp. 618-24 Vol. 1.

28. Said, A., and W. Pearlman, "A New, Fast, and Efficient Image Codec Based on Set Partitioning in Hierarchical Trees," IEEE Transactions on Circuits and Systems for Video Technology, Vol. 6, June 1996, pp. 243-250.

29. Sato, Y., M. Wheeler, and K. Ikeuchi, "Object Shape and Reflectance Modeling from Observation," SIGGRAPH 97, August 1997, pp. 379-387.

30. Shade, J., S. Gortler, L. He, and R. Szeliski, "Layered Depth Images," SIGGRAPH 98, August 1998, pp. 75-82.

31. Shirley, Wang and Zimmerman, "Monte Carlo Methods for Direct Lighting Calculations," ACM Transactions on Graphics, January 1996, pp. 1-36.

32. Stamminger, M., A. Scheel, et al., "Efficient Glossy Global Illumination with Interactive Viewing," Graphics Interface '99, June 1999, pp. 50-57.

33. Stürzlinger, W. and R. Bastos, "Interactive Rendering of Globally Illuminated Glossy Scenes," Eurographics Rendering Workshop 1997, June 1997, pp. 93-102.

34. Udeshi, T. and C. Hansen, "Towards interactive, photorealistic rendering of indoor scenes: A hybrid approach," Eurographics Rendering Workshop 1999, June 1999, pp. 71-84 and pp. 367-368.

35. Wong, T. T., P. A. Heng, S. H. Or, and W. Y. Ng, "Image-based Rendering with Controllable Illumination," Eurographics Rendering Workshop 1997, June 1997, pp. 13-22.

36. Wallace, J., M. Cohen, and D. Greenberg, "A Two-Pass Solution to the Rendering Equation: A Synthesis of Ray-Tracing and Radiosity Methods," SIGGRAPH 87, July 1987, pp. 311-320.

37. Wallach, D., S. Kunapalli, and M. Cohen, "Accelerated MPEG Compression of Dynamic Polygonal Scenes," SIGGRAPH 94, July 1997, pp. 193-196.

38. Walter, B., G. Alppay, E. Lafortune, S. Fernandez, and D. Greenberg, "Fitting Virtual Lights for Non-Diffuse Walkthroughs," SIGGRAPH 97, August 1997, pp. 45-48.

39. Yu, Y., P. Debevec, J. Malik, and T. Hawkins, "Inverse Global Illumination: Recovering Reflectance Models of Real Scenes From Photographs," SIGGRAPH 99, August 1999, pp. 215-224.

Editors' Note: see Appendix, p. 399, 400 for colored figures of this paper

Wavelet Warping

Iddo Drori   Dani Lischinski

School of Computer Science and Engineering
The Hebrew University of Jerusalem, Israel

Abstract. We present *wavelet warping* — a new class of forward 3D warping algorithms for image-based rendering. In wavelet warping most of the warping operation is performed in the wavelet domain, by operating on the coefficients of the wavelet transforms of the images and other matrices defined by the mapping. Operating in this fashion is often more efficient than performing the 3D warp in the standard manner. Perhaps more importantly, operating in the wavelet domain allows one to perform the 3D warping operation progressively and to generate target views at multiple resolutions. We describe wavelet warping of planar, cylindrical, and spherical reference images and demonstrate that the resulting algorithms compare favorably to their standard counterparts. We also discuss and demonstrate utilization of temporal coherence when wavelet-warping image sequences.

1 Introduction

Many image-based rendering algorithms use pre-rendered or pre-acquired *reference images* of a 3D scene in order to synthesize novel views of the scene. The central computational component of such algorithms is 3D image warping, which performs the mapping of pixels in the reference images to their coordinates in the target image.

This paper presents *wavelet warping* — a new class of forward 3D warping algorithms for image-based rendering. We rewrite the 3D warping equations as a pointwise quotient of linear combinations of matrices. Rather than computing these linear combinations in a standard manner, we first pre-compute the wavelet transforms of the participating matrices. Next, we perform the linear combination on the sparse wavelet transform coefficients. Applying the inverse wavelet transform to the resulting coefficients yields the desired linear combinations. Operating in the wavelet domain is advantageous in several aspects:

Sparse representation: The wavelet decomposition of an image or a large matrix is typically much sparser (has fewer non-zero coefficients) than the original direct representation. This property has been utilized to speed up various numerical operations [1, 2]. In our case, a sparse representation of the matrices results in faster computation of their linear combinations since we operate only on the non-zero coefficients.

Multi-resolution and progressive computation: The wavelet decomposition represents each matrix at multiple scales. Such a representation makes it easy to perform the warping operation at multiple resolutions, as well as in a progressive, coarse-to-fine fashion.

Compatibility with emerging standards: Over the past decade the wavelet transform has been recognized as a preferred tool for image and video compression and has been selected as the fundamental building block of the emerging JPEG-2000 standard. Thus, it is very likely that many of the images that we will be working with in the future will be represented in the wavelet domain to begin with. Wavelet domain operations will allow processing of such images without having to reconstruct them first.

114

1.1 Contributions

We describe in detail wavelet warping algorithms for three common types of 3D image warps: planar-to-planar warp, cylindrical-to-planar warp, and spherical-to-planar warp. Cylindrical and spherical panoramas and movies are becoming increasingly common in application areas, such as entertainment, real estate, virtual tourism, and electronic retail. Current viewers allow the user to interactively change the viewing direction, e.g., [4, 9]. By using depth information, a 3D warper enables users to change the *viewing position* (center of projection), in addition to the viewing direction [13]. A fast 3D warper enables users to view a scene interactively. We will show that the wavelet warping algorithm is at least as fast as the most efficient warping algorithm known to date for planar and cylindrical warps, and is nearly twice as fast in the spherical case.

Perhaps more importantly, our wavelet warping algorithms support multi-resolution and progressive rendering. For example, consider an object whose image-based model consists of one or more high-resolution reference images. The high resolution may be necessary for a close-up view of the object, but for most views of a 3D scene containing the object a much lower resolution suffices. Our approach makes it possible to perform the warp at the appropriate coarser resolution, without unnecessarily warping each and every pixel in the reference images. Multi-resolution warping can also be achieved within a standard warping framework by using an over-complete pyramid-based image representation (e.g. a quadtree), but at a cost of increasing the size of the representation. In addition, wavelet warping has the advantage that the computation is progressive: a low resolution result can be progressively refined without redundant computations.

Our final contribution is a new algorithm for 3D warping an entire sequence of images with depth to a novel view. This algorithm is also based on wavelet warping, and it utilizes the temporal coherence typically present in image sequences or panoramic movies to achieve considerable speedups over frame-by-frame warping.

1.2 Related work

The idea of representing a scene as a set of reference images was introduced to computer graphics by Chen and Williams [5] and by McMillan and Bishop [13]. The equations of 3D warping are developed in detail in McMillan's PhD thesis [12]. Mark *et al.* [11] and Shade *et al.* [14] discuss different frameworks for image-based rendering and warping. Dally *et al.* [6] introduce the delta tree, a data structure that represents an object using a collection of images. They divide images into blocks and represent them in the frequency domain using the discrete cosine transform (DCT), but provide little detail regarding the warping of such images.

Smith and Rowe [15] address the issue of processing JPEG-compressed images in the compressed DCT domain. By performing pixel-wise and scalar addition and multiplication on JPEG-compressed images they are able to implement operations such as dissolving between two video sequences and video subtitling very efficiently (compared to uncompressing, processing, and compressing again). In a later paper [16] their methods are extended to the computation of arbitrary linear combinations of pixels in images of motion-JPEG video sequences. However, they do not address 3D warping of images and video sequences.

Their approach is tuned to the particularities of JPEG (block-based DCT, quantization, zig-zag scanning, etc.). The resulting algorithms are quite complicated. In contrast, our approach is applicable to any wavelet transform (although its effectiveness will depend on which transform is actually chosen), and results in very simple algorithms. Another difference between their approach and this work is in the goals. Their primary goal is to process compressed images (or video sequences) directly, without ever leaving the compressed domain. Our primary goal is to provide faster and more flexible operations on ordinary data, by representing the data and/or the operation in the wavelet domain. Our approach is geared towards an interactive setting, where operations are performed in the wavelet domain, but the results are typically reconstructed right away for display.

2   Wavelets

Wavelets are a powerful mathematical tool for hierarchical multi-resolution analysis of functions. They have been effectively utilized in many diverse fields, including approximation theory, signal processing, physics, astronomy, and image processing [10]. Wavelets have also been applied to a wide variety of problems in computer graphics [17]. In this section we briefly review wavelet-related terminology and concepts that will be used later in the paper.

Lifting: The lifting scheme [18] is a method for constructing wavelets in the spatial domain. It consists of three steps: (i) splitting the data into two subsets; (ii) computing the wavelet coefficients as the failure to predict one subset based on the other (high pass); (iii) computing the scaling function coefficients by updating the remaining subset (low pass).

Any discrete wavelet transform can be factored into lifting steps [7], thus allowing: (i) in-place computation of the wavelet transform; (ii) faster computation, asymptotically reducing the complexity by a factor of two; (iii) construction of wavelet transforms that map integers to integers [3].

Integer wavelets: Integer wavelet transforms operate on integer valued signals to produce integer valued wavelet coefficients. Such transforms have been effectively used for lossless compression of images [3]. Calderbank *et al.* [3] describe invertible integer wavelet transforms, but use floating point arithmetic to compute them. In our implementation, the integer transforms are computed using integer arithmetic, with addition, subtraction and shift operations only.

2D transforms: The 2D wavelet transform of a matrix or an image can be constructed using the 1D wavelet transform in two ways: the *standard decomposition* and the *nonstandard decomposition*. The nonstandard decomposition is computed by applying the 1D transform alternating between rows and columns of the matrix. In this paper we use both the 1D wavelet transform and the 2D non-standard wavelet transform.

Linear combinations of matrices

Our approach is based on fast computation of linear combinations of matrices in the wavelet domain. Let $\mathbf{A}$ be a 2D matrix that can be expressed as a linear combination of matrices: $\mathbf{A} = \sum_i \alpha_i \mathbf{A}_i$, and let T be a 2D wavelet transform. Since T is an invertible linear operator, we can express $\mathbf{A}$ as

$$\mathbf{A} = T^{-1}(T(\mathbf{A})) = T^{-1}\left(\sum_i \alpha_i T(\mathbf{A}_i)\right).\tag{1}$$

In other words, $\mathbf{A}$ can be computed in the wavelet domain, by precomputing the wavelet transform (decomposition) of each matrix $\mathbf{A}_i$, linearly combining the resulting wavelet coefficients, and applying the inverse transform (reconstruction). If the wavelet decom-

116

positions $T(\mathbf{A}_i)$ are sparse, this computation can be done rapidly by operating only on the non-zero coefficients of each transform.

3 3D Warping

This section describes the application of our approach to the various 3D warping mappings, which are in the core of most image-based rendering algorithms. We begin by briefly reviewing the 3D warping equations (the reader is referred to McMillan's PhD thesis [12] for detailed derivations). Following the review we show how to express (parts of) the warping operation as a linear combination of matrices, thereby paving the way for *wavelet domain 3D warping*.

Most image-based rendering algorithms use *forward* 3D warping, which maps pixels from a reference (source) image to the desired (target) image, according to the following general equation [12]:

$$\mathbf{p}_2 = \mathbf{M}_2^{-1}\left(\delta\left(\mathbf{p}_1\right)\left(\mathbf{o}_1 - \mathbf{o}_2\right) + \mathbf{M}_1\left(\mathbf{p}_1\right)\right).$$

The 3-vectors $\mathbf{p}_1$ and $\mathbf{p}_2$ are the homogeneous image coordinates of the source and target pixels, respectively. The matrices $\mathbf{M}_i$ map pixel coordinates to 3D rays, and the points $\mathbf{o}_i$ are the centers of projection. The generalized disparity $\delta(\mathbf{p})$ is inversely proportional to the depth at pixel $\mathbf{p}$.

More specifically, the forward mapping from reference image space coordinates (x, y) to target image space coordinates (u, v) is expressed as

$$u = \frac{f_1(x,y)}{f_3(x,y)} \quad \text{and} \quad v = \frac{f_2(x,y)}{f_3(x,y)}, \tag{2}$$

where the functions $f_i(x, y)$ depend on the type of warp. For example, when warping a planar reference image to a planar target image, $f_i(x, y)$ can be expressed as:

$$f_i(x,y) = \begin{bmatrix} p_{i1} & p_{i2} & p_{i3} & p_{i4} \end{bmatrix} \begin{bmatrix} x \\ y \\ 1 \\ \delta(x,y) \end{bmatrix} \tag{3}$$

The scalars p_{ij} are dependent upon the view matrices $\mathbf{M}_1$ and $\mathbf{M}_2$ and the vector $\mathbf{o}_1 - \mathbf{o}_2$ between the two centers of projection. The result is valid when $f_3(x, y) > 0$ (point is in front of camera), and when (u, v) are in the range of target image space coordinates.

When warping a cylindrical reference image to a planar target image, the equations become:

$$f_i(x,y) = \begin{bmatrix} c_{i1} & c_{i2} & c_{i3} & c_{i4} \end{bmatrix} \begin{bmatrix} \sin(2\pi x/w) \\ \cos(2\pi x/w) \\ y_0 + (y_1 - y_0)y/h \\ \delta(x,y) \end{bmatrix} \tag{4}$$

where w and h are the width and height of the image in pixels, and y_0 and y_1 define the vertical field-of-view of the cylindrical image. Similarly, a warp from a spherical reference image to a planar target image is defined by:

$$f_i(x,y) = \begin{bmatrix} s_{i1} & s_{i2} & s_{i3} & s_{i4} \end{bmatrix} \begin{bmatrix} \sin(2\pi x/w)\sin(\pi y/h) \\ \cos(2\pi x/w)\sin(\pi y/h) \\ \cos(\pi y/h) \\ \delta(x,y) \end{bmatrix} \tag{5}$$

3.1 Wavelet warping

In order to perform 3D warping in the wavelet domain, we express the warping equations as element-wise divisions between three linear combinations of matrices. Let $\mathbf{F}_i$ denote the matrix of all the values $f_i(x, y)$, and let $\mathbf{U}$ and $\mathbf{V}$ denote the matrices containing all of the warped u and v target coordinates. Using these matrices we rewrite equation (2) as

$$\mathbf{U} = \frac{\mathbf{F}_1}{\mathbf{F}_3} \quad \text{and} \quad \mathbf{V} = \frac{\mathbf{F}_2}{\mathbf{F}_3},$$

where

$$\mathbf{F}_i = m_{i1}\mathbf{A} + m_{i2}\mathbf{B} + m_{i3}\mathbf{C} + m_{i4}\mathbf{D}. \tag{6}$$

In the planar-to-planar warp, for example, the linear combination coefficients m_{ij} are simply the p_{ij}-s from equation (3), and the matrices are defined as follows:

$$\mathbf{A} = [x]_{x,y} \quad \mathbf{B} = [y]_{x,y} \quad \mathbf{C} = [1]_{x,y} \quad \mathbf{D} = [\delta(x, y)]_{x,y} \tag{7}$$

Thus, the matrix $\mathbf{A}$ is simply a linear ramp, increasing from left to right; all of its rows are the same vector $[0, 1, \ldots, n-1]$. Similarly, the matrix $\mathbf{B}$ is a linear ramp, and all of its columns are the same vector. The matrix $\mathbf{C}$ is constant. The wavelet transform of these matrices is extremely sparse, and the efficiency of our wavelet warping algorithm stems from this sparse representation.

In the cylindrical-to-planar case the matrices $\mathbf{A}, \mathbf{B}$ and $\mathbf{C}$ are slightly more complicated:

$$\mathbf{A} = \left[\sin(2\pi x/w)\right]_{x,y} \qquad \mathbf{B} = \left[\cos(2\pi x/w)\right]_{x,y}$$
$$\mathbf{C} = \left[y_0 + (y_1 - y_0)y/h\right]_{x,y} \quad \mathbf{D} = [\delta(x, y)]_{x,y} \tag{8}$$

Still, note that each of the matrices $\mathbf{A}$ and $\mathbf{B}$ is a function of a single variable x, which means that in each of these two matrices all of the rows are equal. Similarly, $\mathbf{C}$ is a function of y, and therefore all of the columns are equal. Both the standard cylindrical-to-planar warp and our wavelet warping algorithm exploit this structure to save computations.

Finally, in the spherical-to-planar case the matrices are:

$$\mathbf{A} = \left[\sin(2\pi x/w)\sin(\pi y/h)\right]_{x,y} \quad \mathbf{B} = \left[\cos(2\pi x/w)\sin(\pi y/h)\right]_{x,y}$$
$$\mathbf{C} = \left[\cos(\pi y/h)\right]_{x,y} \qquad\qquad \mathbf{D} = [\delta(x, y)]_{x,y} \tag{9}$$

In this case only $\mathbf{C}$ is a function of a single variable y, and therefore all of its columns are equal.

The wavelet warping operation consists of two steps: computation of linear combinations of matrices (equation (6)), followed by clipping and element-wise divide. The first step is carried out in the wavelet domain, as illustrated in Figure 1. Thus, following equation (1), we compute the matrices $\mathbf{F}_i$ as follows:

$$\begin{aligned} \mathbf{F}_i &= T^{-1}T\left(m_{i1}\mathbf{A} + m_{i2}\mathbf{B} + m_{i3}\mathbf{C} + m_{i4}\mathbf{D}\right) \\ &= T^{-1}\left(m_{i1}T(\mathbf{A}) + m_{i2}T(\mathbf{B}) + m_{i3}T(\mathbf{C}) + m_{i4}T(\mathbf{D})\right) \end{aligned} \tag{10}$$

Several things should be noted at this point:

- The matrices $\mathbf{A}$, $\mathbf{B}$, and $\mathbf{C}$ depend only on the type of warp (planar, cylindrical, or spherical), and are independent of the reference or the target images. Consequently, $T(\mathbf{A}), T(\mathbf{B}), T(\mathbf{C})$ are precomputed once for each type of warp, and then reused for all warping operations.

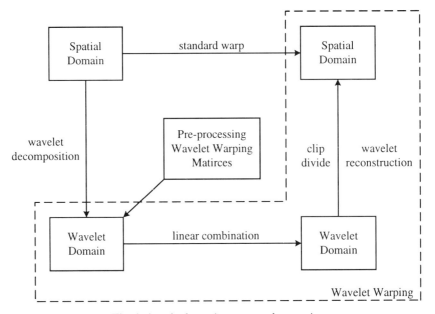

Fig. 1. Standard warping vs. wavelet warping.

- The matrix **D**, which is the disparity image of the reference view is independent of the target view, and $T(\mathbf{D})$ is precomputed once for each reference view.
- The scalars m_{ij} are dependent upon both the reference and the target view, and are calculated once for each target view, the same as in a standard warp.

The pseudocode for the resulting warping algorithm is listed in Figure 2. Note that all wavelet-transformed matrices are represented by arrays containing only the non-zero coefficients. Each entry in such an array has an *index* field indicating position of the coefficient, and a *value* field containing the value of the coefficient. Our implementation uses an integer wavelet transform [3]. Since the disparity values in **D** as well as the entries of **A**, **B**, and **C** (in the cylindrical and spherical cases) contain floating point values, these values are first mapped into an integer range.

3.2 Choice of basis

In order to make our wavelet warping algorithm as efficient as possible, we must choose a suitable wavelet basis. There are two requirements that the chosen basis must satisfy: (i) the transforms $T(\mathbf{A})$, $T(\mathbf{B})$, $T(\mathbf{C})$, and $T(\mathbf{D})$ should be sparse; (ii) the reconstructions $\mathbf{F}_i = T^{-1}(\hat{\mathbf{F}}_i)$ should be fast to compute. After experimenting with several different options, we have chosen a slightly modified version of the second order interpolating wavelet transform, $I(2,2)$ [18]. The modification consists of omitting the update phase of the lifting scheme. The resulting transform requires $\frac{8}{3}n^2$ operations to decompose or reconstruct an $n \times n$ matrix using the 2D nonstandard wavelet transform.

The wavelet coefficients of this transform measure the extent to which the original function fails to be linear. In the case of a planar warp, the matrices **A** and **B** are simply

```
Pre-processing:
    For each type of warp, precompute transforms: T(A), T(B), T(C)
    For each reference image, precompute T(D)
    Store non-zero coefficients in arrays t_A, t_B, t_C, t_D

Input:   Reference image, target view, coefficient arrays t_A, t_B, t_C, t_D
Output: Target image

3D Warp:
    for i = 1 to 3
        Compute m_ij for j = 1 to 4
        foreach coefficient array t
            for l = 1 to length of t
                F̂_i [t[l]. index] = F̂_i[t[l]. index] + m_ij t[l]. value
            endfor
        endfor
        Reconstruct F_i = T^{-1}(F̂_i)
    endfor

Clip and Divide:
    for x = 0 to w − 1
        for y = 0 to h − 1
            w = F_3(x, y)
            if w > 0 then (u, v) = (1/w)(F_1(x, y), F_2(x, y))
            if (u, v) ∈ target image space then target(u, v) = ref(x, y)
        endfor
    endfor
```

Fig. 2. Wavelet domain warping.

linear ramps and matrix $\mathbf{C}$ is constant (eq. (7)). Consequently, the transforms $T(\mathbf{A})$ and $T(\mathbf{B})$ consist of two non-zero coefficients each, and $T(\mathbf{C})$ consists of a single non-zero coefficient. Note that this is *lossless compression* of the three matrices — they can be reconstructed exactly from these sparse transforms.

In the case of a cylindrical warp (eq. (8)) the transforms $T(\mathbf{A})$ and $T(\mathbf{B})$ have fewer than $\frac{1}{9}n^2$ non-zero coefficients each, while $T(\mathbf{C})$ has two non-zero coefficients.

In the case of a spherical warp (eq. (9)) the transforms $T(\mathbf{A})$, $T(\mathbf{B})$ and $T(\mathbf{C})$ have fewer than $\frac{1}{9}n^2$ non-zero coefficients each. Once again, the compression of the matrices is lossless.

As for the disparities matrix $\mathbf{D}$, the number of non-zero coefficients depends, of course, on the reference image. In our experiments, roughly one third of the coefficients of $T(\mathbf{D})$ were non-zero. Although the number of non-zero coefficients can be decreased further by lossy wavelet compression, it is not beneficial to do so. As we shall see in the next section, the computational bottleneck of wavelet warping lies in the reconstruction stage. A slight reduction in the number of coefficients does not significantly improve performance, while a more drastic truncation causes errors in the mapping, resulting in visible artifacts.

4 Analysis and Results

The complexity of the standard 3D warp depends on the type of warp. A planar-to-planar warp computes equation (3) using an incremental loop, which requires a single addition for each increment in x or y, plus an additional multiplication and addition for the generalized disparity term for each f_i [14]. The clipping is followed by two divisions. Thus, the total number of operations to warp an $n \times n$ image is $11n^2$.

In the cases of cylindrical-to-planar and spherical-to-planar warps, the computation cannot be done incrementally. To perform the standard warp efficiently, the terms in matrices $\mathbf{A}$, $\mathbf{B}$, and $\mathbf{C}$ are precomputed and stored in lookup tables (LUT). In the cylindrical-to-planar case, further savings are possible since, as pointed out earlier, there are only n distinct terms in each of the three matrices. Thus, each m_{ij} must be multiplied with only n, rather than n^2 different terms. A similar optimization is performed in the spherical-to-planar case when computing $m_{i3}\mathbf{C}$.

In contrast, since the wavelet warping algorithm performs operations only on the non-zero elements of the transformed matrices, the total number of operations required to compute equation (10) is t multiplications and $t - |T(\mathbf{D})|$ additions (where t is the total number of non-zero wavelet coefficients), plus the cost of the reconstruction step that takes $\frac{8}{3}n^2$ operations in our implementation. We perform three reconstruction steps (one for each $\mathbf{F}_i$), followed by clipping and two divisions per pixel. The results of the analysis are summarized in the following table:

Operation	any wavelet warp	planar	cylindrical	spherical
Addition	$8n^2 + 3(t - \|T(\mathbf{D})\|)$	$6n^2 + 3n$	$6n^2 + 3n$	$9n^2$
Multiplication	$3t$	$3n^2$	$3n^2 + 9n$	$9n^2 + 3n$
Division	$2n^2$	$2n^2$	$2n^2$	$2n^2$
Total	$10n^2 + 6t - 3\|T(\mathbf{D})\|$	$11n^2 + 3n$	$11n^2 + 12n$	$20n^2 + 3n$

As explained in Section 3.2, our choice of wavelet basis results in a total number of $t = |T(\mathbf{D})| + 5$ non-zero coefficients in the wavelet planar warp, $t < \frac{2}{9}n^2 + |T(\mathbf{D})| + 2$ in the cylindrical case, and $t < \frac{1}{3}n^2 + |T(\mathbf{D})|$ in the spherical case. The conclusion from our analysis is therefore that wavelet warping is as fast as the most efficient standard warp in the planar and cylindrical cases, while in the spherical warp we can expect speedups by a factor greater than $20/13$.

4.1 2D vs. 1D decomposition

The standard warping algorithm warps the reference image pixels to their destination one-by-one, so its intermediate storage requirements are $O(1)$. In contrast, the wavelet warping algorithm described above must reconstruct the three matrices $\mathbf{F}_i$ before computing the target pixel coordinates. Thus, it requires $O(n^2)$ intermediate storage. When the warped image is sufficiently large, the intermediate storage requirements may exceed the size of the L2 cache, resulting in a performance penalty. In this case, we use a modified version of the wavelet warping algorithm. This version computes a 1D wavelet decomposition of each row in each of the matrices $\mathbf{A}, \mathbf{B}, \mathbf{C}$, and $\mathbf{D}$ instead of the 2D non-standard wavelet decomposition. The linear combination of the matrices is then computed row-by-row. Now the reconstruction step is performed on one row at a time, and the required intermediate storage is $O(n)$. In addition to avoiding cache misses, this modification also allows us to take advantage of the fact that in many of the matrices the rows are identical, as pointed out earlier for the standard cylindrical and spherical warps. On the other hand, using the 1D transform version slightly increases the number of non-zero coefficients: in our experiments with this method we found that roughly half of the coefficients of $T(\mathbf{D})$ were non-zero (compared to third with 2D decomposition). The 1D version is still faster than the 2D version, but it compromises our ability to perform the warping in a true multi-resolution fashion, as described in the next section. Since memory speed and cache size tend to increase faster than image resolution, it is safe to assume that in the near future it will be possible to use the 2D version even on large images, without incurring a performance penalty.

4.2 Empirical results

The theoretical analysis presented above has been validated experimentally. We have implemented our wavelet warping algorithm, as well as the standard warps: incremental planar-to-planar, LUT-based cylindrical-to-planar and spherical-to-planar, with the optimizations mentioned earlier. The algorithms were implemented in Java. All of the results reported in this paper were measured on a 450 MHz Pentium II processor. In all our comparisons we measured the entire warping time, including reconstruction, clipping, and the divisions by the homogeneous coordinate. The averaged performance of the different warping algorithms (in frames per second) is summarized in the following table.

Type of Warp	standard warp	2D wavelet	1D wavelet
planar (512^2 reference)	6.5	6.5	7
cylindrical (512×256 reference)	12	12	15
spherical (512×256 reference)	7.7	14	14
spherical (1024×512 reference)	4	4	6.5

As predicted by our analysis, in the planar and cylindrical cases, we found wavelet warping to be roughly as fast as the standard algorithms, when 2D decomposition of the matrices was used. Using the 1D decomposition version, we found wavelet warping to be slightly faster (up to 25 percent in the cylindrical case) than the standard algorithms. Note that in the planar case the reference image has twice as many pixels as in the cylindrical case. This is the reason that the number of warps per second in the first row of the table is smaller almost by a factor of two.

As expected, in the spherical case with a 512×256 reference image, wavelet warping outperforms the standard algorithm by a factor of roughly 1.8. When the resolution of the spherical reference image is increased to 1024×512, 2D wavelet warping suffers from cache misses and the performance drops down to the speed of the standard algorithm. The 1D wavelet version, however, still outperforms the standard algorithm by a factor of over 1.6. Figure 3 (see color plates) shows a spherical-to-planar warping example. The two rectangular images on the left show a spherical reference image of a chapel along with the corresponding depth image. The middle image is a planar view of the chapel taken from a slightly displaced view point. Since only one reference image was used, some disocclusion artifacts can be seen. The right image is another planar view of the chapel, taken from the original view point.

5 Multi-Resolution Warping

Suppose that we have an image-based representation of a 3D object and would like to generate a novel view in which the object is farther away from the viewpoint, and thus appears much smaller than in its reference views. Or perhaps, we are interested in rapidly generating lower resolution novel views when the view is constantly changing, and then refine it if the camera stops moving. Our wavelet warping algorithms are well suited for such multi-resolution and/or progressive rendering.

When wavelet-warping a reference image to a target image of lower resolution, we compute the linear combination (10) exactly as before. However, in this case there is no need to perform a full reconstruction of the result. For example, if the target image resolution is twice smaller in each dimension, we stop reconstruction just before processing the wavelet coefficients of the finest level. As a result, the reconstruction step is faster by a factor of four, and there are also four times fewer clip-and-divide operations. The warped coordinates (u, v) are still generated in the original range, so they are shifted right by one bit.

When the target image resolution is lower, we must low-pass filter the color values of the reference image pixels, before copying them to the target image. Therefore, the color channels of the reference image are also represented in the wavelet domain. Prefiltered color values are obtained by reconstructing the image incrementally, as the resolution of the result is progressively refined from coarse to fine.

Figure 4 (see color plates) shows the results of planar-to-planar wavelet warping to different target resolutions. Two 512^2 reference views of a synthetic scene (with depth for each pixel) were warped to a common novel view. Both reference views and their corresponding depth images are shown in the top row. In the bottom row we show the target image generated at quarter (128^2), half (256^2), and full (512^2) resolutions, from left to right. In order to make the differences visible, all three images are shown at the same size in the figure.

When the target image is generated at full resolution, the wavelet warp is performed at roughly 6.5 frames per second (see table in previous section). However, when the target resolution is reduced by half, wavelet warping becomes more than 4 times faster compared to full resolution warping (around 27 frames per second). At quarter resolution, wavelet warping becomes more than 16 times faster.

It should be noted that multi-resolution warping can also be achieved within a standard warping framework by using an over-complete pyramid-based image representation (e.g. a quadtree), but at a cost of increasing the size of the representation by a factor of $4/3$. In addition, wavelet warping has the advantage that the computation is progressive: a low resolution result can be progressively refined without redundant computations, simply by performing one more level of reconstruction. In contrast, in a pyramid-based scheme each level must be warped from scratch.

6 Fast Warping of Image Sequences

When warping an entire sequence of reference images taken using fixed viewing parameters (for example, a sequence that captures a dynamic event as seen from a particular viewpoint), temporal coherence can be utilized to make the computation faster than warping each frame individually. This is particularly easy to see using the matrix notation introduced earlier. The matrices $\mathbf{A}$, $\mathbf{B}$, and $\mathbf{C}$ are the same for any reference image, and the only matrix that differs between successive frames is the disparities matrix $\mathbf{D}$. Let $\mathbf{D}^{(t)}$ denote the disparity matrix of frame t. Each frame of the warped sequence can be computed incrementally as

$$\mathbf{F}_i^{(t+1)} = \mathbf{F}_i^{(t)} + m_{i4}\Delta\mathbf{D}^{(t)}, \qquad \text{where} \quad \Delta\mathbf{D}^{(t)} = \mathbf{D}^{(t+1)} - \mathbf{D}^{(t)}.$$

Thus, if the difference matrices $\Delta \mathbf{D}^{(t)}$ are precomputed, it takes only $3kn^2$ additions, $3kn^2$ multiplications, and $2kn^2$ divisions to forward-warp an $n \times n \times k$ image sequence (saving $3kn^2$ additions compared to warping each frame individually). This is a simple observation, and the improvement is applicable to standard warping, but we have not encountered it in the image-based rendering literature.

Temporal coherence in this case is easily exploited in the context of wavelet warping. We precompute the 2D wavelet transforms $T(\Delta \mathbf{D}^{(t)})$. Each warped frame is then generated as follows:

$$\mathbf{F}_i^{(t+1)} = \mathbf{F}_i^{(t)} + T^{-1}\left(m_{i4}T(\Delta \mathbf{D}^{(t)})\right). \tag{11}$$

In other words, the differences between successive disparity images are multiplied by m_{i4} in the wavelet domain. Since the disparities of many pixels remain unchanged between consecutive frames, the wavelet transform of the differences is very sparse.

Utilization of temporal coherence in wavelet warping is demonstrated in the following "virtual studio" example. In this example we generate a target image sequence by warping sequences of images from three different sources into a common target view. Three source images, one from each source, are shown in the top row of Figure 5 (see color plates). Three of the resulting images are shown in the bottom row. One of the sources is a video sequence of an actor performing in front of a Zcam — a real-time depth-sensing camera [19]. Another source is a synthetic animation of a coffee-table following a circular trajectory. The third source is a still image of a synthetic 3D scene (a room). The target view is different from each of the original views of the three image sources. The three sources are wavelet-warped to the target view, where they are combined using a Z-buffer. The result is a video sequence where the actor is looking at the coffee-table that flies in a circle about him. Using wavelet warping, as described earlier in this section, the target sequence is generated in real time at 15 fps, which is faster by a factor of 2.5 than wavelet-warping each frame individually.

7   Conclusions and Future Work

We have presented a simple way of computing various 3D image warps in the wavelet domain. We have demonstrated (both analytically and experimentally) that performing these warps in the wavelet domain is in many cases faster than their direct computation, particularly in the spherical-to-planar warp case. Furthermore, wavelet warping enables multi-resolution and progressive computations, with no storage or computation overhead. Finally, we have presented a wavelet warping algorithm for image sequences, which utilizes temporal coherence to achieve considerable speedups over frame-by-frame warping. We intend to use this algorithm for 3D warping of spherical depth movies.

In order to extend and improve our wavelet warping approach, we would like to develop an adaptive multi-resolution warping scheme, which would allow to warp different regions of a reference view at different resolutions.

The warping algorithms presented in this paper are one example of a more general approach in which various operations on images are expressed using linear combinations of matrices, and then performed directly in the wavelet domain. In addition to 3D warping we have applied this approach to convolution of images and image sequences [8]. In the future we plan to apply our approach to other types of image and video operations, such as other types of image warping (perhaps using more complicated mappings), and blending of image sequences.

Acknowledgements

This research was supported by the Israel Science Foundation, founded by the Israel Academy of Sciences and Humanities. We would also like to thank 3DV Systems [19] and Eyal Ofek for providing us with the depth video used in Section 6. Finally, thanks to the Siggraph and EGWR anonymous reviewers, whose comments have greatly helped to improve this paper.

References

1. G. Beylkin. On the representation of operators in bases of compactly supported wavelets. *SIAM Journal of Numerical Analysis*, 29:1716–1740, 1992.
2. G. Beylkin, R. Coifman, and V. Rokhlin. Fast wavelet transforms and numerical algorithms I. *Comm. Pure Appl. Math.*, 44:141–183, 1991.
3. R. Calderbank, I. Daubechies, W. Sweldens, and B.-L. Yeo. Wavelet transforms that map integers to integers. *Appl. Comput. Harmon. Anal.*, 5(3):332–369, 1998.
4. S. E. Chen. QuickTime VR — an image-based approach to virtual environment navigation. In *Computer Graphics Proceedings, Annual Conference Series (Proc. SIGGRAPH '95)*, pages 29–38, 1995.
5. S. E. Chen and L. Williams. View interpolation for image synthesis. In *Computer Graphics Proceedings, Annual Conference Series (Proc. SIGGRAPH '93)*, pages 279–288, 1993.
6. W. J. Dally, L. McMillan, G. Bishop, and H. Fuchs. The delta tree: An object-centered approach to image-based rendering. MIT AI Lab Technical Memo 1604, MIT, May 1996.
7. I. Daubechies and W. Sweldens. Factoring wavelet transforms into lifting steps. *J. Fourier Anal. Appl.*, 4(3):245–267, 1998.
8. I. Drori. Image operations in the wavelet domain. Master's thesis, School of Computer Science and Engineering, The Hebrew University of Jerusalem, Israel, Jan. 2000.
9. Internet Pictures Corporation (iPIX). http://www.ipix.com.
10. S. Mallat. *A Wavelet Tour of Signal Processing*. Academic Press, 1998.
11. W. R. Mark, L. McMillan, and G. Bishop. Post-rendering 3D warping. In *Proceedings of the 1997 Symposium on Interactive 3D Graphics*. ACM SIGGRAPH, Apr. 1997.
12. L. McMillan. *An Image-Based Approach to Three-Dimensional Computer Graphics*. PhD thesis, Department of Computer Science, University of North Carolina at Chapel Hill, Chapel Hill, North Carolina, 1997.
13. L. McMillan and G. Bishop. Plenoptic modeling: An image-based rendering system. In *Computer Graphics Proceedings, Annual Conference Series (Proc. SIGGRAPH '95)*, pages 39–46, 1995.
14. J. W. Shade, S. J. Gortler, L. He, and R. Szeliski. Layered depth images. In M. Cohen, editor, *Computer Graphics Proceedings, Annual Conference Series (Proc. SIGGRAPH '98)*, pages 231–242, July 1998.
15. B. C. Smith and L. A. Rowe. Algorithms for manipulating compressed images. *IEEE Computer Graphics and Applications*, 13(5):34–42, Sept. 1993.
16. B. C. Smith and L. A. Rowe. Compressed domain processing of JPEG-encoded images. *Real-Time Imaging*, 2:3–17, 1996.
17. E. J. Stollnitz, T. D. DeRose, and D. H. Salesin. *Wavelets for Computer Graphics: Theory and Applications*. Morgan Kaufmann Publishers, Inc., San Francisco, CA, 1996.
18. W. Sweldens. The lifting scheme: A construction of second generation wavelets. *SIAM Journal of Mathematical Analysis*, 29(2):511–546, 1997.
19. 3DV Systems. http://www.3dvsystems.com.

Editors' Note: see Appendix, p. 401 for colored figures of this paper

Artistic Multiprojection Rendering

Maneesh Agrawala*   Denis Zorin†   Tamara Munzner*

*Stanford University   †New York University

Abstract

In composing hand-drawn images of 3D scenes, artists often alter the projection for each object in the scene independently, thereby generating multiprojection images. We present a tool for creating such multiprojection images and animations, consisting of two parts: a multiprojection rendering algorithm and an interactive interface for attaching local cameras to the scene geometry. We describe a new set of techniques for resolving visibility between geometry rendered with different local cameras. We also develop several camera constraints that are useful when initially setting local camera parameters and when animating the scene. We demonstrate applications of our methods for generating a variety of artistic effects in still images and in animations.

1 Introduction

In computer graphics we typically use a single linear projection – often a perspective projection – to generate a realistic view of a scene. Linear projections achieve this realism at the cost of imposing restrictions on the 2D shape of each object in the image and on the overall composition of the picture. Artists have developed a variety of techniques for composing images of 3D scenes that deviate from the standard perspective projection. One of the most common techniques is to combine multiple projections in a single image.

Artists create such multiprojection images for several reasons, including: expressing a mood, feeling or idea; improving the representation or comprehensibility of the scene; and visualizing information about the spatial relationships and structure of the scene. Multiple projections could similarly enhance computer-generated images and animations, but simple and efficient methods for multiprojection rendering have not been available.

Today, the most common method for creating a multiprojection image requires a combination of 3D rendering and 2D image compositing. The process is a labor intensive cycle that involves rendering multiple views of the scene, transferring the images into a compositing application and then manually merging them into a single multiprojection image. Although some research systems [12, 11] shortcut this cycle by combining rendering and compositing into a single application, resolving visibility between the images remains a manual process. In this paper we present interactive methods for creating multiprojection images and animations. The main technical contributions of our work are new algorithms designed for:

Resolving Visibility: In the multiprojection setting there is no uniquely defined solution to the visibility problem. However, in many cases the user wishes to maintain the visibility ordering of a *master camera* while using different *local cameras* to introduce shape distortions to individual objects. Based on this insight, we propose an algorithm that automatically resolves visibility for most practical cases and allows user adjustments when the automatically computed visibility is not satisfactory.

Constraining Cameras: We suggest a simple and intuitive set of camera constraints allowing the user to choose appropriate projections for a variety of artistic effects. These constraints are particularly effective when initially placing cameras and when animating the scene.

Interactive Rendering: We leverage multipass hardware rendering to achieve interactive rendering rates. The user can immediately see how changing the parameters of any camera or moving any object will affect the final image.

The remainder of this paper is organized as follows. In section 2, we describe artistic uses of multiple projections. After presenting related work in section 3, we describe our multiprojection rendering algorithm with an emphasis on resolving occlusion in section 4. In section 5, we present a set of camera constraints that provide intuitive controls over the camera parameters. Examples of images generated with our system appear in section 6. Finally, section 7 outlines future directions and conclusions.

2   Artistic Uses of Multiple Projections

Using a single projection for an entire scene is restrictive. The ideal projection for one object may not be the best projection for all objects in the scene. Artists have a long history of solving this problem by creating multiprojection images, which generally serve some combination of three functions:

- **Artistic Expression** – Multiple projections help the artist express a mood, feeling or idea.
- **Representation** – Multiple projections improve the representation or comprehensibility of the scene.
- **Visualization** – Multiple projections communicate information about the structure of the objects and spatial relationships in the scene.

In this section, we consider several specific examples of each function. In section 6, we present several images and animations that are based on these examples and were created using our multiprojection rendering tools.

2.1   Artistic Expression

Viewing Anomalies: In Giorgio de Chirico's *The Mystery and Melancholy of a Street*, figure 1(a), the buildings, the van and the ground plane all have different viewpoints. Willats [19] suggests that the melancholy aura is created by the unusual arrangement of the objects which results in an incongruous spatial system. Despite the large disparities between projections, the overall impression of a three-dimensional space remains intact.

Cézanne similarly incorporates multiple viewpoints in *Still Life with Fruit Basket*, figure 1(b). Loran [13] describes how these viewing distortions generate tension between different planes in the image; the distortions flatten some regions of the picture, while enhancing depth in other regions. He explains that the inconsistencies in projection generate an "emotional nonrealistic illusion of space."

Foreground Elements in Animation: In cel-based animations, moving foreground elements sometimes translate across the image with little to no change in parallax (like cutouts or sprites). Equivalently, as the element translates in the scene, its local camera moves with it, thereby maintaining an identical view of the element from frame to frame. Meanwhile, the background is rendered using its own separate projection. Although fixing the view of foreground elements is done primarily to reuse the same drawing from frame to frame, it has become a stylistic convention in hand-drawn animation since the foreground elements appear flatter and more "cartoony."

In contrast to the flattened foreground elements, animators often exaggerate the perspective projection of the background to create a deeper, more dynamic environment. However, such a strong perspective could introduce distortions in the foreground of the image. A fixed view of the foreground objects alleviates this problem.

2.2   Representation

Best Views: Certain viewpoints are better than others for comprehending the overall geometric shape of an object. By using multiple viewpoints the artists can present the best views of all objects in the scene. Graham [5] points out that a single viewpoint is often inadequate for large format pictures like murals, frescoes, or billboards. Such images are often placed above standard eye-level and are seen from a much wider range of viewpoints than smaller format pictures. For these reasons, many large format images are created with multiple projections. As

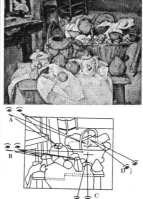

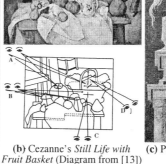

(a) Giorgio de Chirico's *The Mystery and Melancholy of a Street*

(b) Cezanne's *Still Life with Fruit Basket* (Diagram from [13])

(c) Paolo Uccelo's *Sir John Hawkwood*

(e) Artificial Perspective via Multiple Parallel Projections (Chairs from [2], 53rd Street from [6])

Fig. 1. Multiprojection examples (clockwise labeling)

(d) Raphael's *School of Athens*

(a) A different projection is used for each major structure. Note the difference in vanishing points for the buildings, the van, and the ground plane. An exaggerated perspective projection elongates the white building and the ground plane is placed so that the horizon is high up in the image to create the long receding path.

(b) Cezanne incorporates many viewpoints into this still life, of which four are shown in the diagram. Notice how viewpoint **A** is much higher than the other viewpoints, thus the ginger jar and basket appear to be tipped forward. Differences in viewpoint also cause the table to appear to split under the table cloth.

(c) The projection for the base differs from the projection for the horse and rider. In its original setting viewers stood below and to the left of the fresco, so the entire picture was first created for this viewpoint. While the low–set viewpoint was effective for the base, Uccelo found that it exposed too much of the horse's belly and distorted the rider. He repainted the top of the picture and raised the viewpoint of the horse and rider to eliminate the distortion.

(d) The foreground humans would appear distorted if rendered using the projection of the background architecture. Thus, Raphael altered the projections for the humans to give each one a more central projection. Without the correction, the sphere (inset) would appear elliptical rather than circular[10, 21].

(e) Multiple parallel projections can produce an artificial sense of perspective by pointing the receding parallels towards a central vanishing point. Dubery and Willats[2] argue that this technique works better with oblique projections than with axonometric projections. Each building in the illustration of 53rd Street is projected using a different oblique projection. Note how the receding parallels differ for the buildings at the left, right, top, and bottom of the image.

---

large wall-sized displays become more prevalent [8, 16], we expect that multiprojection rendering techniques will be required to reduce perceptual distortions in images generated for such displays. Paolo Uccelo's fresco of *Sir John Hawkwood* is a well-known large format multiprojection example. He used two projections, one for the base and one for the horse and rider, to produce the best view of both elements, as described in figure 1(c).

Reducing Wide-Angle Distortion: A well known problem with wide-angle, perspective projections is that curved objects located near the edges of the viewing frustum, close to the image plane, can appear unnaturally stretched and distorted. The most common technique for decreasing this distortion is to alter the projection for every object to provide a perceptually "correct" view of each one. The deviations in projection are often subtle and in many cases even the artist, focused on producing a comprehensible image of the scene, may not realize he altered the projections. Kubovy [10] shows that the foreground human figures in Raphael's *School of Athens*, figure 1(d), are inconsistent with the strong central perspective projection of the background architecture. The inconsistencies improve the comprehensibility of the figures and make them easier to recognize.

2.3 Visualization

Artificial Perspective via Multiple Parallel Projections: It is possible to create an artificial sense of perspective using multiple axonometric or multiple oblique projections. The "trick" is to orient the receding parallels of each object towards some pre-chosen vanishing point. In the illustration of 53rd Street [6] (figure 1(e)) the buildings are drawn from above in oblique projection. The receding parallels for each building point towards a central vanishing point, thereby creating the illusion of perspective.

An advantage of such artificial perspective over true perspective projection is that objects do not diminish in size as they recede from the viewer. With oblique projections, one face of each object retains its true shape, allowing the viewer to perform some size and area comparisons. Applying this principle to the 53rd Street example, it is possible to visually compare the 2D area covered by each building. The convergence of true perspective would cause displayed rooftop areas to depend on building height, making such comparisons more difficult.

3 Related Work

In computer graphics, alternatives to standard linear projections have been developed in a variety of contexts. Max [14] shows how to project images onto a curved Omnimax screen, while Dorsey et al. [1] present methods for projecting images onto planar screens for off-axis viewing. Zorin and Barr [21] show how to correct perceptual distortions in photographs by reprojecting them. Glaeser and Gröller [3] use cartographic projection techniques to reduce wide-angle distortions in synthetic images. Both Wood et al. [20] and Rademacher and Bishop [15] describe techniques for smoothly integrating all the views for a given camera path into a single image.

Savranksy et al. [17] describe methods for rendering Escher-like "impossible" scenes. They treat geometric transformations between pairs of objects as constraints on the viewing projection and then solve for a single projection that best meets all the constraints. They compute orthographic viewing projections for several "impossible" scenes. It is unclear how well such an approach would extend to perspective projection. They show that the only way to obtain a single projection for Escher-like scenes is by relaxing the constraints, so they remain valid in the 2D image but not necessarily in 3D object space. In fact, many of the "impossible" scenes only appear impossible from a single viewpoint and animated camera paths would destroy the illusion.

Several systems have been developed to allow more general alternatives to planar-geometric projection. Inakage [9] derives mathematical formulations for three alternatives: curvilinear projection, inverted projection and arbitrary 3D warps. However, he does not consider combining multiple projections within a single image. Löffelmann and Gröller [12] explore the use of curvilinear and non-linear projections to create Escher-like images. Levene [11] investigates artistic uses of curvilinear, inverted, and oblique projections as alternatives to planar perspective. He derives a mathematical framework that unifies several classes of projections. The last two systems are notable because they contain mechanisms for specifying multiple projections within a single image. However, to our knowledge, no system adequately addresses the problem of resolving visibility in the multiprojection setting.

We will show in section 4.1 that resolving visibility is perhaps the most difficult problem in generating multiprojection images because visibility ordering between objects is different under each projection. Our solution is to use a master camera to specify visibility ordering while maintaining shape distortions due to local cameras attached to each object. Although Levene uses the concept of a master camera to compose his multiprojection images, he points out that visibility is not properly resolved with his approach and leaves this as an open problem for future work.

The previous multiprojection rendering systems require the user to directly manipulate the parameters of their generalized projections. Such controls are not always natural and their effect on the final image may be unintuitive. In contrast, we provide several novel camera constraints that allow the user to obtain commonly desired effects with relative ease. Users can also directly specify projection parameters when necessary.

Creating a multiprojection image is far easier with interactive rendering so that the user can immediately see how changing a projection effects the final image. Earlier systems [12, 11] use software ray tracing renderers; therefore, image updates are not interactive for typical image sizes. Our system maintains interactive rendering rates by leveraging graphics hardware. Although this restricts our current implementation to linear planar-projections, our visibility ordering algorithms would work with any invertible projection, including the generalized projection formulations proposed by Inakage, Löffelmann and Gröller, or Levene.

4 Multiprojection Rendering

Our multiprojection rendering algorithm includes three computational stages. The input to the algorithm is a set of *camera groups*, each associating a collection of geometric objects with one *local camera*. The user must provide a *master camera* and can optionally specify

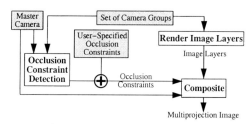

Multiprojection Image

object-level occlusion constraints, both of which are used to resolve visibility. In the block diagram, white boxes represent computational stages of the algorithm, while gray boxes represent user-specified data. The first stage of the algorithm renders each camera group into a separate *image layer*. We then merge the image layers together to form the multiprojection image.

The main difficulty in the compositing stage is the absence of a natural visibility ordering. When visibility ordering differs from camera to camera, there is no unique way to resolve occlusion. Our key observation is that in most multiprojection images, all the local cameras are relatively similar to one another and therefore generate similar visibility orderings. Instead of specifying the occlusion relationship between every pair of objects in the scene, the user simply specifies a master camera (often a local camera doubles as the master). We then use the master camera to resolve visibility through a combination of two automatic techniques: 3D depth-based compositing and standard 2D compositing based on object-level occlusion constraints. If necessary, the user can directly modify the visibility ordering by specifying additional pairwise occlusion relationships between image layers.

4.1 Visibility Ordering

With a single linear projection, visibility is defined unambiguously; the *fibres*, that is, the set of points in 3D space that map to a point on the image surface, are straight lines. For any two points that lie on the same fibre, occlusion is resolved by displaying the

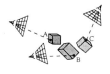

point closest to the center of projection. This approach can resolve occlusion whenever the fibres are continuous curves. With multiprojection images, the fibres generally have a more complicated structure since the mapping from 3D space to the image surface can be discontinuous. Suppose, as in the diagram, that points A, B and C project to the same pixel in their local images. The fibre of the multiprojection image at this pixel consists of the union of the three dotted lines. It is difficult to automatically compute a visibility ordering with complicated fibres because no natural ordering exists for the points on different lines.

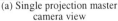

| (a) Single projection master camera view | (b) Multiprojection with depth compositing only | (c) Multiprojection with occlusion constraints and depth compositing |

Fig. 2. To reduce the distortion of the column in the single projection image (a) we alter its projection as shown in figure 5(c). In the multiprojection image, the point on the column (triangle) and the point on the floor (circle) coincide. With depth-based compositing alone (b) the floor point "incorrectly" occludes the column point since it is closer to the master camera. However, the column occludes the floor in the master view. Applying this object-level occlusion constraint during compositing yields the desired image (c).

It may be tempting to resolve visibility for the multiprojection image by directly comparing local depth values stored with each image layer. The rendering algorithm would then be quite simple: we could add the local camera projection to the modeling transformation matrix for each object and render the scene using a standard z-buffer pipeline without resorting to layer based compositing. However, this approach would lead to objectionable occlusion artifacts. Suppose our scene consists of a vase sitting on a table. If we simply add the vase's local camera projection into its modeling transform, in most cases the vase will intersect the table. Our algorithm handles these situations more gracefully by using the master camera to impose visibility ordering while employing local cameras to provide shape distortion. In our example, the master camera would be the original projection, in which the vase and table do not intersect, and the local projection would affect only the shape of the vase without affecting visibility.

Given the master camera, we can define an ordering for any set of points in 3D space based on the distance from each point to the master camera viewpoint. To merge the image layers rendered for each camera group, we transform all the pixels in each image-layer into world space using their pixel coordinates and z-values. We then apply the master camera projection to these world space points and use a standard z-buffer test to determine the frontmost point at each pixel of the master camera image. However, figure 2 shows that the results produced by this depth-based approach are not always satisfactory. The problem occurs because visibility is resolved for each pixel independently, yet we want to preserve object-level occlusion constraints, such as "column occludes floor", that occur in the single projection master camera view. In the next section, we describe a simple algorithm for automatically computing these constraints with respect to the master camera. However, we will also show that visibility can not always be resolved using object-level occlusion constraints alone. Thus, the compositing stage of our algorithm combines two approaches. We use object-level occlusion constraints wherever possible and fall back onto depth-based compositing only when the occlusion constraints are ambiguous.

While additional user intervention is not required, the user may explicitly specify occlusion constraints between pairs of objects. These user-defined occlusion constraints are added to the list of constraints computed via the occlusion detection algorithm. Conflicts between user-specified constraints and computed constraints are resolved in favor of the user and the conflicting computed constraints are removed from the list.

4.2 Object-Level Occlusion Constraints

Object-level occlusion constraints are defined for whole objects rather than individual points of the objects. If every point of object A is in front of object B, we say that A occludes B. To compute the occlusion constraints with respect to the master camera, we must determine for each pair of objects A and B whether A occludes B, B occludes A or neither. Our occlusion constraint detection algorithm is based on an algorithm described by Snyder and Lengyel[18].

Occlusion Constraint Detection Algorithm

Input: Set of Objects,
    Master Camera
Output: Set of Occlusion Constraints

foreach camera group
  Render object using Master Camera into a separate
  buffer storing (Camera Group ID, depth) per–pixel
foreach pixel
  Sort objects in pixel by depth
  foreach pair of objects in sorted list
    if conflicting occlusion constraint appears in list
      Mark object pair as non–ordered
    else
      Add occlusion constraint to list

Object-level occlusion constraints may not provide enough information to merge all the image layers. There are two forms of ambiguity. When the convex hulls of A and B intersect we may find that A occludes B in some regions of the master view, while B occludes A in other regions. Our constraint detection algorithm checks for such binary occlusion cycles and marks the objects as non-ordered. Another type of ambiguity arises when A and B do not occlude one another in the master view at all, but their local image layers do overlap. Our occlusion constraint detection algorithm cannot provide any constraint in this case. We handle these ambiguities during the compositing phase of the algorithm.

4.3 Compositing

The last stage of the algorithm, compositing, combines the multiple image layers produced in the first step into a single image. If two objects map to the same pixel and there is an occlusion constraint between them, we simply use the constraint to determine which object is visible. When no such occlusion constraint is available (as in the cases described in the previous section), we use depth compositing to resolve visibility.

In certain cases, occlusion cycles can pose a problem for our algorithm. Suppose there is a three object cycle[1] in which A occludes B, B occludes C, and C occludes A. Our pixel-by-pixel compositing algorithm will produce the desired multiprojection image regardless of the order in which it considers the objects, unless a single pixel contains all three. While it is possible to detect such loops in the occlusion constraint graph, resolving occlusion in such cases requires an arbitrary choice as to which object in the cycle is visible. In practice, we have found that this problem rarely occurs, and when it does, we provide controls so that the user can choose which object is visible.

5 Camera Constraints

When creating multiprojection images and animations, it is useful to be able to constrain the motions of an object and its local camera in relation to one another. For example, the user may want to dolly the camera closer to its object without changing the object's size in the image plane. This would produce a close-up, wide angle view of the object, thus increasing its perceived depth without changing its relative size in the image. Such camera constraints are indispensable for multiprojection animations, since direct specification of several dependent cameras is quite difficult. The user might keyframe an object motion and with such constraints in place, the cameras would automatically move in relation to the object to enforce the constraint.

We consider three camera constraints we have found particularly useful. Each constraint is a system of equations, relating the camera parameters and object position before and after modification. The system is typically underconstrained and we can choose some of the camera parameters arbitrarily. Once these parameters are chosen, we use the constraints to determine the other parameters.

Notation: Each equation will be preceded by a label (i.e. pos, dir, size, dist) describing the constraint it imposes. We use $'$ to denote the quantities corresponding to the camera and the objects after modification. We denote the vector length as $\|\mathbf{a}\|$ and the vector dot product as $\mathbf{a}\cdot\mathbf{b}$. We use $\pi[x; P, \mathbf{v}, \mathbf{w}, n]$ to denote the world-space coordinates of the projection of a point x into the image plane with a camera defined by parameters $P, \mathbf{v}, \mathbf{w}, n$. The image plane coordinates of the projection of x are denoted $\pi_1[x; P, \mathbf{v}, \mathbf{w}, n]$ and $\pi_2[x; P, \mathbf{v}, \mathbf{w}, n]$, as shown in figure 3.

---

[1]We remove binary cycles as described in section 4.2.

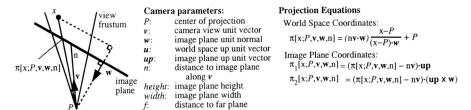

Fig. 3. Camera model and parameters.

5.1 Object-Size Constraint

Normally, as a camera moves towards an object, the projected image size of the object grows and the perspective convergence of the object changes. The goal of the object-size constraint is to keep the object's size and position approximately constant while changing its perspective convergence by dollying the camera towards (or away from) it. We characterize the object's size by the distances between two points on the object, x_1 and x_2. The constraint maintains a constant distance between the projections of the two points and is expressed in the following equation:

size : $\|\pi[x_1; P', \mathbf{v}', \mathbf{w}', n'] - \pi[x_2; P', \mathbf{v}', \mathbf{w}', n']\| = \|\pi[x_1; P, \mathbf{v}, \mathbf{w}, n] - \pi[x_2; P, \mathbf{v}, \mathbf{w}, n]\|$

The simplest way to adjust perspective convergence for an object is to change the near parameter n of the camera model while leaving the *height* and *width* at the near plane unchanged. Suppose, as in figure 4(a), we move the camera towards the center of the object to a new position $P' = P + (x - P)\Delta t$. We assume that the view vector and image plane normal remain fixed (i.e. $\mathbf{v}' = \mathbf{v}$ and $\mathbf{w}' = \mathbf{w}$), and compute the new near distance n':

$$n' = n\frac{\|\pi[x_1; P', \mathbf{v}, \mathbf{w}, n] - \pi[x_2; P', \mathbf{v}, \mathbf{w}, n]\|}{\|\pi[x_1; P, \mathbf{v}, \mathbf{w}, n] - \pi[x_2; P, \mathbf{v}, \mathbf{w}, n]\|}$$

In the film *Vertigo*, Hitchcock uses this technique to give the audience a sense of the vertigo as experienced by the main character. Hitchcock simultaneously dollies the camera and adjusts its focal length (i.e. near distance) to maintain the object-size constraint. The change in perspective, with little or no change in object size and position conveys the impression of dizziness and falling.

Another interesting use of the object-size constraint is constructing artificial perspective by combining multiple oblique projections as described in section 2.3. If we enforce the object-size constraint, move the camera out to infinity, and also force the view vector $\mathbf{v}$ to be parallel to the line between the camera center of projection P and the object center x, we obtain an oblique projection. Although there is no vanishing point for the oblique projections, the receding parallels will point towards the vanishing point of the original perspective projection. By separately applying the constraint to each object in the scene, we combine multiple oblique projections to produce an artificial sense of perspective. We used this approach to create plate 3.

5.2 Fixed-View Constraint

Under a perspective projection, as an object translates parallel to the image plane in world space, different sides of the object are exposed. As the object moves from left to right with respect to the camera center of projection, the intra-object occlusions change.

At times we wish to both maintain a fixed view of an object and move its position in the image plane. The result is an object that translates in the image much like a 2D sprite. However, unlike a normal sprite, an object under the fixed-view constraint continues to move in 3D and can therefore rotate and deform as a 3D body.

As shown in figure 4(b), we must maintain the direction vector between the object center and the camera center of projection. In addition, we would like the size and position of the object in the image plane to be approximately the same as if the camera were not changed. That is, we

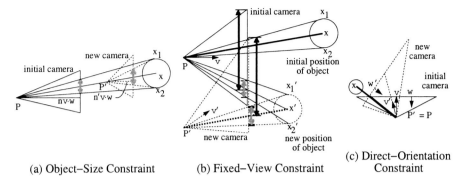

(a) Object–Size Constraint   (b) Fixed–View Constraint

(c) Direct–Orientation Constraint

Fig. 4. Camera constraint diagrams. In (a) the image size (light gray arrow) of the object remains fixed as the camera moves towards it. In (b) as the object translates in world space, its image size (light gray arrow), image position (dark gray arrow) and the direction between it and the center of projection remain fixed. For clarity we introduce a slight separation between the image planes. In (c) the camera is reoriented so the image plane normal $\mathbf{w}'$ matches the direction of the line joining x with P. The distance between the camera and the object's image also remains fixed.

wish to maintain:

$$\mathbf{dir} : \quad \frac{x' - P'}{\|x' - P'\|} = \frac{x - P}{\|x - P\|}$$

$$\mathbf{pos} : \quad \pi_i[x'; P', \mathbf{v}', \mathbf{w}', n'] = \pi_i[x'; P, \mathbf{v}, \mathbf{w}, n] \quad i = 1, 2$$

$$\mathbf{size} : \quad \|\pi[x_1'; P', \mathbf{v}', \mathbf{w}', n'] - \pi[x_2'; P', \mathbf{v}', \mathbf{w}', n']\| = \|\pi[x_1'; P, \mathbf{v}, \mathbf{w}, n] - \pi[x_2'; P, \mathbf{v}, \mathbf{w}, n]\|$$

where, as before, x_1, and x_2 are two points that we use to define the size of the object.

We have found that it is convenient to choose x to be the center of the bounding sphere of an object, and x_1 and x_2 to be the two extremal points of the bounding sphere such that the plane formed by x, x_1 and x_2 is parallel to the image plane. Thus, x_1 and x_2 are the endpoints of an interval centered at x, and their positions with respect to x do not change as the object moves. We assume that both $\mathbf{w}$ and the distance from the center of projection to the image plane remain fixed (i.e. $\mathbf{w} = \mathbf{w}'$ and $n\mathbf{v} \cdot \mathbf{w} = n'\mathbf{v}' \cdot \mathbf{w}$). Then the first constraint equation can be solved for P', and the other two can be solved for $\mathbf{v}'$ in order to determine the new position of the image plane.

5.3 Fixed-Position Constraint

The fixed-position constraint is similar to the fixed-view constraint. Instead of maintaining a particular view of the object, the fixed-position constraint maintains the position of the object in the image plane. As the object translates, different sides of it are exposed, but it remains in the same place in the image plane. While the effect is similar to rotating the camera about the object, this constraint actually produces an off-axis projection. The following constraint ensures that the center of the object remains fixed in the image plane:

$$\mathbf{pos} : \quad \pi_i[x; P, \mathbf{v}, \mathbf{w}, n] = \pi_i[x'; P', \mathbf{v}', \mathbf{w}', n'] \quad i = 1, 2$$

The desired effect is that as the object moves in world space, the window of the image plane through which we see the object shifts with it. However, the image plane does not move. Thus, P and $\mathbf{w}$ remain fixed (i.e. $P' = P$ and $\mathbf{w}' = \mathbf{w}$), while $\mathbf{v}$ and n change.

As with the fixed-view constraint, the distance from the center of projection to the image plane remains fixed, so $n\mathbf{v} \cdot \mathbf{w} = n'\mathbf{v}' \cdot \mathbf{w}$. Assuming no change in camera parameters, we first compute the displacement d of the object's image and then use this displacement to determine the center of the image plane for the new camera $n'\mathbf{v}'$.

$$d_i = \pi_i[x'; P, \mathbf{v}, \mathbf{w}, n] - \pi_i[x; P, \mathbf{v}, \mathbf{w}, n] \quad i = 1, 2$$
$$n'\mathbf{v}' = n\mathbf{v} + d_1 \, \mathbf{up} + d_2 \, (\mathbf{up} \times \mathbf{w})$$

5.4 Direct-Orientation Constraint

In section 2.2, we observed that curved objects can appear extremely distorted under a wide-angle projection. There are several ways to reduce this distortion.

The simplest approach is to use a parallel projection for each distorted object. For example, with a scene consisting of a row of columns, figure 5, we would use the same orthographic camera for all the columns to ensure that they all appear to be the same size. The drawbacks of this approach are that the columns appear flat and that we see each column from exactly the same side.

A better approach is to use the direct-orientation constraint. For each object we create a camera pointed directly at this object. Equivalently, the image plane normal for each local camera is parallel to the direction vector to the object. At the same time, we preserve the position of the object in the image plane. Finally, we try to keep the size of the object approximately constant in the image plane (see figure 4(c)). Instead of using a general equation of the type derived for the object-size constraint, we use a simpler condition requiring that the distance from the camera to the image of the object remains fixed. We obtain the following constraint equations for the camera corresponding to the object located at x:

$$\textbf{dir}: \quad \mathbf{w}' = \frac{x - P}{\|x - P\|}$$

$$\textbf{pos}: \quad \pi_i[x, P, \mathbf{v}', \mathbf{w}', n'] = \pi_i[x, P, \mathbf{v}, \mathbf{w}, n] \quad i = 1, 2$$

$$\textbf{dist}: \quad \|\pi[x, P, \mathbf{v}', \mathbf{w}', n'] - P\| = \|\pi[x, P, \mathbf{v}, \mathbf{w}, n] - P\|$$

Assuming that the up vector $\mathbf{u}$ does not change, these equations uniquely determine $\mathbf{v}'$ and n' when $\mathbf{v}$ and n are known.

6 Results

We have created several images and animations using our multiprojection rendering system as shown in the color plates, figure 5, and the accompanying video[2]. In all our examples, all occlusion relationships were computed by our algorithm. Plate 1 is our reconstruction of de Chirico's *Mystery and Melancholy of a Street*. The scene is modeled as shown in the plan view thumbnail image. The drop shadows from the building are explicitly modeled as polygons. Interactively adjusting the five local cameras took about an hour and a half. Matching the painting took about 20 minutes and the remainder of the time was spent animating the van to move through the scene. We made extensive use of our camera constraints throughout the process. To place the local camera of the brown building, for example, we initially set the image plane of the camera parallel to the front face of the building. We then used the object-size and fixed-position constraints to interactively adjust the vanishing point for its receding faces until they matched the painting. The van was animated to go around the brown building using a combination of object motion and camera motion. Note that as the van moves from being in front of the brown building to going behind it, the occlusion relationship between the two objects is updated automatically.

The multiprojection still life in plate 2 was inspired by Cézanne's *Still Life with Fruit Basket* and adjusting the 10 local cameras took about an hour for this scene. Plate 3 is shows a comparison of an overhead view of a city rendered using multiple oblique projection to create an artificial sense of perspective in (a), and a true perspective projection in (b). There are two advantages to using multiple oblique projections. First, more of the scene is visible; in the true perspective many building extend beyond the field of view the image and there is more occlusion between

---

[2]http://graphics.stanford.edu/papers/mpr/video

buildings than in the multiple oblique view. Second, it is easier to judge the relative rooftop sizes, and the area of the block that each building covers in the multiple oblique view. Plate 4 shows some frames from an animation we created using the fixed-view constraint. In parts (a) and (b) we show how the fixed-view constraint improves the composition of the scene. The fixed-view constraint only affects translational motions. Unlike traditional sprites, objects can rotate and deform as 3D bodies as shown in the frames on left side of plate 4.

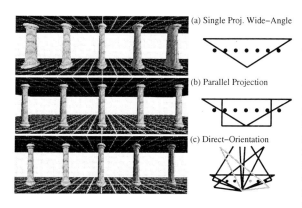

(a) Single Proj. Wide–Angle

(b) Parallel Projection

(c) Direct–Orientation

Fig. 5. Reducing the wide-angle distortion of curved objects

The columns in figure 5(a) appear distorted due to a wide-angle camera. If we use a parallel projection for the columns as in figure 5(b) (see camera schematic), the distortion is corrected, but each column appears flat and the lighting is wrong: every column is lit identically. A better approach is to use the direct-orientation constraint to aim each local camera at its column as in figure 5(c). Since the local cameras all have the same center of projection, we see exactly the same parts of each column as in the original view and the lighting is correct because the visibility is unchanged. We have colored one of the columns and its local camera light gray in the camera schematic to show how the local camera is reoriented.

Our implementation of the multiprojection rendering algorithm uses hardware rendering to maintain an interactive interface. The main bottleneck in the rendering algorithm is this multipass read/write of the framebuffer required before rendering each camera group and resolving visibility. Therefore rendering performance is based on the number of camera groups in the scene and the size of the image. Despite the read/write bottleneck, we are able to achieve interactive framerates for most of our test scenes running on a SGI RealityEngine graphics system. For example, the multiprojection still life contains 10 camera groups and renders at a rate of 3 to 5 frames per second at a resolution of 333 x 256. Other scenes containing fewer cameras render more quickly. The de Chirico scene containing five camera groups renders at 10 - 12 frames per second at a resolution of 402 x 491.

In addition to the interactive interface, we built a script-based animation system for creating keyframed multiprojection animations. Obtaining visually pleasing results with a multiprojection animation is somewhat difficult because animation adds motion parallax as a cue about the spatial relationship between objects. The motion parallax may conflict with the perspective and occlusion cues, disconcerting the viewer. When the entire scene is moved by applying the same transformation to every object in the scene (or equivalently to every camera in the scene), each object will move and scale at a different rate since the local cameras may be very different. We have found that in most cases animating objects in the scene, while holding the background environment fixed, works well. Moving the entire scene tends to only work for relatively small translations and rotations. One notable exception is when all the local cameras have the same center of projection as in the row of columns example in figure 5. In this case, moving the entire scene does not cause any unexpected effects.

7 Future Work and Conclusions

We have presented a multiprojection rendering algorithm as well as a constraint-based camera specification interface. Using this system, it is possible to create a large variety of still and animated visual effects that can not be created with a standard, single projection rendering system.

136

There are several directions in which to expand this work. As we described in the previous section, not all types of animation produce pleasing results. Moreover, animation requires keyframing the motion over every object by hand. While our camera constraints can make it easier to produce certain types of camera motions, the constraints are designed to produce very specific effects. It would be useful to incorporate a more flexible constraint-based interface for cameras, similar to the design of Gleicher and Witkin [4], in both our camera specification interface and our animation system.

It is unclear how to handle lighting effects like shadows and reflection in the multiprojection setting. We currently assume that all lights are specified in the global scene and each camera group is lit based on its local camera viewpoint. The difficulty arises when we try to cast a shadow from one camera group onto another. Despite these issues, multiprojection images are an effective device for creating a variety of artistic effects.

8 Acknowledgements

Thanks to Pat Hanrahan for giving us insightful feedback throughout the course of this work. Gregory Lam Niemeyer's artistic guidance was invaluable during the early stages of the project.

References

[1] J. O. Dorsey, F. X. Sillion, and D. P. Greenberg. Design and simulation of opera lighting and projection effects. In *Computer Graphics (SIGGRAPH '91 Proceedings)*, volume 25, pages 41–50, July 1991.

[2] F. Dubery and J. Willats. *Perspective and Other Drawing Systems*. Van Nostrand, 1983.

[3] G. Glaeser and E. Gröller. Fast generation of curved perspectives for ultra-wide-angle lenses in VR applications. *The Visual Computer*, 15:365–376, 1999.

[4] M. Gleicher and A. Witkin. Through-the-lens camera control. In E. E. Catmull, editor, *Computer Graphics (SIGGRAPH '92 Proceedings)*, volume 26, pages 331–340, July 1992.

[5] D. W. Graham. *Composing Pictures*. Van Nostrand Reinhold Company, 1970.

[6] S. Guarnaccia. 53rd Street Map. In N. Holmes, editor, *The Best in Diagrammatic Graphics*, pages 174–175. Quarto Publishing, 1993.

[7] A. Hertzmann. Painterly rendering with curved brush strokes of multiple sizes. In *SIGGRAPH 98 Conference Proceedings*, pages 453–460. ACM SIGGRAPH, Addison Wesley, July 1998.

[8] G. Humphreys and P. Hanrahan. A distributed graphics system for large tiled displays. *IEEE Visualization '99*, pages 215–224, October 1999.

[9] M. Inakage. Non-linear perspective projections. In *Modeling in Computer Graphics (Proceedings of the IFIG WG 5.10 Working Conference)*, pages 203–215, Apr. 1991.

[10] M. Kubovy. *The Psychology of Perspective and Renaissance Art*. Cambridge University Press, 1986.

[11] J. Levene. A framework for non-realistic projections. M.eng. thesis, MIT, 1998.

[12] H. Löffelmann and E. Gröller. Ray tracing with extended cameras. *The Journal of Visualization and Computer Animation*, 7(4):211–227, Oct.-Dec. 1996.

[13] E. Loran. *Cezanne's Composition*. University of California Press, 1943.

[14] N. L. Max. Computer graphics distortion for IMAX and OMNIMAX projection. In *Nicograph '83 Proceedings*, pages 137–159, Dec. 1983.

[15] P. Rademacher and G. Bishop. Multiple-center-of-projection images. In *SIGGRAPH 98 Conference Proceedings*, pages 199–206, July 1998.

[16] R. Raskar, G. Welch, M. Cutts, A. Lake, L. Stesin, and H. Fuchs. The office of the future: A unified approach to image-based modeling and spatially immersive displays. *Proceedings of SIGGRAPH 98*, pages 179–188, July 1998.

[17] G. Savransky, D. Dimerman, and C. Gotsman. Modeling and rendering Escher-like impossible scenes. *Computer Graphics Forum*, 18(2):173–179, June 1999.

[18] J. Snyder and J. Lengyel. Visibility sorting and compositing without splitting for image layer decomposition. In *SIGGRAPH 98 Conference Proceedings*, pages 219–230, July 1998.

[19] J. Willats. *Art and Representation: New Principles in the Analysis of Pictures*. Princeton University Press, 1997.

[20] D. N. Wood, A. Finkelstein, J. F. Hughes, C. E. Thayer, and D. H. Salesin. Multiperspective panoramas for cel animation. In *SIGGRAPH 97 Conference Proceedings*, pages 243–250, Aug. 1997.

[21] D. Zorin and A. H. Barr. Correction of geometric perceptual distortion in pictures. In R. Cook, editor, *SIGGRAPH 95 Conference Proceedings*, Annual Conference Series, pages 257–264. ACM SIGGRAPH, Addison Wesley, Aug. 1995.

Editors' Note: see Appendix, p. 402 for colored figures of this paper

A Closed-Form Solution for the Irradiance due to Linearly-Varying Luminaires

Min Chen   James Arvo

California Institute of Technology, Pasadena, CA
{chen,arvo}@cs.caltech.edu

Abstract. We present a closed-form expression for the irradiance at a point on a surface due to an arbitrary polygonal Lambertian luminaire with linearly-varying radiant exitance. The solution consists of elementary functions and a single well-behaved special function that can be either approximated directly or computed exactly in terms of classical special functions such as Clausen's integral or the closely related dilogarithm. We first provide a general boundary integral that applies to all planar luminaires and then derive the closed-form expression that applies to arbitrary polygons, which is the result most relevant for global illumination. Our approach is to express the problem as an integral of a simple class of rational functions over regions of the sphere, and to convert the surface integral to a boundary integral using a generalization of irradiance tensors. The result extends the class of available closed-form expressions for computing direct radiative transfer from finite areas to differential areas. We provide an outline of the derivation, a detailed proof of the resulting formula, and complete pseudo-code of the resulting algorithm. Finally, we demonstrate the validity of our algorithm by comparison with Monte Carlo. While there are direct applications of this work, it is primarily of theoretical interest as it introduces much of the machinery needed to derive closed-form solutions for the general case of luminaires with radiance distributions that vary polynomially in both position and direction.

Keywords: Illumination, Rendering, Radiosity.

1   Introduction

The computation of radiant energy transfers is an essential component of physically-based rendering algorithms, both for local and global illumination. In particular, radiative transfers among discrete surface elements arise in finite element methods for global illumination, and in both direct lighting computations and final gathers from coarse global solutions [4, 12, 19]. By far the most ubiquitous computations involve transfers from finite planar areas to differential areas. In diffuse piecewise-constant environments, these transfers correspond to point-to-area form-factors [6], for which a wide assortment of formulas are available [13].

In this paper we present a direct method for computing the irradiance at a differential surface element due to a Lambertian area light source (luminaire) in which the radiant exitance is non-uniform; that is, varying with position over the surface of the luminaire. Few tools currently exist for handling this type of luminaire aside from Monte Carlo or numerical quadrature [10]. We derive our result with an approach similar to that used by Arvo [4]; specifically, we extend the concept of *axial moments* to accommodate a simple class of rational functions over the sphere. This new class of functions allows us to compute irradiance from non-uniform luminaires. One direct application of our result is the exact computation of transfers from linear polygonal elements to differential areas in the context of a collocation-based radiosity method [20].

Common to all methods for computing surface integrals of this nature is Stokes' theorem [18], by which surface integrals can be converted into boundary integrals. Such reductions are generally advantageous, as boundary integrals are better suited for computation [10] and frequently lead to closed-form solutions [4, 17].

Our approach is to use Stokes' theorem to derive a recurrence relation for a tensor form of irradiance; a similar approach was previously used to derive closed-form expressions for simulating glossy reflection and illumination from directional luminaries [4]. Our representation leads to a general boundary integral for expressing irradiance from linearly-varying luminaires. Our approach differs from that of DiLaura [10] in that our boundary integral is defined on the spherical projection of a luminaire, and easily leads to a closed-form solution in the case of polygonal luminaires and polynomial variation. One complication that arises in our solution is the appearance of a *special function* that has no finite representation in terms of elementary functions. This complication also occurs in computing patch-to-patch form factors [17], which requires a special function known as the dilogarithm [14]. Interestingly, the special function encountered in our case can also be evaluated in terms of the dilogarithm, or in terms of a somewhat simpler function known as the Clausen integral.

The specific contributions of this paper are

1. The derivation of a boundary integral for computing the irradiance due to planar luminaires of arbitrary shape and linearly-varying radiant exitance,
2. The derivation of a *closed-form* expression (including one special function) for the restricted case of polygonal luminaires with linearly-varying radiant exitance,
3. An evaluation procedure that is suitable for irradiance computations in image synthesis.

The theoretical contribution of this work is somewhat broader, however, in that the same approach can be applied to luminaires with non-linear spatial variation as well as directional variation. All cases of polynomial variation admit similar closed-form solutions, which rest on the same special function that emerges in the linear case [8].

2 Luminaires with Varying Radiant Exitance

The irradiance ϕ impinging on a differential surface element at the point $\mathbf{o}$ due to a planar Lambertian luminaire L is given by

$$\phi(L) = \int_L \frac{f(\mathbf{x})}{\pi} \frac{\cos\theta_1 \cos\theta_2}{r^2} \, d\mathbf{x}, \tag{1}$$

where $\mathbf{x}$ is a point on L, r is the distance from $\mathbf{o}$ to $\mathbf{x}$, and $f(\mathbf{x})$ is the *radiant exitance* of the luminaire at the point $\mathbf{x}$; thus, $f(\mathbf{x})/\pi$ is the radiance of the surface at $\mathbf{x}$, which is constant in all directions. Here θ_1 denotes the angle between $\mathbf{x} - \mathbf{o}$ and the receiver normal $\mathbf{b}$, and θ_2 denotes the angle between $\mathbf{x} - \mathbf{o}$ and the luminaire normal. Without loss of generality, we shall assume that $\mathbf{o}$ is the coordinate origin throughout the remainder of the paper.

The class of luminaires that we consider are those that are planar, and for which the function f, mapping points on the plane to $\mathbb{R}$, is linear. Therefore,

$$f(\mathbf{x}) = [w_1 \ w_2 \ w_3] \, \hat{\mathbf{x}}, \tag{2}$$

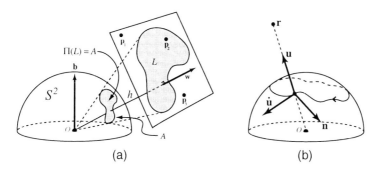

Fig. 1. *(a) The irradiance at* **o** *due to a planar figure* L *with linearly varying radiant exitance is computed by a boundary integral. The radiant exitance variation is uniquely determined by any three non-collinear points* $\mathbf{p}_1$, $\mathbf{p}_2$, *and* $\mathbf{p}_3$ *on the luminaire plane. (b) The outward normal* **n** *is tangent to the sphere and orthogonal to the boundary of the spherical projection.*

where $\hat{\mathbf{x}}$ is the barycentric coordinate vector of $\mathbf{x}$ with respect to any three non-collinear points $\mathbf{p}_1$, $\mathbf{p}_2$ and $\mathbf{p}_3$ on L at which the radiant exitance is w_1, w_2 and w_3. Thus, $\hat{\mathbf{x}}$ is given by

$$\hat{\mathbf{x}} = [\mathbf{p}_1\, \mathbf{p}_2\, \mathbf{p}_3]^{-1}\, \mathbf{x}, \tag{3}$$

where $[\mathbf{p}_1\, \mathbf{p}_2\, \mathbf{p}_3]$ denotes the matrix with $\mathbf{p}_1, \mathbf{p}_2, \mathbf{p}_3$ as its columns. Letting $A = \Pi(L)$ denote the projection of L onto the unit sphere about the origin, equation (1) becomes the integral of a simple rational function over A:

$$\phi(A) = \frac{1}{\pi} \int_A \frac{\langle \mathbf{a}, \mathbf{u}\rangle\, \langle \mathbf{b}, \mathbf{u}\rangle}{\langle \mathbf{w}, \mathbf{u}\rangle}\, d\sigma(\mathbf{u}), \tag{4}$$

where $\mathbf{w}$ is the unit vector orthogonal to the planar luminaire, $\mathbf{a}$ is a constant vector, which we define below, and $\mathbf{b}$ is the receiver normal at the origin. See Figure 1a. The measure σ denotes area on the sphere, and $\langle \cdot, \cdot \rangle$ denotes the standard inner product. The denominator $\langle \mathbf{w}, \mathbf{u}\rangle$ is introduced by expressing $\mathbf{x}$ in equation (3) in terms of the unit vector $\mathbf{u}$; that is, $\mathbf{x} = h\,\mathbf{u}/\langle \mathbf{w}, \mathbf{u}\rangle$, where h is the distance from the origin to the plane containing the luminaire, as shown in Figure 1a. It follows from equations (2) and (3) that the constant vector $\mathbf{a}$ appearing in equation (4) is given by

$$\mathbf{a} = h\,[w_1\, w_2\, w_3]\,[\mathbf{p}_1\, \mathbf{p}_2\, \mathbf{p}_3]^{-1}. \tag{5}$$

3   The General Boundary Integral

Let $A \subset S^2$ denote a region on the sphere with a rectifiable boundary; that is, a boundary for which an outward normal is defined almost everywhere. If A is the spherical projection of a planar Lambertian luminaire with linearly-varying radiant exitance, then it can be shown that the irradiance at the origin, $\phi(A)$, is given by the boundary integral

$$\phi(A) = -\frac{1}{2\pi} \int_{\partial A} \mathbf{M}_{ijk}(\mathbf{w}, \mathbf{u})\, \mathbf{a}_i\, \mathbf{b}_j\, \mathbf{n}_k\, ds(\mathbf{u}) \tag{6}$$

where ds denotes integration with respect to arclength, $\mathbf{M}$ is a 3-tensor that depends on the unit vectors $\mathbf{w}$ and $\mathbf{u}$, and $\mathbf{n}$ is the outward-pointing unit normal of the curve; thus $\mathbf{n}$

is always tangent to the sphere and orthogonal to the curve on the sphere. See Figure 1b. In equation (6), and throughout the paper, we employ the summation convention, where repeated subscripts imply summation from 1 to 3. The tensor $\mathbf{M}$ is given by

$$\mathbf{M}_{ijk}(\mathbf{w}, \mathbf{u}) \equiv \delta_{ik}\mathbf{w}_j + \left[\frac{\delta_{km}\mathbf{u}_i}{\langle \mathbf{w}, \mathbf{u} \rangle} - \delta_{im}\mathbf{w}_k\, \eta(\mathbf{w}, \mathbf{u})\right](\delta_{jm} - \mathbf{w}_j\mathbf{w}_m), \tag{7}$$

where δ_{ij} is the Kronecker delta, and the scalar-valued function η is defined to be

$$\eta(\mathbf{w}, \mathbf{u}) \equiv \frac{\ln \langle \mathbf{w}, \mathbf{u} \rangle}{1 - \langle \mathbf{w}, \mathbf{u} \rangle^2}. \tag{8}$$

Here $\langle \mathbf{w}, \mathbf{u} \rangle > 0$ for the illuminated hemisphere, and we define $\eta = 0$ at the singularity where $\langle \mathbf{w}, \mathbf{u} \rangle = 1$. An outline of the derivation of equation (7) is provided in Appendix A, and a direct proof of the formula using Stokes' theorem is given in Appendix B. The former provides some insight into the process by which such a formula is found, while the latter is a short and purely mechanical verification after the fact.

As a basic test of correctness, observe that for luminaires with constant radiant exitance c, we have $w_1 = w_2 = w_3 = c$, from which it follows that $\mathbf{a} = c\mathbf{w}$ by using the volume of a tetrahedron [7, 9]. Thus, equation (6) simplifies to

$$\phi(A) = -\frac{c}{2\pi} \int_{\partial A} \langle \mathbf{b}, \mathbf{n} \rangle \, ds, \tag{9}$$

which is the continuous version of Lambert's well-known formula for irradiance from a uniform polygonal luminaire [6].

4   Restriction to Polygons

We now specialize the result given in the previous section to spherical polygons, which result from projecting simple planar polygons onto the sphere. The resulting formula will allow us to compute the exact irradiance due to a polygonal luminaire with linearly-varying radiant exitance.

For a spherical polygon P with s edges, the boundary integral in equation (6) can be evaluated along each edge ζ of P, where ζ is a great arc connecting two adjacent vertices. That is,

$$\phi(P) = -\frac{1}{2\pi} \sum_{m=1}^{s} \left[\int_{\zeta_m} \mathbf{M}_{ijk}\, \mathbf{a}_i\, \mathbf{b}_j \, ds\right] \mathbf{n}_k(m), \tag{10}$$

where the normal $\mathbf{n}$ has been moved outside the integral since it is constant along each ζ_m; this is precisely the property that allows us to simplify boundary integrals of this form when applied to polygons. Consequently, each term in equation (10) can be written as

$$\langle \mathbf{a}, \mathbf{n} \rangle \langle \mathbf{b}, \mathbf{w} \rangle \, \Theta_m + \mathbf{b}^\mathsf{T}(\mathbf{I} - \mathbf{w}\mathbf{w}^\mathsf{T})\left[B_1(\zeta_m)\, \mathbf{n} - B_2(\zeta_m) \langle \mathbf{w}, \mathbf{n} \rangle \mathbf{a}\right], \tag{11}$$

where $\mathbf{n}$ depends on the edge ζ_m,

$$B_1(\zeta) = \int_\zeta \frac{\langle \mathbf{a}, \mathbf{u} \rangle}{\langle \mathbf{w}, \mathbf{u} \rangle} \, ds, \quad B_2(\zeta) = \int_\zeta \eta(\mathbf{w}, \mathbf{u}) \, ds,$$

and Θ_m is the arc length of ζ_m. We now parameterize each edge ζ by

$$\mathbf{u}(\theta) = \mathbf{s}\cos\theta + \mathbf{t}\sin\theta,$$

where $\mathbf{s}$ and $\mathbf{t}$ are orthonormal vectors in the plane containing the edge and the origin, with $\mathbf{s}$ directed toward the first vertex of the edge [4]. Using this parameterization, the functions B_1 and B_2 can be simplified to obtain [9]

$$\overline{B}_1(c_1, c_2, \Theta, \phi_1, \phi_2) = \frac{c_2}{c_1}\left[\cos(\phi_1 - \phi_2)\Theta + \sin(\phi_1 - \phi_2)\ln\frac{\cos(\Theta - \phi_1)}{\cos\phi_1}\right]$$

$$\overline{B}_2(c_1, \Theta, \phi_1) = \Lambda(c_1, \Theta - \phi_1) - \Lambda(c_1, -\phi_1),$$

where c_1, c_2, ϕ_1, and ϕ_2 are functions of $\mathbf{s}$ and $\mathbf{t}$ that satisfy

$$(\cos\phi_1, \sin\phi_1) = \left(\frac{\langle\mathbf{w},\mathbf{s}\rangle}{c_1}, \frac{\langle\mathbf{w},\mathbf{t}\rangle}{c_1}\right) \quad \text{where} \quad c_1 = \sqrt{\langle\mathbf{w},\mathbf{s}\rangle^2 + \langle\mathbf{w},\mathbf{t}\rangle^2},$$

$$(\cos\phi_2, \sin\phi_2) = \left(\frac{\langle\mathbf{a},\mathbf{s}\rangle}{c_2}, \frac{\langle\mathbf{a},\mathbf{t}\rangle}{c_2}\right) \quad \text{where} \quad c_2 = \sqrt{\langle\mathbf{a},\mathbf{s}\rangle^2 + \langle\mathbf{a},\mathbf{t}\rangle^2}.$$

The function Λ appearing in the expression for $\overline{B}_2$ is defined by

$$\Lambda(\alpha, \beta) \equiv \int_0^\beta \frac{\ln(\alpha\cos\theta)}{1 - (\alpha\cos\theta)^2}\, d\theta, \tag{12}$$

where $0 < \alpha \le 1$ and $-\pi/2 \le \beta \le \pi/2$. This same integral arises in computing the irradiance from all polynomially-varying Lambertian luminaires [8], and is therefore of practical importance beyond the linear problem we address here. We discuss this integral more fully in the following section.

5 The Special Function Λ

The two-parameter function $\Lambda(\alpha, \beta)$ defined in equation (12) has no finite representation in terms of elementary exponential and logarithmic functions, since it contains Lobachevski's function as a special case [9]. The function Λ therefore qualifies as a *higher transcendental function*, also known as a *special function*. For certain values of the parameters, such as $\alpha = 1$, $\Lambda(\alpha, \beta)$ simplifies immediately to known definite integrals with exact solutions. For example, $\Lambda(1, \beta) = -\beta - \cot\beta\ln(\cos\beta)$. However, to evaluate $\Lambda(\alpha, \beta)$ in general, we reduce it to a well-known special function that can be evaluated to high accuracy, such as the *dilogarithm* $\mathrm{Li}_2(z)$ [16, 14] or *Clausen's integral* $\mathrm{Cl}_2(\theta)$ [1, 5, 14]; these two special functions are closely related, as $\mathrm{Cl}_2(\theta)$ is simply the imaginary part of $\mathrm{Li}_2(e^{i\theta})$ [14, pp.91]. Since $\Lambda(\alpha, -\beta) = -\Lambda(\alpha, \beta)$, we need only consider $\beta \in [0, \pi/2]$. By the change of variable $\tan\theta = \sqrt{1 - \alpha^2}\tan t$, we relate $\Lambda(\alpha, \beta)$ to an intermediate two-parameter function $\Upsilon(\mu, \nu)$ introduced by Arvo [3, pp.112], which can then be expressed in terms of either the dilogarithm with a complex argument, or Clausen's integral with a real argument [3, pp.195]. The latter representation has some advantages, since $\mathrm{Cl}_2(\theta)$ can be easily approximated to high accuracy (with relative error $\le 0.003\%$) using elementary real functions [11]. One such approximation procedure, due to Grosjean [11], is shown in the pseudo-code ApproxClausen in Figure 3b.

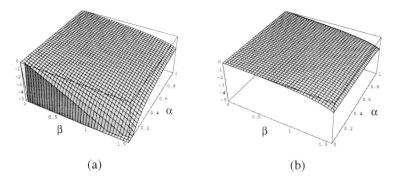

Fig. 2. *(a) The special function $\Lambda(\alpha, \beta)$ defined in equation (12), over the range $0 < \alpha \leq 1$, and $0 \leq \beta \leq \pi/2$. (b)The second component $\Lambda'(\alpha, \beta)$ defined in equation (15), over the range $[0, 1] \times [0, \pi/2]$.*

The key to finding the exact connection between $\Lambda(\alpha, \beta)$ and the Clausen integral is an identity involving the Clausen integral derived by Newman [15, pp.88] in the 19th century. From Newman's result, it follows that

$$\Lambda(\alpha, \beta) = \frac{2(\eta - \mu) \ln \gamma + 2\mathrm{Cl}_2(2\mu) - \mathrm{Cl}_2(4\mu - 2\eta) - \mathrm{Cl}_2(2\eta)}{4\sqrt{1 - \alpha^2}}, \tag{13}$$

where $0 < \alpha < 1, 0 \leq \beta \leq \pi/2$, and

$$\mu(\alpha, \beta) = \tan^{-1}\left(\frac{\tan \beta}{\sqrt{1 - \alpha^2}}\right),$$

$$\gamma(\alpha) = \left(\frac{1 - \sqrt{1 - \alpha^2}}{\alpha}\right)^2,$$

$$\eta(\alpha, \beta) = \tan^{-1}\left(\frac{\sin(2\mu)}{\gamma + \cos(2\mu)}\right).$$

It is not surprising that a special function like $\Lambda(\alpha, \beta)$ appears in the problem we have addressed; integrals of a similar nature have been discovered and studied in connection with radiative transfer for half a century [16]. It is interesting to note that the dilogarithms and related functions like the Clausen integral appear in computing the form factor between two arbitrary polygons, as shown by Schröder and Hanrahan [17].

By using equation (13), $\Lambda(\alpha, \beta)$ can be evaluated directly, where the Clausen integral is computed using a hypergeometric representation [2, pp.102] or a procedure such as ApproxClausen shown in Figure 3b. However, as a more efficient alternative, one can tabulate the function $\Lambda(\alpha, \beta)$ on a regular grid, and retrieve values by direct indexing and bilinear interpolation. Unfortunately, $\lim_{\alpha \to 0} \Lambda(\alpha, \beta) = -\infty$, which makes it impossible to approximate Λ over its entire domain using bilinear interpolation. To remedy this, we may separate a small strip $[0, \alpha_\epsilon] \times [0, \pi/2]$ from the domain, and evaluate $\Lambda(\alpha, \beta)$ using formula (13) inside the strip and use bilinear interpolation over the rest of the domain. We have used this hybrid approach to generate Figures 4 and 5 (see Appendix). By choosing $\alpha_\epsilon = 0.01$ and tabulating Λ over a 300×300 grid, we can achieve a maximum relative error of 0.022%.

ComputeIrrad(P, $\mathbf{p}_1$, $\mathbf{p}_2$, $\mathbf{p}_3$, w_1, w_2, w_3)

> $\mathbf{w} \leftarrow \mathbf{unit}[(\mathbf{p}_2 - \mathbf{p}_1) \times (\mathbf{p}_2 - \mathbf{p}_3)]$
> **if** $\langle \mathbf{w}, \mathbf{p}_1 + \mathbf{p}_2 + \mathbf{p}_3 \rangle < 0$
> > $\mathbf{w} \leftarrow -\mathbf{w}$
> **endif**
> $\mathbf{b} \leftarrow$ *surface normal at the origin* $\mathbf{o}$
> $\mathbf{a} \leftarrow \langle \mathbf{p}_1, \mathbf{w} \rangle [w_1 \ w_2 \ w_3] [\mathbf{p}_1 \ \mathbf{p}_2 \ \mathbf{p}_3]^{-1}$
> $s \leftarrow 0$
> **for each** edge $\mathbf{AB}$ in polygon P **do**
> > $\mathbf{s} \leftarrow \mathbf{unit}[\mathbf{A}]$
> > $\mathbf{t} \leftarrow \mathbf{unit}[(\mathbf{I} - \mathbf{ss}^\mathsf{T})\mathbf{B}]$
> > $a_1 \leftarrow \langle \mathbf{w}, \mathbf{s} \rangle; \quad a_2 \leftarrow \langle \mathbf{a}, \mathbf{s} \rangle$
> > $b_1 \leftarrow \langle \mathbf{w}, \mathbf{t} \rangle; \quad b_2 \leftarrow \langle \mathbf{a}, \mathbf{t} \rangle$
> > $c_1 \leftarrow \sqrt{a_1^2 + b_1^2}; \quad c_2 \leftarrow \sqrt{a_2^2 + b_2^2}$
> > $\phi_1 \leftarrow \mathbf{sign}[b_1] * \cos^{-1}(a_1/c_1)$
> > $\phi_2 \leftarrow \mathbf{sign}[b_2] * \cos^{-1}(a_2/c_2)$
> > $\Theta \leftarrow$ *angle between* $\mathbf{A}$ *and* $\mathbf{B}$
> > $\mathbf{n} \leftarrow \mathbf{unit}[\mathbf{A} \times \mathbf{B}]$
> > $\mathbf{v} \leftarrow (\mathbf{I} - \mathbf{ww}^\mathsf{T})\mathbf{b}$
> > $s_0 \leftarrow \langle \mathbf{a}, \mathbf{n} \rangle * \langle \mathbf{b}, \mathbf{w} \rangle * \Theta$
> > $s_1 \leftarrow \overline{B}_1(c_1, c_2, \Theta, \phi_1, \phi_2) * \langle \mathbf{v}, \mathbf{n} \rangle$
> > $s_2 \leftarrow \overline{B}_2(c_1, \Theta, \phi_1) * \langle \mathbf{w}, \mathbf{n} \rangle * \langle \mathbf{v}, \mathbf{a} \rangle$
> > $s \leftarrow s + s_0 + s_1 - s_2$
> **endfor**
> **return** $-s / 2\pi$
> **end**

ApproxClausen(x)

> $c_1 \leftarrow \quad 3.472222222E - 04$
> $c_2 \leftarrow \quad 9.869604401E + 00$
> $c_3 \leftarrow \quad 5.091276919E + 01$
> $c_4 \leftarrow \quad 1.362943611E - 01$
> $c_5 \leftarrow \ -2.165319440E - 03$
> $c_6 \leftarrow \quad 1.639639947E - 04$
> $c_7 \leftarrow \ -2.471701169E - 05$
> $c_8 \leftarrow \quad 5.538890645E - 06$
> **if** $x == 0$
> > **return** 0.0
> **endif**
> **if** $x > \pi$
> > **return** -ApproxClausen($2\pi - x$)
> **endif**
> **return**
> > $c_1 * x * (c_2 - x^2) * (c_3 + 3x^2)$
> > $+ c_4 * \sin(x) + c_5 * \sin(2x)$
> > $+ c_6 * \sin(3x) + c_7 * \sin(4x)$
> > $+ c_8 * \sin(5x)$
> > $- x * \ln(\sin(x/2))$
> **end**

(a)   (b)

Fig. 3. *(a) Pseudo-code for irradiance at the origin due to a linearly-varying luminaire. (b) Pseudo-code for Grosjean's approximation of Clausen's integral for $x \in [0, 2\pi]$, which can be used to evaluate $\overline{B}_2$.*

Another approach is to split Λ into two parts by replacing $\ln(\alpha \cos\theta)$ in the numerator by $\ln(\alpha) + \ln(\cos\theta)$. This results in

$$\Lambda(\alpha, \beta) = \lambda(\alpha, \beta) + \Lambda'(\alpha, \beta), \tag{14}$$

where we define

$$\Lambda'(\alpha, \beta) \equiv \int_0^\beta \frac{\ln(\cos\theta)}{1 - (\alpha \cos\theta)^2} \, d\theta, \tag{15}$$

and λ can be evaluated exactly as

$$\lambda(\alpha, \beta) = \frac{\ln \alpha}{\sqrt{1 - \alpha^2}} \tan^{-1}\left(\frac{\tan \beta}{\sqrt{1 - \alpha^2}}\right),$$

for $\alpha < 1$, and $\lambda(1, \beta) = 0$. A plot of the new function $\Lambda'(\alpha, \beta)$ for $0 \leq \alpha \leq 1$ and $0 \leq \beta \leq \pi/2$ is shown in Figure 2b. Since Λ' is smooth and bounded, it can be easily computed using numerical quadrature. Furthermore, by tabulating $\Lambda'(\alpha, \beta)$ we can approximate Λ over its entire domain via interpolation.

The pseudo-code for computing the irradiance at the origin $\mathbf{o}$ due to a linearly-varying luminaire P is shown in Figure 3a. Here, $\mathbf{p}_1, \mathbf{p}_2, \mathbf{p}_3$ are any three non-collinear points on P with corresponding radiant exitances w_1, w_2 and w_3. Note that the evaluation of $\overline{B}_2$ in ComputeIrrad may be carried out using any of the methods we have described for Λ, including direct calls to ApproxClausen.

6 Results

Figures 4 and 5 (see Appendix) shows two simple scenes, each illuminated by an area light source with two linearly-varying superimposed colors. This effect is simulated by integrating two linearly-varying scalar values over the luminaire and weighting the corresponding colors by them. Both scenes were rendered using the new technique and also by Monte Carlo for comparison. In implementing our analytical method, several optimizations were employed: 1) the vector $\mathbf{a}$ was computed incrementally [9] rather than inverting a matrix at each receiver point, 2) the vector form of irradiance was used to share most of the computation cost of the two color variations, and 3) bilinear interpolation was used to evaluate the function Λ^1. Stratified sampling within a rectangular region was used for the Monte Carlo solutions. All the images were computed at a resolution of 300×300 on an SGI Indigo2 with a 175 Mhz $R10000$ processor. The numbers beneath each picture indicate the computation time in minutes.

Figure 4 (see Appendix) depicts a box blocker in front of a luminaire. Polygonal occlusions are handled by clipping the luminaire against all blockers and computing the contribution from each visible portion using our closed-form solution. The result clearly matches the Monte Carlo image generated by using 100 stratified samples per pixel, yet is over 20 times faster. Moreover, our method results in much higher quality than simple Monte Carlo, using nearly the same amount of time.

For the leaf-like polygonal luminaire in Figure 5 (see Appendix), our proposed algorithm shows a significant advantage over Monte Carlo in that it can handle non-convex polygons directly, and produce a noise-free image in far less time, as shown in the top row. The Monte Carlo images are rendered by stratified sampling the bounding rectangle of the leaf-shape polygon. The same scene was rendered using a semi-analytical method for further comparison. This latter approach subdivides the luminaire into small pieces and computes the contribution from each piece using Lambert's formula. Although each pixel of the resulting image shown in the right is within 2% of the exact solution, this finite element approach is much slower than the analytic solution.

These experiments provide numerical evidence of the correctness of our formula, and also demonstrate its utility in computing direct illumination. The approach is also applicable to indirect illumination, however, as it provides an analytical means of computing generalized form-factors involving non-constant surface elements [20].

7 Conclusions

We have introduced a new deterministic technique for computing irradiance from polygonal luminaires with linearly-varying radiant exitance. Our solution is closed-form, but includes a single well-behaved special function $\Lambda(\alpha, \beta)$ that can be efficiently approx-

---

[1] Software for evaluating Λ is available at www.cs.caltech.edu/~arvo/software.

imated via numerical quadrature or interpolation, or evaluated exactly in terms of the dilogarithm or Clausen's integral. The approach can be extended to include directional variation as well as more complex spatial variation. Surprisingly, these generalizations all rely on the very same special function Λ [8], and will be described in detail in a subsequent paper.

Acknowledgements

This work was supported by a Microsoft Research Fellowship and NSF Career Award CCR9876332.

Appendix A: A Brief Outline of the Derivation

We briefly sketch the derivation of equations (6), (7), and (8). Complete details are available as a technical report [9]. First, we expand the denominator of the integrand in equation (4) around $\mathbf{u}_0 = \mathbf{w}$ using Taylor's theorem and the binomial theorem, to obtain the infinite series

$$\frac{1}{\langle \mathbf{w}, \mathbf{u} \rangle} = \sum_{n=0}^{\infty} \sum_{k=0}^{n} (-1)^k \binom{n}{k} \langle \mathbf{w}, \mathbf{u} \rangle^k. \tag{16}$$

Accordingly, the integrand $\langle \mathbf{a}, \mathbf{u} \rangle \langle \mathbf{b}, \mathbf{u} \rangle / \langle \mathbf{w}, \mathbf{u} \rangle$ can be expanded into an infinite series, each term of which is a product of three inner products, with one raised to a power. To integrate these terms, we introduce the *triple-axis moment*

$$\bar{\bar{\bar{\tau}}}^{i,j,k}(A, \mathbf{r}, \mathbf{s}, \mathbf{t}) \equiv \int_A \langle \mathbf{r}, \mathbf{u} \rangle^i \langle \mathbf{s}, \mathbf{u} \rangle^j \langle \mathbf{t}, \mathbf{u} \rangle^k \, d\sigma(\mathbf{u}), \tag{17}$$

which is a natural generalization of the *angular moments* used by Arvo [4] for non-Lambertian phenomena. When $j = k = 1$, $\bar{\bar{\bar{\tau}}}^{i,j,k}$ satisfies the recurrence relation

$$(n+3)\,\bar{\bar{\bar{\tau}}}^{n,1,1}(A, \mathbf{r}, \mathbf{s}, \mathbf{t}) = \langle \mathbf{s}, \mathbf{t} \rangle \, \bar{\tau}^n(A, \mathbf{r}) + n \langle \mathbf{r}, \mathbf{t} \rangle \, \bar{\bar{\tau}}^{n-1,1}(A, \mathbf{r}, \mathbf{s})$$
$$- \int_{\partial A} \langle \mathbf{r}, \mathbf{u} \rangle^n \langle \mathbf{s}, \mathbf{u} \rangle \langle \mathbf{t}, \mathbf{n} \rangle \, ds. \tag{18}$$

By representing solid angle $\sigma(A)$ as a boundary integral

$$-\int_{\partial A} \frac{\langle \mathbf{w}, \mathbf{n} \rangle}{1 + \langle \mathbf{w}, \mathbf{u} \rangle} \, ds = \sigma(A), \tag{19}$$

where $\mathbf{w}$ is any unit vector such that $-\mathbf{w} \notin A$, the axial moments $\bar{\tau}^i$ and $\bar{\bar{\tau}}^{i,j}$ can be shown to satisfy simpler recurrence relations [4, 9]. The resulting series for the irradiance $\phi(A)$ can then be simplified by means of assorted binomial identities. Finally, the infinite summation can be reduced to a finite number of terms using the identities

$$\int_{\partial A} \frac{\langle \mathbf{v}, \mathbf{n} \rangle}{\langle \mathbf{w}, \mathbf{u} \rangle^2} \, ds = \langle \mathbf{w}, \mathbf{v} \rangle \int_{\partial A} \frac{\langle \mathbf{w}, \mathbf{n} \rangle}{\langle \mathbf{w}, \mathbf{u} \rangle^2} \, ds, \tag{20}$$

$$\int_{\partial A} \left[\langle \mathbf{v}, \mathbf{n} \rangle - \frac{\langle \mathbf{v}, \mathbf{u} \rangle \langle \mathbf{w}, \mathbf{n} \rangle}{\langle \mathbf{w}, \mathbf{u} \rangle} \right] ds = \int_{\partial A} [\langle \mathbf{v}, \mathbf{w} \rangle \langle \mathbf{w}, \mathbf{n} \rangle - \langle \mathbf{v}, \mathbf{n} \rangle] \frac{\ln \langle \mathbf{w}, \mathbf{u} \rangle}{\langle \mathbf{w}, \mathbf{u} \rangle^2} ds, \quad (21)$$

for an arbitrary vector $\mathbf{v}$ and unit vector $\mathbf{w}$ in S^2. Identities (19), (20) and (21) all follows from Stokes' theorem. Identity (19) can be viewed as a generalization of Girard's formula [7] for the area of spherical triangles.

Appendix B: Direct Proof of Equation (6)

It follows from equations (4) and (6) that the identity to be proved is

$$\int_A \frac{\langle \mathbf{a}, \mathbf{u} \rangle \langle \mathbf{b}, \mathbf{u} \rangle}{\langle \mathbf{w}, \mathbf{u} \rangle} d\omega = -\frac{1}{2} \int_{\partial A} \mathbf{M}_{ijk} \mathbf{a}_j \mathbf{b}_k \mathbf{n}_k \, ds, \quad (22)$$

where the 3-tensor $\mathbf{M}$ is defined in equation (7), which can also be written as

$$\mathbf{M}_{ijk} = \delta_{ik} \mathbf{w}_j + \mathbf{u}_i \frac{\delta_{jk} - \mathbf{w}_j \mathbf{w}_k}{\langle \mathbf{w}, \mathbf{u} \rangle} - \eta \left(\delta_{ij} \mathbf{w}_k - \mathbf{w}_i \mathbf{w}_j \mathbf{w}_k \right). \quad (23)$$

Proof: The proof is done by applying Stokes' Theorem on the right hand side and changing it into a surface integral, which can be accomplished in the four steps:

Step 1: As shown in Figure 1b,

$$\mathbf{n} \, ds = \frac{\mathbf{r} \times d\mathbf{r}}{r^2}, \quad \mathbf{u} = \frac{\mathbf{r}}{r},$$

so we may rewrite the boundary integral on the right hand side in terms of the position vector $\mathbf{r}$ and its derivatives:

$$\int_{\partial A} \mathbf{M}_{ijk} \mathbf{a}_i \mathbf{b}_j \mathbf{n}_k \, ds = \int_{\partial A} \mathbf{M}_{ijk} \mathbf{a}_i \mathbf{b}_j \frac{\varepsilon_{kpl} \mathbf{r}_p \, d\mathbf{r}_l}{r^2} = \int_{\partial A} B_l \, d\mathbf{r}_l, \quad (24)$$

where we have introduced a vector B_l given by

$$B_l = \frac{\varepsilon_{kpl} \mathbf{M}_{ijk} \mathbf{a}_i \mathbf{b}_j \mathbf{r}_p}{r^2}.$$

Step 2: To convert the boundary integral in equation (24) into a surface integral using Stokes' theorem, we must compute the partial derivative of B_l with respect to $\mathbf{r}_m$. By using the fact that

$$\frac{\partial}{\partial \mathbf{r}_m} \left[\frac{\mathbf{r}_p}{r^2} \right] = \frac{\delta_{pm} r^2 - 2 \mathbf{r}_p \mathbf{r}_m}{r^4},$$

$$\frac{\partial}{\partial \mathbf{r}_m} [\mathbf{M}_{ijk}] = (\delta_{jk} - \mathbf{w}_j \mathbf{w}_k) \frac{\delta_{im} \langle \mathbf{w}, \mathbf{r} \rangle - \mathbf{r}_i \mathbf{w}_m}{\langle \mathbf{w}, \mathbf{r} \rangle^2} - \eta_m (\delta_{ij} \mathbf{w}_k - \mathbf{w}_i \mathbf{w}_j \mathbf{w}_k),$$

where η_m denotes the partial derivative of η with respect to $\mathbf{r}_m$. That is,

$$\eta_m = \frac{\partial \eta}{\partial \mathbf{r}_m} = \frac{r^2 - \langle \mathbf{w}, \mathbf{r} \rangle^2 + 2 \langle \mathbf{w}, \mathbf{r} \rangle^2 \ln \langle \mathbf{w}, \mathbf{u} \rangle}{\left(r^2 - \langle \mathbf{w}, \mathbf{r} \rangle^2 \right)^2} \left[\frac{r^2 \mathbf{w}_m}{\langle \mathbf{w}, \mathbf{r} \rangle} - \mathbf{r}_m \right]. \quad (25)$$

It follows that

$$B_{l,m} = \varepsilon_{kpl} a_i b_j \frac{\partial}{\partial \mathbf{r}_m} \left[\frac{\mathbf{M}_{ijk} \mathbf{r}_p}{r^2} \right] = \varepsilon_{kpl} a_i b_j \left[A_1 + A_2 + A_3 \right], \qquad (26)$$

where A_1, A_2, A_3 are given by

$$A_1 = \mathbf{M}_{ijk} \frac{\delta_{pm} r^2 - 2\mathbf{r}_p \mathbf{r}_m}{r^4},$$

$$A_2 = (\delta_{jk} - \mathbf{w}_j \mathbf{w}_k) \frac{\delta_{im} \mathbf{r}_p \langle \mathbf{w}, \mathbf{r} \rangle - \mathbf{r}_i \mathbf{r}_p \mathbf{w}_m}{r^2 \langle \mathbf{w}, \mathbf{r} \rangle^2},$$

$$A_3 = -\frac{\mathbf{r}_p}{r^2} \eta_m (\delta_{ij} \mathbf{w}_k - \mathbf{w}_i \mathbf{w}_j \mathbf{w}_k),$$

and $\mathbf{M}$ and η_m are given by equations (23) and (25), respectively. Thus, we have

$$\int_{\partial A} B_l \, d\mathbf{r}_l = \int_A B_{l,m} \, d\mathbf{r}_m \wedge d\mathbf{r}_l$$

$$= \int_A B_{l,m} \left[\frac{d\mathbf{r}_m \wedge d\mathbf{r}_l - d\mathbf{r}_l \wedge d\mathbf{r}_m}{2} \right]$$

$$= \int_A B_{l,m} \left[\frac{\delta_{sm} \delta_{tl} - \delta_{sl} \delta_{tm}}{2} \right] d\mathbf{r}_s \wedge d\mathbf{r}_t$$

$$= \int_A \varepsilon_{qml} \varepsilon_{kpl} a_i b_j [A_1 + A_2 + A_3] \left[\frac{\varepsilon_{qst} \, d\mathbf{r}_s \wedge d\mathbf{r}_t}{2} \right]. \qquad (27)$$

The transformation above follows from anti-commutativity of the wedge product and the tensor identity

$$\varepsilon_{qml} \varepsilon_{qst} = \delta_{sm} \delta_{tl} - \delta_{sl} \delta_{tm}. \qquad (28)$$

Step 3: Applying identity (28) to the three terms in equation (27), we get [9]

$$\varepsilon_{qml} \varepsilon_{kpl} a_i b_j A_1 = \frac{2\mathbf{r}_q}{r^3} \left[\frac{\langle \mathbf{a}, \mathbf{u} \rangle \langle \mathbf{b}, \mathbf{u} \rangle}{\langle \mathbf{w}, \mathbf{u} \rangle} - \eta \left(\langle \mathbf{a}, \mathbf{b} \rangle \langle \mathbf{w}, \mathbf{u} \rangle - \langle \mathbf{a}, \mathbf{w} \rangle \langle \mathbf{b}, \mathbf{w} \rangle \langle \mathbf{w}, \mathbf{u} \rangle \right) \right],$$

$$\varepsilon_{qml} \varepsilon_{kpl} a_i b_j A_2 = \frac{\mathbf{r}_q}{r^3} \left[-\frac{\langle \mathbf{a}, \mathbf{b} \rangle}{\langle \mathbf{w}, \mathbf{u} \rangle} + \frac{\langle \mathbf{a}, \mathbf{w} \rangle \langle \mathbf{b}, \mathbf{w} \rangle}{\langle \mathbf{w}, \mathbf{u} \rangle} \right],$$

$$\varepsilon_{qml} \varepsilon_{kpl} a_i b_j A_3 = \frac{\mathbf{r}_q}{r^3} \left[\frac{\langle \mathbf{a}, \mathbf{b} \rangle}{\langle \mathbf{w}, \mathbf{u} \rangle} - \frac{\langle \mathbf{a}, \mathbf{w} \rangle \langle \mathbf{b}, \mathbf{w} \rangle}{\langle \mathbf{w}, \mathbf{u} \rangle} + 2\eta \left(\langle \mathbf{a}, \mathbf{b} \rangle \langle \mathbf{w}, \mathbf{u} \rangle - \langle \mathbf{a}, \mathbf{w} \rangle \langle \mathbf{b}, \mathbf{w} \rangle \langle \mathbf{w}, \mathbf{u} \rangle \right) \right].$$

Consequently, equation (27) simplifies to

$$\int_{\partial A} B_l \, d\mathbf{r}_l = 2 \int_A \left[\frac{\langle \mathbf{a}, \mathbf{u} \rangle \langle \mathbf{b}, \mathbf{u} \rangle}{\langle \mathbf{w}, \mathbf{u} \rangle} \right] \frac{\mathbf{r}_q}{r^3} \left[\frac{\varepsilon_{qst} \, d\mathbf{r}_s \wedge d\mathbf{r}_t}{2} \right]. \qquad (29)$$

Step 4: By representing the right hand side of equation (29) in terms of the solid angle 2-form $d\omega$, which is defined as [18, pp.131]

$$d\omega \equiv -\frac{\varepsilon_{qst} \mathbf{r}_q \, d\mathbf{r}_s \wedge d\mathbf{r}_t}{2r^3},$$

148

formula (22) follows easily from equations (24) and (29):

$$-\frac{1}{2} \int_{\partial A} \mathbf{M}_{ijk} \mathbf{a}_i \mathbf{b}_j \mathbf{n}_k \, ds \;=\; -\frac{1}{2} \int_{\partial A} B_l \, d\mathbf{r}_l \;=\; \int_A \frac{\langle \mathbf{a}, \mathbf{u} \rangle \langle \mathbf{b}, \mathbf{u} \rangle}{\langle \mathbf{w}, \mathbf{u} \rangle} \, d\omega.$$

References

1. Milton Abramowitz and Irene A. Stegun, editors. *Handbook of Mathematical Functions*. Dover Publications, New York, 1965.
2. George E. Andrews, Richard Askey, and Ranjan Roy. *Special Functions*. Cambridge University Press, New York, 1999.
3. James Arvo. *Analytic Methods for Simulated Light Transport*. PhD thesis, Yale University, December 1995.
4. James Arvo. Applications of irradiance tensors to the simulation of non-Lambertian phenomena. In *Computer Graphics* Proceedings, Annual Conference Series, ACM SIGGRAPH, pages 335–342, August 1995.
5. A. Ashour and A. Sabri. Tabulation of the function $\psi(\theta) = \sum_{n=1}^{\infty} \sin n\theta / n^2$. *Mathematical Tables and other Aids to Computation*, 10(54):57–65, April 1956.
6. Daniel R. Baum, Holly E. Rushmeier, and James M. Winget. Improving radiosity solutions through the use of analytically determined form-factors. *Computer Graphics*, 23(3):325–334, July 1989.
7. Marcel Berger. *Geometry*, volume 2. Springer-Verlag, New York, 1987. Translated by M. Cole and S. Levy.
8. Min Chen and James Arvo. Closed-form expressions for irradiance from non-uniform lambertian luminaires, Part 2: Polynomially-varying radiant exitance. Technical Report CS-TR-00-04, Caltech, CA, March 2000. (www.cs.caltech.edu/~arvo/papers/TR-00-04.ps.gz).
9. Min Chen and James Arvo. Closed-form expressions for irradiance from non-uniform lambertian luminaires, Part I: Linearly-varying radiant exitance. Technical Report CS-TR-00-01, Caltech, CA, January 2000. (www.cs.caltech.edu/~arvo/papers/TR-00-01.ps.gz).
10. David L. DiLaura. Non-diffuse radiative transfer 3: Inhomogeneous planar area sources and point receivers. *Journal of the Illuminating Engineering Society*, 26(1), 1997.
11. C. C. Grosjean. Formulae concerning the computation of the Clausen integral $Cl_2(\theta)$. *Journal of Computational and Applied Mathematics*, 11:331–342, 1984.
12. David Hart, Philip Dutré, and Donald P. Greenberg. Direct illumination with lazy visibility evaluation. In *Computer Graphics* Proceedings, Annual Conference Series, ACM SIGGRAPH, pages 147–154, August 1999.
13. John R. Howell. *A Catalog of Radiation Configuration Factors*. McGraw-Hill, New York, 1982.
14. Leonard Lewin. *Dilogarithms and associated functions*. Macdonald, London, 1958.
15. Francis W. Newman. *The Higher Trigonometry and Superrationals of Second Order*. Macmillan and Bowes, 1892.
16. E. O. Powell. An integral related to the radiation integrals. *Philosophical Magazine*, 34(236):600–607, September 1943.
17. Peter Schröder and Pat Hanrahan. On the form factor between two polygons. In *Computer Graphics* Proceedings, Annual Conference Series, ACM SIGGRAPH, pages 163–164, August 1993.
18. Michael Spivak. *Calculus on Manifolds*. Benjamin/Cummings, Reading, Massachusetts, 1965.
19. Michael M. Stark, Elaine Cohen, Tom Lynche, and Richard F. Riesenfeld. Computing exact shadow irradiance using splines. In *Computer Graphics* Proceedings, Annual Conference Series, ACM SIGGRAPH, pages 155–164, August 1999.
20. Roy Troutman and Nelson L. Max. Radiosity algorithms using higher-order finite element methods. In *Computer Graphics* Proceedings, Annual Conference Series, ACM SIGGRAPH, pages 209–212, August 1993.

Editors' Note: see Appendix, p. 403 for colored figures of this paper

Exact Illumination in Polygonal Environments using Vertex Tracing

Michael M. Stark and Richard F. Riesenfeld

University of Utah
Salt Lake City, UT
mstark@cs.utah.edu

Abstract. Methods for exact computation of irradiance and form factors associated with polygonal objects have ultimately relied on a formula for a differential area to polygon form factor attributed to Lambert. This paper presents an alternative, an analytical expression based on vertex behavior rather than the edges the polygon. Using this formulation, irradiance values in a scene consisting of partially occluded uniformly emitting polygons can be computed exactly by examining only the set of apparent vertices visible from the point of evaluation without explicit reconstruction of polygon contours. This leads to a fast, low-overhead algorithm for exact illumination computation that involves no explicit polygon clipping and is applicable to direct lighting and to radiosity gathering across surfaces or at isolated points.

1 Introduction and Previous Work

Fast and accurate computation of shadows continues to be one of the more perennial problems in computer graphics. Related problems include form-factor computation, visibility, and image reconstruction. In polygonal scenes, these problems ultimately amount to integration over visible portions of polygons. In this paper we consider the computation of the irradiance due to a collection of partially occluded uniformly emitting polygons. Numerous methods have been used to perform or approximate the integration, such as Monte Carlo integration, ray casting or other structured sampling approaches. Soler and Sillion [18] used the FFT to approximate the convolution integral for an occluded polygon. The hemi-cube and related algorithms can be used in the situation where there are many emitting polygons. Exact evaluation methods generally involve clipping the emitting polygon against all the intervening occluders then applying Lambert's formula. The backprojection method by Drettakis and Fiume [8] first partitions the receiver into regions of topologically equivalent visibility, then the scene is efficiently backprojected onto the emitting polygon. The method of Hart *et al.* [12] exploits scanline coherence to reduce the number of polygons involved in the clipping.

Methods such as the backprojection algorithm are fast, but have significant overhead. Furthermore, in radiosity environments where all the objects are emitters, the methods would have to be applied to each polygon in the scene. Aspect graphs or visibility maps can be used to compute the irradiance in a complex scene, but the entire graph must be constructed before evaluation can take place.

This paper presents an alternative to Lambert's formula, developed by projecting the emitting polygons onto an image plane. The resulting summation is reformulated in terms of the projected vertices and the slope of the "incoming" and "outgoing" edges. We then show how this formula can be used to compute the irradiance due to all the polygons in the scene by examining only the apparent vertices, *i.e.,* the vertices of

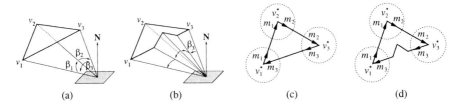

(a)	(b)	(c)	(d)

Fig. 1. (a) The geometry for Lambert's formula. (b) The angles β_i depend on the edges, so if part of the polygon is clipped by an occluder, the terms associated with the vertices of the affected edges have different values. (c) Using Green's theorem in the image plane produces a formula in terms of the local behavior at the vertices. (d) The contributions of the existing vertices are not affected if a bite is taken out of the polygon.

the visibility map, without actually computing the entire structure or performing any polygon clipping.

2   Irradiance from Diffusely Emitting Polygons

We recall that the irradiance from a uniformly emitting surface $\mathcal{S}$, which is not self-occluding as viewed from a point r on a receiver can be computed [2] from the surface integral

$$I(r) = M \int_{\mathcal{S}} \frac{\cos \theta_0 \cos \theta}{d^2} \, dS, \tag{1}$$

where d is the distance from r to a point on $\mathcal{S}$, θ_0 and θ are the angles made by the ray joining r and the point with the receiver normal at r and the surface normal at the point, respectively. The constant M is an emission constant of $\mathcal{S}$.

If the surface is a planar polygon P with vertices $v_1, \ldots, v_n$, the irradiance may be computed from a formula attributed to Lambert:

$$L(r) = \sum_{i=1}^{n} \beta_i \cos \alpha_i, \tag{2}$$

where β_i is the angle subtended by v_i, v_{i+1} from r, and α_i is the angle between the plane containing v_i, v_{i+1}, and r, and the normal to the receiver at r (*e.g.*, [6]). The drawback of (2) is that it depends on the angles between adjacent vertices, and thus requires the complete contour of the polygon to be known. In effect, Lambert's formula is a summation over the edges of the polygon rather than the vertices. Figure 1(a) illustrates the geometry.

Our objective is to construct a formula in terms of the vertices of the polygon P and the local behavior of the incident edges at each vertex. To do this, we project the polygon P through r onto an *image plane*, which is the plane parallel to the surface at r and one unit above (in the direction of the outward normal **n** at r) as shown in Figure 2. This projection does not change the irradiance at r [3].

Lambert's formula shows that the irradiance is invariant under rotation about the normal **n**, so the orientation of the x and y-axes in the image plane is not important. If **u** is an arbitrary unit vector perpendicular to **n**, and $\mathbf{v} = \mathbf{n} \times \mathbf{u}$, the projection of a vertex

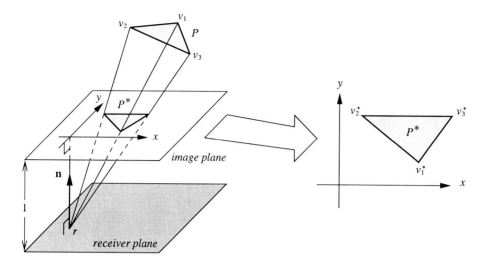

Fig. 2. To apply Green's theorem, the polygon P is projected onto an image plane parallel to the receiver plane, one unit above. The origin of the coordinate system of the image plane lies directly above the point of evaluation r on the receiver. The projection induces a reversal of orientation for front-facing polygons.

v of P may be computed, for example, using the homogeneous transformation

$$v^* = \begin{bmatrix} \mathbf{I} & \mathbf{0} \\ 0\ 0\ 1 & 0 \end{bmatrix} \begin{bmatrix} \mathbf{u} & \mathbf{v} & \mathbf{n} & \mathbf{0} \\ 0 & 0 & 0 & 1 \end{bmatrix}^T \begin{bmatrix} \mathbf{I} & -r \\ \mathbf{0}^T & 1 \end{bmatrix} \begin{bmatrix} v \\ 1 \end{bmatrix}. \tag{3}$$

(In the case of a polygonal receiver, $\mathbf{u}$ can be a normalized edge; for a curved receiver, $\mathbf{u}$ could be the direction of one of the curvilinear coordinates.) In what follows, we shall assume P has been projected onto the image plane forming a new planar polygon P^* having vertices $v_1^*, \ldots, v_n^*$. Each vertex v_i^* of P^* will be treated as a two-dimensional point (x_i, y_i) in image plane coordinates.

2.1 Integration

For the projected polygon P^*, the integral of (1) has a particularly simple form; it reduces to the ordinary plane double integral (omitting the emission constant)

$$I(r) = \int\!\!\int_{P^*} \frac{1}{\left(1 + x^2 + y^2\right)^2}\, dx\, dy. \tag{4}$$

This double integral may be reduced to a contour integral on the boundary of P^* using Green's theorem:

$$\oint_{\partial P^*} F_1\, dx + F_2\, dy = \int\!\!\int_{P^*} \left(\frac{\partial F_2}{\partial x} - \frac{\partial F_1}{\partial y} \right) dx\, dy. \tag{5}$$

The usual convention is counter-clockwise vertex ordering with respect to the outward normal. For a "front-facing" polygon, the angle between the outward normal and the receiver surface normal is negative, so the projected polygon P^* will have a clockwise vertex ordering on the image plane, which means a negatively-oriented boundary contour and the sign of the left-hand side of (5) must be reversed.

Taking $F_2(x, y) \equiv 0$ and $F_1(x, y)$ an anti-derivative of the integrand in (4) with respect to y we obtain from Green's theorem

$$\iint_{P^*} \frac{1}{(1 + x^2 + y^2)^2}\, dx\, dy = \oint_{\partial P^*} F_1(x, y)\, dx = \sum_{i=1}^{n} \int_{E_i^*} F_1(x, y)\, dx.$$

The line integral over each edge can be evaluated by parameterizing the edge with the line equation $y = m_i x + b_i$ and integrating over the domain of the edge $E_i^* = \overline{v_i^* v_{i+1}^*}$

$$\int_{E_i^*} F_1(x, y)\, dx = \int_{x_i}^{x_{i+1}} F_1(x, m_i x + b_i)\, dx = \Omega(x_{i+1}, m_i, b_i) - \Omega(x_i, m_i, b_i)$$

(vertical edges consequently drop out of the summation). Here Ω is

$$\Omega(x, m, b) = \int \left(\int \frac{1}{(1 + x^2 + y^2)^2}\, dy \right) \Bigg|_{y = mx + b} dx,$$

$m_i = (y_{i+1} - y_i)/(x_{i+1} - x_i)$ is the slope of the segment joining v_i^* and v_{i+1}^*, and b_i is the y-intercept of that line.

The irradiance integral may therefore be written as

$$
\begin{aligned}
I &= \sum_{i=1}^{n} \Omega(x_{i+1}, m_i, b_i) - \Omega(x_i, m_i, b_i) \\
&= \Omega(x_2, m_1, b_1) - \Omega(x_1, m_1, b_1) + \cdots + \Omega(x_1, m_n, b_n) - \Omega(x_n, m_n, b_n) \\
&= \sum_{i=1}^{n} \Omega(x_i, m_{i-1}, b_{i-1}) - \Omega(x_i, m_i, b_i)
\end{aligned}
$$

As $b_i = y_i - m_i x_i$ and $b_{i-1} = y_i - m_{i-1} x_i$ the intercept term can be eliminated by introducing a new function $F(x, y, m) = \Omega(x, m, y - mx)$, and the final form of the solution thereby obtained is

$$I = M \sum_{i=1}^{n} F(x_i, y_i, m_{i-1}) - F(x_i, y_i, m_i). \qquad (6)$$

The function F is

$$F(x, y, m) = \frac{Ax}{2} \arctan(Ay) + \frac{C(y - mx)}{2} \arctan\left[C(x + my) \right] \qquad (7)$$

where

$$A = \frac{1}{\sqrt{1 + x^2}}, \qquad C = \frac{1}{\sqrt{1 + m^2 + (y - mx)^2}}. \qquad (8)$$

Equations (6), (7) and (8) provide a formula analogous to Lambert's formula for the irradiance due to a uniformly emitting polygon. The first term in (7) is independent of m, and therefore appears to cancel in the summand of (6) so it is tempting to omit it from F. But recall that terms of F with undefined m are omitted outright, so in the case where only one of m_i and m_{i-1} is undefined, there is nothing to cancel the first term. The terms do cancel if neither incident edge is vertical.

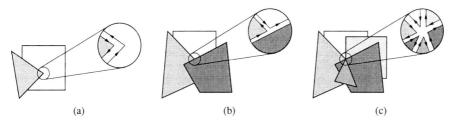

Fig. 3. Common cases of vertex behavior: (a) an intrinsic vertex against a background polygon, (b) an apparent vertex caused by the intersection of two edges against a background polygon, (c) a particularly unfortunate conjunction of three edges and one polygon vertex.

2.2 Remarks

There are several notable points about the result. Most importantly, the formula is a summation over a function of the vertices and the incoming and outgoing slopes m_{i-1} and m_i, respectively, and consequently may be evaluated in any order. In the case of an extraneous vertex, which has the same incoming and outgoing slope, the two F terms cancel and there is no contribution to the sum. Although the formula for F looks complicated, it is fairly easy to evaluate. Both the square root and arctangent functions have desirable computational behavior; note the radicand is bounded above 1.

The formula is valid only for a polygon which lies strictly above the plane of the receiver. As with Lambert's formula, the polygon must be clipped against the receiver plane, but unlike Lambert's formula, the projected polygon must be bounded on the image plane. (Otherwise the foregoing computation would have to be evaluated in the real projective plane.) One solution to this is to clip some small height above the receiver plane, another is to clip against a large bounding square on the image plane. The incurred error, as well as other vertex-based formulations, are discussed in [19].

3 Vertex Tracing and Angular Spans in Polygonal Environments

Equation (6) provides a method independent of vertex order for computing the irradiance due to a polygonal source. In a scene consisting of uniformly emitting polygons and perhaps other opaque occluding polygons, the scene projected onto the image plane consists of a collection of apparent polygons. The cumulative irradiance may therefore be computed at a point by examining only the apparent vertices of these projected polygons. The irradiance contribution at each vertex from (6) is summed over all the projected vertices to compute the total irradiance.

The projection of the scene onto the image plane is equivalent to the construction of the visibility map [16, ?]. That is, once the visibility map is constructed, our formula may be directly applied to compute the irradiance. However, the visibility map by definition includes the complete contour information of the projected polygons, and this defeats the purpose of the vertex formulation.

In this section, we propose a naive algorithm exploiting equation (6) by determining the apparent vertices of the projected scene using path tracing. The method is easily adapted to work with any number of emitting polygons in the scene, and is thus equally applicable to the problem of computing shadows from a single area light source as well as radiosity reconstruction, where every polygon in the scene is assumed to emit. Optimization methods and implementation details are discussed in the next section.

3.1 Visible vertices

Following Arvo [2], there are two types of vertices visible from a point r: *intrinsic* vertices, which are vertices of the original scene polygons, and *apparent* vertices, which are formed by the apparent intersection of two edges. Figure 3 illustrates these types of vertices as they appear from r against a "background" polygon. In Figure 3(a), an intrinsic vertex appears in front of a background polygon. There are two contributions to the irradiance sum in this case, one from the intrinsic vertex, and one from the projected intrinsic vertex onto the background polygon. If the emission constants of the foreground and background polygons are M and M_B, respectively, the contribution to the sum is

$$M\left[F(x,y,m_{\text{in}}) - F(x,y,m_{\text{out}})\right] - M_B\left[F(x,y,m_{\text{in}}) - F(x,y,m_{\text{out}})\right]$$
$$= (M - M_B)F(x,y,m_{\text{in}}) - (M - M_B)F(x,y,m_{\text{out}}).$$

Figure 3(b) shows an apparent vertex, also against a background polygon. The computation of the irradiance contribution is similar, except there is an extra edge, and there is no contribution from the front-most polygon because the incoming and outgoing slopes are the same.

Figure 3(a) and (b) illustrate what are by far the most common situations for visible vertices. However, it is possible that vertices (intrinsic or apparent) may appear to coincide as viewed from the point of evaluation. We will use the term *conjunctive* vertex for this situation, in homage to ancient astronomers. Examples of conjunctive vertices include the apparent intersection of three edges, two intrinsic vertices, or an intrinsic vertex and an apparent vertex [9, 14]. Figure 3(c) shows an example of a conjunctive vertex containing three apparent vertices and one intrinsic vertex. Despite the complexity of the interaction, the local behavior is still sufficient to compute the irradiance contribution. Our method seamlessly handles conjunctive vertices of arbitrary complexity.

3.2 Angular Spans

The zoomed insets of Figure 3 demonstrate how the local behavior at each vertex (intrinsic, apparent, or conjunctive) can be represented using circular sectors, or angular spans. An angular span is a circular sector with emission and depth information. The angular spans for a vertex are naturally represented as a doubly-linked circular list, having nodes of the form

```
struct span {
    double      θ₁    // smaller boundary
    double      z     // depth (set to ∞ for the background)
    spectrum    M     // emission constant (can be zero)
}
```

Each angular span actually has two boundaries, θ_1 and θ_2; the second boundary is the θ_1 field of the next span in the list. (Our implementation uses tandem arrays to store the span list.) Angular spans are similar to linear spans used in scanline rendering (*e.g.*, [23]) except that the opposite ends of a linear scan line do not "wrap around". Angular spans crossing the branch cut at π radians have to be handled properly. The algorithm described below depends on a fast implementation of an angular span insertion algorithm, where the spans may be inserted in random depth order.

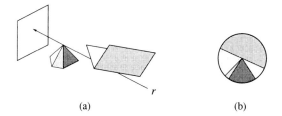

(a)   (b)

Fig. 4. (a) Tracing a conjunctive vertex, and (b) the resulting angular spans.

(a)   (b)

Fig. 5. (a) The span for an intrinsic vertex, (b) the span for an incident edge.

3.3 Naive Vertex Tracing

To compute the irradiance, all the visible vertices in the scene must be examined, which means each intrinsic vertex and all the apparent vertices from apparent edge intersections must be found and tested for visibility. Naively, the apparent vertices can be found by testing each pair of edges in the scene. Visibility is determined by tracing the ray from the point of evaluation r through the projected (intrinsic or apparent) vertex and collecting all vertices, edges and polygons incident on the ray. This way, all the participating polygons in a conjunctive vertex are found during the visibility test. A span list for the vertex is constructed by incrementally adding a span for each object incident on the ray (Figure 4). The depth value z for each span comes from the distance along the ray from r to the point of intersection. When the span list is completed, the contribution for the vertex, consisting of the contributions from all the spans in the list, is added to a master summation of the irradiance. The process is repeated for each vertex in the scene, and upon completion the master sum will equal the total irradiance.

There are two types of spans which will need to be added incrementally: vertex spans and edge spans. For a span at vertex (x_i, y_i), $\theta_1 = \arctan(y_{i-1} - y_i, x_{i-1} - x_i)$ and $\theta_2 = \arctan(y_{i+1} - y_i, x_{i+1} - x_i)$. For an edge span, $\theta_1 = \arctan(y_i - y_{i+1}, x_i - x_{i+1})$ and $\theta_2 = \theta_1 + \pi$, where the points are as in Figure 5. In addition, when a ray hits the interior of a polygon a "full" span, with $\theta_1 = -\pi, \theta_2 = \pi$, is added at the depth of intersection. Once the angular span list has been fully constructed, the contribution of the vertex is computed using the formula

$$\sum_{s \in \text{span list}} (s.M - \text{prev}(s).M) F(x, y, \tan s.\theta_1). \tag{9}$$

Here prev(s) denotes the predecessor of the span s in the span list. Note that a full angular span by itself has no contribution.

Algorithm 1 General vertex tracing

$\Sigma \leftarrow 0$
for each visible vertex v on an unvisited ray **do**
  reset the span list

  for each polygon P which intersects the ray (cone) $\vec{rv}$ **do**
    if $\vec{rv}$ intersects the interior of P **then**
      Add a full angular span for P at the depth z_P of the intersection

    else if $\vec{rv}$ intersects vertex i of P **then**
      add a span for vertex i of P (as in Figure 5(a)) at the depth of the intersection
      mark the ray through (x, y) as visited

    else if $\vec{rv}$ intersects edge i of P **then**
      add a span for edge i of P (as in Figure 5(b)) at the depth of the intersection
      mark the ray through (x, y) as visited
    end if
  end for

  for each span s **do**
    $\Sigma \leftarrow \Sigma + (s.M - \text{prev}(s).M)F(x, y, \tan s.\theta_1)$
  end for
end for

3.4 Conjunctive Vertices and Bookkeeping

Although the angular span method properly handles conjunctive vertices it creates a new problem: the contributions of a conjunctive vertex could be included more than once. For example, if two intrinsic vertices lie on the same ray, the contribution for the resulting conjunctive vertex will be added when the first vertex is traced, then again when the second vertex is traced. Floating-point imprecision complicates this and is discussed in the next section.

In polyhedral environments, where all the objects are closed solids bounded by outward-facing polygons, only silhouette edges and vertices need be examined in the inner loop of the algorithm. However, all vertices and edges are shared, so much more bookkeeping of visited vertices is required unless the environment has more structure than a simple list of polygons. If a winged-edge data structure is used, for example, the vertices and edges are separate data entities, so conjunctive vertices occur only when distinct *shared* intrinsic vertices and/or apparent vertices appear to coincide.

In less structured polygonal environments the back faces of two-sided polygons may be visible and the resulting angular spans have the opposite direction with respect to the contours. In the cases of shared edges and vertices, all the incident polygons will have the same depth. Extra information (such as the normal to the face) is required to assure an invisible polygon does not incorrectly contribute a span. The latter is also an issue for non-convex vertices of closed polygons.

4 Implementation and Efficiency Issues

The naive vertex tracing algorithm does not have good asymptotic behavior. Assuming there are no efficiency structures for ray tracing the scene polygons, the running time could be as large as cubic in the number of scene polygons N (assuming a small upper bound on the number of vertices per polygon) due to the N^2 comparisons of edges to find apparent vertices, and a trace time of $O(N)$ for each vertex. Both can be significantly improved.

Most graphics systems with large numbers of polygons have some efficiency structure already built in. Ray tracing can be certainly made sub-linear, and in the proper environments can have a logarithmic expected running time. If this is the case, the bottleneck will be the N^2 comparison of the scene edges to find apparent vertices. One solution is to use a bounding volume hierarchy: if two volumes do not appear to intersect, then none of their contents can appear to intersect either. Our implementation use a bounding-spheres hierarchy, as the test for apparent intersection is very simple and fast. In our implementation we put a bounding sphere hierarchy on both the faces and the edges of the objects in the scene to accelerate ray tracing and the apparent intersection tests.

4.1 Single-Source Environments

In direct lighting, where there is only one emitting source, several improvements are possible. First, there are really only three distinct depths, for the background, source, and blocker which can be discretely represented. More significantly, only source vertices and vertices which otherwise appear inside the source need be traced. Performance can be improved by *shaft culling* [11] the scene against the source and only tracing un-culled polygons. Additionally the entire scene need not be clipped on the viewing plane—only the source polygon need be clipped.

4.2 Radiosity and Subdivided Environments

In radiosity systems the intrinsic scene polygons are subdivided into many smaller child polygons, often to the extent that the original polygons become vastly outnumbered. This can be exploited in a number of ways by the vertex tracing algorithm. First of all, the ray tracing phase is faster because only the parent polygons need to be ray-traced for visibility. Second, only edges coincident with silhouette edges of the original polygons can appear to intersect, so the number of tests for edge intersections is reduced. Finally, the vast majority of intrinsic vertices are vertices shared by sub-polygons. There is no background polygon in this case, so the angular spans will simply be the edges of the incident sub-polygons and these are straightforward to evaluate.

5 Floating-Point Imprecision and Cone Tracing

The discussion up to now has been entirely mathematical. In an implementation we are forced to contend with the anomalies of finite precision floating-point arithmetic. True conjunctive vertices generally do not occur. Instead the incident edges and vertices will tend to intersect each other at nearby points, or miss each other outright, resulting in erroneous angular spans. Also, nearly parallel edges can result in extraneous apparent intersections.

We solve the conjunctive vertex problem using a variant of *cone tracing* [1]. Rather than tracing a ray through a vertex, a thin cone is traced instead. All faces, edges and vertices which intersect the cone are "snapped" to the axis, forming an approximate conjunctive vertex (Figure 6). Cone tracing is of course more expensive than ordinary ray tracing. However, a second advantage of using bounding spheres is that the cone-sphere intersection test is fast, so tracing a small cone through the interior nodes of

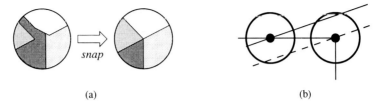

(a)   (b)

Fig. 6. (a) The view of a nearly conjunctive vertex down the axis of the cone; the vertices and edges are "snapped" to the axis. (b) Snapping asymmetry: the line is snapped to the intrinsic vertex cone, but the vertex is not snapped to the apparent vertex cone.

the hierarchy tree is not significantly more expensive than tracing a ray. Nonetheless, testing cone-polygon intersection is a good deal slower than testing ray-polygon intersection. On the whole, our implementation is slowed roughly by a factor of three from tracing cones rather than rays.

Cone tracing does not completely solve the problem of conjunctive vertices. Extra bookkeeping is required to prevent a conjunctive vertex from being counted more than once. Our implementation stores a flag along with each intrinsic vertex that is set when it is visited, or snapped to another vertex. For vertex-edge and edge-edge pairs we use a hash table which stores pairs of pointers. Each pair of objects, including all the edges incident on the intrinsic vertices, are stored in the hash table. The table and vertex flags must then be consulted before tracing a new vertex. The situation becomes even more complicated if a single edge is snapped at more than one point.

Notice that the tables need only be consulted if a conjunctive vertex has been found, and they are found automatically because the cone for each vertex must be traced through the scene anyway. Our implementation starts by assuming there are no conjunctive vertices. If an "unexpected" vertex or edge is found during a simple cone trace, then the evaluation is handed off to a slower more rigorous version which handles the conjunctive vertices properly. Pixels with conjunctive vertices number from a few to a few hundred in a typical scene, depending on the cone nape angle.

This brings up the issue of what nape angle to use. If the angle is too large, there will be too many conjunctive vertices, and larger snaps incur larger approximation error. If the angle is too small, numerical underflow problems surface. Depending on the scene, a nape angle of between 10^{-6} and 10^{-7} (radians) seems to work well.

6 Results

So far we have used the vertex tracing algorithm primarily as a "plug-in" to a ray tracer, as a function to compute lighting. The 512×512 pixel images in Figure 7 were all created using this method, with one sample per pixel. The running times include both setup and rendering time, including top-level ray tracing. All the images were rendered on a single-processor SGI Mips 195MHz R10K workstation with 512 Mbytes of RAM.

We have found that direct lighting in scenes involving a few hundred reasonably well distributed polygons can generally be rendered in under 30 seconds. The bottleneck occurs when there is a lot of shadow interaction, and this happens when the objects appear in front of each other or the source subtends a large solid angle.

Radiosity reconstruction using the algorithm is significantly slower, but faster than gathering from each patch as a single source. One advantage of the algorithm is that the coarse "solution", found in this case by repeated gathering, can be found very quickly as it involves gathering at a relatively small number of isolated points on the surfaces.

It is interesting to note that the aliasing artifacts on the scene geometry, due to the lack of super-sampling, do not appear on the shadow edges; those are already "soft" due to the laws of physics.

7   Conclusion

In this paper we have presented an alternative to Lambert's formula for the exact evaluation of irradiance due to uniformly emitting polygons. The expression is formulated in terms of the local behavior of the edges at the vertices projected onto an image plane. We described an algorithm exploiting this formulation, based on vertex tracing using angular spans at the vertices, applicable to direct lighting and radiosity gathering. The algorithm is relatively simple, incurs a low overhead, and is likely to fit into existing radiosity systems and their efficiency structures. The details of the efficiency of the algorithm have been discussed only loosely, partially because the performance (and implementation, for that matter) depends greatly on the structure available on the geometry of environment.

The algorithm in its purest form is for computing irradiance at isolated points. Performance could certainly be improved by exploiting coherence, or applying some of the many efficient visibility computation schemes in the literature. But there are advantages to having an algorithm tuned for diverse sampling. First, often this is all one needs. Radiosity solutions can be improved by computing exact values at certain points where the geometry becomes messy. Also, numerical derivative and integration methods often rely on exact function values at certain points. Finally, the independence of the algorithm makes it naturally suited to parallelization.

We do not expect this algorithm to immediately replace existing methods for shadow calculation. However, we hope the simplicity and relatively low overhead of the method will make it attractive in circumstances where other methods become cumbersome, such as in situations where it is undesirable to compute the entire visibility mesh or the entire visibility map.

Acknowledgments

This work was supported in part by DARPA (F33615-96-C-5621) and the NSF Science and Technology Center for Computer Graphics and Scientific Visualization (ASC-89-20219). Comments from Brian Smits, Bill Martin, Elaine Cohen and the reviewers were helpful in producing this paper and are gratefully acknowledged.

References

1. John Amanatides. Ray tracing with cones. In Hank Christiansen, editor, *Computer Graphics (SIGGRAPH '84 Proceedings)*, volume 18, pages 129–135, July 1984.
2. James Arvo. The irradiance Jacobian for partially occluded polyhedral sources. In *Siggraph '94*, pages 343–350, July 1994.
3. James Arvo. *Analytic Methods for Simulated Light Transport*. PhD thesis, Yale University, 1995.
4. P. Atherton, K. Weiler, and D. Greenberg. Polygon shadow generation. volume 12, pages 275–281, August 1978.

160

5. Michael F. Cohen and Donald P. Greenberg. The hemi-cube: a radiosity solution for complex environments. *Computer Graphics*, 19(3):31–40, July 1985. ACM Siggraph '85 Conference Proceedings.

6. Michael F. Cohen and John R. Wallace. *Radiosity and Realistic Image Synthesis*. Academic Press Professional, Cambridge, MA, 1993.

7. Robert L. Cook, Thomas Porter, and Loren Carpenter. Distributed ray tracing. In *Computer Graphics (SIGGRAPH '84 Proceedings)*, volume 18, pages 137–45, jul 1984.

8. George Dretakkis and Eugene Fiume. A fast shadow algorithm for area light sources using backprojection. In Andrew Glassner, editor, *Proceedings of SIGGRAPH '94 (Orlando, Florida, July 24–29, 1994)*, Computer Graphics Proceedings, Annual Conference Series, pages 223–230. ACM SIGGRAPH, ACM Press, July 1994. ISBN 0-89791-667-0.

9. G. Drettakis. *Structured Sampling and Reconstruction of Illumination for Image Synthesis*. PhD thesis, University of Toronto, 1994.

10. Frédo Durand, George Drettakis, and Claude Puech. The visibility skeleton: A powerful and efficient multi-purpose global visibility tool. In Turner Whitted, editor, *SIGGRAPH 97 Conference Proceedings*, Annual Conference Series, pages 89–100. ACM SIGGRAPH, Addison Wesley, August 1997. ISBN 0-89791-896-7.

11. Eric Haines and John Wallace. Shaft culling for efficient ray-traced radiosity. In *Eurographics Workshop on Rendering*, 1991.

12. David Hart, Philip Dutré, and Donald P. Greenberg. Direct illumination with lazy visibility evaluation. *Proceedings of SIGGRAPH 99*, pages 147–154, August 1999. ISBN 0-20148-560-5. Held in Los Angeles, California.

13. Paul Heckbert. Discontinuity meshing for radiosity. *Third Eurographics Workshop on Rendering*, pages 203–226, May 1992.

14. Daniel Lischinski, Filippo Tampieri, and Donald P. Greenberg. Discontinuity meshing for accurate radiosity. *IEEE Computer Graphics and Applications*, 12(6):25–39, November 1992.

15. T. Nishita and E. Nakamae. Continuous tone representation of three-dimensional objects taking account of shadows and interreflection. In *Computer Graphics* Proceedings, Annual Conference Series, ACM SIGGRAPH, pages 23–30, July 1985.

16. H. Plantinga and C.R. Dyer. Visibility, occlusion, and the aspect graph. *International Journal of Computer Vision*, 5(2):137–160, 1990.

17. François Sillion and Claude Puech. *Radiosity and Global Illumination*. Morgan Kaufmann, San Francisco, 1994.

18. Cyril Soler and François X. Sillion. Fast Calculation of Soft Shadow Textures Using Convolution. In Michael Cohen, editor, *SIGGRAPH 98 Conference Proceedings*, Annual Conference Series, pages 321–332. ACM SIGGRAPH, Addison Wesley, July 1998. ISBN 0-89791-999-8.

19. Michael M. Stark. Vertex-based formulations of irradiance from polygonal sources. Technical Report UUCS-00-012, Department of Computer Science, University of Utah, May 2000.

20. Michael M. Stark, Elaine Cohen, Tom Lyche, and Richard F. Riesenfeld. Computing exact shadow irradiance using splines. *Proceedings of SIGGRAPH 99*, pages 155–164, August 1999. ISBN 0-20148-560-5. Held in Los Angeles, California.

21. Seth Teller and Pat Hanrahan. Global visibility algorithms for illumination computations. In *Computer Graphics Proceedings, Annual Conference Series, 1993*, pages 239–246, 1993.

22. John R. Wallace, Kells A. Elmquist, and Eric A. Haines. A ray tracing algorithm for progressive radiosity. In Jeffrey Lane, editor, *Computer Graphics (SIGGRAPH '89 Proceedings)*, volume 23, pages 315–324, July 1989.

23. Alan Watt and Mark Watt. *Advanced Animation and Rendering Techniques*. ACM Press, 1992.

24. Andrew Woo, Pierre Poulin, and Alain Fournier. A survey of shadow algorithms. *IEEE Computer Graphics and Applications*, 10(6):13–32, November 1990.

Editors' Note: see Appendix, p. 404 for colored figures of this paper

Wavelet Radiosity on Arbitrary Planar Surfaces

Nicolas Holzschuch[1], François Cuny[2] and Laurent Alonso[1]

ISA research team
LORIA[3]
Campus Scientifique, BP 239
54506 Vandœuvre-les-Nancy CEDEX, France

Abstract. Wavelet radiosity is, by its nature, restricted to parallelograms or triangles. This paper presents an innovative technique enabling wavelet radiosity computations on planar surfaces of arbitrary shape, including concave contours or contours with holes. This technique replaces the need for triangulating such complicated shapes, greatly reducing the complexity of the wavelet radiosity algorithm and the computation time. It also gives a better approximation of the radiosity function, resulting in better visual results. Our technique works by separating the radiosity function from the surface geometry, extending the radiosity function defined on the original shape onto a simpler domain – a parallelogram – better behaved for hierarchical refinement and wavelet computations.

1 Introduction

Wavelet radiosity [12] is one of the most interesting technique for global illumination simulation. Recent research [7] has shown that higher order multi-wavelets ($\mathcal{M}_2$ and $\mathcal{M}_3$) are providing a very powerful tool for radiosity computations. Multi-wavelets can approximate the radiosity function efficiently with a small number of coefficients. As a consequence, they give a solution of better quality in a shorter time.

Multi-wavelets are defined only on parallelograms and triangles. This causes problems for radiosity computations on scenes coming from real world applications, such as architectural scenes, or CAD scenes. In such scenes, planar surfaces have a fairly complicated shape (see figure 1 and 12(a)). To do wavelet radiosity computations on such scenes, we have to tessellate these planar shapes into triangles and parallelograms, which results in a large number of input primitives (see figure 1(b)). Furthermore, this decomposition is purely geometrical and was not based on the illumination, yet it will influence our approximation of the radiosity function. In some cases, this geometric decomposition results in a poor illumination solution (see figure 2(a) and 11(a)).

In the present paper, we separate the radiosity function from the surface geometry. This enables us to exploit the strong approximating power of multi-wavelets for radiosity computations, with planar surfaces of arbitrary shape – including concave contours, contours with holes or disjoint contours. Our algorithm results in a better approximation of the radiosity function (see figure 2(b) and 11(b)) with a smaller number of input primitives, faster convergence and lower memory costs.

---

[1] INRIA Lorraine.

[2] Institut National Polytechnique de Lorraine.

[3] UMR n° 7503 LORIA, a joint research laboratory between CNRS, Institut National Polytechnique de Lorraine, INRIA, Université Henri Poincaré and Université Nancy 2.

162

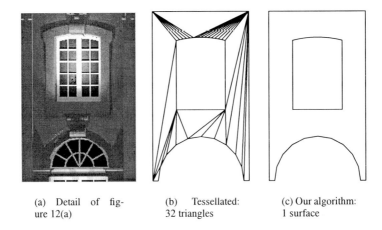

(a) Detail of figure 12(a)

(b) Tessellated: 32 triangles

(c) Our algorithm: 1 surface

Fig. 1. Planar surfaces can have a fairly complicated shape

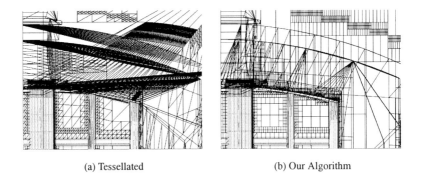

(a) Tessellated

(b) Our Algorithm

Fig. 2. Wavelet radiosity on arbitrary planar surfaces (see also figure 11)

Our algorithm extends the radiosity function defined on the original shape onto a simpler domain, better behaved for hierarchical refinement and wavelet computations. This extension of the radiosity function is defined to be easily and efficiently approximated by multi-wavelets. The wavelet radiosity algorithm is modified to work with this abstract representation of the radiosity function.

Our paper is organised as follows: in section 2, we will review previous work on radiosity with planar surfaces of complicated shape. Section 3 is a detailed explanation of our algorithm and of the modifications we brought to the wavelet radiosity algorithm. Section 4 presents the experiments we have conducted with our algorithm on different test scenes. Finally, section 5 presents our conclusions.

2 Previous work

The wavelet radiosity method was introduced by [12]. It is an extension of the radiosity method [11] and especially of the hierarchical radiosity method [13]. It allows the use of higher order basis functions in hierarchical radiosity.

In theory, higher order wavelets are a very powerful tool to approximate rapidly varying functions with little coefficients. In practice, they have several drawbacks, especially in terms of memory costs. In the early implementations of wavelets bases in the radiosity algorithm, these negative points were overcoming the positive theoretical advantages [19]. Recent research [7] has shown that using new implementation methods [2, 3, 7, 18, 21] we can actually exploit the power of higher order wavelets, and that their positive points are now largely overcoming the practical problems. They provide a better approximation of the radiosity function, with a small number of coefficients, resulting in faster convergence and smaller memory costs.

On the other hand, higher order wavelets, and especially multi-wavelets ($\mathcal{M}_2$ and $\mathcal{M}_3$) are defined as the tensor products of one-dimensional wavelets. As a consequence, they are defined over a square. The definition can easily be extended on parallelograms or triangles, but higher order wavelets are not designed to describe the radiosity function over complex surfaces.

Such complex surfaces can occur in the scenes on which we do global illumination simulations. Especially, scenes constructed using CAD tools such as CSG geometry or extrusion frequently contain complex planar surfaces, with curved boundaries or holes in them.

The simplest solution to do radiosity computations on such surfaces is to tessellate them into triangles, and to do radiosity computations on the result of the tessellation. This method has several negative consequences on the radiosity algorithm:

- It increases the number of input surfaces and the algorithmic complexity of the radiosity algorithm is linked to the square of the number of input surfaces.
- The tessellation is made before the radiosity computations and it influences these computations. It can prevent us from reaching a good illumination solution.
- The tessellation does not allow a hierarchical treatment over the original surface, only over each triangle created by the tessellation. We can not fully exploit the capabilities of hierarchical radiosity, and especially of wavelet radiosity.
- By artificially subdividing an input surface into several smaller surfaces, we are creating discontinuities. These discontinuities will have to be treated at some point in the algorithm.
- Tessellation can create poorly shaped triangles (see figure 1(b)), or slivers. These slivers can cause Z-buffer artifacts when we visualise the radiosity solution, and are harder to detect in visibility tests (*e.g.* ray-casting).

Some of these problems can be removed by using clustering [10, 16, 17]. In clustering, neighbouring patches are grouped together, into a *cluster*. The cluster receives radiosity and distributes it to the patches that it contains. On the other hand, current clustering strategies are behaving poorly in scenes with many small patches located close to each other [14]. It would probably be more efficient to apply clustering to the original planar surfaces instead of applying it to the result of the tessellation.

A better grouping strategy is face-clustering [20]. In face-clustering, neighbouring patches are grouped together according to their coplanarity. Yet even face-clustering depends on the geometry created by the tessellation. Furthermore, it would not allow us to exploit the strong approximating power of multi-wavelets.

```
• if the original planar shape is polygonal:
    – compute its convex hull (in linear time) using the
      chain of points [9].
    – compute the minimal enclosing parallelograms of
      the convex hull (in linear time) using Schwarz et
      al. [15].
    – if the previous algorithm gives several enclos-
      ing parallelograms, select the one that has angles
      closer to π/2.
• if the original shape is a curve, or contains curves:
    – approximate the curve by a polygon
    – compute the enclosing parallelogram of the poly-
      gon
    – compute the extrema of the curve in the directions
      of the parallelogram.
    – if needed, extend the parallelogram to include
      these extrema.
```

Fig. 3. Our algorithm for finding an enclosing parallelogram.

Bouatouch *et al.* [5] designed a method for discontinuity meshing and multi-wavelets. In effect, they are doing multi-wavelets computations over a non-square domain. However, their algorithm requires several expensive computations of push-pull coefficients. Our algorithm avoids these computations.

Baum *et al.* [1] designed a method for radiosity computations with arbitrary planar polygons, including polygons with holes. Their method ensures that the triangles produced are well-shaped, and suited for radiosity computations. Since it is designed for non-hierarchical radiosity, it is done in a preliminary step, before all radiosity computations. Our method, designed for wavelet radiosity, acts during the global illumination simulation, and adapts the refinement to the radiosity.

3   The Extended Domain Algorithm

In this section, we present our algorithm for wavelet radiosity computations on planar surfaces of arbitrary shape. Our algorithm separates the radiosity function from the surface geometry; we introduce a simple domain that will be used for radiosity computations. The radiosity function on the original surface is inferred from the radiosity on the simple domain.

Section 3.1 explains how we select an extended domain for our computations. In section 3.2, we describe how we extend the definition of the radiosity function over this domain. The extended domain is then used in a wavelet radiosity algorithm like an ordinary patch, with some specific adjustments. These adjustments are described in section 3.3.

3.1   Selection of an extended domain

The first step of our algorithm is the choice of an extended domain, which we will use for wavelet radiosity computations. This extended domain must obey two rules:

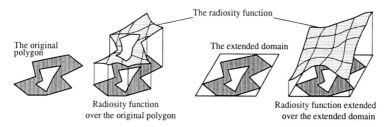

The original polygon

The radiosity function

The extended domain

Radiosity function
over the original polygon

Radiosity function extended
over the extended domain

Fig. 4. Extending the radiosity function over the extended domain.

- it must enclose the original shape,
- it must be well suited for wavelet radiosity computations.

Since multi-wavelets ($\mathcal{M}_2, \mathcal{M}_3$...) are defined as tensor products of one-dimensional wavelets, the second rule implies that the extended domain must be a parallelogram. Moreover, if this parallelogram is closer to a rectangle, there will be less distortions in the wavelet bases, resulting in a better approximation of the radiosity function. So we want the angles of the parallelogram to be close to $\frac{\pi}{2}$.

Since only radiosity computations made on the original shape are of interest, we also want the enclosing parallelogram to be as close as possible from the original shape.

Basically, any parallelogram satisfying these criterions could be used with our algorithm. The algorithm used in our implementation is described in figure 3. The key point is that this algorithm runs in linear time with respect to the number of vertices: the convex hull of a chain of points in 2D can be computed in linear time [9], and Schwarz's algorithm for the enclosing parallelogram is also linear [15].

3.2 Extending the radiosity function over this domain

Once we have an extended domain, we need to define the radiosity function over this domain. This extension of the radiosity function must obey two rules (see figure 4):

- it must be equal to the original radiosity function over the original domain
- it must be as simple and as smooth as possible, to be efficiently approximated by multi-wavelets.

The second point is crucial: we have to compute the radiosity function over the entire domain. Because of the hierarchical nature of wavelets, during the push-pull step radiosity values computed at one point of the domain can influence other points of the domain. So our extension of the radiosity function must be computed with the same precision regardless of whether we are on the original surface or not.

Since the discontinuities of the radiosity function and its derivatives only come from visibility discontinuities, we do not want to introduce more visibility discontinuities in our extension. We define an *extended visibility* function V': the visibility between a point Q in space and a point P on the extended domain is defined as the visibility between Q and P', where P' is defined as the closest point from P on the original planar surface:

$$V'(Q, P) = V(Q, P')$$

Of course, if P is already on the original planar surface, P' is equal to P. In that case, the extended visibility function is equal to the standard visibility function.

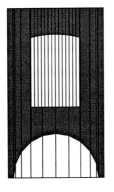

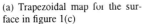

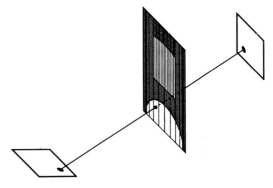

(a) Trapezoidal map for the surface in figure 1(c)

(b) Using the trapezoidal map for visibility queries

Fig. 5. Trapezoidal map of an arrangement of line segments

The radiosity function on the extended domain is then defined as the radiosity function, as computed by the wavelet radiosity algorithm, using this extended visibility function in the radiosity kernel.

3.3   Using the extended domain in the wavelet radiosity algorithm

In this section, we describe our adaptation of the wavelet radiosity algorithm to work with our extended domains. We use a standard wavelet radiosity algorithm [7, 21]. The core of the algorithm is left unchanged (refinement oracle, link storage). We will review here the points that require some special attention:

- reception and push-pull
- visibility
- emission
- refinement

Reception and Push-Pull. The wavelet radiosity algorithm is a hierarchical algorithm. During the push-pull step, radiosity values computed at one point of the patch can influence the representation of radiosity for the entire patch. Hence, we want the same precision for all radiosity computations over the entire patch.

For reception, the extended domain is therefore treated just like an ordinary patch. All parts of the extended domain are receiving radiosity, with the same precision, regardless of whether or not they belong to the original planar surface.

Similarly, we are doing the push-pull step over the entire extended domain, without any reference to the original surface. Since our extended domain is by design a parallelogram, instead of an ordinary polygon, we do not have to compute any expensive push-pull coefficients.

Visibility. For all the visibility computations, only the original planar surface can act as an occluder. The extended domain is never used in visibility computations.

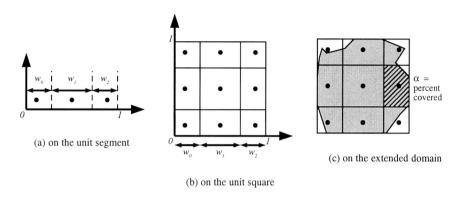

(a) on the unit segment

(b) on the unit square

(c) on the extended domain

Fig. 6. The weights of the quadrature points can be seen as the area of a *zone of influence*.

To detect if the original surface is actually occluding an interaction, we compute the trapezoidal map of an arrangement of line segments [4, 8] over the segments of the contour of the original surface (see figure 5). For each trapeze, we store its status – whether it is inside or outside of the original surface.

Using randomized algorithms, trapezoidal maps can be constructed in time $O(n \log n)$, where n is the number of vertices. Once constructed, they can be queried in $O(\log n)$ time. Since the construction algorithm is randomised, we shuffle the segments of the original surface before building the trapezoidal map.

Visibility queries in our radiosity algorithm are visibility queries between two points, either two quadrature points [7] or the closest point on the original surface from a quadrature point (see section 3.2). We compute the intersection between the ray joining these quadrature points and the supporting plane of the original surface, check whether the intersection point is inside the bounding box of the extended domain, then check whether it is inside the extended domain itself, then query the trapezoidal map to check if it is inside or outside the original surface.

Emission. During the reception, the entire extended domain has received illumination. The radiosity received over parts of the extended domain that are not included in the original surface does not exist in reality, and it should not be sent back into the scene. Otherwise, there would be an artificial creation of energy, violating the principle of conservation of energy.

Because of the hierarchical nature of the wavelet radiosity algorithm, it would be difficult to compute the exact part of this radiosity function that really exists. Instead, we act on the weights of the quadrature points.

In the wavelet radiosity algorithm, all the transfer coefficients between an emitter and a receiver are computed using quadratures. Quadratures allow the evaluation of a complex integral by sampling the function being integrated at the quadrature points, and multiplying the values by quadrature weights. Most implementations use Legendre-Gauss quadratures.

Since the weights are positive and their sum is equal to 1, you can visualise them as being the length of a *zone of influence* for the corresponding quadrature point (see figure 6(a) for the one dimension case). The same applies in two dimensions: the weights of the quadrature points can be seen as the area of a zone of influence (see

```
for each interaction s → r:
    for each quadrature point qᵢ on the emitter s
        Aᵢ = area of influence of qᵢ
        αᵢ ← percentage of Aᵢ that is inside the original emitter
        q′ᵢ = nearest point from qᵢ on the emitter
        for each quadrature point pⱼ on the receiver r
            p′ⱼ = nearest point on the receiver
            V(q′ᵢ, p′ⱼ) = visibility between q′ᵢ and p′ⱼ
            G(qᵢ, pⱼ) = radiosity kernel between qᵢ and pⱼ
            Bᵣ+ = αᵢwᵢwⱼBₛ(qᵢ)V(q′ᵢ, p′ⱼ)G(qᵢ, pⱼ)
        end for
    end for
```

Fig. 7. Pseudo-code for wavelet radiosity emission using the extended domain.

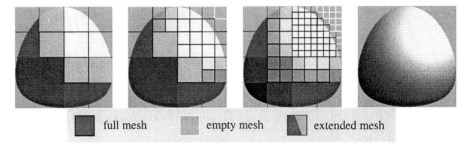

full mesh   empty mesh   extended mesh

Fig. 8. Refinement of the extended domain

figure 6(b)); the weight of quadrature point $p_{i,j}$ is $w_i w_j$. Please note that these zones of influence are not equal to the Voronoï diagram of the quadrature points.

We suggest an extension to the Gaussian quadrature to take into account the fact that the extended domain is not entirely covered by the actual emitter: the weight of a quadrature point is multiplied by the proportion of its area of influence that is actually covered by the emitter. For example, on figure 6(c), the weight of the quadrature point in the hashed area should be $w_1 w_2$. Since the fraction of its area of influence covered by the emitter is α, the weight used in the computation will be $\alpha w_1 w_2$.

Our method allows for a quick treatment of low precision interactions, and for high precision interactions, it tends toward the exact value. The more we refine an interaction, the more precision we get on the radiosity on the emitter. We also get the exact value if the zone of influence is entirely full or entirely empty.

In some cases, it can happen that the quadrature point falls outside the original emitter. We use these quadrature points anyway.

Figure 7 shows the pseudo-code for radiosity emission using the extended domain.

Refinement. As with the original wavelet radiosity algorithm, the extended domain can be subdivided if the interaction needs to be subdivided. The refinement oracle deals with the extended domain as it would deal with any other patch. Because of the hierarchical representation of the radiosity function in the wavelet radiosity algorithm, we must have the same precision on the radiosity function over the entire domain. The push-pull step can make parts of the domain that are not inside the original surface influence our representation of the radiosity function over the entire domain.

Name	# initial surfaces	after tessellation	ratio
Opera	17272	32429	1.88
Temple	7778	11087	1.43
Soda Hall	145454	201098	1.38

Table 1. Description of our test scenes

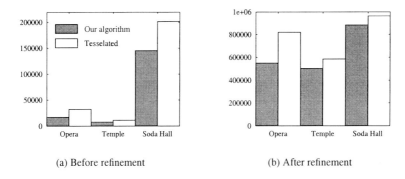

(a) Before refinement   (b) After refinement

Fig. 9. Number of patches in our test scenes

If the extended domain is refined, we deal with each part of the subdivided extended domain as we would deal with the original extended domain. Two special cases can appear (see figure 8):

- if the result of the subdivision does not intersect at all with the original planar surface, it is empty. Therefore it cannot play a role in the emission of radiosity, but we keep computing the radiosity function over this patch.
- if the result of the subdivision is totally included inside the original planar surface. In that case, we are back to the standard wavelet radiosity algorithm on parallelograms.

4 Experiments

We have tested our algorithm for wavelet radiosity on arbitrary planar surfaces on various test scenes (see figure 12 for images of our test scenes, and table 1 and figure 9(a) for their description). We were interested in a comparison between our algorithm and the standard wavelet radiosity algorithm, acting on parallelograms and triangles. All the computations were conducted on the same computer, a SGI Origin 2000, using a parallel version [6] of our wavelet radiosity algorithm [7, 21].

In all these test scenes, the number of surfaces after tesselation is less than twice the number of surfaces in the original scene. Much less than what could be expected from figure 1. Most of the initial surfaces in the scenes are parallelograms or triangles, and don't require tesselation.

The first result is that our algorithm gives better visual quality than doing wavelet radiosity computations on a tessellated surface (see figure 2 and 11). Our separation of the radiosity function from the surface geometry results in a better approximation of the radiosity function.

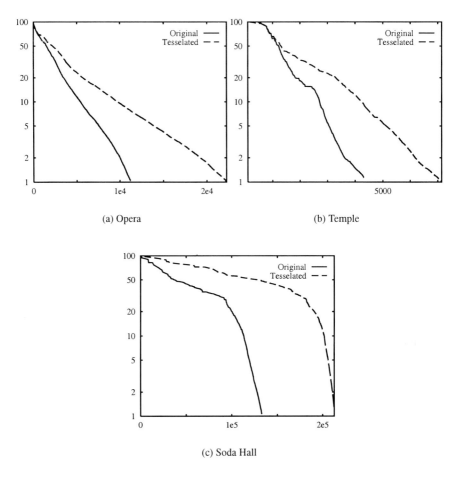

(a) Opera

(b) Temple

(c) Soda Hall

Fig. 10. Convergence rate (un-shot energy over initial energy) as a function of computation time (in seconds).

Beyond this important result, we were interested in a comparison of computation time and memory costs for both algorithms.

Obviously, our algorithm reduces the number of patches, and therefore the memory cost of the initial scene (see table 1 and figure 9(a)). According to our computations, it also reduces the number of patches in the final scene, although not in the same proportions (see figure 9(b)).

The later result was to be expected: the wavelet radiosity algorithm will refine the original scene a lot, resulting in numerous sub-patches. The number of patches in the scene after the radiosity computations is mainly linked to the complexity of the radiosity function itself, and not to the complexity of the scene. However, it appears that our algorithm results in more efficient refinement, since we reach convergence with a smaller number of patches. In some scenes, we can reach convergence with 30 % less patches.

The fact that our algorithm allows for more efficient refinement also appears in the computation times (see figure 10). In our experiments, we measure the energy initially present in the scene and the energy that hasn't yet been propagated in the scene. The ratio of these two measures tells us how far we are from complete convergence. Figure 10 displays this ratio as a function of the computation time, both for our algorithm and for the wavelet radiosity algorithm operating on a tessellated version of the scene. Our algorithm ensures a faster convergence on all our test scenes. The speedup is of about 30 %, which shows that acting on the original planar surface instead of the tessellated surface gives more efficient refinement.

5 Conclusion

In conclusion, we have presented a method to separate the radiosity function from the surface geometry. This method removes the need to tessellate complex planar surfaces, resulting in a more efficient global illumination simulation, with better visual quality. Our method results in faster convergence, with smaller memory costs.

In our future work, we want to extend this algorithm to discontinuity meshing. Discontinuity meshing introduces a geometric model of the discontinuities of the radiosity function and its derivatives, the *discontinuity mesh*. The discontinuity mesh provides optimal meshing for radiosity computations near the discontinuities. The discontinuity mesh is a complicated structure, and it can influence radiosity computations away from the discontinuities, for example because of triangulation. We want to use our algorithm to smoothly integrate the discontinuity mesh in the natural subdivision for multi-wavelet radiosity, removing the need to tesselate the discontinuity mesh.

We also want to explore a combination of our algorithm with clustering techniques. First, our algorithm could be used to group together neighbouring coplanar patches in a natural way. This would help the clustering strategy [14] and give a more accurate result. Second, we would like to integrate our algorithm with face-clustering, bringing multi-wavelets into face-clusters.

Finally, our separation of the radiosity function from the surface geometry could also be used to compute radiosity using multi-wavelets on curved surfaces. There are several parametric surfaces for which the limits of the parametric space are not square. We suggest using our algorithm to enclose these limits into a square limit, making it easier for multi-wavelets.

6 Acknowledgements

Permission to use the Soda Hall model[4] was kindly given by Prof. Carlo Sequin.

Jean Claude Paul has started and motivated all this research. The authors would like to thank him for his kind direction, support and encouragements.

References

1. D. R. Baum, S. Mann, K. P. Smith, and J. M. Winget. Making Radiosity Usable: Automatic Preprocessing and Meshing Techniques for the Generation of Accurate Radiosity Solutions. *Computer Graphics (ACM SIGGRAPH '91 Proceedings)*, 25(4):51–60, July 1991.
2. P. Bekaert and Y. Willems. Error Control for Radiosity. In *Rendering Techniques '96 (Proceedings of the Seventh Eurographics Workshop on Rendering)*, pages 153–164, New York, NY, 1996. Springer-Verlag/Wien.

---

[4]The Soda Hall model is available on the web, at `http://www.cs.berkeley.edu/~kofler`.

172

3. P. Bekaert and Y. D. Willems. Hirad: A Hierarchical Higher Order Radiosity Implementation. In *Proceedings of the Twelfth Spring Conference on Computer Graphics (SCCG '96)*, Bratislava, Slovakia, June 1996. Comenius University Press.

4. J.-D. Boissonnat and M. Yvinec. *Algorithmic Geometry*. Cambridge University Press, 1998.

5. K. Bouatouch and S. N. Pattanaik. Discontinuity Meshing and Hierarchical Multiwavelet Radiosity. In W. A. Davis and P. Prusinkiewicz, editors, *Proceedings of Graphics Interface '95*, pages 109–115, San Francisco, CA, May 1995. Morgan Kaufmann.

6. X. Cavin, L. Alonso, and J.-C. Paul. Parallel Wavelet Radiosity. In *Second Eurographics Workshop on Parallel Graphics and Visualisation*, pages 61–75, Rennes, France, Sept. 1998.

7. F. Cuny, L. Alonso, and N. Holzschuch. A novel approach makes higher order wavelets really efficient for radiosity. *Computer Graphics Forum (Eurographics 2000 Proceedings)*, 19(3), Sept. 2000. To appear. Available from http://www.loria.fr/~holzschu/Publications/paper20.pdf.

8. O. Devillers, M. Teillaud, and M. Yvinec. Dynamic location in an arrangement of line segments in the plane. *Algorithms Review*, 2(3):89–103, 1992.

9. H. Edelsbrunner. *Algorithms in Combinatorial Geometry*, volume 10 of *EATCS Monographs on Theoretical Computer Science*. Springer-Verlag, Nov. 1987.

10. S. Gibson and R. J. Hubbold. Efficient hierarchical refinement and clustering for radiosity in complex environments. *Computer Graphics Forum*, 15(5):297–310, Dec. 1996.

11. C. M. Goral, K. E. Torrance, D. P. Greenberg, and B. Battaile. Modelling the Interaction of Light Between Diffuse Surfaces. *Computer Graphics (ACM SIGGRAPH '84 Proceedings)*, 18(3):212–222, July 1984.

12. S. J. Gortler, P. Schroder, M. F. Cohen, and P. Hanrahan. Wavelet Radiosity. In *Computer Graphics Proceedings, Annual Conference Series, 1993 (ACM SIGGRAPH '93 Proceedings)*, pages 221–230, 1993.

13. P. Hanrahan, D. Salzman, and L. Aupperle. A Rapid Hierarchical Radiosity Algorithm. *Computer Graphics (ACM SIGGRAPH '91 Proceedings)*, 25(4):197–206, July 1991.

14. J. M. Hasenfratz, C. Damez, F. Sillion, and G. Drettakis. A practical analysis of clustering strategies for hierarchical radiosity. *Computer Graphics Forum (Eurographics '99 Proceedings)*, 18(3):C–221–C–232, Sept. 1999.

15. C. Schwarz, J. Teich, A. Vainshtein, E. Welzl, and B. L. Evans. Minimal enclosing parallelogram with application. In *Proc. 11th Annu. ACM Sympos. Comput. Geom.*, pages C34–C35, 1995.

16. F. Sillion. A Unified Hierarchical Algorithm for Global Illumination with Scattering Volumes and Object Clusters. *IEEE Transactions on Visualization and Computer Graphics*, 1(3), Sept. 1995.

17. B. Smits, J. Arvo, and D. Greenberg. A Clustering Algorithm for Radiosity in Complex Environments. In *Computer Graphics Proceedings, Annual Conference Series, 1994 (ACM SIGGRAPH '94 Proceedings)*, pages 435–442, 1994.

18. M. Stamminger, H. Schirmacher, P. Slusallek, and H.-P. Seidel. Getting rid of links in hierarchical radiosity. *Computer Graphics Journal (Proc. Eurographics '98)*, 17(3):C165–C174, Sept. 1998.

19. A. Willmott and P. Heckbert. An empirical comparison of progressive and wavelet radiosity. In J. Dorsey and P. Slusallek, editors, *Rendering Techniques '97 (Proceedings of the Eighth Eurographics Workshop on Rendering)*, pages 175–186, New York, NY, 1997. Springer Wien. ISBN 3-211-83001-4.

20. A. Willmott, P. Heckbert, and M. Garland. Face cluster radiosity. In *Rendering Techniques '99*, pages 293–304, New York, NY, 1999. Springer Wien.

21. C. Winkler. *Expérimentation d'algorithmes de calcul de radiosité à base d'ondelettes*. Thèse d'université, Institut National Polytechnique de Lorraine, 1998.

Editors' Note: see Appendix, p. 405 for colored figures of this paper

Hierarchical Instantiation for Radiosity

Cyril Soler

Max Planck Institut für Informatik

François Sillion

iMAGIS-GRAVIR/IMAG

Abstract.
We present the concept of hierarchical instantiation for radiosity. This new method enables an efficient, yet accurate determination of the illumination in very large scenes, where similar objects are replaced by instances of the same element. Instances are equipped with suitable radiative properties and are used to replace large amounts of geometry at multiple levels of the scene hierarchy. In essence, our algorithm replaces a single very large hierarchical radiosity problem by a collection of hierarchical radiosity problems within small sets of objects at a time, at several hierarchical levels. We prove the applicability of our method on architectural scenes with replicated geometry. However we reach the best time and memory gains on plant models thanks to the high degree of self-similarity in such kinds of scenes. This allows us to compute lighting simulations on scenes including a very large number of polygons in a short time on machines with limited memory.

1 Introduction

In scenes that include a large number of input geometric primitives, hierarchical radiosity algorithms are rapidly limited by their memory and computation costs.

We propose a new radiosity algorithm based on the concept of hierarchical instantiation, which allows this calculation to be performed while dramatically reducing the resources needed as compared to previous approaches. The hierarchical instantiation idea takes advantage of the inherent repetition and structure in a scene, while allowing full differentiation in terms of lighting conditions.

The notion of instantiation refers to the replacement of similar parts of the complete geometrical model by copies of a single geometry. This is commonly used in ray tracing algorithms, where only a geometric transformation needs to be stored with each instance, all ray intersections being computed against the unique geometrical model common to all instances. In a more general approach, the approximate self-similarity in large models lets us use instances to replace parts of the geometry that are largely, although not exactly, identical. At first sight, instantiation does not seem really suitable for radiosity calculations because geometrically similar objects may receive totally different illumination. Therefore our algorithm cleanly separates the representation of the light distribution from the geometry management. Thanks to a well-chosen computation mechanism and associated traversal of the hierarchical structure, only a fraction of the total geometry ever needs to be present in memory, making the algorithm practical even for very large models such as plants. Instantiation also appears to be a promising approach to radiosity simulations in very complex architectural scenes involving some repetition.

The remainder of the paper is organized as follows: we first review existing approaches for lighting simulation with instantiation. Section 3 presents the hierarchical instantiation algorithm in detail, and analyzes the expected benefits of the approach. In Section 4 we propose a complete set of solutions to the different problems arising in the radiosity simulation using hierarchical instantiation. Section 5 presents our results, including the validation of the hierarchical instantiation algorithm and the evaluation of its performance.

2 Previous work

The general principle of *instantiation* is to replace the geometric definition of several identical objects by pointers to a unique original object and the geometric transformation needed to map the original to the instanced object.

Ray-tracing instanced objects simply involves transforming the ray back to the coordinate system of the original object before computing the intersection. Complex models can be ray traced with little memory, since only the geometric representations of original objects must be kept in memory [SB87, KK86]. Applied to plants [Har92] or to fractal objects [BW94] the gain is even more interesting, because the self similarity of such models appears at different levels of their hierarchical representation.

When the objects to be instanced are not exactly identical to a given original object (as is the case for most scenes), approximate instantiation can be used to save memory while ensuring a similar visible result. This has been used to render images of giant outdoor scenes [DHL+98].

Instancing objects for radiosity simulation is a much more difficult problem, because radiosity operates on a representation of illumination traditionally attached to geometry (typically in the form of a mesh). Ouhyoung [OCL96] defined the concept of *re-usable radiosity objects* to share precomputed geometric information between instances of a given object, in order to accelerate the computation of visibility and of the form factors involving these objects. However, the representation of radiosity inside different instances of the same object can not be shared, because it not only depends on internal characteristics of the object but also on its position in the scene. Besides, when dealing with approximate instantiation the geometry of the original can not simply be used as a support geometry for the instances. Therefore this method requires the complete model of all similar objects to be present in memory.

An exception to this rule exists, however, for the case where the radiosity of the instance is not that much influenced by its position in the scene, and it can therefore be considered constant. This is the case for the *canned light sources* objects [HKSS98], for which an inside radiosity solution is precomputed and stored with the model. Such an object can be further instanced and used in any radiosity solution.

3 Hierarchical Instantiation Radiosity

3.1 Using instances in radiosity

Radiosity algorithms compute an explicit representation of illumination, typically associated with the geometry in the form of a mesh. Copies of a given object each have their own, unique illumination. Instantiation for radiosity is therefore more elaborate than for simpler rendering techniques, since it should differentiate between the geometry (that is easily shared) and the illumination (that varies from one instance to another).

Hierarchical radiosity algorithms, especially those using clustering, try to avoid considering the inherent complexity of energy exchanges by computing transfers at fairly high levels of a scene hierarchy. However a complete traversal of the scene is needed to estimate the energy emitted or received by a cluster with any accuracy [SAG94]. The use of meta-objects, or impostors, has been proposed to avoid this descent in the hierarchy, and instead perform the computation with fairly large (and simple) objects [RPV93, OCL96].

This is a very good idea, resulting in important savings, but in order to guarantee a sufficient accuracy these meta-objects should be equipped with very precise radiometric information: they should respond appropriately (i.e. just like their actual contents would do) to incident light, and allow accurate determination of light transmitted through their contents.

An instance should therefore be able to participate in radiosity calculations without accessing its geometric content. In general, for each instance, this requires the knowledge of (a) an outgoing radiance distribution [SDS95], (b) a bidirectional scattering phase function to convert incoming energy into outgoing radiance, and (c) a transmittance function. The phase function of an instanciable object can be sampled by placing an external light source for a number of incoming directions and recording the outgoing radiance after solving for a global energy balance inside its geometry. To compute the outgoing distribution of light of an instance due to incoming energy along a link, we multiply its phase function for the incident direction by the irradiance along the link. For that reason, the phase function can also be called the *reflectance* function of the instance, as an extension to its usual definition on simple surfaces.

Obviously, these characteristics are quite costly to handle, both in terms of computation time and in terms of storage. Meta-objects are therefore especially useful when a sufficient number of such identical objects are present in the scene, since all instances share the same intrinsic characteristics. Phase and transmittance functions are precomputed and stored, and can be accessed whenever needed, to instance a part of the geometry of the scene that corresponds to it.

In summary, instantiation is a key element in making the accurate characterization of simplified objects viable. It is realized by identifying objects (in fact, clusters) that have a similar behavior in terms of light emission, reflection and transmission. Note that the radiometric behavior of an instance can therefore be an approximation of reality, just like its geometry is approximately that of the original. A flexible trade-off is possible between the accuracy of the representation and its compactness, largely controlled by the degree of auto-similarity in the model.

After a radiosity solution is obtained at the level of the instances, the illumination of objects *inside* the instances must still be determined. This involves a local hierarchical radiosity solution in which the contained geometry is subjected to the incident illumination computed for the considered instance. A major potential difficulty is that the contents of the instance might still be too complex to allow a hierarchical radiosity calculation. The hierarchical instantiation algorithm described below provides an elegant and efficient solution to this problem.

3.2 Hierarchical Instantiation

Our aim is to ensure that hierarchical radiosity calculations are always performed on a fairly small scene. To this end, we explore the possibility of creating instances at various hierarchical levels. This is possible whenever different scales of similarity exist in the model. (Plant models are the perfect example of such a property; we will therefore illustrate the idea with the case of plants in the results section).

Structure of the hierarchy. We want to reveal the redundancy present at different scales of the scene hierarchy. This information can easily be extracted from the architecture of plants for instance and we anticipate that it will be possible to obtain it in large-scale architectural scenes as well. If the cluster hierarchy made from *instantiable* clusters still has a large branching factor its efficiency toward hierarchical radiosity must be improved by inserting new levels of (non instantiable) clusters into the hierarchy. This can be done using a constrained clusterizer [HDSD99].

As a result, the entire scene can be described as a hierarchy of clusters, in which instantiable clusters appear at various levels (possibly one included in the other). However, during any call to the computation of a *local* solution using hierarchical radiosity, the part of the hierarchy that is considered always consists of a cluster hierarchy whose leaves are either non opened instances or polygons.

Hierarchical solution. The scene hierarchy is first loaded into memory with a depth limited to the first level of instances. Then it is processed by the hierarchical radiosity solver, which involves iteratively establishing (refining) links between clusters and propagating energy until convergence. Refinement of the links is limited to the level of instances, since their geometry is not available at this time. However the resulting solution is still much more accurate than if we had performed a hierarchical radiosity solution on the entire scene while limiting the link refinement to the level of the instances. This is due to the fairly precise representation of each instance's "phase function" or general reflectance property, which is precomputed and embodies the effect of light propagation and scattering inside the instance. In addition, it should be noted that no self-links are established on instances, because their reflectance function already accounts for internal light scattering.

We then traverse the scene hierarchy, and focus on each instance encountered in the following manner: (a) form in a new hierarchy by loading down to the next instantiation level the geometry contained in the instance, (b) compute a local radiosity solution inside the new hierarchy (with a recursive application of the algorithm) and (c) destroy the new hierarchy and replace it back with the instance. Therefore we essentially perform a depth-first traversal of the scene, always focusing on a given hierarchy of instances.

When we reach a level with no instances below, the algorithm is equivalent to hierarchical radiosity with clustering, and a complete solution is available for the current branch of the scene hierarchy, taking into account contributions from the entire scene.

The solution for the current portion of the hierarchy is accessible at this stage only, because its supporting geometry will be deleted when closing the instance. We thus render the corresponding polygons into an off-screen buffer (or output the results to a file), thereby progressively forming the image during the traversal of the scene.

Opening instances. We detail here the operations involved in the "local" solution computed when opening an instance in the recursive traversal. This process is illustrated in Figure 1. On the left we see a solution computed at a given level. Oval shapes represent objects or clusters, while rectangles represent instances. Links are indicated by arrows, and have been created at varying levels of the cluster hierarchy.

When the lower-right instance is opened, we build a hierarchy with its contents, as shown on the right-hand side of the figure. In order to properly account for all incoming light, we create copies of all links that previously arrived on the instance (marked using dashed lines on the figure) and attach them to the root of the new hierarchy. We also add a self-link to the root if no self link exist on any parent levels, to account for all internal exchanges [Sil95].

We can then apply the solution procedure outlined above, that is first solve for radiosity, then traverse the hierarchy to open instances and recurse. The right side of Figure 1 illustrates the radiosity solution, in the opened level: Dashed links correspond to links that previously arrived at the instance level, and have been refined. Internal links issued from the refinement of the added self link are also represented. The recursion would then continue into the smaller instances before returning to the left-hand situation and opening the other instance.

Note that refinement is constrained in that only elements belonging to the considered hierarchy may be subdivided (either as emitters or receivers). Gathering and push/pull operations are also applied to the local hierarchy only, essentially treating all elements external to this hierarchy as fixed light sources.

Discussion. Our algorithm essentially gains by neglecting the correlation between objects lying in different instances at the same hierarchical level. For two such sibling instances, no link can ever be created between one object from each, because the contents of both instances are never simultaneously present in memory. This ensures that every local solution only involves a small number of objects, at the expense of a small approximation. For the

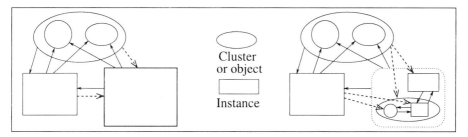

Fig. 1. Two consecutive stages of the recursive computation of the radiosity solution in the hierarchy of instances.

same reason, a complete solution is never present in memory, although every part of the global solution is available at some stage of the calculation. This explains why any results such as images or radiosity values written to a file must be output during the calculation as mentioned earlier.

The same result could be achieved in a normal radiosity algorithm, by preventing the refinement of an emitter if it is an "instantiable" object different from the receiver. However the global accuracy would be lower unless the emitter is already refined enough to obtain a high-quality representation of its internal light distribution. Since the phase functions of the original instances are pre-computed and stored, more computation time can be invested in this process than typically done in a hierarchical radiosity computation. For instance the effects of internal visibility in emitting clusters, which are usually not computed for cost reasons [SD95], are accounted for in our general reflectance functions (See Section 4).

The pseudo-code on Figure 2 summarizes the algorithm.

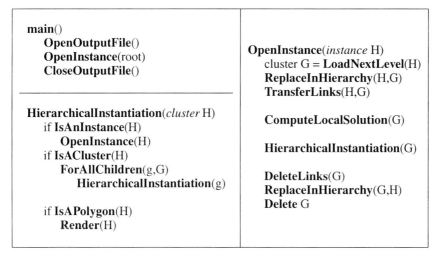

Fig. 2. Pseudo code for the radiosity instantiation algorithm. The generic *Render* procedure replaces any output of the information as rendering the polygon to an off-screen buffer, or saving its radiosity to a file.

3.3 Cost considerations

Simple recursion arguments allow us to evaluate the cost of our algorithm in terms of storage and computation cost. Let us denote the number of instantiation levels by k, the number of elements at each instantiation level by N, and the number of these elements that are instances by p. This model is very simple because it assumes a uniform branching factor among all levels of the hierarchy of instances, and a uniform proportion of instances and polygons at each level of the scene hierarchy. Using these characteristics, the total number of polygons in the scene is :

$$n = (N - p)(1 + p + \ldots + p^{k-1}) + p^k N = O(p^k N) \tag{1}$$

Gain in memory. Let us denote the memory size of a polygon, an instance and an original (instanced) object by ε, I and o.

Assuming r original objects are used to create the p instances, the memory footprint of the scene at the top level of calculation is :

$$M_{inst}(1) = (N - p)\varepsilon + pI + ro$$

Since the algorithm only loads the geometry of the branch of the hierarchy it is descending into, the maximum memory requirement is reached at the bottom of the hierarchy, where it is :

$$M_{inst}(k) = k(N - p)\varepsilon + kpI + kro \tag{2}$$

For the ideal case of a well balanced hierarchy of instances, the memory cost is thus logarithmic in terms of the total number of polygons in the scene. In any case, it is much less than the $O(n\varepsilon)$ memory size of the model itself.

As an example taken from our implementation and real data, consider $o = 1,100$ bytes (an original object holds two sampled directional functions at 528 bytes each), $\varepsilon = 150$ bytes (this rather large size accounts for geometry, radiometric and subdivision information) and $I = 200$ bytes (in our implementation, instances are also clusters and thus contain inherited information). For the tree presented in Figure 5, we have $n = 119,000$, $k = 4$, $r = 5$, $N \approx 30$ and $p \approx 8$. The expected memory size given by Expression 2 is 48 kb, which is much less than $n\varepsilon = 15,085Kb$, the expected size of the entire scene.

Although these numbers do not translate directly into required memory sizes, because of the missing constants and various fixed costs, we will see in Section 5 that a large memory reduction is observed, the gain increasing with scene complexity. It actually becomes feasible to simulate very large scenes that simply could not be treated by previous methods.

Since the accuracy threshold does not change when recursively computing the local solutions, the maximum number of links in memory can be estimated by the number of links that contribute to the illumination of a leaf element in a classical hierarchical radiosity solution on the entire scene, multiplied by the number of leaf elements at the lowest level, $e.g$ $O(N \log n)$. This is much less than the $O(n \log n)$ links of the normal clustering radiosity method.

In scenes with limited instantiation depth ($e.g$ k is small) the logarithmic equivalent does not hold anymore. In the worst case, the gain in memory is the number of instances times the ratio between the memory cost of an instance and the actual geometry.

Computation cost. We consider that a hierarchical radiosity solution in a scene of n elements equipped with a well balanced hierarchy can be performed in $O(n \log n)$ time.

Let $C(i)$ denote the cost of our algorithm for solving level i, then we get :

$$C(i) = N \log(N) + pC(i - 1) \quad \text{and} \quad C(1) = N \log(N)$$

The cost is thus :

$$\begin{aligned} C(k) &= N \log(N) \left(1 + p + \ldots + p^k\right) \\ &= O(p^k N \log(N)) \end{aligned}$$

Considering that $n = O(p^k N)$, the value $C(k)$ appears to be equivalent to $O(n \log(N))$, which is very close to the cost of the classical hierarchical radiosity algorithm. However, our algorithm is faster in practice, as will be discussed in the results section.

4 Implementation

Precomputation and use of instance information. In the general case, we use a directional distribution to represent the transmittance information of an instance. We precompute it using graphics hardware, by rendering the concerned object off-screen in each direction sample and recording the percentage of the bounding box of the object that is not masked by the object itself. In some cases, the transmittance information can preferably be accessed through a simplified geometric representation of the real geometry, especially if the instances replace very simple objects. This representation can still be approximative since we allow the instantiation of not necessarily identical objects.

We compute the phase function by performing a series of accurate lighting simulations for directional incoming illuminations, and recording the distribution of outgoing light. Each lighting simulation is done using hierarchical radiosity. We record the outgoing light by rendering the illuminated object in an off-screen buffer and measuring the average values of pixels in the resulting image, so as to obtain an average radiance value per unit of projected area. One advantage of this technique is to account for self-occlusion for the outgoing light as well as for the incoming light in the objects. However, if instances are used to replace very complex geometry this approach can be costly. In such a case, a recursive application of the Hierarchical Instantiation algorithm with limited depth could be used to improve the computation time of the phase functions. An other possibility is to use generic phase functions, which works well for plant models.

To compute the contribution of an emitting instance to the radiosity of an element in a given direction θ, we then multiply its emmited radiance by the projected area $a(\theta)$ of its geometry in the direction of the receiving element. This projected area is easily deduced from the value of the directional transmittance $\tau(\theta)$, and the projected area $A(\theta)$ of the instance's bounding box:

$$a(\theta) = (1 - \tau(\theta))A(\theta)$$

Visibility computation. Computing visibility using exact geometric information is only viable for clusters that contain a small number of polygons. Therefore the geometric information of simple objects can be kept with the original cluster, for use by all the instances. At higher levels, a formulation based on extinction coefficients [Sil95] works well for isotropic clusters, like the ones we find on plant models. For all other cases, a more complex representation of visibility can be needed depending on the geometric configuration of the energy transfer it is involved in. This can be achieved using a simplified geometry. Indeed, even a highly decimated mesh produces much more realistic shadows than a box equipped with directional transmittance.

When computing the visibility through a blocker that is not an instance, the visibility is recursively computed down to next instances or polygons.

Instantiation policy. The basic principle of instantiation requires that a sufficient number of copies of an instantiable cluster exist in the scene to counterbalance the cost of keeping general reflectance functions of original clusters in the scene. It should be noticed that exact geometric similarity between objects instanced by the same original is not necessarily needed: it is sufficient that they only have similar radiometric properties at the level of the hierarchical radiosity solution they are involved in. After being opened, the instances are automatically replaced by more appropriate geometry. This allows us to instance branches of a plant for instance, whose geometry would differ in details but that still would have the same global shape. In general, a more complete approach would consist in precomputing and storing the necessary information to obtain a bound on the error for energy exchanges that involve approximate instances, and use it to decide whether to use a different but more appropriate original cluster to reduce the error.

Instancing at all levels of the hierarchy is not necessarily a good idea: In some cases in which clusters are too close to each other, replacing both of them by instances would suppress any interaction between pairs of sub-elements in these clusters. This is a common cause of error in hierarchical radiosity algorithms. Besides, clusters that lay too close to each others tend to be associated to poorly approximated form factors, which can cause divergence of the algorithm when a number of them sum up to too large a value. To correct both problems, our implementation allows to skip levels of instantiation to increase accuracy, at the expense of computation time and additional memory cost.

In our first implementation, this strategy is entirely user-defined, which is not acceptable if we want to be able to treat complex scenes automatically. It would also be a good idea to have the instantiation policy depend on the memory currently available by caching instance memory: the program could be allowed to skip instantiation levels whenever needed provided that sufficient memory is available.

5 Results

5.1 Application to classical architectural scenes

In Figure 6 (*See appendix*) we present a solution on a "classical radiosity scene" of $55,000$ polygons, in which all objects have been instanced (*e.g* 24 chairs, 3 tables, 3 orchids and 4 plants. Computation times for each of the four phase functions took between 1mn and 10mn). To be able to generate correct shadows for the instances the transmittance function is computed using a unique and shared copy of the geometry of each object. Note that shadows of external geometry (including instances) on instances themselves are also correctly generated (consider for instance the shadows on tables cast by the orchids).

The solution itself is computed in 8mn using 15MB of memory, whereas the computation time and memory cost of hierarchical radiosity is 45mn/67MB. However, it could be possible to improve the gain in this particular scene, using a higher depth of instantiation on the two plant models but we did not have access to their botanical structure. This raises the question of automatically finding potential instances in a scene.

5.2 Application to plant models

Hierarchical radiosity without clustering is of little help in the case of plants, mainly because the polygons that define the models are always very small, thus raising the cost of initial linking. Radiosity methods with clustering [SAG94, Chr95, Sil95] seem to be very promising since they have a much smaller computation cost, but they still require considering the entire model simultaneously in order to establish links between clusters, which becomes unpracticable for very large plants. Other calculation algorithms based on statistical or continuous approximations have been proposed [Gre89, MMKW97, Gov95], but are ill-suited to simulations at the scale of a few plants, which is more typical in virtual reality and computer graphics applications.

Conversely, our approach works very well because of the high degree of self similarity inside the plant models, and because instances are able to share properties such as phase functions. We observe indeed that phase functions for a given kind of axis (branch, whole plant) tend to reach a "limit" as its age increases. This allows us to instantiate older axes using the precomputed information of medium aged ones. Otherwise, precomputing the phase function of very complex objects (like old trees) using a brute force approach can be even longer than computing the solution for the scene itself. Finally, directional transmittance functions work pretty well because the transmittance of such kind objects is, to a large extent, uniform at the scale of the energy transfers.

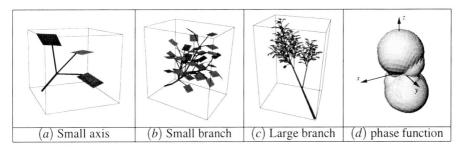

| *(a)* Small axis | *(b)* Small branch | *(c)* Large branch | *(d)* phase function |

Fig. 3. *(a)* to *(c)* : Axes corresponding to three different levels of possible instantiation. Each level also corresponds to a cluster in the hierarchy that defines the tree. *(d)* represents the reflectance function for the axis in *(a)*. The two main bulbs come from the shape of the bounding box and the smaller ones from the common orientation of the polygons in the cluster. See text also.

We import our scenes as a depth-first description of the cluster hierarchy and the geometry. In the case of plants, each cluster (before constraining the hierarchy) corresponds to a plant axis in the architectural sense [dREF+88], and contains information about the kind of axis and its age. We use this information as a criterion of similarity between clusters that can be instantiated. The clusters in Figure 3 represent different levels of instances used for the images of Figures 5 and 7 (*See appendix*). With each of these clusters is also stored its position and orientation in space. Whenever it is deemed possible to instantiate a cluster, its geometric definition is skipped and replaced by an instance with the correct geometrical transformation.

In our current implementation, phase functions only account for incoming light direction in the instances, the outgoing radiance per unit of projected area is assumed to be uniform. This allows us to store only radiosity values on instances instead of complete directional radiance distributions. While incurring some approximations, this allowed us to test our algorithm in a first approach, and does not depend on any limitations of the algorithm itself. Such a phase function is represented in Figure 3d that corresponds to the cluster in Figure 3a.

Finally, leaves are modeled by two-sided polygons with diffuse transparency. The radiosity on one side is computed as the sum of two terms: (1) the irradiance on the same side multiplied by its reflectance, and (2) the irradiance on the other side multiplied by a diffuse transmittance coefficient.

5.3 Comparison with hierarchical radiosity

In Figure 5 (*See appendix*) we compare the results given by our radiosity algorithm to that of a hierarchical radiosity simulation with clustering, performed with the same set of parameters but without instantiation. Three light sources are used (the 3rd one is masked by the tree). The model of the tree is a 30-year old poplar tree (*populus*) consisting of 119 000 polygons. Experiments have been conducted on a *SGI Origin2000* computer.

Although the results seem identical at first sight, some subtle differences can be found, that mainly concern a variation of the energy in some parts of the plant where instantiation has been used. This is due to the fact that the radiosity stored in the instances is not directional but represented as a single value. On the *right* image for instance, the light arriving from the light source on the center of the tree has been distributed behind the instance because of this approximation. As expected by our estimations, the gain is very important (15 times less memory in this particular case), especially considering that there are fixed memory costs (Our radiosity program requires a fixed amount of 5MB of RAM).

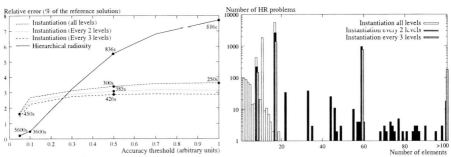

Fig. 4. Left: L^2 *error in percentage of the maximum value of the reference solution (computed using hierarchical radiosity) for various values of the accuracy threshold used in link refinement. The numbers in black on the curves indicate computation times in seconds.* Right: *histogram of the number of hierarchical radiosity solutions on local hierarchies with variable numbers of leaf elements. When instancing at fewer levels, hierarchical radiosity computations tend to involve more elements.*

An important gain in computation time is also apparent (Hierarchical Instantiation is 8 times faster). Since our algorithm does not allow bidirectional refinement of energy links between instances, it refines fewer links and computes fewer form factors. The ratio between the two numbers of links is the average number of elements an emitter is subdivided into. This of course depends on the relative positions of the elements and on the refinement algorithm. If the instances are not too close to each other, we can consider that our algorithm is equivalent to normal refinement; for really close instances it is more approximate. Visibility calculations are also faster with instances, since they do not require geometric operations, instead using the stored mean transmittance value in the relevant directions.

On the left side of Figure 4 we show a comparison of the accuracy of hierarchical radiosity and hierarchical instantiation for values of the accuracy threshold used in the refinement of links, for the scene of Figure 5. It appears that for larger values of the error threshold, hierarchical instantiation is much faster then hierarchical radiosity with a better accuracy. This confirms that using phase functions that accurately account for the internal scattering of light is more efficient than the traditional approximation used for clusters in hierarchical radiosity. For small error thresholds hierarchical radiosity is still more accurate than hierarchical instantiation. We believe that this is caused by the omni-directional approximation of the reflectance functions in our current implementation, which is confirmed by the fact that instancing fewer levels in the hierarchy only marginally increases the accuracy. The repartition of the hierarchical radiosity solutions required by our algorithm corresponding to each case is shown on the right side of Figure 4. It clearly appears that when instancing all levels, only hierarchical radiosity problems with small number of elements occur. When instancing every other level, the average number of elements per hierarchical radiosity problem increases. Finally, when instancing every three levels, the algorithm tends to mainly solve hierarchical radiosity problems with more than 100 leaf elements.

Figure 7 (*See appendix*) presents a lighting simulation in a scene of 1 210 925 input polygons, built using poplar trees of various ages[1]. The simulation took 9 hours and 53 minutes to compute on a *Sgi-Origin 2000* computer, using only 49Mb of memory. When comparing this computation time with the one of the solution on Figure 5, it should be noticed that the source we used here is much more complex (Each bulb contains an average of 1 000 small polygons grouped into clusters) and thus drastically increases the number of links in the scene. Computation time with a single polygon source is less than 2 hours.

---

[1] Models generated by the AMAPHydro software. Courtesy of Pr.Philippe de Reffye and F.Blaise, CIRAD

6 Conclusions and future work

We have proposed a new hierarchical instancing technique that drastically reduces the amount of resources needed for the lighting simulation with hierarchical radiosity in scenes with approximate geometrical redundancy. This enables for the first time the precise simulation of light in very large models, such as entire trees, with limited memory. This instantiation technique essentially bridges the gap between explicit radiosity solutions and view-dependent approaches operating on instanced geometry, allowing a precise calculation in object space with reasonable resources.

Whereas in the case of plants it appears that the phase functions from large models can be approximated by the ones for small models, (*e.g* by the phase functions from instances at lower levels in the hierarchy) this is not true in architectural scenes. Some investigation is required to search for a way to deduce phase functions of large instances without computing a hierarchical radiosity in the entire model. We are thinking about considering an incremental approach, where phase functions are initially considered uniform, but are incrementally updated after opening the corresponding instance.

We have seen in the case of architectural scenes that directional transmittance functions do poorly in the computation of shadows cast by the instances and we used geometry based transmittance. Indeed, in the method we have presented, the instances are "opened" to improve the computation of their internal light distribution only. The regions where shadows are cast by an instance could also be considered as to be improved when opening this instance. Therefore, a formulation of our algorithm based on the accuracy of energy transfer along links that encounter an instance – rather than based on the accuracy of light on approximated geometry – would form a more general approach that could also permit to accurately compute shadows due to the geometry in the instances while keeping an approximate transmittance function within the instance.

The hierarchical instantiation algorithm could perhaps be improved by detecting instances with simple contents receiving a nearly uniform distribution of incoming light. In such cases, a simple hierarchical push/pull may replace the local radiosity solution at a fraction of the cost. Smarter and more generic instantiation policies could be used, especially as we start applying these ideas to scenes with less self-similarity. The vector quantization technique of [DHL+98], based on the difference between phase functions, should prove particularly useful.

As could be observed in the results section, the compromise between storage requirements of the phase functions and the accuracy of the simulation leads to approximations in the solution for highly refined scenes. This choice was not due to a particular restriction of our algorithm but for the sake of simplicity for a first approach. Experiments could be conducted on bidirectional phase functions, and the kind of phase function to use (uniform, mono or bi-directional) could be adapted to the case of each object to be instanced. The precise distribution of illumination computed in our method could also be used to create high quality renderings, using a rendering step in which each leaf is subjected to the irradiance from links but uses a more accurate BRDF, including specular/shiny effects which are visually important despite their limited global impact.

Finally, it is clear that this work has a direct application on physiological plant growth simulation where the precise illumination on leaves is needed to compute the production of vegetal matter. We are currently working on such a project in collaboration with the LIAMA[2] and the CIRAD[3].

---

[2]French-Chinese Laboratory for Computer Science, Beijing, China
[3]International Research Center in Agronomy and Development.

184

References

BW94.   Ph. Bekaert and Y. D. Willems. Raytracing 3d linear graftals. *Winter School of Computer Graphics 1994*, January 1994. Held in held at University of West Bohemia, Plzen, Czech Republic, 19-20 January 1994.

Chr95.   Per Henrik Christensen. *Hierarchical Techniques for Glossy Global Illumination*. Ph.D. thesis, Technical Report, Department of Computer Science and Engineering, University of Washington, Seattle, Washington, 1995.

DHL+98.   Oliver Deussen, Patrick Hanrahan, Bernd Lintermann, Radomr Mech, Matt Pharr, and Przemyslaw Prusinkiewicz. Realistic modeling and rendering of plant ecosystems. *Proceedings of SIGGRAPH 98*, pages 275–286, July 1998. ISBN 0-89791-999-8. Held in Orlando, Florida.

dREF+88.   Ph. de Reffye, C. Edelin, J. Françon, M. Jaeger, and C. Puech. Plant models faithful to botanical structure and development. In *Computer Graphics(Proceedings of SIGGRAPH 88)*, volume 22(4), pages 151–158, 1988.

Gov95.   Y. M. Govaerts. *A Model of Light Scattering in Three-Dimensional Plant Canopies: A Monte Carlo Ray Tracing Approach*. PhD thesis, Departement de Physique, Universitat Catholique de Louvain, Louvain, Belgium, 1995.

Gre89.   Ned Greene. Voxel space automata: Modeling with stochastic growth processes in voxel space. *Computer Graphics (Proceedings of SIGGRAPH 89)*, 23(3):175–184, July 1989. Held in Boston, Massachusetts.

Har92.   J. C. Hart. The object instancing paradigm for linear fractal modeling. In *Proc. of the Graphics Interface '92*, pages 224–231, Vancouver, Canada, 1992.

HDSD99.   Jean-Marc Hasenfratz, Cyrille Damez, François Sillion, and George Drettakis. A practical analysis of clustering strategies for hierarchical radiosity. In *Computer Graphics Forum (Proc. Eurographics '99)*, volume 18(3), September 1999.

HKSS98.   Wolfgang Heidrich, Jan Kautz, Philipp Slusallek, and Hans-Peter Seidel. Canned lightsources. *Eurographics Rendering Workshop 1998*, pages 293–300, June 1998. ISBN 3-211-83213-0. Held in Vienna, Austria.

KK86.   Timothy L. Kay and James Kajiya. Ray tracing complex scenes. *Computer Graphics*, 20(4):269–278, August 1986.

MMKW97.   Nelson Max, Curtis Mobley, Brett Keating, and En-Hua Wu. Plane-parallel radiance transport for global illumination in vegetation. In Julie Dorsey and Phillip Slusallek, editors, *Rendering Techniques '97 (Proceedings of the Eighth Eurographics Workshop on Rendering)*, pages 239–250, New York, NY, 1997. Springer Wien. ISBN 3-211-83001-4.

OCL96.   Ming Ouhyoung, Yung-Yu Chuang, and Rung-Huei Liang. Reusable radiosity objects. *Computer Graphics Forum*, 15(3):C347–C356, C483, September 1996.

RPV93.   Holly Rushmeier, Charles Patterson, and Aravindan Veerasamy. Geometric simplification for indirect illumination calculations. In *Proceedings Graphics Interface '93*. Morgan Kaufmann publishers, 1993.

SAG94.   Brian Smits, James Arvo, and Donald Greenberg. A Clustering Algorithm for Radiosity in Complex Environments. In *Computer Graphics Proceedings, Annual Conference Series, 1994 (ACM SIGGRAPH '94 Proceedings)*, pages 435–442, 1994.

SB87.   John M. Snyder and Alan H. Barr. Ray tracing complex models containing surface tessellations. *Computer Graphics*, 21(4):119–128, July 1987.

SD95.   François Sillion and George Drettakis. Feature-Based Control of Visibility Error: A Multiresolution Clustering Algorithm for Global Illumination. In *Computer Graphics Proceedings, Annual Conference Series, 1995 (ACM SIGGRAPH '95 Proceedings)*, pages 145–152, 1995.

SDS95.   F. Sillion, G. Drettakis, and C. Soler. A clustering algorithm for radiance calculation in general environments. In *Eurographics Rendering Workshop 1995*. Eurographics, June 1995.

Sil95.   François Sillion. A Unified Hierarchical Algorithm for Global Illumination with Scattering Volumes and Object Clusters. *IEEE Transactions on Visualization and Computer Graphics*, 1(3), September 1995.

Editors' Note: see Appendix, p. 406 for colored figures of this paper

A Unified Approach to
Prefiltered Environment Maps

Jan Kautz[†]   Pere-Pau Vázquez[*]   Wolfgang Heidrich[†]   Hans-Peter Seidel[†]

Max-Planck-Institut für Informatik[†] Saarbrücken, Germany	Institut d'Informàtica i Aplicacions – UdG[*] Girona, Spain

Abstract. Different methods for prefiltered environment maps have been proposed, each of which has different advantages and disadvantages. We present a general notation for prefiltered environment maps, which will be used to classify and compare the existing methods. Based on that knowledge we develop three new algorithms: 1. A fast hierarchical prefiltering method that can be utilized for all previously proposed prefiltered environment maps. 2. A technique for hardware-accelerated prefiltering of environment maps that achieves interactive rates even on low-end workstations. 3. Anisotropic environment maps using the Banks model.

1 Introduction

Environment maps [3] are a widely used technique to approximate reflections in interactive rendering. Although environment maps make the assumption that the reflected environment is far away — thus being an approximation — they often nevertheless achieve convincing reflections.

Recently environment maps have been introduced as a means to render glossy reflections [5, 7, 8, 9, 11]. All of these methods prefilter a given environment map with either a fixed reflection model [7, 8, 9] or a certain class of BRDFs (bidirectional reflectance distribution functions) [5, 11]. Although these methods are similar, they have different strengths and weaknesses, which are worthwhile to discuss. In order to be able to compare these methods we present a general notation of prefiltered environment maps, which allows us to classify and contrast all the well-known prefiltering techniques.

Based on the insights we have gained from this comparison we have developed three new techniques:

1. A general *fast hierarchical prefiltering* method that can be used to compute all known types of prefiltered environment maps, and which is much faster than brute force prefiltering.
2. A *hardware-accelerated prefiltering* method that prefilters environment maps at interactive rates even on low-end workstations. It works for all reflectance models that translate to constant and radially symmetric filter kernels (like the Phong model [18] or approximations with the said properties [11]).
3. An *anisotropic environment map*. We use the Banks model [1] to create an anisotropic prefiltered environment map.

After a brief discussion of related work, we introduce our general notation of pre-filtered environment maps and classify the previously proposed prefiltered environment map techniques with regard to that general notation in Section 4. This leads to our new environment map algorithms presented in Section 5. Section 6 concludes the paper with a discussion of the new techniques.

2 Related Work

The environment maps technique to produce mirror-like reflections on curved objects was first introduced by Blinn and Newell [3]. This is the basis on which most environment map methods — including ours — are based on [5, 7, 8, 9, 11]. We will discuss these techniques in great detail in Section 4.

Since environment maps are defined over the sphere, a way has to be found to represent them in two dimensional textures. A commonly used format in software renderers are cube maps, which now also start becoming supported by graphics hardware. A spherical parameterization, which is directly supported by OpenGL, was introduced by Blinn and Newell [3]. Heidrich and Seidel [10] proposed dual paraboloid mapping which uses two texture maps, one for the front facing hemisphere and one for the backfacing. This parameterization is now also supported by a variety of newer graphic boards.

Other techniques have been proposed for the interactive rendering of glossy reflections, which are not based on environment maps. Diefenbach and Badler [6] used multi-pass methods (Monte Carlo integration) to generate glossy reflections. Photon maps were used by Stürzlinger and Bastos [20]; photons were "splatted" and weighted with an arbitrary BRDF. Miller et al. [15] stored precomputed glossy reflections in surface light fields. Bastos et al. [2] used a convolution filter in screen-space to produce glossy reflections. Lischinski and Rappoport [13] used a large collection of low resolution layered depth images to store view-dependent illumination.

3 General Prefiltered Environment Maps

Generally speaking, prefiltered environment maps capture all the reflected exitant radiance towards all directions $\vec{v}$ from a fixed position $\mathbf{x}$:

$$L_{\text{glossy}}(\mathbf{x}; \vec{v}, \vec{n}, \vec{t}) \quad = \quad \int_{\Omega} f_r(\vec{\omega}(\vec{v}, \vec{n}, \vec{t}), \vec{\omega}(\vec{l}, \vec{n}, \vec{t})) L_i(\mathbf{x}; \vec{l}) < \vec{n}, \vec{l} > \ d\vec{l}, \quad (1)$$

where $\vec{v}$ is the viewing direction and $\vec{l}$ is the light direction in world-space, $\{\vec{n}, \vec{t}, \vec{n} \times \vec{t}\}$ is the local coordinate frame of the reflective surface, $\vec{\omega}(\vec{v}, \vec{n}, \vec{t})$ represents the viewing direction and $\vec{\omega}(\vec{l}, \vec{n}, \vec{t})$ the light direction relative to that frame, f_r is the BRDF, which is usually parameterized via a local viewing and light direction. A prefiltered environment map stores the radiance of light reflected towards the viewing direction $\vec{v}$, which is computed by weighting the incoming light L_i from all directions $\vec{l}$ with the BRDF f_r. Note, that L_i can be viewed as the unfiltered original environment map. This map should use high-dynamic range radiance values to be physically correct. As you can see, in the general case we have a dependence on the viewing direction as well as on the orientation of the reflective surface, i.e. the local coordinate frame $\{\vec{n}, \vec{t}, \vec{n} \times \vec{t}\}$.

This general kind of environment map is five dimensional. Two dimensions are needed to represent the viewing direction $\vec{v}$ (a unit vector in world coordinates) and three dimensions are necessary to represent the coordinate frame $\{\vec{n}, \vec{t}, \vec{n} \times \vec{t}\}$; e.g. three angles can be used to specify the orientation of an arbitrary coordinate frame.

The prefiltered environment maps which we will examine usually drop some dependencies (e.g. on the tangent $\vec{t}$) and are often reparameterized (e.g. indexing is not done with the viewing direction $\vec{v}$, but the reflected viewing direction).

4 Classification of Known Techniques

In this section we will classify diffuse environment maps [14], Phong environment maps [9, 14], and environment maps prefiltered with isotropic BRDFs [5, 11]. Note that we will define the BRDFs using global viewing and light directions.

Diffuse Environment Maps. Miller [14] has proposed to use a purely diffuse BRDF to prefilter environment maps. A diffuse BRDF can be written as:

$$f_r(\vec{v}, \vec{l}) \quad := \quad k_d,$$

where $k_d \in [0, 1]$ describes the absorption of the surface. Moving this into Equation 1, we get:

$$L_{\text{diffuse}}(\mathbf{x}; \vec{v}, \vec{n}, \vec{t}) \quad = \quad \int_{\Omega} k_d L_i(\mathbf{x}; \vec{l}) < \vec{n}, \vec{l} > \; d\vec{l}.$$

We can drop all dependencies except the one on the normal $\vec{n}$ and we get the following two dimensional environment map:

$$L_{\text{diffuse}}(\mathbf{x}; \vec{n}) \quad = \quad k_d \int_{\Omega} L_i(\mathbf{x}; \vec{l}) < \vec{n}, \vec{l} > \; d\vec{l}.$$

This environment map accurately stores the diffuse illumination at the point $\mathbf{x}$. It is only two-dimensional and it is indexed by the surface normal.

Phong Environment Maps. Heidrich [9] and Miller [14] used the original Phong model [18] to prefilter environment maps. The Phong BRDF is given by:

$$f_r(\vec{v}, \vec{l}) \quad := \quad k_s \frac{< \vec{r}_v(\vec{n}), \vec{l} >^N}{< \vec{n}, \vec{l} >},$$

where $\vec{r}_v(\vec{n}) = 2(\vec{n} \cdot \vec{v})\vec{n} - \vec{v}$ is the reflected viewing-direction in world-space. The parameters k_s and N are used to control the shape and size of the lobe. Using the Phong model, the Equation 1 becomes

$$L_{\text{phong}}(\mathbf{x}; \vec{v}, \vec{n}, \vec{t}) \quad = \quad \int_{\Omega} k_s \frac{< \vec{r}_v(\vec{n}), \vec{l} >^N}{< \vec{n}, \vec{l} >} L_i(\mathbf{x}; \vec{l}) < \vec{n}, \vec{l} > \; d\vec{l}$$

$$= \quad k_s \int_{\Omega} < \vec{r}_v(\vec{n}), \vec{l} >^N L_i(\mathbf{x}; \vec{l}) \; d\vec{l}.$$

Obviously the tangent $\vec{t}$ is not used and can be discarded. Instead of indexing the environment map with $\vec{v}$ and $\vec{n}$, it can be reparameterized so that it is directly indexed by the reflection vector $\vec{r}_v$:

$$L_{\text{phong}}(\mathbf{x}; \vec{r}_v) = k_s \int_{\Omega} <\vec{r}_v, \vec{l}>^N L_i(\mathbf{x}; \vec{l})\, d\vec{l}.$$

Although the Phong model is not physically based, the reflections make a surface look metallic, only at glancing angles one expects sharper reflections. This indexing via the reflection vector $\vec{r}_v$ is the one used to access environment maps without prefiltering and is therefore supported in OpenGL via the spherical, parabolic and cube map parameterizations.

Miller [14] and Heidrich [9] proposed to use a weighted sum of a diffuse and a Phong environment map to get a complete illumination model. They also propose to add a Fresnel term so that the ratio between the diffuse and glossy reflections can vary with different viewing angles:

$$L_o(\vec{r}_v, \vec{n}) = F_d(<\vec{r}_v, \vec{n}>)L_{\text{diffuse}} + F_p(<\vec{r}_v, \vec{n}>)L_{\text{phong}} \qquad (2)$$

This way a wider range of materials can be created.

Environment Maps with Isotropic BRDFs – I. Kautz and McCool [11] extended the Phong environment maps idea to other isotropic BRDFs by approximating it with a special class of BRDFs:

$$f_r(\vec{v}, \vec{l}) := p(<\vec{n}, \vec{r}_v(\vec{n})>, <\vec{r}_v(\vec{n}), \vec{l}>),$$

where p is an approximation to a given isotropic BRDF, which is not only isotropic, but also radially symmetric about $\vec{r}_v(\vec{n}) = 2(\vec{n} \cdot \vec{v})\vec{n} - \vec{v}$, and therefore only depends on two parameters.

Now consider Equation 1 using this reflectance function:

$$L_{\text{isotropic}}(\mathbf{x}; \vec{v}, \vec{n}, \vec{t}) = \int_{\Omega} p(<\vec{n}, \vec{r}_v(\vec{n})>, <\vec{r}_v(\vec{n}), \vec{l}>)L_i(\mathbf{x}; \vec{l}) <\vec{n}, \vec{l}>\, d\vec{l}.$$

Then the authors make the assumption that the used BRDF is fairly specular, i.e. the BRDF is almost zero everywhere, except when $\vec{r}_v(\vec{n}) \approx \vec{l}$. Using this assumption they reason that $<\vec{n}, \vec{r}_v(\vec{n})> \approx <\vec{n}, \vec{l}>$. Now the equation can be reparameterized and rewritten the following way:

$$L_{\text{isotropic}}(\mathbf{x}; \vec{r}_v, <\vec{n}, \vec{r}_v>) = <\vec{n}, \vec{r}_v> \int_{\Omega} p(<\vec{n}, \vec{r}_v>, <\vec{r}_v, \vec{l}>)L_i(\mathbf{x}; \vec{l})\, d\vec{l},$$

which is only three dimensional. They also proposed to use the following approximation to a given isotropic BRDF:

$$f_r(\vec{v}, \vec{l}) := F(<\vec{n}, \vec{r}_v(\vec{n})>)p(<\vec{r}_v(\vec{n}), \vec{l}>).$$

This approximates a BRDF with a constant lobe (defined by p) that is scaled by a factor which depends on the angle between $\vec{n}$ and $\vec{r}_v(\vec{n})$. An environment map prefiltered with this model is only two dimensional:

$$L_{\text{isotropic}}(\mathbf{x}; \vec{r}_v, <\vec{n}, \vec{r}_v>) = <\vec{n}, \vec{r}_v> F(<\vec{n}, \vec{r}_v>) \int_{\Omega} p(<\vec{r}_v, \vec{l}>)L_i(\mathbf{x}; \vec{l})\, d\vec{l}.$$

It is two dimensional only, because the dependence on $< \vec{n}, \vec{r}_v >$ can be moved outside the integral. It is sufficient to multiply the two factors onto the prefiltered environment map during rendering.

This technique has the big advantage that it can use approximations of arbitrary isotropic BRDFs and achieves interactive frame rates. Off-specular peaks can also be incorporated into this technique. An additional Fresnel factor like Miller [14] and Heidrich [9] proposed is not needed because real physically based BRDFs can be used. The 2D approximation is directly equivalent to Phong prefiltered environment maps with a separate Fresnel factor, but a more generally shaped lobe is used and the Fresnel factor was computed from a real BRDF. In contrast to that, the 3D approximation does not compute a separate Fresnel factor, instead it is incorporated into the approximation, which allows to vary the shape of the lobe not only with a scale factor.

Depending on the BRDF, the quality of the approximation varies. For higher quality approximations Kautz and McCool also propose to use a multilobe approximation, which basically results in several prefiltered environment maps which have to be added.

For instance, if a BRDF is to be used, which is based on several separate surface phenomena (e.g. has retro-reflections, diffuse reflections, and glossy reflections) each part has to be approximated separately, since no radially symmetric approximation can be found for the whole BRDF. This again corresponds to the technique by Miller or Heidrich, just that it is based on a real BRDF, see Equation 2.

Environment Maps with Isotropic BRDFs – II. Cabral et al. [5] use a similar technique, which also assumes an isotropic and radially symmetric BRDF. They prefilter an environment map for different fixed viewing directions, resulting in view-dependent environment maps. In contrast to the previous approach, they actually use a four dimensional environment map:

$$L_{\text{isotropic2}}(\mathbf{x}; \vec{v}, \vec{n}) = \int_{\Omega} p(< \vec{n}, \vec{r}_v >, < \vec{r}_v, \vec{l} >) L_i(\mathbf{x}; \vec{l}) < \vec{n}, \vec{l} > d\vec{l}$$

This four dimensional environment map is sparsely sampled in $\vec{v}$. A two dimensional spherical map is extracted from this four dimensional map for every new viewpoint. This map corresponds to one specific viewing direction and is generated using warping. This new view-dependent environment map is then applied to an object. The warping compensates for the undersampled viewing directions, and no visible artefacts occur.

This method can also use approximations of arbitrary isotropic BRDFs. Using a sparse four dimensional environment map makes it unnecessary to approximate the factor $< \vec{n}, \vec{l} >$. The necessary warping requires high-end graphics hardware to achieve interactive frame rates.

Warping is done based on an assumption what the central reflection direction of the BRDF is (the reflected viewing direction and the surface normal are mentioned). This assumption fails for BRDFs that have off-specular reflections.

Since radially symmetric BRDFs are used, this method has the same difficulties with complex BRDFs as the previous method. Different contributions which add to a BRDF have to be decomposed into their components (e.g. diffuse contribution, glossy contribution, ...), otherwise this technique fails (just like the previous one).

As mentioned before the generated two dimensional environment map is view-dependent, so the reflective object needs to be viewed with an orthographic projection or otherwise the reflections are incorrect, since the reflection directions are computed based on an infinite viewer.

5 New Algorithms

5.1 Fast Hierarchical Prefiltering

All the methods we discussed in Section 4 need a way to prefilter environment maps. Brute force methods are effective but prohibitively slow. We propose a fast hierarchical method, which can be used to filter all types of prefiltered environment map techniques.

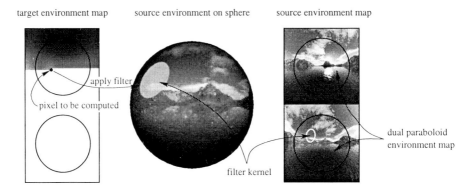

target environment map   source environment on sphere   source environment map

apply filter

pixel to be computed

dual paraboloid
environment map

filter kernel

Fig. 1. *Filtering of an environment map. A pixel in the target environment map is computed by applying a filter to the source environment map. Both are usually given in a representation like the dual paraboloid map. The filter which is defined on the sphere has to be projected to the environment map space.*

Prefiltering of environment maps can be seen as the application of a space variant filter. Every pixel $(p_1, p_2, \dots)$ in the (possibly more than two dimensional) target environment map $E(\mathbf{x}; p_1, p_2, \dots)$ — i.e. the one that we are creating — is a weighted sum of all the pixels of the given specular environment map $L_i(\mathbf{x}; \vec{l})$; see Figure 1. This weighting is given by the two-dimensional Filter $F(p_1, p_2, \dots) := f_r(p_1, p_2, \dots, \vec{l}) < \vec{n}, \vec{l} >$. Note, that the support of the filter F is usually over the hemisphere, unlike in Figure 1, where we used a smaller filter size for demonstration purposes.

The filter F is space-variant because it usually varies for every pixel in the target environment map for two possible reasons. First, the filter is already space-variant on the sphere, i.e. for different $(p_1, p_2, \dots)$ we get a differently shaped filter. Second, any mapping of the sphere to a rectangular texture domain maps a filter that is space-invariant over the sphere to a space-variant filter in the environment map representation.

Prefiltering is often done with a brute force technique. For every pixel in the target environment map, the filter is applied to every single pixel in the source environment map. This makes the prefiltering process very slow, since e.g. even for a two dimensional target environment map $(width \times height)^2$ pixels have to be touched and the same number of BRDF evaluations has to be performed.

Since the filter kernel is basically a two dimensional slice of a reflection model, which is usually a smooth function, we can use a hierarchical method instead.

Our hierarchical prefiltering method first generates a mip-map of the source environment map using a 2×2 box filter. The corresponding two-dimensional filter kernel is generated for every target pixel and a mip-map is built also using a 2×2 box filter (it is actually not necessary to compute the full mip-map, see next paragraph). The computation of one target pixel works as follows. Both, the filter and the environment

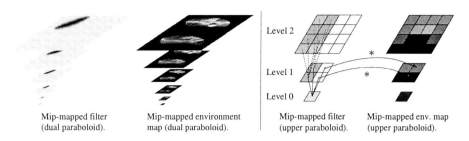

Level 2	Level 1	Level 0

Mip-mapped filter (dual paraboloid).

Mip-mapped environment map (dual paraboloid).

Mip-mapped filter (upper paraboloid).

Mip-mapped env. map (upper paraboloid).

Fig. 2. *Hierarchical filtering of an environment map. The left side shows the mip-maps for the filter and for the environment map. The right side shows how the hierarchical filtering works (for one target pixel). For every value in a mip-map level of the filter (done separately for the upper and lower paraboloid), the difference to the four values in the next higher level is checked. If it is below some threshold the value is used and multiplied with the corresponding value from the environment mip-map. All these contributions are added up and result in a single value for the target pixel.*

map are sampled and mip-mapped in environment map space; see left side of Figure 2. Instead of directly applying the filter kernel to the source environment map, we first check if it is sufficient to apply the coarsest level of the filter kernel (i.e. one sample) to the coarsest level of the source environment map (also one sample). We do this check by computing the differences to the four corresponding values in the next higher mip-map level. If this difference is greater than some threshold value, we go to the next finer level in the mip-map hierarchy and check for each of the four finer-grained parts of the mip-mapped filter kernel (each is one sample) whether the difference to the next higher mip-map level is above or below the threshold. If it is above we go again to the next finer level. If not we apply that part of the mip-mapped filter to the corresponding value from the mip-mapped environment map and add it to our target pixel value; see right side of Figure 2. We do this until all parts of the filter have been applied to the environment map.

The main speed up is due to the fact that the filter is usually very smooth and fades out quickly from its peak (BRDFs tend to have a slim lobe). Furthermore it is not necessary to compute the finest mip-map level(s) of the filter, since it is hardly used. If it is needed, it can either be evaluated on the fly or interpolated from the next coarser level.

In Figure 2 you can see an example for this algorithm. We have used a dual paraboloid environment map, which uses two faces, one for the front-facing part of the environment map and one for the back-facing part.

The right side of Figure 2 shows two steps in the filtering process (for the upper paraboloid). The differences between the pixel in level 0 and the pixels in level 1 are too big, so we cannot multiply the pixel of level 0 with the corresponding pixel of the environment mip-map and use that value, but we have to go to the next level. In level 1 we compute the differences for all four pixels to the pixels from level 2 and find out that the differences for the two white pixels to next level are below the given threshold, so we can multiply them with the corresponding pixels from the environment mip-map and we get the contribution for that region of the environment map. For the other pixels we have to go the next finer levels of the filter mip-map.

It should be noted that this algorithm is biased, since a given sample is used determine what it will be used for [12]. For the application of prefiltering environment maps the introduced bias is not crucial though.

Results. We have validated our algorithm with the Phong model [18] using different exponents. Filtering a parabolic environment map with 128×256 pixels yields the following results (Pentium II with 350Mhz):

exponent	brute force	hierarchical	speed up
10	413	98	4.2
50	442	83	5.3
100	474	61	7.7
250	545	55	9.9
500	552	39	14.1

The table shows the timings in seconds for the brute force method and our new hierarchical method. We used a threshold (difference in BRDF values) of 0.001 for the hierarchical method, which yields the same visual quality as the brute force method, see Figure 4 (color plates).

We have also tested different sizes of environment maps. The results indicate that the brute force method has linear complexity in the number of touched pixels, whereas our hierarchical method is sublinear.

5.2 Hardware accelerated Prefiltering

For interactive applications it would be interesting if environment map prefiltering could be done on the fly, for example using graphics hardware. This means that if the scene changes, glossy reflections change accordingly. In this paper, we will only deal with the accelerated filtering of a given environment map. It has been shown in [19] that environment maps can be generated on the fly. Live video capturing of an environment map is also conceivable. For example the Omnicam [16] directly captures an environment as parabolic map.

As seen in the previous section, environment map prefiltering always uses a two dimensional filter kernel, which is shift-variant in general, but depends on the representation of the environment map. The OpenGL imaging subset only supports shift-invariant two dimensional filters of certain sizes [17]. Hence, for hardware accelerated prefiltering we have to choose an environment map technique that uses only two dimensional environment maps with a BRDF which results in a shift-invariant filter over the hemisphere, and an environment map representation that keeps the filter shift-invariant.

The Phong model has a shift-invariant filter kernel over the hemisphere, since its cosine lobe is constant for all reflected viewing directions $\vec{r}_v$. It is also radially symmetric about $\vec{r}_v$. The filter size can also be decreased if smaller BRDF values are clamped to zero (will be necessary due to the restricted filter size of the graphics hardware). The filter shape is obviously circular, since it is radially symmetric. Therefore Phong environment maps fulfill the necessary requirements for hardware accelerated prefiltering. We still need to find an environment map representation that maps the shift-invariant circular filter kernel from the hemisphere to a shift-invariant circular filter kernel in texture space.

It turns out that the dual paraboloid mapping proposed by Heidrich and Seidel [10] comes close to this desired property. A circular filter kernel which is mapped from the parabolic environment map back to the hemisphere is also (almost) circular. A distortion occurs depending on the radius and the position of the filter. To visualize the distortion, we project a circular filter kernel with a radius of r ($r = 1$ is half the width of the parabolic map) from the parabolic map back to the sphere and measure the error; see right side of Figure 3. We measure how much the distances from the center of the

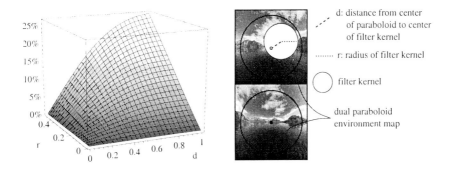

Fig. 3. *Distortion of a circle when projected from a paraboloid map back to the sphere.*

projected circle to its border deviate from a constant radius. The maximum deviation is used as the error, shown on the left side of the same figure. The distortion depends on the radius of the filter kernel and also on the distance d of the filter's center from the parabolic map's center (i.e. the center of the front- or backfacing paraboloid). The distortion goes up to 25% for large radii, but in these cases the prefiltered environment map will be very blurry, so that the distortion will not lead to visible errors. For smaller radii the distortion remains fairly small and again no visible artefacts occur.

Although the shape of the filter almost remains the same in the parabolic space, the radius of the filter kernel varies with the distance d. The ratio between the smallest filter radius and largest filter radius is about 2. We will overcome this problem by generating two prefiltered environment maps, one with the smallest (yields map S) and one with the largest necessary filter size (yields map L). Then we blend between both prefiltered environment maps. The value with which we need to blend between both maps is different for different pixels in the parabolic environment map, but it depends only on the distance d and is always d^2. For a pixel in the center of the paraboloid this means that we use 0% of map L and a 100% of map S; for a pixel with distance $d = 0.5$ to the center of the parabolic map, we use 25% of map L and 75% of map S, and so on.

Algorithm. The actual algorithm is fairly simple. First we create a mip-map of the parabolic environment map, then we load the environment map (plus the mip-map) into texture memory. The user has to specify the Phong exponent to be used and a limit when BRDF values from the Phong model can be clamped to zero, which is used to restrict the kernel size in the first place. Then we compute the two necessary filter radii, r_s for the small filter and r_l for the large filter. If a kernel size is larger then the maximum supported OpenGL kernel size, we scale the environment map and the filter by 0.5 until it is within the supported kernel size. Now we get to the actual filtering part:

1. Set the camera to an orthographic projection (so that we can draw the environment map seen from the top).
2. Draw alpha texture with d^2 to alpha channel
3. *For* both radii r_s and r_l:
4.   *While* r_s (resp. r_l) < hardware supported filter size:
5.   Divide r_s (resp. r_l) by 2. Double the shrink factor.
6.   Draw environment map shrunk by the shrink factor (uses mip-mapping).
7.   Sample Phong model into the filter.
8.   Filter the environment map with it (OpenGL convolution).

9. Store it again as texture map (RGBα texture).
10. Draw environment map S.
11. Blend environment map L with it (using d^2).
12. Store again as a texture map.
13. Set up real camera.
14. Draw reflective object with generated environment map.

One problem arises when the center of the filter kernel is close to the border of the environment map. Part of the filter kernel will be outside the actual environment map, thus including values from outside the environment map. This can be solved by including a large border in the environment map.

It should also be mentioned, that the graphics hardware clamps all numbers to the $[0, 1]$ range, and therefore the original environment map cannot have a high dynamic range.

Results. We have tested our algorithm on an SGI O2 where it achieves interactive rates. All the tests were done with parabolic environment maps with 512×1024 pixels. The border was 64 pixels in each direction (for each face). The maximum kernel size we used was 7 (larger kernel sizes considerably degrade the convolution speed on an O2). We measured the following timings (reflective sphere, 2592 triangles):

exponent	filter size		shrink factor		fps 2-pass	fps 1-pass
	small	large	small	large		
10	174	260	32	64	25	33
50	78	136	16	32	20	33
100	56	100	8	16	16	25
250	36	66	8	16	16	25
500	26	48	4	8	9	11

Please note that filtering was performed for *every* frame, even though the Phong exponent did not change. We have included timings for the two-pass convolution (i.e. using the small and the large filter) and for a one-pass convolution (using only the small filter). Furthermore we have included the filter sizes in pixels that would have been required (the BRDF clamp value was set to 0.1) and the necessary shrink factor to get filter sizes within a maximum size of 7 pixels. You can see that for small Phong exponents hardware prefiltering is very interactive. For larger Phong exponents the rendering speed is slower, because filtering cannot be done with a shrunk environment map. For a visual comparison please see Figure 4 (color plates). You can see that the hardware method generates dark borders, which does not pose a problem since these are not used for rendering. Figure 5 shows renderings with different environment maps and different Phong exponents; they all run at interactive rates.

It should be mentioned that the two dimensional approximation to an isotropic BRDF proposed by Kautz and McCool [11] can also be used, since it also fulfills the necessary requirements (see beginning of this section). Hence their approximation can be used to prefilter environment maps with arbitrary isotropic BRDFs in real-time.

5.3   Anisotropic Environment Maps

So far, there has not been an environment map technique that can also be applied to anisotropic BRDF models. Generally, an anisotropic BRDF depends on many parameters, which then results in a five dimensional environment map, see Section 4.

We need to look for a model which allows to create a lower dimensional environment map. The Banks model [1], which is simple and depends only on dot products, yields a three dimensional environment map if self shadowing is excluded. The BRDF is given by:

$$f_r(\vec{v}, \vec{l}) := \left(\sqrt{1 - <\vec{l},\vec{t}>^2} \sqrt{1 - <\vec{v},\vec{t}>^2} - <\vec{l},\vec{t}><\vec{v},\vec{t}> -s \right) \frac{1}{(1-s)^2},$$

where we have extended the original Banks model with a new parameter $s \in [0,1)$, which allows to have sharper highlights. The environment map equation becomes:

$$L_{\text{banks}}(\mathbf{x}; \vec{v}, \vec{n}, \vec{t}) = \int_{\Omega} \left(\sqrt{1 - <\vec{l},\vec{t}>^2} \sqrt{1 - <\vec{v},\vec{t}>^2} - <\vec{l},\vec{t}><\vec{v},\vec{t}> -s \right)$$
$$\frac{1}{(1-s)^2} L_i(\mathbf{x}; \vec{l}) <\vec{n},\vec{l}> \ d\vec{l}.$$

To decrease the dimensionality of this environment map, we discard the self-shadowing term $<\vec{n},\vec{l}>$, and then reparameterization gives us the following three dimensional environment map:

$$L_{\text{banks}}(\mathbf{x}; \vec{t}, <\vec{v},\vec{t}>) = \int_{\Omega} \left(\sqrt{1 - <\vec{l},\vec{t}>^2} \sqrt{1 - <\vec{v},\vec{t}>^2} - <\vec{l},\vec{t}><\vec{v},\vec{t}> -s \right)$$
$$\frac{1}{(1-s)^2} L_i(\mathbf{x}; \vec{l}) \ d\vec{l}.$$

Now we have an anisotropic prefiltered environment map. In order to render an object using this environment map it is necessary to compute the 3D texture coordinates at every vertex by hand, i.e. the two coordinates of the unit vector $\vec{t}$ and the third coordinate corresponding to $<\vec{v},\vec{t}>$. This anisotropic environment map can then be rendered at interactive rates if the hardware supports three dimensional texturing. In Figure 6 we show a teapot with an anisotropic material, which was done with an anisotropic prefiltered environment.

Since the self-shadowing term is omitted, an object using this environment map does reflect light from behind it. This is usually not noticeable unless a bright light source shines "through".

6 Conclusions

We have proposed a general notation of prefiltered environment maps, according to which we have classified previously proposed prefiltered environment map techniques. We have developed three new techniques. First, we have used a new hierarchical pre-filtering method which is on average about 10 times faster than a brute force prefiltering method. Second, we have proposed a hardware accelerated prefiltering method, which can prefilter environment maps in real-time, if the used reflectance model translates to a constant and radially symmetric filter kernel. Third, we have proposed an anisotropic prefiltered environment map using the Banks model.

Future research should investigate the possibility to use difference pyramids first introduced by Burt and Adelson [4] to further speed-up the hierarchical prefiltering. Anisotropic environment maps using a constant shaped anisotropic lobe (à la Phong) should be researched as a possible alternative to the Banks model.

7 Acknowledgements

We would like to thank Jonas Jax and Jeff Heath who put their beautiful environment maps online. This work was partially supported by the SIMULGEN ESPRIT project #35772 and by the Universitat de Girona under grant BR98/I003.

References

1. BANKS, D. Illumination in Diverse Codimensions. In *Proceedings SIGGRAPH* (July 1994), pp. 327–334.
2. BASTOS, R., HOFF, K., WYNN, W., AND LASTRA, A. Increased Photorealism for Interactive Architectural Walkthroughs. In *1999 ACM Symposium on Interactive 3D Graphics* (April 1999), J. Hodgins and J. Foley, Eds., ACM SIGGRAPH, pp. 183–190.
3. BLINN, J., AND NEWELL, M. Texture and Reflection in Computer Generated Images. *Communications of the ACM 19* (1976), 542–546.
4. BURT, P., AND ADELSON, E. A Multiresolution Spline with Application to Image Mosaics. *ACM Transactions on Graphics 2*, 4 (October 1983), 217–236.
5. CABRAL, B., OLANO, M., AND NEMEC, P. Reflection Space Image Based Rendering. In *Proceedings SIGGRAPH* (August 1999), pp. 165–170.
6. DIEFENBACH, P., AND BADLER, N. Multi-Pass Pipeline Rendering: Realism For Dynamic Environments . In *1997 ACM Symposium on Interactive 3D Graphics* (April 1997), M. Cohen and D. Zeltzer, Eds., ACM SIGGRAPH, pp. 59–70.
7. GREENE, N. Applications of World Projections. In *Proceedings Graphics Interface* (May 1986), pp. 108–114.
8. GREENE, N. Environment Mapping and Other Applications of World Projections. *IEEE Computer Graphics & Applications 6*, 11 (November 1986), 21–29.
9. HEIDRICH, W., AND SEIDEL, H. Realistic, Hardware-accelerated Shading and Lighting. In *Proceedings SIGGRAPH* (Aug. 1999), pp. 171–178.
10. HEIDRICH, W., AND SEIDEL, H.-P. View-Independent Environment Maps. In *Eurographics/SIGGRAPH Workshop on Graphics Hardware* (1998), pp. 39–45.
11. KAUTZ, J., AND MCCOOL, M. Approximation of Glossy Reflection with Prefiltered Environment Maps. In *Proceedings Graphics Interface* (May 2000), pp. 119–126.
12. KIRK, D., AND ARVO, J. Unbiased Sampling Techniques for Image Synthesis. In *Proceedings SIGGRAPH* (July 1991), pp. 153–156.
13. LISCHINSKI, D., AND RAPPOPORT, A. Image-Based Rendering for Non-Diffuse Synthetic Scenes. In *Nineth Eurographics Workshop on Rendering* (June 1998), Eurographics, pp. 301–314.
14. MILLER, G., AND HOFFMAN, R. Illumination and Reflection Maps: Simulated Objects in Simulated and Real Environments. In *SIGGRAPH '84 Course Notes – Advanced Computer Graphics Animation* (July 1984).
15. MILLER, G., RUBIN, S., AND PONCELEON, D. Lazy Decompression of Surface Light Fields for Precomputed Global Illumination. In *Nineth Eurographics Workshop on Rendering* (June 1998), Eurographics, pp. 281–292.
16. NAYAR, S. Catadioptric Omnidirectional Camera. In *Proceedings of IEEE Conference on Computer Vision and Pattern Recognition* (june 1997).
17. NEIDER, J., DAVIS, T., AND WOO, M. *OpenGL - Programming Guide*. Addison-Wesley, 1993.
18. PHONG, B.-T. Illumination for Computer Generated Pictures. *Communications of the ACM 18*, 6 (June 1975), 311–317.
19. SGI. Iris performer. http://www.sgi.com/software/performer/brew/envmap.html.
20. STÜRZLINGER, W., AND BASTOS, R. Interactive Rendering of Globally Illuminated Glossy Scenes. In *Eighth Eurographics Workshop on Rendering* (June 1997), Eurographics, pp. 93–102.

Editors' Note: see Appendix, p. 407 for colored figures of this paper

Antialiasing with Line Samples

Thouis R. Jones, Ronald N. Perry

MERL[1]

Abstract. Antialiasing is a necessary component of any high quality renderer. An antialiased image is produced by convolving the scene with an *antialiasing filter* and sampling the result, or equivalently by solving the *antialiasing integral* at each pixel. Though methods for analytically computing this integral exist, they require the continuous two-dimensional result of visible-surface computations. Because these computations are expensive, most renderers use *supersampling*, a discontinuous approximation to the integral. We present a new algorithm, *line sampling*, combining a continuous approximation to the integral with a simple visible-surface algorithm. Line sampling provides high quality antialiasing at significantly lower cost than analytic methods while avoiding the visual artifacts caused by supersampling's discontinuous nature.

A line sample is a line segment in the image plane, centered at a pixel and spanning the footprint of the antialiasing filter. The segment is intersected with scene polygons, visible subsegments are determined, and the antialiasing integral is computed with those subsegments and a one-dimensional reparameterization of the integral.

On simple scenes where edge directions can be precomputed, one correctly oriented line sample per pixel suffices for antialiasing. Complex scenes can be antialiased by combining multiple line samples weighted according to the orientation of the edges they intersect.

1 Introduction

Aliasing, the masquerading of a signal's high frequencies as low frequencies when the signal is sampled at too low a rate, has plagued computer graphics since its inception. Images (two-dimensional signals) generated from scenes comprised of polygons are particularly prone to aliasing since polygon edges contain infinitely high frequencies which alias as the well-known "jaggies."

The sampling theorem states that a signal can be correctly reconstructed from a regular sampling only if the signal's maximum frequency component is below the Nyquist limit, defined as half the sampling rate. Frequencies above the Nyquist limit appear as low-frequency aliases in the reconstructed signal. The naïve method to reduce aliasing is to represent the signal with more samples (e.g., by adding more pixels to the display), but this is usually unacceptable. The preferred method is to *bandlimit* the signal or image prior to sampling by convolving it with a filter that attenuates the high frequencies. Convolving an image I with a bandlimiting filter F and then sampling at location P can be expressed as the integral

$$S(P_x, P_y) = \iint I(x,y)\, F(x - P_x, y - P_y)\, dx\, dy$$

where S is the resulting sampled image, made up of pixels at the sample points $\{P\}$. We refer to F as the *antialiasing filter*[2] and the equation above as the *antialiasing integral*.

[1] MERL- Mitsubishi Electric Research Laboratory, {rjones,perry}@merl.com

[2] Also known as the *prefilter* or *presampling filter*.

The perfect bandlimiting filter, *sinc*, completely removes frequencies above the Nyquist limit, but has infinite extent and causes "ringing" in images, making it unsuitable for antialiasing in most cases. A smooth, positive filter with finite extent (e.g., a truncated Gaussian) is preferable for efficiency and aesthetics.

There are two common methods for computing the antialiasing integral. *Analytic* methods compute the integral directly from a continuous representation of I. Point sampling methods, or *supersampling*, approximate the integral by sampling I at multiple points around P and computing $S(P)$ as a weighted sum according to F.

For three-dimensional scenes, I is the two-dimensional solution to the visible surface problem. Computing a continuous representation of visible surfaces is non-trivial, which has limited the use of analytic approaches despite efficient methods for computing the integral once visible surfaces are known.

Supersampling results in much simpler visible surface calculations, since visibility need only be determined at independent points. However, supersampling has some negative traits. Since the sampling points are discrete, it is a discontinuous approximation to the antialiasing integral. A small movement of an edge can cause a sample point to change from inside to outside a polygon, resulting in a jump in pixel value. Also, small features can be missed entirely by the sampling. Finally, regularly spaced samples result in patterned aliases, which are easily detected by the human eye. Adaptive and stochastic sampling can alleviate discontinuous behavior and patterned aliases, respectively, but lack a regular structure making them less amenable to efficient implementation.

In this paper we introduce *line sampling*, a new antialiasing method that combines a continuous approximation to the antialiasing integral with a simple visible-surface algorithm. Line sampling computes the antialiasing integral from the intersection of I and a line segment centered at P and spanning the footprint of the filter F, giving a one-dimensional signal that is antialiased analytically according to F. The underlying assumption is that the one-dimensional signal along the line sample is representative of the two-dimensional image I near P. This assumption is valid if the line sample is oriented perpendicularly to nearby edges in I. Unfortunately, determining such a direction is impossible in some cases, and infeasible in general.

In practice, sampling slightly off the optimal direction gives acceptable results, which leads us to taking multiple line samples per pixel and combining their results based on local image features. With two perpendicular line samples, this approach produces high quality antialiased images, comparable to those from analytic methods.

Line sampling's analytic nature with regards to one-dimensional features gives it smooth behavior when those features change slightly, as in animations. This yields much more aesthetically pleasing results, preventing the "twinkling" effects that are visible in animations generated with supersampling (unless a large number of samples are used).

1.1 Related Work

A tutorial on antialiasing is given by Foley in [12], and Joy [16] includes an excellent review of antialiasing methods [1, 4, 5, 6, 7, 8, 9, 11, 17, 23, 26, 27]. More recent work on analytic methods includes [10, 14, 19], all of which assume a precomputed solution to the visible surface problem. Recent work on supersampling includes [20, 21, 22].

An interesting variation of particular relevance is given by Max in [18], which presents a hybrid technique using data from a scanline renderer to antialias scenes, providing a method similar to analytic antialiasing in one direction and regular supersampling in the other. This is roughly equivalent to our method with a single line sample per pixel and each line sample having the same orientation. He extends his method in the

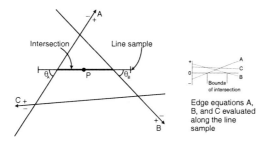

Fig. 1. The intersection of a triangle defined by the edge equations {A, B, C} and a line sample centered at pixel P. The intersection can be computed as the segment along the line sample where the edge equations are all positive, as shown in the graph. θ_A and θ_B are the angles of intersection between the line sample and the edges A and B of the triangle.

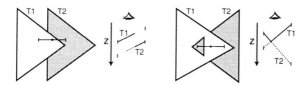

Fig. 2. Visible segment calculation. On the left, triangle T1 partially obscures triangle T2. On the right, T1 and T2 intersect. The depth information is shown in the graphs.

same paper to use data from adjacent scanlines and the slopes of the edges intersected by scanlines to infer a more accurate approximation of the image prior to filtering. An extension of this method is described by Tanaka in [25] in which every polygon's exact coverage is determined by inserting a vertical scanline at each position where an active edge is created, destroyed, or intersects a horizontal scanline. These vertical scanlines are bounded by the two neighboring horizontal scanlines to reduce computational cost. Even so, their method is 4-8 times slower than traditional scanline rendering. Guenter [14] also uses one-dimensional samples, but takes them from a precomputed visible surface solution and uses them to approximate the antialiasing integral via Gaussian quadrature.

We extend Max's work in [18] by using multiple sampling directions simultaneously, by considering independent sampling directions for each pixel, and by combining multiple samples per pixel. We do not use edge slopes in the approximation of I, though our method could be extended to do so. As will be shown (§3.2), our method produces high quality results with a cost of only about twice that of a scanline render.

2   Line Sampling

Computing an approximation to the antialiasing integral at a pixel with line sampling involves three steps: intersecting the line sample (a line segment in the image plane) with polygons in the scene, calculating visible segments along the line sample, and computing the filtered result. These calculations take place after the polygons in the scene have been converted to triangles and transformed to screen space. A line sample can be oriented in any direction; we assume a horizontal sample for the following discussion.

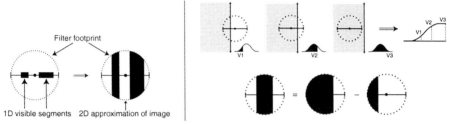

Fig. 3. Left: Extension of visible segments to two dimensions. The visible segments are "stretched" perpendicularly to the line sample within the filter footprint. Right: Computing and applying the one-dimensional summed-area table. The table stores the fraction of the filter covered as a perpendicular edge moves along the line sample. The filtered contribution of any segment can be calculated as the difference of two values from the table.

The intersection of a line sample and a triangle can be calculated by finding the segment of the line sample along which the signed distances to each edge of the triangle are all positive; these distances can be computed via edge equations as in Pineda [24], as shown in Figure 1. Since the edge equations are linear, they need only be evaluated at the endpoints of the line sample[3]. Intersections are calculated for each triangle and buffered for the visibility calculation.

Given the multiple intersections for a line sample, the visible segments along the line sample must be determined. Since depth is a linear function (see Blinn [2]), depth at segment endpoints is sufficient to determine visibility. Segments on a line sample can obscure or intersect each other as in Figure 2, and it is possible that a segment will be split into separate segments by the visibility calculation.

After the visible segments along a line sample are known, the value for the corresponding pixel P is computed as the sum of the filtered contribution of each visible segment. Since the antialiasing filter F is defined in two dimensions but the visible segments are one dimensional, the segments must be extended to two dimensions before filtering. In effect, the line sample acts as a very thin "window" onto the image I from which we must guess the rest of I within the footprint of F. Limited to one-dimensional information, we must assume that I changes only in that dimension, and is static in the other dimension. This is equivalent to "stretching" the visible segments perpendicularly to the line sample as shown in Figure 3.

Rather than computing a two-dimensional approximation of I and then filtering, it is possible to compute the filtered result directly from the visible segments. As shown in Figure 3, the contribution of each visible segment can be calculated using a one-dimensional summed-area table computed from a reparameterization of the antialiasing integral along the line sample.

3 Multiple Line Samples

To properly antialias an image with a single line sample per pixel requires that each line sample be oriented perpendicularly to any nearby edges. This is impossible near corners, and difficult even in simpler cases. Within these limitations, one possible antialiasing method is to render the image without antialiasing and postprocess it with an edge detector to yield approximate edge orientations, similar to the technique used by Bloomenthal [3]. Given these edge orientations, an antialiased image can then be

---

[3] Analogous to [24], a tiebreaker rule must be used when a line sample is collinear with a triangle edge.

rendered with line sampling. However, aliases in the non-antialiased pass can cause the wrong orientation to be chosen for the line samples, leading to aliasing in the final image. Another method to determine edge orientations, given by Fujimoto in [13], is to project all edges regardless of visibility to the screen. The projected edges could then be used to orient line samples for rendering. However, this can result in obscured edges affecting the orientation of line samples, again leading to aliasing.

Rather than attempting to antialias using a single line sample, we extend line sampling to use multiple line samples at each pixel. To determine the number of line samples necessary per pixel, we consider how close to optimal the orientation of a line sample needs to be to still give acceptable results. We have found that near an edge, line sample orientations within 45° of optimal are adequate (§4.1). Therefore, with two perpendicular line samples per pixel, one of the line samples will produce a value suitable for an antialiased image. Thus, we use two line samples, oriented horizontally and vertically; this simplifies implementation and improves efficiency (§3.2).

3.1 Combining Multiple Line Samples

Given two perpendicular line samples at a pixel, some method must be devised to combine their values. Simple averaging of the two values is unacceptable, equivalent in the worst case to averaging an antialiased image with a non-antialiased one. Some method is needed for weighting the two line samples based on how close one or the other's orientation is to optimal. We compute these weights from the edges that the line samples intersect.

For a line sample that intersects an edge, the accuracy of the antialiasing by that sample depends on the relative orientation of the line sample and the edge, with greater accuracy achieved the closer they are to perpendicular. We use $\sin^2 \theta$ as a weight that follows this behavior, with θ the angle between the line sample and the edge, as shown in Figure 1. The relative weights of the two line samples at a pixel are computed as the sum of $\sin^2 \theta$ for every intersection of an edge with either line sample at that pixel. Using $\sin^2 \theta$ rather than $\sin \theta$ normalizes the total weight from a single intersection.

Once we have relative weights for the two line samples, a blending function is used to combine their values. Early experiments showed that simply choosing the value with the higher weight gave good results, but in some cases such a discontinuous blend causes temporal aliasing. Instead, we perform cubic blending[4] of the values from the line samples according to their relative weights, which gives a smooth approximation of the step function.

Obscured, Created, and Shared Edges. Properly weighting line samples based on edges present in the image requires the determination of whether an edge from the scene data is visible in the image or not. As in Figure 2, some edges might be obscured, or two objects that intersect might create a new edge. Finally, some edges might be shared between adjacent triangles in an object, and should contribute to the weights according to the change in color across the shared edge.

Obscured edges and edges created by intersections are handled as follows. For each triangle that a line sample intersects, the orientation of edges crossed by the line sample (e.g., A and B in Figure 1) and the triangle's surface normal are stored. During the visibility calculation, obscured edges are culled by depth comparison. When segments intersect, the orientation of the created edge is calculated from the cross product of the surface normals of the corresponding triangles.

---

[4]The cubic blend of values (v_1, v_2) according to the weights (w_1, w_2) is defined as $v = v_1 + (v_2 - v_1)(w^2(3 - 2w))$ with $w = \frac{w_2}{w_1 + w_2}$.

202

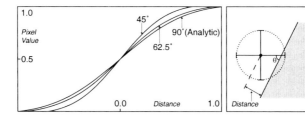

Fig. 4. Plots of line sampling of single edges, oriented at 90°, 62.5°, and 45° relative to one of the line samples. Plots are of pixel value versus distance from the edge to the pixel center, as shown on the right. Two line samples, oriented horizontally and vertically, were used to generate the data for the plots. Because of symmetry, the plots do not depend on which line sample the orientations are measured from.

Detecting shared edges is trivially accomplished by comparing segment endpoints. Determining how much a shared edge should contribute to the weighting calculation requires a heuristic based on the change in color across the edge. We do not explore such a heuristic in this paper, noting that other antialiasing methods such as proper texture filtering are more relevant in these cases.

3.2 Computing Visible Segments Along Scanlines

When using two line samples per pixel, oriented horizontally and vertically, the horizontal line samples are all subsegments of the horizontal scanlines running through those pixels. Likewise, the vertical line samples are subsegments of "vertical scanlines." It is possible to compute visible segments along entire scanlines at a time, as in a standard scanline renderer, and then extract the visible segments for individual pixels.

Such an implementation of line sampling is equivalent to generating two images via scanline techniques, with the weights of the two line samples being used to perform a per-pixel blend of the two images. Each of the two images is antialiased well in one direction and poorly in the other, and the weights indicate which image is better antialiased at a particular pixel.

With such an implementation, the computational cost of line sampling is not much more than twice the cost of a scanline renderer, and the storage required is proportional to the size of the image being rendered (not including short-term storage for the scanline visibility calculation). After taking into account transformations, shading, and other calculations independent of the antialiasing method, line sampling becomes a viable alternative for achieving high quality antialiasing without a large increase in cost.

4 Results

4.1 Error Analysis for Single Edges

Figure 4 shows the behavior of line sampling applied to a single edge for different edge orientations. Each plot shows the pixel value computed for varying distances from the edge to the pixel center. Two line samples, oriented horizontally and vertically, were used to generate the plots, with a Gaussian filter e^{-2r^2} (truncated at $r = 1$ and normalized), and cubic blending used to combine the values of the two line samples.

For edges oriented at 90°, line sampling is equivalent to analytic antialiasing. For 45° and 62.5° edges, the maximum errors compared to the analytic result are 0.09 and 0.03, respectively. The 45° orientation is the worst case for a single edge.

When antialiasing a 45° edge, the result is equivalent to the analytic solution for a filter with $r = \sin 45°$ (≈ 0.71)[5]. In the 62.5° case, the computed value is a blend between two filters, one with $r = \sin 62.5°$ (≈ 0.89) and the other with $r = \sin 27.5°$ (≈ 0.46). Cubic blending ensures that the wider filter dominates.

It is also important to notice the smooth behavior of line sampling in all cases as the distance to the edge changes. This prevents temporal artifacts as edges move slightly in animations.

4.2 Images

Figures 5 and 6 compare different antialiasing methods. Figure 5 is a scene comprised of thin triangles scaled and rotated around a single point; Figure 6 is a triangle comb, where each triangle is 1.01 pixels wide at the base and 100 pixels high. Each figure shows four images, two from stochastic sampling (256 or 16 point samples per pixel, shared during filtering), one from line sampling, and one without antialiasing (regular sampling, one sample per pixel). Supersampling with 256 samples is indistinguishable from the analytic solution for these images.

The stochastic sampling and line sampling images were generated with a Gaussian filter (truncated at $r = 1$ and normalized). Two line samples, oriented horizontally and vertically, were used to render the line sampling images, with cubic blending used to combine the values of the two line samples.

The 256-supersampled and line sampling images compare quite favorably. The Moiré artifacts in the line sampling image in Figure 5 are slightly more pronounced near edges oriented at about 45°; this is due to the effectively narrower filter in those areas (§4.1).

Stochastic noise is quite noticeable in the 16-supersampled images in areas with high frequencies. When animated, these areas "twinkle" distractingly, due to the high frequency content of the closely-spaced parallel edges. Line sampling performs almost as well as analytic antialiasing in those areas, and the same animations generated with line sampling do not suffer from such temporal artifacts.

4.3 Failure Cases

There are some cases where line sampling can fail, primarily because it is unable to properly antialias areas with high-frequency content in multiple near-orthogonal directions. For example, a 90° axis-aligned corner can protrude into a pixel without intersecting either line sample. A slight change in its position can cause it to cover both line samples halfway, resulting in a jump in pixel value. Other cases such as sub-pixel polygons and endpoints on thin rectangular polygons are not properly antialiased by line sampling.

Line sampling can also fail due to interactions of patterned scenes with the pattern of line samples. For example, a geometric (rather than textured) checkerboard tilted at 45° in screen space could appear all white if the line samples and checkerboard squares were to line up perfectly.

5   Conclusions and Future Work

Line sampling provides high quality antialiasing of polygonal scenes without a large increase in the computational cost of rendering. It provides near-analytic antialiasing

---

[5] A single line sample interacts with an edge as if the line sample were perpendicular to the edge, but scaled by $\sin \theta$, where θ is the angle between the edge and the line sample.

on one-dimensional features, and prevents most of the distracting "twinkling" artifacts that occur in animations generated with stochastic sampling. Because one-dimensional features are visually important, line sampling's emphasis on properly antialiasing such features is justified.

In the future, we plan to explore using more line samples at each pixel to improve line sampling's robustness. Some of the failure cases might also be prevented by stochastic line sampling, in which the orientations of line samples are chosen randomly for each pixel. We would also like to investigate the natural extension of line sampling to motion blur. Finally, we note that line sampling's per-pixel memory requirements could be unbounded, similar to Carpenter's A-buffer [4]. Recent work by Jouppi [15] on a simplified A-buffer with fixed per-pixel memory leads us to believe that analogous methods might be applied to line sampling.

Fig. 5. Clockwise from upper left: stochastic sampling (256 samples/pixel), line sampling, regular sampling (1 sample/pixel), stochastic sampling (16 samples/pixel).

Fig. 6. Left to right: stochastic sampling (256 samples/pixel), line sampling, stochastic sampling (16 samples/pixel), regular sampling (1 sample/pixel). In the rightmost image, the thin vertical triangles of the comb break up completely and alias as large triangles.

References

1. Greg Abram, Lee Westover, and Turner Whitted. Efficient Alias-free Rendering Using Bit-Masks and Look-up Tables. *Proceedings of SIGGRAPH 85*, pages 53–59, July 1985.
2. James F. Blinn. Jim Blinn's Corner: Hyperbolic Interpolation. *IEEE Computer Graphics & Applications*, 12(4), July 1992.
3. J. Bloomenthal. Edge Inference with Applications to Antialiasing. *Proceedings of SIGGRAPH 83*, pages 157–162, July 1983.
4. Loren Carpenter. The A-buffer, an Antialiased Hidden Surface Method. *Proceedings of SIGGRAPH 84*, pages 103–108, July 1984.
5. E. Catmull. A hidden-surface algorithm with anti-aliasing. *Proceedings of SIGGRAPH 78*, pages 6–11, August 1978.
6. Edwin Catmull. An Analytic Visible Surface Algorithm for Independent Pixel Processing. *Proceedings of SIGGRAPH 84*, pages 109–115, July 1984.
7. Robert L. Cook. Stochastic Sampling in Computer Graphics. *ACM Transactions on Graphics*, 5(1):51–72, January 1986.
8. F. C. Crow. A Comparison of Antialiasing Techniques. *IEEE Computer Graphics & Applications*, 1(1):40–48, January 1981.
9. Mark A. Z. Dippé and Erling Henry Wold. Antialiasing Through Stochastic Sampling. *Proceedings of SIGGRAPH 85*, pages 69–78, 1985.
10. T. Duff. Polygon Scan Conversion by Exact Convolution. In *Raster Imaging and Digital Typography*, pages 154–168. 1989. ISBN 0521374901.
11. E. A. Feibush, Marc Levoy, and Robert L. Cook. Synthetic Texturing Using Digital Filters. *Proceedings of SIGGRAPH 80*, pages 294–301, July 1980.
12. James D. Foley, Andries van Dam, Steven K. Feiner, and John F. Hughes. *Computer Graphics, Principles and Practice, Second Edition*. Addison-Wesley, 1990.
13. A. Fujimoto, C. Perrot, and K. Iwata. A 3D Graphics Display System with Depth Buffer and Pipeline Processor. *IEEE Computer Graphics & Applications*, 4(6):11–23, June 1984.
14. Brian Guenter and Jack Tumblin. Quadrature Prefiltering for High Quality Antialiasing. *ACM Transactions on Graphics*, 15(4):332–353, October 1996.
15. Norman P. Jouppi and Chun-Fa Chang. Z3: An Economical Hardware Technique for High-Quality Antialiasing and Transparency. In *Proceedings of the 1999 Eurographics/SIGGRAPH Workshop on Graphics Hardware*, pages 85–93. 1999.
16. Kenneth I. Joy, Charles W. Grant, Nelson L. Max, and Lansing Hatfield, editors. *Tutorial: Computer Graphics: Image Synthesis*. Computer Society Press, 1988.
17. Mark E. Lee, Richard A. Redner, and Samuel P. Uselton. Statistically Optimized Sampling for Distributed Ray Tracing. *Proceedings of SIGGRAPH 85*, pages 61–67, July 1985.
18. Nelson L. Max. Antialiasing Scan-Line Data. *IEEE Computer Graphics & Applications*, 10(1):18–30, January 1990.
19. Michael D. McCool. Analytic Antialiasing With Prism Splines. *Proceedings of SIGGRAPH 95*, pages 429–436, August 1995.
20. Don P. Mitchell. Consequences of Stratified Sampling in Graphics. *Proceedings of SIGGRAPH 96*, pages 277–280, August 1996.
21. Don P. Mitchell. Generating Antialiased Images at Low Sampling Densities. *Proceedings of SIGGRAPH 87*, pages 65–72, July 1987.
22. Steven Molnar. Efficient Supersampling Antialiasing for High-performance Architectures. Technical Report 91-023, University of North Carolina, 1991.
23. Alan V. Oppenheim and Ronald W. Schafer. *Digital Signal Processing*. Prentice-Hall, 1975. ISBN 0132146355.
24. Juan Pineda. A Parallel Algorithm for Polygon Rasterization. *Proceedings of SIGGRAPH 88*, pages 17–20, August 1988.
25. Toshimitsu Tanaka and Tokiichiro Takahashi. Cross Scanline Algorithm. *Proceedings of EUROGRAPHICS '90*, pages 63–74, 1990.
26. K. Turkowski. Anti-Aliasing through the Use of Coordinate Tansformations. *ACM Transactions on Graphics*, 1(3):215–234, July 1982.
27. Turner Whitted. An Improved Illumination Model for Shaded Display. *Communications of the ACM*, 23(6):343–349, June 1980.

Comparing Real & Synthetic Scenes using Human Judgements of Lightness

Ann McNamara Alan Chalmers

Department of Computer Science

Tom Troscianko Iain Gilchrist

Department of Experimental Psychology
University of Bristol Bristol
mcnamara@cs.bris.ac.uk

Abstract. Increased application of computer graphics in areas which demand high levels of realism has made it necessary to examine the manner in which images are evaluated and validated. In this paper, we explore the need for including the human observer in any process which attempts to quantify the level of realism achieved by the rendering process, from measurement to display. We introduce a framework for measuring the perceptual equivalence (from a lightness perception point of view) between a real scene and a computer simulation of the same scene. Because this framework is based on psychophysical experiments, results are produced through study of vision from a *human* rather than a *machine* vision point of view. This framework can then be used to evaluate, validate and compare rendering techniques.

1 Introduction

The aim of realistic image synthesis is the creation of accurate, high quality imagery which faithfully represents a physical environment, the ultimate goal being to create images which are perceptually indistinguishable from an actual scene. Rendering systems are now capable of accurately simulating the distribution of light in an environment. However, physical accuracy does not ensure that the displayed images will have authentic visual appearance. Reliable image quality assessments are necessary for the evaluation of realistic images synthesis algorithms. Typically the quality of an image synthesis method is evaluated using numerical techniques which attempt to quantify fidelity using image to image comparisons (often comparisons are made with a photograph of the scene that the image is intended to depict).

Several image quality metrics have been developed whose goals are to predict the *visible* differences between a pair of images. It is well established that simple approaches, such as mean squared error (MSE), do not provide meaningful measures of image fidelity, more sophisticated techniques are necessary. As image quality assessments should correspond to assessments made by humans, a better understanding of features of the **H**uman **V**isual **S**ystem (HVS) should lead to more effective comparisons, which in turn will steer image synthesis algorithms to produce more realistic, reliable images. Any feature of an image not visible to a human is not worth computing. Results from psychophysical experiments can reveal limitations of the HVS. However, problems arise when trying to incorporate such results into computer graphics algorithms. This is due to the fact that, often, experiments are designed to explore a single dimension of the HVS at a time under laboratory conditions. The HVS comprises many complex mechanisms, which rather than function independently, often work in conjunction with each other, making it more sensible to examine the HVS as a whole. Rather than attempting to reuse results from previous psychophysical experiments, new experiments are needed which examine the complex response HVS as a *whole* instead of than trying to isolate features for individual investigations. In this work we study the ability of the HVS to perceive albedo and the impact of rendering quality on *this task*. Rather than deal with atomic aspects of perception, this study examines a complete task in a more realistic setting.

Human judgements of lightness are compared in real scenes, and synthetic images. Correspondence between these judgements is then used as an indication of the fidelity of the synthetic image.

1.1 Lightness Perception

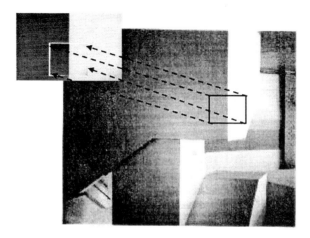

Fig. 1. Importance of depth perception for lightness constancy

Lightness is apparent reflectance, brightness is apparent intensity of the illuminant. Reflectance is the proportion of light falling on an object that is reflected to the eye of the observer. Reflectance (albedo) is constant, the perception of lightness depends of reflectance [1]. Gilchrist [8] showed that the perception of the degree of "lightness" of a surface patch (i.e. whether it is white, gray or black) is greatly affected by the perceived distance and orientation of the surface in question, as well as the perceived illumination falling on the surface - where the latter were experimentally manipulated through a variety of cues such as occlusion, or perspective.

Perception of the lightness of patches varying in reflectance may thus be a suitable candidate for the choice of visual task. It is simple to perform, and it is known that lightness constancy depends on the successful perception of lighting and the 3D structure of a scene, for example figure 1. When viewed in isolation the patches on the top left hand corner appear to be of different luminance. However, when examined in the context of the entire scene, it can be seen that the patches have been cut from the edge of the stairwell, and is perceived as an edge where the entire stairwell has the same luminance. Eliminating the depth cues means the patches are perceived as different, demonstrating the dependency of lightness perception on the correct perception of three dimensional structure, [10]. As the key features of any scene are illumination, geometry and depth, the task of lightness matching encapsulates all three key characteristics into one task. This task is particularly suited to this experimental framework, apart from being simple to perform it also allows excellent control over experimental stimuli. Subsequent sections describe an experimental framework, with such a lightness matching task at the core, to allow human observers to compare real and synthetic scenes.

The remainder of this paper is divided into the following sections. In Section 2, we describe previous research. In Section 3, we describe the steps taken to build the experiment in order to facilitate easy human comparison between real and synthetic scene, we also discuss the actual organisation of participants in terms of scheduling. Section 4 describes the experiment, the results are presented in section 5 and finally, conclusions are drawn in section 6.

2   Previous Work

Models of visual processing enable the development of perceptually based error metrics for rendering algorithms that will reduce the computational demands of rendering while preserving the visual fidelity of the rendered images. Much research investigating this issue is under way.

Using a simple five sided cube as their test environment Meyer et al [13] presented an approach to image synthesis comprising separate physical and perceptual modules. They chose diffusely reflecting materials to built a physical test environment. Each module is verified using experimental techniques. The test environment was placed in a small dark room. Radiometric values predicted using a radiosity lighting simulation of a basic environment are compared to physical measurements of radiant flux densities in the real environment. Then the results of the radiosity calculations are transformed to the RGB values for display, following the principles of colour science.

Measurements of irradiation were made at 25 locations in the plane of the open face for comparison with the simulations. Results show that irradiation is greatest near the centre of the open side of the cube. This area provides the best view of the light source and other walls. The calculated values are much higher than the measurements. In summary, there is good agreement between the radiometric measurements and the predictions of the lighting model. Meyer et al. then proceeded by transforming the validated simulated value to values displayable on a television monitor. A group of twenty experimental participants were asked to differentiate between real environment and the displayed image, both of which were viewed through the back of a view camera. They were asked which of the images was the real scene. Nine out of the twenty participants (45%) indicated that the simulated image was actually the real scene, i.e. selected the wrong answer, revealing that observers were simply guessing. Although participants considered the overall match and colour match to be good, some weaknesses were cited in the sharpness of the shadows (a consequence of the discretisation in the simulation) and in the brightness of the ceiling panel (a consequence of the directional characteristics of the light source). The overall agreement lends strong support to the perceptual validity of the simulation and display process.

Rushmeier et al. [15] used perceptually based metrics to compare image quality to a captured image of the scene being represented. The image comparison metrics were derived from [4],[6], [11]. Each is based on ideas taken from image compression techniques. The goal of this work was to obtain results from comparing two images using these models that were large if large differences between the images exist, and small when they are almost the same. These suggested metrics include some basic characteristics of human vision described in image compression literature. First, within a broad band of luminance, the visual system senses relative rather than absolute luminances. For this reason a metric should account for luminance variations, not absolute values. Second, the response of the visual system is non-linear. The perceived "brightness" or "lightness" is a non-linear function of luminance. The particular non-linear relationship is not well established and is likely to depend on complex issues such as perceived lighting and 3-D geometry. Third, the sensitivity of the eye depends on the spatial frequency of luminance variations. The perceptual metrics derived were used to compare images in a manner that roughly corresponds to subjective human vision, in particular the Daly model performed very well.

The Visible Difference Predictor (VDP) is a perceptually based image quality metric proposed by Daly [4]. Myskowski [14] realised the VDP had many potential applications in realistic image synthesis. He completed a comprehensive validation and calibration of VDP response via human psychophysical experiments. Then, he used the VDP local error metric to steer decision making in adaptive mesh subdivision, and isolated regions of interest for more intensive global illumination computations. The VDP was tested to determine how close VDP predictions come to subjective reports of visible differences between images by designing two human psychophysical experiments. Results from these experiments showed a good correspondence with VDP results for shadow and lighting pattern masking and in comparison of the perceived quality of images generated as subsequent stages of indirect lighting solutions.

McNamara et al [12] built an experimental framework to facilitate human comparison between real and synthetic scene. They ran a series of psychophysical experiments in which human observers were asked to compare regions of a real physical scene with regions of the computer generated representation of that scene. The comparison involved lightness judgements in both the generated image and the real scene. Results from these experiments showed that the visual response to the real scene and a high fidelity rendered image was similar. The work presented in this paper extends this work to investigate comparisons using three dimensional objects as targets, rather than simple regions. This allows us to examine scene characteristics such as shadow, object occlusion and depth perception.

3 Experimental Design

This section outlines the steps involved in building a well articulated scene containing three dimensional objects placed within a custom built environment to evoke certain perceptual cues such as lightness constancy, depth perception and the perception of shadows. Measurements of virtual environments are often inaccurate. For some applications[1] such estimation of input may be appropriate. However, for these purposes an accurate description of the environment is essential to avoid introducing errors at such an early stage. Also, once the global illumination calculations have been computed, it is important to display the resulting image in the correct manner while taking into account the limitations of the display device. As we are interested in comparing different rendering engines, it is vital that we minimise errors in the model and display stages, this means then that any errors arising can be attributed to the rendering technique employed to calculate the image. This study required an experimental set-up comprised of a real

---

[1]The level of realism required is generally application dependent. In some situations a high level of realism is not required, for example games, educational techniques and graphics for web design.

Fig. 2. The test environment showing real environment and computer image.

environment and a computer representation of that three dimensional environment. The measurements required for this study, the equipment used to record them are described herein, along with the rendering process employed to generate the physical stimuli.

3.1 The Real Scene

The test environment was a five sided box shown in figure 2. Several objects that were placed within the box for examination. All interior surfaces of the box were painted with white matt house paint. To accommodate the three dimensional objects, custom paints were mixed, using precise ratios to serve as the basis for materials in the scene. To ensure correct, accurate ratios were achieved, 30ml syringes were used to mix paint in parts as shown in Table 1. The spectral reflectance of the paints were measured using a TOPCON-100 spectroradiometer, these values were transformed to RGB tristimulus values following [16].

Appearance	% White	Reflectance	Patch#	Patch Reflectance
Black	0	0.0471	0	.0494
Dark Gray	10	0.0483	0	.0494
Dark Gray	20	0.0635	2	.0668
Dark Gray	30	0.0779	4	.0832
Dark Gray	40	0.0962	6	.1012
Dark Gray	50	0.1133	7	.1120
Gray	60	0.1383	9	.1224
Gray	70	0.1611	14	1680
Light Gray	80	0.2002	15	.2259
Light Gray	90	0.3286	19	.3392
Light Gray	95	0.4202	23	.4349
Almost White	97.5	0.5292	26	.5512
Almost White	98.25	0.5312	26	.5512
White	100	0.8795	29	.8795

Table 1. Paint Reflectance along with Reflectance of Corresponding Patch

212

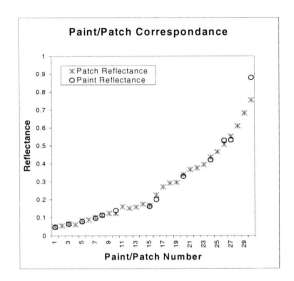

Fig. 3. Correspondence of Patches to Paints

As in [12] a small, front-silvered, high quality mirror was incorporated into the set up to allow the viewing conditions to facilitate alternation between the two settings, viewing of the original scene or viewing of the modelled scene on the computer monitor. When the optical mirror was in position, subjects viewed the original scene. In the absence of the optical mirror the computer representation of the original scene was viewed. The angular sub-tenses of the two displays were equalised, and the fact that the display monitor had to be closer to the subject for this to occur, was allowed for by the inclusion of a +2 diopter lens in its optical path; the lens equated the optical distances of the two displays.

3.2 Illumination

The light source consisted of a 24 volt quartz halogen bulb mounted on optical bench fittings at the top of the test environment. This was supplied by a stabilised 10 amp DC power supply, stable to 30 parts per million in current. The light shone through a 70 mm by 115 mm opening at the top of the enclosure. Black masks, constructed of matt cardboard sheets, were placed framing the screen and the open wall of the enclosure, a separate black cardboard sheet was used to define the eye position. An aperture in this mask was used to enforce monocular vision, since the VDU display did not permit stereoscopic viewing.

3.3 The Graphical Representations

Ten images were considered for comparison to the real scene, they are listed here along with the aims that we hoped to achieve from the comparison.

1. **Photograph**: Comparison to a photograph is needed to enable us to evaluate our method to more traditional image comparison metrics. The reasoning behind this is that most current techniques compare to "reality" by comparing to a captured

image. We wanted to see if this is equivalent to comparing to a real physical environment and so included a photograph, taken with a digital camera, as one of our test images.

2. **Radiance: 2 Ambient Bounces**: A Radiance [17] image generated using 2 ambient bounces is generally considered to be a high quality image. Here we wanted to determine if 2 ambient bounces gives a similar perceptual impression to an 8 ambient bounce image which is more compute intensive.

3. **Radiance: 8 Ambient Bounces**: We wanted to investigate if there was a marked difference using a Radiance image generated using 8 ambient bounces, as this involves considerably more compute time, and might not be necessary i.e. may not provide any more perceptual information than an image rendered using 2 ambient bounces.

4. **Radiance: 8 Ambient Bounces BRIGHT**: This image had its brightness increased manually to see if this affected perception. The brightness was doubled (i.e. the intensity of each pixel was multiplied by 2) to see what, if any effect this had on the perception of the image.

5. **Radiance: Default**: Image generated with the default Radiance parameters. This would determine whether extra compute time makes a significant difference. The default image renders in a very short time, however ambient bounces of light are absent, we wanted to compare this to imagery where interreflections were catered for.

6. **Radiance: Controlled Errors in Estimate Reflectance Values**: The RGB values for the materials were set to equal values to see what difference, if any, this made compared to using measured values. A poor perceptual response to this image would confirm our suspicion that material properties must be carefully quantified if an accurate result is required. This comparison, and the next, was to demonstrate the importance of using exact measurements rather than estimations for material values.

7. **Radiance: Controlled Errors in Estimate of Light Source**: The RGB values for the light source were set to equal values to see what difference this made compared to using measured values. This experiment will show the necessity of measuring emission properties of sources in an environment if an accuracy is the aim.

8. **Radiance: Tone Mapped**: We wanted to investigate the difference tone mapping would make to our test image. Tone mapping transforms the radiance values computed by the rendering engine to values displayable on a display device in a manner that preserves the *subjective* impression of the scene. The Tone Mapping Operator (TMO) used here was introduced by Ferwerda et al. [5]. Although the image examined does not have a very high dynamic range, we were interested to see the effects tone mapping would have on image perception.

9. **Renderpark: Raytraced**: This was a very noisy image generated using stochastic raytracing. This experiment was designed to see how under-sampling would affect perception. Here the effect of under-sampling is exaggerated but might give insights in to how much undersampling a rendering engine can "get away with" without affecting perceptual performance.

10. **Renderpark: Radiosity**: Finally, to investigate the effects of meshing in a radiosity solution, a poorly meshed radiosity image was used. We wanted to demonstrate the importance of using an accuracy meshing strategy when employing radiosity techniques.

These images are shown in the accompanying colour plate.

214

The media used for stimulus presentation was a gamma corrected 20-inch monitor with the following phosphor chromaticity coordinates:

$$x_r = 0.6044 \quad x_g = 0.2808 \quad x_b = .1520 \quad x_w = 0.2786$$
$$y_r = 0.3434 \quad y_g = 0.6016 \quad y_b = .0660 \quad y_w = 0.3020$$

4 Experiment

Eighteen observers participated in the experiment, and were naive of the purpose of the experiment. All had normal or corrected-to-normal vision. Both condition order and trial order were fully randomised across subjects and conditions. Participants were given clear instructions.

4.1 Training on Munsell Chips

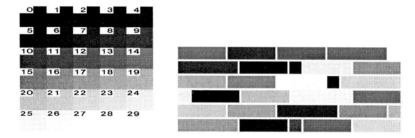

Fig. 4. Patch arrangement used to train participants with Reference Chart)

In [12], the task involved matching regions to a control chart which meant observers had to look away from the scene under examination to choose a match. Moving between scene and chart may affect adaptation to the scene in question, also the view point is not fixed, for this reason we decided to *train* participants on the control patches first. Once trained on the patches participants could then recall the match from memory. Training was conducted as follows. Observers were asked to select, from a numbered grid of 30 achromatic Munsell chips presented on a white background, a sample to match a second unnumbered grid (figure 4) simultaneously displayed on the same background, under constant illumination. The unnumbered grid comprised 60 chips. At the start of each experiment participants were presented with two grids, one an ordered numbered regular grid the other an unordered unnumbered irregular grid comprising one or more of the chips from the numbered grid. Both charts were hung on the wall approximately one meter from the participant. Each participant was asked to match the chips on the unnumbered grid to one of the chips on the numbered grid on the left. In other words they were to pick a numbered square on the left and place it right next to the grid on the right which in the grid would match it exactly. This is done in a random manner, a laser pointer [2] was used to point to the unnumbered chip under examination. Then the numbered chart was removed, and the unnumbered chart replaced by a similar chart but one where the chips had a different order. Participants repeated the task, this time working from memory to recall the number each chip would match to. The results of this training exercise are graphed in figure 5. The graph on the left shows the average

---
[2] non-invasive medium

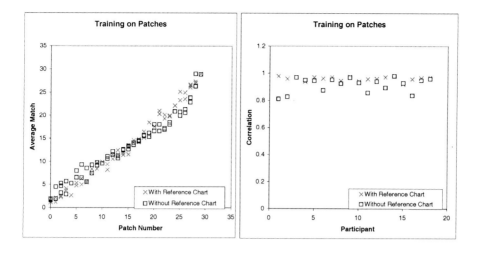

Fig. 5. Average of Matching to Training Patches with and without the reference chart shown on the right along with the Average Correlation for both cases on the left

match across 18 subjects, both with the reference chart and without the reference chart. The graph on the right shows the average correlation. This correlation gives an indication of the extent to which two sets of data are linearly related. A values close to 1 indicates a strong relationship, while a value of 0 signifies there is no linear relationship. A correlation of 1 would result if the participant matched each unnumbered patch to its corresponding numbered patch, in reality this is not the case and some small errors are made, what we need to determine is if the errors made when matching from memory i.e. without the chart are about the same size as the errors made with the reference chart in place. The correlation value when matching the patches with the chart in place is 0.96, and when matching from memory the result is 0.92, indicating a very small difference of 0.04 between the two conditions. From this small difference we can conclude that participants are *just as good* at matching the patches without the reference chart in place. Thus, this training paradigm proved to be reliable and stable. This has the dual benefit of speeding up the time taken per condition, as well as ensuring participants do not need to move their gaze from image to chart, thus eliminating any influence due to adaptation.

4.2 Matching to Images

Each participant was presented with a series of images, in a random order, one of which was the real environment. Participants were not explicitly informed which image was the physical environment. The images presented were the real scene, the photograph and the 9 rendered images. There were 17 different objects in the test environment, subjects were also asked to match the 5 sides of the environment (floor, ceiling, left

wall, back wall and right wall) giving a total of 21 matches. The paints used on the objects match to the training patches as shown in graph 3, and detailed in table 3.1. Participants were asked to judge the lightness of target objects in a random manner.

We chose this particular task - that of matching materials in the scene against a display of originals - because the task has a number of attractive features. First, Gilchrist [9, 7] has shown that the perception of lightness (the perceptual correlate of reflectance) is strongly dependent on the human visual system's rendition of both illumination and 3-D geometry. These are key features of perception of any scene and are in themselves complex attributes. However, the simple matching procedure used here depends critically on the correct representation of the above parameters. Therefore, the task should be sensitive to any mismatch between the original and the rendered scene. Secondly, the matching procedure is a standard psychophysical task and allows excellent control over the stimulus and the subject's response. The task chosen here corresponds closely to the methodology of Gilchrist [2, 9, 7] which permits simple measures (of lightness) to be made at locations in complex scenes. Ultimately, the task was chosen to be simple while also being sensitive to perceptual distortions in the scene.

5 Results

Results for each participant were recorded and analysed independently. The value (or gray level) chosen by each participant in the real scene was compared with the values chosen in the rendered image. For a rendered image to be a faithful reproduction, the values in both cases should be closely related. To examine this relationship we carried out a linear correlation for each subject. This correlation gives an indication of the extent to which two sets of data are linearly related. A values close to 1 indicates a strong relationship, whilst a value of 0 signifies there is no linear relationship. A correlation of 1 would result if the participant chose exactly the same gray level for each object in the real scene and rendered image. Correlation values are shown in table 2, and graphed as shown in the colour plate, the graph on the right shows these values averaged.

To examine *the pattern* of these correlations across participants we carried out ANalysis Of VAriance (ANOVA). ANOVA is a powerful set of procedures used for testing significance where two or more conditions are used, here 10 conditions were examined [3]. A *repeated measures within subjects* ANOVA was used. There was a significant effect of condition:

$$F(9, 153) = 80.3; p < .001$$

This equation can be read as follows, the F statistic equals 80.3, with 9 degrees of fredom (10 images), 153 degrees of freedom for the error term (calculated as a function of image combinations). The P value indicates the probability that these differences occur by *chance*. This is a repeated measures within subjects analysis of variance as each subject performed each condition.

This means there are statistically reliable differences between the conditions. This is to be expected as some images were deliberately selected for variation in quality.

The ANOVA showed there are significant differences in perception across images. Further analyses were carried out to investigate where these differences occur. These analyses took the form of a paired comparison t-test. Here we took the correlation between the real scene and the photograph, and compared it to the correlation of the real scene to the other images. Results from the correlations are shown in the following table.

Image	Mean Correlation with REAL
Photograph	.8918
* 2 Ambient Bounces	.843
8 Ambient Bounces	.884
Brightened 8 Ambient Bounces	.865
* Default	.337
* Controlled Error Materials	.692
Tone Mapped	.879
Controlled Error Illumination	.862
* Raytraced	.505
* Radiosity	.830

Table 2. Comparison of Rendered Images to Real Environment

A star in the table indicates a statistically significant difference, reflecting a reliable decrement in quality when compared to the photograph. The significant t values were as follows:

Two Ambient Bounces: $(t(17) = 3.11; p < .01)$
Default Image: $(t(17) = 12.4; p < .001)$
Guessed Materials Image: $(t(17) = 10.7; p < .001)$
Raytraced Image: $(t(17) = 9.36; p < .001)$
Radiosity Image: $(t(17) = 3.00; p < .01)$

The t statistic equals (take Two Ambient Bounces as an example) 3.11, with 17 degrees of freedom (18 participants). The probability, p of this distribution happening by chance is less than 0.01. This means that while there are some small differences between the results of matching to the photograph and matching to other images, these differences are not significant.

In summary, our results show that there is evidence that the 2 Ambient Bounces image, the Default image, the Controlled Error Materials image, the Raytraced image and the Radiosity image are perceptually degraded compared to the photograph. However, there is no evidence that the others images in this study are perceptually inferior to the photograph. From this we can conclude that the 8 Ambient Bounces image, the Brightened 8 Ambient Bounces image, the Tone Mapped image and the Controlled Error Illumination image are of the same perceptual quality as a photograph of the real scene.

6 Conclusions

We have introduced a method for measuring the perceptual equivalence between a real scene and a computer simulation of the same scene, from a lightness matching point of view. Because this model is based on psychophysical experiments, results are produced through study of vision from a human rather than a machine vision point of view.

By conducting a series of experiments, based on the psychophysics of lightness perception, we can estimate how much alike a rendered image is to the original scene. Results show that given a real scene and a faithful representation of that scene, the visual response function in both cases is similar.

Because the complexity of human perception and the computational expensive rendering algorithms that exist today, future work should focus on developing efficient methods from which resultant graphical representations of scenes yield the same perceptual effects as the original scene. To achieve this the full gamut of colour perception, as opposed to simply lightness, must be considered by introducing scenes of increasing complexity.

References

1. E. H. Adelson, Lightness Perception and Lightness Illusions, 339–351, MIT Press, 1999, pp. 339–351.
2. J. Cataliotti and A. Gilchrist, *Local and global processes in lightness perception*, Perception and Psychophysics, vol. 57(2), 1995, pp. 125–135.
3. H. Coolican, *Research methods and statistics in psychology*, Hodder and Stoughton, Oxford, 1999.
4. S. Daly, *The visible difference predictor: an algorithm for the assessment of ima ge fidelity*, In A. B. Watson Editor, Digital Images and Human Vision, MIT Press, 1993, pp. 179–206.
5. J. A. Ferwerda, S.N. Pattanaik, P. Shirley, and D. P. Greenberg, *A model of visual adaptation for realistic image synthesis*, Computer Graphics **30** (1996), no. Annual Conference Series, 249–258.
6. J. Gervais, Jr. L.O. Harvey, and J.O. Roberts, *Identification confusions among letters of the alphabet*, Journal of Experimental Psychology: Human Perception and Perfor mance, vol. 10(5), 1984, pp. 655–666.
7. A. Gilchrist, *Lightness contrast and filures of lightness constancy: a common explanation*, Perception and Psychophysics, vol. 43(5), 1988, pp. 125–135.
8. A. Gilchrist, S. Delman, and A. Jacobsen, *The classification and integration of edges as critical to the perception of reflectance and illumination*, Perception and Psychophysics **33** (1983), no. 5, 425–436.
9. A. Gilchrist and A. Jacobsen, *Perception of lightness and illumination in a world of one reflectance*, Perception **13** (1984), 5–19.
10. A. L. Gilchrist, *The perception of surface blacks and whites*, Scientific American **240** (1979), no. 3, 88–97.
11. J. L. Mannos and D. J. Sakrison, *The effects of a visual criterion on the encoding of images*, IEEE Transactions on Information Theory **IT-20** (1974), no. 4, 525–536.
12. A. McNamara, A. Chalmers, T. Troscianko, and E. Reinhard, *Fidelity of graphics reconstructions: A psychophysical investigation*, Proceedings of the 9th Eurographics Rendering Workshop, Springer Verlag, June 1998, pp. 237–246.
13. G. W. Meyer, H. E. Rushmeier, M. F. Cohen, D. P. Greenberg, and K. E. Torrance, *An Experimental Evaluation of Computer Graphics Imagery*, ACM Transactions on Graphics **5** (1986), no. 1, 30–50.
14. K. Myszkowski, *The visible differences predictor: Applications to global illumination problems*, Rendering Techniques '98 (Proceedings of Eurographics Rendering Workshop '98) (New York, NY) (G. Drettakis and N. Max, eds.), Springer Wien, 1998, pp. 233–236.
15. H. Rushmeier, G. Ward, C. Piatko, P. Sanders, and B. Rust, *Comparing real and synthetic images: Some ideas about metrics*, Eurographics Rendering Workshop 1995, Eurographics, June 1995.
16. D. Travis, *Effective color displays*, Academic Press, 1991.
17. G. J. Ward, *The RADIANCE lighting simulation and rendering system*, Proceedings of SIGGRAPH '94 (Orlando, Florida, July 24–29, 1994) (Andrew Glassner, ed.), Computer Graphics Proceedings, Annual Conference Series, ACM SIGGRAPH, ACM Press, July 1994, ISBN 0-89791-667-0, pp. 459–472.

Editors' Note: see Appendix, p. 408 for colored figures of this paper

Interactive Tone Mapping

Frédo Durand and Julie Dorsey

Laboratory for Computer Science
Massachusetts Institute of Technology
fredo@graphics.lcs.mit.edu, dorsey@lcs.mit.edu
http://www.graphics.lcs.mit.edu

Abstract. Tone mapping and visual adaptation are crucial for the generation of static, photorealistic images. A largely unexplored problem is the simulation of adaptation and its changes over time on the visual appearance of a scene. These changes are important in interactive applications, including walkthroughs or games, where effects such as dazzling, slow dark-adaptation, or more subtle effects of visual adaptation can greatly enhance the immersive impression. In applications such as driving simulators, these changes must be modeled in order to reproduce the visibility conditions of real-world situations. In this paper, we address the practical issues of interactive tone mapping and propose a simple model of visual adaptation. We describe a multi-pass interactive rendering method that computes the average luminance in a first pass and renders the scene with a tone mapping operator in the second pass. We also propose several extensions to the tone mapping operator of Ferwerda et al. [FPSG96]. We demonstrate our model for the display of global illumination solutions and for interactive walkthroughs.

1 Introduction

The human visual system performs effectively over a vast range of luminous intensities, ranging from below starlight, at $10^{-6}cd/m^2$, to sunlight, at $10^6 cd/m^2$. The visual system copes with the high dynamic range present in real scenes by varying its sensitivity through a process known as *visual adaptation*. Visual adaptation does not occur instantaneously. Hence, the time course of such variations in luminance is also important. The recovery of sensitivity from dramatic light to dark changes, which can take tens of minutes, is known as *dark adaptation*; the faster recovery from dark to light changes or small light decrements, which can take seconds, is known as *light adaptation*. Moreover, our visual system does not function equally at all illumination levels. In dark scenes we are unable to distinguish colors and our acuity is low, while as the luminance is increased, colors become increasingly vivid and acuity increases. Another fascinating feature of vision is *chromatic adaptation*, which allows us to discount the illuminant: a given object seen under sunlight (bluish) or under a tungsten illuminant (yellowish) will be perceived as having a constant color, although the physical stimuli arriving at the eye have objectively different hues. This explains why a variety of photographic films are necessary to obtain a correct color balance.

The ability to simulate the time course of visual adaptation is important for a variety of visual simulation applications. In architectural walkthroughs, for example, the perceptual effects due to lighting variations between different rooms or between interior and exterior spaces must be displayed with good subjective fidelity in order to convey the ambiance of these environments. For driving simulators, the ability to model adaptation is essential not only for providing a sense of immersion but also in accurately reproducing the visibility conditions actually encountered in real scenes. A particular modeling challenge is the slow dark adaptation and dazzling during light adaptation that a driver would face when entering and then leaving a tunnel. In addition, when driving at night, the visibility of traffic signs and traffic lights is a major concern. A similar need for modeling accuracy exists in the case of immersive VR safety training, for example for hazardous factories. The realism of games can also benefit from visual adaptation simulation. Because these applications also rely on 8 bits displays, the dynamic range cannot exceed two orders of magnitude. The use of Digital Mirror Devices or direct projection on the retina to obtain a higher dynamic range has however great potential.

In order to address the problem of mapping image luminances into the displayable range of a particular output device, a variety of *tone reproduction* operators have been developed [TR93, War94, CHS+93, Sch95, FPSG96, WLRP97, GTS+97, PFFG98, THG99, Tum99, TT99]. However, most existing tone mapping operators are based on steady-state viewing conditions and have been developed as post-processes for static images. They therefore do not model the time course of visual adaptation discussed above, with the notable exception of the work by Ferwerda et al. [FPSG96], which introduces a specific case of transient adaptation, and the forthcoming work by Scheel et al. [SSS00] and Pattanaik et al. [PTYG00]. As a result, although lighting simulation methods are able to simulate a variety of lighting effects, the display of the results still lacks an important part of the perceptual experience. In order to address this problem, the time component must be integrated into the tone mapping process to provide a faithful subjective impression for interactive visualization. This involves first understanding and modeling the mechanisms of human perception, and second being able to perform such a tone mapping interactively. The current paper focuses on the latter, while the former will be the subject of a companion paper [DD00].

This paper describes a system that performs tone mapping interactively. We take as input a 3D model with high dynamic range colors at vertices, and tone mapping is performed on-the-fly while the user walks through the scene. We present a simple model of light adaptation, and use flares to increase the subjective brightness of visible light sources, and simulate the loss of acuity in dark conditions.

1.1 Visual adaptation

In this section we briefly review the mechanisms of visual adaptation. More detailed descriptions can be found in [Fer98, FPSG96, HF86, WECaS90].

The human eye has two different types of photoreceptors. *Cones* are responsible for sharp chromatic vision in luminous conditions, or the *photopic* range. *Rods* provide less precise vision but are extremely sensitive to light and allow us to see in dark conditions, or the *scotopic* range. Both rods and cones are active in moderately luminous conditions, known as the *mesopic* range.

Light adaptation, or simply *adaptation*, is the (fast) recovery of visual sensitivity after an increase or a small decrease in light intensity. Otherwise, the limited range of neurons results in *response compression* for (relatively) high luminances. This is why everything appears white during the dazzling observed when leaving a tunnel. To cope with this and to always make the best use of the small dynamic range of neurons (typically 1 to 40 [WECaS90]), sensitivity is controlled through *multiplicative* (gain-control) and *subtractive* mechanisms. In previous work on tone reproduction operators, all of these mechanisms are modeled as multiplicative; we make this general assumption in our work as well. It is reasonable for the steady state, however since subtractive and multiplicative mechanisms have different time-constants and different effects, they should be differentiated for a more accurate simulation of adaptation [DD00].

Dark adaptation is the (slow) recovery of sensitivity after a dramatic reduction in light. It can take up to tens of minutes. The classic example of this is the adaptation one experiences on a sunny day upon entering a theater for a matinée. Initially, everything inside appears too dark, and visual acuity is, at best, poor.

Note that all of these mechanisms are local, i.e. they occur independently for single receptors or for small "pools" of receptors. In this paper, we will however make the assumption of a global adaptation state for the entire image. This is motivated by efficiency considerations, but also because considering local adaptation states is extremely challenging. The interaction between local adaptation and eye-gaze movements is very complex and is left as a subject of future research. However, choosing a single *adaptation level* (or "average" light intensity) is not trivial, as we will discuss in Section 4.

Chromatic adaptation allows us to perceive objects as having a constant color, even if they are observed under illuminants with varying hues. This type of adaptation involves mechanisms in the retina as well as higher level mechanisms [Fai98]. It can be reasonably modeled as a different gain-control for each cone type, which is called *Von Kries adaptation.* Chromatic adaptation can be complete or partial and takes approximately one minute to completely occur [FR95]. One of the fascinating aspects of this type of adaptation is that it is not driven by the average color of the stimulus, but by the color of the illuminant: our visual system is somehow able to distinguish the color of the illuminant and discount it, similar to the function of the white balance feature of camcoders [DL86, Fai98, Bre87].

1.2   Previous work

A comprehensive review and discussion of the issues in tone mapping can be found in the thesis by Tumblin [Tum99]; we review issues pertinent to our operator below.

Tone mapping operators can be classified into two categories: *global* and *local.* Global operators use the same function for each pixel to map physical radiances into image colors, while local operators vary the mapping across the image. The simplicity of global methods makes them more suitable for interactive applications than local methods. The classic tone reproduction process used in photography, film, and printing is global, using an *S*-shaped response [Hun95].

Tumblin and Rushmeier [TR93] brought the issue of tone reproduction to the attention of the graphics community. Their global tone mapping operator preserves the impression of *brightness.* Ward's *visibility* preserving operator [War94] ensures that the smallest perceptible intensity difference ("Just Noticeable Difference") in the real scene will correspond to the smallest perceptible difference in the image.

Ferwerda et al.'s global visibility preserving operator [FPSG96] accounts for the transition between achromatic night vision and chromatic daylight vision. In addition, this model introduces the time course of dark and light adaptation for two specific conditions: 1) the sudden transition from a steady illuminated scene to a dark scene and 2) the transition from a completely dark scene to a steady illuminated scene. This model also simulates the loss of acuity for low-light vision. Our work builds on this operator in several respects. In particular, we introduce a more psycho-physically based formula for mesopic conditions, and add a blue-shift to improve the appearance of dark scenes. We also introduce models for transient light adaptation and chromatic adaptation. Finally, we improve their formula for the loss of acuity.

Ward-Larson et al. [WLRP97] propose a very efficient and elegant tone mapping operator based on histogram adjustment. Tumblin et al. [THG99] present two original methods; in the first one they decompose an image into *layers,* such as reflectance and illumination. They apply a compression of the high dynamic range only to the illumination layer. In the second method, the adaptation level is specified by the area of interest (*fovea*) which the user selects with a mouse.

On the other hand, local operators [CHS+93, Sch95, PFFG98, TT99] use a different mapping for each pixel, typically depending on the intensity of its surrounding pixels. They are more computationally demanding and are currently not well suited for interactive implementations. The method by Pattanaik et al. [PFFG98] is nonetheless of interest for our work, as it is the only operator that takes chromatic adaptation into account.

The modeling of flares and glares [NKON90, SSZG95, WLRP97, MH99] is an additional method to increase the subjective brightness of parts of the image, such as those containing light sources. In addition, they simulate the loss in visual sensitivity in the direction of strong sources.

All the methods presented so far are applied in a post-processing phase, which takes high dynamic range images as input. Recently, Scheel et al. [SSS00] have proposed a system that performs tone mapping on-the-fly for radiosity solutions with high dynamic range colors at the vertices. They compute the adaptation level using samples obtained through ray-tracing and perform interactive tone mapping using the texturing hardware: the tone mapping function is computed for each frame and stored as a texture. We present an interactive system based on an alternative approach. Our system provides a more general tone mapping operator, albeit at the expense of speed. Pattanaik et al. also recently proposed a simplified model of dynamic adaptation [PTYG00]. However, they do not address interactive applications.

2 System architecture

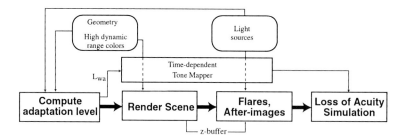

Fig. 1. Architecture of the interactive tone mapping process.

Fig. 1 presents an overview of our interactive system. We take as input a 3D scene with high dynamic range colors at the vertices (typically the output of a lighting simulation, such as radiosity) and a set of point-light sources. We employ a multipass scheme in which we compute the adaptation level, then map this to the displayed colors for each frame, and finally, add flares to improve the appearance of the light sources (Fig. 1). A filtering step is then applied to simulate the loss of acuity due to dim conditions.

As discussed earlier, we consider a single world adaptation level L_{wa} for each frame. This level is computed by first displaying the scene with the log of the colors for each vertex, as will be described in Section 4. This adaptation level is used to drive our time-dependent tone mapping approach that we describe in Section 3. Although we describe our system with this particular tone mapping operator, we have also experimented with other global tone mapping operators [TR93, Tum99, War94, FPSG96, DD00]. Next, we render the actual frame. The scene geometry is sent to the graphics pipeline, and the color of each vertex is mapped on-the-fly (Section 5).

The special case of light sources is crucial to convey a faithful lighting experience. In Section 6 we present our interactive implementation of flares [SSZG95], with a careful treatment of their visibility. Finally, we perform a post-process on the image to simulate the loss of sensitivity due to dim conditions [FPSG96] (Section 7).

2.1 Quantities and units

We briefly summarize the quantities, units, and notation that we will use throughout the remainder of the paper. Quantities corresponding to the scene (world) will have the subscript w, while displayed quantities will have the subscript d. The R and C subscripts will correspond to rods and cones respectively.

For efficiency reasons, our implementation makes the severe assumption that the three RGB components correspond to the three cone types. It is well known that this assumption is not valid for applications where the accuracy of color reproduction is crucial [Hun95, Fai98]. To compensate for this approximation for applications requiring more accuracy, a matrix color transform can be performed at the end of the tone mapping process. The colors in the scene are denoted by r_w, g_w, b_w and are expressed in cd/m^2, the same units as all other quantities. See e.g. [PS86] for conversions. The displayed color is r_d, g_d, b_d.

We use a rod input component s_w for the scotopic range, which in practice is computed using the linear combination given by Pattanaik et al. [PFFG98]. If spectral data are available, a more accurate value could be used (see e.g. [WS82]).

L denotes a luminosity, either the standard formula $L_C = 0.33*r + 0.71*g + 0.08*b$ for the cone system, or $L_R = s$ for the rod system. Adaptation levels will be expressed as L_a, with various subscripts as described above. We use t to represent time, and ε to represent thresholds.

3 Time-dependent tone mapping

The tone mapping operator that we employ builds on the one developed by Ferwerda et al. [FPSG96]. We propose several improvements, including a blue-shift for viewing night scenes and chromatic adaptation. In addition, we extend this operator to time-dependent tone mapping by incorporating a simple model of visual adaptation.

3.1 Review of Ferwerda et al.'s operator

As is the case with Ward's operator [War94], this method uses a global scale-factor: $L_d = m\, L_w$. It is based on *threshold mapping*: the threshold in the real scene $\varepsilon(L_{wa})$ is mapped onto the threshold of the display $\varepsilon(L_{da})$. The scaling factor used is thus $m = \frac{\varepsilon(L_{da})}{\varepsilon(L_{wa})}$. The thresholds for rods and cones respectively are:

$$\log \varepsilon_R(L_{aR}) = \begin{cases} -2.86 & if\ \log L_{aR} \le -3.94, \\ \log L_{aR} - 0.395 & if\ \log L_{aR} \ge -1.44, \\ (0.405 \log L_{aR} + 1.6)^{2.18} - 2.86 & otherwise. \end{cases} \quad (1)$$

$$\log \varepsilon_C(L_{aC}) = \begin{cases} -0.72 & if\ \log L_{aC} \le -2.6, \\ \log L_{wa} - 1.255 & if\ \log L_{aC} \ge 1.9, \\ (0.249 \log L_{aC} + 0.65)^{2.7} - 0.72 & otherwise. \end{cases} \quad (2)$$

Since the observer viewing the display is assumed to be in the photopic state, the scale factor computed for rods uses the threshold of the cones in the display state $m_R = \frac{\varepsilon_C(L_{daC})}{\varepsilon_R(L_{waR})}$.

Two responses are computed: one chromatic for the cone system and one achromatic for the rod system. These responses are then added, and a factor k is used to simulate the loss of rod sensitivity in the mesopic range:

$$r_d = m_C \, r_w + k \, m_R \, s_w$$
$$g_d = m_C \, g_w + k \, m_R \, s_w \qquad (3)$$
$$b_d = m_C \, b_w + k \, m_R \, s_w$$

The original Ferwerda et al. model uses the following formula for k [FP00]: $k = \left(1 - \frac{L_{wa}/2 - 0.01}{10 - 0.01}\right)^2$ clamped to between 0 and 1. However, this formula is an approximation and has no perceptual basis.

3.2 Improvements

We replace their formula for the mesopic factor k by the saturation function used by Walraven and Valeton to fit the rod threshold for higher luminances [WV84]:

$$k = \frac{\sigma - 0.25 \, L_{waR}}{\sigma + L_{waR}}, \qquad (4)$$

clamped to 0, where $\sigma = 100 \, cd/m^2$. (The whole formula (18) of [WV84] could also be used in place of Eq. 1. We have chosen to keep Eq. 1 to minimize the changes to Ferwerda et al.'s operator [FPSG96].)

Night scenes are often represented with a blue hue in paintings and cinema [Mil91]. Indeed, Hunt notes that the subjective hue of colors undergoes a blue shift for dark scenes [Hun52]. Hunt's data show that the subjective color of a white sample in very dark conditions has a CIE hue of $x = 0.3$, $y = 0.3$ — that is, a normalized $RGB = (1.05, 0.97, 1.27)$ on a typical NTSC display. This is further discussed by Trezona [Tre70] who suspects that rod signals are interpreted as slightly bluish. Indeed, rods share many neural pathways with short wavelength cones. Based on these conclusions, we use the following formula to model the blue shift:

$$r_d = m_C \, r_w + 1.05 \, k \, m_R \, s_w$$
$$g_d = m_C \, g_w + 0.97 \, k \, m_R \, s_w \qquad (5)$$
$$b_d = m_C \, b_w + 1.27 \, k \, m_R \, s_w$$

Note that a bluer color can be used for a more dramatic effect.

3.3 A simple model of light adaptation

In this paper we present only a model for light adaptation, since the time constants involved in dark adaptation (up to tens of minutes) make it less important for walk-throughs, unless accurate visibility is required. Moreover, the complex mechanisms required to simulate dark adaptation are beyond the scope of this article.

For simplicity and like previous authors [FPSG96, War94], we simulate both multiplicative and subtractive light adaptation as the multiplicative gain-control m described in the previous section.

The transient recovery of sensitivity is simulated using exponential filters on the values of m: $\frac{dm_R}{dt} = \frac{m_{R\,steady} - m_R(t)}{\tau_R}$ and $\frac{dm_C}{dt} = \frac{m_{C\,steady} - m_C(t)}{\tau_C}$, where m_{steady} is the scaling factor in the steady state (Eq. 2 and 1). Using data from [Ade82, HBH87] we use $\tau_R = 0.4 \, sec$ for rods and $\tau_C = 0.1 \, sec$ for cones.

3.4 A simple model of chromatic adaptation

The achromatic cone scaling factor m_C obtained from the light adaptation must be adapted for each cone type in order to account for chromatic adaptation. We first describe the adaptation correction in the steady state before describing its time-course.

Chromatic adaptation is driven mainly by the chromaticity of the illuminant, or equivalently, by the normalized chromaticity of a white object, (r_{wa}, g_{wa}, b_{wa}). The effect of the reflectances present in the scene is weak [Bre87, Bäu99]. In this paper, we assume a complete chromatic adaptation:

$$r_d = \frac{m_C}{r_{wa}} r_w + 1.05 \, k \, m_R \, s_w$$
$$g_d = \frac{m_C}{g_{wa}} g_w + 0.97 \, k \, m_R \, s_w \qquad (6)$$
$$b_d = \frac{m_C}{b_{wa}} b_w + 1.27 \, k \, m_R \, s_w$$

Chromatic adaptation takes more than one minute to complete, but most of it is complete in a matter of seconds [FR95]. We use an exponential filter on the values (r_{wa}, g_{wa}, b_{wa}) with time constant $\tau_{chroma} = 5 \, sec$.

4 Adaptation level computation

4.1 Interactive implementation

To compute the adaptation level, we first render a version of the scene in which each vertex is assigned a color corresponding to the log of its high-dynamic range color $(\log r_w, \log g_w, \log b_w)$. The log of the rod intensity is mapped to the alpha channel. A lower resolution image can be used for this pass; in practice, we use 64×64 or 128×128. If LODs are available, coarser versions are used for acceleration.

As aforementioned, chromatic adaptation depends on the color of the illuminant, not on the color of the objects of the scene. Brown has moreover shown that the pixels of an image usually do not average to grey [Bro94]. We thus do not exactly use the log of the colors of the vertices. Instead, the chromaticity $(r_{ill}, g_{ill}, b_{ill})$ of the incoming light (irradiance) is instead used together with the luminance of the outgoing light, in a way similar to Neuman et al. [NMNP98]. The color used for each vertex is then:

$$\log\left(\frac{L_w}{L_{ill}} r_{ill}\right), \log\left(\frac{L_w}{L_{ill}} g_{ill}\right), \log\left(\frac{L_w}{L_{ill}} b_{ill}\right)$$

These values are linearly mapped from $[-6, 6]$ to $[0, 1]$. If, following Ward [War94], we use a non-weighted average, we simply compute the mean value of the pixels. Similarly, the histogram of scene values can be computed.

Building on Tumblin et al. [THG99] and Scheel et al. [SSS00], we also can take advantage of the observer's gaze and use a weighted average. For this, we alpha-blend the log-rendered scene with a texture containing the weights. See the following section for a discussion of the metering strategies. The texture is then rendered alone to compute the total of the weights (i.e. the normalization factor). See Fig. 2(a) in the Appendix for an example.

4.2 Exposure metering

As discussed by Scheel et al. [SSS00], computing the adaptation level is very similar to exposure metering for photography. This analogy also shows the complexity of the problem, since metering is one of the hardest tasks a photographer confronts. To illustrate this difficulty, today's state-of-the-art automatic metering system, Nikon's widely acclaimed 3D matrix system [Nik00], collects metering data from eight zones of the picture, computes contrast between these zones, and then uses distance, color, focus information, and a database of 30,000 images to choose the best exposure!

More typical measurements usually involve a centered weighted average. Nikon's weighted centered metering uses 75% of the weight in the 12mm center of a 24x36 film [Nik00]. This is the solution that we generally use, however, spot-centered metering is also available using Gaussian weights.

226

5 On-the-fly tone mapping

Once the adaptation levels have been used to update the tone mapper, the scene is rendered as usual, and the displayed colors of the vertices are computed on-the-fly with our tone mapping operator.

We accelerate tone mapping by caching the function in Look–Up-Tables. This is not crucial for simple tone mapping operators such as the one described in this paper, but it is more important if gamma-correction or more complex operators are used, such as those described in [TR93, DD00]. The tables are re-computed once for each frame and are indexed by the logarithm of r_w, g_w, b_w and s_w. We use 2000 values for the whole 10^{12} range, which provides enough resolution [SFB92]. We thus do not have to use interpolation between the two closest entries in the table.

6 Light sources

6.1 Flares

Flares have been shown to be of great importance in increasing the subjective dynamic range of images [NKON90, SSZG95]. We have implemented an interactive version of the Spencer et al. method [SSZG95]. This method convolves the scene's high-dynamic range pixels with a filter based on psycho-physical models consisting of the following basis functions, where *lambda* is the wavelength in *nm* and θ the angle in *radians*:

$$
\begin{aligned}
f_0(\theta) &= 2.61*10^6 e^{-\left(\frac{\theta}{0.02}\right)^2} & f_1(\theta) &= \frac{20.91}{(\theta+0.02)^3} \\
f_2(\theta) &= \frac{72.37}{(\theta+0.02)^2} & f_3(\theta,\lambda) &= 436.9\frac{568}{\lambda}e^{-(\theta-3\frac{\lambda}{568})^2}
\end{aligned}
\tag{7}
$$

The filter used to convolve the scene is then a weighted average of these basis functions, each f_i having weight w_i. Spencer et al. propose three different filters (i.e. three sets of weights) for photopic, mesopic, and scotopic conditions. Based on their conclusions, we assume that the weights of the different sorts of flares depend on the pupil diameter D (in *mm*). We propose the following formulas, which are linear interpolations between their three sets of weights:

$$
\begin{aligned}
w_1 &= 0.478 & w_2 &= 0.138+0.08(D(L_{wa})-2)/5 \\
w_3 &= 0.033(D(L_{wa})-2)/5 & w_0 &= 1-w_1-w_2-w_3,
\end{aligned}
\tag{8}
$$

where $D(L_{wa}) = 4.9 - 3\tanh(0.4\log(0.5(L_{waR}+L_{waC})+1))$ [SSZG95].

6.2 Interactive Flares

When applied to the whole image, flares are costly and moreover require floating point values for pixels. We thus restrict the addition of flares to light sources. The implementation of interactive flares usually uses textured polygons facing the viewpoint [MH99]. Unfortunately, this causes artifacts since the flares are then tested for occlusion as well, although their visibility should depend only on the visibility of the point light source.

To cope with this, we first render all the geometry, then read the z-buffer and use it in software to query the visibility of the light sources. The hardware z-buffer is disabled, and a flare is rendered only if the pixel corresponding to the point light source has a depth lower or equal to the depth of the light source. Alternatively, ray-casting or, even better, hardware occlusion-culling flags, could also be used if available.

$L_{wa}\ (cd/m^2)$	-3.5	-3	-2.5	-2	-1.5	-1	-0.5	0	0.5	1	1.5	2	2.5	3
$\omega\ (cyc/deg)$	2.1	2.9	4.1	5.5	9	16.3	23.8	32.5	38.5	43.1	46	48	48.8	50

Table 1. Tabulated data from Shaler's acuity experiments [Sha37], expressing maximum visible spatial frequency ω vs. adaptation luminance L_{wa}.

7 Loss of visual acuity

Ferwerda et al. simulate the loss of acuity in low light by applying a 2D Gaussian blur filter g to the image [FPSG96]. They base the size of the filter on data from Shaler [Sha37] (see Table 1). They choose the filter at the given adaptation level L_{waR} such that the highest perceptible frequency $\omega(L_{waR})$ for a grating with high contrast as used by Shaler (black and L_{waR}) is displayed at the scotopic threshold $\varepsilon_R(L_{waR})$. Using capitals for the Fourier transform, this gives:

$$G(\omega(Lwa)) = \frac{\varepsilon_R(L_{waR})}{L_{waR}} \tag{9}$$

Unfortunately, with this formula, blurring does not always increase when the luminance decreases. At very low light levels, $\frac{\varepsilon_R(L_{waR})}{L_{waR}}$ increases with light decrements: $\varepsilon_R(L_{waR})$ becomes constant as absolute sensitivity is reached, and the ratio increases. This means that the cutoff frequency is reduced to a lesser degree, which results in images that are less blurry for darker scenes. To cope with this, we use the constant ratio $10^{-0.395}$ computed from the linear portion of the rod threshold function (Eq. 1).

If $a(L_{waR})$ defines the width of our Gaussian and r is the radius, leaving the parameter L_{waR} for clarity, we have the unit volume 2D Gaussian $g(r) = a^2 e^{-\pi(a r)^2}$, and we want: $G(\omega) = 10^{-0.395}$. Since the Fourier transform of a Gaussian is also a Gaussian[1], we obtain

$$
\begin{aligned}
\frac{1}{a^2} a^2 e^{-\pi \frac{\omega^2}{a^2}} &= 10^{-0.395} \\
\frac{\omega}{a} &= \sqrt{\frac{-\ln 10^{-0.395}}{\pi}} \\
a &= 1.86\,\omega.
\end{aligned} \tag{10}
$$

We use hardware convolution, available in OpenGL 1.2 and on SGI machines, to perform this Gaussian blur. We use the tabulated version of ω given in Table 1 with linear interpolation. The values of a and ω must be converted into pixels using the perspective field of view fov and display resolution $width_{pixel}$.

$$a_{pixel^{-1}}(L_{waR}) = 1.86\,\omega(L_{waR}) * fov/width_{pixel} \tag{11}$$

For efficiency purposes, we apply convolution only when necessary (in practice when $a_{pixel^{-1}}$ is smaller than $1\ pixel^{-1}$), and we interpolate between 1 and 1.1 $pixels^{-1}$ to obtain a smooth transition. The additional cost of convolution could then be compensated for by the use of coarser levels of detail. We plan to implement this solution in the near future.

Like Ferwerda et al., our implementation assumes a fixed distance between the viewer and the display. If a tracking of the observer's position is available (e.g. as in CAVE systems), it can be used to change Eq. 11 for each frame.

---

[1]Note that we use the definition of the Fourier transform given by Bracewell [Bra95] pp. 140-154, which is consistent with our definition of ω.

8 Results

We have tested our system on the output of a radiosity global illumination program. All of the results presented are rendered directly from 3D geometry on a Silicon Graphics Onyx2 Infinite Reality using one R10K processor, with the method described in the paper.

Our examples include a street at night with a car passing by (Fig. 2(a), see Appendix), a walk from the outside to the inside of a house with both yellowish incandescent and neon lighting, an indoor scene with light turned on (Fig. 4) and off. We typically obtain a framerate of 30Hz for the 11,000 triangle scenes, and 6 Hz for a 80,000 triangle model.

Fig. 3 illustrates the importance of using the chromaticity of the light source and not the average chromaticity of the image. The log of the color used in the first pass to compute the adaptation level of Fig. 3(c) is computed with our method.

Our experiments suggest that maintaining a high frame rate (at least 30 Hz) is important. Since light adaptation has small time-constants, a smooth frame rate greatly improves the transient effects. Simple optimizations should be implemented in our system. For example, radiosity meshes are usually too finely subdivided, we use no triangle strips and the levels of detail we use for the adaptation level computation only decrease the polygon count by a factor of 2.

As far as metering is concerned, weighted centered metering is better when the user explores the environment, but uniform average provides a smoother variation of the adaptation level and is more suitable for architectural walkthroughs. Coupling the adaptation level metering with a gaze tracking system would certainly permit optimal results.

The loss of acuity convolution causes the frame rate to drop from 30Hz to 7.5Hz on the gallery scene. It is effective only for dim scenes (below $1.5 \log cd/m^2$, with a $50°$ field of view at video resolution). It is most apparent for high resolution images, as the display resolution is otherwise the major frequency limitation.

9 Conclusions and future work

In this paper we have introduced an interactive tone mapping system, simple extensions to Ferwerda et al.'s operator [FPSG96], and a simplified model of light and chromatic adaptation. Our viewer performs tone mapping for each frame on the high dynamic range colors of the vertices of the 3D geometry. Flares are added to increase the subjective dynamic range of the images, and loss of acuity is simulated.

Our system is obviously slower than the solution proposed by Scheel et al. [SSS00], since they avoid the CPU-consuming on-the-fly mapping that we perform and can instead take advantage of OpenGL display lists. However, their method is unable to use a sophisticated tone mapping such as [FPSG96] or the one described in this paper. Note that some components of the two systems are interchangeable, e.g. their ray-tracing-based adaptation level computation could be plugged into our system and vice-versa.

Our system would greatly benefit from a multiprocessing API using pipelined deferred rendering such as *IRIS Performer* [RH94]. On-the-fly tone mapping could be performed on a separate processor, without impeding the frame rate.

Few restrictions prevent a better hardware integration of tone mapping. Using 12 bits per pixel and a 4th component for rods could be an interesting alternative for specialized hardware, such as driving simulators for which accurate simulation of visual adaptation is important. Textures are currently hard to handle with interactive tone mapping because the hardware performs clamping on vertex colors before texture mapping, rather than on a per pixel basis. A pixel of the texture with value $v < 1.0$ thus cannot be mapped to a color greater than v, preventing the depiction of the white impression due to response compression during dazzling.

Many interesting problems in the area of tone mapping remain. A forthcoming paper will present a more elaborate model of visual adaptation [DD00] for interactive applications. A great deal of work remains to be done, especially for local methods, where the conjugate effect of gaze saccades and local adaptation is quite complicated. Tone mapping in mesopic conditions is another challenging area, as the complex interaction between rods and cones and their effect on the appearance of colors must be simulated.

Acknowledgments

We thank Stephen Duck, Max Chen and Gernot Schaufler for the models that they built for this project, and Jim Ferwerda and Sumant Pattanaik, who kindly answered our questions about their adaptation model. Thanks to the reviewers and Steven Gortler for their advice. This work was supported by an NSF Postdoctoral Research Associates award (EIA-9806139), an NSF CISE Research Infrastructure award (EIA-9892229), an NSF-INRIA Cooperative Research award (INT-9724005), and a grant from Intel.

References

Ade82.   Adelson. Saturation and adaptation in the rod system. *Vision Research*, 22:1299, 1982.

Bäu99.   Bäuml. Color constancy: the role of image surface in illuminant adjustment. *JOSA A*, 16(7):1521, 1999.

Bra95.   R. Bracewell. *Two-Dimensional Imaging*. Prentice Hall, 1995.

Bre87.   Breneman. Corresponding chromaticities for different states of adaptation to complex visual fields. *JOSA A*, 4(6):115, 1987.

Bro94.   Brown. The world is not grey. *Investigative Ophtalmology and Visual Sc,*, 35(Suppl.), 1994.

CHS+93.   Chiu, Herf, Shirley, Swamy, Wang, and Zimmerman. Spatially nonuniform scaling functions for high contrast images. In *Proc. Graphics Interface*, 1993.

DD00.   Durand and Dorsey. A computational model of visual adaptation for time-dependent tone-mapping. *submitted for publication*, 2000. http://graphics.lcs.mit.edu/~fredo.

DL86.   D'Zmura and Lennie. Mechanisms of color constancy. *JOSA A*, 10:1662, 1986.

Fai98.   Fairchild. *Color Appearance Models*. Addison-Wesley, 1998.

Fer98.   Ferwerda. Fundamentals of spatial vision. In *Applications of visual perception in computer graphics*, 1998. Siggraph '98 Course Notes.

FP00.   Jim Ferwerda and Sumant Pattanaik. personal communication, 2000.

FPSG96.   Ferwerda, Pattanaik, Shirley, and Greenberg. A model of visual adaptation for realistic image synthesis. In *Computer Graphics (Proc. Siggraph)*, 1996.

FR95.   Fairchild and Reniff. Time course of chromatic adaptation for color-appearance judgments. *JOSA A*, 12(5):824, 1995.

GTS+97.   Greenberg, Torrance, Shirley, Arvo, Ferwerda, Pattanaik, Lafortune, Walter, Foo, and Trumbore. A framework for realistic image synthesis. In *Computer Graphics (Proc. Siggraph)*, 1997.

HBH87.   Hayhoe, Benimoff, and Hood. The time course of multiplicative and subtractive adaptation process. *Vision Research*, 27:1981, 1987.

HF86.   Hood and Finkelstein. Sensitivity to light. In Boff, Kaufman, and Thomas, editors, *Handbook of Perception and Human Performance*. Wiley and Sons, 1986.

Hun52.   Hunt. Light and dark adaptation and the perception of color. *JOSA A*, 42(3):190, 1952.

Hun95.   Hunt. *The reproduction of Color (5th ed.)*. Kings Langley:Fountain Press, 1995.

230

MH99.   Möller and Haines. *Real-Time Rendering*. A.K. Peters Ltd., 1999.

Mil91.   Millerson. *Lighting for Television and Film, 3rd ed.* Focal Press, 1991.

Nik00.   Nikon. http://www.nikon.ca, 2000.

NKON90.   Nakamae, Kaneda, Okamoto, and Nishita. A lighting model aiming at drive simulators. In *Computer Graphics (Proc. Siggraph)*, 1990.

NMNP98.   Neumann, Matkovic, Neumann, and Purgathofer. Incident light metering in computer graphics. *Computer Graphics Forum*, Dec. 1998.

PFFG98.   Pattanaik, Ferwerda, Fairchild, and Greenberg. A multiscale model of adaptation and spatial vision for realistic image display. In *Computer Graphics (Proc. Siggraph)*, 1998.

PS86.   Pokorny and Smith. Colorimetry and color discrimination. In Boff, Kaufman, and Thomas, editors, *Handbook of Perception and Human Performance*. Wiley and Sons, 1986.

PTYG00.   Pattanaik, Tumblin, Yee, and Greenberg. Time-dependent visual adaptation for realistic image display. In *Computer Graphics (Proc. Siggraph)*, 2000. to appear.

RH94.   Rohlf and Helman. IRIS performer: A high performance multiprocessing toolkit for real–Time 3D graphics. In *Computer Graphics (Proc. Siggraph)*, 1994.

Sch95.   Schlick. Quantization techniques for visualization of high dynamic range pictures. *Eurographics Workshop on Rendering*, 1995.

SFB92.   Stokes, Fairchild, and Berns. Precision requirement for digital color reproduction. *ACM Trans. on Graphics*, 11:406, 1992.

Sha37.   Shaler. The relation between visual acuity and illumination. *J. of General Physiology*, 21:165, 1937.

SSS00.   Scheel, Stamminger, and Seidel. Tone reproduction for interactive walkthroughs. In *Proc. of Eurographics*, 2000. to appear.

SSZG95.   Spencer, Shirley, Zimmerman, and Greenberg. Physically-based glare effects for digital images. In *Computer Graphics (Proc. Siggraph)*, 1995.

THG99.   Tumblin, Hodgins, and Guenter. Two methods for display of high contrast images. *ACM Trans. on Graphics*, 18(1), January 1999.

TR93.   Tumblin and Rushmeier. Tone reproduction for realistic images. *IEEE Computer Graphics and Applications*, 13(6), 1993.

Tre70.   P. W. Trezona. Rod participation in the "blue" mechanism and its effect on colour matching. *Vision Research*, 10:317, 1970.

TT99.   Tumblin and Turk. LCIS: a boundary hierarchy for detail-preserving contrast reduction. In *Computer Graphics (Proc. Siggraph)*, 1999.

Tum99.   Tumblin. *Three methods of detail-preserving contrast reduction for displayed images*. PhD thesis, College of Computing Georgia Inst. of Technology, Sep. 1999.

War94.   Ward. A contrast-based scalefactor for luminance display. In Heckbert, editor, *Graphics Gems IV*, page 415. Academic Press, 1994.

WECaS90.   Walraven, Enroth-Cugell, Hood andMacLeod, and Schnapf. The control of visual sensitivity. In Spillmann and Werner, editors, *Visual Perception, The neurophysiological foundation*. Academic Press, 1990.

WLRP97.   Ward-Larson, Rushmeier, and Piatko. A Visibility Matching Tone Reproduction Operator for High Dynamic Range Scenes. *IEEE Trans. on Visualization and Computer Graphics*, 3(4), 1997.

WS82.   Wyszecki and Stiles. *Color Science: Concepts and Methods, Quantitative Data and Formulae*. Wiley, 1982.

WV84.   Walraven and Valeton. Visual adaptation and response saturation. In A. J. van Doorn, W. A. Van de Grind, and J. J. Koenderink, editors, *Limits in Perception*. VNU Science Press, 1984.

Editors' Note: see Appendix, p. 409 for colored figures of this paper

Modeling and Rendering for Realistic Facial Animation

Stephen R. Marschner   Brian Guenter   Sashi Raghupathy

Microsoft Corporation[1]

Abstract. Rendering realistic faces and facial expressions requires good models for the reflectance of skin and the motion of the face. We describe a system for modeling, animating, and rendering a face using measured data for geometry, motion, and reflectance, which realistically reproduces the appearance of a particular person's face and facial expressions. Because we build a complete model that includes geometry and bidirectional reflectance, the face can be rendered under any illumination and viewing conditions. Our face modeling system creates structured face models with correspondences across different faces, which provide a foundation for a variety of facial animation operations.

1 Introduction

Modeling and rendering realistic faces and facial expressions is a difficult task on two levels. First, faces have complex geometry and motion, and skin has reflectance properties that are not modeled well by the shading models (such as Phong-like models) that are in wide use; this makes rendering faces a technical challenge. Faces are also a very familiar—possibly the most familiar—class of images, and the slightest deviation from real facial appearance or movement is immediately perceived as wrong by the most casual viewer.

We have developed a system that takes a significant step toward solving this difficult problem to this demanding level of accuracy by employing advanced rendering techniques and using the best available measurements from real faces wherever possible. Our work builds on previous rendering, modeling, and motion capture technology and adds new techniques for diffuse reflectance acquisition, structured geometric model fitting, and measurement-based surface deformation to integrate this previous work into a realistic face model.

2 Previous Work

Our system differs from much previous work in facial animation, such as that of Lee et al. [12], Waters [21], and Cassel et al. [2], in that we are not synthesizing animations using a physical or procedural model of the face. Instead, we capture facial movements in three dimensions and then replay them. The systems of Lee et al. and Waters are designed to make it relatively easy to animate facial expression manually. The system of Cassel et al. is designed to automatically create a dialog rather than to faithfully reconstruct a particular person's facial expression. The work of Williams [22] is more similar to ours, but he used a single static texture image of a real person's face and

---

[1]Email: `stevemar@microsoft.com`, `bguenter@microsoft.com`, `sashir@microsoft.com`.

tracked points only in 2D. Since we are only concerned with capturing and reconstructing facial performances, our work is unlike that of Essa and Pentland [6], which attempts to recognize expressions, or that of DeCarlo and Metaxas [5], which can track only a limited set of facial expressions.

The reflectance in our head model builds on previous work on measuring and representing the bidirectional reflectance distribution function, or BRDF [7]. Lafortune et al. [10] introduced a general and efficient representation for BRDFs, which we use in our renderer, and Marschner et al. [15] made image-based BRDF measurements of human skin, which serve as the basis for our skin reflection model. The procedure for computing the albedo map is related to some previous methods that compute texture for 3D objects, some of which deal with faces [16, 1] or combine multiple images [17] and some of which compute lighting-independent textures [23, 19, 18]. However, the technique presented here, which is closely related to that of Marschner [14], is unique in performing illumination correction with controlled lighting while at the same time merging multiple camera views on a complex curved surface.

Our procedure for consistently fitting the face with a generic model to provide correspondence and structure builds on the method of fitting subdivision surfaces due to Hoppe et al. [9]. Our version of the fitting algorithms adds vertex-to-point constraints that enforce correspondence of features, and includes a smoothing term that is necessary for the iteration to converge in the presence of these correspondences.

Our method for moving the mesh builds on previous work using the same type of motion data [8]. The old technique smoothed and decreased motions, but worked well enough to provide a geometry estimate for image-based reprojection; this paper adds additional computations required to reproduce the motion well enough that the shading on the geometry alone produces a realistic face.

The original contributions of this paper enter into each of the parts of the face modeling process. To create a structured, consistent representation of geometry, which forms the basis for our face model and provides a foundation for many further face modeling and rendering operations, we have extended previous surface fitting techniques to allow a generic face to be conformed to individual faces. To create a realistic reflectance model we have made the first practical use of recent skin reflectance measurements and added newly measured diffuse texture maps using an improved texture capture process. To animate the mesh we use improved techniques that are needed to produce surface shapes suitable for high-quality rendering.

3   Face Geometry Model

The geometry of the face consists of a skin surface plus additional surfaces for the eyes. The skin surface is derived from a laser range scan of the head and is represented by a subdivision surface with displacement maps. The eyes are a separate model that is aligned and merged with the skin surface to produce a complete face model suitable for high-quality rendering.

3.1   Mesh fitting

The first step in building a face model is to create a subdivision surface that closely approximates the geometry measured by the range scanner. Our subdivision surfaces are defined from a coarse triangle mesh using Loop's subdivision rules [13] with the

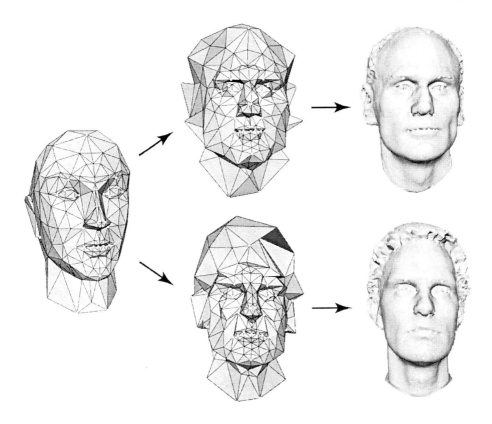

Fig. 1. Mapping the same subdivision control mesh to a displaced subdivision surface for each face results in a structured model with natural correspondence from one face to another.

addition of sharp edges similar to those described by Hoppe et al. [9].[2]

A single base mesh is used to define the subdivision surfaces for all our face models, with only the vertex positions varying to adapt to the shape of each different face. Our base mesh, which has 227 vertices and 416 triangles, is designed to have the general shape of a face and to provide greater detail near the eyes and lips, where the most complex geometry and motion occur. The mouth opening is a boundary of the mesh, and it is kept closed during the fitting process by tying together the positions of the corresponding vertices on the upper and lower lips. The base mesh has a few edges marked for sharp subdivision rules (highlighted in white in Figure 1); they serve to create corners at the two sides of the mouth opening and to provide a place for the sides of the nose to fold. Because our modified subdivision rules only introduce creases for chains of at least three sharp edges, our model does not have creases in the surface; only isolated vertices fail to have well-defined limit normals.

The process used to fit the subdivision surface to each face is based on the algorithm described by Hoppe et al. [9]. The most important differences are that we perform only the continuous optimization over vertex positions, since we do not want to alter the

---

[2]We do not use the non-regular crease masks, and when subdividing an edge between a dart and a crease vertex we mark only the new edge adjacent to the crease vertex as a sharp edge.

connectivity of the control mesh, and that we add feature constraints and a smoothing term. The fitting process minimizes the functional:

$$E(\mathbf{v}) = E_d(\mathbf{v}, \mathbf{p}) + \lambda E_s(\mathbf{v}) + \mu E_c(\mathbf{v})$$

where $\mathbf{v}$ is a vector of all the vertex positions, and $\mathbf{p}$ is a vector of all the data points from the range scanner. The subscripts on the three terms stand for distance, shape, and constraints.

The distance functional E_d measures the sum-squared distance from the range scanner points to the subdivision surface:

$$E_d(\mathbf{v}, \mathbf{p}) = \sum_{i=1}^{n_p} a_i \| p_i - \Pi(\mathbf{v}, p_i) \|^2$$

where p_i is the ith range point and $\Pi(\mathbf{v}, p_i)$ is the projection of that point onto the subdivision surface defined by the vertex positions $\mathbf{v}$. The weight a_i is a Boolean term that causes points to be ignored when the scanner's view direction at p_i is not consistent with the surface normal at $\Pi(\mathbf{v}, p_i)$. We also reject points that are farther than a certain distance from the surface:

$$a_i = \begin{cases} 1 & \text{if } \langle s(p_i), n(\Pi(\mathbf{v}, p_i)) \rangle > 0 \text{ and } \| p_i - \Pi(\mathbf{v}, p_i) \| < d_0 \\ 0 & \text{otherwise} \end{cases}$$

where $s(p)$ is the direction toward the scanner's viewpoint at point p and $n(x)$ is the outward-facing surface normal at point x.

The smoothness functional E_s encourages the control mesh to be locally planar. It measures the distance from each vertex to the average of the neighboring vertices:

$$E_s(\mathbf{v}) = \sum_{j=1}^{n_v} \left\| v_j - \frac{1}{\deg(v_j)} \sum_{i=1}^{\deg(v_j)} v_{k_i} \right\|^2$$

The vertices v_{k_i} are the neighbors of v_j.

The constraint functional E_c is simply the sum-squared distance from a set of constrained vertices to a set of corresponding target positions:

$$E_c(\mathbf{v}) = \sum_{i=1}^{n_c} \| A_{c_i} \mathbf{v} - d_i \|^2$$

A_j is the linear function that defines the limit position of the jth vertex in terms of the control mesh, so the limit position of vertex c_i is attached to the 3D point d_i. The constraints could instead be enforced rigidly by a linear reparameterization of the optimization variables, but we found that the soft-constraint approach helps guide the iteration smoothly to a desirable local minimum. The constraints are chosen by the user to match the facial features of the generic mesh to the corresponding features on the particular face being fit. Approximately 25 to 30 constraints (marked with white dots in Figure 1) are used, concentrating on the eyes, nose, and mouth.

Minimizing $E(\mathbf{v})$ is a nonlinear least-squares problem, because Π and a_i are not linear functions of $\mathbf{v}$. However, we can make it linear by holding a_i constant and approximating $\Pi(\mathbf{v}, p_i)$ by a fixed linear combination of control vertices. The fitting process therefore proceeds as a sequence of linear least-squares problems with the a_i and the projections of the p_i onto the surface being recomputed before each iteration. The subdivision limit surface is approximated for these computations by the mesh at a particular level of subdivision. Fitting a face takes a small number of iterations (fewer than 20), and the constraints are updated according to a simple schedule as the iteration progresses, beginning with a high λ and low μ to guide the optimization to a very smooth approximation of the face, and progressing to a low λ and high μ so that the final solution fits the data and the constraints closely. The computation time in practice is dominated by computing $\Pi(\mathbf{v}, p_i)$.

To produce the mesh for rendering we subdivide the surface to the desired level, producing a mesh that smoothly approximates the face shape, then compute a displacement for each vertex by intersecting the line normal to the surface at that vertex with the triangulated surface defined by the original scan [11]. The resulting surface reproduces all the salient features of the original scan in a mesh that has somewhat fewer triangles, since the base mesh has more triangles in the more important regions of the face. The subdivision-based representation also provides a parameterization of the surface and a built-in set of multiresolution basis functions defined in that parameterization and, because of the feature constraints used in the fitting, creates a natural correspondence across all faces that are fit using this method. This structure is useful in many ways in facial animation, although we do not make extensive use of it in the work described in this paper; see Section 7.1.

3.2 Adding eyes

The displaced subdivision surface just described represents the shape of the facial skin surface quite well, but there are several other features that are required for a realistic face. The most important of these is the eyes. Since our range scanner does not capture suitable information about the eyes, we augmented the mesh for rendering by adding separately modeled eyes. Unlike the rest of the face model, the eyes and their motions (see Section 4.2) are not measured from a specific person, so they do not necessarily reproduce the appearance of the real eyes. However, their presence and motion is critical to the overall appearance of the face model.

The eye model (see Figure 2), which was built using a commercial modeling package, consists of two parts. The first part is a model of the eyeball, and the second part is a model of the skin surface around the eye, including the eyelids, orbit, and a portion of the surrounding face (this second part will be called the "orbit surface"). In order for the eye to become part of the overall face model, the orbit surface must be made to fit the individual face being modeled, and the two surfaces must be stitched together. This is done in two steps: first the two meshes are warped according to a weighting function defined on the orbit surface, so that the face and orbit are coincident where they overlap. Then the two surfaces are cut with a pair of concentric ellipsoids and stitched together into a single mesh.

4 Moving the Face

The motions of the face are specified by the time-varying 3D positions of a set of sample points on the face surface. When the face is controlled by motion-capture data these points are the markers on the face that are tracked by the motion capture system, but facial motions from other sources (see Section 7.1) can also be represented in this way. The motions of these points are used to control the face surface by way of a set of

236

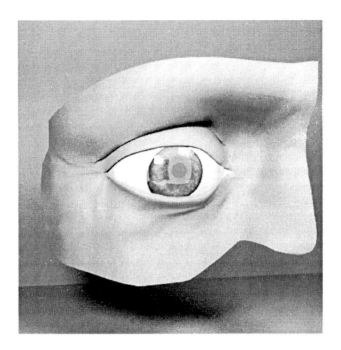

Fig. 2. The eye model.

control points that smoothly influence regions of the surface.

A discussion of the various methods for capturing facial motion is beyond the scope of this paper; we used the method of Guenter et al. [8] to acquire our face motion data.

4.1 Mesh deformation

The face is animated by displacing each vertex w_i of the triangle mesh from its rest position according to a linear combination of the displacements of a set of control points q_j. These control points correspond one-to-one with the sample points p_j that describe the motion. The influence of each control point on the vertices falls off with distance from the corresponding sample point, and where multiple control points influence a vertex their weights are normalized to sum to 1.

$$\Delta w_i = \frac{1}{\beta_i} \sum_j \alpha_{ij} \Delta q_j \quad ; \quad \alpha_{ij} = h(\|w_i - p_j\|/r)$$

$\beta_i = \sum_k \alpha_{ik}$ if vertex i is influenced by multiple control points and 1 otherwise. The parameter r controls the radius of influence of the control points. These weights are computed once, using the rest positions of the sample points and face mesh, so that moving the mesh for each frame is just a sparse matrix multiplication. For the weighting function we used $h(x) = \frac{1}{2} + \frac{1}{2}cos(\pi x)$.

Two types of exceptions to these weighting rules are made to handle the particulars of animating a face. Vertices and control points near the eyes and mouth are tagged as "above" and "below," and controls that are, for example, above the mouth do not influence the motions of vertices below the mouth. Also, a scalar texture map in the region around the eyes is used to weight the motions so that they taper smoothly to zero at the eyelids.

To move the face mesh according to a set of sample points, control point positions must be computed that will deform the surface appropriately. Using the same weighting functions described above, we compute how the sample points move in response to the control points. The result is a linear transformation: $\mathbf{p} = A\mathbf{q}$. Therefore if at time t we want to achieve the sample positions $\mathbf{p}_t$, we can use the control positions $\mathbf{q}_t = A^{-1}\mathbf{p}_t$. However, the matrix A can be ill-conditioned, so to avoid the undesirable surface shapes that are caused by very large control point motions we compute A^{-1} using the SVD and clamp the singular values of A^{-1} at a limit M. We used $M = 1.5$ for the results shown in this paper.[3]

4.2 Eye and head movement

In order to give the face a more lifelike appearance, we added procedurally generated motion to the eyes and separately captured rigid-body motion to the head as a whole.

The eyeballs are rotated according to a random sequence of fixation directions, moving smoothly from one to the next. The eyelids are animated by rotating the vertices that define them about an axis through the center of the eyeball, using weights defined on the eyelid mesh to ensure smooth deformations.

The rigid-body motion of the head is captured from the physical motion of a person's head by filming that motion while the person is wearing a hat marked with special machine-recognizable targets (the hat is patterned closely on the one used by Marschner et al. [15]). By tracking these targets in the video sequence, we computed the rigid motion of the head, which we then applied to the head model for rendering. This setup, which requires just a video camera, provides a convenient way to author head motion by demonstrating the desired actions.

5 Face Rendering

Rendering a realistic image of a face requires not just accurate geometry, but also accurate computation of light reflection from the skin, so we use a physically-based Monte Carlo ray tracer [3, 20] to render the face. This allows us to use arbitrary BRDFs to correctly simulate the appearance of the skin, which is not well approximated by simple shading models. The renderer also supports extended light sources, which, in rendering as in portrait photography, are needed to achieve a pleasing image. Two important deviations from physical light transport are made for the sake of computational efficiency: diffuse interreflection is disregarded, and the eyes are illuminated through the cornea without refraction.

Our reflectance model for the skin is based on the measurements of actual human faces made by Marschner et al. [15]. The measurements describe the average BRDFs of several subjects' foreheads and include fitted parameters for the BRDF model of Lafortune et al. [10], so they provide an excellent starting point for rendering a realistic face. However, they need to be augmented to include some of the spatial variation observed in actual faces. We achieve this by starting with the fit to the measured BRDF of one subject whose skin is similar to the skin of the face we rendered and dividing it into diffuse and specular components, then introducing a texture map to modulate each.

---

[3]The first singular value of A is 1.0.

238

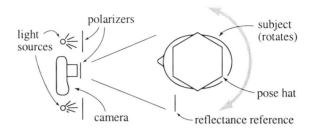

polarizers
light sources
subject (rotates)
pose hat
camera
reflectance reference

Fig. 3. Setup for measuring albedo maps.

The texture map for the diffuse component, or the albedo map, modulates the diffuse reflectance according to measurements taken from the subjects' actual faces as described in the next section. The specular component is modulated by a scalar texture map to remove specularity from areas (such as eyebrows and hair) that should not be rendered with skin reflectance and to reduce specularity on the lower part of the face to approximate the characteristics of facial skin. The result is a spatially varying BRDF that is described at each point by a sum of the generalized cosine lobes of Lafortune et al. [10].

5.1 Constructing the albedo map

We measured the albedo map, which must describe the spatially varying reflectance due to diffuse reflection, using a sequence of digital photographs of the face taken under controlled illumination. (See [14] for a more detailed description of a similar procedure.) The laboratory setup for taking the photographs is shown in Figure 3. The subject wears a hat printed with machine-recognizable targets to track head pose, and the camera stays stationary while the subject rotates. The only illumination comes from light sources at measured locations near the camera, and a black backdrop is used to reduce indirect reflections from spilled light. The lens and light sources are covered by perpendicular polarizers so that specular reflections are suppressed, leaving only the diffuse component in the images.

Since we know the camera and light source locations, we can use standard ray tracing techniques to compute the surface normal, the irradiance, the viewing direction, and the corresponding coordinates in texture space for each pixel in each image. Under the assumption that we are observing ideal Lambertian reflection, we can compute the Lambertian reflectance for a particular point in texture space from this information. Repeating this computation for every pixel in one photograph amounts to projecting the image into texture space and dividing by the computed irradiance due to the light sources to obtain a map of the diffuse reflectance across the surface (Figure 4, top row). In practice the projection is carried out by reverse mapping, with the outer loop iterating through all the pixels in the texture map, and stochastic supersampling is used to average over the area in the image that projects to a particular texture pixel.

The albedo map from a single photograph only covers part of the surface, and the results are best at less grazing angles, so we take a weighted average of all the individual maps to create a single albedo map for the entire face. The weighting function (Figure 4, second row) should give higher weights to pixels that are viewed and/or illuminated from directions nearly normal to the surface, and it should drop to zero well

239

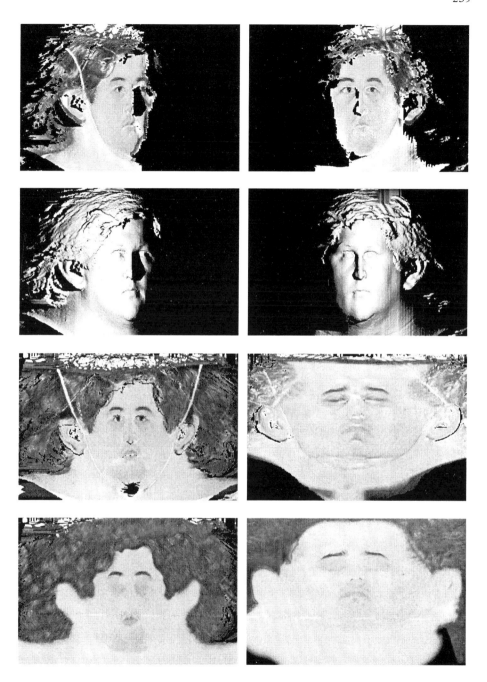

Fig. 4. Building the albedo map. Top to bottom: two camera views of one subject projected to texture space; the associated weight maps; the merged albedo maps for two subjects; the albedo maps cleaned up for rendering.

before either viewing or illumination becomes extremely grazing. We chose the function $(\cos \theta_i \cos \theta_e - c)^p$ where θ_i and θ_e are the incident and exitant angles, and we use the values $c = 0.2$ and $p = 4$.

Before computing the albedo for a particular texture pixel, we verify that the pixel is visible and suitably illuminated. We trace multiple rays from points on the pixel to points on the light source and to the camera point, and mark the pixel as having zero, partial, or full visibility and illumination.[4] We only compute albedo for pixels that are fully visible, fully illuminated by at least one light source, and not partially illuminated by any light source. This ensures that partially occluded pixels and pixels that are in full-shadow or penumbra regions are not used.

Some calibration is required to make these measurements meaningful. We calibrated the camera's transfer curve using the method of Debevec and Malik [4]; we calibrated the light-camera system's flat-field response using a photograph of a large white card; and we calibrated the lens's focal length and distortion using the technique of Zhang [24]. We set the absolute scale factor using a reference sample of known reflectance. When image-to-image variation in light source intensity was a consideration, we controlled for that by including the reference sample in every image.

The texture maps that result from this process do a good job of automatically capturing the detailed variation in color across the face. In a few areas, however, the system cannot compute a reasonable result; also, the strap used to hold the calibration hat in place is visible. We remove these problems using an image editing tool, filling in blank areas with nearby texture or with uniform color. The bottom two rows of Figure 4 show the raw and edited albedo maps for comparison.

The areas where the albedo map does not provide reasonable results are where the surface is not observed well enough (e. g., under the chin) or is too intricately shaped to be correctly scanned and registered with the images (e. g., the ears). Neither of these types of areas requires the texture from the albedo map for realistic appearance—the first because they are not prominently visible and the second because the geometry provides visual detail—so this editing has relatively little effect on the appearance of the final renderings.

6 Results

Figure 5 (in the color appendix) shows several different aspects of the face model, using still frames from the accompanying video. In the top row the face is shown from several angles to demonstrate that the albedo map and measured BRDF realistically capture the distinctive appearance of the skin and its color variation over the entire face, viewed from any angle. In the second row the effects of rim and side lighting are shown, including strong specular reflections at grazing angles. Note that the light source has the same intensity and is at the same distance from the face for all three images; it is the directional variation in reflectance that leads to the familiar lighting effects seen in the renderings. In the bottom row expression deformations are applied to the face to demonstrate that the face still looks natural under normal expression movement.

7 Conclusions

We have described and demonstrated a system that addresses the challenge of modeling and rendering faces to the high standard of realism that must be met before an image as

---

[4]It is prudent to err on the large side when estimating the size of the light source.

familiar as a human face can appear believable. Our philosophy is to use measurements whenever we can so that the face model actually resembles a real face. The geometry of the face is represented by a displacement-mapped subdivision surface that has consistent connectivity and correspondence across different faces, which provides basis functions and a parameterization that form a strong foundation for future work. The reflectance comes from previous BRDF measurements of human skin together with new measurements that combine several views into a single illumination-corrected texture map for diffuse reflectance. The motion comes from a previously described motion capture technique and is applied to the face model using an improved deformation method that produces motions suitable for shaded surfaces.

While many issues remain to be addressed before our model can pass a visual Turing test under close examination, our results demonstrate the value of using measured data in rendering and animating faces. The realism of the renderings is greatly enhanced by using the geometry, motion, and reflectance of real faces in a physically-based renderer.

7.1 Future work

One avenue of future work is to add more features to the face to increase realism: teeth and ears are good candidates. A more difficult but equally important problem is to add hair (including eyebrows, eyelashes, and facial hair if it is present). Another feature that would contribute to realism is the characteristic wrinkles that form in the face as it moves. Since our motion capture data does not resolve these wrinkles, they must be predicted from the face motion and added to the surface. Our consistent parameterization provides a way to position these features automatically on different faces.

An important way to broaden the applicability of our animation technique is to reuse motion data. Since it is inconvenient to do motion capture for each script that needs to be performed for each face, we are investigating ways to transform motion data recorded from one person's face so that it can be used for other people's faces; the correspondence provided by our generic face model is crucial to this effort. It would be even more useful to be able to assemble motion from existing examples for scripts containing arbitrary new speech and expressions, thus avoiding the need to do any new motion capture except for very unusual motions.

The algorithm for deforming the mesh is essentially one of sparse data interpolation, and new ways of solving this problem that use the parameterization and basis functions provided by the subdivision representation are yet another promising future direction.

7.2 Acknowledgements

Thanks to Peter Shirley for the ray tracer Eon, to Hugues Hoppe for many valuable discussions, and to the Cornell Program of Computer Graphics for the skin BRDF data.

References

1. Volker Blanz and Thomas Vetter. A morphable model for the synthesis of 3D faces. In *Computer Graphics (SIGGRAPH 1999 Proceedings)*, pages 187–194, 1999.
2. Justine Cassell, C. Pelachaud, N. Badler, M. Steedman, B. Achorn, T. Becket, B. Douville, S. Prevost, and M. Stone. Animated conversation: Rule-based generation of facial expression, gesture and spoken intonation for multiple conversational agents. In *Computer Graphics (SIGGRAPH 1994 Proceedings)*, pages 413–420, August 1994.
3. R. L. Cook, T. Porter, and L. Carpenter. Distribution ray tracing. In *Computer Graphics (SIGGRAPH 1984 Proceedings)*, pages 165–174, July 1984.

242

4. Paul Debevec and Jitendra Malik. Recovering high dynamic range radiance maps from photographs. In *Computer Graphics (SIGGRAPH 1997 Proceedings)*, pages 369–378, August 1997.

5. Douglas DeCarlo and Dimitris Metaxas. The integration of optical flow and deformable models with applications to human face shape and motion estimation. In *Proceedings CVPR*, pages 231–238, 1996.

6. I. Essa and A. Pentland. Coding, analysis, interpretation and recognition of facial expressions. *IEEE Transactions on Pattern Analysis and Machine Intelligence*, 19(7):757–763, 1997.

7. Andrew S. Glassner. *Principles of Digital Image Synthesis*. Morgan Kaufmann, San Francisco, 1995.

8. Brian Guenter, Cindy Grimm, Daniel Wood, Henrique Malvar, and Frédéric Pighin. Making faces. In *Computer Graphics (SIGGRAPH 1998 Proceedings)*, pages 55–67, July 1998.

9. Hugues Hoppe, Tony DeRose, Tom Duchamp, Mark Halstead, Hubert Jin, John McDonald, Jean Schweitzer, and Werner Stuetzle. Piecewise smooth surface reconstruction. In *Computer Graphics (SIGGRAPH 1994 Proceedings)*, pages 295–302, July 1994.

10. Eric P. F. Lafortune, Sing-Choong Foo, Kenneth E. Torrance, and Donald P. Greenberg. Nonlinear approximation of reflectance functions. In *Computer Graphics (SIGGRAPH 1997 Proceedings)*, pages 117–126, August 1997.

11. Aaron Lee, Henry Moreton, and Hugues Hoppe. Displaced subdivision surfaces. In *Computer Graphics (SIGGRAPH 2000 Proceedings)*, July 2000. (Forthcoming).

12. Yuencheng Lee, D. Terzopoulos, and K. Waters. Realistic modeling for facial animation. In *Computer Graphics (SIGGRAPH 1995 Proceedings)*, pages 55–62, July 1995.

13. Charles Loop. *Smooth Subdivision Surfaces Based on Triangles*. PhD thesis, University of Utah, August 1987.

14. Stephen R. Marschner. *Inverse Rendering for Computer Graphics*. PhD thesis, Cornell University, August 1998.

15. Stephen R. Marschner, Stephen H. Westin, Eric P. F. Lafortune, Kenneth E. Torrance, and Donald P. Greenberg. Image-based BRDF measurement including human skin. In *Rendering Techniques '99 (Proceedings of the Eurographics Workshop on Rendering)*, pages 131–144, June 1999.

16. Frédéric Pighin, Jamie Hecker, Dani Lischinski, Richard Szeliski, and David H. Salesin. Synthesizing realistic facial expressions from photographs. In *Computer Graphics (SIGGRAPH 1998 Proceedings)*, pages 75–84, July 1998.

17. C. Rocchini, P. Cignoni, C. Montani, and R. Scopigno. Multiple textures stitching and blending on 3D objects. In *Rendering Techniques '99 (Proceedings of the Eurographics Workshop on Rendering)*, pages 119–130, June 1999.

18. Holly Rushmeier and Fausto Bernardini. Computing consistent normals and colors from photometric data. In *Proceedings of the Second International Conference on 3D Digital Imaging and Modeling (3DIM '99)*, October 1999.

19. Holly Rushmeier, Fausto Bernardini, Joshua Mittleman, and Gabriel Taubin. Acquiring input for rendering at appropriate level of detail: Digitizing a Pietà. In *Rendering Techniques '98 (Proceedings of the Eurographics Workshop on Rendering)*, pages 81–92, June 1998.

20. Peter Shirley, Changyaw Wang, and Kurt Zimmerman. Monte carlo techniques for direct lighting calculations. *Transactions on Graphics*, 15(1):1–36, 1996.

21. Keith Waters. A muscle model for animating three-dimensional facial expression. In *Computer Graphics (SIGGRAPH 1987 Proceedings)*, pages 17–24, July 1987.

22. Lance Williams. Performance-driven facial animation. In *Computer Graphics (SIGGRAPH 1990 Proceedings)*, pages 235–242, August 1990.

23. Yizhou Yu, Paul Debevec, Jitendra Malik, and Tim Hawkins. Inverse global illumination: Recovering reflectance models of real scenes from photographs. In *Computer Graphics (SIGGRAPH 1999 Proceedings)*, pages 215–224, August 1999.

24. Zhengyou Zhang. A flexible new technique for camera calibration. Technical Report MSR-TR-98-71, Microsoft Research, 1998.

Editors' Note: see Appendix, p. 410 for colored figures of this paper

Real-Time Fur

Jerome Edward Lengyel

Microsoft Research

Abstract. Hair adds compelling richness to computer graphics scenes. This paper describes techniques for lighting and rendering short hair in real-time on current PC graphics hardware. Level-of-detail representations for drawing fur span the viewing distance from close-ups using procedurally generated alpha-blended lines, to mid and far views using volumetric textures, and on to distant views using anisotropic texture map rendering. Real-time lighting with soft-edged shadows is consistent across the level-of-detail representations.

Keywords. I.3.7 Three-Dimensional Graphics and Realism: volume textures, hair shading, soft shadows I.3.3 Picture/Image Generation: item-buffer lightmap I.3.5 Computational Geometry and Object Modeling: procedural geometry, hair modeling

1 Introduction

Make a list of your favorite things, and you will find that many of them are fuzzy. For computer graphics, rendering realistic fuzzy objects has to date required lengthy offline processing per frame, from minutes using line drawing to hours with ray tracing.

Now, with the increase in PC graphics hardware performance, and using techniques described in this paper, convincing hair can be drawn interactively (the Figure 1 example renders at 15 Hz). Once the regime of the problem moves out of offline rendering to interactive camera control, level-of-detail becomes important. The hair must look good over the wide range of scale the interactive viewer might choose.

Fig. 1. Furry Bear with Soft-Edged Shadows

This paper describes new techniques for lighting and rendering hair (and other fuzzy phenomena) in real-time, and makes the following contributions:

- Hair level-of-detail representations that smoothly span the distance from close-ups to distant viewing
- Real-time hair lighting for both line-drawing and volume texture rendering that includes real-time soft-edged shadows

At run-time, we use the standard computer graphics triangle pipeline to composite a textured volumetric representation of hair by rendering a "Russian Doll" of concentric shells generated from an input mesh. For level-of-detail control when moving from near to distant viewing, we decrease the number of levels in the volume representation.

As a pre-process, for smooth transitions from hair geometry to volume data, we filter the procedural geometry of the hair into the volume representation.

Hair lighting that is consistent for both the geometric hair and volumetric hair is calculated at run time, with soft-edged shadows. The combination of smooth level-of-detail with volume textures and real-time lighting makes compelling real-time scenes of furry objects.

2 Previous Work

Computer graphics for hair and fuzzy objects has been around since 1983 when Reeves [20] introduced particle systems. Perlin and Hoffert [18] showed how procedural texturing could be used to render fuzzy objects. Kajiya and Kay [11] introduced the use of 3D texture or "texels" to render hair, which remains one of the most realistic fur rendering techniques. The original Kajiya-Kay system ray-traced a polygonal scene with volumetric texture, generating frames at about 1/7200 Hz.[1] Throughout this paper we use "volume texture" and "texels" interchangeably.

Banks [2] improved the Kajiya-Kay shading model and included a hair self-shadowing term. By using shaded lines, Banks rendered fur nearly 200 times faster than the previous work. We use a modified Banks rendering approach for near views, but add hardware-assisted lighting. The Banks approach did not include level-of-detail.

Anjyo et al. [1] presented a technique for interactively modeling hair using a cantilevered beam physics approximation. The hair model was limited to individual strands and the collision detection was only between hair and special surfaces, such as the scalp. Daldegan et al. [5] improved on this model and added a hair-to-hair repulsive force. We use similar techniques to model the source geometry of the non-tiled hair, which is then filtered into our volumetric representation.

Motion picture special effects have demonstrated high quality hair rendering, such as *Jumanji* by Yost et al. [28]. Goldman presented a simplified model for speeding up the ray-traced rendering of short fur, which was used in *101 Dalmatians* [6]. There are several other proprietary modeling and rendering approaches, such as plug-ins for 3D Studio MAX and the Alias/Wavefront Maya modeling system. These plug-ins typically model the hair with a set of example hairs, and then procedurally fill in the hair during an offline ray tracing. The commercial geometric hair modeling tools are more extensive and polished than our modeling tools, but lack the ability to do fast run-time level-of-detail transitions.

Van Gelder and Wilhelms presented a technique for interactively modeling sparse hair with line rendering [25], which we use during the modeling of the hair distributions.

The texel approach was revisited by Neyret [17] to ray trace such complex phenomena as trees. Chiba et al. presented a ray-tracing approach to model and render landscapes with many trees [4]. Neither of these approaches targeted real-time rendering.

Meyer and Neyret describe how to render texels in real-time on graphics hardware by compositing a set of geometric layers offset from a base mesh [15]. Our work uses the layered volume texture approach extensively and makes several improvements, including better filtering of the source geometry to the volume texture and better hair-specific run-time lighting of the resulting hair volume texture.

Other approaches for rendering hair include the Lumigraph or Lightfield techniques described in 1996 by Gortler et al. [7] and, independently, by Levoy and Hanrahan [14]. This approach takes a dense sampling of views around an object and then uses these views to reconstruct images from novel view positions. The advantages are that many kinds of optical phenomena are represented, including reasonable looking hair. The disadvantage is the huge size of the database required for good fidelity.

Zöckler et al. [29] render streamlines using alpha blending for the width of the streamline. Zöckler et al. use the texture coordinate transformation matrix to encode

---

[1] Kajiya and Kay used enough compute cycles to become members in the "teraflop club." Kajiya and Kay report that they used 12 IBM 3090 and IBM 3081 machines at estimated 40Mflop/s / machine * 12 machines * 40teraflop. On a single Pentium II 300 MHz, tuned to get 100 Mflop/s, the technique would probably take the same amount of time today, 2 to 3 hours.

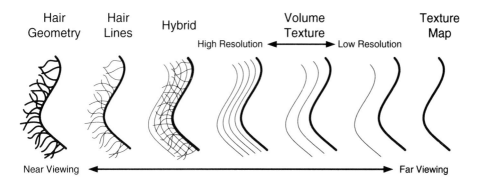

Fig. 2. Level-of-detail representations span near-to-far viewing. For extreme close-ups, the full geometry of the hair is needed. For near views, alpha-blended line segments are used. For intermediate views, volume texture representations range from high to low resolution to capture the needed parallax. For distant views, just one anisotropic texture is needed.

the eye and light position and use a 2D texture to compute the hair lighting. Heidrich et al. [9] use the texture matrix in a similar way to index into a 2D lighting texture to render anisotropic lighting for surfaces as well as lines. We use a similar approach for lighting hair rendered as lines or as volumes but use the half vector H instead of the lighting direction L and wrap the lighting texture differently. We add a second texture for a shadow modulation term on both the lines and the volume texture.

Recently, Kowalski et al. described a system for artistic rendering of foliage and fur based on view-dependent geometry [13]. This approach places procedural geometry to give the appearance of fuzziness. One drawback of this approach is the large amount of temporal aliasing of the procedural features. Our approach uses a similar introduction of procedural geometry for close-ups, but, because of the pre-filtering across level-of-detail representations, there is less temporal aliasing as the filtered volumetric representation of a feature is cross-dissolved with the geometric representation.

3 Level-of-Detail Overview

The key to the success of our approach is to consider the complete range of potential viewing conditions from the outset. To handle the full range of possible viewing configurations, we use view-dependent level-of-detail representations. See Figure 2 for a diagram of the level-of-detail representations and Figure 3 for an example.

For extreme close-ups[2], the full geometry of the hair is needed. For near views, the geometry of each individual hair is modeled with an alpha-blended and textured line, where alpha is mapped to the width of the hair to support subpixel feature size.

As the hair recedes from the viewer, a volume shell representation (similar to [15]) is used which integrates over multiple hairs and captures the aggregate appearance of hair or fur at this scale. The line-drawn hairs are faded from view by scaling alpha down to zero. Concentric, transparent, textured layers render the volume texture. The texel layers are drawn from the skin outwards, since this is the typical viewing direction.

---

[2]The cross-sectional diameter of hair is approximately 7e-5 m (70 microns) and the typical length of the hairs in our examples is about 3e-2 m (3 cm). To cover more than a single pixel at 1024x768, the camera must be zoomed in so that a single hair covers half the screen (1024*70 microns = 7 cm). The current system does not handle extreme close-ups using the full geometry of the hair, but this should be a straightforward addition.

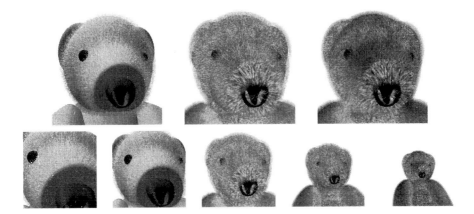

Fig. 3. Level-of-Detail, Bear Example. Row 1: (1a) alpha-blended lines (in contrasting color) (1b) combined lines and volume, (1c) volume texture only. Row 2: Receding viewing distance.

As the object moves further from the camera, the number of concentric shells needed to produce the proper parallax diminishes until a single texture-map suffices (Figure 2, left to right center). The number of mip-map levels within a volumetric layer diminishes in step with the concentric shells. For both the number of samples within a layer, and the number of layers within a volume shell, the levels are powers of 2 of one another. The cross dissolve that blends different scales is analogous to the linear interpolation between layers of the mip-map. At the lowest level of detail a single texture is rendered with an anisotropic model to capture the aggregate lighting (rightmost example in Figure 2).

The choice of which level of detail is active is based on the size of the projected hair features and the resolution of the texture samples. The goal is represent the hair with the smallest number of samples that give a good reconstruction. We keep the texture samples at approximately the same resolution as the screen pixels, which is similar to mip-mapping. (Following standard computer graphics practice, we reconstruct with samples at $1/2$ the frequency Nyquist would suggest.) The level of detail is chosen once per hair tile and is constrained to change smoothly frame-to-frame. The geometry on the left of Figure 2 is needed when the feature size of the hair projects to larger than a single pixel (please see note 2 on the previous page). The line-rendered hair that is second from the left in Figure 2 is used for hair feature sizes of 1 pixel down to approximately $1/2$ pixel. The volumetric representation is the rest of the way down in scale, with the vertical resolution (i.e. the number of concentric layers) tied to the scale of the texture samples.

Since the volumetric hair is a filtered version of the geometric hair, we are free to move forwards or backwards in detail between the representations. If we start from a small patch of hair that is represented by both a volume texture and a procedural hair distribution, then the small patch can be placed on the surface of the input mesh using 2D texture tiling of the input mesh texture domain. The tiling and the procedural hair distribution can then produce the geometric hairs needed for close-up viewing. For the bear example, the same $512 \times 512 \times 16$ level volumetric texture was used for the ears, head, arms, body, and legs. A smaller tile may suffice; experiments are in progress.

Alternatively, if we start with a model of a full head of hair, we can filter the given hair to produce faithful volume representations. Technologically, we are in the same state as when texture-mapping hardware was introduced. Full textures were initially

247

Fig. 4. Example Hair Patches. A wide range of fur is possible from a small set of parameters. The bottom row center, for example, uses a low density and widely spaced seeds to get sparse fur. These small patches of hair render at 50 Hz or better. The underlying geometry is a mesh of 800 triangles, representing the skin. This mesh is extruded along the local normals to produce 16 concentric levels. The volume data is represented on these 16 levels by 512 × 512 textures. The textures were created by placing example hairs on the patch to create a model hair distribution, which was then sampled to the desired density.

too expensive in memory and bandwidth, and so tiled textures were the norm. Then, as graphics memory size and performance increased, full textures for each object were used. The approach described here should scale to allow for the rendering of long hair that flows laterally to track the scalp or skin, where each object in the scene uses a different volumetric texture. General animation of the geometric hair requires re-filtering of the geometry to the volume, which is currently not feasible in real-time. If the animation is limited to deformations of the texel shells, then the level-of-detail approach still works.

This systematic management of level of detail is the key to efficient rendering. Image quality, however, depends on the modeling and shading described in the next sections. Two factors govern the effectiveness of modeling: geometric accuracy and representation. Since the level of detail rendering employs a hybrid of geometric and texel representations, the approximation of geometry with texels must maintain fidelity.

For typical viewing distances, we have found that a combined rendering of volumetric texture and alpha-blended lines gives the best visual result. For the rest of the paper, we will be describing how this combined representation may be used to produce realistic, real-time hair.

4 Geometric Hair Modeling

To geometrically model fur, we first seed the surface with "curl" starting points by painting the seeds directly on the surface of the mesh using a system similar to Hanrahan and Haeberli's direct painting approach [8]. Then we grow the seeds as particle system trajectories, and adjust the hair for the desired effect. The parameters include hair color (black to white to red to brown), hair diameter (wide to narrow), orientation (aim hair in different directions), length (short to long), curliness (straight to twisty), curl radius (small to wide), and curl taper (narrowing or opening out). For quick feedback, we interpolate the seeds to the desired density in a small test patch.

With this simple parametric approach, a wide range of fur is possible. See Figure 4 for examples. By retaining the curl seeds and distribution parameters, the full geometry of the hair can be recreated as needed for closeup views, even if just an initial patch of hair is modeled and then tiled on the surface of the mesh, by transforming the geometric hairs into the local coordinates of the desired tile.

The previous work in individual hair modeling [25] [5] [1] may be used to create an arrangement of the geometric hairs as input to the volume filtering stage.

5 Concentric Shell Generation

To create a coordinate system on which to place the volume textures, we use a simple normal offset of the vertex positions to a user-defined number of levels, m, and scale, h. The connectivity and texture coordinates of the offset mesh are identical to the input mesh. For vertex i of level l,

$$V_i^l = V_i^0 + (hl/m)N_i^0$$

where V_i^0 is the original input vertex position and N_i^0 is the normal per vertex.

For the examples we have tried to date, the simple approach has been satisfactory. Future work will include painting the height of the concentric mesh for varying the application of a volume texture from a hair library, the calculation of the local height needed for a given global arrangement of hair, and smoothing of areas of high curvature to avoid self-intersection of the concentric shells.

6 Volume Filtering

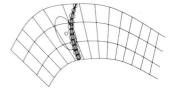

After creating the arrangement of hairs, the next step is to form an accurate volumetric approximation to the hair geometry. Since the hair geometry is at a finer scale than the texel sampling grid, it is represented by a centerline with a varying radius. Each hair's centerline is sampled at high resolution, transformed back into local texture coordinates, and then weighted by the sampling kernel and by the cross-sectional area of the hair. Let S_{ijk} be the texel sample to be filtered, $w_{ijk}(p)$

Fig. 5. The hair is filtered into the texel array by supersampling the centerline and adding weighted contributions to each texel.

be the texel kernel (we use a truncated Gaussian with an overlap of 2 in each sampling direction), and $Area(p)$ be the cross-sectional area of the hair at the sample point.

$$S_{ijk} = \sum_{h \in \text{Hairs}} \sum_{p=Sample(h)} w_{ijk}(p) Area(p) Color(p)$$

This simple approach works well for the irregular and varying sampling kernels needed to filter arbitrary hairs over the concentric shell grids. In Figure 4, a single texel sample is highlighted with a representation of the footprint of the sampling kernel along with a single hair that is to be filtered into the volume. The shape of the sampling kernel is

(skin layer)

Fig. 6. Curly hair filtered into a 16 layer volumetric texture. The sequence of frames (left to right, top to bottom) starts at the skin and moves toward the tips of the hair. The frames shown are the 128×128 cropped center of the volume texture used for the top row, center example in Figure 4.

determined by the sampling density and geometry of the mesh. For the bear example, the resolution of the texel layer is much higher in the plane of the surface geometry, at 512×512 samples, than in the vertical direction with 16 levels. This results in "tall and skinny" filters that project much of the geometry of the hair into each of the texture planes.

The aggregate tangent directions at the vertex positions on the concentric shells are also set by local weighting of the hair tangents, which works for slowly changing tangents. See Neyret [17] for more general normal distribution filtering.

$$T_{ijk} = \text{normalize}(\sum_{h \in \text{Hairs}} \sum_{p=Sample(h)} w_{ijk}(p) Area(p) Tangent(p))$$

Texel layers representing lower levels of detail are derived by filtering their higher resolution predecessors, or by repeating the individual hair integration process with lower sampling resolutions. The latter is more expensive, but overcomes precision problems when the intermediate texel layers are quantized to 24 bits.

250

7 Hair Shading

At run-time, we use the Kajiya-Kay/Banks model on the hair tangents. We use either of two techniques based on previous work, one that works per-vertex and one that works per-pixel. The per-vertex technique chooses the right normal to make standard hardware lighting work by projecting the light vector L and the specular half vector H onto the disk of normals defined by the hair tangent T. E is the eye vector.

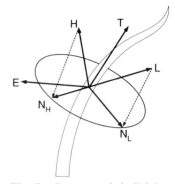

$$H = (L + E)/2$$

$$N_H = H - (T \cdot H)T$$

$$N_L = L - (T \cdot L)T$$

Fig. 7. Per vertex hair lighting projects light L and half vector H onto the disk of normals given by the hair tangent T.

Ideally, the hardware would compute two lighting terms with two normals, one for specular N_H and one for diffuse N_L. Since current graphics hardware is limited to a single normal, we do a weighted combination of the two computed normals, and, following Banks [2], add a portion of the underlying mesh's normal to add the effect of local shading.

$$N = \beta_L N_L + \beta_H N_H + \beta_0 N_0$$

We typically use $\beta_L = 0.5$, $\beta_H = 0.4$, and $\beta_0 = 0.1$. The normal is then given to the graphics hardware to be lit with the typical graphics hardware lighting model. The lighting modulates both the volume texture and the alpha-blended lines. Surprisingly, adding the normals together and then doing the shading gives a reasonable looking result. More comparison to the full shading model is needed to evaluate the quality of this approximation.

With the per-vertex lighting, we noticed some sparkling at the tips of the hair. These may be due to degenerate normals near zero, which are then normalized. In effect, the degenerate normals pick a random direction for the lighting.

The per-pixel technique, which works only for directional lights and a non-local viewer (a single view direction for all the vertices), uses the hardware texture matrix to encode the position of the light and the eye, and a 2D lookup to compute the per-pixel shading [29]. We use H instead of L and wrap the texture rather than offsetting by $1/2$.

$$(u,v) = \begin{bmatrix} T \end{bmatrix} \left[\begin{bmatrix} L/2 \end{bmatrix} \begin{bmatrix} H/2 \end{bmatrix} \right] = (T \cdot L/2, T \cdot H/2)$$

For the shading texture indexed by the (u,v) coordinates computed above, we use the standard ambient K_A, diffuse K_D, and specular K_S constants, the specular exponent n, and the Banks excess brightness diffuse exponent $p = 4.8$ to fill in the shading texture:

$$\text{Shading}(u,v) = K_A + K_D \left(\sqrt{1-d^2} \right)^p + K_S \left(\sqrt{1-s^2} \right)^n$$

$$d = \begin{cases} 2u & 0 \le u < 1/2 \\ 2u - 1 & 1/2 \le u \le 1 \end{cases}$$

$$s = \begin{cases} 2v & 0 \le v < \frac{1}{2} \\ 2v - 1 & \frac{1}{2} \le v \le 1 \end{cases}$$

A low-resolution 32x32 texture suffices to encode the slowly changing lighting. The normalization problem is avoided with the per-pixel approach, since the projection is coded in the texture lookup table and so avoids near-zero-length normals.

Because of limitations with the number of multi-texturing stages available on current hardware, we can use either the per-pixel shading or a lightmap shadow modulation texture described in the next section. When the lightmap shadows are turned on, we use the per-vertex shading. Otherwise, we use the per-pixel shading. Bank's self-shadowing term is modeled by setting the per-concentric-shell material color to be dark near the skin and light near the tips of the hair. This same term is applied each frame to the alpha-blended lines based on the height of the hair from the surface.

8 Soft-Edged Shadows

In addition to using the Banks hair self-shadowing term, we developed a soft-edged shadow rendering technique that adds a feeling of global illumination. For more details see the technical report [12].

In previous work, the shadow map algorithm of Reeves et al. [21] renders a depth map from the point of view of the light and then tests this map against each output pixel when rendering from the camera view. The results of the shadow map test are then filtered to produce a shadow modulation term that attenuates shading per pixel. The width of the shadow map filter is typically small for real-time rendering, and so the shadows have a hard edge. Also, the filtering must be performed every frame, after the depth comparison with the shadow map.

Our technique trades off storage for computation and explicitly stores a shadow modulation texture, or "lightmap", for each mesh (similarly to [23].) The shadow computation is de-coupled from the viewpoint rendering, so the shadows need only be updated when the relative position of the light, object, or occluders changes. We use splatting by the graphics hardware as an alternative to FFT convolution for shadows [23] and avoid the selection-of-blockers problem [23] by letting the rendering hardware select all the blockers simultaneously. Soft edges are much larger than is possible with a reasonable blur kernel size in standard shadow maps [21].

First, the scene is rendered from the point of view of the light using a combined mesh identified/UV texture map [8] (the hair geometry and textures are omitted so only the underlying meshes create the shadows). Each pixel in this view represents a point on each object that is illuminated by the light. Since we have the mesh identifier and the UV coordinates at each point, we can easily map to the lightmap texture on each object.

Second, on the host processor, we make one pass over the light-view rendering, gathering samples that correspond to each mesh. For efficiency, we use a small rendering window of 128x128 pixels, so the number of samples does not fully cover the illuminated region of the object (Figure 10, left, after splatting to the geometry with a single-texel size splat).

Fig. 8. Light-view rendering of uv-coordinates and mesh identifiers

252

Third, for the lightmap of each mesh, we clear to an ambient shadow level. We splat a small Gaussian for each light-view sample to fill light in between the missing samples and to make pleasing soft-edged shadows (Figure 10 right, and Figure 11). The splats are represented with a texture quadrilateral that is composited into each mesh's lightmap using the graphics hardware.

The splat size should depend on the distance along the ray and the local texture sampling rate. Currently, we set splat size once per receiving object to approximate both terms. The desirable blurriness of the shadows comes from two sources, from the Gaussian blur from the textured quadrilateral and from the bilinear reconstruction of the low-resolution lightmap texture.

For global shadowing for the hair drawn as lines, we project each line onto the base mesh to get the appropriate texture coordinates of the base mesh's lightmap. For the volume textures, we use the base mesh's lightmap for each of the successive concentric shells. Because of the soft edges, the translation error in the shadow is not readily apparent on the fur.

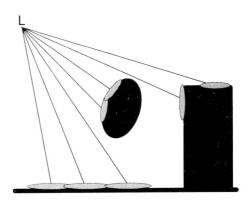

Fig. 9. Soft-Edged Shadow Generation. Rendering from the point of view of the light determines which points on the objects receive light. Then the receiving points are splatted into the shadow maps for each object.

The soft-edged shadow approach needs further investigation. By sampling an area light source and using a fractional splat, we should be able to approximate umbra and penumbra regions in the lightmap. Better shadow-splat pathways are needed that do not require a round-trip to the host, and better shadow-splat sizes should be calculated from the depth channel in the light-view rendering. At 128x128 samples in the view from the light, there is the potential to generate 128x128x2 = 32768 triangles just for the splats. There is also the overhead of rendering the scene triangles from the point of view of the light. Adding these together gives a fairly substantial rendering burden for current graphics hardware. For the bear example, the shadows update at approximately 5 Hz. Improvement of triangle rates in graphics hardware seems to be outpacing the speed increases of the CPU, so our shadowing approach may be more attractive with the next generation of graphics hardware.

9 Examples

All of these examples were rendered on an Intel PIII 733 MHz and a Guillemot 3D Prophet DDR-DVI video card based on the Nvidia GeForce256 chipset, using the Microsoft DirectDraw and Direct3D API's. The filtering of the volume textures for the following examples took several minutes each.

Figure 11 shows a bear that consists of eleven separate meshes, three of which are not textured (the two eyes and nose). The texture coordinates come from the original generalized cylinder model of the bear, so there are singularities at the tips of the arms, head, body, and legs. The fur-covered parts share the same $512 \times 512 \times 16$ level volume texture computed on an initial cube with periodic u and v boundary conditions. The fur

Fig. 10. Lightmap Splat Size. The sampling pattern from the light-viewpoint rendering is visible on the left, but gradually merges together as the splat size increases. The splat also gives the shadow a soft edge.

texture is mapped to each part of the bear as a single, non-tiled texture. The original meshes total 9406 triangles. After offsetting the fur-covered parts to get 16 layers, the total rises to 129466 triangles. The bear renders at 15 Hz. When the light is moved, the frame rate for the bear on the right of Figure 11 drops to approximately 5 Hz.

Figure 4 shows examples of several types of hair possible with the approach. These examples render at 50 Hz. The underlying geometry is a mesh of 800 triangles, representing the skin. This mesh is extruded along the local normals to produce 16 concentric levels (12800 triangles). The volume data is represented on these 16 levels by 512×512 textures.

10 Conclusion

The rendering method presented in this paper gains efficiency through the careful management of level of detail, and yet the results are more realistic than previous interactive methods. This improved quality is a function of both more exact filtering and more full featured shading than previous techniques.

Even as the PC graphics hardware performance continues to increase, there will be the need to filter geometry with fine structure, such as hair, to avoid aliasing artifacts when viewed from a distance, and to handle the large geometric burden that fine structure places on a rendering system.

We anticipate improved modeling and animation tools. One such tool permits "hair distribution painting" (rather than just single seeds) onto a scanned-in geometric mesh, automatically displacing the mesh towards a scalp while adding hair texels.

The concentric shells should include radial fins to provide support for the volume texture near the silhouette edge. Currently, the hair fades out near the silhouette edges as the concentric shell triangles are viewed edge-on. Also near the silhouettes, there are errors in the compositing due to the improper order of the layers. Better sorting is needed.

The concentric shell representation and the simple volume filtering approach work well if the hair is oriented to be mostly normal to the surface, as in the bear example. The higher horizontal resolution (512×512 texture maps) is needed to represent the

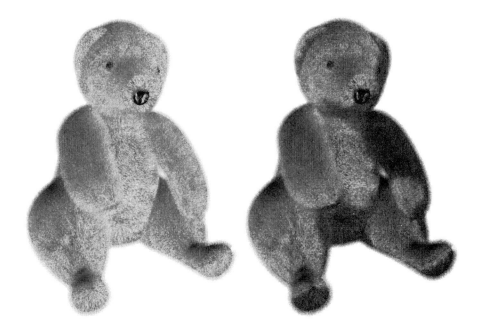

Fig. 11. Soft-edged shadows add realism to the hair rendering. (a) Volume texture only. (b) Modulated by soft-edged shadow map.

fine detail. The low vertical resolution (16 layers) is adequate to sample the slowly changing horizontal trajectory of the hair when viewed from above. For more general hair that flows along the skin, the vertical sampling rate may need to be increased and the orientation of the shells may need to be modified, which may move this approach out of the real-time regime depending on the balance of the graphics system (pixel-fill vs. geometry, i.e. texture resolution vs. number of geometry layers).

Westin et al. [27] sample micro- and milliscale geometry to obtain physically accurate reflectance functions of velvet and other cloth. Our volumetric filtering and lighting models should be tested and improved for photometric validity rather than simply for appearance.

Other future extensions include handling real-time large-scale geometric complexity. The hierarchy of scale works well for hair. Neyret and others have shown that the texel approach works well for offline rendering of such diverse phenomena as trees and buildings [17]. For real-time graphics, it remains to be shown that the hierarchy of detail can be extended to include the recursive filtering of geometry into volume textures, as sketched in Figure 12. From a distance, trees look like hair. When viewed close-up, the needles of a fir branch look like hair. Techniques similar to the ones presented in this paper have the potential to handle the long-standing problem of how to create level-of-detail representations that filter across models rather than per model. Very recent work by Meyer and Neyret [16] is a step in this direction.

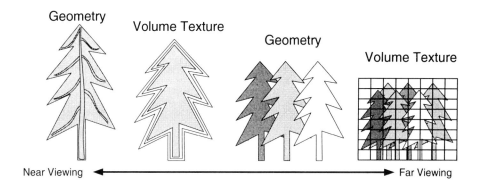

Fig. 12. Future scale hierarchy starts with local geometry and then filters to produce volume texture representations of phenomena such as foliage. As the scale increases further, multiple objects (with volume textures) are merged into a volume texture.

11 Acknowledgements

Thanks to Francois Sillion, Steve Marschner, Peter-Pike Sloan, John Snyder, Jim Kajiya, Michael Cohen, Mike Marr, Sashi Raghupathy, Brian Guenter and the rest of the Microsoft Graphics Group for technical discussions. Thanks to John Snyder and Jim Kajiya for the bear model. For editing help and much more thanks to Allison Hart. For artistic discussions and helpful references thanks to Curtis Christman. Thanks to Turner Whitted for research directions and extensive help with the writing. Thanks to David Thiel for producing and editing the videotapes. Thanks to the anonymous reviewers for helpful suggestions on the writing.

References

1. Anjyo, Ken-ichi, Yoshiaki Usami, and Tsuneya Kurihara. A Simple Method for Extracting the Natural Beauty of Hair, SIGGRAPH 92, pp. 111-120.
2. Banks, David C. Illumination in Diverse Codimensions, SIGGRAPH 94, pp. 327-334.
3. Chen, Lieu-Hen, Santi Saeyor, Hiroshi Dohi, Mitsuru Ishizuka. A System of 3D Hair Style Synthesis Based on the Wisp Model, The Visual Computer, 15 (4), pp. 159-170 (1999). ISSN 0178-2789.
4. Chiba, N., K. Muraoka, A. Doi and J. Hosokawa. Rendering of Forest Scenery Using 3D Textures, Journal of Visualization and Computer Animation, 8 (4), 1997, pp. 191-199.
5. Daldegan, Agnes, Nadia Magnenat Thalmann, Tsuneya Kurihara, and Daniel Thalmann. An Integrated System for Modeling, Animating and Rendering Hair, Computer Graphics Forum (Eurographics '93), 12 (3), pp. 211-221 (1993, Oxford, UK). Blackwell Publishers.
6. Goldman, Dan B., Fake Fur Rendering, SIGGRAPH 97, pp. 127-134.
7. Gortler, Steven J., Radek Grzeszczuk, Richard Szeliski, and Michael F. Cohen. The Lumigraph, SIGGRAPH 96, pp. 43-54.
8. Hanrahan, Pat and Paul Haeberli. Direct WYSIWYG Painting and Texturing on 3D Shapes, SIGGRAPH 90, pp. 215-223.
9. Heidrich, Wolfgang and Hans-Peter Seidel. Realistic, Hardware-Accelerated Shading and Lighting, SIGGRAPH 99, pp. 171-178.
10. Kajiya, James T. Anisotropic Reflection Models, SIGGRAPH 85, pp. 15-21.
11. Kajiya, James T. and Timothy L. Kay. Rendering Fur with Three Dimensional Textures, SIGGRAPH 89, pp. 271-280.
12. Lengyel, Jerome E., Splatting for Soft-Edged Shadows, Microsoft Research Technical Report, 2000.
13. Kowalski, Michael A., Lee Markosian, J. D. Northrup, Lubomir Bourdev, Ronen Barzel, Loring S. Holden, and John Hughes. Art-Based Rendering of Fur, Grass, and Trees, SIGGRAPH 99, pp. 433-438.
14. Levoy, Marc and Pat Hanrahan. Light Field Rendering, SIGGRAPH 96, pp. 31-42.
15. Meyer, Alexandre and Fabrice Neyret. Interactive Volumetric Textures, Eurographics Rendering Workshop 1998, pp. 157-168.
16. Meyer, Alexandre and Fabrice Neyret. Multiscale Shaders for Efficient Realistic Rendering of Pine-Trees, Graphics Interface 2000.
17. Neyret, Fabrice. Synthesizing Verdant Landscapes using Volumetric Textures, Eurographics Rendering Workshop 1996, pp. 215-224 (June 1996, Porto, Portugal). ISBN 3-211-82883-4.
18. Perlin, Ken, and Eric M. Hoffert. Hypertexture, SIGGRAPH 89, pp. 253-262.
19. Poulin, Pierre and Alain Fournier. A Model for Anisotropic Reflection, SIGGRAPH 90, pp. 273-282.
20. Reeves, W. T. Particle Systems - a Technique for Modeling a Class of Fuzzy Objects, ACM Transactions on Graphics, 2 (2), pp. 91-108 (April 1983).
21. Reeves, William T., David H. Salesin, and Robert L. Cook. Rendering Antialiased Shadows with Depth Maps, SIGGRAPH 87, pp. 283-291.
22. Shade, Jonathan W., Steven J. Gortler, Li-wei He, and Richard Szeliski. Layered Depth Images, SIGGRAPH 98, pp. 231-242.
23. Soler, C. and F. X. Sillion. Fast Calculation of Soft Shadow Textures Using Convolution. SIGGRAPH 98, pp. 321-332.
24. Thalmann, N. M., S. Carion, M. Courchesne, P. Volino, Y. Wu. Virtual Clothes, Hair and Skin for Beautiful Top Models, Computer Graphics International 1996. IEEE Computer Society.
25. Van Gelder, Allen and Jane Wilhelms. An Interactive Fur Modeling Technique, Graphics Interface '97, pp. 181-188 (May 1997). ISBN 0-9695338-6-1. ISSN 0713-5424.
26. Watanabe, Yasuhiko and Yasuhito Suenaga. A Trigonal Prism-Based Method for Hair Image Generation, IEEE Computer Graphics & Applications, 12 (1), pp. 47-53 (January 1992).
27. Westin, Stephen H., James R. Arvo, and Kenneth E. Torrance. Predicting Reflectance Functions From Complex Surfaces, SIGGRAPH 92, pp. 255-264.
28. Yost, Jeffrey, Christian Rouet, David Benson, and Florian Kainz. Jumanji, TriStar Pictures, 1996.
29. Zöckler, Malte, Detlev Stalling, and Hans-Christian Hege. Interactive Visualization of 3D-Vector Fields using Illuminated Streamlines, IEEE Visualization '96, pp. 107-114.

Feature-based Displacement Mapping

Xiaohuan Corina Wang[1], Jérôme Maillot[1], Eugene Fiume[2]

Victor Ng-Thow-Hing[2], Andrew Woo[1], Sanjay Bakshi[1]

Abstract.
Displacement mapping was originally created as a rendering tool to provide small-scale modulation of an underlying smooth surface. However, it has now emerged as a sculpting tool, to the extent that complex geometry can effectively be added to a scene at rendering time. The attendant complexity of displacement maps is placing increased demands on rendering systems, from quality, performance, and memory perspectives. While adequate solutions exist within scanline rendering architectures, good general solutions have been difficult to come by in ray-traced or hardware-based environments, or in situations in which a complete displaced surface is desired. We present an approach to the rendering of displacement mapped surfaces that scales with the complexity of the displacement map, with an eye to minimizing the amount of additional geometry generated by the mapping process. We perform a feature analysis of displacement maps, aggregate these features, and map them onto geometry in space. This approach affords a significant degree of complexity control, it permits feature-based tessellation of surfaces, and it is amenable to use in ray-traced, scanline, or hardware accelerated settings. This kind of feature analysis naturally applies to other classes of texture mapping as well.

1 Motivation

The history of rendering in computer graphics is filled with clever ways of adding visual complexity to otherwise smooth geometry. Texture mapping has been used for 25 years to add detail to surfaces [5]. Bump mapping [4] allows one to perturb surface normals to achieve the visual effect of bumps on smooth surfaces. Since the actual surface is not altered, bump mapping has the limitation that artifacts can become apparent when the surface is viewed from certain orientations, especially near the surface silhouette: the geometry remains smooth regardless of the complexity of bump mapping. Furthermore, rendered bump-mapped images will exhibit a lack of shadowing and reflections of features caused by the bumps, even though the self-shadowing problem in bump mapping has been improved by Max [15].

Displacement mapping [6] was introduced to alleviate this limitation, and its use has grown considerably. Technically, a displacement map is a way of specifying an *offset surface*, using a scalar height field $h(x, y)$. Given a surface $\mathcal{S}(x, y)$ with normal field $\mathbf{N}(x, y)$, we can define the offset surface $\mathcal{S}'(x, y) = \mathcal{S}(x, y) + h(x, y)\mathbf{N}(x, y)$. It is possible to generalize this definition to vector displacements independent of the surface normal.

This offsetting operation is seldom easy to perform analytically, except when h and $\mathcal{S}$ are both piecewise linear functions. Furthermore, the representation of both h and $\mathcal{S}$,

---

[1] Alias|Wavefront, 210 King Street East, Toronto, Ontario, Canada, M5A 1J7
[2] University of Toronto, 10 King's College Circle, Toronto, Ontario, Canada, M5S 3G4

as well as their interaction, can result in practical difficulties in getting a good approximation for $S'(x, y)$. In practice, h is often represented by a discrete, parametric texture map, and S is a polygonal mesh, possibly computed from a curved surface representation. It would be natural, therefore, to displace only the vertices in the polygonal mesh according to h. However, if the density of mesh vertices is not commensurate with the complexity of the displacements, the rendered result will be unsatisfactorily coarse and undersampled. On the other hand, if the vertex density is very high relative to the local complexity of the displacement, then one would incur a high cost for unnecessarily large meshes, shading computations, and memory consumption.

In a traditional scanline rendering setting, it is possible to use geometry dicing and texture tiling techniques to localize the amount of extra geometry and displacement information that is produced, to render high-quality displacement mapped surfaces on-the-fly, and to discard any newly-created geometry once it is not needed. However, in cases where a complete mesh is desirable, such as in real time environments or ray-tracing contexts, when high-quality shadows are needed, or when displacement maps are used to produce high quality offset surfaces, an alternative approach is required.

We propose a new displacement mapping technique that is driven by the detection of features in the displacement map, and that causes adaptive refinement of the original surface. Our goal is to match the rendering quality of existing professional rendering packages [1, 17], while maintaining an accurate, minimal mesh that approximates $S'(x, y)$. The approach supports the traditional workflow of layering other texture mapping techniques and shaders on the surface. The technique is robust under significant displacements of the underlying surface. The texture analysis techniques that we present are also amenable to use in a variety of feature based texture-filtering applications.

2 Previous Work

Displacement mapping is credited to Cook in [6]. A follow up paper [7] described an implementation called *REYES*, in which *micropolygon decomposition* is proposed as a general rendering technique. This approach tessellates each surface into polygons that are smaller than a quarter of screen pixel. Because geometry is rendered in surface order, clipped to the size of screen tiles, and then immediately purged once shaded, the practical incurred memory cost of an otherwise explicitly high polygon density from such a tessellation is minimal. Displacement mapping fits naturally into the *REYES* architecture. However, the *REYES* architecture is prone to produce cracks, does not handle rapidly varying displacement maps which produce stretched polygons larger than a quarter of a pixel, and does not easily afford high-quality shadow computation. For the first two cases, some workarounds have been suggested [2]. We view the REYES architecture approach (implemented in Photorealistic Renderman [17]) as setting the reference standard for comparing the rendering quality of displacement maps.

There have been some approaches to accommodate efficient displacement mapping for ray-traced environments. Heidrich and Seidel, for example, employ affine arithmetic to ray trace procedural displacement maps without adding geometry [8]. Pharr and Hanrahan use memory coherence and caching to ray-trace large datasets of displaced geometry [16]. Because our technique actually builds meshes, the work of Pharr [16] can in fact accelerate our rendering, especially in cases where dense meshes are created. Further, Heidrich's work [8] can be a useful substitute for our approach in some cases where the displacement map is uniformly dense and lacking of distinct features.

Another approach to rendering displacement maps would be to treat offset surfaces

1-a: Original mesh, two triangles.

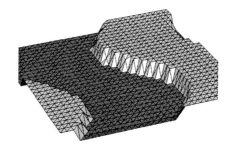

1-b: Fine tessellation, 961 vertices.

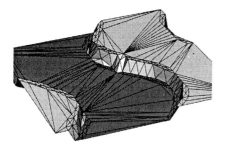

1-c: Our method, initial sample points.

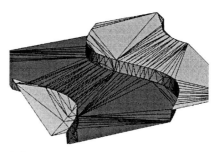

1-d: Our method, final result, 336 vertices.

Fig. 1. Simple examples of results.

as height fields and render them discretely [12]. This could be effective when displacing planar surfaces, but more research would be needed to handle curved ones.

Most practical techniques for ray-traced environments perform some kind of object-space tessellation, perhaps combined with bump mapping to keep the tessellation density low. The problem is that even with high tessellation densities, significant artifacts can arise under displacement. Some commercial graphics system [1] employs a mixture of bump mapping and high tessellation densities to implement displacement mapping, sometimes with unsatisfactory results.

One might suggest using simplification [9, 13] on a dense mesh as a post process. This may help reduce the number of final polygons, but would still require a large amount of temporary memory to store the initial dense mesh. As an example, the single object in figure 13 required 1.1 million micropolygons, which is beyond the limit that most commercial modeling packages can handle. Furthermore, high tessellation densities may be initially encountered, even where the displacement features are sparse.

3   Feature-based displacement overview

The proposed method builds the final displaced object using a minimal set of triangles to reduce memory and computation cost. A complete mesh is constructed so that the triangle density is the greatest where the details are located. These details are found through analyzing the height field described by the displacement function. Furthermore, we will show that we can precisely track features, to a resolution that a brute force micropolygon approach cannot afford, even in conjunction with some mesh reduction.

In most workflows, the original surface geometry is described separately from dis-

260

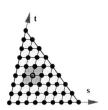 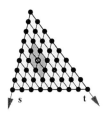

Fig. 2. Uniform generation of grid sample points in the triangle, $n = 8$. The choice of the origin determines the shape of neighbors shown in dark gray. Choosing the origin so that it faces the longest edge makes the first neighbors cell more like a rectangle.

placement and other texture maps. This permits maps and shaders to be layered onto the original surface, usually through a parameterization of the surface. Curved surfaces, like NURBS or subdivision surfaces, are generally tessellated before being rendered. Consequently, we made the assumption that the input surface S is described by a collection of triangles, called the *original tessellation*. We expect the tessellation to be dense enough to represent S, but not fine enough to define displaced S'. We also expect to have a way to compute the height h at each point of S, possibly with some filtering.

Figure 1 illustrates our technique on a simple procedural wave displacement. White areas are high offsets, while black ones remain on S. The original tessellation of the plane is made of two triangles in this case. Figure 1-b shows the displacement using uniform fine sampling. We can see that the geometry does not adequately track the features. Moreover, in most regions, the mesh granularity is far finer than is required.

In our algorithm, we first generate a height map for each triangle in the original tessellation. Section 4 describes how we use uniform sampling of displacement function h in the barycentric domain of the triangle. Then, we compute a feature metric and orientation for every sample point. The meaningful points, visible in figure 1-c, are kept and passed to the next step.

In section 5, we explain how we perturb the remaining points slightly to be better aligned with the feature landscape, as shown in figure 1-d. We also add a few more samples in specific areas to capture the features more precisely. For each original triangle, we then perform a local constrained Delaunay triangulation on these points, to generate a set of sub-triangles.

Finally, we build the output geometry, as described in section 6. For each original triangle, we introduce new tessellation vertices at the feature points, displace them, and build the final tessellation mesh from the sub-triangles. We also compute normals at each vertex on the final mesh using its adjacent triangle normal information and its normal information before displacement.

The proposed approach relates to work in image segmentation and surface reconstruction. The need to extract salient feature in the displacement height field is similar to finding contours in images [11]. The need to create a tessellation from the displaced feature points is similar to surface reconstruction from a cloud of points [10].

4 Generating Feature Point

4.1 Height Map Generation

The height map is built locally by sampling uniformly the barycentric space of every triangle. This step is necessary for generality, because the displacement may be defined by a complex shading network [6], like combination of several textures of various resolutions, or procedural textures. The displacement can also be mapped using any mapping techniques, like uv-mapping or projection mapping. The inverse mapping is not required to exist. Using regularly spaced samples allows a simple and fast feature

Fig. 3. Deviation of height curve from linear height segment. The finite difference approximation in equation (1) corresponds to the distance |**DE**| between the value computed in the mid point and the average of **A** and **B**. This distance is zero, when the curve from **A** to **B** is exactly linear at the sampling resolution, that is when it is not necessary to introduce point **D** to capture the detail in the height field.

detection as described in section 4.2. It also provides a natural filtering size, which can be passed to the sampling method.

The origin of the coordinate system is chosen to be the vertex facing the longest edge in the triangle, to minimize the oblique distortion introduced by the non-orthogonal system (see figure 2). This increases the accuracy of feature computations, which makes use of local neighborhoods. In this coordinate system, we take $n + 1$ samples uniformly along each axis from the origin to produce the $\frac{1}{2}(n + 1)(n + 2)$ sample points $\mathbf{P}_{i,j} = \left(\frac{i}{n}, \frac{j}{n}\right)$, with $i, j \in [0, n]$; $i + j \leq n$. The number n defines the resolution of features that can be detected. For each sample point $\mathbf{P}_{i,j}$, we use barycentric interpolation to compute the rendering attributes, such as texture coordinates and 3D point positions, and sample the displacement function h. This operation may only be a pixel lookup, when the displacement map is a simple texture, but may require a full shading network evaluation for complex displacements. Displacement values are recorded in separate, discretized height maps $h_{i,j} = h(\mathbf{P}_{i,j})$ for each triangle $\mathcal{T}$.

4.2 Feature Map Generation

We use the sampled height map to analyze the displacement features on each triangle. We compute a feature metric $f_{i,j}$ and a feature orientation $\mathbf{o}_{i,j}$ for each sample point $\mathbf{P}_{i,j}$. The metric indicates whether or not there is enough detail at the sample point to require placing a tessellation vertex at that location. The feature orientation is the direction along which the feature points will be adjusted off the regular sampling grid to capture detail well.

Various heuristics can be used to compute $f_{i,j}$, including combinations of the first and second derivatives of h, and f values at the neighboring sample points. After evaluating several approaches, we decided to use the second derivative h'' at the sample point. This is a measure of how much the surface is locally curved. In particular, the h'' vanishes in locally flat areas, and thus identifies vertices of little importance (see figure 3).

In one dimension, the finite difference approximation for the second derivative of a function $h(x)$ can be derived from Taylor's series:

$$h''(x) \approx \frac{h(x + \Delta x) + h(x - \Delta x) - 2h(x)}{(\Delta x)^2} \tag{1}$$

We define $\mathcal{N}(d)$ as a modified d-unit neighborhood of a sample point $\mathbf{P}_{i,j}$, as shown in figure 4. $\mathcal{N}(d)$ contains all points distant by d units or less to $\mathbf{P}_{i,j}$, and not aligned with any point of $\mathcal{N}(d - 1)$. Formally, $\mathcal{N}(d) = \{\mathbf{P}_{i+k,j+l}, |k| < d, |l| < d, k \wedge l = 1\}$, where $k \wedge l$ is the greatest common divisor of k and l.

The feature metric $f_{i,j}$ at $\mathbf{P}_{i,j}$ is computed by summing the four 1-D second derivative approximations (equation (1)) along the directions given by its eight first neighbors

262

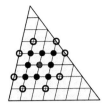

Fig. 4. The gray sample point has 8 first neighbors $\mathcal{N}(1)$ drawn as solid dots. The second order neighborhood $\mathcal{N}(2)$ contains the black circles as well as the solid dots. $\mathcal{N}(2)$ does not contain all the points on the boundary of the 5×5 square, because the directions they represent are already covered by $\mathcal{N}(1)$.

$\mathcal{N}(1)$. The larger the $f_{i,j}$, the more important this point is for capturing the detail in the height field.

$$f_{i,j} = c_{1,0} + c_{0,1} + \frac{1}{2}(c_{1,-1} + c_{1,1}) \tag{2}$$

$$c_{k,l} = |h_{i+k,j+l} + h_{i-k,j-l} - 2h_{i,j}|$$

As we always keep the original triangle vertices to maintain connectivity, we do not need the $f_{i,j}$ values for these vertices. Along the triangle edges, excluding the triangle vertices, some points in $\mathcal{N}(1)$ are outside of the triangle domain. It can be seen in figure 4 that at least $h_{i+k,j+l}$ or $h_{i-k,j-l}$ is valid. We use $c_{k,l} = |2h_{i\pm k,j\pm l} - 2h_{i,j}|$ in those cases, which is equivalent to mirroring the height field along the edge. Any sample point $\mathbf{P}_{i,j}$, having a nonzero feature metric is recorded as a feature candidate. Otherwise, it is discarded. This quickly eliminates samples from the locally planar areas.

We use a discrete gradient computation of h for the feature orientation $\mathbf{o}_{i,j}$. It indicates which direction has the greatest height change, and it is used to determine where to move sample points locally in the second pass. We use the sixteen discretized directions of $\mathcal{N}(2)$ neighborhood, drawn in figure 4, because our algorithm is quite sensitive to $\mathbf{o}_{i,j}$ discretization errors; the eight first neighbors do not produce a precise enough direction.

We fit a linear function, using least squares minimization, to the sixteen samples $f_{i,j}$, weighted by the inverse of the distance. The gradient of this linear function is proportional to

$$\mathbf{o}_{i,j} = \frac{1}{16} \sum_{(k,l)\in\mathcal{N}(2)} (h_{i+k,j+l} - h_{i,j}) \frac{1}{\sqrt{k^2 + l^2}} \begin{pmatrix} k \\ l \end{pmatrix} \tag{3}$$

When $\mathcal{N}(2)$ is not fully contained in the triangle, $\mathcal{N}(1)$ is used instead. This choice was made because testing proved that it is more numerically accurate to ignore the missing directions than to extrapolate the height values outside of the triangle. The $\mathbf{o}_{i,j}$ are not needed along the triangle edges, so $\mathcal{N}(1)$ is well defined, except for points next to the diagonal, where $i + j = n - 1$. In that case, $h_{i+1,j+1}$ does not exist, and we use $\frac{1}{2}(h_{i,j+1} + h_{i+1,j})$ instead as an estimation.

While computing the height and feature maps, we also record the global maximum height difference value $\Delta h_{\max}$, and the maximum feature value $f_{\max}$. A global gradient threshold is then computed as $r\Delta h_{\max}$, $r \in [0,1]$. Parameter r is a user defined ratio that is more intuitive than entering the threshold itself.

At this stage, we can discard all candidate feature points with an average height difference in $\mathcal{N}(1)$ smaller than $r\Delta h_{\max}$. This step allows users to reduce small noise

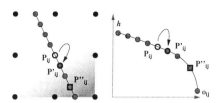

Fig. 5. Adjusting and adding feature points in the $\mathcal{N}(1)$ neighborhood. The black dots are the original samples in the triangle $\mathcal{T}$ around $\mathbf{P}_{i,j}$. Additional samples (gray dots) are taken along $\mathbf{o}_{i,j}$ to determine the new position $\mathbf{P}'_{i,j}$. We also introduce an additional sample $\mathbf{P}''_{i,j}$ at the curvature maximum.

in the displacement. If the displacement map has infinite detail, as does a procedural fractal texture, this threshold can be used to choose the level of detail. We also remove all the points with a feature metric lower than a small percentage of $f_{\max}$. This reduces the number of samples in locally planar areas.

5 Adjusting Feature Points and Triangulation

5.1 Feature Point Adjustment

Once the feature points are identified, we adjust their positions using $\mathbf{o}_{i,j}$ to capture more precisely the displacement shape. After evaluating several approaches, we found that it is particularly important to detect high curvature areas and feature edges. Having samples placed precisely in those locations makes a great difference on the quality of the result.

The figure 1-c shows a mesh generated from the raw feature points. The visible zipper effect is caused by the finite sampling density in each triangle. Refining the sampling grid does not help to capture features that are not grid aligned and it still yields visible step artifacts (albeit at smaller scales). On figure 1-d, the artifacts were removed by the feature point adjustment. Figure 9 is a plane displaced with a ring texture. Artifacts are visible on the top and the bottom of ring. The point adjustment is not enough to capture the top profile, and the curved area along the bottom. Adding vertices at high curvature locations solves the problem, as shown in figure 10.

In order to keep the number of original samples reasonably low, and still capture precisely the shape of the features, we refine locally the position of the samples by moving them slightly toward the features, using the $\mathbf{o}_{i,j}$ direction. If the sample is a triangle edge point, we move along the edge instead to prevent cracks between separate triangles. Our approach is reminiscent of the surface location step in the marching cube algorithm [14].

We take $2m$ samples along the feature orientation at the feature point and try to move this point within its $\mathcal{N}(1)$ neighborhood, as shown in figure 5. We first look for a locally flat area around the sample point, using equation (1) along the sampled line. When $h''(\mathbf{P}_{i,j})$ is below a fixed threshold, we move it to the closest location in which the second derivative is large enough. We also introduce new feature points at extrema of the second derivative along the $\mathbf{o}_{i,j}$ line. Figure 5 shows an example of the moved point $\mathbf{P}'_{i,j}$ and the added point $\mathbf{P}''_{i,j}$.

When the moved and new points are not located precisely enough, the user can repeat the location step k times. This is more efficient than increasing the number m. A $\frac{1}{m}$ smaller search range is used each time. The effective placement resolution is proportional to triangle size divided by nm^k, while using only $O(kmn^2)$ samples instead of $O((nm^k)^2)$ that a brute force micropolygon approach would require.

264

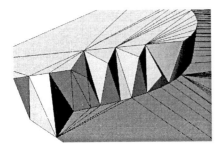 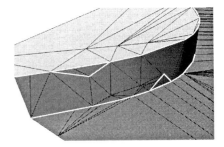

6-a: Default Delaunay triangulation.   6-b: Constrained triangulation.

Fig. 6. The white lines in 6-b are the constraining segments passed to the Delaunay routine. It solves the bad default triangulation problems.

5.2   Constrained Delaunay Triangulation

Once all feature points are correctly placed, for every original triangle $\mathcal{T}$, we gather all the feature points belonging to this triangle. We also include the feature points on the edges that are introduced by adjacent triangles, to prevent cracks along the shared edges. Then, we triangulate locally within $\mathcal{T}$, employing a constrained 2D Delaunay triangulation [19], with the barycentric coordinates of the feature points as its input.[3]

The constraints are defined as line segments $\overline{\mathbf{P}'_{i,j}\mathbf{P}'_{k,l}}$, and are a way to take the height field into account during the triangulation step. Figure 6-a shows the cracks that a standard Delaunay [18] produces. In this case, the problem is that the triangulation in the triangle plane builds triangles joining high and low points. We can avoid this, by forcing the triangulation to include the edges defined by the feature border, as shown in figure 6-b.

To find these border edges, for each feature point, we look for neighbor points in the $\mathcal{N}(2)$ set, with similar height, within a small threshold. When several points match the criteria, we pick the segment which is the most orthogonal to the discrete gradient $\mathbf{o}_{i,j}$. This creates a set of segments, which builds contour lines. Figure 6-b shows the connectivity hints drawn as white segments.

The constrained Delaunay triangulation creates a set of new triangles $\mathcal{T}_i$ to replace $\mathcal{T}$. It may introduce new vertices at the segment intersections if there are any. For example, there are some extra vertices in Figure 6-b, compared to Figure 6-a. Accordingly, we have to sample the displacement map for these new points.

6   Build Final Tessellation To Render

Finally we build all the $\mathcal{T}_i$ triangles into a single object. The vertices along the common edges are shared, to allow a smooth shading. At this stage, we can compute the vertex normals.

To produce sharp feature edges where necessary, each vertex may have multiple normals, depending on its adjacent triangle orientation. We build a partition of the triangles around a vertex by grouping together triangles with similar orientation: two

---

[3]The constrained Delaunay triangulation may create long triangles with bad aspect ratio. Generally, these triangles do not produce visible artifacts when rendering, but adding more feature points (at a cost of creating more triangles) could produce a more balanced triangulation.

 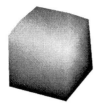  

Fig. 7. Averaging normals if angle is less than α_0. The set of triangles on the left is shaded using three strategies. The second image is the result of using a single averaged normal at the vertex. The third image features a flat shading where each triangle has its own normal. The final image uses our approach to create three distinct normals at the shared vertex corresponding to each of the surrounding partition set of triangles.

8-a: Use triangle normals only.

8-b: Use triangle normals and original vertex normals.

Fig. 8. New vertex normals are computed by averaging the normals. If all three vertices are displaced by equivalent amount, the original vertex normals are used (in 8-b).

triangles are in the same set if their normals form an angle smaller than a given value α_0. We average triangle normals in each set, using the triangle size as weight. Figure 7 compares our approach to other shading strategies. Always using the triangle normals turns out to be unsatisfactory in some cases, as demonstrated in Figure 8-a, where a patch of the polygon sphere is displacement mapped with a checker texture. This is because in cases where all three vertices of a triangle are displaced by the same amount, the original vertex normal before displacement is more accurate than the triangle normal. The improved rendering of using the more accurate normal is shown in Figure 8-b. Figure 11 shows the final rendered result of the simple example we used in figure 1.

7 Results

We implemented our algorithm in *Maya* [1]. The user interface allows the specification of the initial height map sample rate n, the gradient threshold ratio r, the linear sample rate m, the number k of feature point adjustment steps, and the angle α_0 used for averaging the vertex normals. For each triangle, the complexity of our algorithm is $O(kmn^2)$, while reaching a precision equivalent to $(m^k n)^2$ uniform samples.

Images were rendered with *Maya* on a dual Pentium III, 450MHz. In our examples we used $\alpha_0 = 30°$, $k = 2$. The Renderman test was conducted on a R10k Octane. Figure 14 (see Appendix) shows the limitation of the high uniform tessellation method, which exhibits the zipper effect. Our method fixes this problem with much less triangles, as shown in figure 15 (see Appendix). Both images were rendered in Maya. Figure 13 compares our implementation with Photorealistic Renderman version 3.9. A plane is perturbed by a complex vine structure. The displacement map quality of our approach is comparable with what RenderMan generates. With our algorithm, the number of vertices in the final tessellation mesh is 183k. The RenderMan image was produced with 1165k micropolygons, yet still exhibits small zippered artifacts along feature edges, visible in the zoomed images on the right. Reducing these artifacts would require increasing dramatically the number of micropolygons. Figure 12 shows an extreme displacement example with our approach. The spikes of the goblet are created using radial gray scale ramps. The original NURBS surface on the left, rendered 640×480 resolution, took 7 seconds and 100Mb of memory to render. A rendering of the same image, using additional displacement mapping, took 1 minute and 125Mb of memory to render, with 7 seconds spent in performing the algorithm described in section 4, section 5 and section 6. The right image is a close-up rendering of this spiked goblet. Notice the shadows cast by the spikes. Figure 16 (see Appendix) shows a polygonal sphere (30 by 60) displacement mapped with an elevation map of the earth retrieved from [20]. The left image shows the tessellation used for rendering: the vertices are distributed in accordance with the feature landscape. The final rendering is shown on the right. Figure 17 (see Appendix) shows a comparison of two set of cliffs, one with and one without displacement.

8 Conclusion and future work

We have introduced a new approach to the rendering of displacement mapped objects that adaptively refines the original object geometry in a user-controllable manner to the salient features of the displacement map. It offers an alternative to scanline-based micropolygon approaches, and presents a general solution for displacement mapping in ray-tracing, hardware-accelerated rendering (e.g., for games) or when complete meshes are required. If desired, the displacement geometry may be pre-computed and subsequently used as first-class geometric objects.

The speed and locality of this technique opens up possibilities for object sculpting using paint-based techniques. With hardware acceleration, it is possible to paint a displacement map to drive an object sculpting operation in which the geometry adapts in real-time to changes in the map.

The success of this approach suggests numerous new directions to explore. In cases where the inverse parametric map between texture space and object space is known, like a uv-mapped file texture, it would be beneficial to do the feature analysis directly in texture space and back-project the result to object space.

It would be good to have a better criterion to select the feature points than threshold comparison. We generally need a small threshold to capture fine details, which results in too many points. Error accumulation along a Peano curve, or using a probabilistic approach could be more efficient.

Uniform sampling may not be optimal for very long triangles, or when S contains triangles of very different scales. We would like to investigate how to use non-uniform sampling driven by triangle size or aspect ratio.

We focused on techniques which are stable with animation. One could explore view dependent criteria, such as screen space size, to define and adjust the feature points. This would generally produce flickering artifacts in animated sequences, but could be more efficient in cases where a single static image is desired.

267

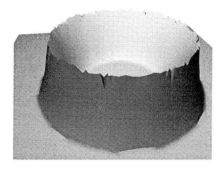

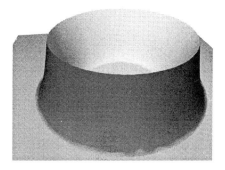

Fig. 9. Uniform sampling, $n = 60$.

Fig. 10. Extra samples. $n = 60$, $m = 30$, $r = 0$.

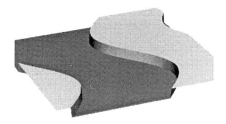

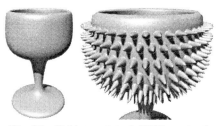

Fig. 11. Final rendered result on the sine wave displaced plane. $n = 30$, $m = 20$, $r = 0$.

Fig. 12. Goblet: original (2286 vertices) and displaced (63992 vertices) with $n = 19$, $m = 0$, $r = 0$, $\alpha_0 = 30$.

Fig. 13. Top: RenderMan result with 3x3 shading samples, generating 1165k micropolygons. Bottom: Our algorithm with $n = 150$, $m = 30$, $r = 0$ produced 183k vertices.

Acknowledgments

We thank the following artists for their imagery: Jason F. Maurer, director of Fathom Studios (Figure 17, apologies for adding the un-displaced cliffs on the right of the scene for comparison), Christine Beaumont (Figure 12), Gary Mundell and Andres Vitale (Figure 13). This work would not have been possible without the valuable insights and feedback from our colleagues at Alias|Wavefront.

References

1. **Alias—Wavefront.** *Maya 2.5 software. http://www.aliaswavefront.com/.*
2. **A.A. Apodaca, L.Gritz.** *Advanced RenderMan.* Morgan Kaufmann Publishers, pages 153 and 155, 2000.
3. **B.G. Becker, N.L. Max.** *Smooth Transitions between Bump Rendering Algorithms.* Computer Graphics (Proc. Siggraph '93), 183-189, August, 1993.
4. **J.F. Blinn.** *Simulation of Wrinkled Surfaces.* Computer Graphics (Proc. Siggraph '78), 286-292, August, 1978.
5. **E. Catmull.** *Computer Display of Curved Surfaces.* Proceedings of the IEEE conference on Computer Graphics, Pattern Recognition and Data Structures, 11, May, 1975.
6. **R.L. Cook.** *Shade trees.* Computer Graphics (Proc. Siggraph '84), 223-231, July, 1984.
7. **R.L. Cook, L. Carpenter, E. Catmull.** *The Reyes Image Rendering Architecture.* Computer Graphics (Proc. Siggraph '87), 95-102, July, 1987.
8. **W. Heidrich, H.P. Seidel.** *Ray-Tracing Procedural Displacement Shaders.* Graphics Interface '98, 8-16, June, 1998.
9. **H. Hoppe.** *Progressive Meshes.* Computer Graphics (Proc. Siggraph '96), 99-108, August, 1996.
10. **H. Hoppe, T. DeRose, T. Duchamp, J. McDonald, W. Stuetzle.** *Surface Reconstruction from Unorganized Points.* Computer Graphics (Proc. Siggraph '92), 71-78, July, 1992.
11. **M. Kass and A. Witkin and D. Terzopoulos.** *Snakes: Active Contour Models.* International Journal of Computer Vision, 1(4), 321-331, 1987.
12. **F. Kenton Musgrave.** *Grid Tracing: Fast Ray Tracing for Height Fields.* Technical Report YALEU/DCS/RR-639, Yale University, Dept. of Computer Science Research, July, 1988.
13. **P. Lindstrom, D. Koller, W. Ribarsky, L.F. Hodges, N. Faust, G.A. Turner.** *Real-Time, Continuous Level of Detail Rendering of Height Fields.* Computer Graphics (Proc. Siggraph '96), 109-118, August, 1996.
14. **W.E. Lorensen.** *Marching Cubes: A High Resolution 3D Surface Construction Algorithm.* Computer Graphics (Proc. Siggraph '87), 163-169, July, 1987.
15. **N. Max.** *Horizon mapping: shadows for bump mapped surfaces.* Visual Computer. 4(2), 109-117, July, 1988.
16. **M. Pharr, P. Hanrahan.** *Geometry caching for ray-tracing displacement maps.* Eurographics Rendering Workshop 1996, Porto, Portugal, Springer Verlag, Vienna, 31-40, June, 1996.
17. **Pixar.** *PRman software.*
18. **J. O'Rourke.** *Computational Geometry in C.* Cambridge University Press, 1994.
19. **J.R. Shewchuk.** *Triangle: Engineering a 2D Quality Mesh Generator and Delaunay Triangulation.* First Workshop on Applied Computational Geometry (Philadelphia, Pennsylvania), pages 124-133, ACM, May, 1996.
20. *http://www.envision.freeserve.co.uk/planets/earth.htm.*

Editors' Note: see Appendix, p. 411 for colored figures of this paper

Soft Shadow Maps for Linear Lights

Wolfgang Heidrich   Stefan Brabec   Hans-Peter Seidel

Max-Planck-Institute for Computer Science
Im Stadtwald
66123 Saarbrücken
Germany
{heidrich,brabec,hpseidel}@mpi-sb.mpg.de

Abstract.   Soft shadows and penumbra regions generated by extended light sources such as linear and area lights are visual effects that significantly contribute to the realism of a scene. In interactive applications, shadow computations are mostly performed by either the shadow volume or the shadow map algorithm. Variants of these methods for soft shadows exist, but they require a significant number of samples on the light source, thereby dramatically increasing rendering times.

In this paper we present a modification to the shadow map algorithm that allows us to render soft shadows for linear light sources of a high visual fidelity with a very small number of light source samples. This algorithm is well suited for both software and hardware rendering.

1   Introduction

Shadows provide important visual cues for the relative position of objects in a scene. Thus, it is not surprising that there has been a lot of work in the computer graphics literature on how to include shadows in interactive applications. Apart from precomputed diffuse shadow textures for each object, and some special purpose solutions like projected geometry [2] for large planar receivers, there are two general purpose shadow algorithms for interactive applications.

The first of these, shadow volumes [5] is an object-space method, while the second one, shadow maps [23] is a purely sampling based approach that works with depth images of the scene. Both techniques have their specific advantages and disadvantages. For example, while the shadow volume algorithm is generally very stable, it can introduce a large number of boundary polygons that significantly increase the geometric complexity of a scene. On the other hand, the shadow map algorithm has a low geometric complexity, however, numerical problems occur quite frequently. Furthermore, the hardware support for shadow maps has so far been restricted to very high end systems so that developers for the low end were forced to use shadow volumes, since these only require a minimal hardware feature set.

Variants to produce soft shadows for linear and area light sources are known both for the shadow volume and for the shadow map algorithm (see, for example [1, 4]) as well as for other texture-based methods [10]. These work by replacing the linear or area light source with a number of point light sources. In many cases, the light source does not subtend a very large solid angle as seen from any object point in the scene. This means that, especially in scenes with mostly diffuse materials, the local illumination caused by different samples of the light source differs only marginally, and thus a small number of light source samples should be sufficient. Nonetheless, the number of samples often has to be quite significant to obtain smooth penumbra regions. This is due to the fact that, with N light source samples, one can only obtain $N+1$ different levels of shadow: fully lit, fully shadowed (umbra), as well as $N-1$ levels of penumbra. Thus we will need to have a large number of light source samples for scenes with large penumbra regions, or the quantization into $N-1$ penumbra regions will become apparent.

So, while a small number of samples would be sufficient for the local shading process, we require a large number of samples to establish the correct visibility in the penumbra regions. This significantly increases the computational cost of soft shadows, and makes them infeasible for many interactive applications.

In this paper, we introduce a new soft shadow algorithm based on the shadow map technique. This method is designed to produce high-quality penumbra regions for linear light sources with a very small number of light source samples. It is not an exact method and will produce artifacts if the light source is so severely undersampled that the visibility information is insufficient (i.e. if there are some portions of the scene that should be in the penumbra, but are not seen by any of the light source samples). However, it produces believable soft shadows as long as the sampling is good enough to avoid these problems. Figure 1 gives a first impression of our technique.

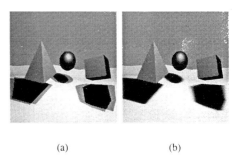

(a)   (b)

Fig. 1. (a): approximating a linear light source with two point lights. (b): our method, also using two light source samples.

The remainder of this paper is organized as follows. In Section 2 we review related work by other researchers. Then, in Section 3, we introduce our soft shadow technique, starting with a simple linear light source with two light source samples, eventually extending the technique to multiple samples.

2 Related Work

Since shadows are such an important visual effect, it is not surprising that a host of literature by many researchers is available on this topic (see [25] for a survey of different methods). In ray-tracing, a shadow ray is cast towards the light source to obtain a boolean visibility flag for point and directional light sources. This method can be extended to distribution ray-tracing for the rendering of soft shadows. This sampling approach, however, suffers from the quantization artifacts similar to the ones mentioned above for the shadow map and the shadow volume algorithm. In other words, with N light source samples we can only discriminate $N-1$ levels of penumbra in addition to the umbra and the completely lit regions. However, this quantization is masked by noise if the sampling pattern on the light source is chosen differently for each illuminated surface point.

To eliminate both quantization and noise, some researchers use a geometrical analysis of the scene to find regions of the scene where the whole light source is visible, the whole light source is occluded (umbra), and regions where part of the light source is visible (penumbra). These methods work in object space by either generating discontinuities on the illuminated objects (discontinuity meshing along the lines of Heckbert [9]), by backprojecting the scene onto the light source (for example Drettakis and Fiume [7] and Stewart and Ghali [21]), or, more recently, by detecting singular points and lines on the light source itself (Ouellette and Fiume [14]).

After the discontinuities have been geometrically analyzed, the actual shading of each point can be performed analytically, or again using sampling. Common to discontinuity meshing and back projection is the large geometric complexity, which makes these approaches ill suited for interactive applications. Recently, there has also been some work by Parker et al. [16] on approximating the penumbra by manipulating the geometry of the occluders, and then assuming a point light source. This work does not yield the exact solution for the penumbra, but results in an approximation of high visual quality. It is similar to our work in that it attempts to render hight quality soft shadows with very few light samples.

Another method of generating soft shadows for off-line rendering is based on convolution, and has recently been introduced by Soler and Sillion [20]. While this method is much faster than the techniques described above, it is still far from interactive.

In the area of interactive computer graphics, we often see special purpose algorithms that are only adequate for very specific situations, such as the projected geometry approach [2], which only works for shadows cast onto large planar objects. In addition to these methods, there has recently been some work on generating shadows from image-based scene representations, for example by Keating and Max [11].

Among the two general purpose algorithms for interactive shadows we find Crow's object space shadow volume method [5]. A variant of this algorithm for graphics hardware using the stencil buffer has later been developed by Diefenbach and Badler [6], and some additional fixes for special situations, where the near plane of the view frustum straddles one of the shadow volumes, have been introduced by Udeshi and Hansen [22]. Soft shadows can be implemented with shadow volumes by sampling the light source with point lights [1], but this bears the above-mentioned sampling problems.

To reduce the geometric complexity of shadow volumes, McCool generates shadow volumes directly from a depth image of the scene in some very recent, unpublished work [13]. He uses an edge detection algorithm to obtain the discontinuities in the depth map, which then act as the boundary polygons of a shadow volume. In this paper, we also use edge detection in the shadow map to obtain discontinuities. However, in contrast to McCool we use this information for rendering penumbra regions rather than extracting shadow volume information.

The other frequently used shadow algorithm in interactive applications are shadow maps [23]. Here, the shadow test is reduced to a comparison of a point's actual depth in the light source coordinate system to a reference value stored in a depth image. In Williams' original paper this reference value is the depth of the visible surface along a ray through the light source position. Reeves et al. improved the shadow map technique by anti-aliasing the shadow boundaries using a technique called *percentage-closer filtering* [17]. Common artifacts of the shadow map algorithm, like self-shadowing of surfaces and missing shadows due to numerical problems in the depth comparison were resolved by Woo [24]. He modified the algorithm to use a shadow map where the reference value is actually a weighted sum of the visible surface and the first surface point behind it. This improved the numerical stability of the shadow map algorithm, because it mostly avoids depth comparisons of very similar values. Finally, Segal et al. [18] introduced hardware support for soft shadows on high-end graphics hardware. Without this dedicated support, shadow maps can be implemented on a fairly standard OpenGL pipeline as described by Brabec et al. [3]. This is the method we use for the hardware implementation of our soft shadow extension to shadow maps.

3 Soft Shadow Maps

For the following discussion, we consider a scene with a single linear light source. As discussed in the Section 1, we want to assume that the visibility term can be separated from the local illumination part, and that the latter is smooth enough to be represented by very few light source samples. The task is then to reconstruct the visibility term with a high quality, while only using a small number of light source samples. For the moment we restrict ourselves to the simplest case where we use only two samples residing at the vertices of the linear light.

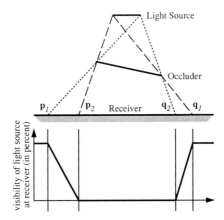

Fig. 2. Top: a simple scene with a linear light source, an occluder and a receiver polygon. Bottom: the percentage of visible portions of the light source as a function of the location on the receiver.

Also suppose for the moment that we have an efficient way of computing for each point in the scene the percentage of the light source visible from that point (Sections 3.1 and 3.2 describe an efficient method for computing an approximation of this term). An example for such a visibility function in a simple 2D scene is shown in Figure 2. In order to render soft shadows in this setting efficiently, we can extend the shadow map algorithm as follows.

First, generate a shadow map for each of the two light samples, considering these as two distinct point lights. Each of the texels in such a shadow map corresponds to one surface point that is visible from the respective light source sample. Now we add a second channel to each of the two shadow maps. This channel describes the percentage visibility of the whole light source for each of these object points. More precisely, this channel has the following properties:

- If a surface point is seen by exactly one of the light samples, the corresponding visibility entry in that shadow map reflects the percentage of the linear light source visible from that point (or an approximation thereof).
- If a surface point is seen by both samples, the sum of the corresponding visibility channels represents the percentage visibility. In the algorithm presented in Section 3.2 we assume that the whole light source is unobstructed if both samples are visible, that is, the visibility is 100%. In our algorithm this means that both maps will get a value of 50%. Note that it would be possible to drop this assumption if a different way of computing the visibility channel was used.

- Surface points not seen by any of the two light samples are not represented in any of the two maps. Therefore these are assumed to be in the umbra.

Put differently, the shadow map not only contains information about *which* object points are visible from a given point light, but also a percentage value that describes *how much* of the whole linear light source can be seen by that point. For any given object point, the sum of these visibility terms from the two point lights should then result in the value of the function plotted at the bottom of Figure 2.

Based on these two-channel shadow maps, we can now formulate a variant of the shadow map algorithm for soft shadows. Let S_1 and S_2 be two shadow maps including such visibility channels V_1 and V_2, one for each of the two point light sources L_1 and L_2. The shading of a particular point **p** in the scene then proceeds according to the following algorithm:

```
shade( p ) {
  if( depth₁(p)> S₁[p] )
    l1= 0;
  else
    l1= V₁[p] * localIllum(p,L₁);

  if( depth₂(p)> S₂[p] )
    l2= 0;
  else
    l2= V₂[p] * localIllum(p,L₂);

  return l1+l2;
}
```

In this piece of pseudo code $S_i[\mathbf{p}]$ means looking up the reference depth value corresponding to **p** in shadow map i. Similarly $V_i[\mathbf{p}]$ means looking up the visibility value for **p**. The depth of a point **p** in the respective light coordinate system is given as depth$_i$(**p**). From this code it is obvious that the proposed method is only marginally slower than shadow mapping with two point lights, assuming that the shadow maps including the visibility channels are provided.

The problem now is to determine how to generate these visibility channels in the first place. In principle, we could use any known object-space algorithm for this, including both analytical methods and sampling. While this may be a feasible approach for static scenes, dynamic environments require faster techniques. For this latter case we chose to use a a linear approximation for the transition in the penumbra regions. In the following we first motivate this approximation, before we describe the details of the method in Section 3.2.

3.1 Linear Interpolation of Visibility

One property of linear lights is that object edges parallel to it do not have a penumbra region. In other words, there is a sharp transition from umbra to fully lit regions for these edges. Furthermore, linear light sources have the advantage that the visibility considerations of a 3D scene can be reduced to 2D scenes. Consider the intersection of the scene with a plane containing the light source. If we can solve the visibility problem for all such planes, i.e. for the whole bundle of planes having the light source as a common line, then we know the visibility of the light source for all 3D points in the scene.

For a motivation of our algorithm for generating the visibility channels, consider the configuration in Figure 2, which contains a linear light source at the top, an occluder and a receiver polygon. In order to compute the correct penumbra, we have to determine for each point on the receiver, which percentage of the linear light source is visible from that point. This percentage is plotted as a function of the surface location at the bottom of Figure 2.

In this simple configuration, it is clear that we have two penumbra regions, one where the visibility varies from 100% at $\mathbf{p}_1$ to 0% at $\mathbf{p}_2$, and similarly from 100% at $\mathbf{q}_1$ to 0% at $\mathbf{q}_2$. In general, the transition from fully visible to fully occluded is a rational function, which becomes obvious by considering the simple case of a single occluder edge, as depicted in Figure 3.

Without loss of generality, the occluder edge is located at the origin (the slope of the occluder is not of importance), the light source is given by the formula $y_1 := mx_1 + t$, and the intersection of the receiver with the 2D plane in consideration is given by $y_2 := nx_2 + s$. From the constraint $x_1/x_2 = y_1/y_2$, which characterizes the point (x_1, y_1) on the light source that is just visible from (x_2, y_2), it follows that

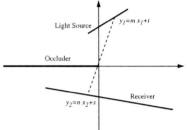

Fig. 3. A simple scene with a single occluder edge that can be used to characterize the change of visibility across a planar receiver that is not parallel to the linear light source.

$$x_1 = \frac{x_2 t}{nx_2 - mx_2 + s}. \qquad (1)$$

This rational function simplifies to a linear one if the slopes m of the light source and n of the receiver are identical, i.e. if light and receiver are parallel as in Figure 2.

If light source and receiver are not parallel, the rational function has a singularity at the point where the receiver polygon intersects the line on which the linear light source resides. However, this is an area where the penumbra region collapses to zero size anyway. On the other hand, the regions for which we expect large penumbra regions are far away from this singularity, and there the rational function from Equation 1 behaves almost like a linear function.

3.2 Generating the Visibility Map

With this observation we can now formulate an algorithm for generating the visibility channels for the two shadow maps. The object points in one of the penumbra regions are of particular interest. In our simple setting, these are the object points seen by one of the two point lights, but not by both.

Now imagine we take the shadow map from the right sample point, triangulate all the depth samples, and warp all the resulting triangles into the view of the left point light, thereby using the depth buffer to resolve visibility conflicts. This is similar to an image based rendering algorithm along the lines of post-rendering 3D warping [12]. The resulting image will consist of two kinds of polygons: those corresponding to the real geometry in the scene, and "phantom polygons", sometimes also called "skins", which result from triangulating across depth continuities. Both types are depicted in Figure 4. The skins are shown as gray lines; the original surfaces are colored black.

While the original polygons are the desired result in image-based rendering and the skins are an artifact, it is the skins that are of particular interest to us. Wherever they are visible in the destination image (i.e. in the image corresponding to the left point light), a penumbra region is located! What is more, we know qualitatively what the visibility value should be for points in this region. Since the skins are generated by depth discontinuities in the source shadow map, they always connect an oc-

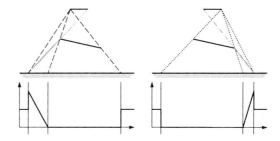

Fig. 4. Top: skin polygons warped from one depth map into the other. Bottom: visibility contributions for both point lights at each point on the receiver, using the presented method to generate the visibility channel of the shadow maps.

cluder polygon and a receiver polygon. Points in the penumbra region that are closer to the occluder in the reprojected image see less of the linear light than points closer to the receiver polygon.

If we assume a linear transition between fully visible and fully occluded, as argued in the previous section, then we can generate the visibility channel as follows: First, we need to find the depth discontinuities in the shadow map of the right point light, which can be done using standard image processing techniques [8], and can be performed at interactive speed. The resulting skins then need to be reprojected and rendered into the visibility channel of the left shadow map. During rendering we Gouraud-shade the skin polygons by assigning the value 0 to vertices on the occluder and the value 1 to vertices on the receiver. This can be done either using a software renderer, or using computer graphics hardware and a depth buffer algorithm. In the latter case, it is possible to generate the visibility channel at interactive frame rates. We repeat the whole procedure to project the discontinuities from the depth buffer of the left point light to the right shadow map.

A final consideration for the generation of the visibility channel is the treatment of completely lit and completely shadowed object points. The latter case is simple. Since points in the umbra are not seen by any of the two light sources, they will fail the shadow map tests for both point light sources, and therefore be rendered black (or with an ambient color only).

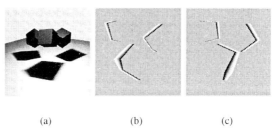

(a)   (b)   (c)

Fig. 5. (b) and (c): the visibility channel for the two point lights for the scene in (a).

Completely lit points on the other hand, are seen by both point lights, and in this case we are going to assume that the whole linear light is visible. Thus, the visibilities for both lights need to sum up to 1. One way of doing this is to give these points a visibility of 0.5 in both shadow maps. This can easily be implemented by initializing all entries in the visibility channel to 0.5 before starting to warp the skin polygons.

Figure 4 shows for both samples on the light source the visibility contribution to each point on the receiver of the 2D scene from Figure 2. These contributions can be generated using the just described algorithm to generate the visibility channels. Furthermore, Figure 5 (b) and (c) show the visibility channels for a linear light source in a 3D scene. The scene itself is depicted in Figure 5 (a).

3.3 Linear Light Sources With More Samples

The restriction of this algorithm for generating the visibility map is that object points seeing portions of the linear light source, but none of the two point lights at its ends, will appear to lie in the umbra. Moreover, there are situations where this results in discontinuities, as depicted in Figure 6. These artifacts result from a severe undersampling of the light source, with the consequence that important visibility information is available in neither of the two shadow maps.

The consequence from this observation is to increase the sampling rate by adding in one or more additional point samples along the linear light source. For example, if we add in a third point light in the center of the linear light, we have effectively subdivided the linear light into two smaller linear lights that distribute only half the energy of the original one. If we treat these two linear light segments independently with the algorithm described in the previous section, we get the situation depicted in Figure 7 for the same geometric setup as in Figures 2 and 4.

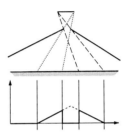

Fig. 6. An example of failure due to undersampling of the light source which causes some portions of the penumbra to end up in full shadow. These artifacts can only be resolved by increasing the sampling rate on the light source.

The top row of the figure corresponds to the rendering of the left half, while the bottom row corresponds to the right half of the linear light. Note that the light source on the right side of the top row, and the one on the left side of the bottom row correspond to the same point light, namely the one inserted at the center of the linear light. Therefore it is possible to combine these two point lights into a single one with twice the brightness, by summing together the visibility channels (the depth channels are identical anyway!).

With this general approach we can add in as many additional sample points on the linear light source as are required to avoid the problems of points in the penumbra that are not seen by any light source sample. To generate the visibility channel for one of the sample points, we need to consider only the depth discontinuities (skins) of those samples directly adjacent to this point. For example, in Figure 7, the discontinuities from the rightmost sample do not play a role for the visibility map of the leftmost sample and vice versa.

4   Results

We have implemented the approaches described in this paper for two different versions. Firstly, we have a software implementation of the method in a ray-tracer, and secondly we also have an implementation that utilizes OpenGL graphics hardware for the rendering. This latter method is an extension of an OpenGL implementation of the standard shadow map algorithm described in [3]. For this hardware-based technique, we use SGI workstations (SGI Octane, O2 and Visual Workstation), which all have support for the

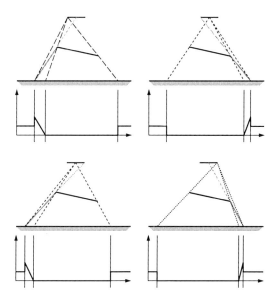

Fig. 7. By inserting an additional point light in the center, we have effectively reduced the problem to two linear lights of half the length and intensity. Top two: left half of linear light. Bottom two: right half.

OpenGL imaging subset [19].

This imaging subset, which allows to perform convolutions of images, is not required for the rendering using an existing shadow map, but it is helpful for generating the visibility channels on the fly in dynamic environments. Remember that this task requires us to find discontinuities in the depth channel of the shadow map in order to determine the skin polygons. Using a convolution with a 3×3 Laplacian-of-Gaussian (LoG) edge detection filter helps us to perform this task very efficiently.

A comparison of the different variants of our soft shadowing algorithm is depicted in Figure 8. The top row shows the images that would be generated by simply approximating a linear or area light source with a number of point lights. The bottom row shows results from our algorithm with the same number of light source samples. It can be seen that the quality of the penumbra regions is much higher in all cases. The left column shows the result from approximating a linear light source with two samples. It has been chosen such that overlapping penumbra regions exhibit the undersampling artifacts described in Section 3.3. These artifacts disappear as a third light source sample is inserted, as shown in the center column.

Finally, in the right column, we have experimented with a triangular area light source, which we have approximated by three linear lights corresponding to the edges of the triangle. As we have shown in Section 3.1, the linear transition of visibility in the penumbra region was an approximation of the true rational function for the case of linear light sources. For area light sources, this transition is, in general, a quadratic rational function, so that the linear approximation of our algorithm is a really crude approximation. Nonetheless, the results seem to indicate that it may still be useful for certain applications. The problem in finding a better approximation is that the shape of the quadratic rational function depends on the shape of the triangle and on the relative orientation of light source and occluder edges. Taking these into account during the

Fig. 8. Comparison of different soft shadow techniques. Top row: simple approximation of the light source by several point lights. Bottom row: the method proposed in this paper. Left column: a linear light source approximated with two samples. Note the artifact introduced where the soft shadows overlap. This is due to undersampling (see Section 3.3). Center: The artifacts disappear as a third light source sample is introduced. Right: Applying the technique to a triangular area light (see text for details).

generation of the visibility channel would slow down the algorithm considerably.

Figure 9 in the color plates compares a high-quality solution for the visibility of a scene with one linear light source, one blocker and one receiver with our method. Figure 9a shows the solution of a ray-tracer using 200 light source samples to determine the visibility in every point on the receiver. Figure 9b depicts the result of a software implementation of our method. In contrast to the OpenGL implementation, the software implementation allows for having the same per-pixel shading as in the ray-traced image. Figure 9c shows a ray-traced solution with 10 uniformly spaced samples for comparison. With a shadow map resolution of 500×500, our method including map generation and rendering of 2×1700 skin polygons takes about as long as ray-tracing with 6 samples.

Figure 10 on the color page shows some more complex scenes rendered with the OpenGL-based implementation. Once the shadow maps are computed, the rendering times using our soft shadow algorithm are identical to those for rendering hard shadows with the same number of point lights. This is true for all scenes. Therefore, our algorithm can be used for interactive walkthroughs with no additional cost. The scenes in Figure 10 can be rendered at about 20 fps, provided the shadow maps do not have to be regenerated for every frame.

Building the shadow maps in a dynamic environment is obviously more expensive for our algorithm, since the visibility channels need to be generated as well. This requires edge detection within the depth maps, as well as rendering a potentially large number of skin polygons. The cost of generating the shadow maps therefore depends on the scene geometry. It varies from $< 1/20$ seconds for the simple scene in Figure 8 to about 2 seconds for the area light source in the jack-in-a-box scene in Figure 10. These numbers include the time for rendering the scene to generate the depth maps.

5 Conclusions

In this paper we presented a new soft shadow algorithm based on the shadow map method. It is designed to produce high-quality penumbra regions for linear light sources with a small number of light source samples. We demonstrated that the method works efficiently and produces high-quality penumbrae for non-trivial scenes. The method can be applied both to software and hardware rendering, and we have demonstrated that it is possible to achieve interactive frame rates in the latter case.

It remains an open research problem to determine the best place to insert samples into a linear light source. Recent work by Ouellette and Fiume [15] seems to be a promising starting point for determining those locations where a new sample point would improve the overall quality of the penumbra regions the most. In the future, it would be interesting to extend the method to area light sources. The key problem there is that a linear visibility transition, as used in this paper, is usually not a good assumption in this case.

References

1. P. Bergeron. A general version of crow's shadow volumes. *IEEE Computer Graphics and Applications*, 6(9):17–28, 1986.
2. James F. Blinn. Jim Blinn's corner: Me and my (fake) shadow. *IEEE Computer Graphics and Applications*, 8(1):82–86, January 1988.
3. Stefan Brabec, Wolfgang Heidrich, and Hans-Peter Seidel. OpenGL shadow maps. Technical Report TR 2000-4-002, Max-Planck-Institute for Computer Science, March 2000.
4. L. S. Brotman and N. I. Badler. Generating soft shadows with a depth buffer algorithm. *IEEE Computer Graphics and Applications*, 4(10):71–81, October 1984.
5. Franklin C. Crow. Shadow algorithms for computer graphics. In *Computer Graphics (SIGGRAPH '77 Proceedings)*, pages 242–248, July 1977.
6. Paul J. Diefenbach and Norman Badler. Pipeline Rendering: Interactive refractions, reflections and shadows. *Displays: Special Issue on Interactive Computer Graphics*, 15(3):173–180, 1994.
7. George Drettakis and Eugene Fiume. A fast shadow algorithm for area light sources using backprojection. In *"Computer Graphics (SIGGRAPH '94 Proceedings)*, pages 223–230, July 1994.
8. Rafael Gonzalez and Richard Woods. *Digital Image Processing*. Addison-Wesley, 1992.
9. Paul Heckbert. Discontinuity meshing for radiosity. In *Rendering Techniques '92 (Proc. of Eurographics Rendering Workshop)*, pages 203–226, May 1992.
10. Paul Heckbert and Michael Herf. Simulating soft shadows with graphics hardware. Technical Report CMU-CS-97-104, Carnegie Mellon University, January 1997.
11. Brett Keating and Nelson Max. Shadow penumbras for complex objects by depth-dependent filtering of multi-layer depth images. In *Rendering Techniques '99 (Proc. of Eurographics Rendering Workshop)*, pages 197–212, June 1999.
12. William Mark, Leonard McMillan, and Gary Bishop. Post-rendering 3D warping. In *Proceedings of the Symposium on Interactive 3D Graphics*, pages 7–16, April 1997.

13. Michael McCool. Shadow volume reconstruction. Technical Report CS-98-06, University of Waterloo, 1998. Available from http://www.cgl.uwaterloo.ca/~mmccool/.

14. Marc Ouellette and Eugene Fiume. Approximating the location of integrand discontinuities for penumbral illumination computation with area light sources. In *Rendering Techniques '99 (Proc. of Eurographics Rendering Workshop)*, pages 213–224, June 1999.

15. Marc Ouellette and Eugene Fiume. Approximating the location of Integrand discontinuities for penumbral illumination with linear light sources. In *Graphics Interface '99*, pages 66–75, June 1999.

16. Steven Parker, Peter Shirley, and Brian Smits. Single sample soft shadows. Technical Report UUCS-98-019, Computer Science Department, University of Utah, 1998. Available from http://www.cs.utah.edu/vissim/bibliography/.

17. William T. Reeves, David H. Salesin, and Robert L. Cook. Rendering antialiased shadows with depth maps. In *Computer Graphics (SIGGRAPH '87 Proceedings)*, pages 283–291, July 1987.

18. Marc Segal, Carl Korobkin, Rolf van Widenfelt, Jim Foran, and Paul Haeberli. Fast shadow and lighting effects using texture mapping. In *Computer Graphics (SIGGRAPH '92 Proceedings)*, pages 249–252, July 1992.

19. Mark Segal and Kurt Akeley. *The OpenGL Graphics System: A Specification (Version 1.2)*, 1998.

20. Cyril Soler and François X. Sillion. Fast calculation of soft shadow textures using convolution. In *Computer Graphics (SIGGRAPH '98 Proceedings)*, pages 321–332, July 1998.

21. James Stewart and Sherif Ghali. Fast computation of shadow boundaries using spatial coherence and backprojections. In *Computer Graphics (SIGGRAPH '94 Proceedings)*, pages 231–238, July 1994.

22. Tushar Udeshi and Charles Hansen. Towards interactive, photorealistic rendering of indoor scenes: A hybrid approach. In *Rendering Techniques '99 (Proc. of Eurographics Rendering Workshop)*, pages 63–76, June 1999.

23. Lance Williams. Casting curved shadows on curved surfaces. In *Computer Graphics (SIGGRAPH '78 Proceedings)*, pages 270–274, August 1978.

24. Andrew Woo. *Graphics Gems III*, chapter The Shadow Depth Map Revisited, pages 338–342. Academic Press, 1992.

25. Andrew Woo, Pierre Poulin, and Allain Fornier. A survey of shadow algorithms. *IEEE Computer Graphics and Applications*, 10(6):13–32, November 1990.

Editors' Note: see Appendix, p. 412 for colored figures of this paper

Interactive Horizon Mapping

Peter-Pike J. Sloan Michael F. Cohen

ppsloan@microsoft.com mcohen@microsoft.com

Microsoft Research

Abstract.
Shadows play an important role in perceiving the shape and texture of an object. While some previous interactive shadowing methods are appropriate for casting shadows on other geometry they can not be applied to bump maps (which contain no explicit geometry.) Horizon Mapping is a technique used to compute shadows for bump-mapped surfaces. We map the technique into modern graphics API's and extend it to account more accurately for the geometry of the underlying surface. We also use it to represent limited self-shadowing for pure geometry. In mapping the algorithm to hardware, we use a novel method to interpolate orientation in tangent space over the surface. We show results of self-shadowing at frame rates.

1 Introduction

Shadows provide important perceptual cues for understanding surface shape. However, it is challenging to display them while maintaining interactivity. An extensive amount of work has been undertaken to develop algorithms to generate shadows in general - see [11] for an excellent survey. Since shadows are essentially a visibility problem, it is not surprising that the most common interactive techniques for generating shadows are variants on the shadow zbuffer [10], (see [9, 12, 6] for implementations that function with modern graphics hardware).

Bump Mapping [2] is a technique to convey surface texture by perturbing the normal vectors of a surface. It is available on most current graphics hardware [5]. The advantage of bump mapping is that it provides a simple way to modulate the shading on a surface. However, since bump mapping does not define any explicit geometry, there are no actual bumps to cast shadows. Thus, interactive shadowing techniques that rely on an explicit representation of the geometry cannot be used to simulate shadows cast by the virtual bumps implied in bump mapping. A concurrent paper [4] presents a way to shadow bump maps by using implicit representations of an ellipse in the tangent plane.

This work is motivated by one particular technique for casting shadows: horizon mapping [7]. The idea behind horizon mapping is to precompute limited visibility from each point on a surface. In particular, the angle to the horizon is encoded in a discrete number of directions to represent at what height something becomes visible from that direction (i.e., pass over the horizon). This parameterization can be used to produce the self-shadowing of geometry as well. Accessibility maps defined by Miller [8] are similar to horizon maps. Accessibility maps only use a scalar value to represent the horizon. In contrast, horizon maps include more detail about the horizon.

In the remainder of the paper we show how horizon maps can be encoded and passed through current APIs to graphics hardware to produce real-time self-shadowing based on bump maps.

2 Bump and Horizon Mapping

Given a surface $P(u, v)$ parameterized on the unit square, a surface normal N is the cross product of the partials of the surface P_u and P_v. Given a bump map $F(u, v)$ a non-negative scalar function parameterized over the same domain, the surface normal N can be modified as follows (after dropping terms of first order):

$$P'_u = P_u + F_u N / |N|, P'_v = P_v + F_v N / |N|, N' = P'_u \times P'_v = N + D$$

where

$$D = (F_u N \times P_v - F_v N \times P_u) / |N|$$

is the perturbation of the normal. Max [7] slightly modfied this so that the bump maps behave properly over the surface. We will use normal mapping as outlined in [5]. This modification effectively deals with parameterization dependency for the illumination, but not for the shadowing.

As in [7] we define a mapping into the local coordinate system of the surface - this is done through the dual of the basis P_u, P_v, N where N is the *unbumpmapped* surface normal (the affine transform C^{-1} Max refers to). This is computed by building a matrix with the basis as columns and inverting it, the rows of this inverse are a scaled version of $N \times P_v$ and $P_u \times N$, along with N itself. A vector in this local frame has an associated orientation in the tangent plane θ and an angle with the normal ϕ.

We are interested in knowing at each pixel whether a light vector when transformed into the local coordinate frame is visible above the horizon. To discover this we build a *Horizon Map*, $\phi_{u,v,\theta}$. The horizon map is tabulated at discrete u, v parameter values, and in a set of directions θ, to represent the azimuth angle ϕ when a light would become visible. Typically u and v are sampled fairly densely (512x512), and θ is sampled more coarsely - 8 sample directions, (N, NE, E, etc.) in both our work and in [7].

In the case of curved surfaces, the precomputed horizon map is created in terms of the local geometry at each discrete (u, v) coordinate. This contrasts with [7] in which there is an essential assumption made that the underlying geometry of the surface is not known when the horizon maps are computed.

Given M sampled directions (8 in our implementation) for θ and the discrete domain coordinates u_i, v_j the horizon angle $\phi(u_i, v_j, \theta)$ for ANY direction at coordinates u_i, v_j can be found by interpolating between the discrete directions as follows:

$$\phi(u_i, v_j, \theta) = \sum_{k=1}^{M} B_k(\theta)\phi(i, j, k) \tag{1}$$

where $B_k(\theta)$ is a basis function for the kth direction, which evaluates to 1 for the corresponding direction and linearly falls of to 0 for the neighboring directions. For example if the kth direction is east, then the value is one when θ equals east and falls off to zero at NE and SE. In other words, the horizon angle ϕ is linearly interpolated between discrete directions, noting that since this is a radial function it wraps around to interpolate between $\phi(i, j, 1)$ and $\phi(i, j, M)$. Similarly, the function $\phi(u, v, \theta)$ is bilinearly interpolated across the parameters u and v.

To test the visibility of a light source, its direction (x, y, z) is transformed into the local tangent frame - a simple affine transform - to provide the local coordinates (u, v, θ). The angle θ could be determined by projecting the transformed vector onto the tangent

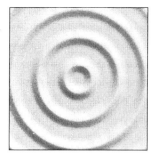

Fig. 1. Normal Map, North Horizon Map, North Basis Texture

plane. Instead, to take advantage of texture mapping hardware as explained later, the first two transformed coordinates are used as a lookup into a table of θ directions encoded as a texture. This is a key element to implementing the shadowing algorithm with current hardware.

3 General Self-Shadowing with Horizon Maps

The tangent plane parameterization and discretization used to compute shadows for bump maps can also be used to store global visibility information about a surface in general. The horizon angles are determined by shooting rays into the object, starting from the horizon and moving towards the surface normal until there is no intersection. This approach has the same limitations that horizon mapping does plus one additional limitation - the largest angle that can be represented in the horizon map is 90 degrees out of the tangent plane. This isn't that significant of a problem when determining shadows from bump maps, but can be a limitation when the gross scale of the features is more significant, for example, when the surface has undercuts.

4 Realizations on Commodity Graphics Hardware

We will now outline the runtime shadowing algorithm and how it is implemented on current graphics hardware. The input consists of:

- a surface geometry with a parameterization in u, v, and
- a scalar valued bump map, $F(u, v)$

4.1 Precomputation

A precomputation step produces:

- a vector valued perturbed normal map, $N'(u, v)$, from the bump map (see Figure 1).
- given M (in our case 8) directions in the tangent plane, $\theta_{k=1..M}$, M horizon maps, $\phi(u, v, \theta_k)$. With the 8 directions we will label each direction θ_k as N, NE, E, etc (see Figure 1). In fact, the 8 horizon maps are collected into only 2 maps by encoding 4 directions into the 4 color channels R, G, B, α. Thus, for example, the first map encodes direction N, NE, E and SE, while the other contains S, SW, W and NW.

- M *basis* maps, $B_k(s,t)$ representing the influence of direction θ_k (note this is independent of the parameterization) (see Figure 1). As in the case of the horizon maps, these are encoded in two maps containing 4 directions each.
- a 1D (arcos) mapping from $cos(\phi)$ to ϕ.

Finally, a per vertex pre-computation is carried out to invert the non-bump mapped local tangent frame $[P_u, P_v, N]^{-1} = [S^T, T^T, N^T]$. This will allow us to quickly transform the light direction onto the local tangent plane of the surface at each frame time. For a planar surface, the local tangent plane is the same for all vertices, but varies at each vertex over a curved surface.

4.2   At each frame time

Given the precomputation above, at each frame time, we first project the light direction onto the local tangent plane at each vertex. The light vector when dotted with the first two components of the inverted frame S and T yields the projection of the light vector into the coordinate space in the tangent plane resulting in the pair, (s,t). The light vector dotted with the normal at each vertex gives $cos(\phi_L)$.

The remainder of the computation is carried out per pixel and is done in hardware using multi-texturing and blending into the frame buffer.

First, set the transformations to render into UV space, (i.e., use (u,v) coordinates as vertex coordinates). Using a blending function to add, and multi-texturing to multiply rendering passes

- Set the multi-texturing to component-wise multiply the textures and sum the results and place them in the α channel
- Accumulate the contribution for the first 4 directions into the frame buffer
  - 1st texture is (E,NE,N,NW) basis map $B_1(s,t)$ (Note the s,t coordinates for each vertex are derived from the light direction.)
  - 2nd texture is (E,NE,N,NW) horizon map, $\phi_1(u,v)$
- Accumulate (i.e., add) the contribution for the next 4 directions
  - 1st texture is (W,SW,S,SE) basis map $B_2(s,t)$
  - 2nd texture is (W,SW,S,SE) horizon map, $\phi_2(u,v)$

The resulting α channel now represents the horizon angle, ϕ, in the direction of the light. Save results to a texture map which we will call $\phi(\theta_{LIGHT})$.

This is followed by three rendering passes with the transformations set to draw into the current camera.

1. First Pass: Draw the model with ambient term only
2. Second Pass: Create a stencil that will only allow non-shadowed pixels to be rendered
   - Set the alpha test to only accept pixels that have non 0 alpha,
   - Set the stencil test to set a bit for any pixel that passes through, and
   - Set color mask to NOT write to color channels to preserve the ambient term of the first pass.
   - Set multi-texturing to subtract (note: negative values are clamped to 0)

- Draw using 2 sets of texture coordinates that will represent the angles to the light and the angle to the horizon. Subtracting the two texture values will yield positive values in the α channel where the surface sees the light and zero (negative values are clamped to zero) where it is in shadow. The two textures to perform this pass are:
  - a 1D texture ($cos(\phi)$->ϕ) (note: $cos(\phi)$ of the light was previous computed at each vertex). This result contains the angle off the normal to the light at each pixel.
  - the 2D texture $\phi(\theta_{LIGHT})$ computed before. This encodes the angle off the normal of the horizon in the direction of the light at each pixel.

3. Third pass to perform normal bump mapped rendering of the model where not in shadow.
   - Turn off alpha test
   - Set color mask to allow writing of color channels
   - Set stencil function to only draw pixels that have the stencil bit set.
   - Set blending to add into the frame buffer to accumulate with ambient term.
   - Draw using normal map - shades non-shadowed regions (i.e., standard bump mapping).

At this point we have an image that displays an ambient only term in shadowed regions and normal bump mapping in non-shadowed regions. We have found that a pleasing minor variant is to create lighter shadows by having the shadowed regions contain a toned down diffuse term rather than ambient only. This can be done in a fourth pass by first setting the stencil function to only draw pixels that do NOT have the stencil bit set and by then drawing the geometry one more time using normal bump mapping, but with a scaled-down diffuse term. This fourth pass can also be combined with the first ambient pass. Iterating on creating the light dependent horizon map and the resulting alpha test can be done if you have multiple lights.

This algorithm can be implemented in any hardware by not leveraging dot product fragment operations, but at a significant performance penalty. It can be coded in D3D using DX7 (using the DOTPRODUCT3 texture mode), but only 3 directions can be packed in a texture, however D3D support rasterizing directly into texture memory and in DX7 this particular function/API is supported on a wider variety of boards. DX8 will provide more general fragment processing than the register combiner extensions.

5   Results and Comments

We have computed normal maps and horizon maps for several surfaces. At 512x512 resolution in texture space it takes approximately two minutes to precompute the object space dependent horizon maps for 8 directions. The current implementation is written in OpenGL and leverages the NVidia register combining extensions [1] to do 4 directions in a single pass. The triangle rendering part of the code has not been optimized to use the vertex array extensions yet. Thus, the geometry can have a significant impact on performance. We have tested the self-shadowing algorithm on three objects: a simple plane (see Figure 2), a cylinder with 160 vertices (158 triangles) (Figure 4, and a tessellated BSpline surface (1600 vertices, 3042 triangles) (Figure 5).

The performance for the plane is around 42hz, 36hz for the cylinder and 33hz for the surface[1]. The main bottleneck is the copy-to-texture space, but the geometry code

---

[1]All timings were taken on a 733mhz PIII using a GeForce based video boards with 32MB of DDR SDRAM

paths are causing a performance hit as well.

The results are very encouraging for shadowing from bump maps. There are several changes to the graphics pipeline that would reduce the number of passes required. The most significant would be putting the alpha and stencil tests after the blending of fragments with the color already in the frame buffer. This way the frame buffer to texture memory copy could be eliminated. This would be done by writing the light direction in tangent space into the alpha channel when the ambient term is written, and then subtracting the contributions from each of the direction passes. This would also eliminate one rendering pass for the geometry. Having a more flexible vertex shader [3] would allow the (s, t) texture coordinates to not be computed on the fly and work optimally with the Transform and Lighting hardware. Also if hardware supported a dependent texture-read[2], the soft shadowing used by Max could be implemented as well.

The most obvious limitation of this method are that it cannot cast bumpy shadows onto other objects, and other objects cast shadows onto the receiving surface as if it was not bumped. For future work, it would be interesting to look at other ways of precomputing self-shadowing. The horizon map is a function over orientation in the tangent plane, there are other functions that could leverage this parameterization we are currently investigating applying it to mip-mapping of normal maps - representing variance as a function of orientation in the tangent plane.

References

1. Nvidia web page. htt://www.nvidia.com.
2. Blinn, J. F. Simulation of wrinkled surfaces. *Computer Graphics (Proceedings of SIG-GRAPH 78) 12*, 3 (August 1978), 286–292. Held in Atlanta, Georgia.
3. D.McCool, M., and Heidrich, W. Texture shaders. *1999 SIGGRAPH / Eurographics Workshop on Graphics Hardware* (August 1999), 117–126. Held in Los Angeles, California.
4. Heidrich, W., Daubert, K., Kautz, J., and Seidel, H.-P. Illuminating micro geometry based on precomputed visibility. *Proceedings of SIGGRAPH 2000* (July 2000).
5. Heidrich, W., and Seidel, H.-P. Realistic, hardware-accelerated shading and lighting. *Proceedings of SIGGRAPH 99* (August 1999), 171–178. ISBN 0-20148-560-5. Held in Los Angeles, California.
6. Heidrich, W., Westermann, R., Seidel, H.-P., and Ertl, T. Applications of pixel textures in visualization and realistic image synthesis. *1999 ACM Symposium on Interactive 3D Graphics* (April 1999), 127–134. ISBN 1-58113-082-1.
7. Max, N. L. Horizon mapping: shadows for bump-mapped surfaces. *The Visual Computer 4*, 2 (July 1988), 109–117.
8. Miller, G. Efficient algorithms for local and global accessibility shading. *Proceedings of SIGGRAPH 94* (July 1994), 319–326. ISBN 0-89791-667-0. Held in Orlando, Florida.
9. Segal, M., Korobkin, C., van Widenfelt, R., Foran, J., and Haeberli, P. E. Fast shad and lighting effects using texture mapping. *Computer Graphics (Proceedings of SIGGRAPH 92) 26*, 2 (July 1992), 249–252. ISBN 0-201-51585-7. Held in Chicago, Illinois.
10. Williams, L. Casting curved shadows on curved surfaces. *Computer Graphics (Proceedings of SIGGRAPH 78) 12*, 3 (August 1978), 270–274. Held in Atlanta, Georgia.
11. Woo, A., Poulin, P., and Fournier, A. A survey of shadow algorithms. *IEEE Computer Graphics & Applications 10*, 6 (November 1990), 13–32.
12. Zhang, H. Forward shadow mapping. *Eurographics Rendering Workshop 1998* (June 1998), 131–138. ISBN 3-211-83213-0. Held in Vienna, Austria.

---

[2]This is available in DX7, but only the Matrox G400 and ATI Rage6 currently supports it

Editors' Note: see Appendix, p. 413 for colored figures of this paper

General calculations using graphics hardware, with application to interactive caustics

Chris Trendall and A. James Stewart

iMAGIS–GRAVIR/IMAG and University of Toronto

Abstract. Graphics hardware has been developed with image production in mind, but current hardware can be exploited for much more general computation. This paper shows that graphics hardware can perform general calculations, which accelerate the rendering process much earlier than at the latter image generation stages. An example is given of the real time calculation of refractive caustics.

1 Introduction

There is much more to graphics than meets the eye — the final image is usually the result of a long series of calculations. Many of these calculations are not directly related to images, but are of a general mathematical character.

Graphics hardware has been developed with image production in mind, but current hardware allows for much more general computation. This paper considers how far back along the long series of calculations the graphics hardware can contribute, and concludes that it can be used for much more than the image generation operations that are currently used.

If current hardware — designed for specific lighting effects rather than general calculations — is already this powerful, it is well worth considering what the next–generation hardware might be able to do if pushed in this direction. This paper considers the limitations of current hardware and discusses potential improvements that could greatly accelerate a more general set of calculations commonly used in graphics.

The paper's contributions are (a) to show how general calculations can be done with current hardware, to evaluate the shortcomings, and to suggest improvements for the future, and (b) to show one example of such a calculation, that of refractive caustics on a pool bottom due to light passing through a time–varying surface.

The paper shows that a time–varying heightfield can be interactively created, and that the refraction, scattering, absorption, and integration of light from this surface can be calculated to render the refractive caustics at the bottom of the pool in real–time.

The real–time computation of realistic caustics is an interesting problem in itself as computing specular lighting in dynamic environments can be computationally expensive. This is the first example of real–time refractive caustic generation.

2 Related Work

2.1 Hardware Rendering

There are many examples of lighting effects that have been computed with algorithms in hardware, but few examples of other types of calculations. What follows is a summary of recent hardware–based calculations.

Heidrich has detailed methods to implement a wider variety of reflection models using multi–pass methods on existing hardware [10, 12, 14], and has discussed the more flexible parabolic parameterization of environment maps [10, 13] which allows multiple viewing directions. His general approach is similar to the approach in this paper: A set of carefully chosen mathematical operations can be combined in order to make a much broader range of calculations.

McCool and Heidrich suggest some basic operations which could be implemented in hardware to support a flexible per–vertex lighting model [10, 19]. Heidrich also shows how specifying a normal map permits the efficient calculation Blinn–Phong lighting using only the imaging part of the graphics pipeline.

In the same spirit, Heidrich also suggests a decoupling of illumination from surface geometry [10, 11]. In this scheme, geometry information is coded into texture maps which treats the texture as a mathematical object rather than a visual one.

Miné and Neyret [20] synthesize procedural textures with graphics hardware using OpenGL. They consider a specific case, and map the Perlin noise function into OpenGL.

Haeberli and Segal [6] show how texture mapping can be used to implement a number of effects, from anti–aliasing to volume rendering. Used in these manners, texture mapping can be thought of as a transfer function between geometry and image space.

In an application which is suggestive of the possibility of using graphics hardware to do more general mathematical calculations, Heidrich [15] shows how the line integral convolutions of a vector field introduced by Cabral *et al.* [4] and further developed by Stalling and Hege [22] can be fully implemented in current hardware. Although a line integral is a general mathematical operation, this research was originally focussed on the *visualization* of the vector field, rather than the merits of performing the calculation itself in hardware. It is exactly this avenue that the present paper explores — more generalized mathematical calculations.

Recently there has been substantial interest in mapping general *shading* operations to graphics hardware. Shading language compilers have been proposed [7, 21] which treat graphics hardware as a SIMD machine and OpenGL as an assembly language.

Several researchers have used graphics hardware for mathematical calculations that are unconnected with image synthesis. Hoff *et al.* [16] leverage z buffering capabilities to calculate Voronoi diagrams, Lengyel *et al.* [18] perform real–time robot motion planning using rasterizing hardware, and Bohn [3] interprets a rectangle of pixels as a four dimensional vector function to do computation on a Kohonen feature map.

2.2 Refractive Caustics

Stam [23] used a probabilistic approach and the wave theory of light to calculate caustics from a randomly varying surface which is correlated in time. The textures are calculated offline, and then rendered in sequence to animate them. This is appropriate for situations which are non–interactive and in which the viewer is unable to correlate the refracting surface with the refracted caustic.

Arvo [1] used backward ray tracing to calculate the position of photons emitted from a light source incident on an object in a scene. Interestingly, he treats texture maps as data structures by using them to accumulate illumination.

Heckbert and Hanrahan [9] leveraged the spatial coherence of polygonal objects by reflecting and refracting beams from the visible surfaces in the view frustum, starting at the eye point. The reverse approach was taken up by Watt [26], who calculated the caustics on the bottom of a swimming pool using backward beam tracing.

Both Watt's approach [26] and Heckbert and Hanrahan's approach would involve rendering multiple polygons and blending them in order to create the refractive caustic, which would require on the order of n passes if the surface was composed of n polygons. This is a result of their discretization. In the present paper, we avoid this problem by making a continuous approximation to the spreading of light after refraction, which leads to an integral that can be discretized.

All the work discussed in Section 2.2 is neither interactive, nor achieved using hardware–based rendering.

3   Mathematical Capabilities of Graphics Hardware

Modern raster graphics implementations typically have a number of buffers with a depth of 32 bits per pixel or more. In the most general setting, each pixel can be considered to be a data element upon which the graphics hardware operates. This allows a single graphics language instruction to operate on multiple data as in a SIMD machine.

Since the bits associated with each pixel can be allocated to one to four components, a raster image can be interpreted as a scalar or vector valued function defined on a discrete rectangular domain in the xy plane. The luminance value of a pixel can represent the value of the function while the position of the pixel in the image represents the position in the xy plane. Alternatively, an RGB or RGBA image can represent a three or four dimensional vector field defined over a subset of the plane.

The beauty of this kind of interpretation is that operations on an image are highly parallelized and calculations on entire functions or vector fields can be performed very quickly in graphics hardware.

One of the drawbacks of current hardware is that only limited precision can be expected due to the limited depth of the buffers. The other major drawback is the lack of signed arithmetic, which leads to much effort in choosing scaling and biasing coefficients to simulate signed arithmetic. This is particularly troublesome as the rendering pipeline clamps the element values to $[0, 1]$ in a number of places.

3.1   Imaging Pipeline

For concreteness, the functionality of OpenGL 1.2 and some of its experimental extensions will be considered. The functions mentioned are all in the rasterization and per–fragment areas of the pipeline, and are performed by moving rectangles of pixels through the imaging pipeline. The details of these functions can be found in [17, 27].

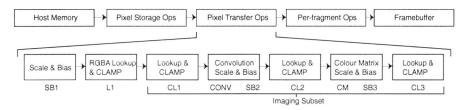

Fig. 1. OpenGl 1.2 imaging pipeline (top) and pixel transfer section (bottom)

The *Scaling and biasing* operation provides a linear transformation, *colour tables* provide arbitrary functions of one variable, a *colour matrix* provides affine transformations, and a *discrete convolution* gives a mechanism for approximating some integrals.

These operations are found in the imaging subset of OpenGL 1.2. [27]

Pixel texturing [17] is part of the per–fragment operations, and performs a mapping between a domain and range of up to four dimensions each. This provides the ability to implement a large class of functions. While this extension is not part of OpenGL 1.2, it exists on several SGI renderers, and equivalent functionality is becoming available on consumer level graphics hardware.

Blending is also part of the per–fragment operations, and provides a mechanism for calculating the product, sum, or difference of functions defined on a rectangular two–dimensional domain.

3.2 Mathematical Operations

General mathematical operations can be built on the hardware capabilities described in the previous section. The mathematical operations detailed below are all used in the refractive caustic demonstration.

Of the possible operations: *convolutions* with limited kernels can be computed directly; *derivatives* of height fields can be computed either by convolution [27] or by blending in the accumulation buffer [2]; *height field normals* can be computed using pixel texturing to normalize the height field derivatives; and *dot products* of a vector field with up to four constant vectors can be computed by the colour matrix. More extensive support for dot products can be found in recent hardware, such as in the NVIDIA register combiner architecture [5].

In order to implement *signed arithmetic* and avoid clamping, functions must be scaled and biased into the range $[0, 1]$. Since clamping always occurs after CL3, BLEND, and prior to enabled colour lookups CLx (see Fig. 1), all values must be properly scaled and biased by the end (respectively beginning) of these operations.

Let $\widetilde{f}$ represent a function f that has been scaled and biased: $\widetilde{f} = \alpha f + \beta$. Such a function is said to have been *adjusted*.

Although proper scaling and biasing requires one to know the approximate bounds of computation beforehand, this is a situation which always exists in computing as all datatypes are finite. It is a somewhat less restrictive issue when the datatype can accommodate a wider range of values but overflow and underflow are always potentially problematic.

In what follows, it is shown how to perform basic arithmetic operations on functions and constants such that the result is correctly adjusted. (The distinction between functions and constants is made because constants are often faster to use in the hardware pipeline.) In some cases, the procedure differs slightly depending on the location of the data — framebuffer or main memory.

Sums and Differences. To sum an adjusted function, $\widetilde{f}$, with an unadjusted constant, c, the programmer must pre–multiply c by the same scale factor which was applied to the function:

$$\widetilde{f + c} = \alpha (f + c) + \beta = \alpha f + \beta + \alpha c = \widetilde{f} + \alpha c.$$

To perform this in hardware, it is sufficient to set the bias to αc at some point in the pipeline and to send $\widetilde{f}$ through the pipeline.

In summing two functions, $\widetilde{f}$ which is adjusted and g which is not, we have the same equation:

$$\widetilde{f + g} = \widetilde{f} + \alpha g.$$

To perform this operation, we must scale g by α and use additive blending. The scaling can be done at one of the scale and bias points, or g can be scaled by a constant user–specified value in the blend equation. Subtraction works the same way with a subtractive blending function.

If both quantities, $\tilde{f}$ and $\tilde{g}$, are already adjusted, we sum them as follows:

$$\widetilde{f+g} \ = \ \alpha(f+g) + \beta \ = \ \alpha f + \beta + \alpha g + \beta - \beta \ = \ \tilde{f} + \tilde{g} - \beta.$$

Thus β must be subtracted from the sum either before or after additive blending, or must be added to the difference after subtractive blending.

The sum and difference of vector functions works in the same manner, except all components must be scaled or biased equally.

Products. Multiplication of an adjusted function $\tilde{f}$ by a constant c is done as follows:

$$\widetilde{cf} \ = \ \alpha\,(c\,f) + \beta \ = \ \alpha\,c\,f + \beta\,c + \beta - \beta\,c \ = \ c\,\tilde{f} + (1-c)\,\beta.$$

This can be done by blending $\tilde{f}$ with a pixel rectangle of constant value β using blend factors c and $1-c$, or by scaling and biasing $\tilde{f}$ by c and $(1-c)\beta$.

This technique also works for vector functions. Each colour component of the constant can be independently modified so as to scale the components of the vector field by different amounts, if wanted.

Multiplication of an adjusted function $\tilde{f}$ by an unadjusted scalar function g can be achieved in a similar manner. Again we have

$$\widetilde{fg} \ = \ g\,\tilde{f} + (1-g)\,\beta.$$

Assuming that $\tilde{f}$ is in the RGB components of the pixel rectangle and that g is in the ALPHA component (which can always be achieved) then a blend as above with a source blend factor of ALPHA and a destination blend factor of $(1 - \text{ALPHA})$ achieves the proper result.

The final case is the multiplication of two adjusted scalar functions, $\tilde{f}$ and $\tilde{g}$. This is performed using the following equation:

$$
\begin{aligned}
\widetilde{fg} \ &= \ \alpha\,fg + \beta \\
&= \ \alpha\,fg + \beta(f+g) + \frac{\beta^2}{\alpha} - \beta\,(f+g) - \frac{\beta^2}{\alpha} + \beta \\
&= \ \frac{1}{\alpha}\,(\alpha^2\,fg + \alpha\beta\,(f+g) + \beta^2) - \frac{\beta}{\alpha}\,(\alpha \cdot (f+g) + \beta - \alpha) \\
&- \ \frac{1}{\alpha}\,(\tilde{f} \cdot \tilde{g}) \quad \frac{\beta}{\alpha}\,(\widetilde{(f+g)} - \alpha).
\end{aligned}
$$

Multiplication of two adjusted functions in this manner is quite expensive, requiring three passes through the pipeline.

4   Refractive Caustics

This section demonstrates a general calculation using the graphics hardware. Refractive caustics will be computed on the bottom plane of a square pond with a time–varying surface height field, as shown in Figure 1 (see Appendix).

Consider light incident on a particular point on the surface, arriving from direction $\hat{\mathbf{L}}_i$. The direction $\hat{\mathbf{L}}_t$ of transmitted light is given by Snell's Law [24]:

$$\hat{\mathbf{L}}_t = \frac{n_i}{n_t} \hat{\mathbf{L}}_i + \Gamma \hat{\mathbf{N}}, \text{ where } \Gamma = \frac{n_i}{n_t} \cos\theta_i - \cos\theta_t, \tag{1}$$

where n_i and n_t are the absolute indices of refraction in air and water, respectively, $\hat{\mathbf{N}}$ is the surface normal, and θ_i and θ_t are the angles of incidence and transmission with respect to $\hat{\mathbf{N}}$. Each of $\hat{\mathbf{N}}$, $\hat{\mathbf{L}}_i$, and $\hat{\mathbf{L}}_t$ is normalized.

If $L_i \, \delta(\theta - \theta_i)$ is the radiance incident on some infinitesimal surface, then the irradiance or flux density at the surface is given by $L_i \cos\theta_i$. Let $L_t \, \delta(\theta - \theta_t)$ be the transmitted radiance. Then $L_t \cos\theta_t$ is the transmitted flux density or exitance, and the ratio between the exitance and the irradiance, averaged over polarizations, is given by the Fresnel transmission coefficient T [8]:

$$T(\theta_i) = 2 \frac{n_t \cos\theta_t}{n_i \cos\theta_i} \left(\left[\frac{n_i \cos\theta_i}{n_i \cos\theta_i + n_t \cos\theta_t} \right]^2 + \left[\frac{n_i \cos\theta_i}{n_t \cos\theta_i + n_i \cos\theta_t} \right]^2 \right).$$

The effect of multiple scattering in the forward direction is empirically modelled by a Gaussian distribution in angle about $\hat{\mathbf{L}}_t$. This Gaussian models the effect of scattering throughout the volume; any scattering that ends up sending light in a forward direction (including photons that backscatter and then reverse direction to go forward, even multiple times) is taken into account in this model:

$$L(\hat{\mathbf{P}}) \sim \exp(-a(1 - (\hat{\mathbf{L}}_t \cdot \hat{\mathbf{P}})^2)).$$

Above, $L(\hat{\mathbf{P}})$ is the radiance in (normalized) direction $\hat{\mathbf{P}}$ and a is a coefficient proportional to the density of particulate matter, which is dependent on the rate of absorption and multiple backscattering.

Attenuation due to absorption is modelled as

$$L(d) \sim \exp(-\varepsilon\, d),$$

where $L(d)$ is the radiance at distance d travelled by the light and ε is the *extinction coefficient*, which is dependent on the absorption and total backscatter in the volume. This type of extinction occurs when the absorption probability is constant with position [24].

Let L_s be the radiance of the point source, which is assumed to be very distant from the surface. Then the incident direction $\hat{\mathbf{L}}_i$ is constant over the surface. Assuming that the surface is nowhere self–shadowing, the irradiance on the bottom plane can be calculated in this model by integrating over the surface of the air–water boundary. If we assume that the bottom plane is perfectly diffuse, and that light reflected from this plane is *not* absorbed by the transmission medium and not reflected from the surface boundary, then this is the image on the plane that would be seen by a viewer in the transmission medium.

Let $(x_0, y_0, -d)$ be some point on the plane at which the irradiance is to be calculated. Let $\vec{\mathbf{P}}$ be the vector from the surface point $(x, y, h(x, y))$ to the point $(x_0, y_0, -d)$. Let $\hat{\mathbf{P}} = \vec{\mathbf{P}}/\|\vec{\mathbf{P}}\|$. Then at the point $(x_0, y_0, -d)$ the irradiance is given by

$$E = L_s \int_\Omega T(\theta_i) \cos\theta_i(\hat{\mathbf{P}}_z) \exp(-a(1 - (\hat{\mathbf{L}}_t \cdot \hat{\mathbf{P}})^2)) \exp(-\varepsilon\|\vec{\mathbf{P}}\|) \, dx \, dy. \tag{2}$$

Evaluation of this integral at discrete points on the bottom plane yields an image of the caustic induced by the height field.

4.1 Discretization and Approximation

The problem to be solved is to evaluate equation (2), which gives the irradiance on the plane $z = -d$. To do so, the integral must be discretized, and a number of approximations must be made in order to achieve real–time performance:

- The surface is represented by a height field h which is a discrete sampling of the continuous surface. It is represented as a texture map $\tilde{h}$ of values in the range $[0, 1]$ with 0.5 representing the zero–height of the surface. The normal $\widehat{N}_{i,j}$ at $h_{i,j}$ is the normal to the plane passing through $h_{i,j}$, $h_{i+1,j}$, and $h_{i,j+1}$, and is computed with finite differences, then normalized with a lookup table.
- The Fresnel transmission coefficient $T(n_i, n_t, \cos\theta_i, \cos\theta_t)$ is discretized as a function of $\cos\theta_i$ and evaluated with a lookup table. This is possible since $\cos\theta_t$ is a function of $\cos\theta_i$, and n_i, n_t are constant.
- In the same manner, the Γ term in equation 1 is discretized as a function of $\cos\theta_i$ and evaluated with a lookup table.

Since the imaging pipeline has the ability to perform convolutions, the integral of equation (2) can be approximated efficiently by phrasing it as a convolution and leveraging the efficiency of the hardware. However, in order to do so, the integrand must be *separable*, i.e. the integral must be expressed as $\int f(x, y)\, g(x - x_0, y - y_0)\, dx\, dy$ so that g can be used as a convolution kernel applied to f. Noting that a product of functions is separable if and only if each function in the product is separable, and recalling the terms in the integrand of equation (2), we have the following components:

- Since $\theta_i = -\widehat{L}_i \cdot \widehat{N}$ and $\widehat{N}$ is a function of $\frac{\partial h(x,y)}{\partial x}$ and $\frac{\partial h(x,y)}{\partial y}$, $T = T(x, y)$ is trivially separable. Similarly, $\theta_i = \theta_i(x, y)$, and $\cos\theta_i$ is trivially separable.
- We make the approximation $d \gg h(x, y)$ so that $-d - h(x, y) \approx -d$. Then $\exp(-\varepsilon \|\vec{P}\|)$ and $\widehat{P}_z$ become functions of $(x_0 - x, y_0 - y)$ and are both trivially separable.

Finally, an approximation is needed for the Gaussian, $\exp(-a(1 - (\widehat{L}_t \cdot \widehat{P})^2))$. We use an exponentiated cosine, $(\widehat{L}_t \cdot \widehat{P})^n$. Keeping the terms to first order in $\widehat{L}_{tx}$ and $\widehat{L}_{ty}$ in the multinomial expansion for $(\widehat{L}_t \cdot \widehat{P})^n$ gives

$$(\widehat{L}_t \cdot \widehat{P})^n \approx (\widehat{L}_{tz}\widehat{P}_z)^{n-1}(\widehat{L}_{tz}\widehat{P}_z + n(\widehat{L}_{tx}\widehat{P}_x) + n(\widehat{L}_{ty}\widehat{P}_y)),$$

which is most accurate for $\widehat{L}_{tz} \gg \widehat{L}_{tx}, \widehat{L}_{ty}$. Since $\widehat{L}_t$ is a function of (x, y) and $\widehat{P}$ is a function of $(x_0 - x, y_0 - y)$ under the approximation above, then the result is the sum of three separable functions.

Combining these results and discretizing makes L a sum of three convolutions:

$$L_{1j} \;=\; L_s \sum\sum \left[T(\cos\theta_i) \cos\theta_t \, (\widehat{L}_{tz})^{n-1} \widehat{L}_{tj} \right] \left[(\widehat{P}_z)^n \widehat{P}_j \, \exp(-\varepsilon\|\vec{P}\|) \right],$$

where $j = x, y, z$. The first term in each is the kernel, and the double sum is over the size of the kernel.

4.2   Hardware Algorithm

The caustic computation algorithm performs the following steps:

Init: Calculate lookup tables, convolution kernels
FOR EACH HEIGHT FIELD IN THE SEQUENCE OF TIME–VARYING HEIGHT FIELDS
  Pass 1: Calculate $\widehat{\mathbf{N}}_{ij}$, vector field of normals to height field
  Pass 2: Calculate $\Gamma \widehat{\mathbf{N}}_{ij}$, a term need to determine $\widehat{\mathbf{L}}_{\mathbf{t}}$
  Pass 3: Calculate $L_s \cos\theta_i \, T(\cos\theta_i)$
  Pass 4: Calculate $\widehat{\mathbf{L}}_{\mathbf{t}} \, (\widehat{\mathbf{L}}_{\mathbf{tz}})^{n-1}$
  Pass 5: Calculate function to be convolved: $(L_s \cos\theta_i \, T(\cos\theta_i)) \cdot (\widehat{\mathbf{L}}_{\mathbf{t}} \, (\widehat{\mathbf{L}}_{\mathbf{tz}})^{n-1})$
  Pass 6: Convolve function using precomputed kernel
REPEAT

In *Pass 1* the heightfield normals are calculated by convolving to get the x and y discrete partial derivatives, and then using pixel texturing to look up the associated normal.

In *Pass 2*, the adjusted function $\widetilde{\Gamma \, \widehat{\mathbf{N}}}$ is calculated by multiplying the adjusted function $\widetilde{\widehat{\mathbf{N}}}$, by an unadjusted scalar function, Γ as described in Section 3.2. In order to achieve this, a pixel rectangle containing the bias value of the adjusted function must first be copied to the framebuffer before blending.

In *Pass 3*, $L_s \cos\theta_i \, T(\cos\theta_i)$ is calculated by multiplying an unadjusted function, $\cos\theta_i T(\cos\theta_i)$, by a function, $L_s{}^1$. Since each of the terms is in the range $[0,1]$, neither scaling nor biasing is necessary, and the result is an unadjusted function.

In *Pass 4*, $\widehat{\mathbf{L}}_{\mathbf{t}} \, (\widehat{\mathbf{L}}_{\mathbf{tz}})^{n-1}$ is calculated by multiplying an adjusted function, $\widetilde{\widehat{\mathbf{L}}_{\mathbf{t}}}$ (see Eq. 1), by an unadjusted function, $(\widehat{\mathbf{L}}_{\mathbf{tz}})^{n-1}$.

In *Pass 5*, the function F to be convolved is calculated. F is the product of the results of Passes 3 and 4 — an adjusted function and an unadjusted function.

In *Pass 6*, the three final convolutions are performed and the results summed in order to give the irradiance, E, on the bottom plane.

4.3   Heightfield Generation

This section describes the real time generation of a height field which represents the surface of the pond. The user can click to create an impulse at a point on the surface (as though dropping a pebble). Over time, the wave propagates, attenuates, and reflects off of the pond walls. Multiple waves are possible with multiple impulses.

Wave height h is a function of time and distance from the original impulse:

$$h(t,d) = \exp(-\beta(f(t) - d)) \exp(-\alpha t) \sin(Kd - \omega t)$$

where $f(t)$ is the distance to the wavefront from the original impulse, α and β are damping constants, K is the wave number and ω the angular frequency. The β term attenuates the wave with distance behind the wavefront, while the α term attenuates it with time. This is a model of wave propagation in a fluid more viscous than water, but it may be replaced by any function of t and d without affecting the hardware computation described below.

---

[1] L_s can vary with surface position as in Fig. 2 (see Appendix).

We precompute and store two functions in textures: $h(t, d)$ and $T(u, v)$. The T texture stores distances from the impulse point as

$$T(u, v) = \sqrt{(u - c_u)^2 + (v - c_v)^2}$$

for (c_u, c_v) the center point of the texture. Then the contribution to the heightfield at position (x, y) due to an impulse at (i_x, i_y) is

$$h(t, T(x - i_x + c_u, y - i_y + c_v))$$

This contribution is easily calculated in hardware by first loading the colour map with one row of h: $h(t, \cdot)$. Then the appropriate rectangle of T is copied to the framebuffer. As the distances of T pass through the colour map, they are replaced with the corresponding heights. The functions h and T must of course be scaled and biased to the range $[0, 1]$.

Multiple impulses are treated by accumulating the results of the individual impulses. Reflections off of the pond walls are simulated by placing, for each impulse, four additional impulses outside of the pond: Each additional impulse is placed at the reflection of the original impulse through one of the four pond walls. (The dimensions of T are four times those of the height field.)

5 Implementation Results

The hardware caustic computation algorithm was implemented in OpenGL on an SGI Indigo 2 with a High Impact renderer and on an SGI Infinite Reality with an Onyx 2 renderer. A separate, completely software implementation was also made to validate the hardware results and to compare frame rates. The caustic algorithms were tested on sequences of height fields generated by the algorithm of Section 4.3. The resulting animation can be found at [25].

The Infinite Reality does not support pixel texturing and, despite the documentation to the contrary, we were unable to enable pixel texturing on the Indigo 2. The pixel texturing was thus simulated in software.

5.1 Frame Rates

Table 1 reports the frame rates for three configurations: The hardware implementation without pixel textures, which gives incorrect images but has times closest to those likely if pixel texturing were indeed supported, the hardware implementation with software pixel textures, which provides a lower bound on the frame rate, and the software implementation.

The frame rates of Table 1 are those required to generate the raster images of caustics from raster images of height fields. Running times for height field generation on an Infinite Reality Onyx 2 are 178 frames per second for a 128×128 heightfield with one impulse (plus four reflected impulses), and 64 frames per second for a 256×256 heightfield with three impulses (plus 12 reflected impulses).

From Table 1, it is clear that interactive rates of between 9 and 15 frames per second can be achieved on the Infinite Reality for a height field of size 256×256. On the Indigo 2, the frame rate drops to between three and four frames per second which, while not interactive, is still reasonable. The software implementation is between 8 and 26 times slower than the hardware implementation.

Table 1. Frames per second for various configurations of the algorithm on height fields of size 128 × 128 and 256 × 256, using a 7 × 7 convolution kernel. HW/No PT: Hardware implementation , pixel texturing disabled. HW/SWPT: Hardware implementation with software pixel texturing. SW: Software implementation. Sizes are in pixels.

Size	Infinite Reality			Indigo2		
	HW/No PT	HW/SWPT	SW	HW/No PT	HW/SWPT	SW
128 × 128	37.9	24.8	2.56	11.9	8.6	1.0
256 × 256	14.9	9.4	0.6	4.2	2.6	0.2

5.2 Correctness

The caustics resulting from one of the more complex height fields were calculated in both software and hardware in order to compare the numerical values of the irradiance. The software implementation made the same approximations as the hardware implementation, but the calculations in software were done in floating point so that the loss of precision due to the limited depth and discretization imposed by the hardware could be measured. For the height field seen in Fig. 1 (see Appendix), the relative RMS error between the two caustics was 26%. The height field which was used is clearly not the the height field in the sequence for which the error is minimal, and was chosen to estimate the worst case bound on the precision error.

6 Discussion

This paper has shown that graphics hardware can be used to perform complex general calculations, and has demonstrated an example of the calculation of interactive caustics. Although the calculation is clearly not as precise as a floating point implementation, there are many situations where current hardware can be used to make such calculations. The likelihood of deeper hardware buffers in the future make this an even more important area of research, as the number of problems that can be approached with these techniques will grow.

The calculation of caustics is particularly suitable for an implementation which lacks precision since visual perception of tones and shades is much less precise than for position, for example. There are many problems in which precision is unnecessary such as initial approximations to mathematical equations, situations where perceptual acuity is limited due to distance, motion, or lighting conditions, and the description of natural phenomena that appear to have an element of randomness. Generally speaking, when speed of calculation is more important than precision, mathematics on current graphics hardware can be very useful.

An increase in numerical precision would, of course, extend the set of problems amenable to this treatment. The implementation of floating point operations in graphics hardware, for example, would greatly enhance the applicability of graphics math. With or without floating point calculations, deeper buffers would increase numerical precision but at the cost of bandwidth. In addition, in lieu of full floating point, a floating point scale and bias prior to the initial quantization to framebuffer resolution would allow for increased dynamic range.

The approximations necessary to implement caustic generation in hardware provide a good clue as to the features which would improve such computations. The most significant approximations involved integration as current hardware is equipped with only a relatively small convolution kernel for implementing this operation. Certainly larger kernels would increase the applicability of this method, but larger kernels are likely to reduce performance, and the size of the kernel is only part of the difficulty: in order to implement integration as convolution, the integrand must be separable. To ease this restriction, operations on the kernel during the convolution would be useful, especially after the multiplication operation and before the summation.

Any reduction of clamping in the pipeline would also be beneficial. A 'wrap-around mode' for table lookups would allow for modular arithmetic, for example, and currently a lookup causes all the colour components to be clamped, even if they aren't used for the lookup, which could be prevented. Lookups are also currently implemented by quantizing and taking the nearest value in the table. This is quite appropriate for linear or near–linear functions with small dynamic range, but highly non–linear functions lose more precision in this algorithm. Interpolation would be a possible remedy to extend the applicability of lookup tables, but one must be careful not to sacrifice too much performance.

Although there is currently some capability in OpenGL for conditional execution such as stencil buffering and min/max functions, extending the scope and functionality of these operations would provide much greater flexibility. This direction has been taken in the register combiner architecture of NVIDIA, where different general combiner computations are allowed depending on one of the inputs to a combiner stage [5].

Programming the graphics hardware to do general mathematics can be quite tedious, which suggests that a computational approach might be suitable. Given a set of operations, software to aid fitting the operations into the pipeline would be quite useful. In addition, the tedium involved in correctly restricting values to $[0, 1]$ could be alleviated by an expression compiler which, given the types and ranges of the components of an expression, automatically computes the appropriate scale and bias. On a larger scale, one could imagine a 'graphics compiler' to analyse both scale and bias and pipeline fitting, and generate the necessary OpenGL code for the hardware in a similar manner to the shading language compilers recently proposed [7, 21].

Given the applications of graphics hardware to problems such as artificial intelligence [3], robot path planning [18], computational geometry [16], and now the creation and rendering of caustics, it is clear that graphics hardware can be used for much more general mathematical purposes than for which it was first intended: graphics hardware is not just for images any more.

6.1 Acknowledgements

We would like to thank all the people at iMAGIS–GRAVIR/IMAG for their kindness during our stay there, especially David Bourguignon for the donation of his machine. Special thanks also to David Torre for his help preparing images.

References

1. James Arvo. Backward ray tracing. *Developments in Ray Tracing. ACM SIGGRAPH Course Notes*, 12:259–263, 1986.
2. David Blythe, Brad Grantham, Mark J. Kilgard, Tom McReynolds, and Scott R. Nelson. Advanced graphics programming techniques using OpenGL. In *SIGGRAPH 99 Course Notes*, August, 1999.
3. Christian-A. Bohn. Kohonen feature mapping through graphics hardware. In *3rd Int. Conf. on Computational Intelligence and Neurosciences*, 1998.

298

4. Brian Cabral and Leith Casey Leedom. Imaging vector fields using line integral convolution. *Computer Graphics (SIGGRAPH '93 Proceedings)*, pages 263–272, August 1993.
5. NVIDIA Corporation. Nvidia OpenGL Extension Specifications. http://www.nvidia.com, April, 2000.
6. Paul Haeberli and Mark Segal. Texture mapping as a fundamental drawing primitive. *Fourth Eurographics Workshop on Rendering*, June:259–266, 1993.
7. Pat Hanrahan, Bill Mark, Kekoa Proudfoot, Svetoslav Tzvetkov, David Ebert, Wolfgang Heidrich, and Philipp Slusallek. Stanford Real–Time Programmable Shading Project. http://graphics.stanford.EDU/projects/shading/, 2000.
8. Eugene Hecht and Alfred Zajac. *Optics*. Addison Wesley Longman, Inc., 1979.
9. Paul S. Heckbert and Pat Hanrahan. Beam tracing polygonal objects. In *SIGGRAPH '84 Proceedings*, pages 119–127, July, 1984.
10. Wolfgang Heidrich. *High–quality Shading and Lighting for Hardware–accelerated Rendering*. PhD thesis, University of Erlangen–Nurenberg, April, 1999.
11. Wolfgang Heidrich, Hendrick Lensch, Michael F. Cohen, and Hans-Peter Seidel. Light field techniques for reflections and refractions. In *Rendering Techniques '99 (Proceedings of the Eurographics Rendering Workshop)*, August, 1999.
12. Wolfgang Heidrich and Hans-Peter Seidel. Efficient rendering of anisotopic surfaces using computer graphics hardware. *Proceedings of the Image and Multi-dimensional Digital Signal Processing Workshop (IMDSP)*, 1998.
13. Wolfgang Heidrich and Hans-Peter Seidel. View-independent environment maps. *Eurographics/SIGGRAPH Workshop on Graphics Hardware*, pages 39–45, 1998.
14. Wolfgang Heidrich and Hans-Peter Seidel. Realistic, hardware-accelerated shading and lighting. In *Computer Graphics (SIGGRAPH '99 Proceedings)*, August,1999.
15. Wolfgang Heidrich, Rudiger Westermann, Hans-Peter Seidel, and Thomas Ertl. Applications of pixel textures in visualization and realistic image synthesis. In *ACM Symposium on Interactive 3D Graphics*, August, 1999.
16. Kenneth E. Hoff III, Tim Culver, John Keyser, Ming Lin, and Dinesh Manocha. Fast computation of generalized Voronoi diagrams using graphics hardware. *Computer Graphics (SIGGRAPH '99 Proceedings)*, pages 277–286, August, 1999.
17. Silicon Graphics Inc. Pixel texture extension. Specification, http://www.opengl.org, 1999.
18. Jed Lengyel, Mark Reichert, Bruce R. Donald, and Donald P. Greenberg. Real–time robot motion planning using rasterizing computer graphics hardware. *Computer Graphics*, 24(4):327–335, August, 1990.
19. Michael D. McCool and Wolfgang Heidrich. Texture shaders. In *SIGGRAPH/Eurographics Workshop on Graphics Hardware*, 1999.
20. A Miné and F Neyret. Perlin textures in real time using OpenGL. Technical Report RR-3713, iMAGIS–GRAVIR/IMAG/INRIA, 1999.
21. Mark S. Peercy, Marc Olano, John Airey, and P. Jeffrey Ungar. Interactive multi–pass programmable shading. In *Computer Graphics (SIGGRAPH 2000 Proceedings)*, July, 2000.
22. Detlev Stalling, Malte Zöckler, and Hans-Christian Hege. Fast display of illuminated field lines. *IEEE Transactions on Visualization and Computer Graphics*, 3(2):118–128, 1997.
23. Jos Stam. Random caustics: Natural textures and wave theory revisited. In *ACM SIGGRAPH Visual Proceedings*, page 151, 1996.
24. Jerry Tessendorf. Simulating ocean water. In *SIGGRAPH 99 Course Notes*, August, 1999.
25. Chris Trendall and James Stewart. An example of hardware mathematics: Refractive caustics. http://www.dgp.utoronto.ca/~trendall/egwr00/index.html, 2000.
26. Mark Watt. Light-water interaction using backward beam tracing. *Computer Graphics*, 24(4):327–335, 1990.
27. Mason Woo, Jackie Neider, Tom Davis, and Dave Shreiner. *OpenGL Programming Guide*. Addison Wesley Longman, Inc., third edition, 1999.

Editors' Note: see Appendix, p. 414 for colored figures of this paper

Dynamic Acceleration Structures for Interactive Ray Tracing

Erik Reinhard, Brian Smits and Charles Hansen

University of Utah

reinhard|bes|hansen@cs.utah.edu

Abstract. Acceleration structures used for ray tracing have been designed and optimized for efficient traversal of static scenes. As it becomes feasible to do interactive ray tracing of moving objects, new requirements are posed upon the acceleration structures. Dynamic environments require rapid updates to the acceleration structures. In this paper we propose spatial subdivisions which allow insertion and deletion of objects in constant time at an arbitrary position, allowing scenes to be interactively animated and modified.

1 Introduction

Recently, interactive ray tracing has become a reality [8, 9], allowing exploration of scenes rendered with higher quality shading than with traditional interactive rendering algorithms. A high frame-rate is obtained through parallelism, using a multiprocessor shared memory machine. This approach has advantages over hardware accelerated interactive systems in that a software-based ray tracer is more easily modified. One of the problems with interactive ray tracing is that previous implementations only dealt with static scenes or scenes with a small number of specially handled moving objects. The reason for this limitation is that the acceleration structures used to make ray tracing efficient rely on a significant amount of preprocessing to build. This effectively limits the usefulness of interactive ray tracing to applications which allow changes in camera position. The work presented in this paper is aimed at extending the functionality of interactive ray tracing to include applications where objects need to be animated or interactively manipulated.

When objects can freely move through the scene, either through user interaction, or due to system-determined motion, it becomes necessary to adapt the acceleration methods to cope with changing geometry. Current spatial subdivisions tend to be highly optimized for efficient traversal, but are difficult to update quickly for changing geometry. For static scenes this suffices, as the spatial subdivision is generally constructed during a pre-processing step. However, in animated scenes pre-processed spatial subdivisions may have to be recalculated for each change of the moving objects. One approach to circumvent this issue is to use 4D radiance interpolants to speed-up ray traversal [2]. However, within this method the frame update rates depend on the type of scene edits performed as well as the extent of camera movement. We will therefore focus on adapting current spatial subdivision techniques to avoid these problems.

To animate objects while using a spatial subdivision, insertion and deletion costs are not negligible, as these operations may have to be performed many times during rendering. In this paper, spatial subdivisions are proposed which allow efficient ray traversal as well as rapid insertion and deletion for scenes where the extent of the scene grows over time.

The following section presents a brief overview of current spatial subdivision techniques (Section 2), followed by an explanation of our (hierarchical) grid modifications (Sections 3 and 4). A performance evaluation is given in Section 5, while conclusions are drawn in the final section.

2   Acceleration Structures for Ray Tracing

There has been a great deal of work done on acceleration structures for ray tracing [5]. However, little work has focused on ray tracing moving objects. Glassner presented an approach for building acceleration structures for animation [7]. However, this approach does not work for environments without *a priori* knowledge of the animation path for each object. In a survey of acceleration techniques, Gaede and Günther provide an overview of many spatial subdivisions, along with the requirements for various applications [4]. The most important requirements for ray tracing are fast ray traversal and adaptation to unevenly distributed data. Currently popular spatial subdivisions can be broadly categorized into bounding volume hierarchies and voxel based structures.

Bounding volume hierarchies create a tree, with each object stored in a single node. In theory, the tree structure allows $O(\log n)$ insertion and deletion, which may be fast enough. However, to make the traversal efficient, the tree is augmented with extra data, and occasionally flattened into an array representation [10], which enables fast traversal but insertion or deletion incur a non-trivial cost. Another problem is that as objects are inserted and deleted, the tree structure could become arbitrarily inefficient unless some sort of rebalancing step is performed as well.

Voxel based structures are either grids [1, 3] or can be hierarchical in nature, such as bintrees and octrees [6, 11]. The cost of building a spatial subdivision tends to be $O(n)$ in the number of objects. This is true for both grids and octrees. In addition, the cost of inserting a single object may depend on its relative size. A large object generally intersects many voxels, and therefore incurs a higher insertion cost than smaller objects. This can be alleviated through the use of modified hierarchical grids, as explained in Section 4. The larger problem with spatial subdivision approaches is that the grid structure is built within volume bounds that are fixed before construction. Although insertion and deletion may be relatively fast for most objects, if an object is moved outside the extent of the spatial subdivision, current structures would require a complete rebuild. This problem is addressed in the next section.

3   Grids

Grid spatial subdivisions for static scenes, without any modifications, are already useful for animated scenes, as traversal costs are low and insertion and deletion of objects is reasonably straightforward. Insertion is usually accomplished by mapping the axis-aligned bounding box of an object to the voxels of the grid. The object is inserted into all voxels that overlap with this bounding box. Deletion can be achieved in a similar way.

However, when an object moves outside the extent of the spatial subdivision, the acceleration structure would normally have to be rebuilt. As this is too expensive to perform repeatedly, we propose to logically replicate the grid over space. If an object exceeds the bounds of the grid, the object wraps around before re-insertion. Ray traversal then also wraps around the grid when a boundary is reached. In order to provide a stopping criterion for ray traversal, a logical bounding box is maintained which contains all objects, including the ones that have crossed the original perimeter. As this scheme does not require grid re-computation whenever an object moves far away, the cost of maintaining the spatial subdivision will be substantially lower. On the other hand, because rays now may have to wrap around, more voxels may have to be traversed per ray, which will slightly increase ray traversal time.

During a pre-processing step, the grid is built as usual. We will call the bounding box of the entire scene at start-up the 'physical bounding box'. If during the animation an object moves outside the physical bounding box, either because it is placed by the user in a new location, or its programmed path takes it outside, the logical bounding box is extended to enclose all objects. Initially, the logical bounding box is equal to the physical bounding box. Insertion of an object which lies outside the physical bounding box is accomplished by wrapping the object around within the physical grid, as depicted in Figure 1 (left).

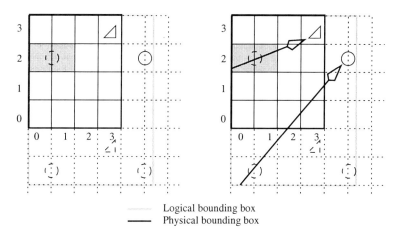

Logical bounding box
Physical bounding box

Fig. 1. Grid insertion (left). The sphere has moved outside the physical grid, now overlapping with voxels $(4, 2)$ and $(5, 2)$. Therefore, the object is inserted at the location of the shaded voxels. The logical bounding box is extended to include the newly moved object. Right: ray traversal through extended grid. The solid lines are the actual objects whereas the dashed lines indicate voxels which contain objects whose actual extents are not contained in that voxel.

As the logical bounding box may be larger than the physical bounding box, ray traversal now starts at the extended bounding box and ends if an intersection is found or if the ray leaves the logical bounding box. In the example in Figure 1 (right), the ray pointing to the sphere starts within a logical voxel, voxel $(-2, 0)$, which is mapped to physical voxel $(0, 2)$. The logical coordinates of the sphere are checked and found to be outside of the currently traversed voxel and thus no intersection test is necessary. The ray then progresses to physical voxel $(1, 2)$. For the same reason, no intersection with the sphere is computed again. Traversal then continues until the sphere is intersected in logical voxel $(4, 2)$, which maps to physical voxel $(0, 2)$.

Objects that are outside the physical grid are tagged, so that in the above example, when the ray aimed at the triangle enters voxels $(0, 2)$ and $(1, 2)$, the sphere does not have to be intersected. Similarly, when the ray is outside the physical grid, objects that are within the physical grid need not be intersected. As most objects will initially lie within the physical bounds, and only a few objects typically move away from their original positions, this scheme speeds up traversal considerably for parts of the ray that are outside the physical bounding box.

When the logical bounding box becomes much larger than the physical bounding box, there is a tradeoff between traversal speed (which deteriorates for large logical bounding boxes) and the cost of rebuilding the grid. In our implementation, the grid is rebuilt when the length of the diagonals of the physical and logical bounding boxes differ by a factor of two.

Hence, there is a hierarchy of operations that can be performed on grids. For small to moderate expansions of the scene, wrapping both rays and objects is relatively quick without incurring too high a traversal cost. For larger expansions, rebuilding the grid will become a more viable option.

This grid implementation shares the advantages of simplicity and cheap traversal with commonly used grid implementations. However, it adds the possibility of increasing the size of the scene without having to completely rebuild the grid every time there is a small change in scene extent. The cost of deleting and inserting a single object is not constant and depends largely on the size of the object relative to the size of the scene. This issue is addressed in the following section.

4   Hierarchical grids

As was noted in the previous section, the size of an object relative to each voxel in a grid influences how many voxels will contain that object. This in turn negatively affects insertion and deletion times. Hence, it would make sense to find a spatial subdivision whereby the voxels can have different sizes. If this is accomplished, then insertion and deletion of objects can be made independent of their sizes and can therefore be executed in constant time. Such spatial subdivisions are not new and are known as hierarchical spatial subdivisions. Octrees, bintrees and hierarchical grids are all examples of hierarchical spatial subdivisions. However, normally such spatial subdivisions store all their objects in leaf nodes and would therefore still incur non-constant insertion and deletion costs. We extend the use of hierarchical grids in such a way that objects can also reside in intermediary nodes or even in the root node for objects that are nearly as big as the entire scene.

Because such a structure should also be able to deal with expanding scenes, our efforts were directed towards constructing a hierarchy of grids (similar to Sung [12]), thereby extending the functionality of the grid structure presented in the previous section. Effectively, the proposed method constitutes a balanced octree.

Object insertion now proceeds similarly to grid insertion, except that the grid level needs to be determined before insertion. This is accomplished by comparing the size of the object in relation to the size of the scene. A simple heuristic is to determine the grid level from the diagonals of the two bounding boxes. Specifically, the length of the grid's diagonal is divided by the length of the object's diagonal, the result determining the grid level. Insertion and deletion progresses as explained in the previous section.

The gain of constant time insertion is offset by a slightly more complicated traversal algorithm. Hierarchical grid traversal is effectively the same as grid traversal with the following modifications. Traversal always starts at a leaf node which may first be mapped to a physical leaf node as described in the previous section. The ray is intersected with this voxel and all its parents until the root node is reached. This is necessary because objects at all levels in the hierarchy may occupy the same space as the currently traversed leaf node. If an intersection is found within the space of the leaf node, then traversal is finished. If not, the next leaf node is selected and the process is repeated.

This traversal scheme is wasteful because the same parent nodes may be repeatedly traversed for the same ray. To combat this problem, note that common ancestors of the current leaf node and the previously intersected leaf node, need not be traversed again. If the ray direction is positive, the current voxel's number can be used to derive the number of levels to go up in the tree to find the common ancestor between the current and the previously visited voxel. For negative ray directions, the previously visited voxel's number is used instead. Finding the common ancestor is achieved using simple bit manipulation, as detailed in Figure 2.

```
bitmask = (raydir_x > 0) ? x : x + 1
forall levels in hierarchical grid
{
  cell = hgrid[level][x>>level][y>>level][z>>level]
  forall objects in cell
    intersect(ray, object)
  if (bitmask & 1)
    return
  bitmask >>= 1
}
```

Fig. 2. Hierarchical grid traversal algorithm in C-like pseudo-code. The bitmask is set assuming that the last step was along the x-axis.

As the highest levels of the grid may not contain any objects, ascending all the way to the highest level in the grid is not always necessary. Ascending the tree for a particular leaf node can stop when the largest voxel containing objects is visited.

This hierarchical grid structure has the following features. The traversal is only marginally more complex than standard grid traversal. In addition, wrapping of objects in the face of expanding scenes is still possible. If all objects are the same size, this algorithm effectively defaults to grid traversal. Insertion and deletion can be achieved in constant time, as the number of voxels that each object overlaps is roughly constant[1].

5   Evaluation

The grid and hierarchical grid spatial subdivisions were implemented using an interactive ray tracer [9], which runs on an SGI Origin 2000 with 32 processors. For evaluation purposes, two test scenes were used. In each scene, a number of objects were animated using pre-programmed motion paths. The scenes as they are at start-up are depicted in Figure 5 (top). An example frame taken during the animation is given for each scene in Figure 5 (bottom). All images were rendered on 30 processors at a resolution of 512^2 pixels.

To assess basic traversal speed, the new grid and hierarchical grid implementations are compared with a bounding volume hierarchy. We also compared our algorithms with a grid traversal algorithm which does not allow interactive updates. Its internal data structure consists of a single array of object pointers, which improves cache efficiency on the Origin 2000.

From here on we will refer to the new grid implementation as 'interactive grid' to distinguish between the two grid traversal algorithms. As all these spatial subdivision methods have a user defined parameter to set the resolution (voxels along one axis and maximum number of grid levels, respectively), various settings are evaluated. The overall performance is given in Figure 3 and is measured in frames per second.

---

[1]Note that this also obviates the need for mailbox systems to avoid redundant intersection tests.

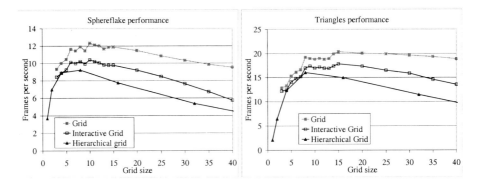

Fig. 3. Performance (in frames per second) for the grid, the interactive grid and the hierarchical grid for two static scenes. The bounding volume hierarchy achieves a frame rate of 8.5 fps for the static sphereflake model and 16.4 fps for the static triangles model.

The extra flexibility gained by both the interactive grid and hierarchical grid implementations results in a somewhat slower frame rate. This is according to expectation, as the traversal algorithm is a little more complex and the Origin's cache structure cannot be exploited as well with either of the new grid structures. The graphs in Figure 3 show that with respect to the grid implementation the efficiency reduction is between 12% and 16% for the interactive grid and 21% and 25% for the hierarchical grid. These performance losses are deemed acceptable since they result in far better overall execution than dynamically reconstructing the original grid. For the sphereflake, all implementations are faster, for a range of grid sizes, than a bounding volume hierarchy, which runs at 8.5 fps. For the triangles scene, the hierarchical grid performs at 16.0 fps similarly to the bounding volume (16.4 fps), while grid and interactive grid are faster.

The non-zero cost of updating the scene effectively limits the number of objects that can be animated within the time-span of a single frame. However, for both scenes, this limit was not reached. In the case where the frame rate was highest for the triangles scene, updating all 200 triangles took less than 1/680th of a frame for the hierarchical grid and 1/323th of a frame for the interactive grid. The sphereflake scene costs even less to update, as fewer objects are animated. For each of these tests, the hierarchical grid is more efficiently updated than the interactive grid, which confirms its usefulness.

The size difference between different objects should cause the update efficiency to be variable for the interactive grid, while remaining relatively constant for the hierarchical grid. In order to demonstrate this effect, both the ground plane and one of the triangles in the triangle scene was interactively repositioned during rendering. The update rates for different size parameters for both the interactive grid and the hierarchical grid, are presented in Figure 4 (left). As expected, the performance of the hierarchical grid is relatively constant, although the size difference between ground plane and triangle is considerable. The interactive grid does not cope with large objects very well if these objects overlap with many voxels. Dependent on the number of voxels in the grid, there is one to two orders of magnitude difference between inserting a large and a small object. For larger grid sizes, the update time for the ground plane is roughly half a frame. This leads to visible artifacts when using an interactive grid, as during the update the processors that are rendering the next frame temporarily cannot intersect this object (it is simply taken out of the spatial subdivision). In practice, the hierarchical grid implementation does not show this disadvantage.

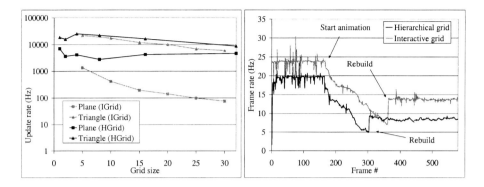

Fig. 4. Left: Update rate as function of (hierarchical) grid size. The plane is the ground plane in the triangles scene and the triangle is one of the triangles in the same scene. Right: Frame rate as function of time for the expanding triangle scene.

The time to rebuild a spatial subdivision from scratch is expected to be considerably higher than the cost of re-inserting a small number of objects. For the triangles scene, where 200 out of 201 objects were animated, the update rate was still a factor of two faster than the cost of completely rebuilding the spatial subdivision. This was true for both the interactive grid and the hierarchical grid. A factor of two was also found for the animation of 81 spheres in the sphereflake scene. When animating only 9 objects in this scene, the difference was a factor of 10 in favor of updating. We believe that the performance difference between rebuilding the acceleration structure and updating all objects is largely due to the cost of memory allocation, which occurs when rebuilding.

In addition to experiments involving grids and hierarchical grids with a branching factor of two, tests were performed using a hierarchical grid with a higher branching factor. Instead of subdividing a voxel into eight children, here nodes are split into 64 children (4 along each axis). The observed frame rates are very similar to the hierarchical grid. The object update rates were slightly better for the sphereflake and triangle scenes, because the size differences between the objects matches this acceleration structure better than both the interactive grid and the hierarchical grid.

In the case of expanding scenes, the logical bounding box will become larger than the physical bounding box. The number of voxels that are traversed per ray will therefore on average increase. This is the case in the triangles scene[2]. The variation over time of the frame rate is given in Figure 4 (right). In this example, the objects are first stationary. At some point the animation starts and the frame rate drops because the scene immediately starts expanding. At some point the expansion is such that a rebuild is warranted. The re-computed spatial subdivision now has a logical bounding box which is identical to the (new) physical bounding box and therefore the number of traversed voxels is reduced when compared with the situation just before the rebuild. The total frame rate does not reach the frame rate at the start of the computation, because the objects are more spread out over space, resulting in larger voxels and more intersection tests which do not yield an intersection point.

Finally, Figure 6 shows that interactively updating scenes using drag and drop interaction is feasible.

---

[2]For this experiment, the ground plane of the triangles scene was reduced in size, allowing the rebuild to occur after a smaller number of frames.

306

6 Conclusions

When objects are interactively manipulated and animated within a ray tracing application, much of the work that is traditionally performed during a pre-processing step becomes a limiting factor. Especially spatial subdivisions which are normally built once before the computation starts, do not exhibit the flexibility that is required for animation. The insertion and deletion costs can be both unpredictable and variable. We have argued that for a small cost in traversal performance flexibility can be obtained and insertion and deletion of objects can be performed in constant time.

By logically extending the (hierarchical) grids into space, these spatial subdivisions deal with expanding scenes rather naturally. For modest expansions, this does not significantly alter the frame rate. When the scenes expand a great deal, rebuilding the entire spatial subdivision may become necessary. For large scenes this may involve a temporary drop in frame rate. For applications where this is unacceptable, it would be advisable to perform the rebuilding within a separate thread (rather than the display thread) and use double buffering to minimize the impact on the rendering threads.

Acknowledgements

Thanks to Pete Shirley and Steve Parker for their help and comments and to the anonymous reviewers for their helpful comments. This work was supported by NSF grants CISE-CCR 97-20192, NSF-9977218 and NSF-9978099 and by the DOE Advanced Visualization Technology Center.

References

1. J. Amanatides and A. Woo, *A fast voxel traversal algorithm for ray tracing*, in Eurographics '87, Elsevier Science Publishers, Amsterdam, North-Holland, Aug. 1987, pp. 3–10.
2. K. Bala, J. Dorsey, and S. Teller, *Interactive Ray Traced Scene Editing using Ray Segment Tree*, in Rendering Techniques '99, pp. 31-44. Springer-Verlag, 1999.
3. A. Fujimoto, T. Tanaka, and K. Iwata, *ARTS: Accelerated ray tracing system*, IEEE Computer Graphics and Applications, 6 (1986), pp. 16–26.
4. V. Gaede and O. Günther, *Multidimensional access methods*, ACM Computing Surveys, 30 (1998), pp. 170–231.
5. A. S. Glassner, ed., *An Introduction to Ray Tracing*, Academic Press, 1989.
6. A. S. Glassner, *Space subdivision for fast ray tracing*, IEEE Computer Graphics and Applications, 4 (1984), pp. 15–22.
7. A. S. Glassner, *Spacetime ray tracing for animation*, IEEE Computer Graphics and Applications, 8 (1988), pp. 60–70.
8. M. J. Muuss, *Towards real-time ray-tracing of combinatorial solid geometric models*, in Proceedings of BRL-CAD Symposium, June 1995.
9. S. Parker, W. Martin, P.-P. Sloan, P. Shirley, B. Smits, and C. Hansen, *Interactive ray tracing*, in Symposium on Interactive 3D Computer Graphics, April 1999.
10. B. Smits, *Efficiency issues for ray tracing*, Journal of Graphics Tools, 3 (1998), pp. 1–14.
11. J. Spackman and P. Willis, *The SMART navigation of a ray through an oct-tree*, Computers and Graphics, 15 (1991), pp. 185–194.
12. K. Sung, *A DDA octree traversal algorithm for ray tracing*, in Eurographics '91, W. Purgathofer, ed., North-Holland, sept 1991, pp. 73–85.

Editors' Note: see Appendix, p. 415 for colored figures of this paper

Direct Ray Tracing of Displacement Mapped Triangles

Brian Smits   Peter Shirley   Michael M. Stark

University of Utah

bes|shirley|mstark@cs.utah.edu

Abstract.
We present an algorithm for ray tracing displacement maps that requires no additional storage over the base model. Displacement maps are rarely used in ray tracing due to the cost associated with storing and intersecting the displaced geometry. This is unfortunate because displacement maps allow the addition of large amounts of geometric complexity into models. Our method works for models composed of triangles with normals at the vertices. In addition, we discuss a special purpose displacement that creates a smooth surface that interpolates the triangle vertices and normals of a mesh. The combination allows relatively coarse models to be displacement mapped and ray traced effectively.

1 Introduction

Visually rich images are often generated from simpler models by applying *displacement maps* to increase surface detail (Figure 1). Displacement maps are a special type of *offset surface*, and are usually assumed to perturb surface positions a small distance using some function. Images with displacement maps are usually computed using explicit subdivision [3]. The displacement is often a semi-random procedural function that uses Perlin-style noise [11]. Somewhat surprisingly, displacement maps are almost never used in ray tracing. This turns out to be for entirely technical reasons; a straightforward implementation would need to store more micropolygons than would fit in main memory on most computers [4]. For this reason, sophisticated caching strategies have been suggested [12]. Although caching strategies work well for a variety of applications they are problematic for applications that resist reordering such as Metropolis Light Transport [16]. Alternatively, explicit numeric root-finding can be used, provided the displacements can be nicely bounded [5, 8]. A third approach that could work for displacement mapped surfaces is the recursive subdivision scheme used for procedural geometry by Kajiya[6]. This approach requires knowing tight bounds over each subdivided region of the displacement function in order to be efficient. Because most global illumination algorithms require ray tracing, it is desirable to find a simple way to add displacement maps to ray tracing programs. This would allow realism in both global lighting complexity and local geometric complexity.

We introduce a method for ray tracing polygonal models with displacements that avoids complex strategies by restricting the allowable base geometry to triangle meshes with vertex normals. Although this is a narrow class of modeling primitive, almost all other modeling primitives can be converted to triangle meshes in a practical manner. The key problem with triangle meshes is the well-known faceting artifacts. However, we show how to use a deterministic spline displacement function to smooth tessellated models. While we have restricted how our base models must be represented, we feel

Fig. 1. *An image of a complex object created by displacement mapping an icosahedron. The figure is ray traced with global illumination. Only twenty triangles are stored.*

the resulting benefits in computation and storage make up for this restriction.

In Section 2 we give an overview of our assumptions on the model and the restrictions we impose for our algorithm. In Section 3 we present the ray intersection algorithm for triangles with displacement functions. The requirements for a displacement function used to smooth triangle meshes is discussed in Section 4. Images resulting from the algorithm are shown in Section 5. Finally, we discuss future directions for the work in Section 6.

2 Overview

The inspiration for our method comes from the *REYES* rendering architecture [3]. That simple architecture has worked well for almost two decades, and relies on three simplifying assumptions related to displacements:

- displacements are bounded in distance,
- base surfaces know how to subdivide themselves,
- subdividing the displaced base surfaces into a net of simple sub-pixel patches provides sufficient accuracy.

We borrow these assumptions directly. By assuming that a finely subdivided model provides sufficient accuracy, we can use micropolygon normals directly, so no derivative properties of the displacement need be known. We also add the assumption that the displacements are along the direction of the interpolated normal. Although this is more restrictive than the displacement mapping found in the REYES architecture, it is

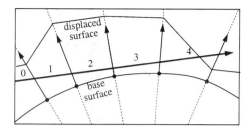

Fig. 2. *A set of points with normals partitions space into cells (one is shaded) which can be traversed in order by a ray. This observation holds in 3D as well. An analogous partition can be added within each cell.*

the type of displacement mapping found in Maya[1]. For the intersection method, first imagine a base surface being "carved up" with a set of vertices and normals (Figure 2). Within each partition we could displace a triangle whose vertices lie along projected normal vectors from the base surface. If one considers a given triangle under all possible displacements, it sweeps out a 3D region in space. For reasonably well-behaved surfaces, adjacent triangles have adjacent regions. The shape of the boundaries between these regions depends on how the normal vectors of base geometry behave. If one imagines all the regions swept out by all triangles, each triangle forming a "column" in space, the possibility of a traversal algorithm presents itself. If the base geometry is a plane then all displacements are perpendicular to the plane and the traversal algorithm would be similar to that usually used for ray intersections with height fields [9], except that the traversed cells would have triangular rather than rectangular cross-sections. We would like to choose a base geometry that is general enough to be geometrically expressive, but restrictive enough that such a traversal algorithm is feasible.

Because they are so often used in practice, three obvious choices are NURBS surfaces, subdivision surfaces, and implicit surfaces such as metaballs. Since all three of these primitive types are quite different from each other, it is desirable to find a common representation that they could all be converted into. The only obvious choice for this common representation is a triangulated mesh, to which it is straightforward to convert for NURBS and subdivision surfaces, and at least feasible for implicit surfaces [15]. For this reason we choose triangles as our base geometry. To ensure that the displaced surface is continuous, we use shared vertex normals and displace along normals computed via barycentric interpolation (i.e., Phong normal interpolation [13]). Although more general displacements are useful [10], we leverage this restriction on the direction of displacement to create a simpler algorithm than would be possible otherwise.

We strengthen the restriction of a bound on the displacement to limit the range of possible displacements so that any resulting displaced surface is unable to intersect itself. Each point in the valid region corresponds to exactly one position and displacement value on the base triangle. This restriction means that each region has only one set of neighbors, another requirement for a simple traversal algorithm. It also means that the first intersection found will be the closest intersection to the ray origin.

Our displacement framework assumes there is a point $\mathbf{p}$ on an underlying surface which is displaced in the direction of the normal vector $\mathbf{n}(\mathbf{p})$ by a displacement function $h(\mathbf{p})$ (Figure 3). For a triangle with points $\mathbf{p}_0, \mathbf{p}_1, \mathbf{p}_2$ and corresponding normals

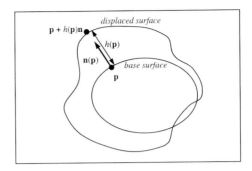

Fig. 3. *A simple displacement by function h in the normal direction creates a new curve in 2D.*

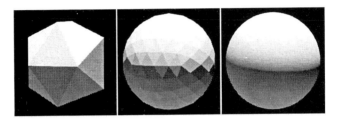

Fig. 4. *Icosahedron with displacement pushing each point to a sphere, $N = 1, 4, 100$.*

n_0, n_1, n_2 the bilinearly interpolated points and normals **p** and **n** are:

$$\mathbf{p} = \alpha\mathbf{p}_0 + \beta\mathbf{p}_1 + \gamma\mathbf{p}_2,$$
$$\mathbf{n} = \alpha\mathbf{n}_0 + \beta\mathbf{n}_1 + \gamma\mathbf{n}_2,$$

where (α, β, γ) are the *barycentric coordinates* on the triangle, so $\alpha + \beta + \gamma = 1$. Our displaced surface $\mathbf{p}_d$ is thus:

$$\mathbf{p}_d = \alpha\mathbf{p}_0 + \beta\mathbf{p}_1 + \gamma\mathbf{p}_2 + h(\alpha\mathbf{p}_0 + \beta\mathbf{p}_1 + \gamma\mathbf{p}_2)(\alpha\mathbf{n}_0 + \beta\mathbf{n}_1 + \gamma\mathbf{n}_2)$$

3 Ray Intersection

Our ray intersection test is similar in spirit to intersecting a ray with a height field using a regular grid over the base plane. We will take advantage of an implicit triangular grid formed by the barycentric coordinates. We choose a subdivision amount N (Figure 4) and use dividing lines $\alpha_i = \gamma_i = \beta_i = i/N$ for $i = 0, ..., N$ which creates N^2 grid cells for each triangle. Each grid cell generates one displaced microtriangle, as shown in Figure 5. The grid is regular on the base triangle, but due to the interpolated surface normals, it is irregular throughout space. Although it is irregular, our restrictions limit the range of the displacement function $h()$ to the interval $[-m, +M]$ where a traversal algorithm is possible.

Much like standard grid traversal algorithms, there are two phases to the algorithm. First the start point must be initialized. Next the grid must be traversed, checking each cell for an intersection with the triangle it contains. The traversal algorithm will be described first in order to determine the quantities that need to be initialized.

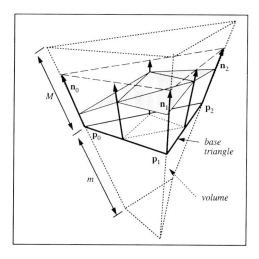

Fig. 5. *The base triangle and four displaced microtriangles generated by setting the subdivision parameter, N, to 2. The volume for the maximum displacement is also shown.*

3.1 Traversal

Assuming we will be able to initialize the traversal algorithm, we focus first on how to do an efficient traversal. This traversal is conceptually simple, however the use of triangles complicates the indexing. For each cell entered, the microtriangle is generated. If it is hit, the traversal is over, if it is missed, the next cell must be determined and a new microtriangle generated. The new triangle will differ from the previous triangle by exactly one vertex. This means that for each step through the grid we need only evaluate the expensive displacement function once.

A position in the grid will be labeled by a triple, (i, j, k), corresponding to the lines of constant barycentric coordinates $\alpha = i/N, \beta = j/N, \gamma = k/N$. The indices sum to either $N - 1$ or $N - 2$ depending upon whether the triangle is a *lower* triangle or an *upper* triangle as shown in Figure 6. The classification into lower and upper determines how the vertices are generated given the indices. For a lower triangle, the barycentric lines corresponding to indices are the edges of the triangle. For an upper triangle, the barycentric lines corresponding to the indices touch the triangle only at the vertices. This is not as neat as other possible numbering schemes, however it means that each triangle differs from its neighbors by one in exactly one index.

Each microtriangle is represented by three displaced points, **a**, **b**, and **c**, with the order chosen such that the ray is assumed to have entered the cell passing through the side corresponding to edge **a**, **b**. The next cell to be tested can be marked based on which index will change and if the index will be incremented or decremented. This flag can be represented as {iplus, jminus, kplus, iminus, jplus, kminus}, and depends upon the orientation of the current triangle and which side of the cell the ray exits through. By knowing how the ray entered the current cell, there are usually only two options for how the ray leaves the cell. The exception for when the ray exits through the face it enters is handled by the initialization code and will be discussed later. These options can be checked by seeing on which side of the line determined by $\mathbf{c} + s\mathbf{n}_c$ (the far point and its normal) the ray passes, as shown in Figure 7. If the above list of choices is viewed as a ring, the next possible choice is either the next flag in the ring, or the

312

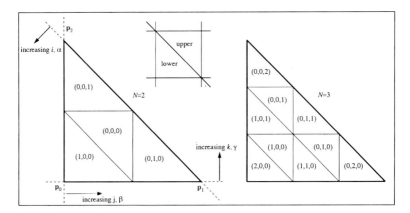

Fig. 6. *Barycentric indexing for $N = 2$ and $N = 3$. When moving between adjacent triangles, exactly one index changes by one. For a given triangle, this change has the same sign for all three edges. The "upper" triangle for a given (j, k) is the one with the smaller i index.*

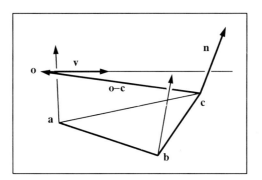

Fig. 7. *The ray $\mathbf{o} + t\mathbf{v}$ passes between the normals at $\mathbf{a}$ and $\mathbf{b}$. It will leave either between the normals at $\mathbf{a}$ and $\mathbf{c}$, or between the normals at $\mathbf{b}$ and $\mathbf{c}$. This can be tested by whether the ray passes left or right of $\mathbf{n}$. It goes to the left of the line $\mathbf{c} + t\mathbf{n}$ if $\mathbf{v} \cdot (\mathbf{n} \times (\mathbf{o} - \mathbf{c}))$ is negative.*

previous flag in the ring.

The traversal can be terminated by checking if the (i, j, k) values are the same as the stop cell (i_e, j_e, k_e) determined by the initialization phase. We also terminate the traversal if the ray exits the volume. The traversal loop can be expressed in pseudocode as follows:

```
Ray ray        // ray, including valid interval for t
Vector3 a,b,c        // microtriangle vertices, ordered
Vector2 uva,uvb,uvc        // (β, γ) for each vertex
Vector3 cNormal        // normal at vertex c
int i, j, k        // indices of current cell
bool rightOfC        // flag used to determine next cell
LastChange change        // where change is one of:
                // {iplus, jminus, kplus, iminus, jplus,kminus}
float delta = 1 / N
while(true)
  if TriangleIntersect(ray, a, b, c)
    intersectionNormal = (b-a) × (c-a)
    return true
  if EndCell(i,j,k) return false
  rightOfC = ((cNormal × (ray.Origin() - c)) * ray.Direction() > 0)
  if(rightOfC)
    a = c,    uva = uvc
  else
    b = c,    uvb = uvc
    // Take advantage of numbering. 5 = −1  mod 6
  change = AdvanceType((change + (rightOfC ? 1 : 5)) % 6)
  if(change == iminus)
    if (−− i < 0) return false
    uvc = Vector2((j+1)*delta, (k+1)*delta)
  else if(change == iplus)
    if (++ i ≥ N) return false
    uvc = Vector2( j*delta, k*delta)
  else if(change == jminus
    if (−− j < 0) return false
    uvc = Vector2( j*delta, (k+1)*delta)
  else if(change == jplus)
    if (++ j ≥ N) return false
    uvc = Vector2( (j+1)*delta, k*delta)
  else if(change == kminus
    if (−− k < 0) return false
    uvc = Vector2( (j+1)*delta, k*delta)
  else if(change == kplus)
    if (++ k ≥ N) return false
    uvc = Vector2( j*delta, (k+1)*delta)
  (c,cNormal) = GetPoint(uvc)
```

3.2   Initialization

The initialization phase of the algorithm must determine where in the grid the traversal algorithm starts and ends. The volume through which the traversal takes place is shown in Figure 5. The top and bottom of the space are bounded by triangles, the sides are bounded by bilinear patches.

Before the start and end cells are determined, the subdivision amount N must be found. This can either be fixed for the displacement map, $N = C$, or made adaptive, based on projected screen area. We allow either, and compute the adaptive size based on the area and an estimate of the distance to the camera, with a user defined N_{max}.

The initialization phase must determine the correct index (i, j, k) for starting the traversal. In standard grid traversal algorithms the traversal may start anywhere inside the grid. This clearly makes sense and would be ideal, but determining the index given an arbitrary point is equivalent to determining the barycentric coordinates and displacement (height) for the point. The computation involves solving a cubic equation, and the method seemed to have numeric problems. Our solution is to treat the ray as an infinite line and find the place where that line enters the volume and where it exits. This can require a longer traversal than necessary, however unlike uniform space subdivision in ray tracing, where the grid bounds the environment or a complex object, the displaced triangle tends to occupy a relatively small fraction of the scene, so most rays will pass completely through the volumes of most triangles.

The start and end points are the smallest and largest intersections of the ray with the volume. If the intersection point is on one of the bilinear side patches, one of the barycentric coordinates is zero, and the u parametric value found while intersecting the side can be used directly to determine the other two. If the intersection point is on one of the triangular end caps, the barycentric coordinates of the intersection point are exactly what is needed. The index for the grid cell is then $(\lfloor \alpha * N \rfloor, \lfloor \beta * N \rfloor, \lfloor \gamma * N \rfloor)$.

The last part of the initialization is to determine which face of the cell the ray entered from, so that the traversal algorithm can determine the appropriate next cell. This is given if the intersection is on one of the bilinear sides, however it is not given for the top or bottom boundaries. In this case, the bilinear walls of the cell can be checked. As the ray entered either the top or the bottom, the side hit will be the side the ray leaves from. It is valid to assume the ray entered from either of the other two sides. If the ray does not hit any sides, then this cell is the end cell as well, so the parameter does not matter.

3.3 Complications

There are some complications created in using a traversal algorithm to walk through an irregular volume filled with many small triangles. The first and most significant is that the sides of the volume are not planar and the ray may intersect one twice. This means that the traversal may exit the grid without reaching the correct stop cell. More importantly, the intersection with the surface may lie in the second interval within the volume. The initialization code can be modified so that if the ray hits one of the bilinear sides twice, and no intersection is found in the first interval, then the traversal is called again with a new start cell determined by the second intersection point.

A second complication occurs due to the sides of the grid cells being non-planar. The first way this could cause problems was briefly mentioned while discussing the traversal. Geometrically, the ray can enter a cell briefly, and then quickly return to the first cell. This does not happen in our algorithm because of the way the traversal chooses the next cell; the ray passes on the same side of both point-normal pairs for that side, so the ray never enters the cell. In terms of Figure 7, although the ray could possibly intersect the bilinear patch along edge **bc** twice, our algorithm ignores the double intersection and chooses the cell on the other side of edge **ac**. For certain extreme

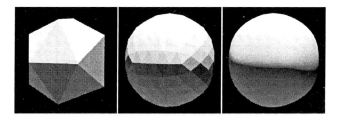

Fig. 8. *An icosahedron with a smoothing displacement that only uses the vertices and vertex normals for the triangle being displaced for* $N = 1, 4, 100$.

configurations, it is possible that the ray may actually intersect the microtriangle in the missed cell. Because the cells in general do not exactly bound the microtriangles, it is possible the ray should have hit the neighbor's triangle even if the ray misses the bilinear wall of the cell. Due to the small size of the microtriangles, and the significantly smaller size of the potentially missed piece, we have not noticed any significant errors caused by this problem. One solution would be to grow the triangle slightly in the triangle intersection test, a solution sometimes used to prevent cracking in simple triangle meshes. We chose not to do this because in our experience, expanding geometry eventually causes it's own set of problems.

A final issue to consider is that this method has the potential to create very small triangles. Some of the standard triangle intersection tests use epsilons that may be not be suitable for the size of the input. This can cause microtriangles to be falsely missed.

The intersection algorithm is implemented entirely using four byte floats. Although there are occasional rays that miss the surface, these problems are about the same frequency as those often found in ray tracers using simple polygonal objects.

4 A Smoothing Displacement Function

Since we have a mechanism to create images with displacements, it is useful to have a displacement that creates a smooth mesh. This would allow rendering smoothed versions of tessellated models with or without additional displacements. To make the problem as local as possible, we would like the smoothing displacement to only have knowledge of a given triangle's vertices and vertex normals. Knowledge about neighboring triangles could allow a smoother surface, but create additional complexities in the representation of the triangle mesh.

Although examining how to smooth triangle meshes has been examined by many researchers (e.g., [7]), this problem is different in that the function must have the algebraic form of a height function in barycentric coordinates with respect to barycentric interpolated normals.

We have created a simple smoothing displacement as a proof of concept. This displacement interpolates the triangle vertices, and has a smooth tangent plane on the transition between two adjacent triangles. This implies a number of constraints:

- the surface must depend only on the vertices and vertex normals,
- the surface must be smooth over the triangle,
- the surface must interpolate the vertices of the triangle,
- the surface normal at each vertex must match the prescribed vertex normals,

- the tangent plane along each edge of the surface must match that constructed on an adjacent triangle, so that joined patches meet with G^1 continuity.

The final requirement listed above is the one which is the most difficult to satisfy, because Hermite (derivative) interpolation is more difficult to enforce over a line than at single points.

We use the Coons patch approach to construct the surface. First, boundary curves and prescribed tangent planes are constructed using ordinary Hermite interpolation. Then three surfaces are constructed which interpolate the boundary curves and tangents along two of the edges. These three surfaces are blended in such a way as to preserve the derivatives and remove the "bad" edges from the final surface. The surface will be constructed in terms of barycentric coordinates. The approach applied to an icosahedron is shown in Figure 8. This displacement function, although useful for eliminating artifacts in certain models, creates objectionable artifacts for other models. More details of the smoothing function are available in a technical report [14].

5 Results

We evaluated our system on models with a large number of displaced triangles. Additionally, we wanted to verify the robustness of the algorithm under fairly extreme displacements. All scenes were rendered in parallel on an SGI O2K with 250 MHZ R1000K processors using a fairly standard Monte Carlo path tracer in order to capture shadows and indirect lighting effects.

The image in Figure 1 shows an icosahedron with high frequency displacements of roughly half the sphere radius. Without a smoothing displacement, the outline of the icosahedron would be visually obvious.

The second example is a piece of pottery containing 4680 initial triangles. The final displaced pottery is shown in Figure 9. For this scene N was fixed at 80. The 4680 initial triangles would have generated 30 million triangles if the geometry had been represented explicitly. Note that instancing would not have helped here. The image shows global illumination and shadowing effects on the grooves that would not have been possible either with bump mapping in a ray tracer, or without a global illumination framework. The 640x480 image was rendered using 256 paths of length 4 per pixel, and took roughly 24 CPU hours to run.

The final example is a small section of terrain data consisting of roughly 55,000 thirty meter cells. The resulting 110,000 triangles have been displacement mapped with an expensive displacement function based on several uses of the turbulence function[11] and is shown in Figure 10. The viewpoint is set near the ground, roughly at eye height for a person. The amount of subdivision was determined adaptively for each triangle. Because of the view, the foreground must be subdivided a large amount. We set $N_{max} = 3162$, resulting in ten million potential microtriangles per input triangle (approximately 1cm wide microtriangles). The maximum N is achieved and needed for the left quarter of the image, where some facets can still be seen. Storing all 10^{12} triangles would have required about 100 terabytes. Our implementation requires roughly 10 megabytes for the terrain data. The 1200x900 image was generated with 36 paths of length 2 per pixel. Total CPU time was 43 hours. We believe that optimizing the algorithm and displacement function could reduce this time, as could changing the assumption in the ray tracer that object intersections are cheap, so testing objects multiple times is acceptable.

6   Discussion

The algorithm presented in this paper can produce ray traced images of displacement mapped geometry without resorting to explicitly stored tessellation or numerical root-finding. The goal of our system is to be able to render models with large amounts of displaced geometry. If the resulting displaced geometry is small, explicitly generating all polygons and putting them into a general acceleration scheme should prove faster. Our approach benefits from processor speeds continuing to grow faster than memory speeds and sizes, and provides a viable alternative to geometry caching schemes and numerical root finding.

We view this work as a proof-of-concept. There are potential numeric stability problems with the traversal. There are many areas where efficiency could be improved. Adaptively determining the subdivision amount, N, provides some performance bene-fits, however, there are two problems that can occur. Changing the level of subdivision for two adjacent pixels may cause some tearing. We are conservative in choosing the subdivision level, and haven't seen any artifacts due to this. A potentially more seri-ous problem occurs when the displacement maps are used to represent surfaces such as brushed or scratched metal. Reducing the subdivision level can result in significant changes in appearance, even if the geometry itself is subpixel. In this case, we would like to carefully replace geometry with BRDF as discussed by Becker and Max [2].

Our current spline-based smoothing displacement function ensures that the base tessellations can be converted to smooth surfaces. The smooth surface is not always desirable, particularly in regions of high curvature or where the triangles have poor aspect ratios. It may take more information about the surface than we allowed in the restrictions from Section 4 to eliminate these problems. A more global interpolation scheme could ensure higher orders of continuity or a more intuitive fit to the data.

Acknowledgments

Thanks to Michael Ashikmin, Mark Bloomenthal, Elaine Cohen and Simon Premoze for helpful discussions. Thanks to Alias|Wavefront for their donation of Maya. This work was supported by NSF grants CDA–96–23614, 97–96136 and 97–31859.

References

1. ALIAS|WAVEFRONT. *Maya v. 1.5*. Toronto, Canada, 1998.
2. BECKER, B. G., AND MAX, N. L. Smooth transitions between bump rendering algorithms. In *Computer Graphics (SIGGRAPH '93 Proceedings)* (Aug. 1993), J. T. Kajiya, Ed., vol. 27, pp. 183–190.
3. COOK, R. L., CARPENTER, L., AND CATMULL, E. The reyes image rendering architecture. *Computer Graphics (SIGGRAPH '87 Proceedings)* (July 1987), 95–102. Held in Anaheim, California.
4. GRITZ, L., AND HAHN, J. K. BMRT: A global illumination implementation of the render-man standard. *Journal of Graphics Tools 1*, 3 (1996), 29–47. ISSN 1086-7651.
5. HEIDRICH, W., AND SEIDEL, H.-P. Ray-tracing procedural displacement shaders. *Graphics Interface '98* (June 1998), 8–16. ISBN 0-9695338-6-1.
6. KAJIYA, J. T. New techniques for ray tracing procedurally defined objects. In *Computer Graphics (SIGGRAPH '83 Proceedings)* (July 1983), vol. 17, pp. 91–102.
7. KRISHNAMURTHY, V., AND LEVOY, M. Fitting smooth surfaces to dense polygon meshes. In *SIGGRAPH 96 Conference Proceedings* (Aug. 1996), H. Rushmeier, Ed., Annual Con-

318

ference Series, ACM SIGGRAPH, Addison Wesley, pp. 313–324. held in New Orleans, Louisiana, 04-09 August 1996.

8. LOGIE, J. R., AND PATTERSON, J. W. Inverse displacement mapping in the general case. *Computer Graphics Forum 14*, 5 (December 1995), 261–273.

9. MUSGRAVE, F. K. Grid tracing: Fast ray tracing for height fields. Technical Report YALEU/DCS/RR-639, Yale University Dept. of Computer Science Research, 1988.

10. PEDERSON, H. K. Displacement mapping using flow fields. In *Proceedings of SIGGRAPH '94 (Orlando, Florida, July 24–29, 1994)* (July 1994), A. Glassner, Ed., Computer Graphics Proceedings, Annual Conference Series, ACM SIGGRAPH, ACM Press, pp. 279–286. ISBN 0-89791-667-0.

11. PERLIN, K., AND HOFFERT, E. M. Hypertexture. In *Computer Graphics (SIGGRAPH '89 Proceedings)* (July 1989), J. Lane, Ed., vol. 23, pp. 253–262.

12. PHARR, M., AND HANRAHAN, P. Geometry caching for ray-tracing displacement maps. *Eurographics Rendering Workshop 1996* (June 1996), 31–40. ISBN 3-211-82883-4. Held in Porto, Portugal.

13. PHONG, B.-T. Illumination for computer generated pictures. *Communications of the ACM 18*, 6 (June 1975), 311—317.

14. SMITS, B., SHIRLEY, P., AND STARK, M. Direct ray tracing of smoothed and displacement mapped triangles. Tech. Rep. UUCS–00–008, Computer Science Department, University of Utah, March 2000.

15. STANDER, B. T., AND HART, J. C. Guaranteeing the topology of an implicit surface polygonization for interactive modeling. In *SIGGRAPH 97 Conference Proceedings* (Aug. 1997), T. Whitted, Ed., Annual Conference Series, ACM SIGGRAPH, Addison Wesley, pp. 279–286. ISBN 0-89791-896-7.

16. VEACH, E., AND GUIBAS, L. J. Metropolis light transport. In *SIGGRAPH 97 Conference Proceedings* (Aug. 1997), T. Whitted, Ed., Annual Conference Series, ACM SIGGRAPH, Addison Wesley, pp. 65–76. ISBN 0-89791-896-7.

Editors' Note: see Appendix, p. 416 for colored figures of this paper

Ray Tracing Point Sampled Geometry

Gernot Schaufler

Massachusetts Institute of Technology

Henrik Wann Jensen

Stanford University

Abstract. We present a novel technique for ray tracing geometry represented by points. Our approach makes it possible to render high quality ray traced images with global illumination using unstructured point–sampled data thus avoiding the time-consuming process of reconstructing the underlying surface or any topological information. Compared with previous point rendering methods, our approach allows for more complex illumination models while still maintaining the simplicity of the point primitive.

Intersections with the point–sampled geometry are detected by tracing a ray through the scene until the local density of points is above a predefined threshold. We then use all the points within a fixed distance of the ray to interpolate the position, normal and any other attributes of the intersection. The considered distance from the ray must be larger than the largest "hole" among the points.

We demonstrate results for soft shadows, reflection and refraction, global illumination and subsurface scattering.

Keywords: points, ray tracing, global illumination

1   Introduction

As geometry is getting more complex, the triangles – today's most popular modeling primitives – are getting smaller and smaller. Soon, the overhead associated with them will no longer be justified, given that they only occupy sub-pixel areas in image space. The alternatives explored currently in the research community are higher order surfaces or simpler primitives such as points.

Points became popular in particular with the introduction of particle systems [17] but have also been used by rendering systems as the final target for subdividing more complex modeling primitives [4]. Today they have seen a comeback in image–based rendering and real-time graphics due to their modeling flexibility, efficiency, and ease of acquisition with digital cameras, 3D scanners and range finders,

Given the simplicity of points and the growing complexity of the geometric models, it seems natural that point geometry will become an important element in modeling and rendering. It is therefore desirable to extend the available rendering algorithms to the realm of photo–realistic image synthesis and physically–based lighting simulation.

This paper extends previous rendering approaches by introducing a method for ray tracing point–sampled geometry. This enables more complex illumination models and even makes it possible to simulate global illumination in scenes containing point sampled geometry. We have developed an intersection technique that uses only a local sampling of the point sampled geometry. This makes it possible to skip the time consuming surface reconstruction step and instead make high–quality renderings directly from the points representing the geometry.

2 Previous Work

To date, direct rendering of points has mostly proceeded in a "forward" fashion using the perspective transformation to map 3D points to 2D image locations. The image-based rendering literature is rich in techniques how to deal with the fact that with this approach not necessarily every output pixel receives a sample. Pioneering work [11] has been done by Levoy and Whitted in 1985, in which they propose points as a universal modeling primitive and present algorithms allowing for anti-aliased rendering of this representation. Cook *et al.* [4] propose to decompose more elaborate primitives to points in image space during rendering. More recent approaches include work by Grossman *et al.* [7], Pfister *et al.* [16], and Rusinkiewicz *et al.* [18]. The differ by how visibility among points is established and how the final image is reconstructed.

In image-based rendering, points are usually organized either into images with depth or layered–depth images [19]. For those images, incremental algorithms can be devised which make use of this particular organization of the points into 2D grids. Chen *et al.* [2] approximate the apparent motion of 3D points using optical flow. Dally *et al.* [5] present a method to build hierarchical object representations from points. Shade *et al.* [19] introduce layered depth images to obtain a complete sampling of the objects rather than just a sampling of the visible surfaces. A recent approach [14] factors the warping equation into two steps simplifying the reconstruction.

Somewhat related to layered-depth images of 3D geometry are volume representations. These have been rendered using "splatting" of individual volume elements as in [25, 10, 12] or with hardware acceleration [24].

All these approaches have one thing in common: no global illumination models can be applied to the geometry. In many cases the color stored per sample is copied into the final image directly. The only global effect reported so far is sharp shadows from point lights using shadow maps [15].

3 Point Sampled Geometry

The most popular sources of point–sampled geometry are 3D scanners and laser range finders. While many scans are usually required to cover the surface of complex objects with samples, there exist efficient methods such as the one by Chen *et al.* [3] and Nyland *et al.* [13] which register multiple scans into a common coordinate system without explicitly reconstructing the surfaces in the scene. In [13] planes are fit to points on known planar surfaces which are aligned between different scans. This approach works best for indoor scenes, where samples on walls are aligned. For scans of smaller objects, background planes can be added to the scanned geometry artificially. We build on the success of such methods and assume registered point samples of complex objects to be available.

In order to unambiguously represent a surface by a sampling of points, this sampling must fulfill a number of requirements in order to distinguish close but different surface portions from each other, and to distinguish holes in the surface from regions of sparse sampling. In particular, the sampling density of the points must be at least twice as high as the minimum distance between different portions of the surface [8], *i.e.* at least as high as the distance to the nearest point on the medial axis of the surface [1].

Our rendering approach assumes that the maximum size of a gap in the samples is known. If the point samples are not that uniformly distributed over the surface, they can be made to be more evenly spaced using an approach described by Szeliski *et al.* [21, 22]. By giving attracting and repulsive forces to the points, points tend to even out the spacing between them. Adding points at gaps along borders can fill holes of a given maximum size.

Like Szeliski *et al.*, we also assume a normal to be available per point. If the 3D scanning process does not provide normal information, it can be estimated by fitting a plane to the points in the neighborhood of each point using least-squares minimization. The nearest neighbor search can be accelerated using spatial data structures such as octrees or bsp-trees, giving normal computation a complexity of $O(n \log n)$ [8]. Note that we do not reconstruct a surface as Hoppe *et al.*but only compute normals from fitting tangent planes to each point. Our implementation is capable of pre-computing on the order of 5000 normals/second for geometry represented by 440000 points on a MIPS R10k processor running at 250MHz. Alternatively, normals can be computed on the fly as intersections are detected.

4 Intersecting a Ray with Point Geometry

Computing an intersection with the point geometry is split into two parts: detecting if an intersection has occurred and computing the actual point and normal of the intersection.

4.1 Intersection Detection

An intersection is reported, if the ray intersects a disk centered at each point. These disks have the same normal as the surface point. The radius r of the disks is set slightly bigger than the radius of the biggest hole in the points' sampling of the surface. We accelerate the search for such a point using an octree. The ray is surrounded by a cylinder of radius r and only those nodes in the tree that intersect the cylinder are traversed. The cylinder is capped off at the origin of the ray and the maximum length of the ray using two planes. Further acceleration is achieved by projecting the cylinder onto two coordinate planes and checking the octree nodes with these projections (see Figure 1).

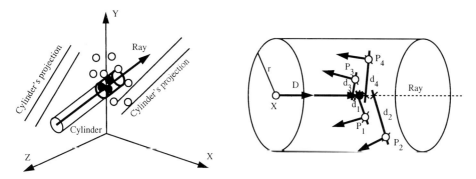

Fig. 1. Left: Cylinder around ray with projections onto coordinate planes. The first disk centered at a point intersected by a ray (black) triggers an intersection. Position, normal and other per-point attributes are interpolated for all points inside the bold cylinder (grey) starting at the first found point. Right: Calculating the intersection point (grey) from four points in the cylinder. Their normals and positions along the ray are weighted by their distance d_i from the ray.

The two planes are chosen based on the largest component of the ray's direction

322

vector. The example in the figure shows a ray with the Y-coordinate largest. Therefore, the cylinder is projected onto the XY- and YZ-planes.

4.2 Intersection Point Computation

Once an intersection is detected, another short cylinder is started at this point along the ray (shown in bold on the left of Figure 1) and all the points within this cylinder are collected. The actual intersection point will be interpolated from these points. We have found our simple interpolation scheme to give visually satisfactory results although higher order interpolation is possible. In particular, the normal of the intersection point is formed by weighting the normals of the points in the cylinder based on the point's distance from the ray. The same weighting is applied to find the actual intersection point along the ray. We intersect the planes formed by each point and its normal with the ray's parametric representation, $ray = X + t * D$, where X and D are the origin and the direction of the ray. The final intersection point is found by interpolating the computed t values, and inserting this value in the ray's parametric representation.

The right of figure 1 shows a 2D example of a ray running through a group of four points. For each point P_i, the normal and local plane are shown which intersect the ray's supporting line at a distance d_i from the point. The normal of the intersection point (shown in grey) is then calculated as in equation (1). In general, any attribute associated with the points can be interpolated this way.

$$attrib = \frac{\sum_i attrib_i * (r - d_i)}{\sum_i (r - d_i)} \tag{1}$$

Points will only be considered if their distance from the ray d_i is smaller than r. Note that the distance is *not* measured orthogonal to the ray but in the plane of the point and its normal to create the circular disks around each point.

This intersection point computation is slightly view dependent. The final position of the surface will vary with the direction of the incoming ray. The variations are small enough that they do not result in visible changes to the surface, but for more complex illumination algorithms this discrepancy must be taken into account as explained in the next section.

5   Rendering with Points

Given a technique for intersecting a ray with points, we can apply more advanced illumination models. We also augment each point with extra information such as texture coordinates, color, diffuse albedo etc. that can be interpolated and used by the ray tracer. Recursive ray tracing considers shadows and reflected and transmitted light. Furthermore, we can use Monte Carlo ray tracing methods to compute global illumination.

As mentioned in the previous section, the computed intersection point is slightly dependent on the direction of the incoming ray. Even though this does not result in visible changes to the surface, it must be taken into account within the ray tracer. This is particularly important for shadow rays where wrong ray-geometry intersections can result in false self-shadowing of the surface. To avoid this problem, we use a shadow offset based on the radius r of the disks. We have found a shadow offset of 1-3 times r to work well in practice. We do not consider this to be a problem of using points since shadow offsets are necessary even for triangle meshes with vertex normals [20]. In addition to the shadow offset we only accept intersections with point–sampled geometry that are at least $2r$ away from the ray origin. This is to prevent wrong intersections for reflected and transmitted rays.

Normals are either computed on the fly or in a pre-processing step. These normals can possibly point into the interior of objects. To prevent this from being a problem in the ray tracer, we flip the point normals such that they always point towards the ray origin, meaning we cannot use the normal to determine whether the ray enters or leaves a given object. For this purpose we use the history of the ray - ie. by counting the number of previous transmissions we can determine whether we are inside or outside a given object.

6 Results

We have implemented the intersection technique for point sampled geometry as a geometry component in our ray tracer. This ray tracer also supports global illumination via stochastic sampling of indirect light optimized with irradiance caching [23] and photon maps [9]. All timings and results were obtained using a dual PII-400MHz.

Our first sequence of images in Figure 2 illustrates how the radius of the cylinder around the ray is approaching the distance between the points. Eventually, the single points join together into a smooth surface. Bigger radii result in more smoothing.

We have also implemented texture coordinate interpolation as another example of a surface attribute specified per point. Figure 3 gives two examples of a texture mapped onto geometry specified as points. Interpolation of texture coordinates in between points is accomplished using Equation 1 from Section 4.

The image in Figure 4 demonstrates global illumination and caustics on point sampled geometry. It is a glass bunny generating a caustic on a wooden bunny. The rendering time for this image was 11 minutes given a resolution of 768x512 and 4 samples per pixel.

Our final example in Figure 5 illustrates our approach on a complex model. It is a scanned version of the head of Michelangelo's David statue. The head has more than two million points. Each point has an additional diffuse albedo attached.

Figure 5(a) shows the head rendered with global illumination and using the interpolated diffuse albedo information as the local surface color. This model was rendered in 1024x1024 with 4 samples per pixel in 61 minutes. For this model we optimized the size of the radius such that the surface just connects, and so we are able to capture every fine detail of the model. We precomputed the normals using the 3-6 nearest neighboring points.

Figure 5(b) shows an example of a complex translucent illumination model applied to the head. We rendered the head using subsurface scattering with multiple scattering [6] based on highly translucent artificial volumetric marble. Notice how the point sampled surface provides enough information to perform this simulation. The image does have a few artifacts in areas with holes in the model (such as in the nose and in the hair), but the overall appearance is captured faithfully. The image was rendered in 1024x1024 with 4 samples per pixel in approx. 4 hours.

To test the speed of our point intersection code we compared it with triangles in a number of simple test scenes: one containing the bunny and one containing the Buddha appearing in the video. Table 1 shows the resulting timings. The points code has not yet been optimized, and it can be observed from the table that our optimized triangle intersection code is approximately 3-4 times faster. For the triangle meshes we used a hierarchical grid. We believe that most of this overhead is due to traversing the octree.

(a) Bunny: 500 points, r = 0.04   (b) Bunny: 1900 points, r = 0.03   (c) Bunny: 34800 points, r = 0.014

Fig. 2. Rendering a bunny with a variety of point counts and cylinder radii.

Fig. 3. Interpolation of texture coordinates in between points.

Fig. 4. A caustic from a glass bunny onto a wood bunny.

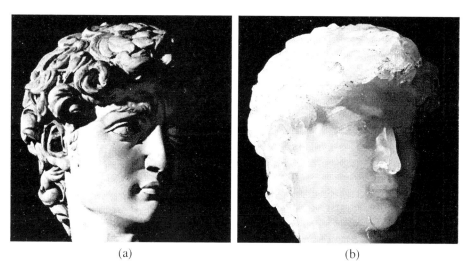

(a)   (b)

Fig. 5. The head of the David rendered from 2 million points. (a) Global illumination using points with color information, (b) Subsurface scattering using artificial volumetric marble.

Model	Points/Triangles	Render time (sec.)	Rays/sec.
Bunny (points)[a]	34834	23.1	34204
Bunny (points)[b]	34834	24.5	32142
Bunny (triangles)	69451	8.4	93809
Buddha (points)[b]	543652	46.1	12309
Buddha (points)[c]	543652	36.1	15731
Buddha (triangles)	1087716	8.6	63300

[a]5 octree levels
[b]6 octree levels
[c]7 octree levels

Table 1. Intersection timing (points vs. triangles).

7 Discussion

In the process of trying to obtain these results we considered a number of simpler intersection techniques that did not work quite as well as the method we decided to use.

We tried the following alternative approaches:

- **Using a sphere around each point.** This method grows the object by the radius of the spheres. It requires a large number of spheres to make the surface appear mostly smooth – too few spheres will make the surface bumpy. The normals generated at intersection points are determined by where each sphere is hit and exhibit discontinuities between spheres.
- **Using an octree with non–cube shaped leaf nodes.** Within each leaf node the local subset of points can be used to construct a small surface patch (a plane or a higher order surface) which will possibly cause an intersection with the ray in this part of space. This technique suffers from lack of continuity between the leaf nodes. Moreover, the border of the patch is determined by the faces of the octree node. In many cases the patch will inappropriately extend into the corners of nodes.
- **Using an oriented disc at each point.** This approach is closest to what we currently apply for ray intersection, but without interpolation between points, it will not give a smooth surface. As other attributes are not interpolated, normals or color per point and texture mapping will not work as expected. The disks will appear as flat-shaded patches.

In our approach we use a cylinder to locate the points from which attributes are to be interpolated. This results in a visually smooth surface – its smoothness can be controlled by varying the disk radius. As pointed out, our definition of the ray-point geometry intersection causes the obtained surface to be slightly view-dependent. The interpolation of the ray-parameter t, from which the exact point of intersection is derived, will be different for different directions of incidence of the ray. However, in the animations we have rendered, this did not cause any visually distracting artifacts. We attribute this to the fact that the shading of the surface is mostly determined by the normal, which is unaffected by the exact location of the intersection.

An interesting question is how direct use of point sampled geometry compares to using triangles. As our timings statistics in table 1 indicate our intersection code for point sampled geometry is approximately 3-4 times slower than our optimized triangle intersection code. This is not bad considering that the points intersection code is the first rough implementation which has not been optimized. We believe that the point-geometry intersection is no more complicated than triangles since the disk test is much simpler than the barycentric test used for triangles. In addition most complex models have fewer points than triangles (the bunny has approximately 70000 triangles but only 35000 points). Memory usage is similar for the two methods; points use slightly less memory since they do not require connectivity information.

Another advantage with points is that it is easy to make hierarchical simplifications by merging neighboring points. As demonstrated in a recent splatting approach [18] it is possible to build a highly efficient hierarchical representation of point sampled geometry for use with very complex models (more than hundred million points). The complete model of the David has on the order of 1 billion points. A hierarchical point sampled representation may be the most efficient way to deal with a model of this complexity. Since we already use an octree to locate the points for our intersection computation is should be straightforward to test this concept.

Currently, we use a fixed radius to locate neighboring points. This assumes a similar density of points over the surface. For some objects it might be advantageous to wary the density of the points to capture certain local variations such as edges in the geometry more efficiently. For this purpose we would like to include an adaptive radius where the local density of points is used to adjust the size of the region from which points are used.

Our intersection routine for points is slightly view dependent. This has not caused problems in the models that we have rendered, but it would be nice to have completely consistent geometry. We have considered using a fixed direction for the cylinder that collects points (for example based on the normal of the first disk that is intersected). Another alternative would be to collect points using a sphere around the first intersection point.

8 Conclusion and future work

In this paper we demonstrate how global illumination effects can be achieved on geometry represented only by a sampling of 3D points. We formulated a method to intersect a ray with such a surface representation and smoothly interpolate surface attributes across it. By that we have extended the usefulness of this type of object representation to the field of realistic image synthesis and physically-based light transport.

In the future we would like to compute a more accurate surface intersection based on an adaptive local sampling of the points. In addition, we would like to make better use of our octree hierarchy and sample the geometry at a level which reflects the level of detail at which the point sampled geometry is observed. This could be done by storing filtered attributes at the interior nodes of the point hierarchy using a filtering similar to mip-mapping.

Even though it is still faster to use triangles for rendering our scanned models we believe that direct ray tracing of point sampled geometry has significant potential in particular as our models become more complex.

9 Acknowledgments

Thanks to Szymon Rusinkiewicz and Justin Legakis for helpful comments on the paper. The dataset of David's head appears courtesy of Marc Levoy and is part of the ongoing Digital Michelangelo Project. Other models appear thanks to their availability in the Stanford 3D Scanning Repository. This work was funded by DARPA DABTB63-95-C0085.

References

1. Nina Amenta, Marsahll Bern and Manolis Kamvysselis: "A new Voronoi-based surface reconstruction algorithm", *Proc. SSIGGRAPH '98*, pp 415-421, 1998.
2. E. Chen and L. Williams: "View Interpolation for Image Synthesis", *Proc. SIGGRAPH '93*, pp 279-288, 1993.
3. Yang Chen and Gérard Medioni: "Object Modeling by Registration of Multiple Range Images", *Proceedings of the International Conference on Robotics and Automation*, 1991.
4. Robert L. Cook, Loren Carpenter and Edwin Catmull: "The Reyes Image Rendering Architecture", *Proc. SIGGRAPH '87*, pp 95-102, 1987.

5. William J. Dally, Leonard McMillan, Gary Bishop, and Henry Fuchs: "The Delta Tree: An Object-Centered Approach to Image-Based Rendering", *MIT AI Lab Technical Memo 1604*, May 1996.

6. Julie Dorsey, Alan Edelman, Henrik Wann Jensen, Justin Legakis and Hans Køhling Pedersen: "Modeling and Rendering of Weathered Stone", *Proc. SIGGRAPH '99*, pp 225-234, 1999.

7. J. P. Grossman and W. Dally: "Point Sample Rendering". *Rendering Techniques '98*, Springer, Wien, Vienna, Austria, pp 181-192, 1998.

8. H. Hoppe, T. DeRose, T. Duchamp, J. McDonald, and W. Stuetzle: "Surface reconstruction from unorganized points", *Proc. SIGGRAPH '92*, pp 71-78, 1992.

9. Henrik Wann Jensen: "Global illumination using photon maps". *Rendering Techniques '96 (Proceedings of the Seventh Eurographics Workshop on Rendering)*, Springer Verlag, pp 21-30, 1996.

10. David Laur and Pat Hanrahan: "Hierarchical Splatting: A Progressive Refinement Algorithm for Volume Rendering", *Proc. SIGGRAPH '91*, pp 285-288, 1991.

11. M. Levoy and T. Whitted: "The Use of Points as Display Primitives", *Technical Report TR 85-022*, The University of North Carolina at Chapel Hill, Department of Computer Science, 1985.

12. K. Mueller and R. Yagel, "Fast Perspective Volume Rendering with Splatting by Utilizing a Ray-Driven Approach", *Visualization '96*, pp 65-72, 1996.

13. Lars Nyland, David McAllister, Voicu Popescu; Chris McCue and Anselmo Lastra: "Interactive exploration of acquired 3D data". *Proceedings of SPIE Applied Image and Pattern Recognition Conference (AIPR99)*, Washington DC, October, 1999.

14. Manuel M. Oliveira, Gary Bishop, David McAllister: "Relief Texture Mapping". *to appear in Proc. SIGGRAPH 2000*, July 2000.

15. Manuel M. Oliveira and Gary Bishop: "Dynamic Shading in Image-Based Rendering". *UNC Computer Science Technical Report TR98-023*, University of North Carolina, May 31, 1998.

16. Hanspeter Pfister, Matthias Zwicker, Jeroen van Baar and Markus Gross: "Surfels: Surface Elements as Rendering Primitives", *to appear in Proc. SIGGRAPH 2000*, July 2000.

17. W. T. Reeves and R. Blau: "Approximate and Probabilistic Algorithms for Shading and Rendering Structured Particle Systems". *Proc. SIGGRAPH '85*, pp 313-322, 1985.

18. Szymon Rusinkiewicz and Marc Levoy, "QSplat: A Multiresolution Point Rendering System for Large Meshes", *to appear in Proc. SIGGRAPH 2000*, July 2000.

19. J. Shade, S. Gortler, L. He, and R. Szeliski: "Layered Depth Images", *Proc. SIGGRAPH '98*, pp 231-242, 1998.

20. John M. Snyder and Alan H. Barr: "Ray Tracing Complex Models Containing Surface Tessellations", *Proc. SIGGRAPH '87*, pp 119-128, 1987.

21. Richard Szeliski and David Tonnesen: "Surface modeling with oriented particle systems", *Proc. SIGGRAPH '92*, pp 185-194, 1992.

22. Richard Szeliski, David Tonnesen and Demitri Terzopoulos: "Modeling surfaces of arbitrary topology with dynamic particles". *IEEE CVPR 1993*, pp 82-87, 1993.

23. Greg Ward, Francis M. Rubinstein, and Robert D. Clear. "A Ray Tracing Solution for Diffuse Interreflection". *Proc. SIGGRAPH '88*, pp 85-92, 1988.

24. Rüdiger Westermann and Thomas Ertl: "Efficiently using graphics hardware in volume rendering applications", *Proc. SIGGRAPH '98*, pp 169 - 177, 1998.

25. L. Westover: "Footprint Evaluation for Volume Rendering", *Proc. SIGGRAPH '90*, pp 367-376, 1990.

Editors' Note: see Appendix, p. 417 for colored figures of this paper

Tapestry: A Dynamic Mesh-based Display Representation for Interactive Rendering

Maryann Simmons and Carlo H. Séquin

U.C. Berkeley, Berkeley CA, USA
simmons@cs.berkeley.edu

Abstract.
This paper presents a new method for interactive viewing of dynamically sampled environments. We introduce a 3D mesh-based reconstruction called a *tapestry* that serves both as the display representation and as a cache that supports the re-use of samples across views. As the user navigates through the environment, the mesh continuously evolves to provide an appropriate image reconstruction for the current view. In addition, the reconstruction process provides feedback to the renderer to guide adaptive sampling.

We present our implementation of an interactive application utilizing the RADI-ANCE lighting and simulation system to generate the samples. Our approach offers several advantages. The 3D mesh supports an extended cache life for samples and generates a complete image, even with a sparse sampling density. Through efficient use of ubiquitous OpenGL hardware, we provide smooth progressive refinement and resolution-independent viewing. With this framework, we achieve interactive performance on a two-processor machine running a single ray tracing process, even at a resolution of 3000 × 1000 pixels.

1 Introduction

Interactive, realistic rendering of complex environments, real and virtual, is a long-standing goal in the field of computer graphics. The capability exists to calculate full global illumination solutions, producing the complex lighting effects necessary to impart a realistic percept of an environment. Graphics hardware advances allow interactive exploration of complex polygon-based environments. Incorporating both of these capabilities into a single system, however, continues to pose a challenge.

Interactive ray-based renderers offer one class of solutions to this problem. Unfortunately, high quality rendering comes at a cost, and it is typically not possible to produce samples fast enough to fill a high-resolution window at interactive frame rates. For many applications, for the sake of interactivity, it is acceptable that intermediate frames present only an approximation of the final solution, as long as the image converges to the correct solution if the observer lingers long enough at a particular view. Given this environment, the challenge is to reconstruct the best possible image from a given sample set, both for a static view and in an interactive setting with a dynamic observer and/or world. In addition, in consideration of the limited sample budget per frame, the renderer should be directed to focus sampling on the regions of highest visual priority.

This paper presents a new method for interactive viewing of dynamically sampled environments. We introduce a 3D mesh-based reconstruction called a *tapestry* that serves both as the display representation and as a cache that supports the re-use of samples across views. A tapestry is a dynamic 3D triangle mesh with vertices corresponding to the sample points. A Delaunay condition is maintained on the projection of the mesh relative to the viewpoint both to improve image quality and to achieve robustness of the meshing code. As the user navigates through the environment, the mesh continuously evolves to provide an appropriate reconstruction for the current view given the available samples. In addition, the reconstruction process provides feedback to the renderer to guide adaptive sampling of locations most in need of more resolution.

We present our implementation in an interactive application utilizing the RADIANCE [22] lighting and simulation system to generate the samples. Our approach offers several advantages. The 3D mesh supports an extended cache life for samples and provides a complete reconstruction, even with sparse sampling density. The display representation is progressively refined depending on the available resources for generating samples, and on how long the user lingers at a particular view. Through efficient use of ubiquitous OpenGL hardware, we provide smooth progressive refinement, and achieve resolution-independent viewing. With this framework, we have obtained interactive performance on a two-processor machine running a single ray tracing process, even at a resolution of 3000×1000 pixels.

1.1 Related Work

Due to the prohibitive computational cost of high quality rendering, it is only recently that hardware capabilities have made interactive ray tracing a possibility. Parker et al [12] have demonstrated a "brute force" approach that can achieve interactive results on a high end multi-processor machine. In practice, however, these resources are not yet readily available. Even as processor speeds increase, so will the demand for ever more complex environments and rendering paradigms. Most systems, therefore, must rely on other techniques to achieve interactivity.

Several techniques have been explored in the literature, and many approaches utilize some combination of these, including: adaptive sampling to provide fast visual convergence, reconstruction to support sparse sampling, exploitation of available polygon-based rendering pipelines, and caching to allow re-use of samples/rays across frames. Our approach incorporates all of these techniques: the adaptive progressive refinement of the image is guided by a cache that also acts as the display representation, taking advantage of hardware rendering at many stages in the algorithm. In the remainder of the section, we will discuss some of the more relevant work.

For progressive refinement of a single view, the RADIANCE *rview* program employs a quadtree in the image plane as its display representation. Painter and Sloan [11] use a 2D k-D tree and a measure of variance estimates of the nodes to guide the sampling. They demonstrate a piecewise constant reconstruction based upon the k-D cells, but suggest a Delaunay triangulation would provide a higher quality interpolant. Subsequent approaches utilize the Delaunay reconstruction [2, 13] and base the adaptive sampling on vertex color discontinuities and triangle size. A priority queue is maintained to determine which triangles to sample next. Pighin et al [13] present a more sophisticated constrained triangulation that improves the quality with constraint edges inserted at image plane discontinuities in a preprocessing stage, and by special processing of high frequency regions in the image. These approaches are also relevant in the transmission of images over slow media [20]. Our approach improves on this basic model by even further exploiting the rendering hardware, and more importantly, it allows interactive motion by re-using the reconstruction across subsequent frames.

Several other approaches exploit frame-to-frame coherence to allow an interactive viewer in situations where the rendering engine cannot keep up [1, 19, 9, 7, 21, 24]. Our method is most closely related to the render cache [21] and the holodeck [7, 23]. Both techniques support interactive viewing through the use of a cache. In the render cache, a fixed size cache is maintained, and samples are re-projected and re-used between frames. The reconstruction is based on interpolation and smoothing in a pixel's 3×3 neighborhood. A priority image generated from the cache samples is used to guide adaptive sampling. The main difference from our approach lies in the reconstruction technique. Our tapestry technique has the advantage over the render cache in that it does not depend on a dense sampling to produce an image without holes. In addition, while the render cache is suitable for a purely software-based implementation, we exploit rendering hardware in several stages of our algorithm.

The holodeck [7, 23], is a four-dimensional ray-caching data structure that serves as a rendering target and caching mechanism. The system supports multiple display drivers; the simplest one is based on the *rview* quadtree reconstruction technique. Another driver draws 3D cones that produce a constant interpolation of the Voronoi regions of the sample points in the image plane [4]. Scene geometry is rendered into the back buffer, and the depth buffer is used to identify depth discontinuities in the image. This information is used to constrain the cone drawing along discontinuity edges. The third display representation is a spherical Delaunay mesh [18], which acts as a first-level cache on top of the holodeck cache. Only limited viewpoint motion is supported by the spherical mesh: it must be completely rebuilt after large view motions. Our tapestry reconstruction is a direct extension of this technique. The tapestry mesh presented here is fully dynamic, and thus better exploits frame-to-frame coherence. Another advantage of the tapestry approach over the holodeck system is that it supports adaptive sampling, and therefore can present higher quality reconstructions with fewer samples. In addition, the user can move about freely. The holodeck assumes the viewer will remain within predefined grid cells.

1.2 Algorithm Overview

Our algorithm must perform the following tasks: sample location selection, sample generation, mesh construction and display. Our application heavily exploits the availability of OpenGL accelerated hardware. The hardware is utilized to a) generate a priority image for adaptive sampling, b) do the triangle-based point location required for mesh insertion, c) perform barycentric interpolation of sample points for reconstruction, and d) do re-projection and occlusion culling. Figure 1 illustrates the logical processes and flow of information between each. In practice, the hardware rendering tasks are staggered to allow the ray tracer to run concurrently. This is discussed in more detail in Section 5. The following steps are performed each frame based on the view:

- Choose next n image locations to sample based on priority image.
- Generate samples with RADIANCE *rtrace* process.
- Incorporate new samples into the display representation.
- Render new display representation.

Figure 2 illustrates the relevant tapestry components. When the viewpoint is moving, the following steps are also necessary:

- Delete invalidated samples from the cache.
- Perform fix-up on display representation to maintain required invariants.

Since the tapestry mesh is utilized both to guide sampling and as the display representation, we will first describe the construction and display of the mesh, and then

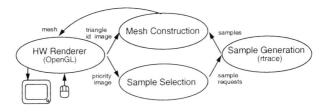

Fig. 1. Algorithm overview.

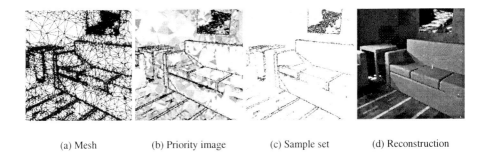

| (a) Mesh | (b) Priority image | (c) Sample set | (d) Reconstruction |

Fig. 2. Tapestry components. An example view of a reconstruction after 2% of the pixels have been sampled. Darker areas on priority image indicate higher sampling priority.

discuss how the resulting reconstruction is used to guide sampling. We first describe the approach in the context of a single view, and then address how view motion is supported in this same infrastructure.

2 Image Reconstruction

Given a single view, we construct the 2D Delaunay triangulation of the projected samples. In previous approaches [2, 13], the image plane was used as the projection surface. To avoid having to re-construct the mesh each frame, the projected points can be utilized to determine the mesh topology in 2D, while still retaining the 3D information at the vertices. The resulting mesh can be viewed from alternate (nearby) viewpoints using the rendering hardware [17, 3, 16]. Artifacts will appear as soon as the viewer moves enough off the initial view to reveal the 2.5D nature of the mesh.

The tapestry representation utilizes the unit sphere centered at the viewpoint as the logical projection surface. A icosahedral base mesh is created to cover the surface of the sphere. Given a new sample, we perform point location to find the existing spherical mesh triangle that encloses its projection. The sample is inserted into this triangle, creating three new triangles if the new sample falls interior to an existing triangle or four if it falls on an edge. The Delaunay condition is tested for each new triangle and reasserted if necessary. Sample points may also be deleted from the mesh. In this case, the sample is removed and the Delaunay condition reasserted locally. The following sections describe the point location and Delaunay test in more detail. A more complete discussion is found in [18]. In Section 4 we describe how the mesh is evolved to handle viewer motion.

2.1 Point Location

Once the base mesh has been initialized, new samples can be inserted incrementally. Given a sample point we must first determine which mesh triangle encloses the point on the projection sphere. One approach is to randomly select a triangle in the mesh and test if the projection of the new sample lies within the spherical triangle. We compare the position of the point relative to each of the planes forming the pyramid with apex at the viewpoint, and defined by the edges of the world space triangle, or equivalently, against the great circles forming the spherical triangle. If the point lies inside of all three planes, it is accepted as being inside the triangle. If any one of the three tests fail, the test traverses to the triangle adjacent to the current one across the plane(edge) for which the test failed. With this approach, we are guaranteed to find the appropriate triangle. Firstly, there will be a triangle, since the surface of the view sphere is completely tiled with spherical triangles. Secondly, because of the spherical Delaunay topology, we are guaranteed to converge upon the correct triangle, without re-visiting any mesh triangles along the way.

If the mesh is large, the initial choice of triangle will greatly affect the performance of the point location. If the mesh elements are inserted into a spatial data structure, the point location time can be greatly reduced. We have chosen instead to utilize a hardware accelerated point location scheme. Each frame, the current mesh is rendered into the back buffer, using the triangle identifier as part of the color value. This information is read back into a triangle-id image. Given the sample's image space location x, y, it is then a constant time operation to identify the triangle that mapped to that same pixel. If the rendering hardware is exact and the mesh is a height field relative to the view, this operation would be sufficient to perform point location. Since the former is not true, and we would like the option to relax the latter (see Section 4), we use the triangle-id buffer location to initialize our walk as described above.

In addition, since we are changing the mesh with each sample added, and are rendering the id information only once for each set of samples, the id returned by the triangle-id buffer may no longer be the correct triangle. To address this, given a set of samples to add, we first assign each sample to the triangle stored at the corresponding x, y pixel location. If a triangle is deleted during the insertion of a sample, all of its associated samples that have not yet been inserted are redistributed to the new triangles replacing the original one. This approach comes at the cost of having to render the mesh into the back buffer. In the same pass, we also render triangle priorities, which are used to guide adaptive sampling. In addition, this approach makes it feasible to relax the height field constraint on the mesh. While the rendering hardware is performing the point location, other work can be done concurrently.

2.2 Delaunay Condition

We maintain a Delaunay condition on the mesh to improve image quality and robustness of the representation. In addition to providing a reasonable interpolation of sample values, such a triangulation has the property of maximizing the minimum angle and therefore minimizes rendering artifacts caused by long, thin triangles. Such triangles can also prove problematic during the computation and manipulation of the mesh, as they are prone to producing round-off error and inconsistencies in the calculations. We have adapted a planar Delaunay algorithm [8, 18] to work on the sphere.

After any changes to the mesh topology, a test is performed to verify whether the Delaunay condition still holds. A triangle satisfies the Delaunay condition in 2D if the circumcircle of the triangle contains no other sample points [14]. In the spherical environment, we utilize a point-in-cone test to verify the Delaunay condition. When a new sample is added to the mesh, the Delaunay test is performed against the sample point and all adjacent triangles. If the test fails, an edge swap is performed in the quadrilateral formed by the two adjacent triangles. These new triangles are then added to the list of triangles that must be tested against their neighbors to determine if the Delaunay condition is maintained.

2.3 Display

Since the tapestry is a 3D triangle mesh, display is straightforward: the mesh is transformed and displayed by the OpenGL hardware for each requested view. If the mesh is maintained as a height field, depth testing can be disabled. In addition, for a static viewpoint, since each batch of new triangles will overwrite the image of the triangles that they are replacing, it is sufficient to do an incremental render update each frame.

3 Adaptive Sampling

Given the limited number of samples that can be generated for each frame, it is important to generate those samples that contribute the most to the visual quality of the current image. Our approach assigns a priority to each triangle. Each frame, the triangles are rendered into the back buffer, packing the priority as part of the color component (in addition to the triangle id). This priority image is then utilized to select the next n sample locations for processing, which are placed in a queue and sent to the *rtrace* process to generate the appropriate sample rays. Initially, (and after every view change), a request is first made for the 12 samples corresponding to the base icosahedron mesh on the view sphere. This provides values for the initial base mesh, and also ensures that the mesh cannot "collapse" upon itself during motion.

3.1 Priority Assignment

When a triangle is created, it is assigned a priority. The priority is an estimate of how well the Gouraud-shaded triangle approximates the corresponding portion of the sampled environment relative to the current view. Our implementation uses a simple heuristic based upon the difference between the vertex colors and depths.

We utilize a contrast measure for color differences. This metric was shown to be a good measure of perceived color distance when weighted according to the visual system's relative sensitivity to red, green, and blue [10]. The individual components are also weighted by the average value, to prevent over sampling when the color values are small. The resulting priority p_c is calculated as follows, where $min, max,$ and avg are calculated over the three triangle vertices :

$$p_c = 0.4 \frac{r_{max} - r_{min}}{r_{max} + r_{min}} * r_{avg} + 0.3 \frac{g_{max} - g_{min}}{g_{max} + g_{min}} * g_{avg} + 0.6 \frac{b_{max} - b_{min}}{b_{max} + b_{min}} * b_{avg}$$

We also incorporate a term p_d based on the depth difference of the vertices relative to the current view:

$$p_d = 1.0 - \frac{d_{min}}{d_{max}}$$

The final priority is a weighted sum of p_c and p_d, clamped to $[0.0, 1.0]$: $p = w_c p_c + w_d p_d$. In practice, we have found weights of $w_c = 0.9, w_d = 0.1$, respectively, to work

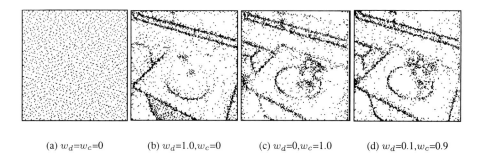

(a) $w_d=w_c=0$　　　(b) $w_d=1.0,w_c=0$　　　(c) $w_d=0,w_c=1.0$　　　(d) $w_d=0.1,w_c=0.9$

Fig. 3. Adaptive Sampling based on priority image generated by OpenGL. Values for contrast weight w_c and depth ratio weight w_d are indicated below each figure. See rightmost image in Figure 4 for reference image.

well. It is not necessary to include an area term, as area is implicitly weighted in the sample selection process described in the next section. Previous methods [2, 13] did not incorporate the depth because geometric discontinuities may or may not make any marked visual contribution to a static image. When moving, however, these edges are extremely important visually. Also, they often correspond to color discontinuities as well, so the weighting scheme works well in both dynamic and static viewing conditions.

We also want a relatively uniform distribution of sample priorities from frame to frame, due to the limited bit bandwidth to store the priority value in the frame buffer (from 5 bits to 12 bits on the configurations we have tested). The maximum priority value is calculated for each frame, and used to weight the next set of priorities such that priorities with a value equal to the maximum priority of the previous frame will scale to 1.0.

3.2 Sample Selection

Priorities are assigned at the triangle level, but the actual choice of sample locations for each frame is based on the projected priority image. This method is appropriate in our approach, since for any particular view, the germane choice of high priority samples is image space dependent, not object space dependent. Not all triangles will be visible in any particular view. In addition, the projected area of each triangle is automatically weighted by this scheme, as a triangle that is large in the current view will map to more pixels in the image and have a higher probability of being selected.

For each frame, we would like to choose n of the highest priority pixels, but we also want good coverage of the image, and do not want to have to sort pixels, or even have to look at all of the pixels each pass. We choose the quasi-random Sobol sequence [15] as our base sampling pattern. A Sobol sequence generates numbers between zero and one, and has the property of filling in space uniformly on a progressively finer grid. We utilize a two-dimensional Sobol sequences to generate the (x, y) pixel coordinates of the next candidate for sampling. The implementation is very efficient, involving only bitwise operations.

Each frame, the Sobol sequence produces the next candidates for selection one at a time. The priority of the pixel is compared to the average priority of pixels examined in the last frame and only accepted if it is above some threshold. Figure 3 illustrates

336

the results of the adaptive sampling process. The leftmost figure shows the samples selected by the Sobol sequence. The next two figures show the effect of weighting the sample choice by depth difference only ($w_c = 0.0, w_d = 1.0$), and color contrast only ($w_c = 1.0, w_d = 0.0$), respectively. The final figure is the result of a combined weighting scheme ($w_c = 0.9, w_d = 0.1$); it is driven primarily by color contrast, but the addition of w_d results in slightly more emphasis along the depth discontinuities.

4 Dynamic Mesh Evolution

Thus far we have described the tapestry mesh in the context of a static viewpoint. We now discuss how the mesh is evolved to handle user motion, and then address how the motion affects the assignment of priorities and sample selection as described above.

If we require the mesh to be a height field relative to the current viewpoint, we must fix-up the mesh to ensure this invariant is satisfied as the viewer moves. This requires deleting all triangles that would become back facing in the new view. To make this operation efficient, when each triangle is created, we store the maximum Euclidean distance d_n that the viewer could move in any direction, and still have the triangle be front facing. After the viewer's position has moved a distance Δd, only those triangles with $d_n > \Delta d$ are considered as candidates for removal.

In addition, when adding samples to the mesh, we enforce a minimum allowable spherical separation between projected points on the view sphere to ensure stability of the meshing code, as well as a minimum vertex-edge distance. To ensure that these constraints are maintained after motion, we also do a Δd calculation for these angles and calculate the maximum (conservative) distance d_e the viewer could move and still have the constraints satisfied. The minimum d of the normal calculation d_n and 6 projected angle calculations d_e is stored with the triangle. The triangles are binned by d_e so that only a small fraction of the triangles need to be considered for removal each frame of motion.

To maintain the quality of the mesh, we also perform Delaunay testing of the triangles relative to the new view. If the number of triangles is large, it is preferable to do this lazily, only updating those vertices and triangles that are touched in subsequent mesh operations. We can also relax the height field assumption for efficiency, as the mesh update is expensive and therefore can degrade the performance for large meshes. During point location and Delaunay testing, a check is performed to see if the corresponding walks are traversing around "corners" in the mesh onto back facing triangles. If this occurs, the current operation is abandoned. In this case the hardware point location is very valuable, as the only constraint it places on the underlying representation is that it can be rendered by the graphics hardware. A main caveat to this relaxation is that it is no longer possible to make guarantees about the robustness of the representation. With the height field and Delaunay invariants, and a minimum sample separation on the view sphere, it is possible to verify that the mesh construction will be robust under any view motions [18].

4.1 Cache Management

Samples are deleted from the cache if the cache size limit is reached, and also should be deleted if the sample value is no longer valid in the current view. In practice, we set the maximum number of mesh vertices equal to the output pixel resolution plus 12 (for the icosahedron vertices). As mentioned in the previous section, samples are removed from the cache if any of the adjacent triangles become back-facing during motion. A sample from a previous view might cause an occlusion error if a new surface has now come into view that should be in front of the existing mesh surface, but it has not been sampled yet. In addition, on specular surfaces the color of the sample will change with the view. If dynamic objects are in the environment, the sample geometry will be invalidated as well.

We have implemented a simple cache replacement scheme. Samples are incrementally aged when the viewpoint changes. A triangle's priority is scaled by the age of its three vertex samples. If a new sample is inserted into a triangle and its addition would add a color or depth discontinuity to the existing triangle, and any of the triangles vertex samples are older than the current sample, the older adjacent samples are marked for removal. Each pass, a subset of aged samples is selected for removal. In the case of a height field, it is also possible to just re-sample the pixel location in the current view without performing deletion. There is a tradeoff in that case of quality vs. speed: it is much faster to just update the sample value rather than remove the sample and update the mesh, but there may be a higher priority location to sample which would produce a better reconstruction. If one of the icosahedral base mesh samples is marked for deletion, re-sampling is always preferred over deletion to maintain the structure of the mesh.

We do not currently handle a dynamic environment, but it could be incorporated if the moving objects were identified a priori, and all samples corresponding to the object invalidated each frame. We could also use object space information to mark those surfaces that are specular, and therefore likely to need re-sampling more often than those that are purely diffuse.

5   Results and Discussion

We have implemented a simple interactive application that utilizes a single RADIANCE *rtrace* process to generate samples. When the viewpoint is static, the mesh is first rendered into the back buffer to create the triangle-id and priority image for the new view. This information is read into a single buffer which is used by both the point location and sample selection. Next, sample locations are selected for ray tracing and put into a queue which is passed to a *rtrace* process. While the *rtrace* process is filling that request, the rendering hardware runs in parallel and displays the mesh from the previous frame in the new view. Once the hardware rendering is complete, the main process collects the finished queue of samples (and blocks if they are not ready). These samples are then added to the mesh. If the view is changing, a request is first made for the icosahedral base samples for the new view: the main process blocks until these samples are ready. A mesh update is then performed to guarantee that the mesh will remain valid in the new view. We do not perform re-projection or Delaunay fix-up at this stage: as the mesh is further processed, touched portions are updated lazily. The remainder of the frame is processed as in the static case.

Figure 4 contains images and results from a timing session. We collected results on two different Silicon Graphics machines: an Octane workstation with SI graphics and 175 MHz R10k processors, and an Onyx2 with IR2 graphics and 195 MHz R10k processors. The graph shows the breakdown of per-frame running times on the Onyx2 (the shape of the graphs for the Octane was similar). The output resolution was 512×512, and 50 samples were added per frame (giving an average frame time of 6.5 fps on the Onyx2 and 1.8 fps on the Octane). The animation contains 1600 frames total: in 76% of the frames the viewpoint was static (including rotations), in 24% the viewpoint location moved. The first row of images shows the three frames indicated on the graph.

The second row shows the reconstruction quality when 5 samples are added per frame (at 26.8 fps average on the Onyx2 and 8.5 fps on the Octane).

We reduced the number of samples requested per frame until *rtrace* was no longer the bottleneck. Overall, the frame time increases with the number of triangles(samples) in the mesh, with spikes occurring at cases when the clean-up must process many triangles. The worst case frame is 1.4 seconds and occurs when moving through the door into the bathroom: it coincides with the maximum number of deletions for a frame, with 5128 triangles removed. On average for the moving frames, 89 triangles were removed. Due to the fixed cache size, the render time will not continue to grow as the program is run for longer sessions.

In addition to total frame time, the graph also shows the running times of various subcomponents of the algorithm: **Render**: rendering the mesh; **Sample**: selecting sample locations, including rendering into the back buffer to create priority/triangle-id image; **Meshing**: maintaining the mesh, including point location and insertion, Delaunay fix-up, priority and visibility assignment; **Moving clean-up**: removing triangles that would be invalidated in new view; **Blocked1**: waiting for *rtrace* when requesting the next batch of samples; **Blocked2**: waiting for *rtrace* when asking for icosahedral base samples during motion.

The Render time and Blocked1 time together give an indication of how the algorithm may perform with an alternate sample generator. Currently, since the rendering and sample generation are done in parallel for the batch requests, the Render time bounds the optimal sample generation time: if the sample generation time is greater than the render time (as is in the earlier part of the animation) the main process will have to wait. If the sample generation time is much less than the render time, the sample generator will be under-utilized. The dotted line graph indicates the running time of the algorithm minus blocking, assuming a better time-matched sample generator, achieving a hypothetical average frame rate of 7.2 fps.

A main advantage of our approach is that it can be used with large output resolutions and still produce a full image reconstruction each frame. We ran the same motion path as tested in the above session on the Onyx2, but this time with an output resolution of 1000×1000 pixels, and a different run at output resolution 3000×1000 pixels, and achieved frame rates of 5.8 and 4.6 fps, respectively. With larger resolution and lower sample rate, it requires longer for an image to converge to high quality, but it is possible to increase the output resolution with no apparent degradation in performance.

Our approach offers advantages over other methods, but presents new challenges – not all of which have been solved by this prototype implementation. In this implementation, the application (decoupled from sample generation time) is primarily render-bound: the mesh overhead is negligible, except when large changes of topology occur during motion. A spatial data structure on the samples would permit efficient software view frustum culling to reduce the render load. If the height field constraint is maintained we can do incremental rendering in static frames. The approach could also benefit from a geometric simplification technique once the triangles reach a certain resolution (e.g. as in Pighin et al[13]). It would also be desirable to go to a different, sample-based representation at high resolution to allow an anti-aliasing step, and to guarantee that the solution will converge to the correct image.

While the strict height field constraint results in performance and rendering optimizations, maintaining strict constraints on the mesh topology is also prohibitive when the mesh becomes large. In this prototype implementation we have enforced most of the constraints on the topology of the mesh, and as a result frame rate can become highly variable during motion if the mesh becomes very large and frequent verification of the topological constraints is required. This shortcoming could be addressed with lazy re-assertion of the additional constraints (e.g. in the same spirit as was done with the Delaunay and sample re-projection) during motion.

The main artifact in the image quality is the lack of sharp edges at discontinuities. The adaptive sampling helps minimize the impact of these artifacts, but does not eradicate them until the sampling becomes fairly dense. The reconstruction would benefit from a constrained triangulation that incorporated discontinuity edges. The discontinuity meshing of Pighin et al [13] and the holodeck Voronoi driver [23] both achieve enhanced results at the cost of preprocessing the model in the former and rendering much of the geometry each frame in the latter. An approach that could approximate such edges without a priori knowledge as they became apparent in the reconstruction in an efficient manner would greatly improve the quality of the reconstruction. The adaptive sampling could also be improved if it was possible to differentiate between edges and high frequency textured information locally.

Our goal was to design an interactive system that could be run even with limited resources, but we would also like to be able to exploit more powerful systems if available. The minimally parallelized model of sample request and collection could be extended to support multiple CPUs. The meshing code should also be able to benefit from additional CPUs, but the parallelization potential is less obvious.

6 Conclusion

We have demonstrated the effectiveness of the tapestry display representation with a simple prototype application. The tapestry method offers a novel solution to the dynamic reconstruction problem, making it possible to display the results of a high quality renderer in an interactive setting in a manner that is relatively insensitive to sampling rate or output resolution. Such an application makes interactive rendering possible even on low end machines. The tapestry cache has an advantage over previous approaches in that the samples can have a longer cache life, allowing re-use over multiple frames. In addition, since it is a full geometric representation, the 3D mesh surface removes many of the occlusion errors that are the bane of any re-projection scheme. The prototype we have presented is modular, and allows exploration of different sampling schemes and rendering engines (e.g. photon maps [5] and path tracing [6]). We would like to incorporate more sophisticated perceptually-based priority assignment schemes and reconstruction techniques. We also see our approach as complementary to the holodeck, as its 4D caching structure could be utilized as a secondary cache to the tapestry mesh.

Acknowledgments

This research was supported by ONR (MURI grant #FDN00014-96-1-1200). The author would like to thank Laura Downs, Henrik Wann Jensen, Sara McMains, Tomas Möller, Greg Ward, and Mike Wittman for engaging in numerous discussions regarding this work, the reviewers for their helpful suggestions and critiques, and the Stanford University Graphics Lab for the use of their Onyx2.

References

1. G. Bishop, H. Fuchs, L. McMillan, and E. J. S. Zagier. Frameless rendering: double buffering considered harmful. In *Computer Graphics (Proceedings ACM SIGGRAPH)*, pages 175–

    176, July 1994.

2. L. Darsa and B. Costa. Multi-resolution representation and reconstruction of adaptively sampled images. In *SIBGRAPI*, pages 321–328, 1996.

3. L. Darsa, B. Costa, and A. Varshney. Navigating static environments using image-space simplification and morphing. In *Symposium on Interactive 3D Graphics*, pages 25–34, 1997.

4. Paul Haeberli. Paint by numbers: Abstract image representations. In *Computer Graphics (Proceedings ACM SIGGRAPH)*, pages 207–214, 1990.

5. Henrik Wann Jensen. Global illumination using photon maps. In *Eurographics Rendering Workshop 1996*, pages 21–30, New York City, NY, June 1996. Eurographics, Springer Wien.

6. J. T. Kajiya. The rendering equation. In *Computer Graphics (Proceedings ACM SIG-GRAPH)*, pages 143–150, August 1986.

7. Greg Ward Larson. The holodeck: A parallel ray-caching rendering system. In *Proceedings Eurographics Workshop on Parallel Graphics and Visualization*, September 1998.

8. Dani Lischinski. *Incremental Delaunay Triangulation*, pages 47–49. A P Professional, 1994.

9. W. R. Mark, L. McMillan, and G. Bishop. Post-rendering 3d warping. In *Proceedings Symposium on Interactive 3D Graphics*, pages 7–16, April 1997.

10. D. P. Mitchell. Generating antialiased images at low sampling densities. In *Computer Graphics (Proceedings ACM SIGGRAPH)*, pages 65–72, July 1987.

11. James Painter and Kenneth Sloan. Antialiased ray tracing by adaptive progressive refinement. In *Computer Graphics (Proceedings ACM SIGGRAPH)*, pages 281–288, July 1989.

12. S. Parker, W. Martin, P. J. Sloan, P. Shirley, B. Smits, and C. Hansen. Interactive ray tracing (color plate S. 229). In *Proceedings of the Conference on the 1999 Symposium on interactive 3D Graphics*, pages 119–126, New York, April 26–28 1999. ACM Press.

13. Frederic Pighin, Dani Lischinski, and David Salesin. Progressive previewing of ray-traced images using image-plane discontinuity meshing. In *Proceedings 8th Eurographics Workshop on Rendering*, pages 115–124, June 1997.

14. F. P. Preparata and M.I. Shamos. *Proximity: Fundamental Algorithms*, pages 204–223. Springer-Verlag, New York, NY, 1985.

15. W. H. Press, S. A. Teukolsky, W. T. Vetterling, and B. P. Flannery. *Quasi-(that is sub-)random sequences*, pages 309–314. Cambridge University Press, New York, NY, 1992.

16. K. Pulli, M. Cohen, T. Duchamp, H. Hoppe, L. Shapiro, and W. Stuetzle. View-based rendering: Visualizing real objects from scanned range and color data. In *Rendering Techniques (Proceedings of the Eurographics Workshop)*, pages 23–34, June 1997.

17. François Sillion, G. Drettakis, and B. Bodelet. Efficient impostor manipulation for real-time visualization of urban scenery. In *Computer Graphics Forum (Proceedings Eurographics)*, pages 207–218, 1997.

18. M. Simmons. A dynamic mesh display representation for the holodeck ray cache system. Technical Report CSD-00-1090, University of California, Berkeley, January 13, 2000.

19. Seth Teller, Kavita Bala, and Julie Dorsey. Conservative radiance interpolants for ray tracing. In *Eurographics Rendering Workshop 1996*, pages 257–268, June 1996.

20. P. J. L. van Beek and A. M. Tekalp. Object-based video coding using forward tracking 2-d mesh layers. In *Proceedings SPIE Visual Communications and Image Processing*, pages 699–710, 1997.

21. B. Walter, G. Drettakis, and S. Parker. Interactive rendering using the render cache. In *Rendering Techniques 99: Proceedings 10th Eurographics Workshop on Rendering*, pages 19–30, June 1999.

22. G. Ward. The RADIANCE lighting simulation and rendering system. In *Computer Graphics (Proceedings ACM SIGGRAPH)*, pages 459–472, 1994.

23. Greg Ward and Maryann Simmons. The holodeck interactive ray cache. *to appear: ACM Transactions on Graphics*, 2000.

24. Michael Wimmer, Markus Giegl, and Dieter Schmalstieg. Fast walkthroughs with image caches and ray casting. In *Virtual Environments '99. Proceedings of the Eurographics Workshop in Vienna, Austria*, pages 73–84, 1999.

Editors' Note: see Appendix, p. 418 for colored figures of this paper

Rendering Iridescent Colors of Optical Disks

Yinlong Sun, F. David Fracchia, Mark S. Drew, Thomas W. Calvert

School of Computing Science, Simon Fraser University, Burnaby, BC, Canada V5A 1S6

Abstract: Iridescent colors of optical disks are caused by light diffraction from their surface microstructure. This paper proposes a diffractive illumination model for optical disks based on their physical structure and the superposition principle of light waves. This model includes contributions due to diffractive and non-diffractive factors. For the diffractive part, we first model the pit periodicity for optical disks by using identical spheres and then simplify their distribution by uniform groups of spheres. We also propose and prove the condition for highlights on illuminated grooved surfaces; this condition provides the non-diffractive contribution. The rendered images using this model achieve excellent agreement with photographs of real optical disks.
Keywords: iridescent colors, optical disks, diffraction, illumination, spectral rendering.

1 Introduction

Iridescent colors are commonly observed on optical disks such as CD-ROMs and writable CDs. When illuminated by a white light source, an optical disk typically demonstrates a bright rainbow-like strip called the *major strip* across the disk center, and two *minor strips* of weaker intensities whose colors vary from bluish to dark brown in the *transverse* direction (cf. Color Plate 1). The colors and positions of the strips change sensitively with both illuminating and viewing directions.

Recently, Stam [Stam99] pointed out that the iridescent colors are caused by light diffraction and derived the reflectance using Beckmann's solution of electromagnetic scattering on rough surfaces, which approach was previously proposed for developing illumination models [He91]. However, his rendered images of optical disks show *many strips* under a directional light source, which does not agree with the real appearance that a disk typically demonstrates only *one major strip*. Also, it is our opinion that Beckmann's solution is not appropriate for the case of optical disks because it requires two conditions: the curvature radius of the boundary surface is much larger than the wavelength and the boundary surface is perfectly conducting (see pages 20 and 28 in [Beckmann63]). Unfortunately, neither condition necessarily holds for optical disks (see [Sun99] for a detailed explanation).

This paper proposes a new approach to the problem – deriving an illumination model for optical disks based on their physical microstructure and the superposition principle of light waves [Sun99]. This model includes contributions from both diffractive and non-diffractive factors. For the diffractive part, we first model the pit periodicity for optical disks by using identical spheres and then approximate their distribution as uniform groups of spheres. We also propose and prove the condition for highlights on illuminated grooved surfaces, and this condition provides the non-diffractive contribution. The rendering is done completely based on spectral information, to which we apply the *composite model* [Sun99] that represents a spectrum as a smooth background plus a series of spikes. The composite model is accurate, compact and efficient, and is especially capable of handling spectral peaks that are dynamically created by light diffraction. Our rendered images of optical disks closely match the corresponding photographs and achieve good realism.

342

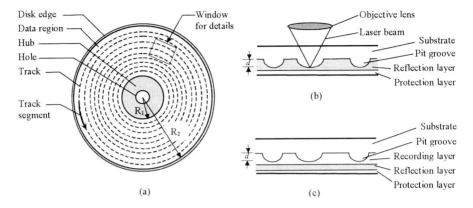

Fig. 1: Physical structure of optical disks: (a) The surface organization. (b) Cross-section of a CD-ROM. (c) Cross-section of a writable CD.

Fig. 2: Photograph of the surface of an optical disk taken with an electron microscope (courtesy of Christian Noldeke) [Noldeke90]. The oval shapes correspond to pit grooves. The track separations and pits widths are uniform, but the lengths and separations of pit grooves vary as *multiples* of a unit length.

2 Physical Structure and Model

Fig. 1 schematically describes the physical structure of optical disks. The disk surface consists of three regions: the *data region* (between R_1 and R_2), the *hub* (below R_1) and the *disk edge* (above R_2). The data region, where the iridescent colors occur, is structured with pits along a slowly extending spiral, which can be approximately regarded as concentric tracks. The hub and disk edge areas are flat. The diagrams in (b) and (c) are cross-sectional views of a CD-ROM and a writable CD along a track segment, e.g. along the curved arrow shown in (a). The multi-layered structure includes a *substrate* (polyvinyl chloride, PMMA or glass), a *reflection layer* (aluminum), and a *protection layer* (lacquer) [Schwartz93]. A writable CD has an additional *recording layer* where pits are burned with laser beams [Purcell97].

Since our goal focuses on rendering the iridescent colors, the most important information is the 2D distribution of pits. Fig. 2 shows an electron microscope photograph [Noldeke90] of a small surface area, as indicated by the rectangular window (exaggerated) in Fig. 1(a). Note that the relative positions of pits are not synchronized amongst different tracks. In other words, given a track, we may regard the start position of a pit as random. The relevant macroscopic and microscopic parameters of CD-ROMs are given in Tables 1 and 2.

Thus we model the hub and disk edge areas as cylinder shells of homogeneous transparent material with smooth surfaces, and the data area as a simple surface (instead of multiple layers) decorated with a partially periodic microstructure.

Table 1: CD ROM's macroscopic parameters. **Table 2**: CD ROM's microscopic parameters

Parameter	Value (mm)
Disk radius	60
Hole radius	7.5
R_1	19
R_2	58.5
Thickness of CD-ROMs	1.1

Parameter	Description	Value (nm)
b	Track spacing	1600
a	Pit length step	300
s	Pit separation	900-3300
l	Pit length	900-3300
w	Pit width	600
d	Pit depth	120

3 Illumination Model

3.1 Diffractive Contribution

For a structure to cause significant diffraction under incoherent lights such as daylight or incandescent lamps, it must satisfy two conditions [Born75, Hecht98]. First, the structure must be periodic or partially periodic. Second, the periodic spacing must be comparable to the wavelengths of light. An optical disk satisfies both conditions.

Consider light diffraction due to a small neighborhood area of point P as shown in Fig. 3(a). We assume that the light source at S and the camera at C are both far away enough from P. Let $\hat{\sigma}$ and $\hat{\tau}$ denote the unit vectors of the radian and track directions for such a neighborhood area (we use hatted symbols to denote unit vectors and bold font to denote vectors). Since the size of the shaded rectangle is very small, we can regard $\hat{\sigma}$ as the direction from the disk center to point O and $\hat{\tau}$ as the track direction at point O. Fig. 3(b) shows the coordinate frame constructed for the shaded rectangle, with x, y and z-axes along $\hat{\tau}$, $\hat{\sigma}$, and the disk surface normal, respectively.

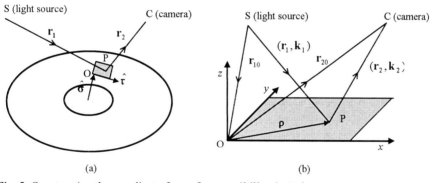

(a)	(b)

Fig. 3: Constructing the coordinate frame for a small illuminated area.

According to optics, the intensity of a light wave is proportional to the product between light field and its complex conjugate

$$I \propto |E|^2 = E \cdot E^*, \tag{3.1}$$

where E is the light field and for a monochromatic light of wavelength λ it can be expressed as a plane wave (as point S and C are far away from P):

$$E(\mathbf{r}) = E_0 e^{i\mathbf{k}\cdot\mathbf{r}}, \tag{3.2}$$

where $\mathbf{r}$ is the location, $\mathbf{k}$ is the wave vector ($\mathbf{k} = k\hat{\mathbf{k}}$, with $k = 2\pi/\lambda$ and $\hat{\mathbf{k}}$ is the unit vector along the propagation direction), and E_0 is the amplitude (independent of **r** and **k**). Thus, the field at the camera location C contributed by the path S-P-C is

$$E(\mathbf{\rho}) = E_0 e^{i(\mathbf{k}_1 \cdot \mathbf{r}_1 + \mathbf{k}_2 \cdot \mathbf{r}_2)}, \qquad (3.3)$$

where **ρ** denotes location P in the xy-plane, $\mathbf{r}_1$ and $\mathbf{r}_2$ are spatial vectors from S to P and from P to C, and $\mathbf{k}_1$ and $\mathbf{k}_2$ are the corresponding wave vectors. From Fig. 3(b), we have $\mathbf{r}_1 = \mathbf{r}_{10} + \mathbf{\rho}$ and $\mathbf{r}_2 = \mathbf{r}_{20} - \mathbf{\rho}$. Thus

$$E(\mathbf{\rho}) = E_0 e^{i(\mathbf{k}_1 \cdot \mathbf{r}_{10} + \mathbf{k}_2 \cdot \mathbf{r}_{20})} \cdot e^{i(\mathbf{k}_1 - \mathbf{k}_2) \cdot \mathbf{\rho}} = E_0' e^{i(\mathbf{k}_1 - \mathbf{k}_2) \cdot \mathbf{\rho}} = E_0' e^{i\mathbf{q} \cdot \mathbf{\rho}}, \qquad (3.4)$$

where $\mathbf{q} = \mathbf{k}_1 - \mathbf{k}_2$ and E_0' combines E_0 and the first exponential factor, which is independent of **ρ**. According to the superposition principle, the field at C contributed by the whole shaded rectangle is

$$E = \iint E(\mathbf{\rho}) dx dy, \qquad (3.5)$$

where the integrals are over the shaded rectangle.

Let us decompose this field as

$$E = E_{\text{track}} + E_{\text{land}}, \qquad (3.6)$$

where E_{track} and E_{land} are the contributions from the tracks and the rest area (called the *land area*). Since the land area is flat, it behaves like a mirror and hence merely contributes to the specular reflection. For diffraction we only need to focus on E_{track}.

Our approach is to model a pit groove using identical spheres of diameter a (see Table 2). In Fig. 4, (a) is an original layout of pit grooves and (b) is the corresponding representation by our model. A pit groove is thus represented by a group of consecutive shaded spheres and an empty space between two pit grooves in a track is represented with a group of unshaded spheres. In Fig. 4(b), we have also taken into account the staggered distribution of pits among different tracks; that is, the centers of the first spheres (the spheres lying on the y-axis) in different tracks have different unrelated x coordinates.

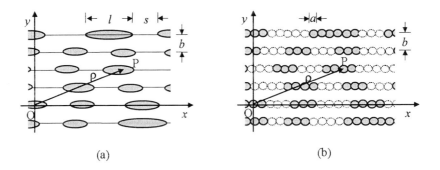

(a)   (b)

Fig. 4: Representing pit distribution in terms of identical spheres.

Following Eq. (3.4) and using the superposition principle of light waves, E_{track} is

$$E_{\text{track}}(\mathbf{q}) = E_{\text{sphere}} \sum_{l,m} c(l,m) e^{i\mathbf{q} \cdot \mathbf{\rho}(l,m)}, \quad l,m = 0, \pm 1, \pm 2 \dots \qquad (3.7)$$

where E_{sphere} represents the common factor of the contributions of spheres, integers l and m are the indexes of a sphere, $c(l,m)$ is 1 (with pit) or 0 (without pit), and $\rho(l,m)$ denotes the center location for a sphere at (l,m). Referring to Fig. 4(b), $\rho(l,m)$ can be further written as

$$\rho(l,m) = \rho_x(l,m)\hat{x} + \rho_y(l,m)\hat{y}, \tag{3.8}$$

with

$$\begin{cases} \rho_x(l,m) = la + \delta_m \\ \rho_y(l,m) = mb \end{cases}, \quad l,m = 0,\pm1,\pm2,... \tag{3.9}$$

where δ_m represents the staggered shift for the first sphere in a track and is assumed *random* within $[-a/2, a/2]$. (Strictly speaking, δ_m is not purely random, as pit lengths and separations are in steps of a along a spiral. However, since a track cycle consists of many various pit lengths and separations, the regularity of δ_m is almost lost.) Combining Eqs. (3.7), (3.8) and (3.9), we obtain

$$E_{\text{track}}(\mathbf{q}) = E_{\text{sphere}} \sum_m e^{imb\mathbf{q}\cdot\hat{y} + i\delta_m \mathbf{q}\cdot\hat{x}} \sum_l c(l,m) e^{ila\mathbf{q}\cdot\hat{x}} \tag{3.10}$$

Now considering the case of perfect periodicity, that is, $c(l,m) = 1$ and $\delta_m = 0$, Eq. (3.10) reduces to

$$E_{\text{track}}(\mathbf{q}) = E_{\text{sphere}} \sum_m e^{imb\mathbf{q}\cdot\hat{y}} \sum_l e^{ila\mathbf{q}\cdot\hat{x}}, \tag{3.11}$$

and each summation generates a delta-function

$$\sum_l e^{ila\mathbf{q}\cdot\hat{x}} = \delta[a\mathbf{q}\cdot\hat{x} - 2\pi n], \quad n = 0,\pm1,\pm2,... \tag{3.12}$$

$$\sum_m e^{imb\mathbf{q}\cdot\hat{y}} = \delta[b\mathbf{q}\cdot\hat{y} - 2\pi n], \quad n = 0,\pm1,\pm2,... \tag{3.13}$$

These equations imply that lights after diffraction appear only in discrete spatial directions for which the delta functions do not vanish. (This is similar to the X-ray diffraction pattern of crystal lattice [Kittel76].) Eq. (3.12) is equivalent to

$$a\mathbf{q}\cdot\hat{x} - 2\pi n = 0, \quad n = 0,\pm1,\pm2,... \tag{3.14}$$

or

$$(\hat{k}_1 - \hat{k}_2)\cdot\hat{x} = \frac{n\lambda}{a}, \quad n = 0,\pm1,\pm2,... \tag{3.15}$$

To study the real distribution of $c(l,m)$, let

$$f(\mathbf{q},m) = \sum_l c(l,m) e^{ila\mathbf{q}\cdot\hat{x}} \ . \tag{3.16}$$

Although $c(l,m)$ takes 1 or 0 *randomly*, $f(\mathbf{q},m)$ still behaves like a delta function

$$f(\mathbf{q},m) \approx \sum_l e^{ila\mathbf{q}\cdot\hat{x}} = \delta[a\mathbf{q}\cdot\hat{x} - 2\pi n], \quad n = 0,\pm1,\pm2,... \tag{3.17}$$

because the harmonics of different values of l tends to cancel with each other except for the constructive conditions specified by the delta function.

However, $c(l,m)$ should take on values 1 or 0 in *groups* of consecutive spheres.

346

Referring to Table 2, the pit lengths and separations are between 900 and 3300 nm and in steps of $a=300$ nm. To reflect this distribution effectively, we simplify the distribution by modeling pits using uniform groups, as shown in Fig. 5. In the simplified representation, every group consists of four spheres because the average lengths of pit grooves is $4a$ (see the Appendix).

(a)

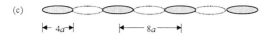

(b)

(c)

Fig. 5: Row (a) is an original distribution of spheres with various group sizes. Row (b) simplifies (a) with every group consisting of four spheres. In row (c), the spheres in a group are merged into a single entity, represented by an ellipsoid.

Thus $f(\mathbf{q},m)$ can be written as

$$f(\mathbf{q},m) = f(\mathbf{q}) \approx C_{\text{ellip}} \sum_{l} e^{il(8a)\mathbf{q}\cdot\hat{\mathbf{x}}} = C_{\text{ellip}}\delta[8a(\mathbf{q}\cdot\hat{\mathbf{x}}) - 2\pi n], \tag{3.18}$$

where C_{ellip} represents the common factor for the contributions of ellipsoids (or groups of spheres) and $8a$ is the periodic spacing between solid ellipsoids. Since this result is independent of m, we can write $f(\mathbf{q},m)$ as $f(\mathbf{q})$. The first two minor strips on both sides of the major strip correspond to $n = \pm 1$

$$8a(\mathbf{q}\cdot\hat{\mathbf{x}}) \pm 2\pi = 0 \tag{3.19}$$

or

$$(\hat{\mathbf{k}}_1 - \hat{\mathbf{k}}_2)\cdot\hat{\mathbf{x}} = \pm\frac{\lambda}{8a} \tag{3.20}$$

Thus a light with larger λ will have a larger value of $|(\hat{\mathbf{k}}_1 - \hat{\mathbf{k}}_2)\cdot\hat{\mathbf{x}}|$. Recalling that the location of the major strip is given by the condition $(\hat{\mathbf{k}}_1 - \hat{\mathbf{k}}_2)\cdot\hat{\mathbf{x}} = 0$, the larger value of $|(\hat{\mathbf{k}}_1 - \hat{\mathbf{k}}_2)\cdot\hat{\mathbf{x}}|$ implies that the red components of the minor strips are farther from the major strip while the blue components are closer. This explains the color change in minor strips.

Combining Eqs. (3.1), (3.10) and (3.16), we have

$$I(\mathbf{q}) \propto |E_{\text{track}}(\mathbf{q})|^2 \propto |g(\mathbf{q})|^2 \cdot |f(\mathbf{q})|^2, \tag{3.21}$$

where we define

$$g(\mathbf{q}) = \sum_{m} e^{imb\mathbf{q}\cdot\hat{\mathbf{y}} + i\delta_m\mathbf{q}\cdot\hat{\mathbf{x}}} \tag{3.22}$$

3.2 Non-Diffractive Contribution

The appearance of an optical disk also relies on a non-diffractive factor. Fig. 6 shows a photograph of a vinyl record with a CD-ROM placed on top of it. Note that the bright strip on the vinyl record aligns with that on the CD-ROM. Because there is no diffraction on the vinyl record, the bright strip on the vinyl record must be caused by some non-diffractive mechanism, which should also apply to a CD-ROM as well.

Fig. 6: Photograph of a vinyl record with a CD-ROM on the top shows the aligned bright strips due to the non-diffractive effect.

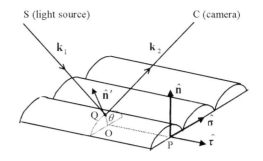

Fig. 7: Reflection on a cylindrically grooved surface.

The concentric tracks can be characterized as parallel cylindrical surfaces as shown in Fig. 7. (We describe the surface details with *raised* cylindrical surfaces although tracks of optical disks are in fact concave – this is just for clarity of illustration and will not affect the derived result.) We claim that *the necessary and sufficient condition for generating a bright strip on a surface with such a parallel cylindrical structure is*

$$(\hat{\mathbf{k}}_2 - \hat{\mathbf{k}}_1) \cdot \hat{\boldsymbol{\tau}} = 0, \tag{3.23}$$

where $\hat{\boldsymbol{\tau}}$ is the longitudinal direction for the cylindrical surfaces oriented in parallel, and $\hat{\mathbf{k}}_1$ and $\hat{\mathbf{k}}_2$ are the incident and reflective directions. To prove sufficiency, we must show that if $\hat{\mathbf{k}}_1$ and $\hat{\mathbf{k}}_2$ satisfy Eq. (3.23) then the received light is a highlight. To do so, we only need to show that there exists a small neighborhood area (but still containing many cylindrical surface pieces) for the illuminated point P such that the local surface normal direction $\hat{\mathbf{n}}'$ (primed) at a point Q within the neighborhood area is parallel to the midway vector $\hat{\mathbf{k}}_2 - \hat{\mathbf{k}}_1$ for the reflection. According to Eq. (3.23), $\hat{\mathbf{k}}_2 - \hat{\mathbf{k}}_1$ has no component along the $\hat{\boldsymbol{\tau}}$ direction and therefore it can be written as

$$\hat{\mathbf{k}}_2 - \hat{\mathbf{k}}_1 = \hat{\boldsymbol{\sigma}} \cos\theta + \hat{\mathbf{n}} \sin\theta. \tag{3.24}$$

At point Q with the same polar angle θ, the local surface normal direction $\hat{\mathbf{n}}'$ will be parallel to $\hat{\mathbf{k}}_2 - \hat{\mathbf{k}}_1$. Thus we have proved sufficiency. To show necessity, suppose that we have a bright strip. Then there exists a point Q in the neighborhood area such that at this point the perfect specular reflection holds. In other words, $\hat{\mathbf{k}}_2 - \hat{\mathbf{k}}_1$ is parallel to the surface normal direction $\hat{\mathbf{n}}'$ at point Q. Since $\hat{\mathbf{n}}'$ is on the plane formed by $\hat{\boldsymbol{\sigma}}$ and $\hat{\mathbf{n}}$, so is $\hat{\mathbf{k}}_2 - \hat{\mathbf{k}}_1$. Thus Eq. (3.23) holds.

In practical computations, it is necessary to express condition (3.23) through a smooth peak function. Similar to the idea of the Phong model [Phong75], we replace Eq. (3.23) by making reflected light intensity behave as

$$I \propto |(\hat{\mathbf{k}}_1 - \hat{\mathbf{k}}_2) \cdot \hat{\boldsymbol{\tau}}|^{\beta}, \tag{3.25}$$

where β is a positive integer. This equation can be regarded as an extension of the Phong model to anisotropic surfaces. Note that at the macroscopic scale, the groove direction $\hat{\boldsymbol{\tau}}$ depends on the surface location. For an optical disk, $\hat{\boldsymbol{\tau}}$ is along the tangent direction of concentric tracks.

Poulin and Fournier [Poulin90] have modeled anisotropic surfaces with consideration of surface details including presence of flat lands and structural dimensions. Their work is useful for evaluating the accuracy of Eq. (3.25) and deriving value of parameter β for specific anisotropic surfaces.

3.3 Combined Illumination Equations

Combining the results of the previous subsections, we write the total intensity of reflected light from the surface of an optical disk as

$$
\begin{aligned}
I_{\text{total}}(\mathbf{k}_1, \mathbf{k}_2) &= I_{\text{non-diff}}(\mathbf{k}_1, \mathbf{k}_2) + I_{\text{diff}}(\mathbf{k}_1, \mathbf{k}_2) \\
&= I_{\text{non-diff}}(\mathbf{k}_1, \mathbf{k}_2) + c_0 \,|\,(\hat{\mathbf{k}}_1 - \hat{\mathbf{k}}_2) \cdot \hat{\boldsymbol{\tau}}\,|^\beta \cdot |\,g(\mathbf{q})\,|^2 \cdot |\,f(\mathbf{q})\,|^2,
\end{aligned}
\tag{3.26}
$$

where c_0 is a positive constant, $\hat{\boldsymbol{\tau}}$ is the track direction at the illuminated point, and $\mathbf{q} = \mathbf{k}_1 - \mathbf{k}_2$. It is often useful to rewrite this equation in the following form

$$
I_{\text{total}}(\mathbf{k}_1, \mathbf{k}_2) = I_0(\lambda)[R_{\text{non-diff}}(\mathbf{k}_1, \mathbf{k}_2) + R_{\text{diff}}(\mathbf{k}_1, \mathbf{k}_2)],
\tag{3.27}
$$

where $I_0(\lambda)$ is the incident intensity, and $R_{\text{diff}}(\mathbf{k}_1, \mathbf{k}_2)$ and $R_{\text{non-diff}}(\mathbf{k}_1, \mathbf{k}_2)$ are

$$
R_{\text{diff}}(\mathbf{k}_1, \mathbf{k}_2) = c_0 \,|\,(\hat{\mathbf{k}}_1 - \hat{\mathbf{k}}_2) \cdot \hat{\boldsymbol{\tau}}\,|^\beta \cdot |\,g(\mathbf{q})\,|^2 \cdot |\,f(\mathbf{q})\,|^2
\tag{3.28}
$$

and

$$
R_{\text{non-diff}}(\mathbf{k}_1, \mathbf{k}_2) = c_{\text{diffuse}} \cdot (\hat{\mathbf{k}}_2 \cdot \hat{\mathbf{n}}) + c_{\text{specular}} \cdot |\,\hat{\mathbf{q}} \cdot \hat{\mathbf{n}}\,|^\alpha,
\tag{3.29}
$$

where $\hat{\mathbf{n}}$ the disk surface normal. Furthermore, we can use delta-functions to approximate $|\,f(\mathbf{q})\,|^2$ and $|\,g(\mathbf{q})\,|^2$

$$
|\,f(\mathbf{q})\,|^2 \approx c_1 \sum_{n=-\infty}^{\infty} \delta[8a \cdot (\mathbf{q} \cdot \hat{\boldsymbol{\tau}}) - 2\pi n] + c_2,
\tag{3.30}
$$

and

$$
|\,g(\mathbf{q})\,|^2 \approx c_3 \sum_{n=-\infty}^{\infty} \delta[b \cdot (\mathbf{q} \cdot \hat{\boldsymbol{\sigma}}) - 2\pi n] + c_4,
\tag{3.31}
$$

where c_1, c_2, c_3, and c_4 are positive constants. For a more precise description we should let the peaks have finite widths. This can be done by replacing every delta-function with a Gaussian function of the form

$$
p(t, t_0) = \frac{\sqrt{\pi}}{2w} e^{-4(t - t_0)^2 / w^2}
\tag{3.32}
$$

where t_0 and w represent the center and width of the peak. The purpose of the factor in front of the exponential is to normalize the Gaussian. Thus $|\,f(\mathbf{q})\,|^2$ can be modeled by a multiple-peak function as

$$
|\,f(\mathbf{q})\,|^2 = h(t) = c_1 \sum_{n=-\infty}^{\infty} p(t, 2\pi n) + c_2 = \frac{c_1 \sqrt{\pi}}{2w} \sum_{n=-\infty}^{\infty} e^{-4[8a \cdot (\mathbf{q} \cdot \hat{\boldsymbol{\tau}}) - 2\pi n]^2 / w^2} + c_2,
\tag{3.33}
$$

where $t_0 = 8a \cdot (\mathbf{q} \cdot \hat{\boldsymbol{\tau}})$. Similarly we can model $|\,g(\mathbf{q})\,|^2$. Fig. 8 shows the profiles of the multiple-peak function $h(t)$ in the range $[0, 4\pi]$ with fixed c_1 and c_2, and various peak widths w.

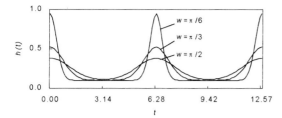

Fig. 8: Profiles of multiple peaks with different peak widths $w = \pi/6, \pi/3, \pi/2$.

Finally, we have some general comments. First, c_2 and c_4 will be zero if the disk surface structure is perfectly periodic. However, they should be positive constants because pits are *partially* periodic. The periodicity imperfection results in scattering in all spatial directions, which effect is included in the diffuse term in Eq. (3.29). In the case that the surface structure is completely random and the surface is regarded as entirely diffuse, all the delta-function terms vanish. Second, to conserve energy, we should relate constant c_1 with c_2 as well as c_3 with c_4 so that the profiles shown in Fig. 8 maintain the same underneath areas. Also, our model obeys the reciprocity principle because, if we switch the incident and reflected directions, the result due to diffraction is the same according to Eq. (3.28), that is, $R_{\mathrm{diff}}(-\mathbf{k}_2, -\mathbf{k}_1) = R_{\mathrm{diff}}(\mathbf{k}_1, \mathbf{k}_2)$. Finally, this paper focuses on *relative* light intensity distributions because calculating the absolute values of light intensities involves more low-level physical information such as exact pit shapes, which deviates too much from our main interest – generating iridescent strips of optical disks. Thus in rendering, we will adjust the relevant intensity constants to obtain the appropriate relative intensities among the major strip, minor strips and the rest area. But in principle it is possible to determine these intensity constants from low-level physical information such as the percentage area covered by pit grooves and exact pit shapes.

4 Rendering

Although diffraction involves phases of light waves, Eqs. (3.27)-(3.29) show that it can be rendered based on *spectral* information. The rendering process can be divided into three stages. First, we generate a *spectral image* using the spectral information based on local and global illumination models. A spectral image is similar to a color image except that for every pixel the information is a spectral power distribution instead of a color. In our rendering, we use Eqs. (3.27)-(3.29) for local illumination and ray tracing for global illumination. A ray tracer provides all the required information for our illumination model, including the illuminating and viewing directions and the illuminated point. Hence we need simply follow the standard raytracing procedure (cf. p780 in [Foley96]) except that we must shade according to Eqs. (3.27)-(3.29) if the intersected point is in the data region of an optical disk. In the second stage, we transform the spectral image into a generic color image described with colors in the CIE XYZ model. In the last stage, we derive the final RGB image by clipping the CIE XYZ colors into an RGB gamut. Various algorithms are available for the color clipping [Hall89]. We will use the simplest algorithm: whenever an RGB component derived from a CIE XYZ color is above 1 or below 0, we reset the value to 1 or 0, respectively. This method however may result in shift of hue. Better results can be obtained by using other clipping methods such as desaturating or uniformly downscaling the colors that are outside the RGB gamut.

Spectral representation is a critical question. Although sampling is commonly used, it does not work well for computing light diffraction. As shown above, light diffraction involves delta functions that generate sharp peaks. To accurately describe a sharp peak with the sampling method, we have to use *many* sample points, which is disadvantageous in both memory and performance. Our approach is to represent all spectra with the *composite model* [Sun98]. Its basic idea is to decompose a spectral function into its *smooth background* and a collection of *spikes*. The smooth component can be represented through sampling while a spike can be simply described through its location and weight (or height). It is straightforward to implement the samples of the smooth background with an array and spectral spikes with a linked list. (Usually the accuracy is sufficient if we use 10 sample points for the smooth background [Sun98].) This model is accurate, compact and efficient, and is flexible to add or manipulate spikes created dynamically by light diffraction. Fig. 9 describes how to handle related spikes. Note that when two light rays overlap and their intensities contain spikes at same or very close wavelengths, the spikes will be merged into a single one. This prevents spike proliferation as well as optimizes the representation with respect to compactness and performance.

```
double temp = b * fabs(              // "fabs" is for absolute value
    (unitVector_k1 - unitVector_k2) * diskRadianDir ); // dot product
int n = 1;                           // initialize for the 1st-order construction
double spike_wl = temp / n;          // spike wavelength

while (spike_wl > 400)               // if spike_wl below 400, no contributions
{
    if (spike_wl < 700)              // spike_wl in visible range
    {
        get incident_SPD at spike_wl;    // incident_SPD is known from input
        compute f_square at spike_wl;    // |f|^2 at spike_wl
        compute pitShapeFactor;          // according to Eq (3.25)
        double spike_value = incident_SPD * f_square * pitShapeFactor; // Eq (3.28)
        CSpike spike(spike_wl, spike_value); // create a new spike instance
        add spike to the reflective intensity
    }
    n++;                             // next order construction
    spike_wl = temp / n;             // new spike wavelength
}
```

Fig. 9: Pseudocode for adding contributions of delta-functions as spikes.

Color Plate 1 displays two rendered images of a CD-ROM corresponding to the photographs. The rendered images match the photographs very well including both colors and orientations of the major and minor strips. (Here, one may question that Eqs. (3.12), (3.13) and (3.23) are three conditions on three parameters, namely the wavelength and two parameters for location, and therefore a rendered CD ROM should show single monochromatic highlights instead of strips. However, Eq. (3.23) corresponds to the case of $n=0$ of Eq. (3.12) and should not be regarded as an independent condition.)

An important characteristic in the appearance of an optical disk is its sensitive dependency on the illuminating and viewing directions. Color Plate 2 shows a series of rendered images for different illuminating angles with the camera fixed (animations can be viewed at http://www.cs.sfu.ca/~graphics/pubs/EGRW00). The point light source moves up along the z-axis and the eight images correspond to different heights of the light source.

Color Plate 3 shows a rendered optical disk illuminated by *three* point sources with similar illumination directions. The result looks more like what we observe in reality, as a real source always has a finite area. This shows the possibility of using a cluster of point sources to represent a *surface* light source.

The rendered image in Color Plate 4 demonstrates an interesting interaction between a CD-ROM and a plastic sphere. We can recognize the major and minor strips of the reflected image of the CD-ROM on the sphere, except that the strips are curved due to the spherical surface. Note that the strip colors shown on the sphere are different from those shown on the CD-ROM itself because the viewing directions relative to the CD-ROM for the two cases are different. This image shows that our illumination model also works well in multiple-object environments.

5 Future Directions and Conclusion

The core idea of our diffractive illumination model, i.e. deriving the light intensity distribution based on structural periodicity and the superposition principle of light waves, would work equally well for other diffractive structures. For instance, it also applies to artificially structured textures of decorations, stickers, or artwork. Films of certain types of liquid crystals contain layer gratings and can cause both reflected and transmitted diffraction [Nassau83], and our model also applies to such films. Notably, some of the most outstanding colors on natural objects are associated with light diffraction, often along with interference [Williamson83, Nassau83]. For example, the iridescent colors of mother-of-pearl are attributed to a combination of diffraction and interference. Another example is the spectacular colors of a gemstone opal, often called "opalescence". In particular, the surface of certain beetles and wasps has a hard corrugation arranged in closely spaced rows, which can cause significant diffraction (see page 111 and plate 16 in [Williamson83]).

In conclusion, we have proposed an illumination model to handle light diffraction at the microstructure of optical disks. This model is based on the physical structure of optical disks and the superposition principle of light waves. The calculations are straightforward, analytic, and self-contained. We have also discussed the non-diffractive factor due to surface anisotropy and derived the general condition for surface highlights. In spite that our modeling process involves light wave phases, the final result of our model can be completely described in terms of spectra. This allows us to render diffraction based on spectral information, which can be effectively represented with a composite model proposed in our early work. The images that we rendered using a ray tracer have an excellent agreement with their corresponding photograph counterparts and have achieved good realism in general.

Appendix

Here we prove that the average length of pit grooves is $4a$. Randomly we pick a pit groove. Since the minimum length is $3a$ [Noldeke90], the probability for this groove to be $3a$ long, i.e. the fourth sphere being *empty* in Fig. 4, is 0.5 because of the equal probabilities for the fourth sphere to be solid and empty. Similarly, the probability for this groove to be $4a$ long is 0.5×0.5, the probability for the fourth sphere to be *solid* times the probability for the fifth sphere to be *empty*. Similar argument also works for other lengths. Thus, the average pit length is the sum of all possible pit lengths times their corresponding probabilities

$$\bar{l} = \sum_{k=3}^{\infty} (ka) \cdot \frac{1}{2^{k-2}} = a \sum_{k=1}^{\infty} \frac{k+2}{2^k} = a \sum_{k=1}^{\infty} \frac{k}{2^k} + 2a \sum_{k=1}^{\infty} \frac{1}{2^k} = 2a + 2a = 4a.$$

References

Beckmann63   P. Beckmann and A. Spizzichino, *The Scattering of Electromagnetic Waves from Rough Surfaces*, Macmillan, New York, 1963.

Born75   M. Born and E. Wolf, *Principles of Optics: Electromagnetic Theory of Propagation, Interference and Diffraction of Light*, Pergamon, Oxford, 1975.

Foley96   J. D. Foley, A. van Dam, S. K. Feiner, and J. F. Hughes, *Computer Graphics Principles and Practice*, Second Edition, Assison-Wesley, Reading, MA, 1996.

Hall89   R. A. Hall, *Illumination and Color in Computer Generated Imagery*, Springer-Verlag, New York, 1989.

He91   X. D. He, K. E. Torrance, F. X. Sillion, and D. P. Greenberg, "A Comprehensive Physical Model for Light Reflection," *Computer Graphics, Proc. of ACM SIGGRAPH 91*, ACM Press, New York, 1991, pp. 175-186.

Hecht98   E. Hecht, *Optics*, Third Edition, Addison-Wesley, Reading, MA, 1998.

Kittel76   C. Kittel, *Introduction to Solid State Physics*, 5th Edition, John Wiley & Sons, New York, 1976.

Nassau83   K. Nassau, *The Physics and Chemistry of Color: The Fifteen Causes of Color*, John Wiley & Sons, New York, 1983.

Noldeke90   C. Noldeke, "Compact Disc Diffraction," *The Physics Teacher*, Oct. 1990, pp. 484-485.

Phong75   B. Phong, "Illumination for Computer Generated Images," *Communications of the ACM*, Vol. 18, No. 6, 1975, pp. 311-317.

Poulin90   P. Poulin and A. Fournier, "A Model for Anisotropic Reflection," *Computer Graphics, Proc. of ACM SIGGRAPH 90*, ACM Press, New York, 1990, pp. 273-282.

Purcell97   L. Purcell and D. Martin, *The Complete Recordable-CD Guide*, Sybex, San Francisco, 1997.

Schwartz93   K. Schwartz, *The Physics of Optical Recording*, Springer-Verlag, Berlin, 1993.

Stam99   J. Stam, "Diffraction Shaders," *Computer Graphics, Proc. of ACM SIGGRAPH 99*, ACM Press, New York, 1999, pp. 101-110.

Sun98   Y. Sun, F. D. Fracchia, and M. S. Drew, "A Composite Model for Representing Spectral Functions," *Simon Fraser University, Technical Report SFU CMPT TR 1998-18*, 1998. Available at ftp://fas.sfu.ca/pub/cs/TR/1998/.

Sun99   Y. Sun, F. D. Fracchia, M. S. Drew, and T. W. Calvert, "Rendering Iridescent Colors of Optical Disks," *Simon Fraser University, Technical Report SFU CMPT TR 1999-08*, (1999). Available at ftp://fas.sfu.ca/pub/cs/TR/1999/.

Williamson83   S. J. Williamson and H. Z. Cummins, *Light and Color in Nature and Art*, John Wiley and Sons, New York, 1983.

Editors' Note: see Appendix, p. 419 for colored figures of this paper

A Physically-based BRDF Model for Multilayer Systems with Uncorrelated Rough Boundaries

Isabelle Icart, Didier Arquès

Université de Marne-La-Vallée
5, boulevard Descartes, Champs-Sur-Marne
77454 Marne-La-Vallée CEDEX 2, FRANCE
Tel: +33-1-49-32-90-11, +33-1-49-32-90-10
icart@univ-mlv.fr, arques@univ-mlv.fr

Abstract. This paper presents a new BRDF model allowing the simulation of the optical behaviour of multilayer systems formed of homogeneous and isotropic thin films with random rough boundaries. The boundaries are supposed to be locally smooth and generated by a stationary and isotropic Gaussian process. Moreover, it is assumed that they are mutually independent from the statistical point of view. The BRDF is composed of three terms: specular, directional diffuse and uniform diffuse terms, and accounts for interference, diffraction and polarization effects. The expressions for the specular and directional diffuse components are derived analytically, by means of the Abelès formalism, within the framework of the Kirchhoff theory of diffraction. We present pictures of composite multilayer materials obtained by incorporating this model in a spectral ray-tracing algorithm.

1. Introduction

Multilayer materials are very common in our environment. Nature provides us with numerous and sometimes spectacular examples of multilayer systems such as nacre layers or pearls that can be found inside seashells, natural oxide layers, or the iridescent scales that adorn the wings of the graceful Morpho butterfly. They have numerous applications in various domains including: anti-reflection coatings, dielectric mirrors, interference filters, car paints (metallic [4] and nacreous), and multilayer optical disks. Despite this, there have been only a few computer graphics papers dealing with multilayer materials. This might be explained by the difficulty to characterise completely the interactions which take place in the core of such systems (surface and bulk scattering, interference). On belief that it might be easier to deduce the macroscopic properties of materials from their microscopic behaviour, some authors turned to simulation methods (Monte-Carlo), which yielded particularly convincing results. This allowed Hanrahan and Krueger [8] to simulate efficiently subsurface scattering inside inhomogeneous non-Lambertian multilayer materials such as leaves and skin. Later, Gondek, Meyer and Newman [7] proposed an extension of classic Monte-Carlo approaches to model interference effects in layered media (nacre, paints).

In this paper, we propose a new analytic approach to the problem of reflection by rough multilayers, which consists in deriving an analytic expression for the bidirectional reflectance distribution function (BRDF) related to homogeneous and isotropic multilayer systems with uncorrelated rough boundaries. Analytic reflection models have already been proposed by several authors for bare surfaces (see [10] for isotropic surfaces and [18] for an extension to the anisotropic case), but none of these

354

takes into account interference. It is therefore impossible to model the optical behaviour of complex multilayer systems such as those previously mentioned. Building on the classic Kirchhoff theory of diffraction [3] and previous work in physics [2][15], our work extends existing surface BRDF models and peculiarly the model of He et al.[10] and the one recently proposed by Icart and Arquès for a system of substrate-identical thin film [12], to the case of rough multilayers.

After setting up the problem and hypotheses (Section 2), we present the Abelès matrix formalism used to derive expressions for the local reflection coefficient of the multilayer system (Section 3). As this general expression is too complex to integrate in the Helmholtz-Kirchhoff integral, we expand it to the second order (assuming that the RMS height of surface irregularities is small compared to wavelength), which allows us to evaluate the components of light reflected by the system (Section 4) and to deduce the expression of the BRDF (Section 5). Pictures obtained by incorporating this model in a spectral ray-tracing algorithm are displayed and discussed in the last part of this contribution. Finally, we present the conclusions and future work.

The derivation presented in Sections 1-4 is quite mathematical, and may require some background in physics and random processes theory. In order to make the derivations more understandable, we have provided some additional computation results in Appendix A and B and a table of symbols in Appendix C. We invite the reader who is mainly interested in the implementation to turn directly to Section 5 where we summarised the whole results.

2. Problem and hypotheses

In this section, we state the problem, make some assumptions on the system and give the general form of our BRDF.

2.1 Components of the BRDF

Like the one proposed by previous authors ([10], [12]), our BRDF (denoted ρ_{bd}) divides into three terms (Fig. 1). The specular component, $\rho_{bd,sp}$, corresponds to light coherently reflected by the system in the specular direction. The directional diffuse term, $\rho_{bd,dd}$, represents light scattered by surface irregularities in the whole hemisphere, whereas the uniform diffuse component, $\rho_{bd,ud}$ accounts for multiple surface (metals) or bulk scattering phenomena (inhomogeneous transparent media).

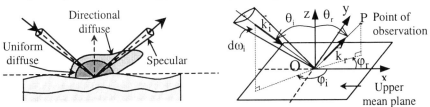

Fig. 1. Components of the BRDF   **Fig. 2.** Geometrical parameters

The BRDF can be written in the form:

$$\rho_{bd}(\theta_i,\varphi_i,\theta_r,\varphi_r)=\rho_{bdsp}+\rho_{bddd}+\rho_{bdud}, \text{ with } \rho_{bd}(\theta_i,\varphi_i,\theta_r,\varphi_r)=\frac{dL_r(\theta_i,\varphi_i,\theta_r,\varphi_r)}{L_i(\theta_i,\varphi_i)\cos\theta_i d\omega_i} \quad (1)$$

355

where $d\omega_i$ represents the solid angle of the incident light and L_i and dL_r represent the radiance incident from the direction (θ_i, φ_i) and reflected in the direction (θ_r, φ_r) respectively (Fig. 2). To evaluate the BRDF, it is necessary to find the electric field scattered by the system in the direction (θ_r, φ_r), which will be done in Section 3 of this contribution.

2.2 Hypotheses and notations

Let us consider a stack of p random rough thin films deposited on a substrate (Fig. 3). The materials forming the films and the substrate are linear, homogeneous, isotropic and non-magnetic, and both the ambient (air) and the substrate are supposed to be semi-infinite. Let n_j be the refractive index of the jth layer (complex, to account for absorption, and wavelength-dependent), t_j its mean thickness (thickness between the mean planes of the layer) and ζ_j the elevation of the jth boundary over its reference plane (Fig. 3). Let us assume that a plane electromagnetic wave with wave vector $\vec{k}_i$ is incident under the angle θ_i upon the mean levels of the boundaries (Fig. 3).

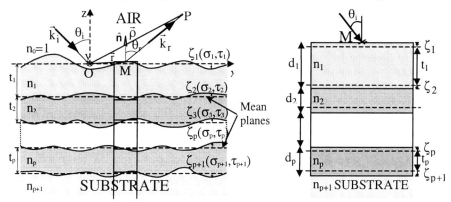

Fig. 3. Uncorrelated multilayer system   **Fig. 4.** local view of the multilayer

In addition, we also introduce the following assumptions:

- The random variables ζ_j, j=1...p+1 are statistically independent, Gaussian (zero mean value), with RMS height σ_j and correlation length τ_j.
- The incident wave is monochromatic (wavelength λ) and plane-polarised, with electric field either parallel ($\|$) or perpendicular ($\perp$) to the plane of incidence.
- The boundaries of the system are locally smooth [15].
- The dimensions of the irradiated parts of the mean planes (2X and 2Y) are much greater than the correlation lengths of the boundaries.
- The point of observation P is in the Fraunhofer diffraction zone, in the direction (θ_r, φ_r) (Fig. 2).

Within these assumptions, the system is represented locally (at point M: Fig 3, 4) by a multilayer formed of wedges. For the sake of simplicity, we assume that the slopes of the boundaries are so small that they can be neglected in the calculations. The system is thus represented locally by a plane parallel multilayer (Fig. 3, 4).

2.3 Problem

Within scalar diffraction theories, the electric field E(P) scattered by the system at point P (Fig. 2 and 3) is given by the Helmholtz-Kirchhoff integral ([3] p. 377):

$$E(P) = \frac{1}{4\pi} \iint_{\Sigma} \left[E(M) \frac{\partial \psi}{\partial \hat{n}} - \psi \frac{\partial E(M)}{\partial \hat{n}} \right] d\Sigma \quad \text{with: } \psi = \frac{e^{ik\rho} e^{-i\vec{k}_r \cdot \vec{r}}}{\rho} \quad \text{and} \quad k = \left\| \vec{k}_i \right\| = \left\| \vec{k}_r \right\| = \frac{2\pi}{\lambda} \quad (2)$$

where $\mathbf{k}_r$ is the reflected wave vector, E(M) and $\partial E(M)/\partial \hat{n}$ are the local electric field and its normal gradient at point M on the upper boundary, $\vec{r}$ is the vector from the origin O to M, ρ is the distance from O to P, ψ is the Green function ([3] p. 379) and Σ represents the irradiated part of the upper boundary. If the incident wave (pulsation $\omega = 2\pi c/\lambda$ where c is the celerity) is represented by the scalar electric field E_i, the electric field and its normal gradient at point M may be expressed as:

$$E(M) = (1+R) E_i \qquad \partial E(M)/\partial \hat{n} = i(1-R) \vec{k}_i . \hat{n} . E_i, \quad \text{with: } E_i = E_0 e^{i(\vec{k}_i \cdot \vec{r} - \omega t)}, \qquad (3)$$

where R is the local reflection coefficient of the system (parallel or perpendicular component). Assuming that all processes are stationary, eq. (3) becomes:

$$E(P) = \frac{ie^{ik\rho} E_0}{4\pi\rho} \iint_{\Sigma} (R \, \vec{v} - \vec{p}) \hat{n} \, e^{i\vec{v} \cdot \vec{r}} . d\Sigma \qquad (4)$$

where $\vec{v}$ and $\vec{p}$ are vectors defined by: $\quad \vec{v} = \begin{pmatrix} v_x \\ v_y \\ v_z \end{pmatrix} = \vec{k}_i - \vec{k}_r \qquad \vec{p} = \begin{pmatrix} p_x \\ p_y \\ p_z \end{pmatrix} = \vec{k}_i + \vec{k}_r \quad (5)$

Assuming a constant normal, this can be rewritten as:

$$E(P) = K_0 \iint_{\Sigma} (R - p_z / v_z) . e^{iv_z \varsigma_1} . e^{i(v_x x + v_y y)} d\Sigma \quad \text{with: } K_0 = ie^{ik\rho} E_0 v_z / 4\pi\rho \qquad (6)$$

Computing integral (6) requires the evaluation of the local reflection coefficient, R, which is the aim of the next section.

3. Local reflection coefficient

The expression of the local reflection coefficient of the multilayer system is easily obtained within the framework of the Abelès matrix formalism. After introducing the main results and notations, we derive a general expression of the reflection coefficient of the system, which is expanded to the second order in the small random variables ζ_j/λ, j=1...p+1, assuming that the height of the irregularities of each boundary is small compared to wavelength.

3.1 The Abelès matrix formalism

The matrix formalism introduced by Abelès in 1948 [1] has become a standard for the study of stratified media in physics. Writing the boundary conditions at the interface between two dielectric media, Abelès showed that each layer j of a multilayer (thickness d_j, refractive index n_j) could be assigned a characteristic matrix defined by:

$$M_{j\perp or\parallel} = \begin{bmatrix} \cos\varphi_j & A_{j\perp or\parallel}\sin\varphi_j \\ -\dfrac{1}{A_{j\perp or\parallel}}\sin\varphi_j & \cos\varphi_j \end{bmatrix} \quad \text{(for } j=1\ldots p+1) \tag{7}$$

with: $A_{j\perp} = i\sqrt{\mu_0/\varepsilon_0}/J_j$, $A_{j\parallel} = in_j^2\sqrt{\varepsilon_0/\mu_0}/J_j$, $\varphi_j = 2\pi d_j J_j/\lambda$ and $J_j = \sqrt{n_j^2 - \sin\theta_i^2}$ (8)
where θ_i is the angle of incidence of the wave upon the system. Simple recursion formulas show that the characteristic matrix C of the whole assembly (p layers) expresses as the ordered product of the p characteristic matrices (for the parallel or perpendicular component):

$$C = \begin{bmatrix} C_{11} & C_{12} \\ C_{21} & C_{22} \end{bmatrix} = M_1.M_2...M_j...M_p \tag{9}$$

The amplitude reflection coefficient R of the multilayer is thus given by (we refer the reader to [1] or to [11] pp. 373-375 for details on the derivation):

$$R = \frac{\Gamma_1(C)}{\Gamma_2(C)} \quad \text{with:} \quad \begin{cases} \Gamma_1(C) = Y_0 C_{11} + Y_0 Y_S C_{12} - C_{21} - Y_S C_{22} \\ \Gamma_2(C) = Y_0 C_{11} + Y_0 Y_S C_{12} + C_{21} + Y_S C_{22} \end{cases} \tag{10}$$

and: $Y_{0\perp} = \sqrt{\varepsilon_0/\mu_0}\cos\theta_i$, $Y_{S\perp} = \sqrt{\varepsilon_0/\mu_0}J_{p+1}$, $Y_{0\parallel} = \sqrt{\mu_0/\varepsilon_0}\cos\theta_i$, $Y_{S\parallel} = J_{p+1}\sqrt{\mu_0/\varepsilon_0}/n_{p+1}^2$

3.2 Expansion of the reflection coefficient

Let us consider the plane parallel multilayer depicted on Fig. 4. It can be seen that the local thickness d_j, of the jth layer is a function of the random variables ζ_j and ζ_{j+1}:

$$d_j = t_j + \zeta_j - \zeta_{j+1}, \tag{11}$$

As the phase shift φ_j (eq. (8)) involves d_j, we can deduce (eq. (9)-(10)) that the characteristic matrix of the multilayer, and thus the reflection coefficient is a function of the p+1 random variables ζ_j, j=1...p+1. Evaluating the Kirchhoff integral with the full expression of R is a difficult task, but if we assume that $\zeta_j/\lambda \ll 1$ for all j, we can limit ourselves to a second order expansion in ζ_j/λ. Expanding the characteristic matrix of the jth layer to the second order gives:

$$M_j = N_j + O_j\Delta\varphi_j - \frac{1}{2}N_j\Delta\varphi_j^2 + o(\Delta\varphi_j^2)1_2 \tag{12}$$

with: $N_j = \begin{bmatrix} \cos\varphi_{0j} & A_k\sin\varphi_{0j} \\ -\dfrac{1}{A_k}\sin\varphi_{0j} & \cos\varphi_{0j} \end{bmatrix}$, $O_j = \begin{bmatrix} -\sin\varphi_{0j} & A_k\cos\varphi_{0j} \\ -\dfrac{1}{A_k}\cos\varphi_{0j} & -\sin\varphi_{0j} \end{bmatrix}$, $1_2 = \begin{bmatrix} 1 & 1 \\ 1 & 1 \end{bmatrix}$ (13)

and: $\varphi_{0j} = 2\pi t_j J_j/\lambda$, $\Delta\varphi_j = 2\pi(\zeta_j - \zeta_{j+1})J_j/\lambda$ (14)

Making the product of the p characteristic matrices (eq. (12)), we draw:

$$C \approx r_0 + r_1\frac{\zeta_1}{\lambda} + \sum_{j=2}^{p+1} r_j\frac{\zeta_j}{\lambda} + \left(\sum_{j=2}^{p+1} q_j\frac{\zeta_j}{\lambda}\right)\frac{\zeta_1}{\lambda} + p_{1,1}\frac{\zeta_1^2}{\lambda^2} + \sum_{j=2}^{p+1} p_{j,j}\frac{\zeta_j^2}{\lambda^2} + \sum_{j=2}^{p}\sum_{m=j+1}^{p+1} p_{j,m}\frac{\zeta_j\zeta_m}{\lambda^2} \tag{15}$$

The expressions for the matrices (r_j and $p_{j,j}$, j=1...p+1) involved in the above equation are fully specified in Appendix A (eq. (35)-(38)). We do not provide the expressions for the other coefficients, as they do not appear in the final expression of the BRDF (eq. 31-34 below). Formula (10) finally allows us to obtain:

$$R \approx R_0 + R_1 \frac{\zeta_1}{\lambda} + \sum_{j=2}^{p+1} R_j \frac{\zeta_k}{\lambda} + \left(\sum_{j=2}^{p+1} Q_j \frac{\zeta_j}{\lambda} \right) \frac{\zeta_1}{\lambda} + P_{1,1} \frac{\zeta_1^2}{\lambda^2} + \sum_{j=2}^{p+1} P_{j,j} \frac{\zeta_j^2}{\lambda^2} + \sum_{j=2}^{p} \sum_{m=j+1}^{p+1} P_{j,m} \frac{\zeta_j \zeta_m}{\lambda^2} \quad (16)$$

The coefficients of eq. (16) are functions of the parameters of the layers (mean thicknesses, optical constants of the materials) and of the angle of incidence. Their expression is fully specified in Appendix A (eq. (39) and (40)).

4. Derivation of the components of the BRDF

Substituting R by formula (16) in the Helmholtz-Kirchhoff integral allows us to evaluate the electric field reflected at point P. From the rendering point of view, we are specifically interested in bidirectional reflectances (ratio of the outgoing radiance to the incoming irradiance). In this paragraph, we perform the calculation of the radiances reflected coherently and incoherently from the system, which leads us to the full expression of the BRDF (Section 5).

4.1 Components of light reflected by the system

The electromagnetic power reflected from a rough surface is usually resolved into a coherent component, which results from the superposition of constructively interfering waves and an incoherent part, composed of waves originating from the whole system, with no phase relationship (see e.g. [2] or [14] pp.4-7). As the power carried by an electromagnetic wave is proportional to the square modulus of the electric field (flux of the Poynting vector [11] p.44), the radiances (power per unit solid angle per unit foreshortened area [5]) reflected coherently (dL_{rcoh}) and incoherently (dL_{rinc}), and the incident radiance, L_i, express as (Fig. 2):

$$dL_{rcoh} = \frac{\rho^2}{A \cos \theta_r} \langle E(P) \rangle \langle \overline{E}(P) \rangle, \quad dL_{rinc} = \frac{\rho^2}{A \cos \theta_r} \left(\langle E(P) \overline{E}(P) \rangle - \langle E(P) \rangle \langle \overline{E}(P) \rangle \right), \quad L_i = \frac{E_0^2}{d\omega_i} \quad (17)$$

where $A = 4XY$ is the area of the upper mean plane of the system. The symbol <> denotes statistical averaging and $\overline{Z}$, the complex conjugate of the complex variable Z. In the following, these two components will be evaluated separately.

4.2 Coherent (specular) component

Replacing R by expression (16) in formula (6), we draw:

$$\langle E(P) \rangle = K_0 \int_{-X}^{X} \int_{-Y}^{Y} \left\{ \underbrace{S_0 \langle e^{iv_z \zeta_1} \rangle}_{\{1\}} + \underbrace{R_1 \left\langle \frac{\zeta_1}{\lambda} e^{iv_z \zeta_1} \right\rangle}_{\{2\}} + \underbrace{\sum_{j=2}^{p+1} R_j \left\langle \frac{\zeta_j}{\lambda} e^{iv_z \zeta_1} \right\rangle}_{\{3\}} + \underbrace{P_{1,1} \left\langle \frac{\zeta_1^2}{\lambda^2} e^{iv_z \zeta_1} \right\rangle}_{\{4\}} + \underbrace{\sum_{j=2}^{p+1} Q_j \left\langle \frac{\zeta_1 \zeta_j}{\lambda^2} e^{iv_z \zeta_1} \right\rangle}_{\{5\}} \right.$$

$$\left. + \underbrace{\sum_{j=2}^{p+1} P_{j,j} \left\langle \frac{\zeta_j^2}{\lambda^2} e^{iv_z \zeta_1} \right\rangle}_{\{6\}} + \underbrace{\sum_{j=2}^{p} \sum_{m=j+1}^{p+1} P_{j,m} \left\langle \frac{\zeta_j \zeta_m}{\lambda^2} e^{iv_z \zeta_1} \right\rangle}_{\{7\}} \right\} e^{i(v_x x + v_y y)} dx dy \quad (18)$$

with: $S_0 = R_0 - p_z / v_z$. As the random variables are mutually independent, $\{3\}$, $\{5\}$ and $\{7\}$ average to zero. Equation (18) becomes (see Appendix B, eq. 41-45 for details on the computation of the averages):

$$\langle E(P) \rangle \approx K_0 \int_{-X}^{X} \int_{-Y}^{Y} \left\{ S_0 + iv_z \frac{\sigma_1^2}{\lambda} R_1 + P_{1,1} \frac{\sigma_1^2}{\lambda^2} + \frac{1}{\lambda^2} \sum_{j=2}^{p+1} P_{j,j} \sigma_j^2 \right\} \cdot \chi_{1,1}(v_z) e^{i(v_x x + v_y y)} dxdy \quad (19)$$

where $\chi_{1,1}$ is the characteristic function (see e.g. [14] p.17) of the distribution of ζ_1 (Gaussian). Integrating (eq. 19) and keeping terms up to the second order in σ_j / λ, we find (the characteristic function was replaced by its second order expansion):

$$\langle E(P) \rangle \approx K_0 F_0 A \sin c(v_x X) \sin c(v_y Y) \quad (20)$$

with: $F_0 = S_0(1 - g_1/2) + (P_{1,1} + i\lambda v_z R_1)\frac{\sigma_1^2}{\lambda^2} + \sum_{j=2}^{p+1} P_{j,j} \frac{\sigma_j^2}{\lambda^2}$ and $\sin c(x) = \frac{\sin x}{x}$, x real (21)

Finally, the coherent radiance is obtained in the form:

$$dL_{rcoh} = \frac{v_z^2}{16\pi^2 \cos\theta_r} FA \left(\sin c(v_x X).\sin c(v_y Y) \right)^2 L_i d\omega_i \quad (22)$$

with: $F = |S_0|^2 + \left[2Re(\overline{S}_0 P_{1,1}) + -2\lambda v_z Im(\overline{S}_0 R_1) - (\lambda v_z)^2 |S_0|^2 \right] \frac{\sigma_1^2}{\lambda^2} + 2\sum_{j=2}^{p+1} Re(P_{j,j} \overline{S}_0) \frac{\sigma_j^2}{\lambda^2}$ (23)

In the case when $X \gg \lambda$ and $Y \gg \lambda$, the coherent radiance is zero in all directions excepted in the specular cone and can therefore be identified with the specular component of our BRDF. If we label dL_{rsp} the specular radiance, we get ([10] p. 186):

$$dL_{rsp} = F\Delta L_i \quad (24)$$

where Δ is a function which is unity in the specular cone and zero otherwise.

4.3. Incoherent (directional diffuse) component

Let us denote $\zeta_j = \zeta_j(x,y)$ and $\eta_j = \zeta_j(x',y')$ for all j. We can write:

$$\langle E(P)\overline{E}(P) \rangle = |K_0|^2 \left\langle \int_{-X}^{X} \int_{-Y}^{Y} \int_{-X}^{X} \int_{-Y}^{Y} \left| R - \frac{p_z}{v_z} \right|^2 e^{iv_z(\zeta_1 - \eta_1)} e^{i(v_x(x-x') + v_y(y-y'))} dxdx'dydy' \right\rangle \quad (25)$$

Expanding formula (25) and eliminating the terms with zero mean value, we find:

$$\langle E(P)\overline{E}(P) \rangle = |K_0|^2 \int_{-X}^{X} \int_{-Y}^{Y} \int_{-X}^{X} \int_{-Y}^{Y} fe^{i(v_x(x-x') + v_y(y-y'))} dxdydx'dy' \quad (26)$$

with: $f = f_1 + 2Re(f_2 + f_3 + f_4) + f_5$ and : $f_1 = |S_0|^2 \left\langle e^{iv_z(\zeta_1 - \eta_1)} \right\rangle$, $f_2 = S_0 \overline{R}_1 \left\langle \frac{\eta_1}{\lambda} e^{iv_z(\zeta_1 - \eta_1)} \right\rangle$

$f_3 = S_0 \overline{P}_{1,1} \left\langle \frac{\eta_1^2}{\lambda^2} e^{iv_z(\zeta_1 - \eta_1)} \right\rangle$, $f_4 = S_0 \sum_{j=2}^{p+1} \overline{P}_{j,j} \left\langle \frac{\eta_j^2}{\lambda^2} e^{iv_z(\zeta_1 - \eta_1)} \right\rangle$ $f_6 = \sum_{j=1}^{p+1} |R_j|^2 \left\langle \frac{\zeta_j \eta_j}{\lambda^2} e^{iv_z(\zeta_1 - \eta_1)} \right\rangle$

Making the change of variables $\{ x - x' = r'\cos\theta, y - y' = r'\sin\theta \}$ in integral (26) and using the computation results summarised in Appendix B (eq. 46-50), we draw:

$$\langle E(P)\overline{E}(P)\rangle = |K_0|^2 \int_{-X}^{X}\int_{-Y}^{Y}\int_{0}^{\infty}\int_{0}^{2\pi} g(r')\chi_{2,1}(v_z,-v_z,r')e^{i(v_x r'\cos\theta + v_y r'\sin\theta)}dxdydr'd\theta \quad (27)$$

where $\chi_{2,1}$ is the 2D characteristic function of ζ_j and η_j (Gaussian) and:

$$g(r') = |S_0|^2 + 2\lambda v_z (1 - C_1(r'))\text{Re}(S_0\overline{R}_1)\frac{\sigma_1^2}{\lambda^2} + 2\sum_{j=1}^{p+1}\text{Re}(S_0\overline{P}_{j,j})\frac{\sigma_j^2}{\lambda^2} + \sum_{j=1}^{p+1}|R_j|^2\frac{\sigma_j^2}{\lambda^2}C_j(r')$$

C_j is the correlation function of ζ_j and η_j (see [2]), which was taken in the form:

$$C_j(r') = e^{-r'^2/\tau_j^2} \quad (28)$$

Subtracting $\langle E(P)\rangle\langle E(P)\rangle$ from eq. (27) where $\langle E(P)\rangle$ is given by eq. (19), and dropping terms higher than second order in the small variables σ_j/λ we get the expression for the incoherent (or directional diffuse) radiance:

$$dL_{rinc} = \frac{v_z^2}{16\pi\cos\theta_r}GL_i d\omega_i \quad (29)$$

$$G = |R_1 + i\lambda v_z S_0|^2\left(\frac{\sigma_1\tau_1}{\lambda}\right)^2 e^{-\frac{(v_x^2+v_y^2)\tau_1^2}{4}} + \sum_{j=2}^{p+1}|R_j|^2\left(\frac{\sigma_j\tau_j}{\lambda}\right)^2 e^{-\frac{(v_x^2+v_y^2)\tau_j^2}{4}} \quad (30)$$

5. Expression for the BRDF

From the previous results (equations (1), (23), (24), (29) and (30)), we can build a combined expression for the BRDF:

$$\rho_{bd} = \rho_{bd,sp} + \rho_{bd,dd} + \rho_{bd,ud}, \text{ with: } \rho_{bd,sp} = \frac{S.\Delta}{\cos\theta_{ik}\omega_{ik}}\left\{\frac{F_\perp + F_\parallel}{2}\right\} \text{ and: } \quad (31)$$

$$\rho_{bd,dd} = \frac{v_z^2.S}{16\pi\cos\theta_i\cos\theta_r}\left\{\frac{G_\perp + G_\parallel}{2}\right\}, \quad \rho_{bd,ud} = \frac{|R_0(\theta_i=0)|_\perp^2 + |R_0(\theta_i=0)|_\parallel^2}{2\pi} \quad (32)$$

$$F = |S_0|^2 - \left[2\lambda v_z\text{Im}(\overline{S}_0 R_1) + (\lambda v_z)^2|S_0|^2\right]\frac{\sigma_1^2}{\lambda^2} + 2\sum_{j=1}^{p+1}\text{Re}(\overline{S}_0 P_{j,j})\frac{\sigma_j^2}{\lambda^2}, \quad S_0 = R_0 - p_z/v_z \quad (33)$$

$$G = |R_1 + i\lambda v_z S_0|^2\left(\frac{\sigma_1\tau_1}{\lambda}\right)^2 e^{-\frac{(v_x^2+v_y^2)\tau_1^2}{4}} + \sum_{j=2}^{p+1}|R_j|^2\left(\frac{\sigma_j\tau_j}{\lambda}\right)^2 e^{-\frac{(v_x^2+v_y^2)\tau_j^2}{4}} \quad (34)$$

The expressions for the coefficients involved in the above equations are given in Appendix A and S is the shadowing function of Smith (see [10], equations (23)-(25)). It should be noted that the uniform diffuse term, which results from multiple reflection phenomena was modelled by a classic Lambert term.

6. Results and discussion

The following pictures (Fig. 5 and 6: See Color Plate) were obtained by integrating the previous BRDF model (eq. 31-34) in a spectral ray-tracing algorithm working on four wavelengths, according to G. Meyer's [13] recommendations. The materials are represented by their complex refractive indices (on the sampling wavelengths), drawn from experimental data [16]. Optical data are still scarce, and available only for a small number of materials in the literature (mainly oxides and metals), and for restricted ranges of wavelengths, this explains why we have taken only four wavelengths for rendering. The pictures could probably be improved by using more well-chosen sampling wavelengths [17], provided we find the values of the complex refractive indices of the materials for each one of these wavelengths. In this section, we study both the influence of the multilayer composition (number and stacking order of layers) and the effect of a variation of the surface parameters.

6.1 Influence of the number and order of layers

Pictures 5a)–f) represent various mono or multi layer systems formed of a titanium substrate coated with an alternance of thin zirconium dioxide (ZrO_2) and tantalum oxide (Ta_2O_3) layers. The statistical parameters (σ,τ) of the boundaries are fixed and the mean thickness of each layer varies slightly varies from e_{min} at the top of the pitcher to e_{max} at the bottom (Fig. 5). The system is lit by several white light sources.

The first picture (5a)) displays a single layer of zirconium dioxide on titanium. As the thickness of the layer varies, fringes of interference can be observed in the diffuse patch. Let us add a layer of tantalum oxide. We can notice that the result strongly depends on whether we insert this layer on (picture 5c)) or under (picture 5b)) the previous one. Now if we add one more ZrO_2 layer on the Ta_2O_3 film (picture 5d)), the pitcher takes a dark plum colour (the uniform diffuse term depends on the multilayer composition: see formula 40) and the fringes of interference become brighter and more numerous. Adding some more layers (pictures 5e) and 5f)) results in a change in the contrast of the fringes and increases their number.

6.2 Influence of the roughness parameters

Consider a system consisting of a thin film of aluminium oxide deposited on a copper substrate (Fig. 6). The mean thickness of the oxide film varies between 400 and 800 nm and we study the evolution of the optical behaviour of the system as a function of roughness parameters of each boundary (pictures 6a)-f)). The parameters are initially set to the values $(\sigma_1,\tau_1)=(30nm,900nm)$ for the ambient-film boundary and $(\sigma_2,\tau_2)=(50nm,900nm)$ for the substrate-layer boundary. Decreasing the RMS height σ_1 from 30 nm to 0 nm slightly reduces the contrast and dimensions of the diffuse spot. As the RMS height of the substrate diminishes to zero (pictures 6c)-f)), light energy tends to concentrate progressively in the specular direction and the system becomes perfectly specular. When the RMS roughness of both boundaries is zero ($\sigma_1=\sigma_2=0$ in eq. (23), (24), (29), (30)), the reflected radiance is purely specular and corresponds to the radiance reflected by the corresponding smooth system (reflection coefficient R_0). Similarly, it can be shown that increasing the correlation length while keeping the RMS height constant tends to make the system more specular.

7. Conclusions and future work

We have presented a new theoretical BRDF model which allows one to simulate the optical behaviour of composite multilayer systems. Derived from physical optics, it extends models previously proposed by some authors for a rough surface [10] and for a single rough thin film [12] and constitutes an original analytic approach to multilayer systems in computer graphics. We have demonstrated some interesting properties of multilayer stacks (the number of interference fringes increases with the number of layers, the reflectance greatly depends on the thickness, order, number and nature of the layers), that have to be verified experimentally. We are currently working on an experimental validation of the model.

This model could prove very useful in predicting the appearance of complex multilayer materials used in industry (such as the pigments involved in nacreous and interference paints) or in simulating the aging of materials [6] (in particular corrosion or oxidation). Conversely, it might help to characterise some physical properties (refractive index, thickness) of given multilayers. An interesting direction for further research is to find a method for taking into account analytically bulk scattering in the case of inhomogeneous multilayer systems (in contrast with Monte-Carlo approaches [7], [8], [9]). We are also planning to generalise the model to the case of multilayer systems with partially correlated rough boundaries, and to systems formed of non isotropic rough boundaries (generalisation of [18]).

References

1. F. Abelès, "Sur la Propagation des Ondes Electromagnétiques dans les Milieux stratifiés", Ann. De Phys., $12^{\text{ème}}$ série, vol. 10, pp. 505-581 , 1948.
2. P. Beckmann and A. Spizzichino,. "The Scattering of Electromagnetic Waves from Rough Surfaces", Pergamon Press, 1963.
3. M. Born and E. Wolf, Principles of Optics-Electromagnetic Theory of Propagation, Interference and Diffraction of Light, sixth (corrected) edition, Pergamon Press, Oxford, 1980.
4. P. Callet, "Physically Based Rendering of Metallic Paints and Coated Pigments", Visualization and Modelling, R. Earnshaw, John Vince and Huw Jones, Academic Press, pp. 287-302, 1997.
5. Commission Internationale de l'Eclairage, International Lighting Vocabulary, CIE 17 (E-1.1), Paris, Troisième édition, 1970.
6. J. Dorsey, A. Edelman, J. Legakis, H. W. Jensen, H. K. Pedersen, "Modeling and Rendering of Weathered Stone", ACM SIGGRAPH' 99 Conference Proceedings, 1999.
7. J. S. Gondek, G. W. Meyer and J. G. Newman, "Wavelength Dependant Reflectance Functions", Proceedings of Siggraph'94, p. 213-220, Orlando, Florida, 1994.
8. P. Hanrahan and W. Krueger, "Reflection from Layered Surfaces due to Subsurface Scattering", Proceedings of SIGGRAPH '93, pp. 165-174, 1993.
9. H. W. Jensen, J. Legakis and J. Dorsey, "Rendering of wet materials", Rendering Techniques '99, Proceedings of The Eurographics Workshop, Grenada, 1999, pp.273-280.
10. X. D. He, K. E. Torrance, F. X. Sillion et D. P. Greenberg, "A Comprehensive Physical Model for Light Reflection", Computer Graphics Vol. 25(4), ACM SIGGRAPH'91 Conference Proceedings, 1991.
11. E. Hecht, Optics, Addison-Wesley Publishing Company, 1987.
12. I. Icart and D. Arquès, "An Illumination Model for a system of Isotropic Substrate-Isotropic Thin Film with Identical Rough Boundaries", Rendering Techniques '99, Proceedings of The Eurographics Workshop, Grenada, 1999, pp.261-272.
13. G. W. Meyer, "Wavelength Selection for Synthetic Image Generation", Computer Vision, Graphics and Image Processing, vol. 41, 57-69, 1988.
14. J. A. Ogilvy, Theory of Wave Scattering from Random Rough Surfaces, Institute of Physics Publishing, Bristol and Philadelphia 1991.
15. I. Ohlídal and K. Navrátil, "Scattering of Light from Multilayer Systems with Rough Boundaries", Progress in Optics, 34, Elsevier Science, 1995.
16. E. D. Palik, Handbook of Optical Constants of Solids, Academic Press, 1997.
17. G. Rougeron and B. Péroche, "Color Fidelity in Computer Graphics:a survey", Computer Graphics Forum, 17, pp.1-13, 1998.
18. J. Stam, "Diffraction Shaders", Proceedings of SIGGRAPH '99, pp. 101-110, 1999.

Appendix A: Coefficients involved in the second order expansions

In this Appendix, we give the expressions for the coefficients involved in equations 18 and 19. For the sake of simplicity, we only provide the expressions for the coefficients involved in the final expression of the BRDF (Section 5, eq. 31-34).

- **Expansion of the characteristic matrix (Formula 15)**

Let us denote (see formula (13)):

$$B = \prod_{i=1}^{p} N_i \quad \text{and} \quad C(j) = \prod_{i=1}^{p} Q_i(j) \quad \text{where:} \quad \begin{array}{l} Q_i(j) = O_i \text{ if } i = j \\ Q_i(j) = N_i \text{ if } i \neq j \end{array} \tag{35}$$

$$D(j,m) = \prod_{i=1}^{p} S_i(j,m) \quad \text{with:} \quad \begin{array}{l} S_i(j,m) = O_i \quad \text{if } i = j \text{ or } i = m \\ S_i(j,m) = N_i \quad \text{otherwise} \end{array} \tag{36}$$

After some calculations, we found the coefficients of equation (15) in the form:

$$r_0 = B \quad r_1 = 2\pi C(1)J_1 \quad p_{1,1} = -2\pi^2 J_1^2 B \quad r_{p+1} = -2\pi C(p)J_p \quad p_{p+1,p+1} = -2\pi^2 J_p^2 B \tag{37}$$

and, for $j = 2...p$: $r_j = 2\pi\left(J_j C(j) - J_{j-1}C(j-1)\right)$ $\quad p_{j,j} = -2\pi^2\left((J_j^2 + J_{j-1}^2)B + 2D(j-1,j)J_{j-1}J_j\right)$ (38)

- **Expansion of the reflection coefficient (Formula 16)**

If we set (see formula (10)): $a_j = \Gamma_1(r_j) \quad c_{j,j} = \Gamma_1(p_{j,j}) \quad \alpha_j = \Gamma_2(r_j) \quad \gamma_{j,j} = \Gamma_2(p_{j,j})$ (39)

then we find: $R_0 = \dfrac{a_0}{\alpha_0}$ and for $j = 1...p+1$: $R_j = \dfrac{\alpha_0 a_j - a_0 \alpha_j}{\alpha_0^2}$, $P_{j,j} = \dfrac{c_{j,j}}{\alpha_0} - \dfrac{a_0 \gamma_{j,j} + a_j \alpha_j}{\alpha_0^2} + \dfrac{a_0 \alpha_j^2}{\alpha_0^3}$ (40)

Appendix B: Computation of the averages (eq. 18 and 26)

- **Equation 18**

Since we supposed that the random variables ζ_j, $j = 1...p+1$ were Gaussian (with zero mean value) and mutually independent, we have the following properties:

$$\text{For } j = 1...p+1: \langle \zeta_j \rangle = 0 \text{ and } \langle \zeta_j^2 \rangle = \sigma_j^2 \text{ and for } i \neq j, \langle \zeta_i \zeta_j \rangle = \langle \zeta_i \rangle \langle \zeta_j \rangle = 0 \tag{41}$$

Using these properties and some results evident from the Fourier theory, the terms involved in eq. 21 can be computed as follows:

$$\{1\} = S_0\left\langle e^{iv_z\zeta_1} \right\rangle = S_0\chi_{1,1}(v_z) \text{ (characteristic function)}, \{2\} = \left\langle \frac{\zeta_1}{\lambda}e^{iv_z\zeta_1} \right\rangle = -\frac{i}{\lambda}\chi'_{1,1}(v_z) = iv_z\frac{\sigma_1^2}{\lambda}\chi_{1,1}(v_z) \tag{42}$$

$$\{3\} = \left\langle \frac{\zeta_j}{\lambda}e^{iv_z\zeta_1} \right\rangle = \left\langle \frac{\zeta_j}{\lambda} \right\rangle\left\langle e^{iv_z\zeta_1} \right\rangle = 0, \{5\} = \left\langle \frac{\zeta_1\zeta_j}{\lambda^2}e^{iv_z\zeta_1} \right\rangle = \left\langle \frac{\zeta_j}{\lambda} \right\rangle\left\langle \frac{\zeta_1}{\lambda}e^{iv_z\zeta_1} \right\rangle = 0 \quad (j \neq 1) \tag{43}$$

$$\{4\} = \left\langle \frac{\zeta_1^2}{\lambda^2}e^{iv_z\zeta_1} \right\rangle = -\frac{1}{\lambda^2}\chi''_{1,1}(v_z) = \frac{\sigma_1^2}{\lambda^2}(1-g_1)\chi_{1,1}(v_z) \approx \frac{\sigma_1^2}{\lambda^2}\chi_{1,1}(v_z) \tag{44}$$

$$\{6\} = \left\langle \frac{\zeta_j^2}{\lambda^2}e^{iv_z\zeta_1} \right\rangle = \left\langle \frac{\zeta_j^2}{\lambda^2} \right\rangle\left\langle e^{iv_z\zeta_1} \right\rangle = \frac{\sigma_j^2}{\lambda^2}\chi_{1,1}(v_z), \{7\} = \left\langle \frac{\zeta_j\zeta_m}{\lambda^2}e^{iv_z\zeta_1} \right\rangle = \left\langle \frac{\zeta_j}{\lambda} \right\rangle\left\langle \frac{\zeta_m}{\lambda} \right\rangle\left\langle e^{iv_z\zeta_1} \right\rangle = 0 \ (j \neq m) \tag{45}$$

- **Equations 26**

We provide below some details on the computation of the averages involved in eq. 26:

$$f_1 = |S_0|^2 \left\langle e^{iv_z(\zeta_1 - \eta_1)} \right\rangle = |S_0|^2 \chi_{2,1}(v_z, -v_z, r') \quad \text{(2D characteristic function of } \zeta_1 \text{ and } \eta_1) \tag{46}$$

$$f_2 = S_0 \overline{R}_1 \left\langle \frac{\eta_1}{\lambda} e^{iv_z(\zeta_1 - \eta_1)} \right\rangle = S_0 \overline{R}_1 i v_z \frac{\sigma_1^2}{\lambda} (C_1(r') - 1) \chi_{2,1}(v_z, -v_z, r') \tag{47}$$

$$f_3 = S_0 \overline{P}_{1,1} \left\langle \frac{\eta_1^2}{\lambda^2} e^{iv_z(\zeta_1 - \eta_1)} \right\rangle \approx S_0 \overline{P}_{1,1} \frac{\sigma_1^2}{\lambda^2} \chi_{2,1}(v_z, -v_z, r') \tag{48}$$

$$f_4 = S_0 \sum_{j=2}^{p+1} \overline{P}_{j,j} \left\langle \frac{\eta_j^2}{\lambda^2} e^{iv_z(\zeta_1 - \eta_1)} \right\rangle = S_0 \sum_{j=2}^{p+1} \overline{P}_{j,j} \left\langle \frac{\eta_j^2}{\lambda^2} \right\rangle \left\langle e^{iv_z(\zeta_1 - \eta_1)} \right\rangle = S_0 \sum_{j=2}^{p+1} \overline{P}_{j,j} \frac{\sigma_j^2}{\lambda^2} \chi_{2,1}(v_z, -v_z, r') \tag{49}$$

$$f_5 = \sum_{j=1}^{p+1} |R_j|^2 \left\langle \frac{\zeta_j \eta_j}{\lambda^2} e^{iv_z(\zeta_1 - \eta_1)} \right\rangle = |R_1|^2 \left\langle \frac{\zeta_1 \eta_1}{\lambda^2} e^{iv_z(\zeta_1 - \eta_1)} \right\rangle + \sum_{j=2}^{p+1} |R_j|^2 \left\langle \frac{\zeta_j \eta_j}{\lambda^2} \right\rangle \left\langle e^{iv_z(\zeta_1 - \eta_1)} \right\rangle$$

$$= \left[|R_1|^2 \frac{\sigma_1^2}{\lambda^2} \left(C_1 + g_1(C_1 - 1)^2 \right) + \sum_{j=2}^{p+1} |R_j|^2 \frac{\sigma_j^2}{\lambda^2} C_j \right] \chi_{2,1}(v_z, -v_z, r') \approx \sum_{j=1}^{p+1} |R_j|^2 \frac{\sigma_j^2}{\lambda^2} C_j \chi_{2,1}(v_z, -v_z, r') \tag{50}$$

Appendix C: Table of symbols

	General			
A	$=4XY$: area of the upper mean plane		λ	Wavelength
C	characteristic matrix of the multilayer (eq. 10)		ρ	distance from O to field point P
$d_1, \ldots, d_p$	local thicknesses of the multilayer (Fig. 4)		σ_j	standard deviation (j^{th} boundary)
$E(M)$	scalar electric field at point M		τ_j	correlation length (j^{th} boundary)
$h_{1,1}$	probability density of the random variable ζ_1		Σ	irradiated surface (eq. 2)
$h_{1,2}$	joint probability density of ζ_1 and η_1		ψ	Green's function
i	unit imaginary number ($i^2 = -1$)		ω	pulsation of the wave
k	wave number		$d\omega_i$	solid angle of incident light
$\vec{k}$	wave vector		**Subscripts**	
L	radiance		bd	bidirectional
$n_1, \ldots, n_{p+1}$	complex refractive indices of the materials		coh	coherent
$\hat{n}$	local normal (unit vector)		dd	directional diffuse
O	origin of the reference frame (Fig. 3)		i	incident
p	number of layers		inc	incoherent
$\vec{p}$	sum of the incident and reflected wave vectors		r	reflected
$\vec{r}$	position vector (Fig. 3)		sp	specular
R	local reflection coefficient (eq. 19)		ud	uniform diffuse
S	Smith's shadowing function		$\parallel$	parallel component
$t_1, \ldots, t_p$	mean thicknesses of the layers		$\perp$	perpendicular component
$\vec{v}$	wave vector change (eq. 6)		**Special**	
X, Y	dimensions of the mean planes		$\overline{Z}$	complex conjugate of Z
ε_0, μ_0	permittivity (resp. permeability of free space)		$|Z|$	modulus of Z
$\zeta_1, \ldots, \zeta_{p+1}$	Gaussian distributed random variables		$\|\vec{z}\|$	magnitude of $\vec{Z}$
$\eta_1, \ldots, \eta_{p+1}$	Gaussian distributed random variables		Re(Z)	real part of Z
$\theta_i, \varphi_i, \theta_r, \varphi_r$	polar and azimuthal angles (Fig. 2)		Im(Z)	imaginary part of Z

Editors' Note: see Appendix, p. 420 for colored figures of this paper

Interactive Rendering with Real-World Illumination

Simon Gibson and Alan Murta

Advanced Interfaces Group
Department of Computer Science
University of Manchester, UK.
{sg,amurta}@cs.man.ac.uk

Abstract.
We propose solutions for seamlessly integrating synthetic objects into background photographs at interactive rates. Recently developed image-based methods are used to capture real-world illumination, and sphere-mapping is used illuminate and render the synthetic objects. We present a new procedure for approximating shadows cast by the real-world illumination using standard hardware-based shadow mapping, and a novel image composition algorithm that uses frame-buffer hardware to correctly overlay the synthetic objects and their shadows onto the background image. We show results of an OpenGL implementation of the algorithm that is capable of rendering complex synthetic objects and their shadows at rates of up to 10 frames per second on an SGI Onyx2.

1 Introduction

The seamless integration of synthetic objects into real photographs or video images is a common requirement in fields such as augmented reality and digital visual effects. Achieving a high degree of realism in such applications requires first matching the geometric characteristics of both the synthetic and real cameras, and then shading the synthetic objects so that they appear to be illuminated by the same lights as the other objects in the background image. By rendering the synthetic objects with the same illumination, important visual cues are provided that increase the apparent accuracy of the integration, and aid the user's judgement of spatial layout.

In the field of augmented reality, many researchers have focussed on the first of these problems, namely camera calibration and registration (for example, see [27, 1]). Few methods, however, have been proposed for solving the problem of illuminating the synthetic objects in a realistic and believable way. This is mainly due to the enormous complexities of real-world illumination, which includes both direct and indirect illumination from complex light-sources, shadows, and glossy reflections and refractions. Global illumination algorithms (e.g. [16]) simulate these effects using complex and time consuming approaches that are not suitable for interactive augmented reality applications.

In this paper, we provide solutions for illuminating and integrating synthetic objects into real-world images at interactive rates. Our method combines the image-based capture and rendering of real-world illumination with a novel shadow generation and image composition algorithm that uses computer graphics hardware to generate photo-realistic images containing both real and synthetic objects.

2 Background and Related Work

One of the earliest algorithms for compositing synthetic objects into background images was proposed by Nakamae *et al.* [20]. Their solution involved estimating the location of the sun and levels of ambient light to illuminate synthetic architectural models rendered onto background photographs.

Fournier *et al.* [9] proposed using an approximate model of the scene to generate estimates of diffuse reflectance characteristics, and radiosity algorithms [11] to illuminate synthetic objects. Using this approach, a re-calculation of the radiosity solution must be performed whenever any form of interaction with the synthetic objects occurs. Radiosity algorithms were also employed by Drettakis *et al.* [8] and Loscos *et al.* [19], who proposed solutions for providing common illumination between real and synthetic objects in an interactive setting. Their approach extended the work of Fournier *et al.* by employing a semi-automatic algorithm for constructing the model of the environment, and an incremental radiosity algorithm for the rapid update of illumination for moving objects.

One of the disadvantages with the approaches described above is that they require a model of the entire environment in order to illuminate the synthetic objects. In many situations (for example, a complex outdoor scene), it is both difficult and time-consuming to construct such a model. In [5], Debevec proposed a different approach to capturing real-world lighting. Instead of storing illumination details on a model of the scene, he captured an omni-directional image (or *radiance-map*) that represented the incident illumination at a single point in the scene. This radiance-map was then used to construct a very simple light-based model of the parts of the scene which were distant from the synthetic objects. An approximate, material-based model of the environment near the synthetic objects was then built, and the synthetic objects were composited into the background image using the RADIANCE global illumination system [31] and a differential rendering algorithm [5]. A similar algorithm has also been proposed by Sato *et al.* [25], who use a hemispherical fish-eye camera lens and stereoscopic reconstruction algorithm to capture illumination and model the distant parts of the environment respectively.

Debevec and Malik [6] have also addressed the problem of representing the dynamic range of real-world lighting conditions. By capturing images at different levels of exposure, the response function of the imaging system may be recovered, and the images combined into a single high-dynamic range photograph.

All of these algorithms use expensive global illumination techniques to illuminate the synthetic objects. With the exception of Drettakis *et al.* [8], these techniques are not applicable when any form of interaction is required. The incremental algorithm employed by Drettakis was reported to provide updates on the order of two to three seconds per frame for a simple environment, but is only capable of modelling diffuse illumination, and so cannot accommodate the wide variety of reflection characteristics we see in real-world images.

Walter *et al.* [30] proposed using hardware-based lighting calculations to approximate reflections from glossy surfaces during an interactive walk-through of a pre-computed global illumination solution. A multi-pass algorithm was also developed by Diefenbach and Badler [7] that used the rendering pipeline to provide high-quality images containing shadows, reflections and refractions.

More recently, Heidrich and Seidel [15] published algorithms for performing realistic shading calculations using computer graphics hardware. They proposed using multi-pass methods for high-quality local illumination with physically-based reflection models, as well as techniques for pre-integrating omni-directional images in order to render objects with complex material characteristics using *sphere-mapping* [2, 12]. In parallel, Cabral *et al.* [4] also developed similar techniques. They pre-integrated an omni-directional image with a surface BRDF to form a sphere-map.

Finally, optimisation processes have previously been used by Poulin *et al.* to find reflectance and shadow properties of scenes [21, 22].

3 Overview

In this paper, we present an algorithm that enables complex synthetic objects to be realistically illuminated and seamlessly combined with background images at interactive rates. Currently, our implementation is restricted to rendering images from a single viewpoint, but we briefly discuss possible extensions at the end of the paper.

Like Debevec [5] and Sato *et al.* [25], we partition the environment into three sections: the *synthetic objects* are the objects we wish to add into the image, the *local scene* is the part of the environment that the local objects will interact with[1], and the *distant scene* comprises the parts of the environment considered to be far enough away that the effect the synthetic objects have on them is negligible.

Instead of employing expensive global illumination algorithms, we utilise recent advances in hardware-based rendering [4, 15] to model the way the distant scene illuminates the synthetic objects. The illumination in an environment is first captured in the form of an omni-directional image using a camera, and then a series of high-dynamic range *basis radiance-maps* are pre-computed. Combinations of these maps are used at run-time to approximate the illumination for different synthetic materials using sphere mapping. We currently ignore inter-reflection effects between the synthetic objects, as well as reflections of the synthetic objects in the local scene.

We also introduce a new approach for modelling the shadows that the synthetic objects cast onto the local scene (and vice versa) as well as self-shadowing effects on the synthetic objects. By analysing the omni-directional image captured by the camera, we automatically position a number of representative directional light-sources around the synthetic objects so that the accumulated effect of the shadows from each light-source approximates those cast by the real-world illumination. We also present a novel image composition algorithm that is capable of merging both the synthetic objects and shadows into the background image at interactive rates.

The remainder of this paper is organized as follows. In the next section we briefly outline how the omni-directional images that store illumination are captured. Following that, we describe how sets of basis radiance-maps are generated in Section 5. Our image composition algorithm is then discussed in detail in Section 6, and Section 7 presents our optimisation methods for selecting the position and intensity of the representative light-sources. Finally, we give results in Section 8 and describe areas for future research in Section 9.

4 Illumination and Image Acquisition

We utilise recent advances in the image-based capture and storage of illumination [6, 5] to correctly illuminate synthetic objects. Currently, we only capture illumination at a

---

[1]A geometric model of the local scene is constructed as a pre-process, using semi-automatic photogrammetry techniques

single position in the scene, and assume that this is a good approximation of the actual light illuminating each synthetic object.

The acquisition process begins with the capture of the background image. We also employ a standard calibration algorithm to determine the position and orientation of the camera [29]. Following that, we construct a high-dynamic range omni-directional image that represents the illumination in the scene. This is achieved in a similar fashion to [6, 5], whereby multiple images of a shiny metallic sphere are captured at different exposure levels. These images are then combined into a single high-dynamic range (HDR) photograph. Further details of the capture process are available in [10].

5   Basis Radiance-Maps

Once an omni-directional radiance-map has been captured, it must be manipulated into a form suitable for rendering with computer graphics hardware. As each synthetic object is drawn, we use hardware-accelerated sphere-mapping [2, 12] to approximate the appearance of the object under the captured illumination conditions.

In [12, 4, 15], it was proposed that an omni-directional radiance-map could be pre-integrated with a BRDF (bi-directional reflectance distribution function) to generate a sphere-map that stores the outgoing radiance for each surface normal direction. This pre-integration, which needs to be performed for each different BRDF, is too slow whenever an application requires the interactive manipulation of materials[2].

As an alternative approach, we propose that a small number of *basis radiance-maps* (storing incoming radiance) may be pre-computed for a specific local reflection model. In the examples presented in this paper, we have used the physically plausible Phong reflectance model [18]. We pre-compute a diffuse irradiance map, as well as specular maps for varying values of the surface roughness parameter. At run-time, we combine these basis maps according to the particular reflection model coefficients associated with each material, and generate the appropriate sphere-map. Whenever a material changes, or a new one is introduced, all that is required is that the appropriate basis maps are re-combined according to the new coefficients. Further details of this process are presented in [10]. The final stage of sphere-map generation is the application of the camera response function [6] to translate the radiance-map into a texture map that can be utilised by computer graphics hardware.

6   Image and Shadow Composition

In this section, we present a multi-pass algorithm that uses sphere-mapping [2, 12], shadow-maps [24, 26] and accumulation-buffer hardware [13] to overlay the synthetic objects and their associated shadows on the background image.

It is important that the synthetic objects cast believable shadows onto the local scene in order to improve a user's perception of spatial layout [28]. The synthetic objects should also be shadowed by the objects in the local scene, and the local scene must not cast shadows onto itself since these are already present in the background image. Self-shadowing is, however, required on the synthetic objects. We must take care that this self shadowing only occurs on parts of the synthetic objects that are facing *towards* the source of illumination, because the reduction in radiance on back facing sections has

---

[2]On a single 250MHz R10000 MIPS processor, we have found that the time required to integrate a 256x256 radiance-map is approximately 4 minutes.

already been accounted for within that object's sphere-map during the pre-integration process.

We approximate shadows cast by the real-world illumination using a small number of *representative directional light-sources*. Rather than considering these as sources of light, we will instead consider them as sources of shadow, because they will be used to subtract light from the already illuminated background image. Each 'shadow-source', i, has associated with it a direction ω_i, a colour I_{i_λ} where $\lambda = (R, G, B)$, and a *shadow ambient* factor [17] α_i, where $(0 < \alpha_i < 1)$. These control the position, colour and darkness of its shadows respectively. In Section 7 we will discuss how these parameters may be chosen so as to best approximate the shadows cast by the real-world illumination.

The generation of a single frame begins with the shadows cast by each shadow source being summed into the accumulation buffer. Once all shadow-sources have been processed, the contents of the accumulation buffer are blended with the background image and synthetic objects. This composition process is illustrated diagrammatically in Figure 1, and is implemented entirely using hardware-accelerated OpenGL features.

Due to the restrictions of shadow-mapping, the shadows cast by a single source must be generated in two stages: firstly, we generate all the shadows in the scene – those cast by the synthetic objects onto themselves and the local scene, and the shadows cast by the local scene onto itself and the synthetic objects. This is an estimate of the shadowing situation we want to see in the final image. Following that, we remove the shadows cast by the local scene onto itself, since these are already present in the background image.

6.1 Stage One: Addition of All Shadows

Stage one of the shadow generation process for a single source begins with the construction of a *shadow-map* [24, 26]. This is produced by rendering the local scene and synthetic objects into the depth-buffer, from the point of view of the shadow-source. The local scene is then drawn from the camera viewpoint, with the shadow-map activated and lighting turned off. All local scene triangles are assigned the colour of the shadow-source, meaning that areas in shadow are rendered with a colour $\alpha_i I_{i_\lambda}$, and those not in shadow with a colour I_{i_λ} (Figure 1a). Note that we have artificially reduced the value of α_i in these images in order to ensure the shadows are more easily identifiable.

The synthetic objects are then be drawn, again using the shadow-map. If this is done in the same way as for the local scene, however, self-shadowing artifacts on back-facing triangles will be present in the image (these are unwanted for the reasons outlined above). To avoid these, we render the synthetic objects so that only triangles facing towards the source have shadows cast upon them. This is achieved by placing an OpenGL light-source the same direction as the shadow-source, and rendering each synthetic object with a material that has ambient and diffuse components of zero, a specular component of I_{i_λ}, and a Phong exponent of zero. This ensures that triangles facing away from the shadow source are rendered in black, and so have no shadows cast upon them (Figure 1b). The resulting image (Figure 1c) is then added to the current contents of the accumulation buffer, as shown in Figure 1d[3].

---

[3]Note that the contents of accumulation buffer can take on values in the range [-1:1]. We have therefore scaled the buffer contents to the range [0:1] for illustration purposes in Figures 1d and h.

370

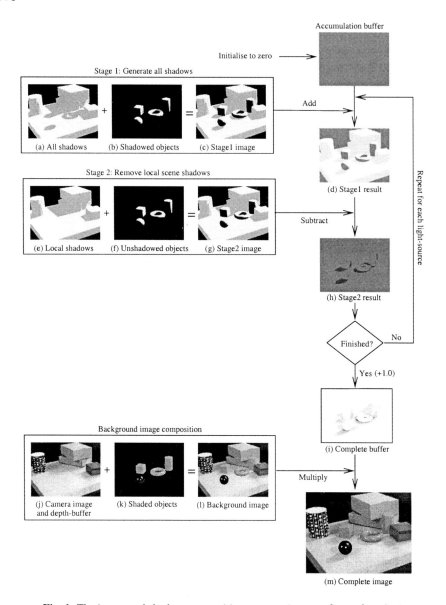

Fig. 1. The image and shadow composition process (see text for explanation).

6.2 Stage Two: Removal of Local Scene Shadows

Stage two of the shadow generation process is required to remove shadows cast by the local scene onto itself. Again, a shadow-map is constructed, but this time only using the triangles in the local scene. The local scene is then rendered from the point of view of the camera, using this shadow-map and a colour of $\alpha_i I_{i_\lambda}$ (Figure 1e). Shadowing is then disabled, and the synthetic objects are drawn so that those triangles facing away from the shadow-source are black (Figure 1f). The resulting image is then subtracted[4] from the accumulation buffer, resulting in an image similar to that shown in Figure 1h.

The overall effect of this sequence of operations is to add $I_{i_\lambda}(\alpha_i - 1)$ to regions in the accumulation buffer that are occluded from shadow-source i. Regions that are not in shadow remain unaffected. Shadow generation may be continued for any number of additional shadow-sources simply by repeating the two-stage process outlined above, using the current contents of the accumulation buffer as the starting point for the next source. Once all shadow-sources have been processed, we add 1 to each pixel in the accumulation buffer, resulting in an image similar to that shown in Figure 1i. If we denote the occlusion of a pixel x to source i as $g(x, i)$, where $g(x, i)$ is 1 if the pixel is shadowed, and 0 otherwise, then the contents of the accumulation buffer after M sources, and the final addition, will be:

$$1 + \sum_{i=1}^{M} I_{i_\lambda}(\alpha_i - 1)g(x, i) \tag{1}$$

Pixels not shadowed from any source will have a value of 1, and pixels in shadow will have values in the range $[0 : 1]$, depending upon the number and intensities of the occluded sources.

The last stage of the image composition process is the construction of the background image. This is achieved by rendering the camera image into the colour buffer, and the local scene geometry into the depth buffer (Figure 1j). The synthetic objects are then drawn, using their appropriate sphere-maps. Finally, the contents of the accumulation buffer is used as a weighting factor to scale the background image. This multiplication is achieved using standard OpenGL blending operations, and the result (Figure 1m) is displayed on screen.

Note that the contents of the accumulation buffer before the final multiplication is only an approximation to the correct weighting factors. Ideally, the image generated after stage one (Image c) should be divided by the image generated for stage two (Image g), and not be subtracted. Because a hardware buffer division is not available, we use the subtraction as an approximation.

7 Shadow-Source Positioning

In this section, we discuss how suitable directions, colours and shadow ambient factors may be determined for any number of shadow-sources. In [5], shadows cast by the synthetic objects were generated using time-consuming ray-tracing techniques [31]. We use similar Monte-Carlo ray-tracing techniques to generate a reference image of the shadows cast by a simple object (e.g. a sphere) onto a diffuse horizontal plane on which the object is resting. A multi-dimensional optimisation is then performed, which selects shadow-source parameters giving the best fit to the target reference image.

---

[4]Since data may only be added into the accumulation buffer, this subtraction is in fact achieved by scaling the image by -1.0 and adding.

The reference image is generated by calculating an occluded radiance estimate, $L_o(x)$, for each pixel x

$$L_o(x) = \rho \int_\Omega L(\omega)(1 - g(x, \omega))(N \cdot \omega)d\omega \tag{2}$$

and an unoccluded radiance estimate, L_u (which is independent of pixel position),

$$L_u = \rho \int_\Omega L(\omega)(N \cdot \omega)d\omega \tag{3}$$

where ρ is the diffuse reflectance of the horizontal plane (we assume a constant value of 0.5), Ω is the upper hemisphere of the omni-directional image, $L(\omega)$ is the radiance stored in direction ω, N is the normal of the horizontal plane, and $g(x, \omega)$ is 1 if the ray from x in direction ω is occluded by the sphere, and 0 otherwise.

We then determine a *reference weighting factor*, $\tau_\lambda(x)$ that gives the ratio of the occluded and unoccluded pixel intensities for channel λ:

$$\tau_\lambda(x) = \frac{R_\lambda(L_o(x), \epsilon)}{R_\lambda(L_u, \epsilon)} \tag{4}$$

where $R_\lambda(L, \epsilon)$ is the camera response function [6] for channel λ, which maps radiance L to a pixel intensity, assuming an exposure of ϵ.

Assume we want to position M shadow-sources, each of which has an associated direction ω_i, colour I_{i_λ}, and shadow ambient factor α_i. The choice of M directly affects the frame time, and so should be kept small enough to maintain interactivity (we currently use between four and eight sources, depending upon the contents of the omni-directional image). From Equation 1, the accumulated effect of these M shadow-sources will be to multiply a background pixel by an *approximate weighting factor*, $\sigma_\lambda(x)$, where

$$\sigma_\lambda(x) = 1 + \sum_{i=1}^{M} I_{i_\lambda}(\alpha_i - 1)g(x, \omega_i) \tag{5}$$

The shadow-source parameters must therefore be chosen such that

$$\sigma_\lambda(x) \approx \tau_\lambda(x) \tag{6}$$

for all x in the reference image. We propose that this may be cast as a multi-dimensional optimisation problem, which attempts to minimise the RMS difference between the image of reference weighting factors, $\tau(x)$, and the image of approximate weighting factors, $\sigma(x)$. Rather than employing complex global minimisation algorithms to solve this problem, we have found that reliable and repeatable results may be obtained using the much simpler Downhill Simplex method [23] and a bounded linear least-squares solver [3], in conjunction with a stratification of the problem domain. For source i, we will derive a direction ω_i and quantity C_{i_λ}, where

$$C_{i_\lambda} = I_{i_\lambda}(\alpha_i - 1) \tag{7}$$

From C_{i_λ}, the colour and ambient shadow factor of each source can then be found

$$I_{i_\lambda} = C_{i_\lambda}/m_i$$

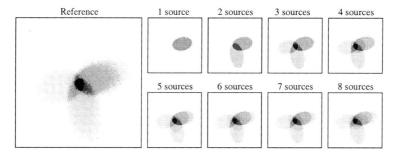

Fig. 2. Shadow approximation using representative sources. An optimisation procedure positions M directional shadow-sources so as to best fit the reference image, shown on the left. Results are given on the right for between one and eight sources.

$$\alpha_i = 1 - m_i \qquad (8)$$

where $m_i = \max_\lambda(C_{i_\lambda})$. The optimisation process for each shadow-source is split into two phases: the first phase chooses a direction ω_i and the intensity (luminance) of C_{i_λ} using the Downhill Simplex method. The second phase then determines the best values for C_{i_λ} for $\lambda = (R, G, B)$ using a bounded linear least-squares solver.

The optimisation process is started by positioning a single shadow-source in a random direction ω_1, and assigning $C_{\lambda_1} = 1/(2M)$ for all λ (we have found this to be a useful initial guess for the shadow intensity). The Downhill Simplex algorithm is then run to find the parameters for this single shadow-source that provide the best fit of $\sigma_\lambda(x)$ to the reference weighting factors, $\tau_\lambda(x)$ for all x.

Once the direction ω_1 and intensity of C_{λ_1} have been chosen, we determine the optimal values of C_{i_λ} for all points x_i ($i = 1 \dots N$) in the reference image, and all m sources positioned so far (i.e. $m = 1$ initially) by solving

$$\text{minimize } \|\mathbf{b} - \mathbf{A}\mathbf{x}\|_2 \quad \text{subject to } (-1 < C_{i_\lambda} < 0) \qquad (9)$$

where

$$\mathbf{A} = \begin{bmatrix} g(x_1, \omega_1), & g(x_1, \omega_2), & \cdots & g(x_1, \omega_m) \\ g(x_2, \omega_1), & g(x_2, \omega_2), & \cdots & g(x_2, \omega_m) \\ \vdots & \vdots & \ddots & \vdots \\ g(x_N, \omega_1), & g(x_N, \omega_2), & \cdots & g(x_N, \omega_m) \end{bmatrix}$$

$$\mathbf{x} = [C_{\lambda_1}, C_{\lambda_2}, \dots, C_{\lambda_m}]^T$$

$$\mathbf{b} = [\tau_\lambda(x_1) - 1, \tau_\lambda(x_2) - 1, \dots, \tau_\lambda(x_N) - 1]^T \qquad (10)$$

Once the values of C_{λ_1} have been chosen, we add a second shadow-source (again, with random direction and $C_{\lambda_2} = 1/(2M)$), but use the results of the first optimisation as the new starting conditions for the first shadow-source. The Downhill Simplex algorithm is repeated to choose parameters for both these sources, and Equation 9 solved for $m = 2$. This process is repeated until all M shadow-sources have been positioned, each time using the results of the previous optimisation, along with one random direction ω_m and $C_{\lambda_m} = 1/(2M)$, as the new initial estimates.

Figure 2 shows the results of this optimisation process for the omni-directional image used throughout the paper. On the left-hand side we show the reference weighting factors, $\tau_\lambda(x)$ for all pixels x. The approximate factors, $\sigma_\lambda(x)$, for the sequence of

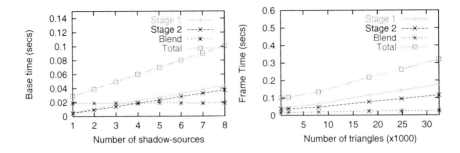

Fig. 3. Timing breakdowns for a single frame.

optimisations $1 \leq m \leq M$ that result from positioning 8 shadow-sources are shown on the right. Overall, the time required to perform this sequence of optimisations was approximately two minutes on a single 250MHz R10000 MIPS processor. Although we have no direct proof that these results represent the true global minimum of the problem, we have found that they are repeatable and, importantly, independent of the initial random positioning of each source. Also, since the time required to render each frame is directly affected by the number of shadow-sources, we are able to use the intermediate results for fewer sources if the frame-time with all M becomes too great.

8 Results

We have implemented this algorithm in OpenGL on a Silicon Graphics Onyx2 workstation with a single InfiniteReality2 rendering pipeline and one 250MHz MIPS R10000 processor. Figure 4 gives a side-by-side comparison of a ray-traced image and one generated in real-time using the techniques presented here. The ray-traced image was produced using the RADIANCE global illumination software [31], and differential rendering techniques similar to those developed by Debevec [5]. The total time required to produce this image was approximately 2 hours. The image on the right was rendered at a sustained rate of almost 10 frames-per-second (fps) on the Onyx2. Eight shadow-sources were used to generate the shadows in this image. It is clear from this comparison that the real-time shadows are a good match for those obtained using expensive ray-tracing algorithms, although differences do exist. Most noticeably, the shadow cast by the cylinder onto a vertical side of the box is not as dark as it should be. This is due to the fact that the shadow intensities are calculated for a horizontal plane with its normal facing upwards, and will differ for vertical surfaces. This situation could be improved by choosing the 'best-fit' shadow intensities for a range of surface orientations. A second example is given in Figure 5 for a different set of illumination conditions. The benefit of introducing shadows into the image, in terms of image fidelity, is clear to see.

Figure 6 compares real-time self-shadowing effects against those produced using ray-tracing. The synthetic object in this image contains almost 50,000 triangles, and was rendered at almost 2 fps with eight shadow-sources. The shadow intensities are generally a good match, but again, differences due to surface orientation and accessibility are visible. Also, because the real-time shadowing only modifies pixel colours, specular highlights from an occluded light-source appear incorrectly in the image.

Finally, Figure 3 gives timing breakdowns for a single frame. On the left we plot the total time required to generate a frame that contains no synthetic objects (and therefore represents the total cost of the image-processing operations we perform), for between 1 and 8 shadow-sources. This represents the minimum frame-time that we can achieve (over 16 fps with 4 shadow-sources, almost 10 fps with 8 sources). Also plotted are the total times for both stages of shadow generation, and the time required to generate and blend the background image. On the right, we show how frame-time increases for larger numbers of synthetic objects (this graph was produced using 8 shadow-sources). We have found that the time required to render a single frame increases linearly as the number of triangles increases. For 32,500 triangles, the frame-rate drops from almost 10 fps to just over 3 fps.

9 Conclusion

In this paper we have presented new algorithms that enable synthetic objects to be integrated into background images at interactive rates. We have combined recent advances in the image-based capture and storage of real-world illumination with novel shadow generation and image composition algorithms. Overall, we are able to manipulate complex synthetic objects at rates of several frames-per-second using a single graphics pipeline.

We have ignored inter-reflections between synthetic objects as well as reflections of the synthetic objects in the local scene. Also, our method is currently restricted to a static viewpoint. Camera movement could be allowed for using real-time tracking techniques, and by warping sphere-maps according to the changing camera orientation. Alternatively, view-independent environment map representations, such as the parabolic maps introduced in [14] could be employed.

Acknowledgements

The authors would like to thank their colleagues in the Advanced Interfaces Group for helpful discussions regarding this work, and the conference reviewers who provided many useful comments. The model shown in Figure 6 was constructed by the Stanford University Computer Graphics Laboratory using a Cyberware 3030MS optical triangulation scanner, and is available from http://www-graphics.stanford.edu/data/3Dscanrep. This research was supported by EPSRC grant number GR/M14531, entitled 'REVEAL: Reconstruction of Virtual Environments with Accurate Lighting'.

References

1. Azuma, R. T. A survey of augmented reality. *Presence: Teleoperators and Virtual Environments 6*, 4 (August 1997), 355–385.

2. Blinn, J. F., and Newell, M. E. Texture and reflection in computer generated images. *Communications of the ACM 19*, 10 (October 1976), 542—546.

3. Boisvert, R. F., Howe, S. E., and Kahaner, D. K. NBS core math library (CMLIB), April 1998. Version 3.0, Center for Applied Mathematics, NBS, http://lib.stat.cmu.edu/cmlib.

4. Cabral, B., Olano, M., and Nemec, P. Reflection space image based rendering. *Proceedings of SIGGRAPH 99* (August 1999), 165–170.

5. Debevec, P. Rendering synthetic objects into real scenes: Bridging traditional and image-based graphics with global illumination and high dynamic range photography. *Proceedings of SIGGRAPH 98* (July 1998), 189–198.

6. Debevec, P. E., and Malik, J. Recovering high dynamic range radiance maps from photographs. *Proceedings of SIGGRAPH 97* (August 1997), 369–378.

7. Diefenbach, P. J., and Badler, N. I. Multi-pass pipeline rendering: Realism for dynamic environments. *1997 Symposium on Interactive 3D Graphics* (April 1997), 59–70.

376

8. Drettakis, G., Robert, L., and Bougnoux, S. Interactive common illumination for computer augmented reality. *Eurographics Rendering Workshop 1997* (June 1997), 45–56.

9. Fournier, A., Gunawan, A. S., and Romanzin, C. Common illumination between real and computer generated scenes. In *Proceedings of Graphics Interface '93* (San Francisco, CA, May 1993), Morgan Kaufmann, pp. 254–262.

10. Gibson, S., and Murta, A. Interactive Rendering with Real-World Illumination. Technical Report UMCS-00-3-2, University of Manchester, Department of Computer Science, March 2000. http://www.cs.man.ac.uk/cstechrep/Abstracts/UMCS-00-3-2.html

11. Goral, C. M., Torrance, K. E., Greenberg, D. P., and Battaile, B. Modelling the interaction of light between diffuse surfaces. In *Computer Graphics (ACM SIGGRAPH '84 Proceedings)* (July 1984), vol. 18, pp. 212–222.

12. Greene, N. Environment mapping and other applications of world projections. *IEEE Computer Graphics and Applications 6*, 11 (November 1986), 21–29.

13. Haeberli, P., and Akeley, K. The accumulation buffer: Hardware support for high-quality rendering. *Computer Graphics (Proceedings of SIGGRAPH 90) 24*, 4 (August 1990), 309–318.

14. Heidrich, W., and Seidel, H.-P. View-independent environment maps. *1998 SIGGRAPH / Eurographics Workshop on Graphics* (August 1998), 39–46.

15. Heidrich, W., and Seidel, H.-P. Realistic, hardware-accelerated shading and lighting. *Proceedings of SIGGRAPH 99* (August 1999), 171–178.

16. Kajiya, J. T. The rendering equation. In *Computer Graphics (ACM SIGGRAPH '86 Proceedings)* (August 1986), vol. 20, pp. 143–150.

17. Kempf, R., and Donnelly, J. H. OpenGL on Silicon Graphics systems, June 1998. http://toolbox.sgi.com/TaseOfDT/documents/OpenGL/OGLonSGS.

18. Lewis, R. R. Making shaders more physically plausible. In *Fourth Eurographics Workshop on Rendering* (Paris, France, June 1993), no. Series EG 93 RW, pp. 47–62.

19. Loscos, C., Frasson, M.-C., Drettakis, G., Walter, B., Granier, X., and Poulin, P. Interactive virtual relighting and remodeling of real scenes. *Eurographics Rendering Workshop 1999* (June 1999).

20. Nakamae, E., Harada, K., Ishizaki, T., and Nishita, T. A montage method: The overlaying of the computer generated images onto a background photograph. *Computer Graphics (Proceedings of SIGGRAPH 86) 20*, 4 (August 1986), 207–214.

21. Poulin, P., and Fournier, A. Painting surface characteristics. *Eurographics Rendering Workshop 1995* (June 1995), 160–169.

22. Poulin, P., Ratib, K., and Jacques, M. Sketching shadows and highlights to position lights. *Computer Graphics International 1997* (June 1997).

23. Press, W. H., Teukolsky, S. A., Vetterling, W. T., and Flannery, B. P. *Numerical Recipies in C: The Art of Scientific Computing*, 2nd ed. ed. Cambridge University Press, Cambridge, NY, 1992.

24. Reeves, W. T., Salesin, D. H., and Cook, R. L. Rendering antialiased shadows with depth maps. *Computer Graphics (Proceedings of SIGGRAPH 87) 21*, 4 (July 1987), 283–291.

25. Sato, I., Sato, Y., and Ikeuchi, K. Acquiring a radiance distribution to superimpose virtual objects onto a real scene. *IEEE Transactions on Visualization and Computer Graphics 5*, 1 (January - March 1999), 1–12.

26. Segal, M., Korobkin, C., van Widenfelt, R., Foran, J., and Haeberli P. E. Fast shadows and lighting effects using texture mapping. *Computer Graphics (Proceedings of SIGGRAPH 92) 26*, 2 (July 1992), 249–252.

27. State, A., Hirota, G., Chen, D. T., Garrett, B., and Livingston, M. Superior augmented reality registration by integrating landmark tracking and magnetic tracking. *Proceedings of SIGGRAPH 96* (August 1996), 429–438.

28. Thompson, W. B., Shirley, P., Smits, B., Kersten, D. J., and Madison, C. Visual glue. Technical Report UUCS-98-007, University of Utah, March 1998.

29. Tsai, R. Y. A versatile camera calibration technique for high accuracy machine vision metrology using off-the-shelf TV cameras and lenses. *IEEE Journal of Robotics and Automation 3*, 4 (August 1987), 323–344.

30. Walter, B., Alppay, G., Lafortune, E. P. F., Fernandez, S., and Greenberg D. P. Fitting virtual lights for non-diffuse walkthroughs. *Proceedings of SIGGRAPH 97* (August 1997), 45–48.

31. Ward, G. J. The RADIANCE lighting simulation and rendering system. *Proceedings of SIGGRAPH 94* (July 1994), 459–472.

Editors' Note: see Appendix, p. 421 for colored figures of this paper

Walkthroughs with Corrective Texturing

Marc Stamminger   Jörg Haber   Hartmut Schirmacher   Hans-Peter Seidel

Computer Graphics Group
Max-Planck-Institut für Informatik
Im Stadtwald, 66123 Saarbrücken, Germany
Email: {stamminger, haberj, htschirm, hpseidel}@mpi-sb.mpg.de

Abstract.   We present a new hybrid rendering method for interactive walkthroughs in photometrically complex environments. The display process starts from some approximation of the scene rendered at high frame rates using graphics hardware. Additional computation power is used to correct this rendering towards a high quality ray tracing solution during the walkthrough. This is achieved by applying corrective textures to scene objects or entire object groups. These corrective textures contain a sampled representation of the differences between the hardware generated and the high quality solution. By reusing the textures, frame-to-frame coherence is exploited and explicit reprojections of point samples are avoided. Finally, we describe our implementation, which can display interactive walkthroughs of fairly complex scenes including high quality global illumination features.

1 Introduction

Photorealistic rendering has a major drawback: its performance is far from interactive. In contrast, hardware-assisted rendering allows walkthroughs in complex environments at interactive frame rates, but lacks the visual complexity and quality of sophisticated global illumination solutions.

Approaches exist for pushing photorealistic rendering towards interactivity, as well as for increasing the realism of interactive hardware-assisted visualization systems. Both directions of research have advanced drastically over the past few years. Yet it can be foreseen that even with the fast increase of computation power and graphics hardware capabilities, the gap between interactive rendering and global illumination will not vanish in the near future.

In this paper, we propose a way to bridge this gap. A scene is first rendered by means of graphics hardware. This rendering can include global illumination effects, e.g. shadows, but most importantly, it guarantees a certain frame rate. Although this approximate rendering contains all geometric features of the scene (which is important for navigation), it can in general not cover the whole range of lighting effects, as for example multiple reflections and refractions, or complex reflection characteristics. In the following we will refer to this rendering as the *interactive solution*.

More desirable, however, is a *high quality solution*, which is typically obtained by ray tracing-based algorithms. Depending on the employed technique, these high quality solutions exhibit both important and subtle global illumination effects, usually at high computational costs. Clearly, we cannot trace every pixel in an interactive display loop, but we can use additional computation power — in between the display of frames or, if available, on parallel processors — to *correct* the interactive solution towards a photorealistic, view-dependent image.

378

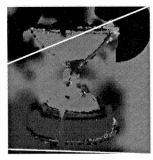

Fig. 1. Corrective texturing example. Left: *interactive solution* that can be displayed at high frame rates. Center: *high quality solution* obtained by applying corrective textures that represent the differences between the interactive solution and the high quality samples. Right: *corrective texture* of the hourglass.

To this end, high quality samples are acquired asynchronously. The resulting error values, i.e. the differences between these samples and the interactive solution, are stored in *corrective textures* which are mapped onto the corresponding object during the interactive display process (cf. Fig. 1).

Using textures has three major advantages. First, corrections are restricted to the object (or cluster) the texture is assigned to. Second, intra-frame coherence is exploited, since the texture resolution can be adapted to match the current sample density from the high quality solution, and a single corrective texel can affect several pixels, using the graphics hardware for texture reprojection and filtering. Finally, inter-frame coherence is also exploited, since the corrections will not change drastically for small camera movements. This is why we can reuse most of the textures, and only need to adapt some of the corrections for each new view point.

2 Previous Work

Allowing interactive exploration of high quality global illumination solutions (so-called walkthroughs) is an important goal in many application areas (e.g. architecture, lighting design, simulation). Two major problems have to be addressed: *geometric* complexity, which is the number of geometric primitives to be processed for a view, and *photometric* complexity, which is the time needed for computing the actual view-dependent appearance of a surface. The latter can be split further into the *local illumination* computation (called *shading*) and the determination of *global illumination* effects such as indirect illumination.

A photometrically simple kind of a walkthrough scene consists of purely diffuse polygonal objects, e.g. the solution of a hierarchical radiosity computation [3]. Since the appearance of the objects does not depend on the viewpoint, this kind of scene can be rendered at high frame rates using off-the-shelf graphics hardware.

Unfortunately, the number of polygons the graphics hardware can render at a certain frame rate is limited. Geometry-based or image-based *level-of-detail (LOD)* techniques can be used to reduce the polygon count. *Impostors* [13, 18, 5, 20], for example, replace a number of distant objects by a single textured polygon. The impostor assignment has to take into account the depth range and apparent size of the objects. LOD techniques generally only take into account geometric properties and not *photometric* features.

Another way of increasing the frame rate for rendering is given by techniques like *post-rendering 3D warp* [15, 14]. Here the display process generates additional in-between frames by reprojecting from neighbouring images. However, only a relatively small speedup is achieved and a number of warping artifacts are introduced.

A variety of methods exists for computing high quality non-diffuse global illumination effects, see for instance [8] for a good overview. Since most of them perform a large number of view-dependent computations and trace light paths through the scene, these algorithms require computation times which are far from interactive frame rates. Several techniques have been proposed that decouple view-independent (e.g. diffuse) and view-dependent (e.g. specular, glossy) global illumination effects and employ some kind of *multi-pass global illumination* technique [23, 21, 12]. Despite a considerable speedup, most of these methods are still not fast enough for interactive use.

With increasing bandwidth and additional features in todays graphics hardware, more and more high quality shading effects can be computed at interactive frame rates using *multi-pass OpenGL rendering*. This includes different types of shadows, specular and glossy reflections on planar and curved objects, sampled approximations of arbitrary reflection functions, and bump maps and normal maps [19, 16, 6, 10, 2, 24, 1]. Each of theses techniques solves a very special subset from the broad range of lighting effects, and it is not always obvious how to combine them all. Usually a number of constraints are imposed on the scene, e.g. number and shape of light sources and reflectors, distance between objects and the reflected environment, and so on.

Finally, some viewing applications perform *massively parallel computations*, sometimes loosely coupled with a *progressive display process* [17, 27]. Udeshi and Hansen use a combination of hardware-assisted techniques for shadow and indirect lighting, plus ray tracing for specular objects [22]. They exploit both parallel CPU power and parallel graphics pipelines, and reuse results from the hardware-assisted rendering for speeding up the software ray tracing step.

Walter *et al.* [25] describe a fully decoupled display process, the so-called *render cache*, which maintains and reprojects the current set of samples and replaces outdated samples by newer ones from the ray tracing clients using a sophisticated importance-weighted, diffusion-like sampling strategy. The render cache can be used for nearly any kind of per-pixel global illumination computation. The down side of this is that during camera motion, a large fraction of the pixels appear as black holes, as long as no information is available for them from the ray tracing processes. The work presented in this paper was motivated by the results of the render cache. Our goal was to build a similar system, that avoids these warping holes by rendering the scene in hardware with full geometric detail, and adding the lighting obtained by ray tracing.

3   Corrective Texturing

Corrective texturing provides a means for refining an approximate, *interactive* solution with corrective samples obtained from a *high-quality* global illumination computation. In our approach, we maintain a set of textures that represent the difference between those two computations. The corrective textures are updated through an adaptive and lazy sample tracing. The actual display process draws the approximate interactive solution, augmented by the corrective textures.

Our method consist of several collaborating tasks that are sketched in Figure 2:

- the *sample clients* deliver high quality samples using a ray tracing-based approach;

380

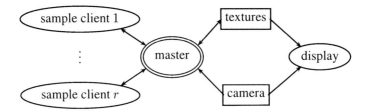

Fig. 2. The main components of our rendering system. The master task keeps track of the camera movements and requests high quality samples from the sample clients. Furthermore, it inserts the resulting samples into the textures which are used by the display task for correcting the approximate solution.

- the *master task* adaptively requests and collects the samples, and assigns, creates, and updates the corrective textures;
- the *display task* renders the hardware-accelerated fast approximation of the scene and applies the corrective textures.

The master task uses an adaptive scheme to request high quality ray samples in image regions where the error of the current scene rendering is probably large. It processes the data returned from the tracing clients and finds the texture assigned to the sample's corresponding scene point. Next, it computes the error of the currently displayed value with respect to the high quality sample and splats the corresponding correction into the texture. The texture resolution is adapted to the chosen sample density, and textures are assigned to scene objects or clusters based on their appearance in the current view. The master also "ages" the texels with respect to the amount of camera movement, so that fresh samples replace older ones.

3.1 Why Textures?

The corrective textures are used to spread corrections across several pixels within the same frame (intra-frame coherence), as well as for reusing the same corrections in further frames until fresher samples are acquired (inter-frame coherence). Our approach of using textures brings along advantages over approaches like the render cache [25], which stores point samples that have to be reprojected and splatted for every frame.

First, the performance of our rendering process is almost independent of the screen resolution due to the use of hardware texture mapping. A single corrective texel can affect several pixels through the use of hardware-assisted texture reprojection and filtering.

Second, we remove the problem of holes in the displayed image caused by under-sampling and missing information. The interactive solution visualizes *all* geometric features of the scene, and the corrective textures always map a *dense* set of corrections onto the objects. By using separate textures for different objects, these corrections are restricted to the object boundaries. This guarantees that the corrections will not be mapped onto the wrong object, as it can occur with warping approaches if the visibility situation changes. However, this also requires a well chosen hierarchy for the texture assignment (see below).

Third, we can afford to splat new samples adaptively into their corrective texture and to blend the new samples with their neighbours, resulting in visually pleasant, smooth textures. These relatively expensive operations cannot be employed if the point samples have to be reprojected and splatted for every new frame as in warping-based display algorithms. Furthermore, the texture resolution can be adapted to match the density of the high quality samples.

3.2   Texture Projection

We use two different modes for applying textures to their associated scene objects, both based on texture projection. Projective texture mapping [19] projects the texture onto the specified scene objects from some virtual point or direction (for perspective or parallel projections, respectively). The projection can either be attached to the object's coordinate system (object-local) or to the current camera system (camera-local).

For flat objects, i.e. objects with only slightly varying normal, we use object-local parallel projection along the surface normal. By this, we have a simple automatic way to parameterize entire object groups (e.g. many triangles in a mesh). Because of the object-local projection, the texture is "glued" onto the object. This means that view independent corrections (e.g. caustics on diffuse surfaces) are reprojected correctly into novel views.

If the textured object is not flat or not even convex, an object-local projection leads to serious problems, since any texel may map to multiple scene points, and surfaces parallel to the projection direction are undersampled.

Instead, for such non-flat objects as well as for object clusters we employ a camera-local texture projection. By placing the center of projection into the current eye point, ambiguity problems are avoided completely. Only visible parts of the scene are assigned corrective samples (which makes the mapping bijective), and one single texture is sufficient per object. We define our texture mapping by projecting a bounding volume of the object into camera space and then using its bounding rectangle on the image plane as the valid texture coordinate domain. This is a sheared perspective transformation which can be applied by the graphics hardware. Furthermore, for camera-local textures we can easily adjust the texture sampling rate to match that of the image.

Our texturing approach shares some ideas with image impostor methods [13, 18], but instead of replacing an object cluster by a single textured polygon, we augment the original geometry and appearance by a *photometric* correction texture. Note that the two approaches fit together well, allowing photometric corrections on simplified geometry.

The drawback of camera-local projection is that it changes with the view point, which means that the texture floats in front of the object rather than sticking onto it. If the object is concave, the correspondence between texel and surface point can even be discontinuous. This is weakened by the fact that typical camera movements in a walkthrough application only lead to a very small texture flow. Furthermore, this kind of artifact mainly affects clusters close to the viewer. Such clusters, however, tend to be split and textured on a lower level (see next Section 3.3).

3.3   Texture Assignment

Textures are not only assigned to single geometric primitives, but also to composite scene objects and object clusters, e.g. provided by spatial subdivision schemes and the scene's modeling hierarchy.

The assignment of textures to scene nodes is adapted on the fly for each novel view point by traversing the scene hierarchy top-down and verifying the validity of the current allocation. The observed motion of a point depends on that point's distance to the camera, so different parts of the object move in a different way (parallax effect). Using a single image-plane texture would cause the texture to float on the geometry.

To avoid this artifact, we estimate the parallax effect by computing the depth range Δr of the textured object in relation to its distance d to the viewer. An object is assigned a single texture if $\Delta r/d < \epsilon$, with ϵ being a parallax threshold. In our tests, values of $\epsilon = 0.2\ldots0.5$ led to parallax distortions that were hardly visible. The threshold is used to control the number of allocated textures, which is reduced further by simple visibility frustum culling. Figure 5 depicts the textures assigned to various objects on a table, with a constant threshold of $\epsilon = 0.3$.

Also the projected size of the object can be included into this test. In this way, also for a large object with no parallax artifacts several textures will be assigned. If the sample density is strongly varying over the object, the texture resolutions can thus be selected separately for different parts of the object (see below).

Building a proper hierarchy for this process is a difficult problem on its own, which has a large impact on the quality of the results. We use the modeling hierarchy for this purpose or a modified hierarchical bounding volume method that does not only consider spatial criteria, but also material properties.

3.4 Sample Insertion

Every texture contains color correction values ΔL_i which approximate the difference between the high quality solution L_i and the basic interactive solution L_i': $\Delta L_i \approx L_i - L_i'$. When a new sample is to be inserted, it should affect a certain texture area rather than a single texel, because we assume some amount of spatial coherence of the approximation error. Ideally, the sampling density determines how far the correction is spread. Therefore we restrict the splat region of a sample to its cell in a Voronoi diagram of the sample points on the texture.

This can be achieved rather easily by an approach similar to the discrete Dirichlet domain creation described in [11]. Every texel i is assigned a validity value v_i, which is basically the *negative* distance of the texel to the sample that is responsible for the texel's value. If we want to insert a new sample, the corresponding texel is inserted with maximum validity 0. Then neighbored texels j with distance d are examined. If the validity of j is smaller than $-d$, the texel gets replaced with the new, more appropriate sample and new validity $-d$. This is continued for growing distances d until for one neighborhood ring no texel could be updated. We call the radius of the last updated ring *splat radius* r. Blending between new and old values according to their respective validity smoothes out harsh boundaries between the splats. Figure 3 shows an example obtained by splatting 20 and 100 samples into a texture.

3.5 Texel Aging

In addition to this purely distance-based splatting criterion, the age of the existing texels has to be taken into account. To avoid updating every texel for each new view point, every texture has one current global maximum validity value $v_{\max}$. The validity/distance values for inserting new texels start with $v_{\max}$ rather than 0 at the sample's center texel, so that newer texels gain priority over the rest of the texture.

If the camera changes, $v_{\max}$ is modified accordingly. The offset reflects both the texture flow appearing for projected textures and an estimated possible change of the correction due to the new viewing directions. The first is zero for object-local projections. For floating projections, it is estimated by the ratio of the visual depth over the distance to the viewer. The latter is estimated by the maximum change of the object's

Fig. 3. Sample insertion: Splatting 20 (left) and 100 (center) samples into a texture using our validity measure. Right: reference solution containing exactly one sample per texel.

BRDFs. We use heuristics for combining these two. This way glossy surfaces age quickly, whereas textures on diffuse objects with fixed textures do not age at all, and the samples remain valid for all possible new view points.

3.6 Texture Resolution

The average splat radius of the last samples inserted into a texture is a valuable hint about the relation between sample density and texture resolution. If the radius is large, the texture resolution is probably too high compared to the number of samples. As a result, inserting a single sample is expensive. On the other hand, a very small average splat radius indicates that the texture resolution is too low, so information gets lost if two samples share one texel.

After each sample insertion, we test the average of previous splat radii against a lower and an upper threshold value. If one threshold is exceeded, the resolution of the texture is increased or decreased by a factor of two. This way, the initially coarse textures become finer the higher the density of the received samples is. If the splat size increases again, for example after aging (cf. Sec. 3.4), this indicates that there is no high frequency detail in the texture, and so the resolution is decreased again to speed up the splatting process. For those textures mapped into the image plane directly (cf. Sec. 3.2), the maximal texture resolution can be derived from twice the sampling rate of the the the screen. By using bilinear interpolation for texture refinement and box filtering for texture coarsening a smooth transition between the resolution levels is obtained.

3.7 Adaptive Sample Acquisition

For acquiring the necessary high quality samples at a reasonable rate, it is imperative to use an adaptive scheme that focuses on image regions with large error. It is important to account for the present approximate correction value ΔL_i. Therefore we measure the error $E_i := L_i - (L_i' + \Delta L_i)$, which is the difference of the high quality sample L_i and the value of the currently displayed and corrected pixel $L_i' + \Delta L_i$. Note that in this step we have to check whether the object visible through that pixel is the same in the interactive and in the high-quality solution. In order to converge against the desired solution, the sampling scheme must make sure to cover all pixels of the image if the user stands still long enough.

The heart of the master process is a priority queue that contains sampling requests, sorted according to their anticipated importance for an improved solution. Each request L_i in this queue contains a sampling direction, a *domain radius* s_i, which denotes the size of the image domain this request represents, and its priority value.

The queue is initially filled with several requests of high priority which are uniformly distributed over the image. The domain radius of these requests is given by their average distance. Then the master iteratively removes the sampling request with the highest priority from the queue and sends it to the sample tracer(s). The new correction value ΔL_i gets splatted into the appropriate texture.

After request L_i has been processed completely, we generate a number of N child requests that cover the affected domain more densely. The domain radius s_c of such a next-generation request c is set to $s_i/\sqrt{N}$, since the domain area is inversely proportional to the number of requests. The product of the parent's correction error E_i and the new radius s_c yields the new priority for request c. If this priority is too small, the request is discarded, otherwise it is inserted into the priority queue.

For each frame, a number n_{sig} of the most *significant* samples are memorized separately, where the sample's significance is determined by its correction error E_i alone. Each time the camera changes, these significant samples are reprojected into the novel view and added to the priority queue as requests (cf. Fig. 4) with high priority. Thus the sampling is directed into regions exhibiting large errors in the previous frame.

If the queue has been processed completely, new randomly positioned global requests with high priorities are inserted with the goal to detect new features that require correction.

```
              start
                |
    +----> add n_glob global requests <----+
    |           |                          |
    |   process & update request queue     |
    |           |                          |
    +----< camera changed? >---------------+
                | y                      n
         clear request queue
                |
         add n_sig significant samples
```

Fig. 4.: The sampling process adds global requests and processes the request queue as long as the user stands still. If the camera moves, some significant samples from the previous frame are reused to yield a faster update in visually important regions.

If the camera stands still long enough, every pixel of the image finally corresponds to the value of the high-quality solution. We use a mask of sampled pixel positions to immediately discard new requests belonging to already sampled pixels. So after a region is sampled at image resolution, the sampling also spreads to less erroneous parts of the image. If most pixels of the image are covered, the sampling process creates a special queue containing the remaining pixels, thereby avoiding to spend too much time on finding free pixel positions for the last few requests.

4 Implementation

4.1 Interactive and High Quality Solutions

In our implementation we display the result of a hierarchical radiosity preprocess as the interactive solution, which can be rendered at high frame rates by the graphics hardware. It contains soft shadows, but completely lacks effects like glossy highlights, mirroring, and refraction.

For the high quality samples, we use standard distributed ray tracing [4], i.e. at non-diffuse surfaces an eye ray spawns several reflection rays which are traced recursively up to a user defined depth. Illumination due to area light sources is computed by casting stochastic shadow rays.

For each high quality sample, the difference to the interactive solution is required. Unfortunately, reading back the frame buffer content is still a fairly expensive operation on almost all current graphics platforms. To avoid this step, we compute the difference value for each high quality sample by performing the Gouraud interpolation of the radiosity value in software.

Using the above setting reveals an interesting effect. Because we use Monte-Carlo sampling for the area light sources in the high quality solution, the penumbra regions are noisy and mostly less accurate than in the radiosity solution. Especially the noise in the "reference" solution imposes severe problems, because it is considered as fine detail in the illumination. As a result, many high quality samples are wasted to capture this supposed detail. Furthermore, the splatting of the noisy corrections produces visually unsatisfactory results, unless the entire penumbra is sampled densely.

The first solution is to increase the number of shadow rays, which works well, but has to be bought by more expensive high quality samples. For performance critical scenes, we solve the problem differently: The high quality ray tracing step itself reuses the diffuse components computed in the radiosity precomputation and only computes specular reflection additionally. This implies that the radiosity solution is precise enough. Furthermore, with this combination it can be guaranteed that all corrections are positive, which speeds up hardware rendering significantly on some platforms (see Sec. 4.3).

4.2 Parallelization

We have tested our implementation of the components sketched in Figure 2 on several different machines running under either IRIX or Solaris. In our computing environment, we use a single-processor `sgi` Octane (MIPS R12000) with hardware-supported texture mapping (EMXI graphics board) as the display process host. The master process and the ray tracing processes run on either a cluster of `sgi` workstations connected to a common 100 MBit-Ethernet, or on a Sun Enterprise 10000 server with 8 available processors and shared-memory communication. The communication between the master process and the ray tracers is implemented using the Message-Passing Interface [9] for both the cluster and the shared-memory approach. Due to the lack of interoperability between different vendor implementations of MPI, we use a standard UNIX protocol and sockets for the communication between the master and the display process. This communication is mostly unidirectional: only upon camera movement, a message containing the new camera parameters has to be sent from the display process to the master. The master process, on the other hand, sends all the ray traced samples along with their texture coordinates to the display process.

4.3 Texturing

The corrective texturing has been implemented through the basic blending functions provided by OpenGL. More specifically, we use an additional blending equation provided by the `blend_subtract` OpenGL extension. This approach requires the scene to be drawn three times: first with the original color and texture, a second time for adding *positive* correction values, and a third time for *subtracting* corrections where the approximation appears too bright. While this method runs on all contemporary `sgi` machines, it has of course the drawback of requiring three rendering passes of the scene. If the interactive solution and the high quality solution are selected appropriately (see above), all corrections will be positive, so the third pass can be omitted. Some newly available graphics boards such as the NVIDIA GeForce system support multi-texturing with general combiner functions. In that case the entire rendering, including additive and subtractive correction, only requires a single rendering pass, and should allow considerably higher frame rates.

5 Results

To test our implementation, we have created several scenes of different geometric complexity. The number of geometric primitives (i.e. the objects our ray tracer can handle as entities) in our test scenes varies between 3,500 and almost 60,000. The corresponding number of triangles generated by our hierarchical radiosity algorithm lies between 15,000 and 415,000. All our test scenes contain several photometrically complex materials with properties such as anisotropic reflection [26], perfect mirroring, and refractive transmission.

We displayed the scenes on a single processor sgi Octane R12000 with EMXI graphics board at a resolution of 1024×1024 pixels. The master process and the sample clients ran on a remote Sun Enterprise 10000 with 8 processors available (cf. Sec. 4.2). Our ray tracer uses BSP trees [7] for spatial subdivision and distributed ray tracing [4] for light rays and reflection rays.

Using all of the 8 processors on the Sun we were able to move through our scenes at a frame rate of 1.5–5 fps. The lower frame rate is achieved for our most complex scene with 4,000 samples being traced and splatted within each frame, while the higher frame rate corresponds to 1,000 samples per frame and our simplest scene. As soon as the camera stopped moving, the displayed images started converging at a frame rate of 2–6.5 fps.

The percentage of time for rendering, sampling and texture update (splatting the samples, refining and coarsening) within each frame depends heavily on the complexity of the scene and the number of ray traced samples. As long as the geometric complexity of the scene is not too high, the balance of rendering : sampling : texture update is about 30:60:10 for 1,000 samples and 10:70:20 for 4,000 samples. For our most complex scene we obtained a balance of 60:30:10 for 1,000 samples and 35:50:15 for 4,000 samples.

The convergence of our method is visualized in Figure 6. Starting from a radiosity solution, more and more samples are traced and added into the corrective textures. The last image in this series is visually almost identical to a fully converged image. Note that our ray tracer can handle shadows of transparent objects and therefore brightens the dark shadow of the glass from the radiosity solution.

In Figure 7, the same scene is first rendered from a a particular point of view. Then the view changes without updating the corrective textures. The next image has been generated after tracing 10,000 new samples. The distribution of these new samples is visualized in the last image. One can clearly see that most of the samples concentrate on the image regions where the error is large.

During an interactive session, the displayed solution can suffer from texture update artifacts. Especially corrective textures that change rapidly with a new view point (for instance on mirroring or refractive objects) need to be updated with quite a few samples. If not enough time is available for acquiring these samples, flickering in the textures becomes visible. Similar effects appear if small lighting details are missed by the initial samples. Such effects then suddenly pop up later on, when they are hit by accident.

6 Conclusions and Future Work

We presented a technique for augmenting hardware-accelerated rendering by results obtained from expensive pixel-based ray tracing methods. The corrections are applied to the objects through textures that are continuously adapted during a walkthrough. By this, we always have full geometric detail, whereas the richness of lighting depends on the available additional computation power. We thus blend between the interactive and the high quality solution. In the worst case, the user sees the interactive solution, but the more computation power is available, the closer we get to the desired high quality solution.

With our resulting system we achieve good frame rates, but if not enough computation power is available and the sampling is too coarse, the lighting still changes visibly. After rapid view changes, it takes about one second until the lighting converged visually, so that later corrections are still noticeable, but subtle.

Our method is in the spirit of the render cache or the Holodeck. However, we additionally exploit graphics hardware, and only spend additional computation power where the hardware-based solution is erroneous. Working with this approach revealed several benefits, but also some limitations.

One major feature is that we can incorporate arbitrary interactive lighting algorithms and exploit the high pixel fill rates from graphics hardware. In contrast to previous approaches, we removed the need of reprojecting samples and filling holes manually. From this point of view, our method is well suited for high screen resolution as long as the graphics hardware supplies sufficiently high frame rates. On the down side, for some interactive rendering methods our approach forces a frame buffer read-back, which is expensive for technical reasons.

In our implementation, we avoid reading the framebuffer by recomputing the framebuffer values for desired samples on the fly. For more sophisticated interactive rendering methods this is probably not feasible. For complex test scenes with about half a million polygons, the interactive rendering time becomes the limiting factor in our implementation. However, this limit could be pushed a lot using more recent graphics hardware (fewer rendering passes), and an improved rendering method (e.g. visibility/occlusion culling). We also did not yet integrate more elaborated interactive rendering techniques, e.g. geometric level-of-detail methods, or multi-pass OpenGL rendering for special lighting effects.

Acknowledgments

The work was supported in part by the ESPRIT Open LTR Project #35772 SIMULGEN "Simulation of Light for General Environments".

References

1. R. Bastos, K. Hoff, W. Wynn, and A. Lastra. Increased Photorealism for Interactive Architectural Walkthroughs. In *1999 Symp. Interactive 3D Graphics*, pp. 182–190, April 1999.
2. B. Cabral, M. Olano, and P. Nemec. Reflection Space Image Based Rendering. In *Computer Graphics (Proc. SIGGRAPH '99)*, pp. 165–170, August 1999.
3. M. F. Cohen and J. R. Wallace. *Radiosity and Realistic Image Synthesis*. Academic Press, London, 1993.
4. R. L. Cook, T. Porter, and L. Carpenter. Distributed Ray Tracing. In *Computer Graphics (Proc. SIGGRAPH '84)*, pp. 137–145, July 1984.

388

5. X. Decoret, G. Schaufler, F. X. Sillion, and J. Dorsey. Multi-Layered Impostors for Accelerated Rendering. In *Computer Graphics Forum (Proc. Eurographics '99)*, volume 18, pp. C61–C72, September 1999.

6. P. J. Diefenbach and N. I. Badler. Multi-pass Pipeline Rendering: Realism For Dynamic Environments. In *1997 Symp. Interactive 3D Graphics*, pp. 59–70, April 1997.

7. H. Fuchs, Z. M. Kedem, and B. F. Naylor. On Visible Surface Generation by a priori Tree Structures. In *Computer Graphics (Proc. SIGGRAPH '80)*, pp. 124–133, July 1980.

8. A. S. Glassner. *Principles of Digital Image Synthesis*. Morgan Kaufmann Publishers, San Francisco, CA, 1995.

9. W. Gropp, E. Lusk, and A. Skjellum. *Using MPI — Portable Parallel Programming with the Message-Passing Interface*. The MIT Press, Cambridge, MA, 1994.

10. W. Heidrich and H.-P. Seidel. Realistic, Hardware-accelerated Shading and Lighting. In *Computer Graphics (Proc. SIGGRAPH '99)*, pp. 171–178, August 1999.

11. K. E. Hoff III, T. Culver, J. Keyser, M. Lin, and D. Manocha. Fast Computation of Generalized Voronoi Diagrams Using Graphics Hardware. In *Computer Graphics (Proc. SIGGRAPH '99)*, pp. 277–286, August 1999.

12. D. Lischinski and A. Rappoport. Image-Based Rendering for Non-Diffuse Synthetic Scenes. In *Proc. 9th EG Rendering Workshop*, pp. 301–314, June 1998.

13. P. W. C. Maciel and P. Shirley. Visual Navigation of Large Environments Using Textured Clusters. In *1995 Symp. Interactive 3D Graphics*, pp. 95–102, April 1995.

14. Y. Mann and D. Cohen-Or. Selective Pixel Transmission for Navigating in Remote Virtual Environments. In *Computer Graphics Forum (Proc. Eurographics '97)*, volume 16, pp. 201–206, August 1997.

15. W. R. Mark, L. McMillan, and G. Bishop. Post-Rendering 3D Warping. In *1997 Symp. Interactive 3D Graphics*, pp. 7–16, April 1997.

16. E. Ofek and A. Rappoport. Interactive Reflections on Curved Objects. In *Computer Graphics (Proc. SIGGRAPH '98)*, pp. 333–342, July 1998.

17. S. Parker, W. Martin, P.-P. J. Sloan, P. Shirley, B. Smits, and C. D. Hansen. Interactive Ray Tracing. In *1999 Symp. Interactive 3D Graphics*, pp. 119–126, April 1999.

18. G. Schaufler. Dynamically Generated Impostors. In *Proc. GI Workshop MVD'95*, pp. 129–136, November 1995.

19. M. Segal, C. Korobkin, R. van Widenfelt, J. Foran, and P. Haeberli. Fast Shadows and Lighting Effects Using Texture Mapping. In *Computer Graphics (Proc. SIGGRAPH '92)*, pp. 249–252, July 1992.

20. J. W. Shade, D. Lischinski, D. H. Salesin, T. DeRose, and J. Snyder. Hierarchical Image Caching for Accelerated Walkthroughs of Complex Environments. In *Computer Graphics (Proc. SIGGRAPH '96)*, pp. 75–82, August 1996.

21. W. Stürzlinger and R. Bastos. Interactive Rendering of Globally Illuminated Glossy Scenes. In *Proc. 8th EG Rendering Workshop*, pp. 93–102, 1997.

22. T. Udeshi and C. D. Hansen. Towards Interactive, Photorealistic Rendering of Indoor Scenes: A Hybrid Approach. In *Proc. 10th EG Rendering Workshop*, pp. 63–76, June 1999.

23. J. R. Wallace, M. F. Cohen, and D. P. Greenberg. A Two-Pass Solution to the Rendering Equation: A Synthesis of Ray Tracing and Radiosity Methods. In *Computer Graphics (Proc. SIGGRAPH '87)*, pp. 311–320, July 1987.

24. B. Walter, G. Alppay, E. P. F. Lafortune, S. Fernandez, and D. P. Greenberg. Fitting Virtual Lights for Non-Diffuse Walkthroughs. In *Computer Graphics (Proc. SIGGRAPH '97)*, pp. 45–48, August 1997.

25. B. Walter, G. Drettakis, and S. Parker. Interactive Rendering using the Render Cache. In *Proc. 10th EG Rendering Workshop*, pp. 27–38, June 1999.

26. G. J. Ward. Measuring and Modeling Anisotropic Reflection. In *Computer Graphics (Proc. SIGGRAPH '92)*, pp. 265–272, July 1992.

27. G. Ward Larson. The Holodeck: A Parallel Ray-Caching Rendering System. In *Proc. 2nd EG Workshop on Parallel Graphics and Visualization*, pp. 17–30, September 1998.

Editors' Note: see Appendix, p. 422 for colored figures of this paper

Appendix: Colour Images

Fig. 4. These clouds are not a texture.

Fig. 5. The scene *Invisible Date* with smoke, lit through the door slit.

Fig. 6. The *Stiftsplatz* in a foggy atmosphere.

Fig. 7. A close-up of figure 6 featuring a volume caustic.

Fig. 8. The scene of figure 6 with an inhomogeneous medium.

Fig. 5. Caustics cast by an egg illuminated by two light sources. About half the number of photons were stored compared to the standard photon map method, without visible differences.

Fig. 6. Visualization of the caustic map convergence criterion. (Blue: Required density reached, Green: required density not reached, but other illumination high enough to mask the errors, Red: density too low.

Fig. 7. Image computed using a global photon map constructed with importance driven density control. For the glossy reflection on the pad, the global map was used directly on the reflected surfaces.

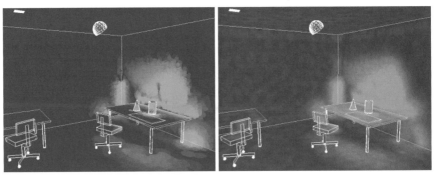

Fig. 8. Required density determined by a path based importance function stored in an importance map. The above image shows the view of the camera.

Fig. 9. Actual density of the global photon map used to generate the above image. About 5 times less photons were stored in the global map than would be stored with a standard photon map method.

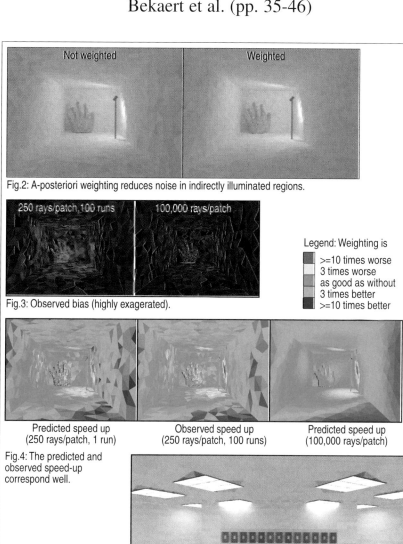

Fig.2: A-posteriori weighting reduces noise in indirectly illuminated regions.

Fig.3: Observed bias (highly exagerated).

Legend: Weighting is
- >=10 times worse
- 3 times worse
- as good as without
- 3 times better
- >=10 times better

Predicted speed up
(250 rays/patch, 1 run)

Observed speed up
(250 rays/patch, 100 runs)

Predicted speed up
(100,000 rays/patch)

Fig.4: The predicted and observed speed-up correspond well.

Fig.5: Hierarchical Stochastic Jacobi Radiosity: without weighting (top) and with weighting (bottom): Weighting reduces high variance on small elements created during refinement and appears to compensate for shadow leaks.
Scene modelled after a photograph of the museum of comtemporary arts Antwerp (MUHKA).

Granier et al. (pp. 47-58)

 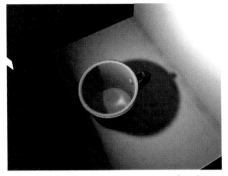

Fig. 5. Interactive walkthroughs using hardware rendering (simple transparency; no refraction). (Left) Soda Shoppe (right) scene with mug; the light source can be moved ~ 2 sec/frame.

Fig. 6. (left) A general view and (Right) a closeup of the bar. Light simulation took 17 m 22 s.

Fig. 7. Soda Shoppe scene with all-indirect light (lights point towards the walls): (Left) computed with our method in 9 min 2 sec; (Right) Particle tracing solution computed in 8 min 2 sec.

Fig. 8. Two frames from a Render Cache interactive session running at 2 Hz, using the output of our system. We are turning left; some artifacts remain where samples are not yet available.

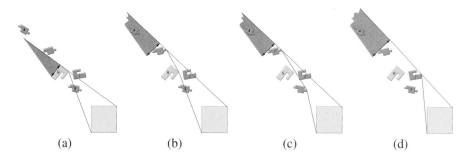

(a) (b) (c) (d)

Fig. 3. Growing the virtual occluders by intersecting objects with the active separating and supporting lines.

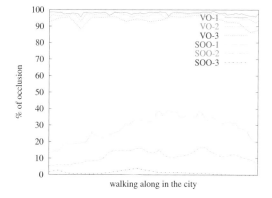

Fig. 8. A comparison between the occlusion of individual occluders and virtual occluders. The graph displays the percentage of occlusion for all viewcells along a path across the London model. Different colors correspond to different cell sizes. Red corresponds to cells of size 160x100 meters; green for 320x200 meters; blue for 640x400.

Fig. 9. A top view of central London. Virtual occluders (in red) are placed around the viewcell (red square). Only a small set of buildings remains potentially visible (colored in black) after using just eight virtual occluders.

Fig. 10. A viewcell (marked in light green) and one of the corresponding virtual occluders (the long red rectangle piercing through the buildings). The buildings that are occluded by this virtual occluder are colored in blue.

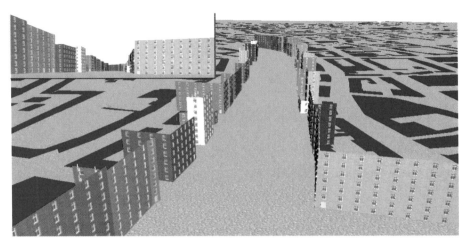

Figure 1. Views from the 8 million polygon model of the city of Vienna used in our walkthrough application. The inset in the upper left corner shows a typical wide open view, while the large image shows the portion of the scene rendered after occlusion culling. Note how occlusion fusion from about 200 visible occluders allows to prune over 99% of the scene.

Figure 7. Overview of the 8 million polygon model of the city of Vienna used as a test scene. Note that the city is modeled in very high detail – every window, for example, is modeled separately with 26 polygons

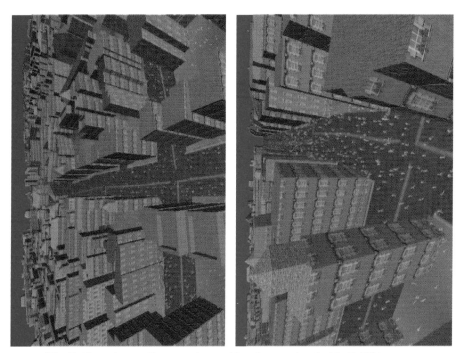

Fig. 5. Views from a distance, of central London populated with 10,000 humans

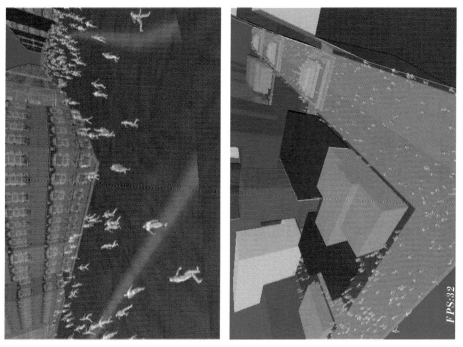

Fig. 6. On the left is a view from closer down at Regent Street and on the right we see climbing of stairs, done using only information from the height-map

Leblanc and Poulin (pp. 89-100)

A: 37424 triangles (204 occluders)

B: 83600 triangles (1140 occluders)

C: 51296 triangles (549 occluders)

D: 741 triangles (119 occluders)

E: 14453 triangles (549 occluders)

F: 642 triangles (203 occluders)

Fig. 5. Test scenes

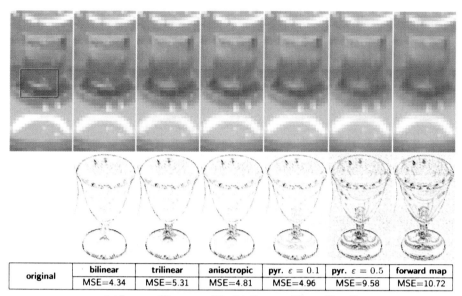

original	bilinear	trilinear	anisotropic	pyr. $\varepsilon = 0.1$	pyr. $\varepsilon = 0.5$	forward map
	MSE=4.34	MSE=5.31	MSE=4.81	MSE=4.96	MSE=9.58	MSE=10.72

(a) Images (Close-up of Parfait Stem and Error Signal)

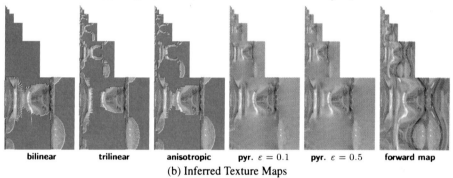

bilinear	trilinear	anisotropic	pyr. $\varepsilon = 0.1$	pyr. $\varepsilon = 0.5$	forward map

(b) Inferred Texture Maps

Fig. 6. Texture Inference Results: (a) shows close-ups of the projected texture, compared to the original rendering on the far left. The highlight within the red box is a good place to observe differences. The next row shows the inverted error signal, scaled by a factor of 20, over the parfait. The bottom row contains the mean-squared error (MSE) from the original image. (b) shows corresponding texture maps. Pink regions represent undefined regions of the texture.

Original	MPEG-view, 361:1, MSE=10.9	Laplacian SPIHT, 361:1, MSE=10.3

Fig. 7. Demo2 Compression Results

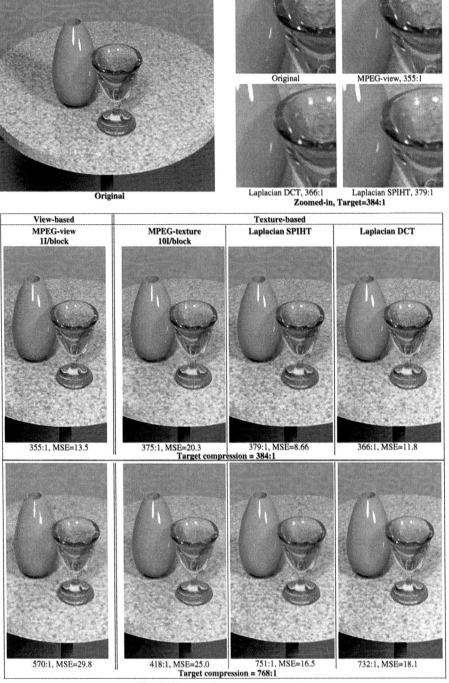

Fig. 8. Demo1 Compression Results

Fig. 3. Spherical-to-planar image warping.

Fig. 4. Multi-resolution wavelet warping.

Fig. 5. Real-time wavelet warping with temporal coherence.

Agrawala et al. (pp. 125-136)

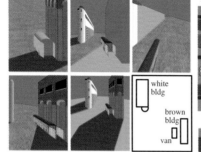

Plate 1. Our reconstruction of Giorgio de Chirico's *Mystery and Melancholy of a Street*. The thumbnails show the 5 local camera views, with attached geometry highlighted in green.

Plate 2. A multiprojection still life containing 10 camera groups took about an hour to create with our system. The impressionist style painting was created in a post-process using Hertzmann's [7] image processing algorithm.

(a) Multiple Oblique Projections

(b) True Perspective Projection

Plate 3.Multiple oblique projections create an artificial sense of perspective, but still allow some area comparisons. In (b) the pink building's rooftop area (arrow) is exaggerated. In (a) it correctly appears to be about the same size as the gray rooftop next to it.

(a) Fixed View Constraint on Car   (b) Single Projection

Plate 4.Our fixed-view constraint can improve composition and give scenes a "cartoony" feel. In (a) it is possible to see the faces of both characters. In (b) the sitting character's face is not visible. The constraint only affects translational motion, so objects can rotate and deform as 3D bodies. In the animation frames to the left, the fixed view constraint is enforced on both cars. In the first and last frame the views of the cars are the same, but when the blue car turns to pass the red car in the middle two frames, we can see the tires rotate and the blue character's uniform becomes more visible than that of the red character.

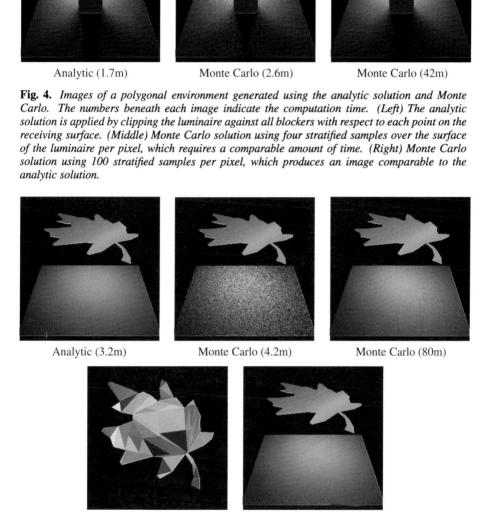

Analytic (1.7m)   Monte Carlo (2.6m)   Monte Carlo (42m)

Fig. 4. *Images of a polygonal environment generated using the analytic solution and Monte Carlo. The numbers beneath each image indicate the computation time. (Left) The analytic solution is applied by clipping the luminaire against all blockers with respect to each point on the receiving surface. (Middle) Monte Carlo solution using four stratified samples over the surface of the luminaire per pixel, which requires a comparable amount of time. (Right) Monte Carlo solution using 100 stratified samples per pixel, which produces an image comparable to the analytic solution.*

Analytic (3.2m)   Monte Carlo (4.2m)   Monte Carlo (80m)

Triangulation (68 patches)   Semi-Analytic (12.5m)

Fig. 5. *Non-convex polygonal luminaires with linearly-varying colors can be efficiently handled with our proposed algorithm. (Top Row) Comparison similar to that shown in Figure 4. (Bottom Row) Image generated by subdividing the luminaire into small regions that are treated as constant. Although each pixel of the resulting image is within 2% of the exact solution, this approach is slower than the analytic solution. Moreover, the accuracy depends on an appropriate level of subdivision.*

Stark and Riesenfeld (pp. 149-160)

(a)

(b)

(c)

(d)

(e)

(f)

Fig. 7. 512×512 single-sample ray-traced images rendered using the algorithm. (a) Evenly arranged occluding objects (32s) producing interference patterns. (b) A particularly difficult scene (shadow image only) of 1000 thin triangles under a large crescent-shaped source (280s). Notice the shape of the source creeping in. (c) a multi-polygon source (98 seconds) and a more pronounced "pinhole" effect. (d) Direct lighting of a self-shadowing object (21s). (e) A coarse one-bounce approximation (321 patches, 1s), and (f) the indirect lighting reconstruction (48m). Image (f) was rendered ignoring conjunctive vertices, yet there are only a few erroneous pixels.

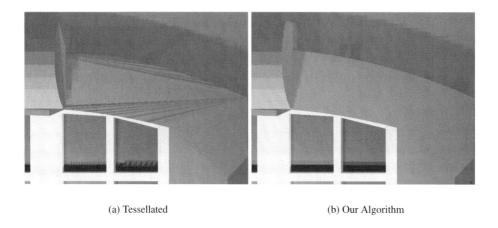

(a) Tessellated   (b) Our Algorithm

Fig. 11. Using our algorithm for wavelet radiosity on arbitrary planar surfaces (see also figure 2)

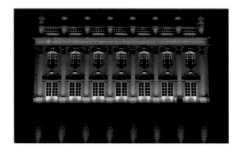

(a) Opera

(b) Temple   (c) Soda Hall

Fig. 12. Our test scenes

H.Radiosity (**119***mn***/123***MB*)   H.Instantiation (**14***mn***/8***MB*)

Fig. 5. *Comparison between hierarchical radiosity and hierarchical instantiation*

Fig. 6. *Application of our algorithm to a "classical radiosity scene".*

Fig. 7. *Hierarchical Instantiation on a scene of* 1M *input polygons.* **9***h***53***mn***/49***MB.*

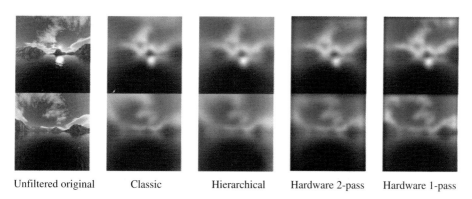

| Unfiltered original | Classic | Hierarchical | Hardware 2-pass | Hardware 1-pass |

Fig. 4. *Comparison of the different filtering methods. Filtering was done with the Phong model and an exponent of 100. From left to right: Unfiltered, the classic method, our new hierarchical method, the hardware accelerated method with two and one pass(es). The original environment map is 128 × 256 pixels in size with a border of 16 pixels.*

N = 50. 20 Hz.   N = 500. 9 Hz.   N = 50. 20 Hz.   N = 500. 9 Hz.

Fig. 5. *Two scenes rendered with a glossy reflective torus (SGI O2). Filtering is done with the Phong model (exponent of 50 and 500) for every frame, but interactive rates are still achieved. The original environment maps are 512 × 1024 pixels in size with a border of 64 pixels.*

Fig. 6. *The two images on the left, show a teapot with an anisotropic environment map using the Banks model ($s = 0.99$). The images on the right show slices of the three dimensional environment map (for $\sphericalangle(\vec{v}, \vec{t}) = 44°, 39°, 35°$).*

Mc Namara et al. (pp. 207-218)

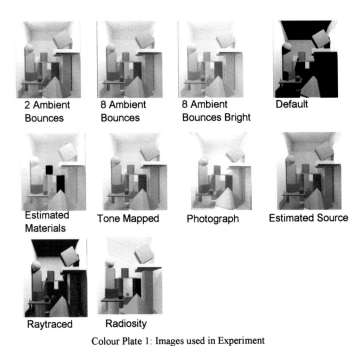

Colour Plate 1: Images used in Experiment

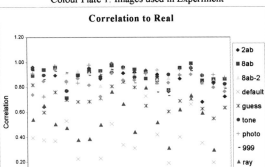

Colour Plate 2: Correlation to Real

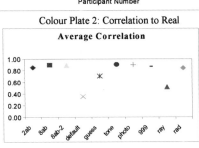

Colour Plate 3: Average Correlation by Image

(a)   (b)

Fig. 2. (a) Our interactive tone mapper for a street scene (70 ktri, 6Hz). The upper left window displays the scene with log colors. The window on the right is used to compute the normalization factor for the weighted average.Below is the histogram of scene luminance. (b) House scene (80 ktri, 6.6Hz). Top: Living room (1 4 $\log cd / m^2$). Note the bluish lighting of the adjacent bathroom. Bottom: Bathroom after chromatic adaptation (1 8 $\log cd / m^2$).

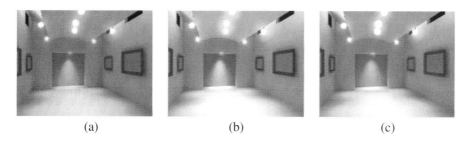

(a)   (b)   (c)

Fig. 3. Chromatic adaptation for a scene with yellowish light sources (10 ktri, 30Hz). (a) No chromatic adaptation. (b) Adaptation to the image chromaticity; since the objects are reddish, the image looks too blue. (c) Adaptation to the source chromaticity.

Fig. 4. Light adaptation when primary lights are turned on (from 1 4 $\log cd / m^2$ to 1 9 $\log cd / m^2$, 10 ktri, 30Hz). Frames are 30ms apart.

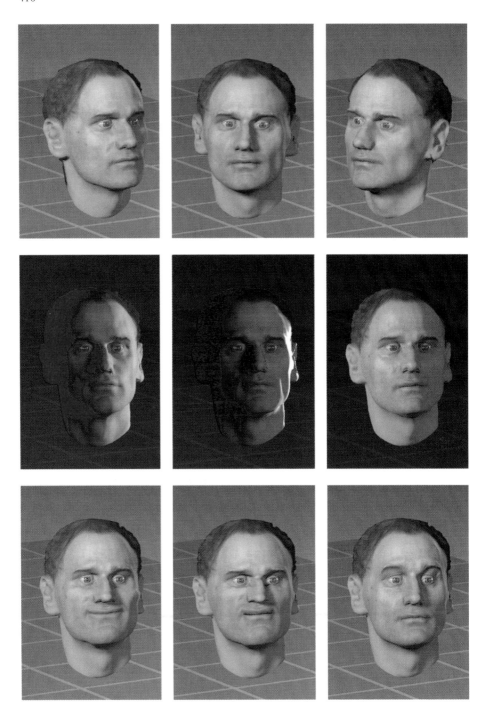

Fig. 5. Renderings of the face model in different orientations, under different lighting, and with different expressions.

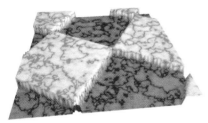

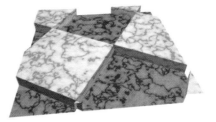

Fig. 14. Brute force approach. 100×100 mesh, 10,201 vertices.

Fig. 15. Our algorithm. 1×1 mesh, 1,477 vertices. $n = 100$, $m = 10$, $r = 0$.

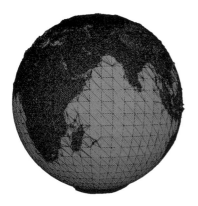

Fig. 16. Displaced 30×60 earth with $n = 10$, $m = 0$, $r = 0.01$. Rendering the 640×480 image took 22 seconds and 127Mb of memory, with 6 seconds spent in the algorithm described in section 4, section 5 and section 6.

Fig. 17. Symmetrical cliffs, with and without displacement. Rendering the 720×389 image took 1 minute and 48 seconds and 139Mb of memory, with 14 seconds spent in the algorithm described in section 4, section 5 and section 6.

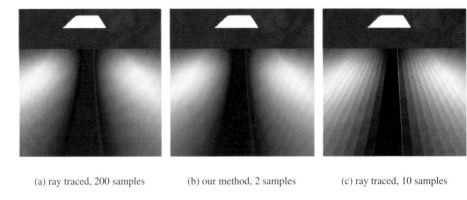

  (a) ray traced, 200 samples   (b) our method, 2 samples   (c) ray traced, 10 samples

Fig. 9. A comparison of ray-traced images and our method for a scene with one blocker and one linear light (not visible).

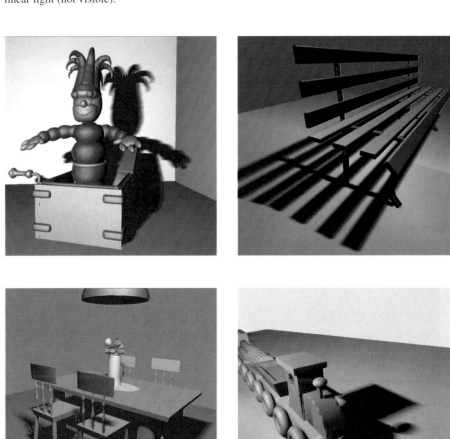

Fig. 10. Some more examples of our method with two samples per light.

Fig. 2. Plane no shadow, dense shadow, light shadow

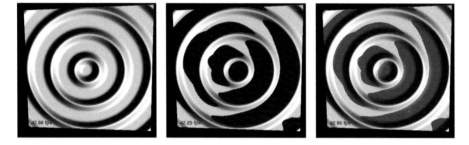

Fig. 3. Different light angle and more extreme bump height, tough case for 8 directions

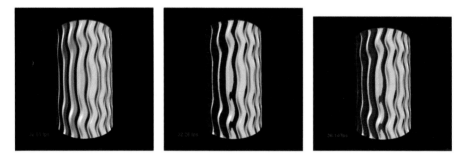

Fig. 4. Cylinder no shadows, cylinder dense shadows, cylinder light shadows

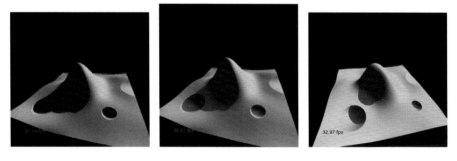

Fig. 5. Surface dense shadow, light shadow, different view light shadow

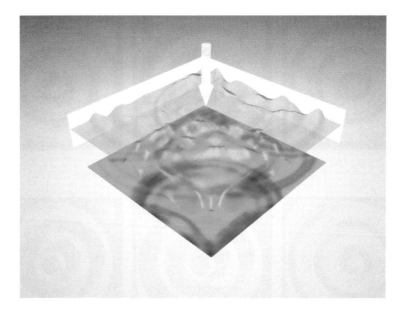

Fig. 1. The water surface/height field is shown in transparent blue, bounded by two white pool borders in a cutaway view. The angle of the incident light is shown by the yellow arrow. The resulting caustics appear on the floor plane below the surface.

Fig. 2. The caustics resulting from surface illumination which varies with position.

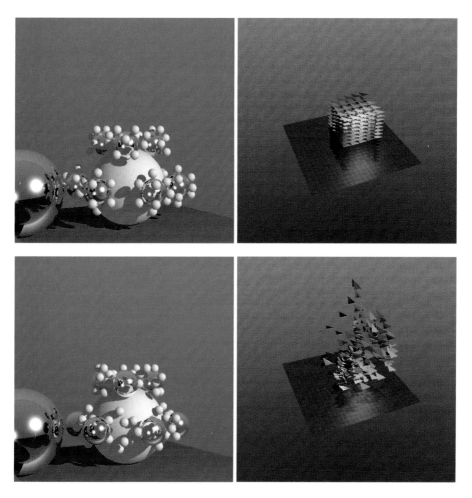

Fig. 5. Test scenes before any objects moved (top) and during animation (bottom).

Fig. 6. Frames created during interactive manipulation.

Smits et al. (pp. 307-318)

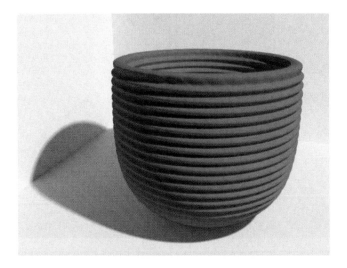

Fig. 9. *A vase modeled with 4860 triangles showing interreflection effects. Generating all displaced microtriangle would have resulted in 30,000,000 triangles.*

Fig. 10. *A terrain dataset with 110,000 initial polygons shown without displacements on the left. Right, with $N_{max} = 3162$ and a procedural displacement map. Instantiating all the geometry would have resulted in more than 1,000,000,000,000 triangles.*

Fig. 4. A caustic from a glass bunny onto a wood bunny.

(a)   (b)

Fig. 5. The head of the David rendered from 2 million points. (a) Global illumination using points with color information, (b) Subsurface scattering using artificial volumetric marble.

Simmons and Séquin (pp. 329-340)

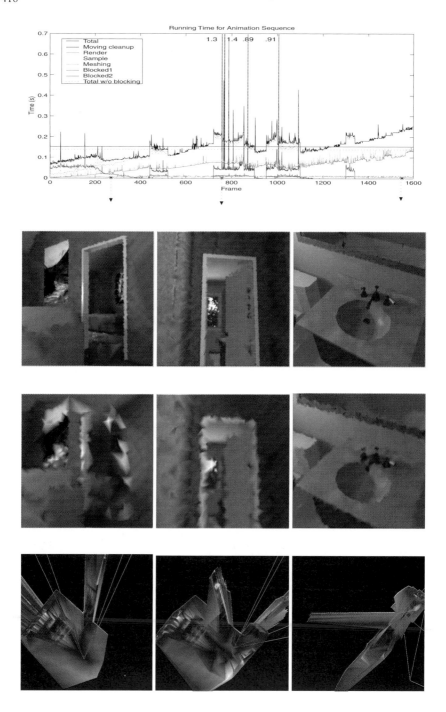

Fig. 4. Results from fixed path timing session: The graph shows the per-frame running time on an Onyx2, as well as the contributions of various algorithm subcomponents (see text for explanation). The first row of images shows reconstruction for 3 selected frames with 50 samples added per frame, and the second row for 5 samples per frame. The first image was captured after a series of rotations from the initial view. The second image occured after moving forward for 120 frames, and the final image was captured after remaining static at the final view for 200 frames. The bottom row shows a top-down view of the mesh and view frustum for each selected frame.

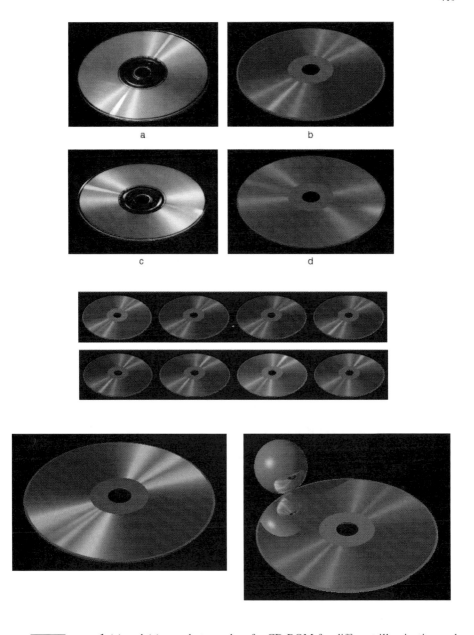

1 (a) and (c) are photographs of a CD-ROM for different illuminating and viewing directions, and (b) and (d) are the rendered images corresponding to (a) and (c). 2 The rendered images for a point light source with different illuminating angles. 3 A rendered CD-ROM under illumination of three point light sources. 4 Interaction between a CD-ROM and a white plastic sphere.

Icart and Arquès (pp. 353-364)

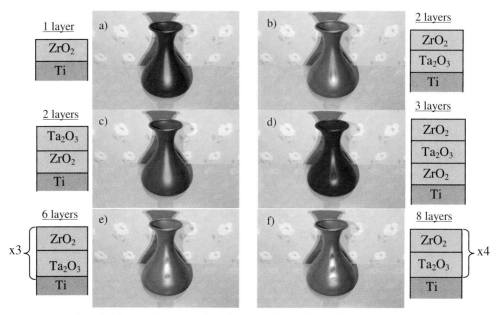

Fig. 5.: Alternate layers of zirconium dioxide (ZrO_2) and tantalum oxide (Ta_2O_3) on a titanium substrate. Statistical parameters of the boundaries :
oxide/oxide and oxide/ambient : $\sigma=50nm$; $\tau=800nm$ substrate/oxide : $\sigma=30nm$; $\tau=800nm$.
thicknesses : ZrO_2 films : 500-650 nm. Ta_2O_3 films : 600-800 nm.

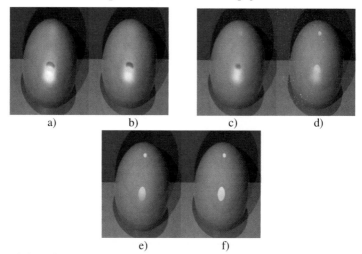

Fig. 6.: Variation of the RMS height parameters for a monolayer system of copper coated with a thin film of aluminium oxide (thickness 400-800 nm).
oxide film parameters : (σ_1, τ_1) (nm); substrate parameters : (σ_2, τ_2) (nm).
a) $(\sigma_1, \tau_1)=(30, 900)$, $(\sigma_2, \tau_2)=(50, 900)$ b) $(\sigma_1, \tau_1)=(0, 900)$, $(\sigma_2, \tau_2)=(50, 900)$
c) $(\sigma_1, \tau_1)=(0, 900)$, $(\sigma_2, \tau_2)=(40, 900)$ d) $(\sigma_1, \tau_1)=(0, 900)$, $(\sigma_2, \tau_2)=(30, 900)$
e) $(\sigma_1, \tau_1)=(0, 900)$, $(\sigma_2, \tau_2)=(15, 900)$ f) $(\sigma_1, \tau_1)=(0, 900)$, $(\sigma_2, \tau_2)=(0, 900)$

Fig. 4. Comparison of ray-traced (left) and hardware generated images (right). The ray-traced image was generated using the RADIANCE lighting-simulation software [31] in approximately 2 hours. The right-hand image was rendered at almost 10 frames-per-second.

Fig. 5. An example of synthetic objects rendered under different lighting conditions, with and without shadows.

Fig. 6. Comparison of self-shadowing produced using ray-tracing (left) and hardware-based rendering (right).

Stamminger (pp. 377-388)

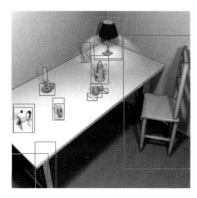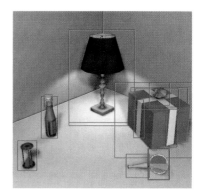

Fig. 5. Adaptive texture assignment according to the relative depth range of scene objects according to the depth range of the objects.

Fig. 6. A radiosity solution (left) is corrected towards a ray tracing solution using 5,000 (0.48 % of all pixels), and 20,000 (1.9 %) ray tracing samples (center and right).

Fig. 7. Exploitation of frame-to-frame coherence: The top left view is obtained with corrective textures. By moving the camera without updating the textures, the top right image is obtained. The bottom left image shows the same view after shooting 10,000 samples (0.95 % of all pixels), the distribution of which is visualized in the bottom right image.

SpringerEurographics

Jurriaan D. Mulder,

Robert van Liere (eds.)

Virtual Environments 2000

Proceedings of the Eurographics Workshop in
Amsterdam, The Netherlands, June 1–2, 2000

2000. X, 217 pages. 95 partly coloured figures.
Softcover DM 98,–, öS 686,–, (recommended retail price)
ISBN 3-211-83516-4. Eurographics

From the Contents
- Practical Calibration Procedures for Augmented Reality
- Evaluation of Rotation Correction Techniques for Electromagnetic Position Tracking Systems
- A 'Plug and Play' Approach to Testing Virtual Environment Interaction Techniques
- Developing Effective Navigation Techniques in Virtual Environments
- The Effects of Group Collaboration on Presence in a Collaborative Virtual Environment
- An Asynchronous Architecture to Manage Communication, Display, and User Interaction in Distributed Virtual Environments
- Time Critical Computing and Rendering of Molecular Surfaces Using a Zonal Map
- A Volumetric Virtual Environment for Catheter Insertion Simulation
- Interacting with Simulation Data in an Immersive Environment
- ERGONAUT: A Tool for Ergonomic Analyses in Virtual Environments
- Accelerometer-Based Motion Tracking for Orchestra Conductor Following

For further information please visit our homepage: **www.springer.at**

 **Springer**WienNewYork

A-1201 Wien, Sachsenplatz 4–6, P.O.Box 89, Fax +43.1.330 24 26, e-mail: books@springer.at, Internet: **www.springer.at**
D-69126 Heidelberg, Haberstraße 7, Fax +49.6221.345-229, e-mail: orders@springer.de
USA, Secaucus, NJ 07096-2485, P.O. Box 2485, Fax +1.201.348-4505, e-mail: orders@springer-ny.com
Eastern Book Service, Japan, Tokyo 113, 3–13, Hongo 3-chome, Bunkyo-ku, Fax +81.3.38 18 08 64, e-mail: orders@svt-ebs.co.jp

SpringerEurographics

Willem Cornelis de Leeuw,
Robert van Liere (eds.)

Data Visualization 2000

Proceedings of the Joint Eurographics – IEEE TCVG Symposium on
Visualization in Amsterdam, The Netherlands, May 29–31, 2000

2000. XI, 296 pages. 166 partly coloured figures.

Softcover DM 118,–, öS 826,–

(recommended retail price)

ISBN 3-211-83515-6. Eurographics

It is becoming increasingly clear that the use of human visual percep-
tion for data understanding is essential in many fields of science. This
book contains the papers presented at VisSym'00, the Second Joint
Visualization Symposium organized by the Eurographics and the IEEE
Computer Society Technical Committee on Visualization and Graphics
(TCVG).
It reports on 27 new algorithms, techniques and applications in the area
of data visualization. The topics are scientific data visualization and
information visualization.
It gives practitioners and visualization researchers an overview of the
state of the art and of future directions of data visualization.

Contents
• Information Visualization
• Large Datasets and Multi Resolution
• Volume and Flow Visualization
• Visualization Systems
• Applications and Case Studies

SpringerWienNewYork

A-1201 Wien, Sachsenplatz 4–6, P.O.Box 89, Fax +43.1.330 24 26, e-mail: books@springer.at, Internet: **www.springer.at**
D-69126 Heidelberg, Haberstraße 7, Fax +49.6221.345-229, e-mail: orders@springer.de
USA, Secaucus, NJ 07096-2485, P.O. Box 2485, Fax +1.201.348-4505, e-mail: orders@springer-ny.com
Eastern Book Service, Japan, Tokyo 113, 3–13, Hongo 3-chome, Bunkyo-ku, Fax +81.3.38 18 08 64, e-mail: orders@svt-ebs.co.jp

SpringerEurographics

David J. Duke,
Angel Puerta (eds.)

Design, Specification and Verification of Interactive Systems '99

Proceedings of the Eurographics Workshop in
Braga, Portugal, June 2–4, 1999

1999. IX, 280 pages. 89 figures.
Softcover DM 118,–, öS 826,–
(recommended retail price)
ISBN 3-211-83405-2. Eurographics

The collection of papers in this volume covers specification methods
and their use in design, model-based tool support, task and dialogue
models, distributed collaboration, and models for virtual reality input.
Strong emphasis is laid on formal representations and modelling techniques and their use in understanding interaction and informing the
design of artefacts.

From the contents
Invited Talks
• Haptic Interactions in the Real and Virtual Worlds (M. Srinivasan)
• Matching Technology to People for Telepresence (M. Hollier)
Papers Presented
• An Analysis and a Model of 3D Interaction Methods and Devices for
  Virtual Reality (C. A. Wüthrich)
• Towards Hybrid Interface Specification for Virtual Environments
  (M. Maasink, D. J. Duke, S. Smith)
• Contrasting Models for Visualization (Seeing the Wood through the
  Trees) (C. Roast, J. Siddiqi)

For further information please visit our homepage: **www.springer.at**

SpringerWienNewYork

A-1201 Wien, Sachsenplatz 4–6, P.O.Box 89, Fax +43.1.330 24 26, e-mail: books@springer.at, Internet: **www.springer.at**
D-69126 Heidelberg, Haberstraße 7, Fax +49.6221.345-229, e-mail: orders@springer.de
USA, Secaucus, NJ 07096-2485, P.O. Box 2485, Fax +1.201.348-4505, e-mail: orders@springer-ny.com
Eastern Book Service, Japan, Tokyo 113, 3–13, Hongo 3-chome, Bunkyo-ku, Fax +81.3.38 18 08 64, e-mail: orders@svt-ebs.co.jp

SpringerEurographics

Nadia Magnenat-Thalmann,
Daniel Thalmann (eds.)

Computer Animation and Simulation '99

Proceedings of the Eurographics Workshop in
Milano, Italy, September 7–8, 1999

1999. X, 230 pages. 148 partly coloured figures.
Softcover DM 89,–, öS 625,–
(recommended retail price)
ISBN 3-211-83392-7. Eurographics

The 20 research papers in this volume demonstrate novel models and concepts in animation and graphics simulation. Special emphasis is given on innovative approaches to Modelling Human Motion, Models of Collision Detection and Perception, Facial Animation and Communication, Specific Animation Models, Realistic Rendering for Animation, and Behavioral Animation.

Contents
- Virtual Humans
- Collision Techniques
- Facial Animation and Communication
- Animation Models
- Realism
- Behavioral Animation
- Appendix

SpringerWienNewYork

A-1201 Wien, Sachsenplatz 4–6, P.O.Box 89, Fax +43.1.330 24 26, e-mail: books@springer.at, Internet: www.springer.at
D-69126 Heidelberg, Haberstraße 7, Fax +49.6221.345-229, e-mail: orders@springer.de
USA, Secaucus, NJ 07096-2485, P.O. Box 2485, Fax +1.201.348-4505, e-mail: orders@springer-ny.com
Eastern Book Service, Japan, Tokyo 113, 3–13, Hongo 3-chome, Bunkyo-ku, Fax +81.3.38 18 08 64, e-mail: orders@svt-ebs.co.jp